THE LIFE OF

MATTHEW FLINDERS

For Arvid, Erik and Axel
and also
To the memory of the brave men who sailed on unknown seas
to discover the shape and form of our world

Contents

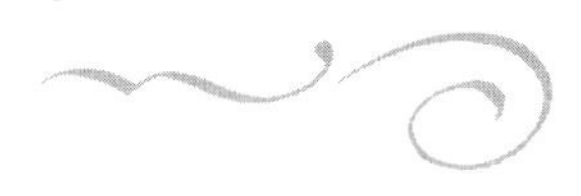

Acknowledgements

The inspiration for this book lay in three areas: a love of ships and the sea that stemmed from family circumstance, a fascination with history and a desire to bring to life an Australian explorer who did not always receive his due in history books in Australia or elsewhere. The work of Matthew Flinders came towards the end of the story of the men and ships who sailed uncharted seas to discover the shape and form of our world. Yet his achievement was considerable: he was the first true circumnavigator of the Australian continent and the first to chart and otherwise record great sections of its shoreline. An intriguing personality as well, he can fluently tell much of his story in his own words.

The track I followed in tracing the life of Matthew Flinders led me, not surprisingly, across the face of the world—to England's little Lincolnshire towns where he was born and grew up, and to London, to explore the streets and squares that he knew and a Thames River that he would have recognised despite the changes. In Mauritius there were the Port Louis harbour, the mountain peaks and the waterfalls he described. I followed long stretches of the Australian coast that he charted—from King George Sound, Western Australia and Tasmania to Cape York and the Torres Strait Islands—and wandered downtown Sydney to mentally reconstruct the settlement he had known. There were visits to existing ships of the period or their replicas and interviews with knowledgeable sailors. Across the world, too, I spent long periods in libraries, archives and museums with their masses of pertinent documents—logs, diaries, letters, certificates, pictures. From all of this there emerged a vivid image of Matthew Flinders and a sweeping picture of the people and circumstances of his life.

I owe very special thanks to Pamela Cook of Flinders's birthplace of Donington, Lincolnshire, whose enthusiasm and effort opened unexpected avenues of information, and to David Simpson of Boston,

Lincolnshire, who left his own pursuits to share his time and expertise. I owe much appreciation to M. R. Barnsdale of Donington, to Lisette Flinders Petrie of Arlington, Polgate, East Sussex, to Robert Perry and Ursula Perry of Lympstone, Devon, and to Nicole Sullivan of Yamba, New South Wales, all of whom in various ways shared with me their particular family ties with the life of Matthew Flinders. I am grateful for the important assistance of Motee Ramdass, Minister of Arts and Culture, Republic of Mauritius, for the efforts of Patrice Curé, Mauritian High Commissioner in Australia, and for the cooperation of the Mauritius Tourism Promotion Authority. For numerous instances of guidance and information on many things Mauritian, I thank Dr Edward Duyker of Sylvania, New South Wales, and Huguette Ly-Tio-Fane Pineo of Beau-Bassin, Mauritius. There is much appreciation also for valued information from Dr Stephen Markey, Southport, Queensland; Dr Axel Estensen, Brisbane, Queensland; Dr Brian Crozier, Curator of Social History, Queensland Museum, Brisbane; Bill Kitson of the Museum of the Department of Mapping and Surveying, and Iain Davis, former Senior Lecturer in the Department of Geographical Sciences and Planning, now Honorary Research Consultant, University of Queensland. For the inspiration of their own enthusiasm for Flinders's voyages, many thanks to Jan and Bern Cuthbertson of Sandy Bay, Tasmania, and to Lyn and Tex Battle of Sweers Island, Gulf of Carpentaria.

To Paul Brunton, Senior Curator, Mitchell Library, Sydney, I owe a special debt for sharing with me his own Flinders research, for answering my many questions and requests with unfailing generosity. I thank the readers of my manuscript who gave time and attention to make valuable suggestions for the shape and content of my story. And not least, my sincere appreciation once again to John Iremonger, Publisher, Allen & Unwin, for the interest, guidance and encouragement that made this book possible.

And there were many more who made their contributions than I can possibly enumerate here. I am grateful to each one.

The great treasuries of information from which I have drawn the principal substance of this book lie in libraries, archives and museums in Australia and overseas. I owe much to the attention I have received from the staffs of the La Trobe Collections, State Library of Victoria;

the National Library of Australia, especially the Pictorial Section; the John Oxley and James Hardie Libraries, State Library of Queensland; the South Australian Maritime Museum; the Queensland Museum; Tourism Queensland; the National Maritime Museum, Sydney; the Powerhouse Museum, Sydney; State Records of South Australia; the Lincolnshire Archives, Lincoln, UK; the British Library, London; the Natural History Museum, London; the Museum of London; the East Riding Archives, Hull, UK; the Public Record Office, Kew, Richmond, UK; the National Maritime Museum, Greenwich, UK; the Fryer Library, University of Queensland; and the Mitchell and Dixson Libraries, State Library of New South Wales, where my countless requests met with ready cooperation from so many, including Jennifer Broomhead, Elizabeth Ellis, Arthur Easton, Warwick Hurst and Martin Beckett. I thank sincerely the trustees of those institutions that provided permission to reproduce in my book quotations and pictures from their collections.

And to my husband and our sons, my utter gratitude for patience, contributions, and every possible kind of support and cooperation.

Conversions

Length

1 inch = 2.54 centimetres
1 foot = 30.48 centimetres
1 yard = 0.91 metres
1 fathom = 1.83 metres or 6 feet
1 chain (surveyor's or Gunter's chain) = 66 feet or 20.1168 metres
1 mile = 1.61 kilometres
1 league = varied in different countries and periods, but usually estimated at approximately 3 miles or 5 kilometres

Weight/Mass

1 ounce = 28.3 grams
1 pound = 454 grams
1 ton = 1.02 tonnes

Temperature

Fahrenheit = 9/5 degrees Centigrade + 32

Area

1 acre = 0.4 hectares

Volume

1 pint = 0.568 litres
1 quart = 1.1 litres
1 gallon = 4.55 litres

Currency

1 shilling = 12 pence
1 pound (£) = 20 shillings
1 guinea = from 1771 21 shillings; not issued after 1813
1 dollar = term generally used by English-speaking people for the Spanish peseta or peso, international currency at the time; the peseta was issued in Spain, the peso generally in Spanish American colonies.

Note: Modern values for currency in use in the past can only be estimated.

Illustrations

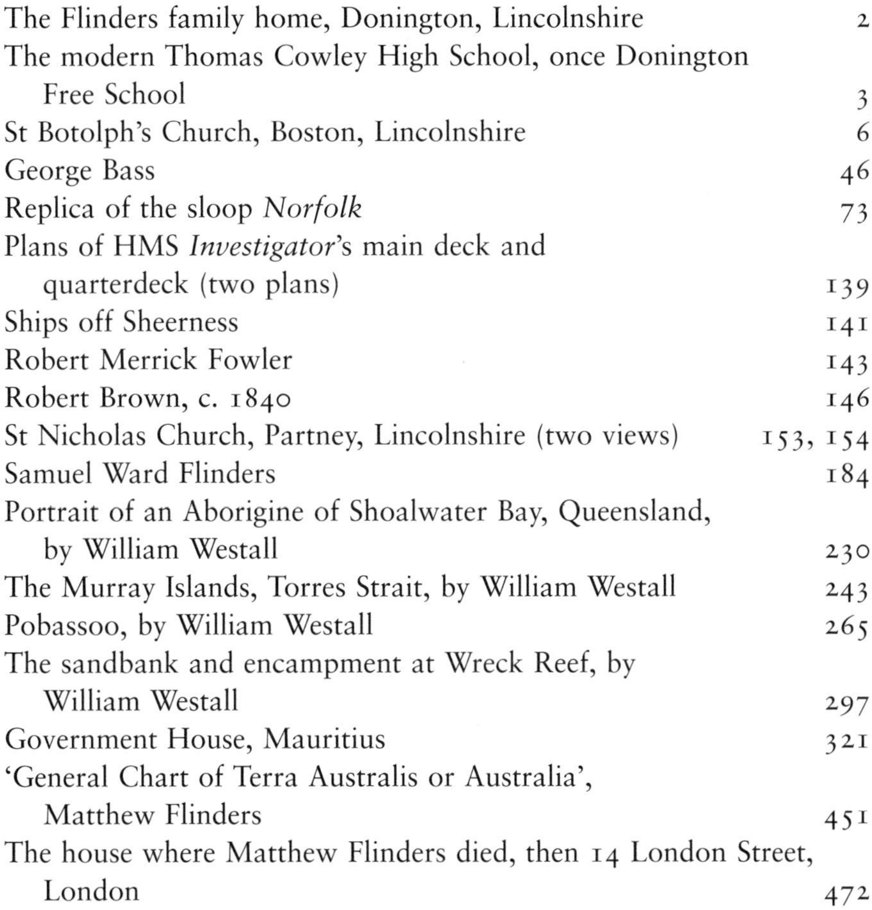

Colour plates

Glossary

ALOFT—up above; up a mast or yard or high in the rigging

ANCHORS—bower, the biggest anchors; stream, the next largest anchors; kedge, smaller anchors for special purposes, usually stored below

AZIMUTH COMPASS—a compass that measure azimuth or bearing clockwise from due north

BARICA—a small barrel

BEAT—sailing as closely as possible to the wind by alternating tacks

BILGE—the curved part of a ship's hull next to the keel

BILGED—when the bilge is broken

BREAKER—a small water cask

BRIG—a two-masted square-rigged ship

CHAINS—the leadman's station under the bowsprit

COLLIER—a ship for carrying coal

CRANK—liable to heel too easily, top-heavy and unable to carry much sail

DRAUGHT—the depth of water needed to float a boat or ship

EPHEMERIS—a table showing the position of a heavenly body on a number of dates in orderly sequence

FLAG RANK, FLAG OFFICER—an admiral's rank, an admiral

FLOG AROUND THE FLEET—to be whipped on board each of a series of ships

HEAVE—to haul in

HEAVE DOWN—to pull over a boat or ship to inspect or repair the bottom

HOGSHEAD—52 gallons; cask or other container with 52 gallon capacity

INDIAMAN—a large merchant ship in trade with India

IN ROOM OF—in place of, instead of

LEAD—a cone or pyramid-shaped piece of lead with a line secured at the top and a small hole in the bottom for picking up samples of the sea floor formation; with measurement markings used to take soundings

LEADSMAN—a sailor stationed in the chains under the bowsprit to heave the lead

LITTORAL—coast or shore

MAKE WATER—to leak

PAY A SHIP'S SEAMS—to seal a ship's seams with pitch after they have been filled with oakum or cotton

PUNCHEON—a large cask, usually with a capacity for 500 litres

QUIRE—a set of uniform sheets of paper of a specific number

ROAD, ROADSTEAD—an anchorage that is some distance from shore

ROOM—space, place; in room of—in place or instead of

SHIPS-OF-THE-LINE—the largest naval warships; also called 'line of battle ships'

SNOW—a small sailing ship resembling a brig

STAND FOR—to sail onwards

STAND OFF AND ON—to sail towards and then away in order to maintain position; usually at night or while waiting

STEM—the vertical timber at the bow of a ship that supports the bow planks

STREAK, STRAKE—a ship's side plank

STRIKE—to lower, e.g. strike into the bold

SUPERCARGO—an officer on a merchant ship who is in charge of the cargo and commercial concerns of the trip

SWEEP—a large oar

SWING ONTO A LEG—to turn onto one of the straight runs that make up the zigzag course of a ship as it tacks

SWIVEL GUN—a gun mounted so that it can be swung from side to side

THEODOLITE—an instrument for measuring horizontal or vertical angles

TREENAILS, TRUNNELS—wooden pegs used in place of metal nails

TREND—to tend to take a particular direction

WATCH ON WATCH—shifts in which watches alternate every four hours

WEIGH—to raise anchor

WOODING—obtaining firewood

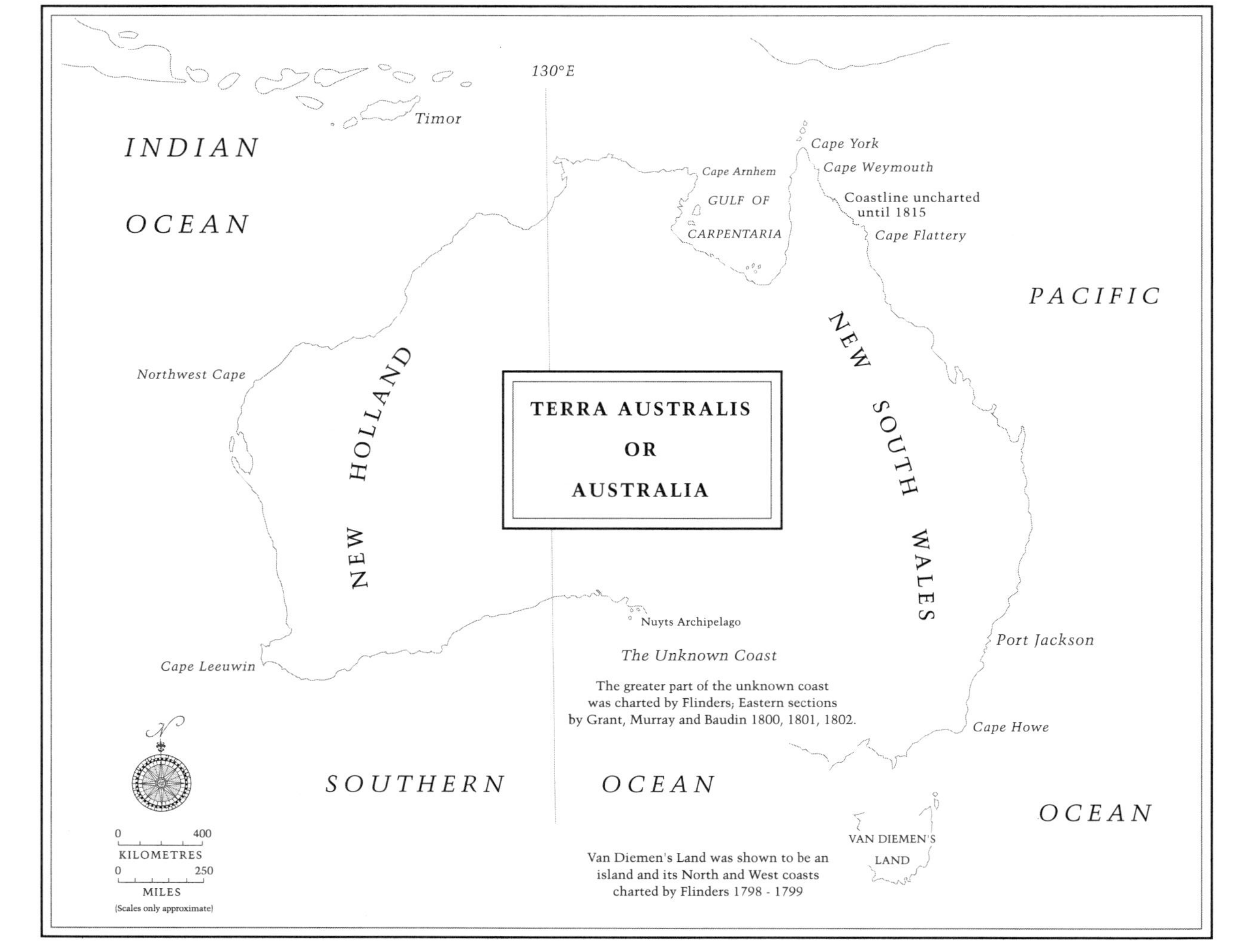

TERRA AUSTRALIS
OR
AUSTRALIA
130°E
Timor
INDIAN
OCEAN
Cape York
Cape Weymouth
Cape Arnhem
GULF OF
CARPENTARIA
Coastline uncharted
until 1815
Cape Flattery
PACIFIC
NEW HOLLAND
NEW SOUTH WALES
Northwest Cape
Nuyts Archipelago
The Unknown Coast
The greater part of the unknown coast
was charted by Flinders; Eastern sections
by Grant, Murray and Baudin 1800, 1801, 1802.
Port Jackson
Cape Leeuwin
Cape Howe
SOUTHERN
OCEAN
OCEAN
VAN DIEMEN'S
LAND
Van Diemen's Land was shown to be an
island and its North and West coasts
charted by Flinders 1798 - 1799
0
400
KILOMETRES
0
250
MILES
(Scales only approximate)

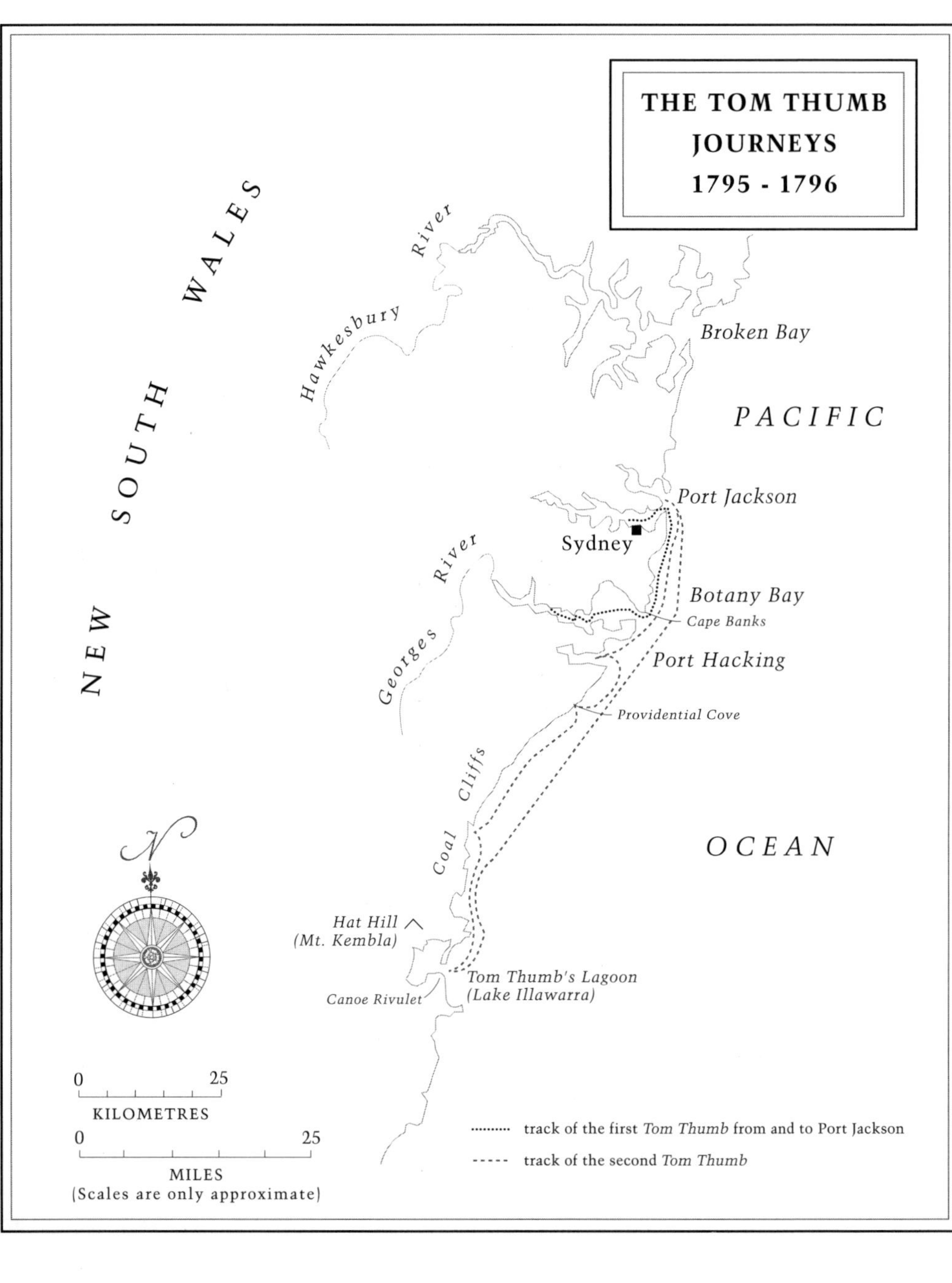
THE TOM THUMB JOURNEYS 1795 - 1796
NEW SOUTH WALES
Hawkesbury River
Broken Bay
PACIFIC
Port Jackson
Sydney
Georges River
Botany Bay
Cape Banks
Port Hacking
Providential Cove
Coal Cliffs
OCEAN
Hat Hill
(Mt. Kembla)
Tom Thumb's Lagoon
(Lake Illawarra)
Canoe Rivulet
0 25
KILOMETRES
0 25
MILES
(Scales are only approximate)
track of the first Tom Thumb from and to Port Jackson
track of the second Tom Thumb

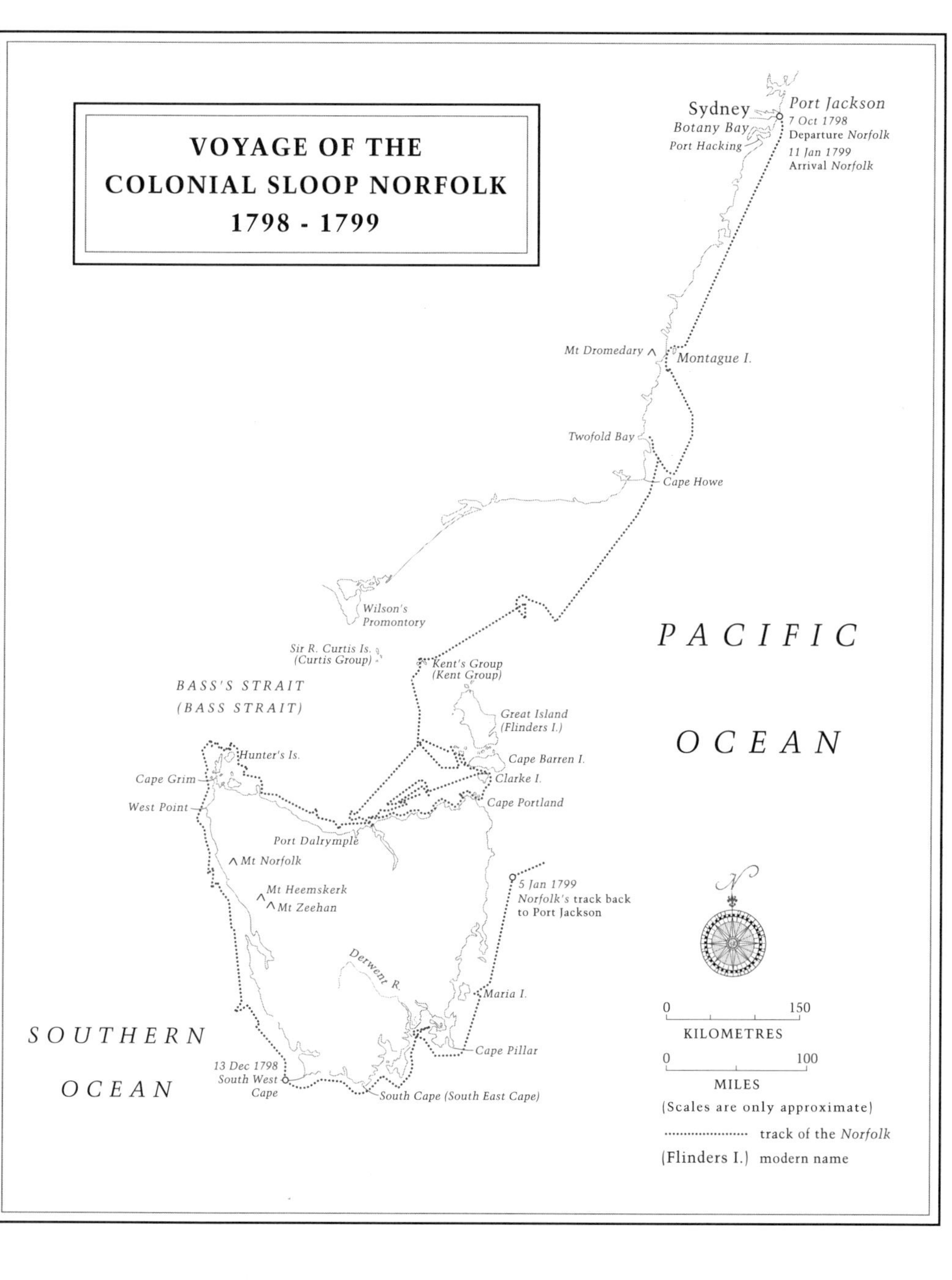
VOYAGE OF THE
COLONIAL SLOOP NORFOLK
1798 - 1799
Sydney
Port Jackson
7 Oct 1798
Departure Norfolk
11 Jan 1799
Arrival Norfolk
Botany Bay
Port Hacking
Mt Dromedary
Montague I.
Twofold Bay
Cape Howe
Wilson's
Promontory
PACIFIC
OCEAN
Sir R. Curtis Is.
(Curtis Group)
Kent's Group
(Kent Group)
BASS'S STRAIT
(BASS STRAIT)
Great Island
(Flinders I.)
Hunter's Is.
Cape Barren I.
Cape Grim
Clarke I.
West Point
Cape Portland
Port Dalrymple
Mt Norfolk
5 Jan 1799
Norfolk's track back
to Port Jackson
Mt Heemskerk
Mt Zeehan
Derwent R.
Maria I.
SOUTHERN
OCEAN
Cape Pillar
13 Dec 1798
South West
Cape
South Cape (South East Cape)
0
150
KILOMETRES
0
100
MILES
(Scales are only approximate)
track of the Norfolk
(Flinders I.) modern name

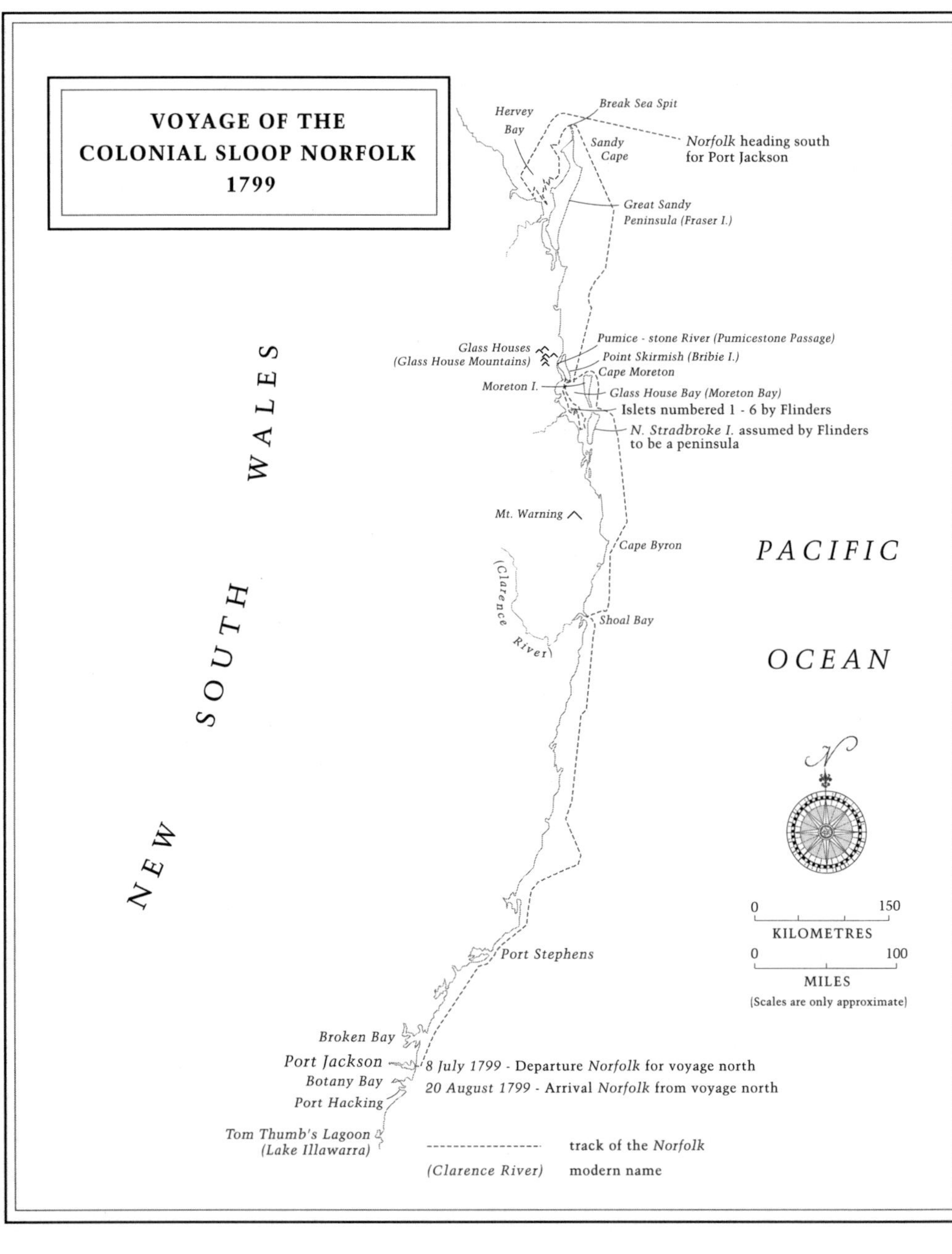

VOYAGE OF THE
COLONIAL SLOOP NORFOLK
1799
Hervey Bay
Break Sea Spit
Sandy Cape
Norfolk heading south for Port Jackson
Great Sandy Peninsula (Fraser I.)
Glass Houses (Glass House Mountains)
Pumice - stone River (Pumicestone Passage)
Point Skirmish (Bribie I.)
Cape Moreton
Moreton I.
Glass House Bay (Moreton Bay)
Islets numbered 1 - 6 by Flinders
N. Stradbroke I. assumed by Flinders to be a peninsula
NEW SOUTH WALES
Mt. Warning
Cape Byron
PACIFIC OCEAN
(Clarence River)
Shoal Bay
N
0 150
KILOMETRES
0 100
MILES
(Scales are only approximate)
Port Stephens
Broken Bay
Port Jackson
Botany Bay
Port Hacking
Tom Thumb's Lagoon (Lake Illawarra)
8 July 1799 - Departure Norfolk for voyage north
20 August 1799 - Arrival Norfolk from voyage north
track of the Norfolk
(Clarence River) modern name

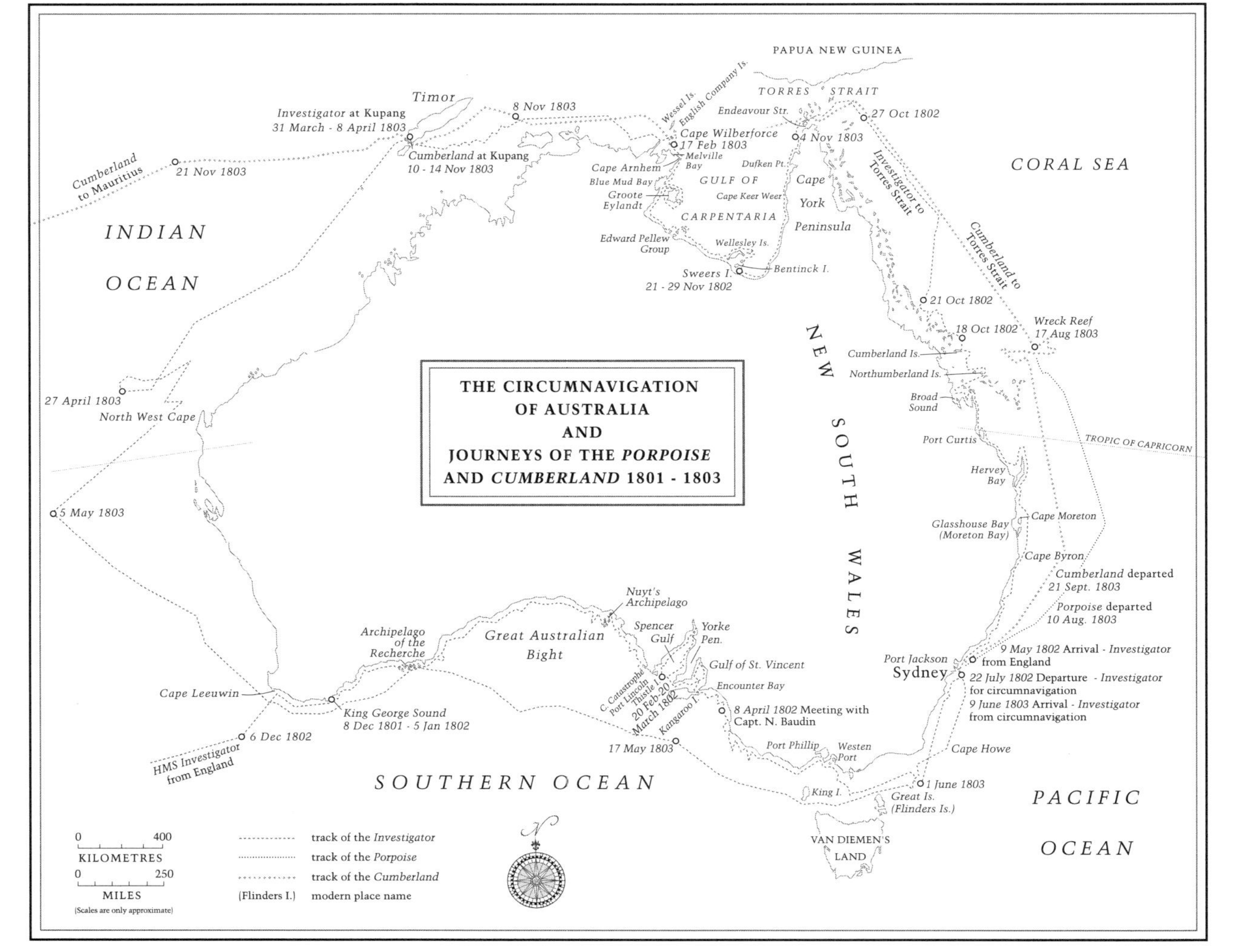

THE CIRCUMNAVIGATION OF AUSTRALIA AND JOURNEYS OF THE *PORPOISE* AND *CUMBERLAND* 1801 - 1803
PAPUA NEW GUINEA
TORRES STRAIT
CORAL SEA
INDIAN OCEAN
SOUTHERN OCEAN
PACIFIC OCEAN
NEW SOUTH WALES
VAN DIEMEN'S LAND
Timor
Investigator at Kupang 31 March - 8 April 1803
Cumberland at Kupang 10 - 14 Nov 1803
Cumberland to Mauritius
21 Nov 1803
8 Nov 1803
Wessel Is.
English Company Is.
Endeavour Str.
Cape Wilberforce 17 Feb 1803
4 Nov 1803
27 Oct 1802
Melville Bay
Cape Arnhem
Blue Mud Bay
Groote Eylandt
GULF OF CARPENTARIA
Dufken Pt.
Cape Keer Weer
Cape York Peninsula
Edward Pellew Group
Wellesley Is.
Bentinck I.
Sweers I. 21 - 29 Nov 1802
Investigator to Torres Strait
Cumberland to Torres Strait
21 Oct 1802
18 Oct 1802
Wreck Reef 17 Aug 1803
Cumberland Is.
Northumberland Is.
Broad Sound
Port Curtis
TROPIC OF CAPRICORN
Hervey Bay
Cape Moreton
Glasshouse Bay (Moreton Bay)
Cape Byron
Cumberland departed 21 Sept. 1803
Porpoise departed 10 Aug. 1803
9 May 1802 Arrival - *Investigator* from England
22 July 1802 Departure - *Investigator* for circumnavigation
9 June 1803 Arrival - *Investigator* from circumnavigation
Port Jackson
Sydney
Cape Howe
1 June 1803
Great Is. (Flinders Is.)
King I.
Port Phillip
Westen Port
8 April 1802 Meeting with Capt. N. Baudin
Encounter Bay
Gulf of St. Vincent
Yorke Pen.
Spencer Gulf
Nuyt's Archipelago
C. Catastrophe
Port Lincoln
Thistle I.
20 Feb-20 March 1802
Kangaroo I.
17 May 1803
Great Australian Bight
Archipelago of the Recherche
King George Sound 8 Dec 1801 - 5 Jan 1802
Cape Leeuwin
6 Dec 1802
HMS Investigator from England
5 May 1803
27 April 1803
North West Cape
0 400 KILOMETRES
0 250 MILES
(Scales are only approximate)
track of the *Investigator*
track of the *Porpoise*
track of the *Cumberland*
(Flinders I.) modern place name
N

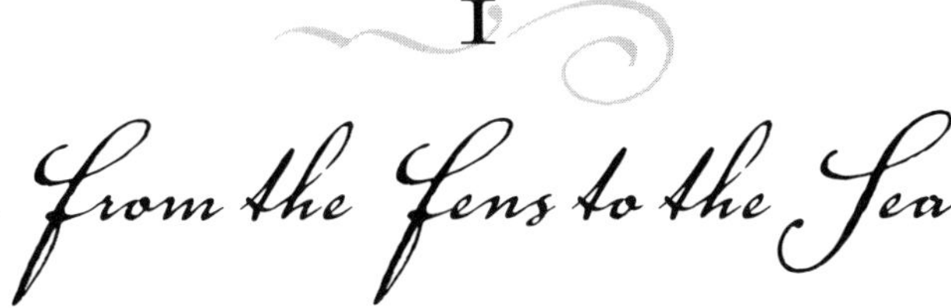

The fenlands of eastern England came out of the sea over thousands of years of natural change and human endeavour. As level as the ocean itself, they are tied to the sea by the flow of rivers and rills, and the rhythm of the tides. Landward the reclaimed earth is a pattern of green fields, rosy brown soil, and windmills and church spires against the sky. Seaward a marshy foreshore slants almost imperceptibly towards the strange blending of land and water that is the Wash, a deep indentation of the North Sea. Along the Witham River lies the town of Boston, marked by the ornate lantern tower of St Botolph's Church.

In 1774 Matthew Flinders was born in the Lincolnshire fenlands town of Donington, some eleven miles south of Boston. Twenty-nine years later he had circumnavigated the little known continent of Australia, had charted thousands of miles of unrecorded coastlines, and had shown the southern continent to be a single great landmass, not two, as had been speculated. The purpose to which he welded his life took him to seas and shores as different and distant as possible from the world in which he grew up, but the bond to the sea was rooted in the fenlands.

The name Flinders may have originated with 16th and 17th century immigrants from Flanders. By the early 17th century Thomas and William of Flanders, or Flinders, were living in Nottinghamshire, and in about 1700 John Flinders, farmer, settled in Donington. By the late 1700s an extended English Flinders family had been established for several generations in southeastern Lindolnshire.

In 1770 a surgeon, Matthew Flinders, set up his practice in Donington. Although no longer the commercial centre it had been in the

The Flinders family home on the town square in Donington, Lincolnshire, where Matthew Flinders was born on 16 March 1774. The ground floor annexe to the right was his father's surgery and apothecary shop. (Courtesy of M. R. Barnsdale, Donington, Lincolnshire)

Middle Ages, Donington had its Saturday markets, and held regular fairs for the sale of livestock, flax, hemp, and quills and feathers from huge flocks of geese. Importantly, it manufactured rope for the British Navy. In the larger town of Spalding the surgeon's father, John Flinders, also practised medicine, and numerous relatives owned farms and small businesses throughout the area.

Matthew Flinders married Susanna Ward, and in Donington's cobblestone town square the young couple occupied a brick house of two floors and an attic and, at one end, a ground floor annexe for the surgery and the doctor's apothecary shop. Their first child was born on 16 March 1774, a boy who was baptised Matthew in the 500-year-old parish church of St Mary and the Holy Rood. As was customary, the child was put out to nurse. A year and a half later a daughter, Elizabeth, was born, and in subsequent years the family grew with the arrival of Susanna, John and Samuel Ward. The mother bore ten children, of whom these five lived.

The modern appearance of the Donington Free School where Matthew Flinders was enrolled at age six. Founded in 1719 by Thomas Cowley, a Donington landowner and businessman, the school is now the Thomas Cowley High School. The façade of this modern building repeats that of the original. (Photo by David Simpson, Boston, Lincolnshire)

Dr Flinders was a short, active man, brown-haired and grey-eyed, with many interests. Occasionally he made modest but generally successful financial investments. He read and greatly enjoyed his garden, at times employing a gardener, while a manservant and a maid were normally part of the household. For housecalls and local travel he kept a mare. He took a scientific interest in the appearance one winter of the Aurora Borealis, in a solar eclipse and in a lunar eclipse he had the opportunity to observe through a telescope. He rode to Boston to estimate the size of a whale stranded in the Witham River. He was a frugal man, keeping detailed monthly accounts, which he totalled at the end of each year.

His attitude towards his children was solidly responsible, if sternly realistic. In his diary he recorded the cost of keeping the newborn with a nurse, and the trouble of having the child home months or even a year or two later. Twice there were stillborn twins, and he expressed his gratitude to Divine Mercy for having been spared the expense of additional children. The surviving children, however, were each to be prepared to earn a respectable living. Susanna Ward Flinders died early in 1783 after the birth of her last child, the boy Samuel Ward. The doctor grieved sincerely, but within the year had married a widow, Elizabeth Weekes Ellis of Spilsby.

The oldest boy, Matthew, was small but lively and healthy. Shortly before his sixth birthday he was enrolled for reading in the Donington Free School founded in 1719 by Thomas Cowley for parish children, and the following year went on to writing and Latin. The boy was bright. His father, remarking that he performed better than had been expected, decided to continue his education. At twelve Matthew was sent as a boarder to the Reverend John Shinglar's grammar school, newly opened in Horbling, a village some seven miles from Donington. Although the small school was expensive, his father wrote that it was time for the boy to be 'from home', adding that he understood his son to be academically 'first Boy except one'.[1] Matthew remained with Shinglar for eighteen months. No school records survive, but his father noted that the school 'improves him much in his Learning'.[2] Matthew's later skill in mathematics and his ability to write clear, correct English suggest that he learned well.

Social rounds were part of Donington life. Christmas parties took place in early January. In 1789 Donington exuberantly celebrated 'His Majesties happy recovery of his Mental Faculties'.[3] Relatives visited, and the Donington family travelled on horseback or in a hired chaise on dirt roads to Spalding, Spilsby and other villages. At Spilsby Mrs Flinders's sister Hannah was married to Willingham Franklin, a shop owner, and with the family including twelve lively youngsters, the red brick house in High Street became a gathering place for games and dances, the young people of this close, congenial group referring to each other simply as brothers and sisters. At some point, probably through church activities, Ann Chappelle of nearby Partney, the step-daughter of the Reverend William Tyler, rector of Braytoft, became a particular friend of the Franklin girls and thus a member of the group.

Dr Flinders intended his eldest son to follow family tradition and become a surgeon and, shortly before the lad turned fourteen, began training him to assist in the shop. Other things, however, held the boy's imagination. England had been at war with France since 1778, the French supporting Britain's American colonies in their War of Independence, and ten years after the war ended with the Peace of Paris in 1783, the conflict was renewed. Donington observed the war's events. In 1798 the news of Nelson's victory in the Battle of the Nile was greeted with enthusiasm.

Dr Flinders's nephew John, son of an older brother, joined the Royal Navy in 1780 as a thirteen-year-old captain's servant, one of the 'young gentlemen' intended for eventual Admiralty-commissioned officer rank. Soon after, John's ship, HMS *Apollo*, saw sharp action against a French frigate, and at the end of the year John, no doubt a family hero, visited, before departing again 'to go fight the perfidious Dutch'.[4] Four years later John returned from America, undoubtedly with tales that held the wide-eyed attention of his ten-year-old cousin. By 1788 John's sister Henrietta was a governess in the household of a naval captain, Thomas Pasley, RN. Stories of the sea, too, would have stirred the imagination of almost every boy in Britain as accounts circulated of the great 1768 to 1779 ocean voyages of James Cook.

Young Matthew knew the port of Boston. He knew the wharves along the river, the bulk and smells of cargoes. He had watched ships come alive as their sails filled and they sheared their way downriver towards the Wash, the sea, and somewhere else in the world. He read Daniel Defoe's *Robinson Crusoe*, which enthralled him. Later in life, completing a questionnaire for a biographical sketch on himself in the *Naval Chronicle*, he answered a question on why he had chosen to go to sea: 'Induced to go to sea against the wishes of friends from reading *Robinson Crusoe*'.[5] A naval career was a prospect infinitely more intriguing than the grind of his father's occupation.

For advice Matthew turned to John Flinders. John pointed out the slowness of promotion in the navy without a highly placed patron. Despite some nine years of service at the time, John was yet to sit his examination for lieutenancy. Nevertheless, he suggested that Matthew study geometry, trigonometry and navigation, and may have loaned the youngster some professional books. Tradition holds that on his own Matthew mastered *John Robertson's The Elements of Navigation: &c.*, and John Hamilton Moore's *The New Practical Navigator; being an Epitome of Navigation*, but it is doubtful that even a clever fifteen-year-old could have done so without help. Realistically, with

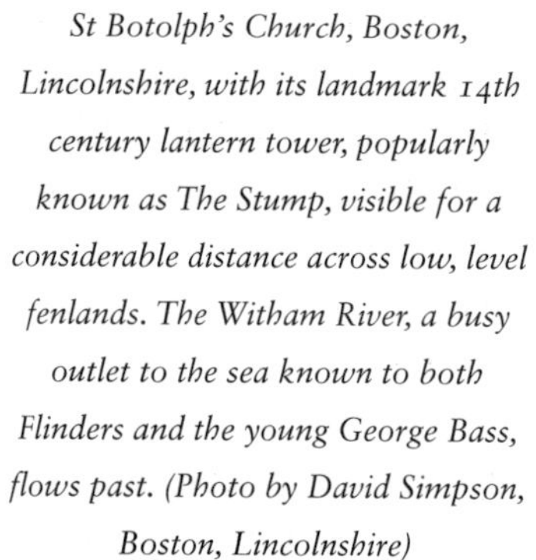

St Botolph's Church, Boston, Lincolnshire, with its landmark 14th century lantern tower, popularly known as The Stump, visible for a considerable distance across low, level fenlands. The Witham River, a busy outlet to the sea known to both Flinders and the young George Bass, flows past. (Photo by David Simpson, Boston, Lincolnshire)

characteristic persistence Matthew could have acquired some basic understanding of navigational theory. John Flinders went a step further. He wrote to a friend, Robert Laurie, acting lieutenant on HMS *Alert* in the West Indies, asking him to accept Matthew as his 'servant', thus placing the boy's name on the ship's muster list while he remained at home in Donington.

This was a common, if illegal, practice in the navy. Commissioned officers were entitled to accept as servants young boys headed for lieutenancy, and although the youngster might not be physically present, his name on the ship's books gained him seatime towards the six years required before he could sit for his lieutenant's Passing Certificate. With the 'servant's' name on the books, the officer drew the lad's allowance for him. If the servant was absent, the officer generally pocketed the allowance. Robert Laurie obliged. On 23 October 1789 the name of Matthew Flinders was entered on the muster roll of the *Alert*, where it remained until his official discharge from the ship on 4 August 1790.[6]

By then Matthew had actually been on board his first ship, HMS *Scipio*, for almost three months. A letter from John would have reached his friend asking that Matthew's name be removed from the muster book. A neat notation then showed him to have been 'discharged'.

Henrietta Flinders, John's sister, made a further contribution to their cousin's aspirations. She brought Matthew's name and his eagerness to join the Navy to the attention of her employer, Captain Thomas Pasley. No real evidence exists for Matthew's having visited the Pasley residence, but Captain Pasley apparently accepted Henrietta's warm recommendation of her cousin and promised Matthew a place on his ship, the *Scipio*.

Dr Flinders, meanwhile, continued his attempt to bring his son into his own profession. He arranged for a position for Matthew with Joseph Dell, a surgeon and apothecary in Lincoln, at a welcome salary of ten guineas a year, and on 26 April 1790 Matthew set off on a hired horse for the great cathedral town. At home a lad would be engaged to take his place in assisting with the practice, and Dr Flinders noted that he would have to make his daughter Elizabeth as 'useful' in the shop as he could.

In less than a fortnight, no doubt 'against the wishes of friends', Matthew had returned to Donington. His father then wrote briefly that he accompanied Matthew to Spalding to take the coach for London and Rochester near the Chatham naval base, in order to 'embark in the Scipio 64 Guns it has long been his Choice, not mine . . . I suppose he will be in the capacity of a Midshipman. The Stipend of which is but bare subsistence. I shall heavily miss him'.[7] He recorded cash paid to Matthew to cover his tailor's bill and the considerable expense of £30 to fit him out for sea. Thus at sixteen, somewhat old to enter his profession as a 'young gentleman', Matthew Flinders began his naval career.

By 1790 the mounting force of the French Revolution was impacting upon Britain. By the Treaties of Paris and Versailles seven years earlier, Britain had conceded the independence of thirteen American colonies, the loss of Tobago in the West Indies and Senegal in Africa to France, and the return of Florida and Minorca to Spain. Britain had, however, acquired some valuable trading rights, and in subsequent years its economic growth accelerated and prosperity rose to unprecedented levels. The nation of 1790 was sufficiently wealthy to carry massive expenditures for wartime military and naval expansion. Between 1789 and 1815 the British army increased sixfold to about 250 000 men, while the Royal Navy grew from 16 000 men before the wars with revolutionary France to more than 140 000 in 1815.

In Britain the outbreak of the French Revolution in 1789 was received by some with considerable enthusiasm. The sweeping reforms of the National Assembly convinced many that a government not unlike Britain's would emerge. Idealists believed that in a bright new democratic age an enlightened republican France would spark needed political, social and religious reform in Britain. Further, the weakening of an old rival power by internal dissension encouraged the prospect of a period of peace.

Away from Europe Britain was occupied with other dispositions. In 1791 Canada became the colonies of Upper Canada and Lower Canada. In India the British government and the powerful East India Company had achieved a partnership in ruling large parts of the subcontinent. On the farthest side of the world Britain's infant colony, New South Wales, was in its third year, clinging precariously to the rim of an alien continent.

In May 1790 Matthew Flinders saw London for the first time as he travelled to Rochester and the neighbouring naval base. On the Medway River, just above its confluence with the Thames, the port of Chatham sprawled around its dockyards, crowding the river with black and yellow warship hulls, a forest of masts and spars, and countless small craft moving about insect-like on the water. Here Flinders joined the *Scipio*, apparently as a midshipman.

Only days later he felt the chill damp wind of the Channel and the ceaseless rise and fall of the deck as the *Scipio* cruised the Downs, off the east coast of Kent. Now there was the daily naval routine to learn, the thousands of parts of a full-rigged warship to memorise, work to be done at swaying, terrifying heights, monotonous food, and dark, crowded quarters filled with the stench of unwashed bodies, wet clothing and vermin seen and unseen.

Soon after, Pasley received command of the *Bellerophon*, 74 guns, and took Matthew with him as an able-bodied seaman. Three days later Matthew Flinders was entered on the *Bellerophon*'s books as a midshipman.

The *Bellerophon* was launched in 1786. Eventually it took part in Horatio Nelson's battles of the Nile and Trafalgar, and in 1815 became famous as the vessel on which Napoleon surrendered to the British after his defeat at Waterloo. In July 1790, however, the ship mainly patrolled the Narrow Seas separating England from continental Europe and from Ireland. In August Matthew received leave to visit Donington. His father wrote, 'he is grown, and much altered by his Uniform and dress . . . he appears satisfied with his Situation, I pray God he may be prosperous'.[8]

2

The Voyage with Bligh

In March 1790 Lieutenant William Bligh returned to England from the *Bounty* expedition to Tahiti and the mutiny, the 3600-mile open-boat voyage from the mid-Pacific to Timor, and the journey home on a Dutch vessel. On 22 October Bligh was court-martialled for the loss of his ship and honourably acquitted. Adulation now surrounded Bligh for his courage and seamanship in completing the longest and most desperate journey by boat in naval records. Rapid promotions, finally to post captain, followed; he was presented to the king and the first part of his account of his astonishing sea adventure was published. In March 1791 the Admiralty approved a second attempt to transplant breadfruit from Tahiti to the West Indies. A month later Bligh was appointed to HMS *Providence* and commissioned to undertake the task. A powerful patron and one determined to carry out the breadfruit experiment lay behind Bligh's remarkable success. This was his friend, Sir Joseph Banks, a wealthy Lincolnshire landowner, president of the Royal Society, a botanist and a dedicated patron of the natural sciences.

Captain Pasley evidently became aware of plans for Bligh's voyage and, seemingly on his advice and certainly with his approval, Flinders applied to join the *Providence*. For many Europeans the voyages of James Cook and Louis Antoine de Bougainville had evoked a vision of the South Pacific as a paradisiacal island world, enhanced by a popularised version of the philosophical concept of the 'noble savage'. For a seventeen-year-old the prospect of a long sea voyage into the Pacific would have been irresistible. Somewhere in his imagination there probably still hovered the image of Robinson Crusoe striding along the beach of his solitary island.

Flinders was accepted. He served briefly on HMS *Dictator*, then transferred his gear to the *Providence* and left on leave for a short visit home to Lincolnshire. His father wrote:

> He is going with Capt. Bligh in the Providence to circumnavigate the Globe . . . and will be near 3 years performing this great under taking . . . God only knows what may be the event of such a long voyage may He prosper and befriend him in every Country, Climate and People . . . he has made much improvement in his knowledge of Navigation and is thanks be to God well and in good spirits . . .[1]

Back on the *Providence*, Flinders wrote to share the news of his acceptance for the voyage with Pasley and before the expedition sailed received Pasley's encouraging reply:

> *Bellerophon* Spithead, June 3rd, 1791
>
> Dear Flinders,
>
> I am favoured with your letter on your return from visiting your friends at the country, and I am pleased to hear that you are so well satisfied with your situation on board the *Providence*—I have little doubt of your gaining the good opinion of Capt. Bligh if you are equally attentive to your duty there as you were in the *Bellerophon*—All that I have to request in return for the good offices I have done you, is, that you never fail writing me by all possibile opportunitys during your Voyage; . . . do this, my young friend, and you may rest assured that my good offices will not be wanting some future day for your advancement.—all on board are well—present my kind remembrances to Captain and Mrs. Bligh, and believe me
>
> Yours very sincerely
> Thos. Pasley
>
> P. S. When do you expect to sail from Deptford?[2]

Preparations for the voyage took several months, mainly at the Deptford shipyard on the Thames, with its docks and slipways, its huge storehouse and long rows of workshops. Bligh received two ships. One was the 28-gun, three-decked *Providence*, a new West Indiaman, designed to carry large cargoes. She was of 406 tons burden,[3] with a complement of 200 that included twenty marines, a security Bligh did not have on the *Bounty*. The second was the small, two-masted brig *Assistant* to serve as tender, with 27 men, among them four marines, all commanded by Lieutenant Nathaniel Portlock, an experienced and science-minded sailor. The two ships would work extremely well together, never out of sight of each other throughout the long journey. Bligh's instructions were to reach Tahiti by way of the Cape of Good Hope, Van Diemen's Land and New Zealand, and to return via Torres Strait, where he was to explore for an easier, faster route than those already known to navigators.

Bligh's plans to engage in hydrography are evident in his substantial requests for navigational and surveying instruments, existing charts, drawing equipment and stationery. However, he received no instructions on surveying. The purpose of the voyage was the safe transport of breadfruit plants to West Indian destinations.

Joseph Banks was much in evidence in the preparations. Banks was personally renowned for his travels as a naturalist and for his dedicated promotion of science. The immense scope of his work, combined with notable government connections, gave him a position of unofficial pre-eminence in certain areas of the administration. The introduction of breadfruit to the West Indies as cheap food for slaves had been suggested by plantation owners there in the early 1770s, and Banks's interest in economically useful plants became a major factor in realising the project. Through his influence two botanists, James Wiles and Christopher Smith, were assigned to care for the breadfruit plants and others, especially any unusual specimens for the Royal Gardens at Kew.

Each ship received a twelve-month supply of food, the traditional navy fare of salt pork and salt beef to be served on alternate days; a gallon of beer per man per day, replaced by wine or brandy when the beer turned bad; sauerkraut, biscuit, pease, oatmeal, cheese and a little butter. In quantity the navy's food was usually sufficient, but nutritionally it was poor, largely due to the primitive methods of preservation used at the time. As a result it was frequently deficient enough in nutrition to make dysentery and especially scurvy commonplace.

Scurvy results from an insufficiency of vitamin C, ascorbic acid, which the human body requires in relatively large amounts.[4] By the

17th century many captains recognised that fresh foods were important in combating the disease, but long periods at sea and landings on barren or hostile coasts could make obtaining them extremely difficult. The remarkable efficacy of citrus fruits was demonstrated in 1747 by the Scottish naval surgeon James Lind, but his findings were not universally accepted, nor was citrus always available in northern Europe. Another assumed remedy was an inspissated juice of malt known as wort, but in fact malt does not contain vitamin C. Spruce beer, brewed from evergreens, was evidently a better anti-scorbutic. Deficiencies of other vitamins, such as those of the B group, also created a range of symptoms from digestive disorders to neurological problems, none understood as to cause.

The expedition sailed from Deptford on 2 August 1791. Its first stop was at Santa Cruz, Tenerife, off North Africa, where the island's 12 718-foot peaks astonished the lad from the fens. He wrote home enclosing a small map of the journey so far, and sketches of the islands and coast. He also sent his first letter to Pasley, describing the streets with balconied houses and the 'merry, good-natured people', as well as a small adventure shared with the botanist, Christopher 'Paddy' Smith, and some of the other young men from the ship:

> We visited a nunnery of the order of St. Dominic. In the chapel was a fine statue of the Virgin Mary, with four wax candles burning before her. Peeping through the bars, we perceived several fine young women at prayers. A middle-aged woman opened the door half-way, but would by no means suffer us to enter this sanctified spot. None of the nuns would be prevailed upon to come near us. However, they did not seem at all displeased with our visit, but presented us with a sweet candy they called Dulce, and some artificial flowers, in return for which Mr. Smith gave them a dollar.[5]

This was indeed something new for an English country boy raised in the established church.

Flinders formed firm friendships with the botanists Smith and Wiles. In the youthful Flinders there were evidently already the qualities that would win him loyal friends over the years—his own loyalty, his generally very principled behaviour and, when he felt at ease, the ability to be a congenial and entertaining companion.

For over a month in the Atlantic Bligh was so seriously ill with high fever and severe headaches that he had Portlock from the *Assistant* assume temporary command of the *Providence*. Gradually, as the ships made their way into cooler latitudes, Bligh improved.

The Cape of Good Hope was reached in October. From the bay where the ships dropped anchor, Cape Town presented a 'pretty appearance' with trees and handsome buildings. The ships remained a welcome two months for repairs and to replenish their supplies of water, firewood and provisions. Flinders wrote again to his father and to Pasley with long, frank and sometimes amusing descriptions of sights and people.

Also at the Cape was a Dutch ship, the *Waaksamheid*, with Captain John Hunter and his crew on board as passengers, en route from Sydney to England. Hunter had commanded HMS *Sirius* in the First Fleet sent out only four years earlier to establish an English colony in New South Wales under Captain Arthur Phillip. The *Sirius* was wrecked at Norfolk Island in 1790, a terrible loss to the struggling colony and, as was required of every commander who lost a ship, Hunter was to face court martial in England. The very junior Midshipman Flinders did not mention meeting the ranking officer who, in a few years, would be his staunch supporter. Refitted and reprovisioned, the *Providence* and the *Assistant* continued uneventfully across the Indian Ocean. The days were filled with watchkeeping, the daily holystone and sand scrubbing of decks, the continual tasks of navigation, the noonday routine of taking the sun's altitude, pronouncing the hour twelve and thereby formally beginning a new nautical day. On Sundays the men were mustered and inspected—every man to be 'clean dressed'—and Bligh performed Divine Service. The sounds and smells of the ship became routine—the heavy creak of straining timbers, the changeable song of wind in the rigging, the odour of live animals on deck and rotting food below, and the pervading stench of rats, alive and rustling, and dead and decomposing in hidden recesses. By night a fire burned in the galley to dry and clean the air.

Flinders learned the realities of trying to shoot the sun, holding a heavy brass sextant as the deck under him pitched and rolled, and to correctly mark the ship's position on a chart, with every loose object on the table sliding about. He became alert to the significance of the vessel's sounds and movement, and saw what experienced men did when something went wrong. He learned to watch the sky for weather and the sea for approaching dangers. He copied for himself the ship's Standing Orders, the instructions designed to keep crew and ship as healthy, clean and disciplined as possible, and noted how the ship's log and other records were kept. Many of these were things Bligh had learned from Cook, and Flinders was learning in turn. He also learned to deal with his own short stature, climbing when necessary to see over the bulkheads.

From Adventure Bay in Van Diemen's Land, he kept a precise log of his own, briefly recording all the daily detail of a ship at sea: course, position, astronomical observations, weather, sail adjustments, cleaning, punishments, sightings and remarks, with small profile sketches of some islands.

The ship's Tobacco List records his purchase of tobacco for £1/2/2, and quite surely he retreated from time to time with his long-stemmed pipe to the brick-lined galley where smoking was permitted. On duty he no doubt preserved his young dignity, but in his journal his sense of wonder slips through in the doubly underlined adjective when one night a 'blazing meteor . . . enlighten'd the whole Atmosphere'.[6] Tiny islands seen in passing, native boats and people, the care of breadfruit seedlings—his journal describes them in fascinated detail.

The extent of Flinders's navigational and hydrographic work on the *Providence* cannot be determined with any certainty. His father, having received Matthew's letters from Tenerife, wrote in his diary, 'with pleasure I note his being in favour with Capt. Bligh. he says he works observations for him, & that the Capt. intrusts him with his Time Keepers'.[7] This was perhaps a proud parent's interpretation of some more general remark. Of the six midshipmen, Flinders was one of the most junior. As his reliability was noted, it is possible that he was assigned to winding the chronometers and comparing their daily rates, but it is more likely that he assisted a senior midshipman. Similarly, as his flair for mathematics became recognised, he might have shared in working out some of Bligh's observations. Three midshipmen were usually employed to read the time from the timekeepers as the captain observed, and evidently to work out these observations. It is possible that he occasionally was one of them. A captain's duty included instructing his midshipmen, and Bligh took this obligation seriously.

Flinders's first sight of the great southern continent was the rugged coast of what Abel Tasman in 1642 had called Anthoony van Diemenslandt. A century and a half later the misty, forested land still held its secrets. No one knew what lay inland, or even whether what they were seeing was part of the Australian mainland. Smoke rising above the trees came from campfires, Flinders was told, or land being burnt off by the inhabitants.

On 9 February 1792 the *Providence* and the *Assistant* anchored in the quiet, dark green water of Adventure Bay, with its pale sand beach backed by forest. Bligh had been there with Cook and with the *Bounty*, and as soon as the anchors were let go, he went ashore to locate his previous firewood and watering sites, and any remnants from his previous visits. He found the blazed trees and the saw-pit, now partially filled in, and one surviving but little-grown apple tree. Undeterred, Bligh had his botanists set into the Australian earth nine little English oaks along with figs, quinces, pomegranates, strawberries, rosemary and, in a little rivulet, some watercress. After a half day's rest, shore parties went to work felling trees for firewood and filling casks with clean, sweet water, while some fished and others landed the ship's goats on a small island for a chance to graze. Groups took turns to bathe and to wash stained and salt-stiffened clothes in the streams.

Several officers explored the beaches, while the botanists ranged through the bush, collecting several new plant species. Notes were taken and drawings made of wildlife. A few animals were shot and examined, among them an echidna. Although the visitors came across some small, deserted huts, encounters with the Aborigines were few, brief and wary, with little exchange of any kind. The Europeans marvelled at the trees, towering into a green canopy far overhead and filling the shadows below with the curious scent of their leaves. There was snow on today's Mt Wellington, and rain and cloud hampered surveying and the observations necessary for checking the rates of the timepieces. Despite the problems, Bligh, an enthusiastic map-maker, produced two charts of the area.

In the early evening of 24 February the *Providence* and the *Assistant* moved out of Adventure Bay. They shaped their course to the east-southeast and then south to just beyond 48°S latitude, circumventing New Zealand. The weather deteriorated and for two weeks ships and men fought cold, gale-force winds.

At approximately 140°W longitude the ships turned north. The weather warmed, and it was often hazy but with fresh winds. An unknown island was charted. Boat crews practised handling small arms, and the marines did target practice. The men washed and mended their clothing, scrubbed their hammocks and, in preparation for associating with the Tahitians, the ship's surgeon examined each man for venereal disease, which Bligh did not want transmitted to the islanders. Bligh's record named five infected men, including Lieutenant George Tobin, but Tobin, writing five years later, stated that there were only two. Flinders noted approvingly that the examination would keep the ship's company from guilt in communicating the disease. Twelve days after landing, however, Bligh wrote in his journal of its prevalence in Tahiti, but common and little understood as the infection was, the general attitude towards it was fairly blithe. George Hamilton, surgeon on HMS *Pandora*, commented good-naturedly in his journal on the 'warm tokens of their affection' left with the crew by the ladies of Tahiti.[8]

Bligh issued special orders on dealing with natives, which Flinders copied into his journal. Trading was to be done only through an assigned person from the ship. The islanders were to be treated with good will and no violence used, even to retrieve stolen objects. No firearms were to be taken ashore without the captain's permission. Several paragraphs stressed the importance of watching for theft, particularly of weapons, tools or other implements, and using tact and firmness to prevent such incidents. No one was to mention the killing in Hawaii of Captain Cook, whom the Tahitians revered, the loss of the *Bounty* or the fact that this expedition, too, had come for breadfruit plants.

Bligh's ships anchored in Tahiti's Matavai Bay on 10 April 1792 following a passage from England of 36 weeks. To Flinders the scene would have been idyllic—canoes with tall, narrow sails, a sandy beach, palms, breadfruit trees, clusters of thatch huts, jungle-mantled peaks against the sky.

Crowds of Tahitians enthusiastically welcomed the ships, and island dignitaries, warmly disposed towards Bligh from his previous visit, came on board with gifts of bark cloth, fruit and pigs. The principal chief and his most important queen were constant guests, while a stream of exotic foods reached the vessels—breadfruits, plantains, a kind of mango, taro, coconuts.

There were some surprises. The British learned that after the *Bounty* mutineers had set adrift Bligh and the eighteen men loyal to him, they had returned briefly to Tahiti, where some chose to remain when the *Bounty* sailed, eventually for Pitcairn Island. Those on Tahiti had been picked up by HMS *Pandora* to be taken to England for trial, but Bligh's company were unaware that the *Pandora* had already foundered on Australia's Barrier Reef, taking with her to the bottom 35 men, four of them mutineers. On Tahiti, however, were most of a wrecked English whaler's crew, thirteen of whom joined the *Providence*. Bligh discovered that the people of Matavai were at war with those of a neighbouring district, and worried that the situation would interfere with acquiring breadfruit plants. This, however, did not eventuate.

The expedition remained in Tahiti for three months. Bligh established a post on a rise near the beach and had it fenced and equipped with huts and a long shaded area for the plants. Crews and officers were kept busy with the routine of securing fresh water and firewood, with salting pork, fishing, repairing the ships and constructing the ship's greenhouse. Some soundings of Matavai and other bays were made (in which Midshipman Flinders might have taken part) and, Bligh having made his breadfruit requests to the chiefs with due diplomacy, available men were set to work with the botanists, potting and caring for the mounting hundreds of young plants.

Petty theft was a recurring problem, Flinders recording in one instance 'a large Bag of dirty Linnen' taken by night from beside the second quartermaster's bed, despite 'four Sentries placed about the Tent.'[9] Bligh lost his pistols when the guide leading him through some underbrush disappeared among the trees with them.

Frequently Bligh was seized by his 'scarce bearable' headaches, which made the many ceremonious courtesies and lengthy hospitality required in dealing with the Tahitians very difficult to endure. Nor would pain have improved the temper of an already irascible captain. Expressions of his outrage were deafening. As his condition improved, however, a small observatory was set up, and he began to make daily observations.

In Bligh's journal, references to venereal infections now appeared more or less regularly. One man received twelve lashes for 'having connection with a Woman while he was infected . . .'[10] The list climbed to twenty-two and, suspecting that some of the men were not reporting their symptoms, Bligh had the ship's company again undergo an examination by the surgeon. The boatswain and an unnamed midshipman were found to be among the infected.

Treatment usually involved forms of mercury, which evidently relieved the symptoms, although its true curative effect is doubtful. While officers apparently made private arrangements with the surgeon, all others, including midshipmen, were recorded as having been charged the equivalent of two weeks' pay for a 'cure'. Flinders did not escape. The pay-book of the *Providence* reveals that the young midshipman was debited twice, 30 shillings, for venereal disease treatments. When these treatments took place is not indicated, but with over a quarter of the ship's company undergoing 'cures' when the *Providence* sailed from Tahiti, it would seem that at least one was performed at that time. The second treatment might have been given after any of the longer stays in port. In 1795 the practice of recording payment for venereal disease treatments was discontinued.

By early July Bligh anxiously decided that the young breadfruit plants were strong enough to be brought on board. Both ships' lower decks were stripped and washed with boiling water to kill the cockroaches—'very numerous and very troublesome'—and otherwise prepared for the precious cargo. One thousand two hundred and eighty-one pots, tubs and boxes ferried to the ships contained an estimated 2126 little breadfruit trees and some 500 other plants. They filled the great cabin of the *Providence* and shelters built on both sides of the after part of the quarterdeck, with narrow passages left for the men to slip through.

Several days were then taken up with farewells and final exchanges of gifts. On the 19th the two ships moved out through the bay, followed for some distance by canoes filled with loudly lamenting islanders, some of whom tore at their heads with sharks' teeth so the blood ran.

The ships sailed west. After a 24-hour stop at Aitutak in the Cook Islands, there were sightings of the Tonga archipelago and then the islands of Fiji, which Bligh had seen from the *Bounty*'s launch and which were now methodically charted. Their beauty was spectacular—volcanic peaks and the incredible greenness of forests and cultivated slopes. Flinders was enchanted. Of Ngau he wrote, 'This is the most beautiful island we have yet seen . . . worthy to be called Paradise Island'.[11]

Four sets of up to eleven charts each were drawn, based on surveys ranging from the island of St Paul in the South Atlantic, to Van Diemen's Land and the Pacific islands to Torres Strait and Kupang on Timor. Bligh signed these charts, but much of the drawing was done by his officers. Flinders merited a minor part in the cartography. Working with the senior midshipmen, his skill evidently improved to the point where he was permitted to draw small, simple plans. Seven such plans can be identified as his because on each he inserted his initials joined in a miniscule monogram, MF.

For himself Flinders drew one chart. This was a chart of Torres Strait, which was intended to accompany his log and was completed well after the journey. This one he signed 'M. Flinders'. His log contained five track charts, the quality of the work improving as the journey progressed.

Bligh entered Torres Strait to the north. Before him lay a labyrinth of waterways threaded among islands, rocks and reefs, which to his knowledge had been traversed only three times previously—in 1606 by the Spanish explorer Luis Baéz de Torres, in 1770 by James Cook in the *Endeavour* and, nineteen years later, by himself in the *Bounty*'s launch. No one in this expedition knew that almost exactly a year before, the survivors of HMS *Pandora* had begun making their way through the strait.

On 3 September they steered through what still appears on maps as Bligh's Entrance. For seventeen days the ships edged forward, anchoring at night, often with the ominous sound of breaking surf around them, and at dawn sending out the boats to search for passageways to the west for the ships to follow. In what appeared to be a safe channel, sudden hazards could force the vessels back. It was slow, arduous work, Bligh often conning his ship himself from the masthead.

On the third day the whaleboat and cutter were sounding a few miles ahead of the ships. At mid-morning the whaleboat was heading back to report what appeared to be a navigable passage. The cutter, with Lieutenant Tobin, a midshipman and seven crew, had remained behind when they sighted four large sailing canoes, in Flinders's words, 'about fifty feet in length, . . . [apparently] hollowed out of a single tree . . . and . . . fitted with an outrigger on each side . . .'[12] On the lead canoe there rested a kind of platform on which stood a palm thatch shelter. As they approached, Tobin tried to signal the whaleboat to return, but it was nearing the ships and his signal went unanswered. Tobin and his men loaded their muskets. The lead canoe was now in the cutter's wake, and its black, naked people were waving for the Europeans to stop.

Another canoe, with fifteen paddlers and raised sail, was rapidly closing in, the men making signs for the cutter to stop. Tobin kept on course. Then, with the lead canoe paddling a few yards away across the bows of the cutter, one of its men, with what appeared to be friendly gestures, held out a green coconut. Tobin imitated the gestures but, wary of so many men, made signs for them to go to the ship while his crew continued pulling. At that, a warrior sitting on top of the thatch shelter spoke to the others, and immediately bows and arrows were handed from inside the shelter. Two men had fitted their arrows and were taking aim as the rest were swiftly stringing their bows. Tobin ordered his men to fire. The islanders fell flat into the bottom of the canoe. As soon as the smoke had cleared a little, the coxswain fired at the man on the shelter. He fell. The canoe dropped behind the cutter, but most of its men bobbed up again, apparently unhurt, and with the three other canoes gathering speed, all four surged after the boat, apparently to cut it off from the ships.

The musket fire was heard on board the *Providence*. Bligh instantly ordered the pinnace, well-manned and armed, to reach the cutter. As it approached, the warriors in the canoes hoisted their sails and steered away for nearby Darnley's Island. Flinders, who had watched from the deck of the *Providence*, later wrote:

> No boats could have been manoeuvred better in working to windward, than were these long canoes by the naked savages. Had the four been

> able to reach the cutter, it is difficult to say, whether the superiority of our arms would have been equal to the great difference of numbers; considering the ferocity of the people, and the skill with which they seemed to manage their weapons.[13]

He was incensed at the action of the coxswain, who 'did not fail to brag about it when he got on board . . . [The] Lieut. did not fire before it was absolutely necessary . . . but to fire after they saw the poor Fellows so frightened, when they had given up the Contest, was not much better than Murder at least it was Cruelty . . .'[14] Flinders conceded, however, that the seamen believed they were being attacked by cannibals.

Bligh was angry and disappointed, believing his hopes of friendly dealings with the islanders had been lost for himself and possibly for others coming after him. This, however, proved not to be so. Over the next few days the ships were approached by canoes, their occupants clapping their hands on their heads, a sign of friendship, as they repeatedly called out a word that the explorers understood to mean iron, and for hatchets and large nails they bartered spears, heavy casuarina clubs, strong, split-bamboo bows and yard-long cane arrows with, as Bligh commented, 'great fairness'. A few were persuaded to board the *Providence*, and Flinders, greatly intrigued, described their appearance at length in his journal—their solid build, woolly hair and beards, nasal septums pierced with rings of bone or shell, earlobes pierced and stretched to accommodate shell and grass ornaments, and nakedness except for cowrie necklaces and pearl oyster shells hung around their necks.

Another amicable exchange took place on the beach of Dalrymple's Island, where the people ran into the water to meet the ships' boats, some climbing into them. 'These people', wrote Flinders, '. . . appeared to be dextrous sailors and formidable warriours; and to be as much at ease in the water, as in their canoes'.[15] For the moment, the passage of the little fleet seemed safe.

Then, on 11 September, there was a complete reversal of events. The two ships were making their way between Dungeness and Warrior Islands, the *Assistant* ahead as usual, her cutter alongside, when a fleet of warrior-filled canoes attacked. Two men in the cutter and one on the deck of the brig were immediately struck by arrows. The brig's crew began firing.

The guns were heard on the *Providence*. The marines rushed for arms and Bligh ordered the quarterdeck guns loaded with round and grapeshot. Now canoes were coming towards the *Providence*. A musket was fired at a large leading craft with some twenty warriors, but at this, all the canoes paddled furiously forward with a great shout. Flinders wrote, 'we fired away upon them as fast as we could load . . . the second great shot that was fired, struck the rear of the large Canoe, and must have raked her nearly fore and aft'.[16] The men leapt into the sea and swam for the other boats 'like so many Porpoises'.

The two ships moved slowly forward. Passing the splintered canoe they saw one man still sitting in it. Flinders watched as other canoes reached the lone warrior, but then left him. There had been no injuries aboard the *Providence*. To Flinders, the encounter was intensely exciting, but sobering. Of their opponents' injuries and possible deaths, he wrote 'they certainly deserved it'.[17]

Shortly before noon on 16 September the vessels anchored in latitude 10°3'S and longitude, by the timekeeper, 142°14'E. Here Bligh landed Lieutenant James Guthrie and a small party on a deserted islet, where in a brief ceremony they took possession of the strait and its islands for King George III. Some coconuts and plum-like fruit were taken, and a knife and other trifles left in exchange.

There was one more sighting of the islanders when three canoes, each with seven or eight men, approached the ships' boats. A musket shot over their heads did not deter them, but on the firing of a swivel gun across their path, they hauled to the south and were not seen again.

A day later, after an anxious, gale-swept night, the ships made their way through a narrow rock- and reef-bound passage until, to the west, neither shoals nor islands could be seen. By noon on 19 September no land was in sight. Flinders wrote:

> Thus was accomplished, in nineteen days, the passage from the Pacific, or Great Ocean, to the Indian Sea . . . Perhaps no space of 3½° in length, presents more dangers than Torres' Strait; but, with caution and perseverance, the captains Bligh and Portlock proved them to be surmountable; and within reasonable time . . .[18]

This was a rare tribute to Bligh, for Flinders had built up considerable resentment against his captain and a lasting conviction that Bligh disliked him. Bligh was not an easily served commander. He was fiery-tempered and could be savagely critical; he was overbearing, entirely lacking in modesty and his recurring illness exacerbated his cranky disposition. Yet he had personally selected or approved his officers, and at the end of the voyage duly recommended his senior midshipmen for promotion to lieutenant. Of Flinders and the other junior midshipmen not yet eligible to take the examination for lieutenancy, he made no mention. Yet when Flinders took his examination in 1791, he was able to present to the board a certificate from Bligh that favourably described his 'diligence, sobriety and obedience to command' and his possession of the skills necessary for an officer.[19] And Flinders fully recognised Bligh's competence. In the treacherous waters of Torres Strait he wrote, 'we trust the Abilities of our Captain, which I believe we may safely rely upon will extricate us from all Difficulties and bring us safe thro' the Strait . . .'[20]

Flinders was not the only person on board to dislike Bligh. The lieutenants also had cause for complaint. The much-abused first lieutenant, Francis Godolphin Bond, son of Bligh's half-sister, wrote to his brother of the captain's unrelenting 'insolence and arrogance' and 'the fury of an ungovernable temper . . .'[21] Nevertheless, after the voyage Bligh and Bond resumed a friendly correspondence.

Some of the discontent during the homeward voyage related to keeping the breadfruit saplings and some 500 other plants watered. Bligh put each man on an allowance of a pint of drinking water per day 'exclusive of his grog', and water used in pea soup and gruel was reduced by more than half. Many suffered desperately from thirst, and one account states that Flinders 'and others would lie on the steps, and lick the drops of the precious liquid from the buckets, as they were conveyed by the Gardener to the Plants'.[22] Despite all efforts, however, plants in over 600 containers perished during the voyage.

Midshipman Flinders was too disciplined to let his feelings show at the time, but some thirteen years later his dislike of Bligh surfaced in letters to Sir Joseph Banks. Bligh, he wrote, had been prejudiced against him, which he felt would rob him of credit for any good work if he again served under his former captain.

The ships steered for the Dutch settlement of Kupang on Timor, which Bligh had reached three years before in the *Bounty*'s launch. Now a salute of friendly guns greeted his little squadron. Flinders wrote, 'This town as we approached it had more the appearance of an Indian Village than an European Settlement and but for the Dutch fort and Colours . . . it would scarcely have been taken for one'.[23]

Ashore the expedition received the shocking news of the sinking of HMS *Pandora*, whose 99 survivors had reached Kupang a year before, going on from there on a Dutch vessel. On his chart of Torres Strait Flinders would later add in red ink the track of the unfortunate *Pandora*.

Bligh's ships remained at Kupang for eight days, taking on wood, water and 92 additional pots of plants. Provisions were scarce owing to drought and the quantities taken by the *Pandora* survivors. Bligh was hospitably received, but the intense heat and exposure to disease took their toll. William Terry, quartermaster, wounded in Torres Strait, died painfully; others came down with dysentery and fever, probably malaria, two of them eventually dying. Bligh himself was tormented by his blinding headaches and intermittent fever.

From Kupang the two ships crossed the Indian Ocean, rounded the Cape of Good Hope and stopped briefly at the island of St Helena. On 17 December the anchors splashed down in Kingstown Bay at the West Indian island of St Vincent. A share of the plants was delivered to an enthusiastically welcoming community, but another crewman was lost when a sailor fell overboard and drowned.

The ships arrived in Jamaica on 4 February. Bligh now followed naval procedure at the end of exploration journeys and confiscated the officers' and midshipmen's journals. Flinders was upset: '. . . as I had not another Book to proceed with, a Stop was totally put to my writing any more Account of the Voyage . . .' When, six months later, the ship left the West Indies and the books were temporarily returned, he had to reconstruct his record from 'Memory and the Ships Log Book', adding tartly, '(which I cannot say much for the Accuracy of) . . .'[24] It angered him not to be able to complete as precisely as he wished the account of his first long journey.

The plants were discharged at Jamaica's Port Morant and other West Indian ports. At Jamaica James Wiles accepted the offer of a job as superintendent of the government's botanical gardens. Christopher Smith remained on board to bring to the gardens at Kew a collection of 1283 plants.

In the midst of this activity the packet *Cumberland* arrived with news: England was at war with revolutionary France. The explosive violence of the French Revolution and French military operations in neighbouring territory, together with inflammatory expansionist propaganda, had moved Britain into preparing for hostilities. On 1 February 1793 the National Convention in Paris declared war on Britain and Holland. A few days later Britain declared war on France.

Bligh's ships were assigned to the area's British naval command, and began several months of wartime duty, escorting convoys and capturing French vessels. Flinders was disrated to Able Seaman. Such downrating, usually temporary, was a common naval practice. Pay and messing with other midshipmen in the gun room remained unchanged, the main disadvantage being less prize money, at a time when prizes were being taken.[25] Flinders may also have been removed from navigational duties, which were important to him. The excitement of his first experience of war at sea was shadowed by disappointment.

Expected naval reinforcements arrived and early in June 1793 Bligh's ships were directed to return to England. A week later they sailed in convoy and on 7 August the *Providence* moored at Deptford, two years and five days from the date of her departure. A few weeks later Bligh delivered to the Admiralty all logs and journals together with his charts. On 12 September 1793 Matthew's father wrote in his diary:

> By the Mercy and Divine Providence of God—my Son hath safe returned from his Long & Perilous Voyage. [C]ompleating it in little more than 2 Years... —his Captain latterly was not on the best terms with him, which was an unpleasant Circumstance... it is not my intention to enter into the particulars of the Voyage.[26]

Flinders never explained why Bligh disliked him. There were undoubtedly minor transgressions, but there is no evidence of anything that would have been remarkable in a group of young sailors. Why Bligh should resent this particular midshipman—if indeed he did—remains an unanswered question.

Flinders had discovered his intense interest in the scientific aspects of navigation and exploration. Bligh's expedition was commercial in purpose, but was also heavily weighted in favour of science, for instructions from the Royal Society covered many parts of the undertaking. The surveying, the botanists' careful study and record-keeping and the astute observations of Bligh himself deeply impressed Flinders.

Flinders was now nineteen years old and five feet seven inches tall, with a slim, wiry body and a light, buoyant step. He was dark-haired, his face pale and thin, the features neatly chiselled, with a slightly aquiline nose and somewhat jutting chin, his mouth rather small and very firm, his eyes dark, bright and steady. There was an alertness about him, his movements were quick and sure, and he gave the impression of possessing deep springs of energy. Already he had formed an almost rigid concept of duty and honour, from which he would only rarely deviate, and a stubborn, unforgiving dedication to the goals he was beginning to set for himself.

3 War

By 1793 the excesses of the French Revolution had shaken all of Europe. France was wracked by massacres and imprisonments, by provincial rebellions, by the execution of the king and queen. Even more alarming was French aggression outside its borders. French troops invaded the Austrian Netherlands, today's Belgium. Savoy, Nice and the papal fief of Avignon were annexed. Territorial aggrandisement was rationalised by propaganda decrees issued by the National Assembly as part of a great crusade pledged to sweep aside existing social and political systems. To the legitimate governments of Europe, revolutionary France had become a devastating threat to all established societies.

At war with France, Britain joined a coalition of European powers, notably Austria and Prussia, which for diverse reasons were already fighting the new republic. Within the British cabinet, however, the strategic prosecution of the war became a matter of sometimes bitter dissension, mainly between those who advocated a large-scale continental campaign and those who supported a trade and colonial war that would carry the conflict away from Europe. Both strategies were seriously handicapped by the country's lack of preparation for hostilities. Early British offensives were minor, with little effect beyond local harassment.

Despite administrative inertia and corruption, the Royal Navy had nevertheless been undergoing certain valuable reforms in battle tactics and signalling, and fighting ships were under construction. By 1793 Britain had 175 large ships-of-the-line[1] and many hundreds of smaller vessels. From that point some £30 million would be spent each year for a naval force that would expand almost ninefold by 1815. Its commitments were global, from the Caribbean Sea to the fledgling colony in Australia. In Europe its role was to blockade enemy coasts and to guard island Britain. The Channel Fleet, under Admiral Lord Howe, patrolled the sea between England and the continent, forming Britain's principal line of home defence.

Thus in August 1793 the men of Bligh's expedition came ashore to find their home ports alive with wartime activity, supplies and equipment arriving at the dockyards, ships undergoing repair and refitting, new vessels taking shape on the stocks, others putting to sea. Before sailing up the Thames to Deptford the *Providence* anchored for a day in the offshore waters of the Downs. Flinders took the opportunity to write a letter to Captain Pasley, then at Plymouth. Pasley promptly replied:

> *Bellerophon*
> Augt 7th 1793
>
> Dear Flinders,
>
> I am favoured with your very acceptable letter from the Downs, and I believe all yours from the different places you wrote me . . . I do not know what are your plans now you are returned back to England. I expect to sail in a day or two to join my Lord Howe on board the *Bellerophon*. I shall receive you with pleasure after so long an absence. You will no doubt wish to see your friends [and] pay them a short visit and return to join me, by that time I shall possibly be returned into Port . . .[2]

A chance to serve with Captain Pasley again, to win prize money, promotion and glory was a thrilling prospect. Flinders rejoined the *Bellerophon* on 7 September as an able seaman and on 1 October appeared on her books as a midshipman. Despite the noisy, crowded, extremely uncomfortable conditions and the long, often erratic hours kept by a young officer on a ship of war, Flinders immediately began writing a journal and eventually filled 40 foolscap pages. Four days after joining the ship, he wrote, no doubt with pride, 'Wednesday, 11th (September 1793) a.m. Hoisted a broad pennant by order of Lord Howe, Capt. Pasley being appointed a commodore of the fleet'.[3]

Very shortly after Flinders returned with the *Providence* he apparently met Joseph Banks. Flinders carried a letter from James Wiles asking Banks, who handled such financial details for the voyage, to entrust an unpaid part of Wiles's salary to the bearer, 'a messmate and most intimate Acquaintance of mine . . . who will deliver it safe into my father's hands'.[4] The letter survives, and a notation in Banks's hand reads, 'Delivered by a Mr. Flinders, who is on board the *Bellerophon*, C. Pasley, Augt. 15 93'. The date suggests a meeting in London, just before Banks and his household undertook their annual migration to his country estates, which usually happened in mid-August. While Flinders had not yet actually transferred to the *Bellerophon*, Banks, at least, seems to have regarded this as an accomplished fact. Flinders may have met Banks previously at some point during the preparations for the *Providence*'s voyage. Certainly he had heard much about the great patron of botany from Smith and Wiles.

In late September Matthew was on leave and in Donington with souvenirs to show and the account of a thrilling journey to tell. The English autumn was cold, and he arrived feverish but recovered quickly. To Matthew the village, the house—even his father—probably seemed smaller and greyer than he remembered. His sister Elizabeth, Ann Chappelle and Mary Franklin were young women in long, high-waisted dresses and beribboned poke bonnets. Only a month before, Susanna, fourteen, friendly, clever and fond of writing, had been boarded at the home of her father's brother, to be taught by her aunt. Samuel was still a lively small boy who was learning to dance, but John, a little older, rudely behaved and increasingly difficult, was clearly of serious concern to his parents. There were also two little half-sisters, and friends and relatives who flocked to see the young sailor. At about this time, however, word arrived that Matthew's cousin John Flinders, finally a lieutenant, had died of fever in the West Indies aboard HMS *Hannibal*. He was 26 years old.

Matthew Flinders now pursued a second errand involving James Wiles. On 21 October 1793 he presented himself at Revesby Abbey, the manorial country seat of Sir Joseph Banks, some 25 miles north of Donington, probably seeing for the first time the impressive house amid trees and wide lawns. On leaving the *Providence* at Jamaica, James

Wiles had been in debt to Flinders for a loan of £30, and it was through Sir Joseph Banks that Flinders was reimbursed.

The forebears of Joseph Banks were of yeoman stock, the first Joseph Banks, an attorney, moving from Nottinghamshire to establish his family in Lincolnshire by buying several country estates, including Revesby Abbey. Son followed father in what became a family tradition of entering politics as local members of parliament, and of shrewdly investing in farm properties and other businesses. Profitable marriages added to the wealth and holdings of the family, and London residences and cultural interests became part of their lives.

The fourth Joseph Banks was born in London in 1743, an only son and the heir to the considerable Banks fortune. Young Joseph made little academic progress either at Harrow or at Eton. A big strong lad, good-natured and popular, he was wholly occupied with sports and the brawling, rough and tumble life of an 18th century boys' school. His erratic spelling and almost non-existent punctuation remained with him all his life.

The story is that one summer evening, returning from a swim in the river, he noticed the flowers growing alongside the path. Taken by their beauty, he decided that he would learn about plants. This seemingly unlikely interest was as complete as it was sudden. Hunting indefatigably not only for plants but also for insects, shells and fossils, he amassed large collections and later organised a small group of students to join him in the serious study of natural history.

Banks's father died in 1761 and, on coming of age three years later, Joseph inherited some 9000–10 000 valuable acres. With an income of about £6000 a year he was among the 400 wealthiest men in England. Leaving Oxford, he devoted himself to social activities, the administration of his estate and study with the day's leading scientists. In 1766, at the age of 23, he was nominated to the prestigious Royal Society and in the same month set off on a scientific excursion to Newfoundland and Labrador. Two years later, he joined the Society-sponsored expedition to the Pacific, and as the group's naturalist, became part of Cook's voyage around the world.

In 1793 Banks was 50 years old. He had been president of the Royal Society for fifteen years and was an active member of many other learned organisations and scientific bodies, some connected with government.

He was a friend and scientific adviser of the king, George III, and corresponded with some of Europe's most eminent scholars. In London his house in Soho Square was the meeting place of scientists, explorers, foreign savants and a great variety of others whom Banks found interesting. The collections in his library and herbarium were outstanding. His access to information was encyclopaedic. Although Banks's greatest personal interest was always botany, he extended his intellectual domain to all aspects of natural history.

He had also become the particular patron of distant Australia, an association that began with his journey up the continent's east coast with Cook in 1770. The connection took further shape in 1779 when, as the principal authority on the far-off country, he advocated before a committee of the House of Commons the establishment of a convict colony at Botany Bay.

The expansion of science into the natural world was a powerful intellectual force in the 18th century, and the navy had the facilities to carry these investigations beyond Europe. Over the years Banks established firm relationships with the men who directed naval policies and operations. New South Wales was a virtually untouched storehouse of some extraordinary natural phenomena, over which Banks extended a protective and proprietory wing, which no one ever contested. His involvement never lost its emphasis on scientific investigation, but his authority on things Australian widened into the colony's social and administrative life as well.

The completion of the second breadfruit voyage was, for Banks, the culmination of five years of careful planning and political manoeuvring, and from Revesby Abbey he wrote letters complimenting Bligh for his achievement and recommending Portlock for promotion. As a member of the expedition, Matthew Flinders would have been well received.

On 22 October Flinders left Donington to return to his ship. Less than a month later Pasley's squadron joined the main group at sea under the command of Admiral Lord Richard Howe. Flinders's journal became a long, detailed account of naval warfare, a relatively objective effort by a writer who had just turned twenty.

> Monday, November 18th. Saw nine or ten sail, seeming large ships, standing towards us. The admiral made the *Russell* and *Defence* signals

> to chase, also the *Audacious*; and soon after ours . . . At 9 the Admiral made the sign for the strange fleet being an enemy . . . At 10 the signal to engage . . . We were now the headmost line of battle ship and gaining fast upon the enemy; but the main part of our fleet seemed rather to drop from them.[5]

A few shots were exchanged, but darkness came on with heavy rain and thick haze, and the French ships vanished into the gloom.

In December 1793 the *Bellerophon* returned for the winter to the naval anchorage at Spithead, in the strait between the Isle of Wight and the English mainland. The ship's refit began: repairs, replacements, sides and stern repainted. Flinders recorded a cold winter, squally, with sleet and snow in January.

In April 1794 Captain William Pasley was promoted to rear-admiral, and Flinders, still with him on the *Bellerophon*, became an aide-de-camp.

Events began to build up to a major naval battle, the first of the war, between the Channel Fleet under Admiral Lord Howe and the French fleet stationed at Brest under Admiral Louis Villaret de Joyeuse. Richard Howe, at 68, was nearing the end of a long and successful naval career. Villaret de Joyeuse was one of the better officers to have survived the decimations of the French Revolution, and his task now was of extreme importance to the country. France was suffering from food shortages amounting to near-famine, for in addition to the disruptions of foreign war and domestic upheavals, the harvests had failed. Thus a convoy of 120 merchant vessels with grain from America was awaited with extreme anxiety. Destroying it, or the French naval squadrons that would attempt to meet and guard it into port, would be a major success for the British.

On 2 May the Channel Fleet put to sea. Twenty-nine large ships-of-the-line and fifteen frigates spread their great white sails and in a magnificent procession of towering, wind-filled canvas and flying pennants, surrounded by scores of lesser craft, passed out of Spithead. On the 16th the French fleet sailed from the port of Brest with 26 ships-of-the-line and numerous smaller vessels. Howe's patrols on the Atlantic yielded no sighting of the convoy and, leaving nine warships to continue the ocean watch, Howe brought his battle fleet back to the coast, to discover that the enemy's ships had left Brest. Howe went in pursuit.

On the 28th sails came into view, and each side was able to confirm that it was looking at the enemy. The wind was strong with gusting rain, and heavy swells rolled across the ocean. In a flurry of flying signals whipping in the wind, Howe ordered his ships to chase, and when the long, close line of the enemy's sails began to tack away from possible action, he signalled an attack. In its own concerted din of bellowing voices, running feet and beating drums, with men pouring onto the decks and into the rigging, each ship prepared to attack, the *Bellerophon* among them.

Galley fires were doused, sand flung across the decks, nettings raised, bulkheads brought down. Gun ports were flung open and the cannon unlashed and, with heavy rumbling, run out, while powder and cartridges arrived clutched in the arms of pale, terrified youngsters from the magazines below, and men shoved shot, tubs of sand and water, and the long, slow-burning matches into place beside the cannons. On the quarterdeck in a milling crowd of seamen, officers and marines stood Pasley, a solid figure in blue and white. Around him were his aides-de-camp, among them Flinders, white-faced with excitement.

Cleaving through the rough sea, the fast-sailing *Bellerophon* came first within striking distance and opened fire at a large frigate. The frigate rapidly made sail and went to windward, and the *Bellerophon* found itself confronted with an enormous black hull and towering pyramid of sail, the three-decker *Révolutionnaire*, 110 guns and 1000 men, 'on whom', Flinders wrote, 'we immediately pointed our guns. In a few minutes she returned it with great spirit, our distance from her being something more than a mile'.[6] Flashes across the water multiplied, strangling black smoke surged across the decks and the deafening roar of guns shook the air itself. Cannon balls crashed into the *Bellerophon*. The maincap was hit and the main topsail had to be dragged in. A sheet block suddenly exploded into dagger-like splinters. The sky bloomed through black-edged holes in the great white curves overhead. Amid the uproar carpenters were battling with knives and axes to clear the decks of a nightmare of collapsed canvas and tangled, broken spars and rigging.

Lord Howe signalled other ships to assist the *Bellerophon* and, as the evening lengthened, more of the British fleet came up. The *Bellerophon* was now so battered she could barely respond to command. Lord Howe signalled the ship to retire into his wake, and other ships fended off a determined attacker as *Bellerophon*'s company flung themselves into bringing a manageable ship out of the terrible shambles on her decks. In the long, gentle twilight of the late spring night, firing continued. The *Révolutionnaire* became a floating wreck and was towed to a French port the next day. The English *Audacious*, 74 guns, damaged beyond ability to fight, limped home. Darkness spilled over sky and sea, lanterns were lit and, carrying their pinpoints of light, both fleets rested on the ocean.

At daybreak the enemy's line was sighted about two nautical miles away. Howe signalled to form the line of battle and subsequently to penetrate the enemy line and cut off the rearmost ships. After some delay, the British ships moved into point-blank range, with enemy shot falling thickly about them. In return the British ships 'began a severe fire, giving it to each ship as we passed'.[7] The *Bellerophon* then sailed between the second and third ships at the end of the French line, firing and receiving fire amid the crashing of timber and the cries of men. One of the French ships lost its fore and maintop masts as they groaned, cracked explosively and fell over the side, each dragging down a twisted mass of timber, line and men; 'she was silenced for a while but it was only till we had passed her',[8] Flinders wrote.

Bellerophon's forward rigging was entirely cut to pieces, and in the high wind the wildly flapping, useless foresail was frenziedly cut away as the ship hove to, again to make repairs. At five-thirty, with some of the rigging restored and a new foresail bent, the *Bellerophon* rejoined Howe's group. Around them Flinders saw the disabled vessels of both navies lying to, struggling in the heavy sea to repair their damage.

The next day fog lay thick and soft upon the sea. The French had vanished. Of the British ships, the *Bellerophon*'s lookout could see only four grey shadows suspended in nothingness. On the *Bellerophon*, 'People employed repairing Sails, rigging etc. with all Expedition'.[9] Through the day and the next morning the fog held, thinning a little from time to time so the closest British ships, 'none of them more than a Cable's length from us', became visible, and eventually '30 Sail of our own Ships'.[10]

In the afternoon of 1 June it began to clear, and the long French battle line was sighted 'to leeward 8 or 9 Miles distant',[11] but by sunset it had still not been possible to bring on a general action, and another night was spent waiting on the sea. At dawn, which by naval reckoning was still the first of June, the sky was cloudy but the breezes fresh. The French were not in sight. Making more sail, the British line came together, steering northwest, and when, just before six o'clock, the French ships were sighted, Howe, with flags streaming in the wind, signalled to attack on a diagonal course from the windward side, to break through the enemy's centre and attack individual ships from the leeward.

Second in the line of the British van, and just two cables' length from her immediate opponent, the *Bellerophon* opened fire shortly after eight o'clock and in passing through her designated gap between enemy ships went so close to the French three-decker *Eole* that the curved sides of the two ships almost touched, each thunderously pouring broadsides into the other amid thickening curtains of black smoke and choking powder fumes. According to one story, when the quarterdeck gun crews were called off to trim sails, Flinders seized a lighted match and fired the primed guns into the enemy's stern. Whatever the truth of this, Flinders burned with excitement and passion as in the turmoil he raced to do Pasley's bidding.

The hot, fierce fighting became general, duels breaking out throughout the fleets. Continuous gunfire from the *Eole* and the nearby *Trajan* pounded the *Bellerophon*. The ship's rigging dissolved into shreds, spars shattered and tumbled down in jagged sections that burst into lethal splinters, the boats were crushed, and men dropped, smashed to the deck, speared by timber fragments, crumpled in reddening heaps. Just before eleven o'clock an 18-pound shot crashed through the quarterdeck barricading and struck Pasley, taking off his leg. A horrified Flinders watched as, streaming blood, he was carried below to the hellish cavern of the surgeon's cockpit. Captain William Hope instantly took command and, with the numbness of shock, Flinders mechanically sprang back into duty.

The ferocious battling continued, ships firing changeably when, in the constant manoeuvring, their guns could be brought to bear on some foe. Demasted ships on both sides continued firing on any opponent that came near them. *Bellerophon*'s fore and main topmasts were gone, almost every main shroud was cut through and torn sails sagged against the main and foremasts. Captain Hope signalled for assistance, and the *Bellerophon* drew off to make what repairs it could. The firing became sporadic. Shortly after one o'clock it ceased almost entirely. The best-conditioned French ships and a few of the disabled moved off, sinking into the horizon, the rest of the severely damaged left behind. '. . . never I believe was such a scene of ruin and devastation seen before . . . eleven ships now laying without a mast standing; several of the French ships that were dismasted continued with invincible obstinacy to fire on our ships',[12] commented Henry Waterhouse, the *Bellerphon*'s first lieutenant. Flinders wrote:

> We were now employed knotting, splicing, repairing, etc., the rigging, cutting away the wrecks of the fore and main topmasts, and securing the lower masts. Fortunately no accident happened with the powder, or with guns bursting. We had but three men killed outright (a fourth died of his wounds very soon after) and about 30 men wounded, amongst whom five lost their limbs, and the other leg of one man was so much shattered as to be taken off some time later. Our brave Admiral was unfortunately in the list . . . [13]

Twelve French ships had surrendered, although one sank within hours, taking some 600 men with her, and five later escaped to rejoin Villaret de Joyeuse, who, with the remainder of his command, retreated with no further challenge into Brest. The exhausted Howe withdrew his fleet towards home. He had fought the first naval battle of the war with an innovative tactical plan, repeatedly piercing the enemy line from windward and bringing on a fierce melee of individual ships, and he had fashioned a victory for the navy, the island nation's pride and bulwark of safety.

All England was jubilant. 'Victory over the French Fleet—June 1, 1794',[14] Matthew's father wrote in his diary. It was 'the glorious First of June'. Meanwhile, the provision ships from America that Villaret de

Joyeuse had fought to protect came through untouched in what for France was an important strategic success.

Twelve days later the Channel Fleet and its prizes, six captured ships, anchored triumphantly at Spithead, many still bearing the scars of battle. Portsmouth celebrated, the town illuminated by evening, streets and pubs alive until late, port women swarming onto the ships. Two weeks later the king arrived. The incredible thunder of combined 21-gun salutes roared through the fleet, and Flinders watched as a colourful procession of elegant barges came across the harbour, a stream of fluttering flags and pennants, of sweeps flashing as they smartly cut the water—Lord Howe's barge, the barges of the Admiralty, of admirals and captains and, with the Royal Standard of Great Britain flying at the stem, the royal barge bearing the King and Queen and their family. Cheers broke from the ships as they passed on to the *Queen Charlotte* where in a glittering levee, the King awarded Howe a diamond-studded sword, and the crowd of officers received peerages, baronetcies, gold medals and promotions.

As the thrill of victory subsided, Flinders soberly assessed his future. It was not promising. Without the required six years of sea duty, he was not eligible for promotion to lieutenant, and a midshipman's prize money of £10 would not go far. More important, the battle had in effect taken his patron from him, for Sir Thomas Pasley would probably never again walk the deck of a fighting ship, and Flinders, with no other connections, needed an active war commander to provide the kind of opportunities and recognition that allowed a young officer to rise. Probably the depressing memory of his cousin John Flinders, so many years a midshipman, came flooding back.

4
The Colony of New South Wales

Suddenly there was an intriguing new possibility. Preparations were under way for the departure for New South Wales of Captain John Hunter, who a few months earlier had become governor-designate—Captain-General and Governor-in-Chief—of the distant British colony. He was to assume the authority held by officers of the New South Wales Corps as acting governors since the departure of Arthur Phillip in December 1792.

Hunter had accompanied Phillip in founding the colony, but returned to England in 1792 after the loss of the *Sirius* on Norfolk Island. He had taken part in the First of June battle, and three weeks later received official instructions for his new position. Late in 1793 the Navy Board had purchased two ships, the *Reliance*, a merchant vessel of 394 tons burden and 90 feet in length, and the *New Brunswick*, renamed the *Supply*, 382 tons and American-built of black birch, for the voyage to the colony and for service there. For months the ships had been undergoing unhurried surveys and refitting at the Deptford and Woolwich shipyards, and in March 1794 were finally commissioned. Lieutenant William Kent received command of the *Supply*. Command of the *Reliance* went to Nathaniel Portlock.

For reasons not now known, Portlock later declined to undertake the voyage. The appointment as second captain, Hunter being the first, then went to Henry Waterhouse, first lieutenant of the *Bellerophon*. It was probably Waterhouse who told his young shipmate Matthew Flinders of the possibility of going to New South Wales, and on 10 August Flinders was appointed to the *Reliance* as senior master's mate. Later he wrote that he was 'led by his passion for exploring new countries, to embrace the opportunity of going out upon a station, which of all others, presented the most ample field for his favourite pursuit.'[1]

Dreams of adventure and achievement, the prospect of patronage from Hunter—all of this must have come together as he looked up at the dark hull and white masts and spars of HMS *Reliance*.

Flinders received three weeks' leave and travelled home to Donington. He was now not only a man who had seen some of the farthest reaches of the world, but also a hero of the Glorious First of June, and was about to sail on yet another voyage to a distant place that his friends and family could barely imagine. 'We had not much of his Company',[2] his father observed. The country roads to and from the towns and villages around Donington were evidently busy as Matthew joined in the visiting back and forth of the crowd of young friends and relations.

Life in the Flinders household at Donington had not stood still. Elizabeth, closest to Matthew in age and his favourite sister, was nineteen and sometimes at odds with her stepmother, as at times was Susanna. John, sulky, rebellious and a constant worry, was home after two years at a boarding school in Deeping, where he had been sent to separate him from undesirable friends. At eleven, however, Matthew's youngest brother, Samuel, was clearly taken with the general acclaim and enthusiasm for the Royal Navy, probably regarding Matthew with both envy and admiration.

Their father wrote in his diary that Matthew was going 'on another long Voyage—the Station will be for 4 or 5 years—wch. is a long time—but he thinks he has a better Chance of Promotion . . .' He was also faced with the loss of another son to the sea:

> My son Samuel having for some time expressed a desire for the sea—and Mattw. wishing to take him & Capt W- being consulted & willing to take him also, I have advanced £30 to Matthew to Fit him out and he is gone with him & is to go this Voyage—Pray Heaven bless them both . . . he is very young (12 in Nov.) but if we had missed this opportunity several years must have passed—before so good an opportunity might again occur, & Mattw. has often lamented he did not go sooner as he thinks he should now have been promoted to a Lieutenancy . . .[3]

Flinders went aboard the *Reliance* at the Deptford dockyard on 3 September 1794, and Samuel shortly joined him as a 'volunteer', earning £6 a year. The normal activity of a ship preparing for sea was heightened by the prospect of the exceptionally long voyage and unusual destination that lay ahead. The refitting continued at Spithead. By the end of 1794 the *Reliance* and the *Supply* were in Plymouth Sound, part of a vast assembly of merchant vessels and naval ships waiting to be escorted beyond the range of possible French attack by Lord Howe's warships. The winter was unusually severe. The Thames froze over, snow mantled London's rooftops and the dome of St Paul's, while at Plymouth the waiting ships rocked ceaselessly in rain and bitter cold. In the chill, damp confines of the ship, Matthew wrote sentimentally of 'the comforts of a Spilsby fire side, the agreeable chat and lively jest . . .'[4]

On 16 February 1795 the huge fleet finally left port, a magnificent mass of over 500 sail moving westward. Two days later Howe's Channel Fleet returned to stations off the French coast, and the convoy broke up, ships and groups of ships heading for their separate destinations like white birds dispersing over the ocean.

Hunter laid his course for Tenerife and Rio de Janeiro, and then across the southern Atlantic and Indian Oceans directly to New South Wales. He was avoiding the usual stop at the Cape of Good Hope, concerned that French successes in the Netherlands could mean their sudden seizure of the Dutch-held Cape. A French republican army had, in fact, just entered Amsterdam.

The stop at Tenerife was brief. Flinders seized the opportunity to send letters home, in one letter addressing the 'Misses [Ann] Chappelle and M. [Mary] Franklin' as 'My charming sisters'. He thanked 'Miss Chappelle' for her kind letter and reproved his 'dear Mary' for failing to write him before he left England, 'but perhaps we sailed but a day before it might arrive'. He urged everyone to direct 'as many sheets of paper to me as your pen can run over . . . the greater quantity I hope to receive . . . the greater will be my happiness'. Of his young brother he wrote fondly, if somewhat paternally:

> My little Samuel on board the *Reliance* stood the gales of wind exceedingly well; he is in high spirits, and has lost no part of that enterprising

> spirit which brought him on board with me. I hope he'll make a good sailor, a good officer, and a good man, which last is the groundwork of the other two, and the foundation of all happiness.

England, in contrast to the barren, volcanic peaks of the Canaries, was a rich and fruitful country, he said, but he could not resist a teasing comment on the islands' 'charming climate . . . while you in England with your double fortified great coats can scarcely keep out the cold, we with the slightest covering are almost too warm . . .'[5] The letters were shared and sometimes joint replies sent by the young girls and others of the group.

Early in May the ships entered Rio de Janeiro's Guanabara Bay. Brazil was a colony of Portugal, traditionally an ally of Britain, but Hunter felt the chill of ambiguous loyalties. Attempting to call upon the viceroy, he was put off for six days, finally being received at seven o'clock in the evening. Nevertheless, the ships spent three weeks taking on water, fresh provisions and, at high prices, a few barrels of salted pork for Sydney.

Hunter, a very capable hydrographer himself, seems to have taken time during the voyage to instruct his younger officers in charting techniques, and Flinders seized every opportunity to improve his skills. From the *Reliance* he used a sextant and timekeeper to observe locations on the Canary and Cape Verde Islands and at Cape Frio in Brazil. At Rio de Janeiro he received permission to land on little Ilha das Enxadas in the middle of the bay, and at the summit carried out a series of eleven altitudes with the artificial horizon for latitude, and fifteen sets of lunar distances for longitude. His observed position was 22°53'37"S latitude, 42°55'23"W longitude, his latitude in error 0.6 miles and his longitude about 15 miles. It was an acceptable result for an inexperienced navigator.

By the 1790s the availability and popularity of the marine chronometer—or timekeeper—for observing longitude was such that they were carried by most captains, frequently as a personal possession. Obtaining a clock reading of Greenwich time and comparing it to the time at sea at the same moment allowed the navigator to convert the difference into degrees of longitude east or west of the Greenwich meridian.

Obtaining Greenwich time by the method of lunar distances was by contrast a long and involved process. It was based on the premise that the moon, moving across a starry sky or in company with the sun, could be used as a clock, and required measuring the angular distance between the moon and the sun or one of several selected stars observed by the navigator. The time of the observation was noted and mathematical procedures were applied to clear the angles of the effects of refraction caused by the object's nearness to the horizon, and parallax, an apparent displacement owing to the object's being observed from the surface, not from the centre of the earth. The navigator then consulted tables in the *Naval Almanac*, which provided the time in Greenwich when the same measurement would have occurred, and the difference between that time and local time gave the ship's position in longitude. The method was tedious and allowed the possibility of mistakes in its several stages. Nevertheless, it was commonly used, whether or not the vessel was equipped with a chronometer, and as that valuable item was not readily exposed to unnecessary risk, the cheaper equipment for obtaining lunar distances, a sextant and a set of lunar distance tables, was often provided for unpredictable situations or inexperienced navigators working without supervision.

The *Reliance*'s second lieutenant, Nicholas Johnson, left the ship at Rio. Waterhouse noted, 'A Mr. Flinders is appointed our 2nd Lieut. in the room of the one left at Rio de Janeiro'.[6] Flinders was thus promoted to a temporary and acting position, not yet having passed his examination for that rank, and Waterhouse confirmed his position as acting lieutenant of the *Reliance* six months later, when he had completed the required six years of service at sea. Flinders had been promoted in preference to the master, Henry Moore, who evidently had also not passed the examination for lieutenant. Despite the rank of lieutenant, Flinders's position remained that of Moore's senior master's mate.

Four months later their father in Donington noted the arrival of letters from Matthew and 'my little Saml', sent from Rio.

The fourteen-week passage to Sydney was rough but without serious incident. In the crowded confines of the ship, the men quickly came to know each other, and in general it was a congenial company. At its periphery stood the new governor, John Hunter, a man of 57 with a strong, open, weathered face framed in fine white hair. He spoke with a Scots brogue and a directness that matched the look he gave those he addressed, and although first and foremost a sailor, he was also a very capable maritime surveyor, a keen natural historian and an accomplished artist. The son of a merchant ship captain, he had grown up in Leith, the port of Edinburgh, and at seventeen joined the Navy. In 1793 Hunter had written, largely illustrated and published the journal of his earlier experiences at Port Jackson and Norfolk Island. A former commander, Sir Roger Curtis, had supported his appointment as governor of New South Wales, with assurances of Hunter's incorruptible integrity, his sound judgement, zeal and knowledge of the new country. Hunter was a solid and dedicated officer, a man sincerely interested in the southern continent, but whose ability to govern a strange and difficult colony was yet to be tested.

Flinders's promotion at Rio created some tension between him and his immediate superior, the master, Henry Moore. Moore was an experienced naval seaman, very capably handling the multiple responsibilities of his position. His working relationship with his mate was necessarily close, and that his junior, an ambitious 21-year-old, should have received a commission in preference to himself was disturbing. There is no mention of open antagonism between the two, but years later Flinders's friend Christopher Smith wrote to him of meeting Moore in Amboina, now Ambon, in the Moluccas, today's Maleku: 'I plainly saw that you were not a favourite of his . . .'[7] Evidently Flinders reciprocated Moore's dislike. Writing to George Bass some years later he referred to the 'rank pride' of an 'acquaintance' he cryptically identified as Moore.

Smith had also noted disapprovingly that Moore was 'a violent Republican'. Governor John Hunter was well aware of Moore's political views. The master, he wrote to the Navy Board, 'affected to be a great Democrat', but was 'perfectly adapted' to service in the faraway colony.[8] It would seem that in Hunter's opinion, such people could serve their country best away from Britain, a view perhaps heightened by wartime concerns.

There was on board another advocate of serious political reform. This was Daniel Paine, a young man travelling as a supernumerary to Sydney to take up an appointment as the colony's boat builder. In May 1794 Hunter had written to Under Secretary John King of the Home

Office: 'I have found a clever young man from Deptford Yard to fill the office of boatbuilder, etc., at Port Jackson...'[9] Paine, 25, had worked at the yard from the age of fifteen, and now was moved by 'Curiosity and a desire to see Foreign Climes...'[10] He was a non-conformist who attended Congregational and Baptist churches and had some radical political leanings as well. In Henry Moore he found someone of similar views, and their conversations no doubt centred on questions of improving society and government, and the political action necessary to accomplish this. Flinders stayed well away from these discussions. Aside from inevitably being aware of Moore's personal resentment, Flinders avoided criticism of the establishment. He had other interests, and the opportunities he sought lay in his own dedicated service and with the recognition and approbation of his superiors. He found a more interesting friend in John Shortland, the first lieutenant, who had sailed to New South Wales with the First Fleet.

Another passenger on the *Reliance* was the Australian Aborigine Bennelong, an Eora man who in 1792 had been taken to England by Captain Phillip, together with a youth, Yemmerrawannie. The two were presented to George III and possibly, at a later reception, to the queen, but two years later Yemmerrawannie was dead, and Bennelong depressed and ill. Arrangements were made for his return home on the *Reliance*, but the many delays distressed him further, and he came aboard at Portmouth a sick man. Hunter reported to King, 'disappointment has much broken his spirit, and the coldness of the weather here has so frequently laid him up that I am apprehensive his lungs are affected—that was the cause of the other's death'.[11]

However, the ship's surgeon, George Bass, undertook his care and, as the journey progressed, Bennelong's health improved and he gradually regained his naturally vigorous and assertive character. Probably in his early thirties at this time, Bennelong has been described as 'of good stature and stoutly made, with a bold intrepid countenance which bespoke defiance and revenge'.[12] With time on his hands, Daniel Paine set about learning the language of Port Jackson from him. Another man with occasional free time also undertook to learn the language. This was George Bass.

Bass was 24 years old, six feet tall, a physically strong, handsome man, the son of a Lincolnshire farmer who died when the boy was six,

George Bass (1771–c. 1803), c. 1800, engraving. Bass arrived in Port Jackson as surgeon on HMS Reliance *and from 1795 to 1799 shared in Flinders's early explorations in the little* Tom Thumbs *and on the sloop* Norfolk. *He disappeared at sea in 1803. (ML Ref: P1/B Mitchell Library, State Library of New South Wales)*

and a firm, devoted mother who saw to it that he received a surgeon's education before he fulfilled a long-held desire to go to sea. In 1789 he became a surgeon in the Royal Navy and for five years served on a series of ships before being posted to the *Reliance*. He was a young man of immense energy and enthusiasm, with a fine sense of humour and a lively, discerning intelligence, who welcomed almost any physical or intellectual challenge. Hunter would later write that he had 'much ability in various ways out of the line of his profession . . .'[13] Bass and Flinders soon discovered that they came from almost neighbouring parts of Lincolnshire. Bass was born in Aswarby, some eleven miles from Donington, and grew up in Boston, a town Flinders knew well.

Flinders was profoundly impressed with Bass. Years later he wrote:

> In Mr. George Bass, surgeon of the *Reliance*, I had the happiness to find a man whose ardour for discovery was not to be repressed by any obstacles, nor deterred by danger; and with this friend a determination was formed of completing the examination of the east coast of New

> South Wales, by all such opportunities as the duty of the ship, and procurable means, could admit.[14]

In Flinders Bass found much to complement his own interests. Younger by three years, Flinders was nevertheless as strong-minded, determined and willing to accept danger as Bass. Although short and slight, Flinders possessed endurance and a physical toughness that would match Bass's.

Before sailing Moore and Bass had applied for a personal servant each and for payment of their wages. The Admiralty granted this, and in London Bass hired a thirteen-year-old lad, William Martin. Almost nothing is known of young Martin's background other than that he was baptised at Dartford, Kent, on 4 March 1781. On board the boy attended Bass personally and assisted in the surgery. As Bass was to discover, young Martin was strong, quick and eager, and readily learned to handle a boat.

The gregarious Bass also formed a lasting friendship with the ship's commander, Henry Waterhouse, a very capable and experienced officer with a genial, straightforward manner, at this point a well-contained fondness for drink, and a good sense of humour. Writing to Arthur Phillip at the end of the voyage, he commented on the *Reliance*, 'I never sailed in so complete a tub'.[15]

Gathered in the gun room or on deck, sometimes around the accessible and affable Hunter, the young officers talked constantly about the land they were on their way to serve, the novices, Flinders and Bass, pelting those who had been there with endless questions.

In the early morning light of 7 September 1795 the long, level line of the cliffs guarding the entry to Port Jackson were seen from the decks of the two ships. Some time after eight o'clock their sails, minute and white against the horizon, were sighted from the lookout station at South Head, and flags signalling their approach fluttered up the flagstaff. A boat with several officers and the pilot came out to meet the ships.

With the massive, fissured headlands slipping past, the ships entered the great bay, the shoreline falling back in coves and promontories and small white beaches. Seven years before, with his friend and commander Arthur Phillip, Hunter had been in one of the three pinnaces that entered a waterway only mentioned by Cook, seeking a site more suited for settlement than Botany Bay. With immense satisfaction they had found, as Phillip wrote, 'the finest harbour in the world...'[16] Now Hunter was returning, bearing the hopeful, anxious weight of governorship, responsible not only for preserving and nurturing this isolated, impoverished convict colony, but also for opening up a strange, difficult land, of which he knew so very little.

An opposing wind slowed the ships. The *Supply* reached the anchorage at Sydney Cove at sunset. The *Reliance* splashed down her anchor at about eight o'clock that evening. Behind them a pinpoint of firelight glowed in the darkness. This was the nightly beacon on South Head, a fire burning in an iron basket on a tripod. Before them the town of Sydney lay dark and quiet. The journey of almost seven months was over.

At daybreak the men on the ships saw the distant range of hills, the nearer sweep of silver-green forest and across the calm waters of the cove the little settlement of Sydney strung along the shore of an inlet bordered on either side by rocky, bush-covered promontories. They saw stretches of cleared land and patches of cultivation and, among scattered tree stumps, dead trees and dirt paths, some rows of small houses, a few low brick buildings and, on rising ground that sloped down to the beach, a two-storey, brick and stone house with an attempt at a formal garden in front: the governor's residence. Behind broad mudbanks a creek emptied into the cove. This was Tank Stream, with clustered ferns and wandering pigs along its banks and a log bridge near its outlet. It was the town's main source of fresh water. Two small jetties extended into the cove's clear waters, with people now gathering on them and on the shore in between. From two or three canoes black-skinned fisherfolk also watched. Cannon boomed in welcome, and in full uniform the governor and his officers came ashore in the longboat.

Four days later, on 11 September, Hunter officially assumed his position as Captain-General and Governor-in-Chief of New South Wales. Before a semicircle of troops, free settlers and convicts, the judge-advocate, David Collins, read out Hunter's commission from the king, and the new governor spoke about his expectations of everyone's good conduct and the importance of all supporting the colony's government. He was then sworn into office, and a gun salute onshore was answered from the ships. The territory assigned to the governorship of John

Hunter extended from the northern extremity of the continent at Cape York to its southern extremity at South Cape in Van Diemen's Land, including 'all the adjacent islands in the Pacific Ocean'[17] between those parallels, and inland to 135° east of the Greenwich meridian, a boundary evidently guided by a Dutch demarcation line between New Holland and the rest of the continent, then labelled Terra Australis, as it appeared on a 1663 map of Melchisédec Thévenot. On a modern map it runs approximately from the Glyde River in Arnhem Land to the town of Elliston on the eastern side of the Great Australian Bight.

Hunter's immediate domain, however, extended only some distance inland from Sydney itself. Here rough trails skirted the gallows and a swamp to reach areas of farmland. A better road ran through a brick-making neighbourhood to the smaller settlements of Parramatta and Toongabbie. A month after his arrival Governor Hunter wrote to the Secretary of State for the Home Office, William Henry Cavendish Bentinck, Duke of Portland, that the British populations of Sydney, Parramatta, Toongabbe, now Toongabbie, and the banks of the Hawkesbury River totalled 3211.[18]

Hunter was aware of the enormous difficulties that would beset his administration. Distance from Britain was a factor, especially the months of sailing required between the colony and the homeland for supplies, equipment and mere communication. Distance, too, could affect the consideration given to a faraway settlement by ministers more concerned with the immediate political fray and the exigencies of war.

The colony suffered from disease, crimes of every description and a desperate lack of supplies. On the arrival of the new governor David Collins wrote, 'we had only gained a few barrels of provisions salted at Rio de Janeiro; a town clock; the principal parts of a large windmill . . .'[19] It was food that the settlement wanted. This very quickly became Hunter's own overwhelming concern. On the day he officially assumed office, he wrote to the Duke of Portland, 'I look every day for the arrival of the two provision ships . . .'[20]

New South Wales had no treasury and no official local money. Commerce took place through a cumbersome process by which the colony's commissariat store fed and clothed the settlement's population through local and overseas purchases for which it paid in bills on the British treasury, redeemable by the British government. Similarly, the New South Wales Corps paymaster drew bills on the regiment's banker-agents in London. The only coinage in circulation was that brought in by individuals. Commerce was further hampered by extensive government restrictions designed to protect the interests of the East India Company, a strong faction in English politics.

There were other difficulties. Since the departure of Phillip four years earlier, civil government had given way to a military administration that had acquired a number of advantages for itself, which it would not surrender easily, and Hunter would come to see the military as the despoiler of his administration. Paradoxically, however, it was the energetic drive for wealth of some of these officers that established the colony's first commerce by bringing in from abroad saleable cargoes, of which spirits were only part. Trade became the premise, as well, of public servants, settlers and emancipists. It drew outside investment, such as from Campbell, Clark and Co. of Calcutta. Inevitably, however, aspects of such enterprise clashed with what the new governor saw as the interests and objectives of his administration. Hunter's entire governorship would be interminably burdened with these conflicts, for which he had neither solutions nor the power or ability to enforce even such remedies as he believed possible.

In his known writings Matthew Flinders never offered any comment on the colony's socioeconomic conditions. They were, of course, entirely outside the duty of a junior naval officer and probably of minor interest to a young man who was seeing before him the glowing possibility of realising long-held dreams of exploration. Nor would Flinders have regarded the presence of crime and squalor as entirely exceptional. He had seen the port areas and poorer districts of English cities; in the colony the same conditions were simply more severe. There were also the tensions of a community in which acknowledged offenders made up the greater part of society, controlled by a small group through a system of harsh punishment, while the ruling clique itself felt continually under threat from rebellion and from divisions within its own ranks. Isolation raised the susceptibility of all to dread and suspicion. Months went by when there was no news of the outside world, no word from families, no response to their own distress. They clung to the edge of a land that itself so often seemed hostile and incomprehensible.

To Flinders, whose interests lay entirely in what he could accomplish with a vessel, the familiar and orderly world of the ship was infinitely preferable. He knew that he depended on the cooperation and good will of the governors, John Hunter and later Philip Gidley King, for the achievement of his goals, and for this reason, too, he may have kept his opinions to himself, whatever he saw or felt away from the decks of the *Reliance*. There was a single-mindedness in the young Flinders that excluded many things that might intrude upon his own particular objectives.

5 The Tom Thumb Adventures

During the long voyage from England Matthew Flinders and George Bass had immersed themselves in the exciting possibilities of their own explorations in New South Wales. The continent's eastern seaboard had been generally charted by Cook, and in 1788 and 1789 Port Jackson, Botany Bay and Broken Bay had been surveyed in detail, mainly by Hunter. But, as Flinders wrote:

> It appeared that the investigation of the coast had not been greatly extended beyond the three harbours . . . Jervis Bay . . . had been entered . . . Port Stephens had lately been examined . . . but the intermediate portions of the coast, both to the north and south, were little further known than from captain Cook's general chart; and none of the more distant openings, marked but not explored by that celebrated navigator, had been seen.[1]

Bass's and Flinders's eagerness to explore now took definite shape. From the hunters who provided game for the settlement they learned that a large, navigable river existed inland, which the hunters believed emptied into Botany Bay. Was it a continuation of the George's River, shown on a chart drawn by Hunter in 1788? It was a question that needed an answer. 'The furor of discovery', Flinders wrote, '. . . is perhaps as strong and can overlook obstacles, as well as most other kinds of mania'.[2] They went to the governor and presented their plan to investigate by boat the upper reaches of the George's River. Hunter hesitated.

Flinders remarked, 'Projects of this nature, when originating in the minds of young men, are usually termed romantic; so far from any good being anticipated, even prudence and friendship join in discouraging, if not in opposing them'.[3]

And, Hunter reminded them, the only available boats in Sydney were those belonging to and certainly needed by the *Reliance.* It was probably Bass who overwhelmed this argument. They 'turned their eyes', and obviously Hunter's attention, '. . . towards a little boat of about eight feet keel and five feet beam, which had been brought out by Mr. Bass and others in the Reliance, and from its size had obtained the name of Tom Thumb'.[4] Length of keel, however, does not necessarily mean overall length. An encyclopaedia of 18th century ship design suggests that with an 8-foot keel and 5-foot beam, the *Tom Thumb* may have been 9–10 feet long overall.[5]

In this little craft the two men and Bass's boy servant, William Martin, could make a worthwhile journey in just a few days. Hunter agreed. Waterhouse gave his permission, and the boat was quickly loaded with a few basic supplies. The next morning, 26 October, the *Tom Thumb* sailed out through the Heads with her happy and excited company of three. No mention is made of a sail, but almost certainly the boat had been fitted with mast, sail and oars, and Flinders and Bass would have tried her out on the waters of Port Jackson, perhaps with the 'others', never identified, who had 'brought out' the little craft.

On the swells and winds of the open sea the *Tom Thumb* sailed south past a seemingly deserted coastline. They rounded Cape Banks into Botany Bay and travelled up the George's River as far as John Hunter had surveyed it. From here they pushed on some 20 miles farther than the *Tom Thumb* 'could go', evidently on foot. The river banks were wooded and the soil seemed fertile. They scratched out notes, sketched the river's course, and returned to Port Jackson after nine days. The expedition was essentially a reconnaissance, and the young men's report to Hunter, particularly its reference to good soil, encouraged the governor to make his own visit to the area and, two years later, to establish a riverside community, Banks Town. In addition, their handling of the excursion lifted Hunter's confidence in their abilities. For the young explorers themselves it was an exhilarating and productive adventure that had proven their skills and competence, and now fired their eagerness for further discoveries.

Naval duties, however, intervened. Matthew Flinders's activities during the final months of 1795 were mostly confined to the *Reliance*, at anchor in Sydney Cove. The life of the colony ran on around him.

The wheat harvest failed. The final deaths of the year brought the colony's total to 26, including several executions. Bennelong lived a divided life in and out of the settlement, visiting the governor at intervals and disappearing among his own people for periods of time.

Occasionally Flinders would have shared in community events. On a warm Saturday evening in mid-January Sydney's first playhouse opened with a presentation of Edward Young's 'The Revenge' and a farce called 'The Hotel', the entire production the work of convicts and the performance 'far above contempt,' according to David Collins. Flinders may well have joined the enthusiastic crowd, guarding the possessions he carried from the pickpockets around him. Unfortunately, on the second night of the plays, homes of families attending the performance were robbed, a problem that eventually led to closing down the theatre. On 18 January the queen's birthday was celebrated as a 21-gun salute from each of the king's ships reverberated across the cove. At some point Flinders had a sudden attack of what appeared to be a kidney problem, and presumably George Bass offered what medication he could. The ailment passed.

The *Reliance* sailed for Norfolk Island, 1041 miles from the Australian mainland, in January 1796 with stores from England and Captain George Johnston of the New South Wales Corps, who was to replace the island's ailing commandant, Philip Gidley King. Flinders had his first sighting of the cliffs, rainforests and tall Norfolk pines seen by Cook the year Matthew was born.

In 1788 Arthur Phillip had established a subsidiary penal colony on the uninhabited island, Lieutenant Philip Gidley King arriving with 22 settlers. Despite periods of considerable hardship, by 1796 Norfolk Island was a modestly successful agricultural community of eight hundred and eighty-seven.[6] King, since 1791 lieutenant governor of the island, was on his second tour of duty.

Apparently Governor Hunter had asked that the *Reliance* bring back to Sydney cannons from the *Sirius*, wrecked in 1788, and on the reef at low tide, the men worked to free the guns from sand and sea-shattered timbers. On occasion King and his wife, Anna Josepha, would have received the officers at Government House.

The *Reliance* returned to Sydney on 5 March 1796. Captain Johnston, who himself had become ill, was on board, leaving Lieutenant Governor King still in command on the island.

On its arrival in Sydney the *Reliance* immediately underwent a much needed refit. For three weeks Flinders was fully occupied on the ship, while Bass gave his time to the hospital, where Joseph Gerrald and William Skirving, two of the four so-called Scottish martyrs, political prisoners transported for sedition, lay terminally ill. Bass visited them twice daily until their deaths.

Bass and Flinders's spare time, however, went mainly into plans for their second expedition. They had spoken at length with the colony's game hunter, Henry Hacking, and had learned of a river not indicated on Cook's charts but seen inland, which was thought to reach the sea a little south of Botany Bay. Central to their plan was the use of 'another boat of nearly the same size . . . built since at Port Jackson . . .'[7] This second boat was probably constructed at the Cove's eastern shore boat-yard by or under the supervision of Daniel Paine, the settlement's official boat builder. It has been argued that it must have been considerably larger than the first, as at one point during the subsequent voyage there were seven people in it. This, however, occurred on a shallow river, not at sea. Paine's journal noted, 'Two gentlemen of the Reliance Lieutenant Flinders and Mr Bass Surgeon coasted about ninety miles and in returning were very near being lost the Boat not being above twelve feet long . . .'[8]

The craft was fitted with mast and sail, probably a lug sail, with a stone for an anchor. Honouring their first little vessel, Flinders and Bass called the boat the *Tom Thumb*. There is no further mention of the first *Tom Thumb*. The second *Tom Thumb* was almost certainly government-owned. Hunter discouraged the private ownership of boats, in some of which convicts had escaped, and the following year issued a public order 'strictly to forbid' the building of boats for private use.[9]

In the early evening of 24 March 1796, Bass, Flinders and young William Martin pushed the second *Tom Thumb* away from the steep wooden side of the *Reliance* and crossed the harbour to spend the night at Sharks Bay, 2 miles from the entrance of Port Jackson. They had provisions for ten days, two muskets, ammunition, a watch and two pocket compasses.

At three in the morning they pulled out from between the heads, raised the sail in a moderately stiff west-southwest breeze and set a course to the south. At daybreak the wind dropped and the *Tom Thumb*'s crew rowed southward in sultry heat. Their water supply, they discovered, had gone bad, having been mistakenly put into a wine barica, and they eased their thirst with some of their five watermelons. To determine their position they watched for landmarks described by Cook or seen from the *Reliance*, and in the afternoon were startled to realise that a prominence among the hills to the west was Cook's Hat Hill, today's Mt Kembla. A strong current had carried them 18 to 20 miles beyond their destination just south of Botany Bay, and wind and rising swells prevented their turning north. As the sea grew increasingly rough, they steered for land.

At eight o'clock and by moonlight, they approached the shore, where the ghostly white surf was clearly too high to risk a landing. They had a 'miserable supper', which included 'drinking a melon', and settled into the bottom of the *Tom Thumb* for the night 'as well as three people may be supposed to in so small a space'.[10]

By morning the explorers were desperately thirsty. Although the sea was breaking heavily on reefs fringing the shore, they had to find water. At a spot where the sea inside the reef seemed quieter, they dropped their anchor stone and veered in to the edge of the surf. Bass flung the barica overboard, sprang in after it and swam to shore. Flinders began hauling the boat away from the surf and towards their anchor, but the stone lifted. A large wave seized the boat and flung her onto the beach. Terrified of losing their craft, the three used the next wave to rush the *Tom Thumb* up on the sand. The little craft was nearly full of water, with muskets, ammunition, clothes and provisions afloat. Hurriedly, they unloaded and baled out the boat. Natives south of Botany Bay were said to be especially fierce, possibly cannibals, and they saw columns of smoke some three miles away.

The most spoilable of their possessions were heaved back in, and the boat run into the water. Bass remained on shore while Flinders and Martin pulled the boat out beyond the surf. Then, with the oars and mast for rafting and Bass stripped and swimming back and forth, the remaining gear was floated across. The incident had been costly. The muskets were full of sand and two of three horns of powder, a watch and two pocket compasses were wet. Of their provisions there remained only some pieces of salt meat, some rice, a little sago, and a few potatoes caught in the bottom boards of the boat. By 3.30 in the afternoon everything that could be salvaged was aboard and they got under sail at once. They were about 44 miles south of Port Jackson and three miles north of modern-day Wollongong.

With twilight creeping across the ocean they searched for a landing place on one of today's Five Islands, but surf broke heavily on every side. Finally, dropping their anchor just off the mainland, they made what meal they could and, wet and chilled, huddled again in the bottom of the *Tom Thumb*. Bass was intensely uncomfortable, painfully sunburned from five hours spent naked in the water and midday sun, rafting their possessions to the boat.

With dawn came the unexpected appearance on the beach of two Aborigines, calling and offering fish and water in the language of Port Jackson, which Bass partially understood. They were, they said, from Botany Bay. Cautiously, Flinders and Bass rowed in and received two fish and a small amount of water for two handkerchiefs and a few potatoes. Other Aborigines now appeared, and the *Tom Thumb*'s crew retreated, coming ashore just to the south in a small, empty cove. Here they cooked a meal and began drying their clothes.

The problem of securing fresh water remained. Thus, when the two Botany Bay natives reappeared, they agreed to be guided to a river. With their pilots in the boat, they steered before the wind, amused by assurances that at the river they would be brought two white women now living with the Aborigines, plenty of black women, and quantities of fish and ducks. Flinders's narrative records that while at the cove he had shorn with scissors the hair and beards of the two natives, apparently entertaining everyone, but how this came about he did not explain.

At noon they reached a small tidal stream cutting across the beach from a lagoon farther inland. Precariously, the *Tom Thumb* nosed through the surf and up the rivulet, with their guides, now joined by eight or ten strangers, walking alongside on the sand. Bass and Flinders rowed about a mile upstream, the bottom of the boat occasionally bumping on the riverbed.

Meanwhile, the group of men around them had grown alarmingly to nearly twenty, with others still arriving. Outnumbered, with useless weapons and in danger of being unable to get the boat out again, they felt distinctly unsafe. As well, their request for fresh water was not met. To leave promptly seemed increasingly urgent. They landed and spread their gunpowder in the sun, but a move to clean the guns caused alarm. Instead, Bass got some of the Aborigines to help him mend an oar. Fresh water suddenly became available from just a few yards away.

The two men who had had their hair and beards clipped were now showing the results to their fellows, urging them to do likewise. The idea was well received and, scissors in hand, Flinders began work

> ... upon the eldest of four or five chins presented up to me; and as great nicety was not required, got on with them to the number of eleven or twelve ... Some of the more timid were alarmed at a double-jawed instrument coming so near to their noses and could scarce be persuaded by their shaven friends to allow the operation to be finished.[11]

Despite some wild stares and forced smiles, the chins were finally trimmed. Bass, meanwhile, was rapidly gathering the dried powder, stowing the water cask and readying the boat.

Now escape seemed imperative. The Aborigines were insisting forcefully that they continue up to the lagoon. Their two guides were the most vehement, and their earlier promises of women and food now seemed sinister. Pretending to move the boat to another spot for the night, the explorers shoved off, but the natives followed, four of them jumping into the boat and others splashing alongside in the shallow water, shouting, singing and dragging the boat. The three young explorers joined in the noisy shouting and singing, although their situation 'was far from being pleasant'.[12]

When they reached the place they had indicated for the night, it took a show of anger before the Englishmen managed to pull away. They headed downstream as rapidly as possible, but at the river entrance found their escape blocked by wind and surf. Watched from the shore, they anchored inside the breakers in fairly deep water. As the sun sank behind the hills another group of Aborigines approached, and having by now gotten the guns in order, Flinders fired a shot. The group stopped, then walked away, and presently the others left, one of the Botany Bay natives being the last. By ten o'clock the moon had risen, and wind and surf abated. They rowed back to the little islands of the previous night and again got what rest they could in the bottom of the boat.

Flinders later described the area they had quitted as low and sandy near the stream he called Canoe Rivulet. About 4 miles to the north-west lay a large lagoon and behind it a semicircle of hills, the highest of which was Cook's rounded Hat Hill. The lagoon, which Flinders later named Tom Thumb's Lagoon, is now Lake Illawarra and Canoe Rivulet probably part of the lake's present exit to the sea.

The next morning they steered north, coming ashore after midday on a beach under some cliffs. Here they noticed some black, slate-like lumps of stone, but only food and rest interested them. That night they slept stretched out on the soft sand, 'to us a bed of down', although Bass still suffered, his back one continuous blister.

After a happy, solid breakfast they pulled out at seven o'clock and began rowing north on a calm sea. By noon, however, a strong northerly wind had set in. Unable to make headway, they dropped their stone in the water alongside the cliffs. When, towards evening, the wind switched to the south, they weighed immediately and headed north. Darkness fell. The sky filled with pendulous black clouds through which lightning was running in all directions, and the growl of thunder penetrated the sounds of the sea. Then the wind burst into gale force. The boat raced before it, the sail straining. The sea rose, heaving into high, spume-whitened crests, whipping arms and faces with biting spray. Frighteningly, they could hear the surf thundering against cliffs. There was as yet no moon, and the *Tom Thumb* was flying through blackness. Bass 'kept the sheet of the sail in his hand . . . I was steering with an oar . . . a single wrong movement, or a moment's inattention, would have sent us to the bottom. The task of the boy was to bale . . .'[13]

Suddenly breakers appeared ahead, without the dark bulk of the cliff behind them. Certain that the sea would soon overwhelm them, they gambled. Approaching the edge of the breakers at what seemed the right moment, 'we brought the boats head to the sea,—had the mast and sail down in a trice, and got upon our oars'. With each surge of the waves they pulled towards the reef, rode into its lee and, within minutes, 'were in smooth water, and out of danger'. A blur of white ahead held them in suspense until they saw that it was a sandy beach. 'We thought Providential Cove a well-adapted name for this place . . .'[14] They were about 22 miles south of Port Jackson in the area now called Wattamolla.

At daybreak they explored a barren, sandy shoreline. There were signs of people, but they saw no one. By nine o'clock the *Tom Thumb* was at sea, heading north in a light southerly breeze, and before noon they steered through a mile-wide entrance into the much indented waterway of Port Hacking, their original destination. Camping on the north shore, they dried and put their possessions in order. Two Aborigines appeared but were friendly. In the evening they amused themselves by fishing from the boat, but without success, owing, perhaps, to the many sharks swimming about them. Only innumerable mosquitos kept it from being a restful night.

They spent a day exploring Port Hacking, concluding that the shoals made it mostly unsuitable for shipping, and early the next morning they were again heading north. Shortly after sunset the three young discoverers were back on board the *Reliance*.

Flinders's manuscript journal of the voyage concludes with a table of related distances and bearings. These do not all reconcile well with modern charts, and must be viewed in terms of pocket compass bearings, computed distances and an inexperienced explorer. Nevertheless, their report pleased Hunter, particularly the mention of good soil. Flinders's own feeling was that he had once more met the demands and perils of exploration and learned skills he would need again—the handling of a boat in surf and heavy weather, dealing with natives on their own ground and gathering geographical information with minimal equipment. And there were the exhilarating thrills and excitement of danger. But there was more.

Flinders was filled with the 'furor of discovery'. Once again he had glimpsed the great sprawl of land beyond the beaches, a strange, unrecorded world that he regarded with a fascination that could be 'termed romantic'.

He had also made a practical start in hydrography. His eye-sketch survey was taken to England by Major William Paterson of the New South Wales Corps, together with some topographical surveys by the colonial surveyor, Charles Grimes. In March 1799 these were published by the cartographer Aaron Arrowsmith, under the title *A Topographical Plan of the Settlement of New South Wales. Including Port Jackson, Botany Bay and Broken Bay. Surveyed by Mssrs Grimes and Flinders—Communicated by Lt. Col. Paterson of the New South Wales Corps.* For a youthful surveyor it was an achievement, and it also brought his name before a number of men interested in the colony, among them Sir Joseph Banks.

6

'No Ship Ever Went to Sea So Much Lumber'd'

Flinders resumed his normal duties on the *Reliance*. With time on his hands, Bass turned to land exploration. The spread of the settlement at Sydney was barred to the west by a range of mountains that had defied attempted crossings since 1790. Speculation as to what lay on the other side ranged from great deserts to a seaway that divided the continent. For the colony, the most important possibility was a region of cultivable land to produce foodstuffs for a growing community located largely on poor soil. Expeditions had penetrated the lower hills, but the long, hazy spine, known as the Blue Mountains, seemed a permanent barricade. In June 1796 Bass undertook a crossing. With two companions and some of his own especially designed equipment, he attacked the almost demented formations of the mountain chain. What seemed a passage ended in an unscalable rock wall or plunged over a precipice into a chasm from which there was no outlet. They found no water and no food. Finally, seeing only the same tortuous ridges extending endlessly west, they acknowledged defeat.

Hunter, meanwhile, had decided upon another means of increasing the colony's food-producing potential. Recent letters had informed him of the British takeover from the Dutch of the Cape of Good Hope, a move Hunter had long urged, fearing French occupation of the Cape, a vital station on the long passage between Britain and the East and Australia. In August 1796 Hunter wrote to Under Secretary Nepean, 'In consequence of that information, I avail myself of the approaching season to send the King's ships, the Reliance and Supply, to the Cape, in order to execute that part of my instructions from his Majesty which relates to the stocking this colony with live cattle'. Both ships, however, were in poor condition. The *Reliance* was receiving what repairs the settlement could provide, but remained 'extremely weak . . .' A further blow to the ship and her company was the loss of her longboat with five or six men. Sent to Botany Bay to fish, they never returned. Hunter continued, 'but the defect of the Supply, whose commander will not complain whilst he can make her swim, is of such a nature as we cannot repair. Her beams, knees, and timbers are exceedingly rotten and decayed. I have inspected them myself . . .'[1]

Nevertheless, two weeks later Hunter stated that the ships 'are now upon sailing', and on 20 September the *Supply* departed for Norfolk Island, to be joined in mid-October by the *Reliance*, the colonial schooner *Francis*, and the chartered transport *Britannia*, which was taking home to England the invalided Major William Paterson and the judge-advocate, David Collins. The ship now took on board the ailing Lieutenant Governor King and his family. On the 25th the ships made sail, the *Francis* returning to Sydney, the others setting forth on their separate journeys. Driven by the westerlies, the *Reliance* and the *Supply* traversed the South Pacific, rounded Cape Horn, and crossed the South Atlantic to arrive in Table Bay at the Cape of Good Hope on 16 January 1797.

Flinders had now more than completed the six years' seatime and two years' service as a midshipman required for promotion and, shortly after their arrival, Waterhouse recommended him to Rear-Admiral Thomas Pringle, commanding at the Cape, for the examination for lieutenancy. Before a board of officers Flinders was put through an oral test on practical seamanship and basic navigation. He did well and received his certificate on 24 January, although as Admiralty approval was required, his seniority as a lieutenant was dated 21 January the following year. Both Matthew and Samuel sent letters home from the Cape.

Heavy work followed as the ships were refitted, water, firewood and fresh provisions taken on, bales of hay loaded and livestock lifted on board in slings. Figures differ, but the *Reliance* embarked about 49 cattle, including three bulls and six calves, just over 100 sheep and a few goats. While most of these were purchased by the commissary for the government, several cows, three horses, some two-thirds of the sheep and all the goats were bought privately by officers. Bass bought a cow and nineteen sheep, but Flinders decided against the investment. About 40 cattle, five mares and over 40 sheep were taken on board the *Supply*.

A small flock of Spanish merino sheep had been bred at the Cape by the commander of the Dutch garrison, the Scots-descended Dutch-born Colonel Robert Jacob Gordon, who, unable to bear the disgrace of surrender, had shot himself. Some of the ships' officers visited his widow. Seeing their interest in the sheep, she offered the animals for sale to the New South Wales Commissary, John Palmer. Busily bargaining for cattle, Palmer declined. Instead, Waterhouse and Kent together bought 26 of the sheep at four guineas each. Six others were presented to King and Paterson when they reached the Cape on the *Britannia*.

Aboard the *Reliance* and the *Supply*, the crowding of men and animals was incredible, with lowing and bleating creatures packed into straw-filled pens on the forward decks and the officers' cows and sheep herded into their cabins. The ships reeked, and Waterhouse wrote to his father, 'I believe no ship ever went to sea so much lumber'd'.[2] The problems of the *Supply* were compounded by her extremely unseaworthy condition. Knowing the importance of the livestock to Hunter, her captain, William Kent, refused a survey, which would probably have recommended that the ship not sail.

On 11 April 1797 the two vessels left Table Bay, shaping their course eastward across the Indian Ocean. Six days out the *Supply* was in serious trouble:

> ... the stern worked loose ... the sides open'd and took in considerable quantities of water, so as to oblige us to keep almost constantly pumping. Storms were expected and ... every precaution for the safety of the ship was taken; ... the jibboom and spritsail yard were got in, the topgallant masts taken on deck, the bows covered all over with new canvas, tar'd ...[3]

The storms came, but through the sheer determination of her captain and his men, the decaying ship survived and, on the evening of 16 May, struggled into Port Jackson. Despite many losses, it landed, according to one source, 27 cows and 35 sheep. The ship itself was a ruin, 'a complete mass of rotten timber',[4] which an official survey condemned as 'irreparable in this port or any other and . . . unfit to proceed to sea'.[5] The *Supply* was dismantled and anchored in Sydney Cove as a hulk.

For the *Reliance* the usual 36- to 40-day run became a storm-ridden nightmare of 78 days. In mountainous seas and manic winds the crew fought the wheel, struggled with the pumps, battled ripped canvas and broken, flying timber, while terrified and injured animals were flung against the bulkheads and each other. Waterhouse wrote, 'We met with one gale of wind, the most terrible I ever saw or heard of, expecting to go to the bottom every moment . . .'[6] Towering seas smashed the jolly boat, which hung on davits over the ship's stern, and stove in the cabin deadlight. The sea poured in to ruin bread and biscuits, and water, sloshing among the animals, ran underfoot in filthy, stinking streams. In the chaos the animals 'liv'd upon air part of the time'.[7] The *Reliance* reached Sydney on 26 June. Waterhouse commented to his father, 'something more than I can account for preserved us. Possible', he added wryly, 'I may be intended to be hung in the room of being drown'd'.[8]

The surviving livestock was debarked. Several officers sold their animals profitably, but Waterhouse evidently established his merinos on a land grant of 25 acres at Liberty Plains, between present-day Strathfield and Bankstown. John Macarthur, farmer and officer of the New South Wales Corps, eventually bought some of Waterhouse's merinos, a little flock of storm-battered animals that became the foundation of an industry of incalculable wealth for the emerging nation. For the Sydney community there was soon the benefit of having enough cattle for teams of six or eight to replace men in pulling the wagons.

Flinders was immediately involved in the major refitting of the *Reliance*. A survey recommended replacements and reinforcements almost throughout, and that the ship be hove down for complete recaulking, while new boats, 'sufficient for any rough work',[9] were built, despite serious lacks in Sydney's naval stores.

While Flinders had not invested in livestock, he returned to Sydney with one live acquisition. In the middle of the Indian Ocean the *Reliance*'s ship's cat gave birth to a litter of kittens. Despite desperate activity in a fiercely storm-ridden sea, Flinders adopted one, calling him Trim after an appealing character in Lawrence Sterne's novel *Tristram*

Shandy. Ashore and at sea the little black cat with white paws remained with Flinders for years to come.

During the night after the arrival of the *Supply*, a small fishing boat pulled into Sydney Cove, the fishermen shouting for help. They had with them three survivors from the wreck of a merchant vessel, the *Sydney Cove*, which in sinking condition had been run onto the beach of an island in the Furneaux group, between New South Wales and northeast Van Diemen's Land. Seventeen men had set off in the longboat for Port Jackson. Wrecked on modern Victoria's Ninety Mile Beach, they walked north for two months along some 400 miles of the continent's trackless edge. Some died; others, exhausted and wounded in Aboriginal attacks, could go no farther. The mate, Hugh Thompson, was speared and ordered the supercargo, William Clarke, to continue with two remaining men. On 15 May 1797, some miles south of Botany Bay, they were sighted by the fishermen. A whaleboat sent to find Thompson and a sick man with him found only bloodied remains.

Hunter dispatched the colonial schooner *Francis* and the decked longboat *Eliza* to the wreck site, now Preservation Island. These small vessels could take only part of the salvaged cargo, and six of the *Sydney Cove*'s seamen were left to guard the remainder. The *Francis* reached Sydney. The *Eliza* never arrived.

Clarke mentioned to Hunter that some 18 or 19 miles south of Botany Bay he had kept his fire going with pieces of coal from a seam in the cliff face. Sent with Clarke to examine the claim, George Bass found some of the veins of coal that eventually became part of the modern industrial complex at Wollongong and Port Kembla.

The wrecking of the *Sydney Cove*, along with the discovery of coal, further impressed upon Hunter the importance of extensive hydrographic surveys of the New South Wales coast. He wrote to Joseph Banks earnestly pressing for a maritime surveyor for the colony. The wreck had also revived the question of whether Van Diemen's Land was or was not separate from New South Wales, for the Furneaux Islands lay directly east of where a strait could be assumed to be. Captain Tobias Furneaux of the *Adventure*, part of Cook's second expedition, had stated positively that there was no strait. The ship's astronomer disagreed, as did others, including John Hunter, who had observed the rapidity and easterly set of the currents.

The importance to the colony of such a passage was enormous. Invaluable time would be saved by a shorter route from the Cape or India to Port Jackson. It could mean a safer journey, the ships avoiding the cold, rough seas south of Van Diemen's Land. And there was also the need to complete the geographical picture of Australia's east and south coasts for scientific purposes. In late 1797 Hunter decided to settle the question with what resources he had, and the man he chose for this expedition was George Bass.

Flinders was tied to the tedious tasks of the *Reliance*'s repairs but Bass, as Hunter wrote, assured the governor 'that nothing could gratify him more effectually than my allowing him the use of a good boat and . . . volunteers from the King's ships . . . I accordingly furnished him with an excellent whaleboat, well-fitted, victualled, and manned to his wish for the purpose of examining along the coast to the southward of this port, as far as he could with safety and convenience go'.[10]

Flinders, no doubt painfully disappointed in not being free to go as well, accepted the situation generously.

7
Van Diemen's Land—An Island?

The Sydney-built whaleboat assigned to Bass was just under 29 feet long, with six volunteer naval seamen and stores for six weeks. On 3 December 1797 Bass and his crew sailed from Port Jackson and seventeen days later rounded Cape Howe. Sailing westward they were soon off an unknown coast. Storms held them for ten days in Wingan Inlet, but at daylight on the last day of the year they pulled out and continued west.

On 5 January 1798 they entered a large circular bay. Bass described the surrounding country as low but hilly, luxuriant with grass and ferns, and lightly timbered. He named the place Western Port.

The expedition spent twelve days at Western Port. They had been away seven weeks, and their supplies were extremely low. The whaleboat, battered by the sea, was leaking. Reluctantly they retraced their journey, largely in foul weather. Bass and his crew entered Sydney Heads on 25 February. They had been away for 84 days. Later Flinders wrote in praise of his friend: 'A voyage *expressly* undertaken for discovery in an open boat, and in which six hundred miles of coast, mostly in a boistrous climate, was explored, has not perhaps its equal in the annals of maritime history'.[1]

George Bass presented his brief journal to Hunter. He was not a skilled cartographer and mapping from a pitching whaleboat or on a rainswept beach was more than difficult. At Western Port he had walked along the shore in a high wind and produced, as he said, 'a sketch, which I am sorry to say, after all the vexation I have had with it, is but very imperfect'.[2] Accuracy was altogether out of his reach. Nevertheless, his 'eye sketches' were useful for details in other charts. His journal, kept by Hunter, was borrowed years later by Flinders when writing his own account of explorations in that area. On 1 January 1798, in recognition of their various efforts, Hunter granted Bass, Flinders and John Shortland 100 acres each in the new settlement of Banks Town.

One detail Bass omitted from his log but recounted to Hunter was finding, on a small island in the present Glennie group, seven sick, starving and nearly naked convicts. Escapees from Sydney, they had been marooned by their companions, who judged their boat too small for all of them.[3] Now the seven wanted only to return to Sydney and, as Hunter put it, throw themselves on His Majesty's mercy. Bass's whaleboat could not take all seven, but he got them to the mainland and took on board the two most ill. To the rest he gave a share of his provisions, a musket and ammunition, a compass, fish-hooks, lines and articles of clothing contributed by his crew, together with instructions to follow the coast north some 500 miles to Port Jackson. The five were never seen again.

Bass's whaleboat, beached at Sydney Cove, became an object of popular admiration. On the visit of the French explorer Baudin in 1802, Governor King presented him with a fragment of wood from the boat, mounted in a silver case engraved with the main facts of the subsequent Bass Strait discovery. In early 1798, however, Bass knew full well that although he had extended European exploration of the south coast considerably, he had not established that there was a sea passage. But as Flinders wrote, Bass 'entertained no doubt of the existence of a wide strait, separating Van Diemen's Land from New South Wales . . .'[4] What remained was to prove it.

In the meantime, six crewmen of the *Sydney Cove* and part of its cargo remained on Preservation Island. Three weeks before Bass returned, Governor Hunter ordered the schooner *Francis* south to complete the rescue.

Repairs to the *Reliance* were now well under way, and Flinders asked to join the *Francis*. To his immense delight, Hunter agreed. Flinders wrote that he was sent 'for the purpose of making such observations, serviceable to geography and navigation, as circumstances might permit; and the master of the schooner was ordered to assist in forwarding those views'.[5] In a dispatch to London Hunter described Flinders as 'a young man well qualifyed' to undertake this task.[6]

Flinders went as a passenger, but he was carrying out his first independent and relatively important hydrographic survey, an opportunity to gain practical experience in an area he considered of extreme importance to himself. Afterwards, his sketch survey was combined on one map with George Bass's discoveries and sent to England.

The *Francis* left Port Jackson on 1 February, following the coast south, and twelve days later reached the wreck site. The *Sydney Cove* still stood, 'but the sea thrown in by westerly gales had, in great measure, broken her up, and scattered beams, timbers, and parts of the cargo upon all the neighbouring shores'.[7] Of the six men left to guard the cargo, one had died, but the rest remained in reasonable health.

For several days rough seas and repairs to the *Francis*'s boat restricted Flinders's surveying to Preservation Island. As soon as weather and boat repairs permitted, he set off with four crewmen on a five-day excursion among the rocky, brush-covered islands, seeking a safe anchorage for ships and landing to climb hills with his instruments to measure line-of-sight distances and angles. He sketched and named new geographical features, among them a high, round hill in the Kent group, which he called Mount Chappelle, and some small nearby islands, the Chappelle Isles, for Ann in faraway Lincolnshire.

He took notes on the wildlife, vegetation and types of rock. There were large colonies of two kinds of seals, some of which the sailors bludgeoned for meat and skins, as well as kangaroos and echidnas—'the flesh has a somewhat aromatic taste, and was thought delicious—'[8] and a 'little bear-like quadruped . . . its flesh resembles lean mutton in taste . . .'[9] This was Flinders's first encounter with a wombat. Huge numbers of birds nested on the islands—geese, Mount Pitt birds, penguins and sooty petrels, which for months had fed the stranded crew of the *Sydney Cove*. There was no sign of other human habitation.

Flinders's surveying was hampered by the schooner's poor steering compass, the lack of an azimuth compass and a chronometer, and the fact that the expedition was primarily a salvage operation. Nevertheless, he produced a chart of the area and 22 quarto pages of careful description and comment. He noted that, inexplicably, his bearings 'showed that a change in the course steered produced an alteration in the compass'.[10] This was a problem of magnetic deviation that he would help to solve years later. Watching the tides and currents, he believed that he had found additional evidence for a strait between Van Diemen's Land and New South Wales.

Flinders returned to Sydney with the *Francis* on 9 March. George Bass was already back from his whaleboat voyage, and the two friends had a joyful meeting. On board the *Reliance* they examined each other's notes and sketches, discussed the indications of a strait and reached the same exciting conclusion: the evidence pointed to a strait and, this being so, they should find it and finally prove that Van Diemen's Land was an island—or group of islands—or a part of the mainland.

At his desk in Government House Hunter wrote to Joseph Banks. Commenting on the rescue of men and cargo from an island shipwreck, he remarked that he had sent 'the Second Lt. of the Reliance with directions to make such observations among the islands as he could'.[11] He did not name the second lieutenant, but Banks would have known who it was. He would have seen the surveys by Flinders and Grimes brought to England by Paterson, and probably had heard the name in discussions with Philip King and David Collins, both of whom reached England in 1797. Recurringly now, references to a young, capable officer and navigator, eagerly interested in exploration, were reaching Banks.

While exploration was indeed on Flinders's mind, other duties intervened. The *Reliance* was again fit for sea and in late May sailed for Norfolk Island with soldiers, officers, convicts, 1200 bushels of wheat and 100 casks of salt meat. In August Flinders sat as a member of the Vice-Admiralty Court of New South Wales to try a case of mutiny, the accused being members of the New South Wales Corps, who were acquitted. Nor was it a time for exploration. The winter months were unusually cold, with frequent storms in the south.

By September, however, Hunter was arranging for a conclusive investigation of the waters between Van Diemen's Land and New South Wales. Van Diemen's Land had been an enigma since its European discovery by Tasman, its insularity a question for over 150 years. Its northern waters had been approached from the east by Tobias Furneaux in 1773, and at a later date from the west by a Captain William Reid of the sealing schooner *Martha*, but just how far Reid sailed is not known. Sealers were often secretive about their hunting grounds.

In sending to the Admiralty the chart that combined the findings of Flinders and Bass, Hunter commented to Secretary Nepean:

> From this little sketch it will appear . . . that the high land in latitude 39° 00' . . . is the southern extremity of this country, and that the land called Van Dieman's is a group of islands . . . probably leaving a safe and navigable passage between; to ascertain this is of some importance. I am endeavouring to fit out a deck'd boat of about fifteen tons burthen for that purpose, in which I propose to send the two officers above mentioned.[12]

The search for a suitable boat met with prompt and unexpected success. Captain John Townson of the New South Wales Corps, King's successor as commandant at Norfolk Island, had attempted to solve the problem of poor communication with Sydney by building a 25-ton sloop of local pine, presumably Norfolk Island pine (*Araucaria heterophylla*).

As the island had no proper harbour, the little craft was launched from the shore without testing, and leaked badly on her journey across the Tasman Sea. Nevertheless, when she arrived in Sydney, Hunter, who disapproved of boat-building on Norfolk, immediately saw the vessel he needed. Anticipating the Admiralty's approval, he named the sloop *Norfolk* and ordered her fitting-out for the voyage.

The *Norfolk*, about 35 feet in length and 11 feet of beam, was small for an extended voyage, but there was no argument from Flinders and Bass. Flinders, whose notice of promotion to lieutenant had been received in Sydney, was now qualified for the command, which he received together with orders to sail south to the Furneaux Islands and then west and, as he wrote:

> . . . should a strait be found, to pass through it and return by the south end of Van Diemen's Land; making such examinations and surveys on the way as circumstances might permit. Twelve weeks were allowed for the performance of this service, and provisions for that time were put on board; the rest of the equipment was completed by the friendly care of captain Waterhouse of the Reliance. I had the happiness to associate my friend Bass in this new expedition.[13]

A modern replica of the sloop Norfolk, *in which Matthew Flinders and George Bass circumnavigated Tasmania in 1798, proving it to be an island. The voyage showed Bass Strait to be a shorter, safer passage from the Pacific to the Indian Ocean than the route around the south of Tasmania. In the* Norfolk *Flinders then explored Australia's east coast north of Sydney as far as Hervey Bay. (Photo by Michael Tierney, Stanley, Tasmania)*

For Flinders this was a triumph. The plan for the voyage was precisely what he wanted and he had at his disposal a ship and crew to direct as he wished. Moreover, the crew of eight volunteers were chosen from the *Reliance* and the *Supply*, experienced seamen who knew each other and their two young officers. Navigational equipment, including a brass sextant, theodolite, azimuth compass and an artificial horizon, was provided from the *Reliance*. Flinders was not, however, given a time-keeper, a lack he remarked upon several times in his reports. Regardless, he hoped to make an important discovery and thereby win the commendation and further support of Hunter, and a reputation as an explorer that would reach the Admiralty.

Some six months earlier a small, three-masted snow, the trading vessel *Nautilus*, had entered Port Jackson. Sailing from Canton, now

Guangzhou, to North America, the ship had been virtually driven back across the Pacific by an almost unrelenting series of typhoons until, severely damaged and with pumps going day and night, she struggled into Sydney. The two merchant adventurers aboard, Charles Bishop, her captain and owner, and Roger Simpson, supercargo, managed to sell their freight, and with Hunter's consent the ship was repaired and provisioned from government stores. The two men met Flinders and Bass, and hearing from Flinders of huge seal populations on the southern islands, evidently decided to recoup their fortunes by seal hunting.

The *Norfolk* cleared Sydney Heads on 7 October 1798 in company with the *Nautilus*. Near Cape Howe deteriorating weather and a south-west wind held them for six days in Twofold Bay. Bass explored the surrounding countryside while Flinders, assisted by Roger Simpson, surveyed. On the long northern beach they laid a base line of 116 chains, took the necessary angles and established a triangulation grid over the bay. Their approach to the beach had startled a group of native women and children, who fled with cries. Flinders wrote:

> Soon afterward a man made his appearance. He was of middle age, unarmed, except for a *whaddie*, or wooden scimitar, and came up to us seemingly with careless confidence. We made much of him, and gave him some biscuit; and he in turn presented us with a piece of gristly fat, probably of whale. This I tasted; but watching an opportunity to spit it out when he should not be looking, I perceived him doing precisely the same thing with our biscuit . . . The commencement of our trigonometrical operations was seen by him with indifference, if not contempt; and he quitted us, apparently satisfied that, from people who could thus occupy themselves seriously, there was nothing be be apprehended.[14]

The next day, although the sun was visible, squalls blotted out the horizon. To observe for latitude, Flinders resorted to his artificial horizon, which entailed pouring mercury from a small flask into a shallow pan, which he positioned so the sun was reflected in the liquid but was also in his own direct view. Sighting through his sextant, he then brought the image of the actual sun to coincide with its reflection. With some mathematical corrections he could then obtain the necessary measurements of degrees.

As Flinders began his preparations, however, the group was startled by the calls of seven or eight native men who appeared upon the bank above them,

> ... holding up their open hands to shew they were unarmed. We were three in number, and, beside a pocket pistol, had two muskets. These they made no objection to our bringing, and we sat down in the midst of the party. It consisted entirely of young men, who were better made, and cleaner in their persons than the natives of Port Jackson usually are; and their countenances bespoke both good will and curiosity, though mixed with some degree of apprehension. Their curiosity was mostly directed to our persons and dress, and constantly drew off their attention from our little presents, which seemed to give but momentary pleasure. The approach of the sun to the meridian calling me down to the beach, our visitors returned to the woods, seemingly well satisfied with what they had seen. We could perceive no arms of any kind among them; but I knew these people too well not to be assured that their spears were lying ready, and that it was prudent to keep a good look out upon the woods, to prevent surprise whilst taking the observation.[15]

The two ships left Twofold Bay in the morning of 14 October, and six days later reached the Furneaux Islands, where the *Nautilus* moored in Kent's Bay, off Cape Barren Island. The sealers set up camp and began their five-month hunting season. With strong winds blocking a westerly course, Flinders explored some of the surrounding channels and islands, adding to the chart he had made aboard the *Francis*. On 1 November he steered the *Norfolk* west toward the northeasternmost point of Van Diemen's Land, later named Cape Portland by Governor Hunter.

The *Norfolk* now followed an uncharted coast, and Flinders knew the thrill of standing on the deck of his first command, watching land and sea no known navigator had traversed before. Matthew Flinders possessed a strong sense of humanity, but as a commander he never forgot that the effective functioning of the ship was essential to the success of his task, and that his task was paramount. There would be firmness, fairness, stringent demands on his crew when necessary, but nothing he was not prepared to undertake himself. Floggings or other corporal punishment were only employed as absolutely required for discipline. To his own work as a scientific navigator he would give unstinting effort, absolute dedication. It was a prescription that would win him the affection and loyalty of many, but could be painfully exacting of himself and of others.

Without the specific duties of a ship's officer, Bass was available and invariably willing to be of help in any way at all. As important, he was a competent navigator and seaman whose thinking in many ways paralleled Flinders's own. In many situations Bass capably took charge of the sloop while Flinders explored in the boat.

On his own Bass investigated rivers and bushland, applying his scientific knowledge to this new natural world. He discovered two new species of eucalypts. He watched the behaviour of hundreds of black swans on the rivers and examined some for the contents of their stomachs. He dissected a wombat and wrote the first anatomical description of the animal. The explorers saw natives only once, and fleetingly, but Bass studied the construction of their deserted huts, their shell middens and the animal bones in the hearths, and noted the absence of canoes.

On its third day off the north coast of Van Diemen's Land, the *Norfolk* entered the estuary of the Tamar River, named by William Paterson when establishing a colony there in 1804. Numerous inlets reached into lightly wooded hill country, the river itself flowing from the southeast. A chain of mountains rose in distant blue peaks. Flinders spent seventeen days in the estuary, moving the *Norfolk* about to expedite his surveying, or going in the boat to explore shoals, creeks and river banks. The weather was changeable, with strong winds, hail and rain, or thick fog and calms that meant manning the sweeps to shift the sloop. Flinders's observations of latitude, often done with the artificial horizon, were generally quite close to modern values, but longitude, observed by sets of lunars, was frequently out by many miles.

On 20 November the *Norfolk* beat out of the river against a strong northwesterly. Thick, rainy weather shrouded the little sloop during the night and by daybreak gale winds were driving out of the west. Great sprays poured over her bows, and as darkness came on, the storm-jib split. Yet she 'performed wonderfully'. Seas that were apparently 'determined to swallow her up she rode over with all the ease and majesty of an old experienced petterel'.[16]

Unable to continue westward, Flinders returned to the Furneaux Islands. A windy day was spent at Preservation Island, drying and repairing sails. At night Flinders watched an eclipse of the moon through the telescope of his sextant and used its timing and the altitudes of the stars Rigel and Sirius to calculate the island's longitude. He found that it differed 37' from the results of his previous lunar distances.

The *Norfolk* then joined the *Nautilus* in Kent's Bay, where Bishop's sealing was going well. On his return to Sydney with a shipload of skins, Bishop delivered to Hunter Flinder's report on the promising new harbour on the Van Diemen's Land coast. The governor named the site Port Dalrymple, for Alexander Dalrymple, the navy's hydrographer.

That evening a favourable breeze sprang up, and risking the hazards of sailing by night, Flinders headed back to Van Diemen's Land. For days strong contrary winds again frustrated the drive westward. Time was running out. Of the twelve weeks Hunter had allotted for the voyage, eight had expired. Then the winds moderated and the *Norfolk* pressed on. Anxiously, Flinders watched the coast trend northwest, as if to meet the New South Wales shore. The water discoloured, as at the head of a bay. On an island consisting of three almost barren hummocks, Flinders and Bass landed to look for food. They found nothing edible, but noticed that although the tide had been running from the east all afternoon, there was, 'contrary to expectation . . . near low water on the shore'.[17] The flood tide, then, must come from the west and, if so, there was a passage.

Passing around a point of land, they saw ahead a long, heavy swell from the southwest, breaking in masses of flying surf upon a small reef. This was an ocean swell, and the *Norfolk*'s company erupted into delighted shouts and laughter. Flinders wrote: 'Mr. Bass and myself hailed it with joy and mutual congratulation, as announcing the completion of our long-wished-for discovery of a passage into the Southern Indian Ocean'.[18]

Bass found further confirmation from a high, steep-sided little island crowded with seals and albatrosses. The coast trended to the south. A few miles farther they saw the dark headland that is Tasmania's north-westermost point. Flinders called it Cape Grim but the triumphant fact was that it undoubtedly showed Van Diemen's Land to be an island.

For the next four days the sloop sped southward under a cloudy sky along a bleak and mountainous coast. Accustomed to the flat fenlands of England and the level, open space of the sea, Flinders wrote apprehensively:

> The mountains which presented themselves to our view . . . were amongst the most stupendous works of Nature I have ever beheld, and, at the same time, are the most dismal and barren that can be imagined. The eye ranges over these peaks . . . with astonishment and horror . . . [19]
>
> . . . as there is no known place of shelter upon this coast, it becomes extremely dangerous to approach it . . . Judging from appearances, the west coast of Van Diemen's Land is as dreary, and as inhospitable a shore, as has yet been discovered . . . [20]
>
> We carried every sail the sloop had to set . . . [21]

From well offshore, Flinders made a running sketch survey, with little detail and hazy hidden sections left as blank spaces. Just two sightings of smoke suggested that the land was sparsely inhabited. He recorded few place names. One peak about 8 miles inland he called Mt Norfolk, for his little command. Two others on the skyline he named Mt Heemskirk and Mt Zeehan, for Tasman's two ships.

At four o'clock in the morning of 13 December, four days and some 220 miles south of Cape Grim, the *Norfolk* was steering for a high, jagged, steep-sided promontory curving into the sea like a giant reptile's tail, which Flinders identified as the southwest cape of Van Diemen's Land, seen by Furneaux from the *Adventure* in 1773. The *Norfolk* had passed from virtually unknown waters to a coastline previously seen by several explorers. Flinders noted with satisfaction that despite the difficulties of surveying, 'yet had the chain of angles been never wholly broken from that part of the coast near the N. E. Cape, where Capt. Furneaux left it, round to the S. W. Cape, where his examination commenced'.[22]

As darkness gathered, a sudden storm from the west engulfed the *Norfolk* in thunder and gushing rain. Had the wind come from the south, they would probably have been smashed under the cliffs of South Cape, their bones left to bleach, as Flinders later remarked, while the separation of Van Diemen's Land from New Holland remained only a conjecture. But in about an hour the storm was over.

The large sheltered bays of Van Diemen's Land's southeast corner were a welcome change. This was the deeply indented coast known to Tasman, Cook, Hayes, Furneaux, Bligh and D'Entrecasteaux. Here was Adventure Bay, where in 1791 a youthful Matthew Flinders had gone ashore. Now, unaware that Joseph-Antoine Raymond de Bruny d'Entrecasteaux had explored the area in 1792, Flinders examined the French admiral's North Bay, today's Frederick Henry Bay, and its inner cove, which he called Norfolk Bay. Several islands bore evidence of Aboriginal visits but, strangely, no evidence of canoes. On Christmas Day Flinders carried his survey up the Derwent River, while Bass climbed the forested slopes of today's Mt Wellington. When the river became too shallow for the *Norfolk*, Flinders, joined by Bass, continued upstream in the boat.

Here they found additional signs of inhabitants but only once were able to make contact. Two women fled but a middle-aged man remained, apparently unafraid, and with open pleasure accepted the gift of a swan. 'He seemed entirely ignorant of muskets, nor did anything excite his attention or desire except the swan and the red kerchiefs about our necks; ... the quickness with which he comprehended our signs spoke in favour of his intelligence'.[23] However, no conversation was possible. The Aborigine understood none of the Port Jackson dialects or common Pacific island words Bass and Flinders tried.

By the first few days of the new year, 1799, the *Norfolk*'s provisions were running out, and the time allotted to the expedition had expired. The *Norfolk* headed north, and at ten o'clock in the evening of 11 January came to rest in the sheltered waters of Sydney Cove. She had exceeded her assigned time by just eleven days.

Flinders went to work on a fair copy of his journal and the completion of his chart. The lack of a chronometer during the voyage continued to rankle. His charts were not perfect, in part because 'no time-keeper could be procured'.[24] He retained any nomenclature given by his predecessors, adding mainly descriptive names to some of his own findings—Cape Barren Island, Pyramid, Swan Isles. Neither Flinders nor Bass named any geographical feature for himself. Hunter, however, made additions. Of the strait they had discovered, Flinders wrote, 'his Excellency the Governor named it Bass's Strait, after my worthy friend and companion, as a just tribute to the extreme dangers and fatigues he had undergone in first entering it in the whaleboat'.[25] Years later, Flinders added that the name had been given on his recommendation.

To a letter of 15 August 1799 to Secretary Evan Nepean, Hunter added a postscript:

> P. S.—I transmit by this conveyance a copy of the rough survey which I had made of the strait which I in a former letter had occasion to say I believ'd to exist between Van Diemen's Land and the southern promontory of this country. Lt. Flinders and Mr. George Bass, late surgeon of the Reliance, were the officers I employed upon this service, and they completely circumnavigated Van Diemen's Land, formerly consider'd a part of this country.[26]

The 'rough survey' was Flinders's manuscript chart of Van Diemen's Land.

If Hunter's comments on an important achievement seem inadequate, they came from a man, naturally bluff, who was beset with the problems of the colony and seriously concerned with his own situation as its governor. Nevertheless, Hunter would have been delighted at having his firm conviction proven. Besides solving a long-standing mystery and adding significant geographical information to the record, the discovery of the strait had shortened the route from the Cape of Good Hope to Port Jackson by over 600 miles, roughly a week's sailing. While Bass Strait was frequently rough, it was not subject to the subantarctic storms of the southern route, which caused serious delays, expensive wear on ships and possible damage to cargoes, all important factors to shipowners.

Writing as a naturalist, Bass filled his account of the journey with observations on plant and animal life and geological features. David Collins later drew extensively from it in his *An Account of the English Colony in New South Wales*. Bass, however, now had something else on his mind. The possibility of a profitable commercial enterprise centred on Port Jackson had captured his interest.

8 Colonial Affairs

By the end of the 18th century Britain had not investigated to any great extent the considerable territory claimed for her by James Cook. The governors of New South Wales were encouraged to examine their coasts whenever vessels could be spared, but practical difficulties restricted the efforts of administrations left so much on their own.

The colony's strategic value had been noted. Writing to the Duke of Portland, Secretary of State, on 1 May 1799, Governor Hunter observed, 'this colony may prove at some future period, from its situation, a settlement of much importance in case of either a Dutch or Spanish war'.[1] In London, however, commercial possibilities were of greater interest. The Colonial and Home Office urged hemp and flax production and the development of timber and coal industries for export, while trade with Asia and Alaska was considered promising.

Despite these potentials, the Australian continent did not compete with India or the West Indies as a region of strategic or commercial importance. Possibly the very size of the continent fostered a casual attitude towards its possession. Cook had claimed for Britain the east coast, which, at some 2000 miles, was of immense length, and the territory defined by Britain as the colony of New South Wales extended to 135°E longitude, a north–south line running almost through the centre of the continent. Yet the remainder of the country was still so large that a foreign colony on another section of coast would have mattered very little, especially in this land of seemingly small value. Even the possibility of a French settlement was viewed in London with fairly marginal concern.

There was also the importance attached to science and scientific discovery. Foreign expeditions to the Australian coasts, charged by their governments to explore for the purposes of natural history and geography, were tolerated, even assisted by the British government. Inevitably, however, there were hidden threads of strategic rivalry, even colonial ambition, in the fabric of these expeditions. European powers in the late 18th and early 19th centuries were intermittently locked in wars in which mercantile and colonial interests played a very large part, and the proximity of Port Jackson to the Spice Islands, its possibilities for trade with China and its position on the rim of the Pacific Ocean, with all of Spanish America on the other side, gradually increased in significance.

With Britain at war in 1799, Terra Australis had slipped well down on any scale of priorities. Nevertheless, Flinders's circumnavigation of Van Diemen's Land had reinforced Britain's claim upon the continent. Further, with the awareness of Bass Strait as an improved route from Britain to New South Wales and the Pacific, the strategic importance of the south coast and Van Diemen's Land grew.

In the colony, however, daily life remained subject to deprivation, crime and harsh punishments, and its administration was more and more acrimoniously discordant and divided. The discovery of Bass Strait was a rare bright ray in the increasingly dark and bitter world of Governor John Hunter. He wrote to the Duke of Portland, 'I cannot help observing in this place, my Lord, that the prying eye of envy and ill-nature will never be at a loss to distinguish in the best designs or most commendable actions some blemish or censure, some conspicuous fault, on which they may glut the desire of a malevolent disposition'. His attempts to improve conditions were repeatedly met with deliberate opposition, 'untill the weight shou'd be felt too heavy for me singly to bear'.[2]

Hunter's ill-trained and uninterested officials offered little support. Others were protecting and expanding their own fortunes and influence and, when his efforts stood in their way, waged ruthless campaigns within the colony and by letter to England to destroy the credibility of his rule. Prime among these was the well-to-do landowner, pastoralist and officer of the New South Wales Corps, John Macarthur. The colonial office extended little sympathy. It had its own complaints, assailing Hunter with questions and criticism on the cost of running the colony and on his irregular methods of reporting and handling finances.

Hunter also wrote to Banks. Their association probably went back to the preparations for the First Fleet in 1786, and in subsequent years Banks was a persevering friend and supporter of John Hunter. However, he could offer little encouragement: 'the situation of Europe is at present so critical, and his Majesty's Ministers so fully employed in the business of the deepest importance, that it is scarce possible to gain a moment's audience on any subject but those which stand foremost in their minds, and colonies of all kinds, you may be assured, are now put into the background'. Hunter's colony, Banks assured him, was 'already a most valuable appendage to Great Britain, and . . . we shall before it is long see her Ministers made sensible of its real value'. But in response to Hunter's immediate problems, Banks could only urge, 'Persevere, my good sir . . .'[3]

Violence and disorder continued. Late one warm night in February, Sydney's sky glowed red as the log-built gaol was burned down. Seven months later flames engulfed the thatch-roofed church and schoolhouse. Along the Hawkesbury River, Aboriginal attacks on settler farms had become frequent, together with retaliation by the settlers. Months of drought and bushfires were followed by torrential rains and devastating flood.

Flinders conscientiously pursued his duty in his regulated naval world, but at times his imagination strayed. Someone had brought from England Ann Radcliffe's recent novel, *The Mysteries of Udolpho*, one of the writer's immensely popular tales of terror, suspense and romance. Probably passed around, the book reached Flinders, and when he could, he set aside his work and immersed himself in the haunted atmosphere of the lonely, menacing castle of Udolpho, high in the Italian Apennines. An imagination that had followed the brave and ingenious activities of a solitary Robinson Crusoe was apparently caught up no less by the terrifying events surrounding an entrapped heroine. Despite the overwhelming importance to him of scientific pursuits, Flinders shared the late 18th century's emotional world and its espousal of sensitivity of feeling, or sensibility, and demonstration of that feeling. To Ann Chappelle he would write of his 'unveiled heart' as not 'very insensible'.

In March Flinders sat as a member of a court of criminal judicature for the trial of Isaac Nichols, an emancipist charged with having received 'One Basket of Brazil Tobacco',[4] which he knew to have been stolen. For his previous good conduct Governor Hunter had appointed Nichols a superintendent of public works. He gained a spirit licence, opened a grog shop in George Street and, when granted 50 acres near the town, developed a farm and built a house. In the process he opposed the military and became a target of their anger. Trials were frequent occurrences in Sydney but the circumstances of Isaac Nichols's alleged crime attracted widespread interest and brought out the colony's deep divisions, the governor believing passionately that Nichols had been maliciously framed, while the new deputy judge advocate, Richard Dore, stubbornly maintained the man's guilt. Dore, a lawyer, had arrived in the colony several months before, and relations between him and the governor soured very quickly. Hunter found Dore dishonest, an inebriate and a man determined to mould the administration to his own views.

The court consisted of two irreconcilable groups: three officers of the New South Wales Corps, who voted for Nichols's conviction; and three naval men, Flinders, Waterhouse and Kent, who believed the evidence either false or insufficient. The presiding officer, however, was Dore, and he sided with the military. The accused was convicted and sentenced to fourteen years on Norfolk Island. Hunter was furious, suspended the sentence and ordered a Court of Inquiry. He then dispatched the relevant documents to London for a final decision. In the meantime, Nichols was freed and returned to his job. Three years later he received a full pardon from the king.

Unusually, Matthew Flinders had allowed himself to become personally involved in the Nichols case, a matter not specifically related to himself or to his career. Like other naval officers, Flinders had routinely served on trials, performing his duty but no more. Yet this case moved him to abandon his usual detachment from the colony's civil affairs.

Observations and letters of comment written by Kent and Waterhouse shredded the general credibility of the evidence against Nichols. Flinders gave especially minute attention to the details as they came before him over the four days of the trial, and subsequently wrote a lengthy memorandum not only analysing the evidence point by point but also examining the background of the case and the persons involved. On the basis of his findings, Flinders wrote, 'I could not possibly find him guilty . . .'[5] He then submitted copies of his conclusions to Dore and Hunter. Four days later he examined the minutes of the trial and wrote some additional remarks, which Waterhouse approved and Flinders gave to Richard Dore. With that, however, Flinders apparently felt he had gone as far as he wished and his involvement ceased.

Perhaps it was the crude falsity and blatant unfairness of the case that had aroused Flinders's concern. Perhaps it was something in the quality of the man Nichols; Flinders noted the evidence given by others for the man's good character. Or possibly Flinders wanted to show support for his friend and patron, the beleaguered governor. Underlying his actions at this time, however, was a tumult of personal feeling that could have surfaced indirectly in his concern with the Nichols affair.

Through the first months of 1799 Matthew Flinders felt a recurring discontent with his career. Seemingly, the ideals of the past years were being confronted with the changing values and aspirations of his growing maturity. In March he turned twenty-five. He had served in the navy for nine years, and the thought of a more liberated life in a wider world was intruding upon his earlier conviction that adventure and the pursuit of fame were the goals of his life. Despite the achievement of having proven the existence of Bass Strait and having circumnavigated Van Diemen's Land, there had been neither reward nor recognition beyond the friendly commendations of his immediate superiors. It is obvious that he had become very much aware of the importance of wealth for a life of independence and comfort. His income remained the inadequate stipend of a lieutenant's pay, without the possibility of prize money. Even marriage on such an income was scarcely to be considered.

9

'Sea, I Am Thy Servant'

On 16 March, his birthday, and the day after the Nichols case concluded with a guilty verdict, Flinders began a letter to Ann Chappelle, with whom he had corresponded intermittently over the years. He had just finished reading the first volume of *The Mysteries of Udolpho*, and its final scene, in which the lovers tearfully separate, had reminded him of their own parting four years earlier. 'Fatal, enervating moment!' he wrote. 'I have never since been satisfied with my profession; and, strange as it may appear when mature deliberation was called, to decide upon the question, it aided the sentiment, and condemned the sea . . . to be cooped up in a wooden box; year after year; one decade after another; and the ultimate object not a bit more forward! . . . forgotten . . .'[1] Was this the expression of the emotions of the moment, an overflow of loneliness and thwarted ambition, directed at someone—'a friend who can feel'— from whom he could expect a sympathetic hearing?

He asked Ann, 'How comes it that I selected thee, of all people in the world, for such a recital? Why not my sister, or my friend Thomas, or my father; or why not Mary?' Apparently there had been some disagreement with Mary Franklin, who would now be 'too much embittered to hear my tale with patience', and he could not write in this way to another man. His sister Elizabeth was married and 'another has a just claim to even a superior share of her affection!' Thus, of his 'sisters', it was Ann to whom he unburdened himself:

> *Sea*, I am thy servant, but thy wages must afford me more than a bare subsistence. I do not mean to be always insulated. Thou art but a rough master, hast little mercy upon the lives and limbs of thy followers, but

> sometimes thou bestowest favours. Half my life I would dedicate to thee, but the whole I cannot. If thou keepest me in penury all the morning and noon of life.[2]

Here was a blunt but negotiable demand: 'half my life', but not the whole, unless for greater financial reward and status. Wealth and position, highly significant in 18th century society, had suddenly become important to Matthew Flinders.

George Bass was now weighing the possibility of going into business with the shipowner Charles Bishop, and shared his ideas with Flinders. Flinders was keenly interested. Leaving the navy for a different career at sea, such as operating his own ship in trade with China and India, seemed to him a means to both money and independence. In April 1799 he wrote to his friend the botanist Christopher Smith, then working at the Botanic Gardens in Calcutta, asking for information and his opinion on such a venture. Smith's reply was not encouraging. 'Continue with the Navy', the botanist wrote; Flinders would become 'a great man yet'.[3] The letter, however, apparently did not reach Flinders for many months, and Matthew remained undeterred. In fact, the arrival in February 1800 of a luxurious and unexpected gift of Madeira wine, spirits, shirts, towels and silk neckerchiefs from Smith prompted him further. On 14 February, two days after Smith's gift was delivered, Flinders wrote again:

> The thing is, my dear friend, I am tired of serving for a pittance, and as it were living from hand to mouth, whilst others with no better claim are making hundreds and thousands. The examples which have occurred in this place have opened my eyes a little to my own interest; and besides, I want to be my own master, and not to be subject to the caprices of whomsoever the Lords above may please to set over me . . . Between ourselves, I have some hopes that my relations in England will advance me two or three thousand pounds to forward my mercantile plans, which if they do, and moderate success should attend me, a few years will probably see me independent of the world . . . As I sincerely believe you wish me well, I make no scruple to ask for any information you can get, and to point out any opening that may be suited to my capacity.

He added that an unnamed Irish gentleman would make available to him on his arrival in England 'the command of a sum of money... which will enable me to enter upon certain speculations and give me the command of a ship'.[4]

Flinders did not say who was making 'hundreds and thousands', but probably had in mind those public officials and officers of the New South Wales Corps who had become well-to-do, even wealthy, on spirits and other commodities purchased from incoming merchant ships or brought in by privately chartered vessels and resold at high prices. A few settlers and even former convicts were also building thriving businesses. Whalers and sealers made substantial profits after a good hunting season. However, Flinders was perhaps exaggerating his own possibilities. That he could expect 'two or three thousand pounds' from his relatives in England may have seemed possible from the distance of New South Wales, but was scarcely realistic. He had no even moderately wealthy family connections. Although generally successful with a number of small investments, his father was a frugal man who noted with regret the premiums paid for his children's apprenticeships and often lamented in his diary the burden of impecunious relatives. And as Matthew would discover, his father believed unshakably that adult children should not turn to aging parents for financial assistance. Flinders did not mention again the loan promised by the Irish gentleman.

On 15 February 1800, the day after writing to Smith, Flinders wrote similarly to Bass, who had left New South Wales:

> Your promised information relative to our mercantile pursuits will be very acceptable, as I think it probable that a part of my future life will be dedicated to speculations in that way; for I am fully determined never to serve as a common lieutenant in a common ship, unless in case of necessity; and I am doubtful, whether even a vessel upon the survey of New Holland, unaccompanied by promotion, or emolument superior to the general run of service, will tempt me. However, should this doubtful case really occur, I mean to bring some body who shall do a little business for me, possibly in such a way, that the survey of New Holland may be the last survey I shall want to make, unless of my own estate: this is between ourselves.[5]

Of his father, he wrote that he would perhaps 'try him about advancing a thousand or two to forward my plans ...'

Bass, already committed to Bishop and, evidently, others, perhaps doubtful of Flinders's suitability for trade, had not asked that Flinders join him in business.[6] Flinders continued:

> It has been my wish, and I have more than once hinted so much to you, that our speculations might fit in and be carried on together; but as this did never appear to meet your approbation, no direct proposal was made; and I now mention the circumstance only, that if you should be in want of a partner and think me qualified for the task, you know when to pitch upon a willing one, should no other plans of mine have proceeded too far for retraction.[7]

In the same letter Flinders referred to occasions when, keenly sensitive to Bass's criticism, he had felt that his friend's treatment of him was 'such as said to me, "you are unworthy of being my friend ..." '

By early 1799 George Bass had decided to leave New South Wales. Several factors probably played their part in this decision. For some time he had apparently not been well. Although no specific ailment is mentioned, he was declared medically unfit for duty and subsequently given a year on half pay to recuperate.

The voyage around Van Diemen's Land had been a high point of adventure and achievement, probably never to be matched. There had followed five months of idleness on a vessel moored safely in port, facing a future as a surgeon on a mundane succession of ships. Bass's acquaintance with Charles Bishop had thrown before him another kind of challenge. Bishop's sealing expeditions to the Furneaux Islands had been very successful. In two return trips to Port Jackson he had landed 9000 first quality skins and several tons of oil, which he planned to sell in China at considerable profit. Before this, the *Nautilus* had been lucratively chartered to deliver to Norfolk Island a cargo of English goods. For Bass, all this suggested intriguing financial possibilities that he discussed with Flinders.

Bishop's immediate plans went only as far as Macau and Guangzhou, where he intended to sell the ship. Travelling as far as China with Bishop, Bass evidently planned either to return to Port Jackson with saleable merchandise, or to continue to England. To assist him

Flinders provided a letter of introduction to Christopher Smith in Calcutta.

On Sunday 17 May 1799 Henry Waterhouse assembled his ship's company on the deck of the *Reliance* to bid farewell to Bass, who went ashore together with his servant, William Martin, now eighteen years of age. Two days later they sailed from Port Jackson on the *Nautilus*.

Flinders's feelings on the departure of Bass are not recorded but the loss of his closest friend would have been painful. Flinders's admiration of Bass was profound. Bass was daring and courageous. He was also a charming, gregarious man, impressive in appearance and bearing, intelligent and eager for knowledge; in many ways he was what the short, slight, reserved and relatively single-minded Flinders was not. In an age when voyages at sea lasted many months and families at home were frequently not seen for years, shipmates provided the grounding of friendship, loyalty, trust and affection that made harsh and hazardous conditions bearable and were sometimes essential to mental and physical survival. Flinders's letter to Bass of February 1800, written nine months after Bass had left Port Jackson, discussed the publication of their charts, mutual acquaintances in Port Jackson and Flinders's own interest in a commercial investment. He then wrote of the excellent friends he had acquired: '—Franklin—Wiles—Smith—Bass, are names which will be ever dear to my heart'.[9] He went on as if seeking to analyse an earlier period in his life when, as he wrote in the somewhat ornate language of thc time:

> I was so completely wrapped up in you, that no conversation but yours could give me a degree of pleasure; your footsteps upon the quarter-deck over my head, took me from my book, and brought me upon deck to walk with you; often, I fear, to your great annoyance...
>
> ...your apparent coolness towards me, and the unpleasant manner you took to point out my failings, roused my pride and cooled my ardour...it is not clear to me that I love you entirely; at least, my affection for Wiles reaches farther into my heart,—I would take him into the same skin with me! Perhaps it is not in human nature to preserve an entire friendship for another, that one knows to be so superior... There is one circumstance that will always keep you from me; your thirst after knowledge and information will not permit you to

> have the necessary consideration for one, who not only cannot afford you these; but has a far less stock than yourself.

That Flinders was somehow retaliating for Bass's criticism by writing warmly of Wiles would have been contrary to his nature. Letters of the time were effusive in style, and Flinders went on to write of Bass's 'knowledge and abilities . . . uprightness, integrity and humanity'. There is no vindictiveness in Flinders's correspondence.

Flinders sailed for England with the *Reliance* less than a month after writing the letter. As no ship had sailed from Sydney for Europe during that period,[9] it seems likely that Flinders left the letter for Bass to pick up on his return, possibly with a James Williamson, who had previously held Bass's mail. On 18 September 1800, however, six months after Flinders's departure, Williamson left New South Wales on HMS *Buffalo*, which was taking Governor Hunter to England. This was sixteen months after Bass had sailed and, perhaps assuming or hearing that Bass was in England, Williamson—or someone else—might have taken it with him. The *Buffalo* reached Spithead on 26 May 1801. Bass had sailed for New South Wales the previous December. His letter would then have been delivered to his wife.

That the letter eventually reached Elizabeth Bass is clear, and it drew from her a remarkable expression of dislike for Flinders. On the address wrapper is a note in ink, in her hand and signed by her. It reads: 'this George is written by a Man that bears a bad Character no one has seen this letter but I could tell you many things that makes me dislike him rest ashured he is no friend of yours or any ones farther than his own interest is concerned'. In pencil, there is a further notation: 'To be directed for Mr. Bass, when . . . where he is to be found—from Mr. Flinders'.[10]

These extraordinarily antipathetic comments are hard to explain. Elizabeth was newly married to George Bass. She was Henry Waterhouse's sister and, as Flinders had known Waterhouse at least from his service on the *Bellerophon* in 1793–94, it is likely that they had met. However this may be, Elizabeth's knowledge of Flinders would have come mainly from her brother and her husband, both Matthew's longtime friends. What were the 'many things' that made her dislike him? What had convinced her of his 'bad Character'?

It seems possible that Elizabeth was deeply jealous of the bond between Flinders and Bass. Elizabeth had been married only two months before surrendering her husband to the world of sea and ships that George shared with Matthew. Possibly she resented Flinders's clear affection and admiration for Bass. Flinders had also expressed his interest in Bass's commercial plans. Was this a sensitive issue with Elizabeth? It was Bass's business venture that had taken him from her. Or had some bit of inimical gossip reached her?

In 1803 there were in Sydney unsubstantiated allegations of financial misconduct against Flinders, and some years later he spoke of 'enemies', but that any serious opposition existed this early in his career seems doubtful. Any answers to these questions must be purely speculative. Equally unanswered is the question of whether the letter ever reached Bass. If it did, Elizabeth's comments apparently had no effect on the friendship of the two men, who continued to correspond as before. Flinders's final letter to Bass, which Bass never received, ended with a promise to see 'your wife, if in London, as well as her family'.[11]

Whatever Elizabeth Bass's feelings about Flinders, he was generally well liked in Sydney. A courteous and well-spoken young man with a growing reputation as a successful navigator, he was welcomed by Sydney's small elite. In a relaxed atmosphere he could show a winning sense of humour and, where there was no intrusion upon his own goals, genuine sympathy and helpfulness. He visited William Paterson of the New South Wales Corps and his attractive and sociable wife, Elizabeth. Paterson had administered the colony from December 1794 to John Hunter's arrival the following year. His great interests, however, were exploration and botany, and while in England on sick leave, he renewed an early friendship with Joseph Banks and was elected to the Royal Society. Returning to Sydney in late 1799 as a lieutenant colonel in command of the Corps, he was a handsome and decisive-looking figure, resplendent in red and gold, all belying a well-meaning but unassertive nature that increasingly took refuge from the realities of the colony in excessive drinking.

Flinders was also a friend of John and Elizabeth Macarthur. Macarthur had held the unpaid office of Inspector of Public Works, which gave him control of the colony's labour resources and leadership of Sydney's trading community. At first on good terms with Hunter,

Macarthur soon quarrelled with him and years of bitter recriminations, charges and countercharges followed. Elizabeth Macarthur was a cultured and intelligent woman, warmly appreciative of her adopted land. She was also unswervingly loyal to her husband, sharing his ambitions for wealth and power. That Flinders admired Elizabeth Macarthur is evident from his later correspondence with her. Holding himself apart from the hatreds and conflicts of the colony perhaps won and kept his welcome in the various homes.

What other associations he may have had are not recorded. Young men off the ships very commonly formed liaisons with convict women. That Flinders's good friend John Shortland did so and became the father of a son is attested by the fact that a land grant of January 1800 specified that 100 acres of the total were granted to his son. Prior to his marriage, Philip Gidley King, the colony's lieutenant governor, had lived for three years with Ann Inett, a convict woman who bore him two sons. Flinders, who had had relationships in Tahiti, could well have had similar involvements in the more than four years he spent in New South Wales.

10

North on the East Coast, 1799

Despite the distractions of war in Europe, a certain amount of pressure to make further useful discoveries in New South Wales was being exerted from England. There was an awakening interest in the colony's possible mineral wealth, particularly in coal seen in 1791 and 1797 at the Hunter River and in 1797 by George Bass along the sea south of Botany Bay.

More importantly, there was the geographically fundamental and potentially significant political question of whether Terra Australis was divided by a sea passage separating New South Wales from New Holland. The continent's entire interior was an enigma. Repeated efforts to reach it by land had failed, and hopes for its exploration shifted to an approach from the sea, with rivers as the pathways inland. However, interest in the question emanated principally not from the Home Office, but from Joseph Banks. Banks was at this time at the height of his power in influencing, and through that even controlling, certain colonial affairs, and from 1779 when he advised the government on founding a convict colony at Botany Bay, virtually every matter relative to New South Wales was referred to him for guidance and determination. His personal experience of the continent was limited to his voyage along its east coast in 1770, but his investigations at the time into a natural world new to science and his continued interest in the country, to which he devoted both time and funds, gave him the status of a savant where Australia was concerned.

On 15 May 1798 Banks wrote to Under Secretary John King:

> We have now possessed the country of New South Wales more than ten years, and so much has the discovery of the interior been neglected

> that no one article has hitherto been discover'd by the importation of which the mother country can receive any degree of return for the cost of founding and hitherto maintaining the colony.
>
> It is impossible to conceive that such a body of land, as large as all Europe, does not produce vast rivers, capable of being navigated, that such a country, situate in a most fruitful climate, should not produce some native raw material of importance to a manufacturing country as England is.[1]

In his letter Banks informed King that he had contacted the explorer Mungo Park, who in 1794 had located the source of the Niger River and become famous through the publication of the narrative of his harrowing journey. Thus Banks now wrote that Park 'offers himself as a volunteer to be employed in exploring the interior of New Holland, by its rivers or otherwise . . .' Banks continued:

> He will want a deck'd vessel of about 30 tons, under the command of a lieutenant, with orders to follow his advice in all matters of exploring . . . and Lieutenant Flinders—a countryman of mine, a man of activity and information, who is already there—will, I am sure, be happy if he is intrusted with the command, and will enter into the spirit of his orders, and agree perfectly with Park.

Further negotiations with Park, however, failed. Park had married and perhaps for personal reasons declined to go to New South Wales. The opportunity for a great voyage of discovery along Australia's coasts awaited another explorer.

Early in July 1799 the *Reliance* was not required for service. With time available and perhaps feeling the emptiness left by Bass's departure, Flinders pressed the governor for a chance to investigate the coast to the north of Sydney. Two large indentations in that coast had been noted but not explored by Captain Cook. The first of these, travelling north, Cook had called Glass-House Bay, which could be identified, he wrote, 'by 3 Hills which lay to the Northward of it in the Lat. of 26°53'S . . . they are very remarkable on account of their Singular form of Elivation, which very much resembles Glass Houses, which occasioned my giving them that Name'.[2]

Even at a distance the peaks were clearly extraordinary, sharp, pyramid-shaped and distinct against the sky in an otherwise flat countryside, evidently reminding Cook of the glass furnaces of his native Yorkshire. Cook had continued north and four days later sighted a large bay to the southwest, which he did not enter but named Hervey's Bay for Admiral Augustus John Hervey.

It was these two bays, of which only the entrances were charted, that Hunter now decided to have Flinders explore. Rivers as navigable access ways for inland exploration were on Hunter's mind, and Flinders wrote, 'I had some hope of finding a considerable river discharging itself at one of these openings, and of being able by its means to penetrate further into the interior of the country than had hitherto been effected'.[3]

To his great satisfaction Flinders was again assigned the sloop *Norfolk*, with much the same volunteer crew as had accompanied him on the circumnavigation of Van Diemen's Land. In addition he took with him his sixteen-year-old brother Samuel, now a midshipman of the *Reliance*, and Bongaree, a Port Jackson Aborigine 'whose good disposition and manly conduct has attracted my esteem'.[4] This is the first of Flinders's many references to Bongaree, who would also be part of his great 1801–03 circumnavigation of Australia.

Bongaree appears to have come from somewhere on the shores of Broken Bay to the north of Port Jackson, where a broad expanse of shallow, dark green water spreads inland. From the west flows a river that has run some 330 miles through clefts and gorges from the mountains that form its source. For thousands of years coastal people had come and gone on these shores, small groups living on seafood, game and foraged roots, berries, grubs, honey and birds' eggs. In fair weather they slept on the earth around a small fire. On cold or rainy nights they sheltered in caves, below rock ledges or in huts of bark and branches.They were members of the Ku-ring-gai language speakers, who lived along the Pacific coast from north of Port Jackson to today's Lake Macquarie.

It is impossible to determine the year of Bongaree's birth, but probably a few years before the first arrival of the Europeans at Port Jackson the boy was growing up along the bay. With other boys he played at war and hunting, swam, fished, learned the ways and skills of his people and, perhaps around the age of thirteen, was initiated into manhood. In 1788, within weeks of landing his little community at Sydney Cove, Governor Phillip led a small expedition in two boats into Broken Bay, to be met by a large crowd of excited but amicable Aborigines. The following year he returned to explore the river he named the Hawkesbury. The presence of the strangers had become a fact of life for the people of Broken Bay.

At some point, together with members of his family, Bongaree arrived in Sydney. By 1799 Flinders was obviously sufficiently acquainted with him to have formed a definite opinion of his character. Bongaree was then a robust young man who readily accustomed himself to an alien way of life at sea and who, over several years, would take part in other English explorations. To his account of preparations for the voyage, however, Flinders added, 'Of the assistance of my able friend Bass I was, however, deprived'[5], and in with the gear that went on board he put his cat Trim. Governor Hunter allotted Flinders six weeks for his voyage, but against unforeseen delays provisions were supplied for eleven weeks. In addition, he allowed Flinders to take with him the *Reliance*'s timekeeper.

The *Norfolk* slipped out of Port Jackson on 8 July 1799 and, with all sails set, bore away northward along the coast Cook had charted 29 years before. Flinders began a running sketch survey of his own. He brought his vessel as close to the coast as possible, four to five miles or less offshore, particularly where Cook had passed by night. With measured stretches of the vessel's track as base lines, he took angles on the most pronounced features of a low, green coast. Where Cook's results did not agree with his own, he invariably offered explanations. James Cook remained the image on which Matthew Flinders wanted to pattern his professional life.

Two days later the wind had pushed the *Norfolk* to some 18 miles from shore. More alarmingly, the sloop had sprung a leak, with so much water coming in that one pump had to be kept constantly at work. The necessity of dealing with this in some sheltered harbour now overshadowed other considerations. Flinders closed with the coast: 'Low land, the shore sandy beaches separat'd by rocky Hds'.[6] At sunset they entered a wide, shallow bay and anchored.

The bay's entrance lay between a sandy point covered with low green brush to the north and a higher, more substantial promontory to the south. At daybreak the boat was lowered. Flinders took bearings from the southern promontory and began exploring the bay. The pale, shifting colours of shallow water lay in serpentine channels between huge sandbanks crowded with pelicans and silver gulls. To the west, masked by sand bars, spits and thick beach vegetation, a large, unseen river emptied into the bay. Flinders did not realise that he was exploring the extensive estuary of today's Clarence River, the first important river that he would fail to identify on this voyage. Flinders named the inlet 'Shoal Bay, an appellation which it but too well merited'.[7]

They found no place suitable to heave down the *Norfolk* for repairs. Flinders returned to the south head to make his noon observations, probably from the ridge that is today occupied by the streets and buildings of the township of Yamba. Here the men found the trees noisy with parakeets, crows and white cockatoos. There were three small round huts framed with heavy, crisscrossed vines tied at intersections with wiry grass and overlaid with a compact covering of soft bark. A small, angled entrance passage kept out wind-driven rain, one of them opening into a kind of double hut with two alcoves. Bongaree was impressed, acknowledging that the huts were better constructed than any in the Port Jackson area, and took with him 'a small hand basket, made of some kind of leaf, capable of containing five or six pints of water'.[8] It resembled containers Flinders had seen in Kupang on Timor. At one o'clock with the tide rising, the men were again aboard the *Norfolk*.

The next day the sloop passed what would eventually be mapped as mainland Australia's most easterly point, Cape Byron, a bold, thickly wooded headland named by Cook for John Byron, circumnavigator of the globe in 1764–66. To the northwest, behind a line of white beaches and wooded hills, a blue mountain range rose into the crooked peak of Cook's Mt Warning.

A day later the *Norfolk* was outside what Cook had called Morton Bay, and Flinders closed in to study the wide, shallow curve facing the Pacific. From farther out to sea, Cook had seen an unbroken shoreline, but Flinders sighted a small, shoal-shielded opening between two sandy points and what appeared to be a large expanse of water beyond. Cook had named the bay for the president of the Royal Society, James Douglas, Earl of Morton, but working from a chart edited by John Hawkesworth in 1775, Flinders copied Hawkesworth's misspelling and wrote the name on his own chart as Moreton Bay. Now he continued north and rounded Cook's Cape Morton. At dusk the pointed peak of one of Cook's Glass Houses appeared small and sharp against the evening sky. At eight o'clock, in darkness and a chilly southerly breeze, the *Norfolk* dropped her anchor at the entrance to Glass-House Bay.

In the morning the bay was a broad sheet of blue water with low, wooded land on either side dissolving into the distance. As the *Norfolk* moved on, five native men appeared at the water's edge, calling and gesturing, one of them holding a green branch at arm's length, which he swung in an arc from side to side, while others ran into the water, striking the surf with sticks. Behind them another group of five, probably women, stood watching. In their calls there seemed to be a word similar to one used by the natives of Port Jackson, and their behaviour was taken to be friendly. However, Flinders went past, and by evening was about two miles from a low sandy point west of the entrance.

At first light the *Norfolk* came around the point and Flinders saw an opening in the shore, a river-like passage running north towards low, level green-wooded land from which rose four or five tiny, extraordinarily shaped blue peaks. Reefs and shallows obstructed the *Norfolk*'s entry into the passage. Flinders had his breakfast; then, in the boat with Bongaree and the rowers, he approached the point. A wall of eucalypts and undergrowth rose behind a beach of soft white sand.

Dogs appeared, and then several Aborigines, most of them carrying fishing nets on their shoulders. The seamen rested their oars, and there was an exchange in sign language across the intervening water. The mood seemed friendly and, seeing that the natives carried pieces of firewood but apparently no weapons, Bongaree decided to meet them. The seamen readied their muskets, backed in the boat, and with his usual fearlessness, Bongaree, naked and unarmed, jumped onto the sand.

The men on the beach seemed shy, but Bongaree's yarn belt was soon exchanged for a headband of kangaroo hair. Flinders stepped ashore. He laid his gun down on the sand and, with friendly gestures, offered a woollen cap. One man took it, but when Flinders indicated that he should have his net bag in return, the man signed that he wanted Flinders's broad-brimmed hat, woven from the white fronds of the cabbage tree. Flinders shook his head. The man then tossed the woollen cap safely behind him and came forward, laughing and talking, clearly intent on getting either the hat or the gun or both. Flinders picked up his gun and, with Bongaree, moved slowly towards the boat. The group now pushed close. One man, laughing, tried to lift the hat off Flinders's head with a long, hooked stick, which produced general laughter. Another reached for the hat but did not dare to come near enough to touch it.

Flinders and Bongaree got into the boat and the sailors pushed off into deep water. Clearly displeased, the Aborigines gestured for the strangers to return. When they remained at a distance, one man threw his piece of firewood at them. It fell short, splashing into the water, and there was more laughter. Another then ran into the water and threw his piece of wood. When it too fell short, he grabbed the hooked stick, somehow removed the hook and produced a spear. Wading out to his waist, he hurled it. The spear shot across the boat just above the gunwale, missing the men.

Flinders, angry and alarmed, then snapped his musket at the spear-thrower, but the flint, damp from lying on the beach, failed to ignite. Momentarily he was tempted to fire buckshot into the entire group, all clearly unaware of the danger they were in, but instead aimed once more at the man who had flung the spear and who, standing in the water, had turned to call to his companions. Again the gun misfired. Flinders fired a third time, and the gun went off. The man in the water toppled over. Those on shore fell flat on their faces, but instantly scrambled up and ran for the trees, some on all fours. Someone in the boat fired. Again the group fell flat, rose immediately and fled into the forest. The man in the water also rose and waded onto the beach, peering over his shoulder as if to see whether a spear was lodged in his back, and stooping, possibly hurt, disappeared into the scrub. Seeing another man still watching from among the trees, Flinders fired twice. One ball touched the edge of the sandbank in front of the man. The other flew over. Later Bongaree claimed that a man's arm had been broken by the second shot from the boat.

In his later account Flinders described the incident as 'an unfortunate occurrence', and on his map wrote 'Skirmish Point' across the southern end of what is now Bribie Island. He hoped, however, that rather than having provoked the continued enmity of the local people, he had impressed them with his power as a deterrent to any interference, for he needed to explore the bay and, above all, to lay the *Norfolk* on shore. He then landed once more, intending to take by way of punishment any fishing nets left behind. None had been left and, with the rustlings of an unknown number of adversaries still running about among the trees, he ordered Bongaree and a seaman back to the boat, and then returned to it himself. Bongaree, whose eyes were more discerning than those of the British, said later that the natives were running to conceal themselves, but there was no certainty about this.

They then rowed into the river-like opening. On the eastern beaches quantities of light, porous pumice stone lay along the high-water mark, which Flinders linked to the idea that the peaks were volcanic, a notion that excited his curiosity even more. Large trees grew right down to the water. Nearby stood several huts, elongated archways of branches, closed at one end. In one they saw a small shield, and in another an old fishing net with a net bag, knotted just as a European seine-maker would have done. On his map, Flinders named the waterway Pumice-stone River. It is, in fact, a narrow strait, now Pumicestone Passage, separating Bribie Island from the mainland.

The crew on the *Norfolk*, meanwhile, had found the loosened plank that caused the leak and filled the crevice with oakum. It was a temporary solution to the problem but, lying quietly, the sloop was making very little water. Flinders decided to postpone the exploration of the Pumice-stone River and survey the bay itself.

In the chilly dawn of 17 July the *Norfolk* was under way south on the rising tide. At mid-morning they landed near some steep red cliffs. In a deserted hut they found a remarkable seine, not more than three feet wide but some fourteen fathoms long, possibly used to trap fish in some semicircular enclosures of woven branches that they saw on a shoal. This was a method of fishing entirely different from those used by the Aborigines around Port Jackson, where fishing was done by spear or with a line and shell hook. Flinders speculated that fishing as he saw it here, with heavy bundles of nets to be carried, would have led to living more permanently in one place, hence the superior construction of the huts. Intrigued by the workmanship of the seine and the ingenuity of what he assumed to be the method of its use, Flinders took the net, leaving a hatchet in exchange. So the people would understand the use of the tool, he chopped down some branches to leave in front of the hut.

For two days the *Norfolk* worked her way up the bay. Little wooded islands ringed by mud flats and mangroves led into shimmering blueness. Flinders sketch-mapped their positions and numbered them. From near the third, now Green Island, the men saw again the opening between the bay they were exploring and Cook's Morton Bay, with the Pacific beyond. Flinders's observed latitude of 27°27'16"S confirmed the observation he had taken outside the opening on the 14th. The land assumed by Cook to be a peninsula was, in fact, an island, which Flinders called Moreton Island, 'supposing it would have received that name from Captain Cook had he known of its insularity'.[9]

Alarm swept the *Norfolk* when at some distance a line of about twenty Aborigines seemed to be advancing toward the sloop as they apparently stood in canoes, in perfect concert aggressively paddling with poles or spears first to one side and then the other. The *Norfolk* was put under easy sail, the deck cleared and the men handed guns, balls and buckshot. Curiously, the Aborigines did not seem to be coming any closer despite their energetic poling. Then, to their enormous relief the Europeans saw that these were fishermen, standing in the water on a mud flat, splashing the water with sticks, first to one side and then the other, to drive fish into their nets.

At dusk the *Norfolk* caught the incoming tide. Through cool darkness the leadsman sounded and eyes strained to see dim outlines as Flinders tacked back and forth. A little before midnight he dropped anchor just northeast of the sixth island, and in the morning moved the *Norfolk* closer to today's Coochiemudlo islet. The high centre was luxuriously covered with large trees, an exposed section of the hill dropping sharply down to the beach, a distinctive slash of dark red earth.

Flinders and a small party splashed ashore. Birds shrieked and flitted among the trees, and rats scurried into the underbrush. There were dog tracks and several places where campfires had burned. Pandanus nuts appeared to have been a food source that drew visitors. Southward the east and west shores of the bay came together 'in the form of a river; but the entrance was too full of shoals to leave a hope of penetrating by it far into the interior, or that it could be of importance to navigation . . .' Further, the *Norfolk* was again taking water. 'I returned on board to seek in Pumice-stone River for a place to stop the leak, and the means of visiting the Glass Houses'.[10]

On his regional chart Flinders represented the bay as ending south of Coochiemudlo, a broken line indicating his uncertainty. Actually, the bay extends well to the south, and a few miles beyond the sixth island, the present Logan River empties. Already Flinders had failed to detect the navigable Brisbane River, which flows into the bay roughly opposite his first and second islands.

Now the *Norfolk* sailed north on a following wind and by sunset of the next day, Saturday, 20 July, was anchored within two miles of Pumicestone Passage.

Early on Sunday Flinders took the boat into the passage to search for a channel deep enough for the sloop. Some six miles up, two Aborigines appeared on the beach, waving to them; Flinders landed out of spears' range. Bongaree went forward and gifts were traded, but when Flinders advanced with gun in hand, the two protested vociferously. The events of Skirmish Point six days earlier were clearly known at this distance from where they had taken place.

On the next morning's high tide Flinders took the *Norfolk* up the passage, steering among sandbanks and mangroves like round, green tufts on the water. About five miles above Skirmish Point the sloop was swung up to a small beach and made fast to the trees. The next day she was cleared of her contents, except for a few tons of ballast, heeled over on her bilge and hauled as high up on the beach as the strength of the crew could take her. Through the day the men worked on the loose plank, caulking the seam, nailing the board back in place and covering the entire section with tarred canvas and sheet lead. Others dug for fresh water, finding only a thick, unappetising ooze until one man, wandering incautiously into the woods, came upon a hole of very good water, with which the breakers were filled.

Flinders hunted for swans and was astonished by the sight of several very large, bulky, blunt-headed animals that came up to the surface of the water to breathe, much as did seals. He fired three musket balls into one, and Bongaree threw his spear into another, but the dugongs sank and were not seen again.

Three Aborigines suddenly appeared on the beach. Unarmed, they eagerly accepted knitted caps, pork and biscuits, and with only Bongaree and Flinders near them, were cheerful, singing and breaking into a dance. As the seamen approached, however, they became alarmed. To restore good feeling, Flinders asked the three Scotsmen in the crew to dance a reel. They did, but without music it was a poor performance, 'which was contemplated by the natives without much amusement or curiosity'[11] before they departed good-naturedly.

The *Norfolk* was righted on the evening's high tide, and at 1 o'clock in the morning was afloat. At sunrise Flinders brought her alongside an embankment, and the men began the task of loading breakers and restowing the sloop's gear and provisions.

To the north, seemingly at the end of the waterway's gleaming path, the pale blue shapes of the Glass House Mountains remained unexplained. Now impatient with curiosity, Flinders took the *Norfolk* some 2–3 miles farther up the channel. White beaches backed by forest lined the waterway on either side. There were innumerable birds of seemingly countless varieties—oystercatchers, ibises, pelicans, curlews, fastidiously stalking stilts, an osprey diving into the water after its prey. The *Norfolk* anchored for the night near the western shore, where they saw the small red glow of a fire and heard young female voices drifting out over the water.

In the morning Flinders, Bongaree and a crew rowed upstream in the *Norfolk*'s boat. From a still, woods-surrounded inlet on the western side, they saw the mountains straight ahead, steep-sided, green and brown. Flinders, Bongaree and two crewmen continued on foot through a swamp and onto stony ground. A great, forested mound was the closest eminence, and Flinders headed for today's 912-foot Mt Beerbarrum. Here they plunged into a tangle of vegetation—tall trees shutting out the sunlight, exposed roots like tentacles over grey rock, shadowed creepers and fallen branches. Nine hours after leaving the boat, they reached the summit. The view was magnificent—flat woodland with smoke rising from several places, the waterway and the ocean eastward, a low mountain range westward. To the north the Glass Houses jutted from the earth as from a carpet, the nearest one a startling sight, a huge, thick tower of dark, almost sheer-sided rock, patched with green near the roughly flattened top. Fascinated, the group descended the hill and headed for what is now known as Mt Tibrogargan, 1194 feet, one of ten similar formations.

As the sun sank into the treetops they stopped beside a little stream, the dark mass of Tibrogargan visible behind a shadowy tracery of trees. Enveloped by the night sounds of the forest, they slept on the ground around a small fire.

At seven o'clock the next morning they stood beneath the great perpendicular rock face of Mt Tibrogargan, sheer, deeply fissured, impossible for them to climb. Flinders had believed that the mountains were volcanic, but now 'could not distinguish any traces of scoria, lava, basalts, or other igneous remains'.[12] He was, however, partly right. The peaks are volcanic plugs 25–30 million years old, composed mainly of trachyte, which has survived the weathering away of softer material.

Flinders led his group back to the boat. There the waiting sailors had just finished cooking a black swan, which the hikers welcomed with ravenous appetites. By evening they were all aboard the sloop.

On the next morning's ebb tide the *Norfolk* moved down the waterway. Unable to get out of the passage on one tide, they anchored about a mile from the entrance. A number of Aborigines had followed their progress, sometimes singing and dancing and urging them to land. On the eastern shore Flinders had his men cut a log from a type of pine that he wanted to show carpenters at Port Jackson, and although startled when the tree crashed noisily to the ground, the onlookers remained, and Bongaree, after demonstrating their use, gave them one of his spears and a throwing-stick, a device evidently new to them.

Heavy rain and squally winds held the sloop at this anchorage for two days. Aborigines came and went on shore, sometimes singing and dancing, at other times fishing with scoop nets. Flinders also saw some large-meshed nets, possibly designed to catch turtles and the big seal-like animals he had seen. When the rain stopped, he sent a party ashore to gather firewood, and for the first time the Aborigines allowed the sailors to advance carrying their muskets. The encounter settled into an exchange of entertainment, the natives singing in a manner the visitors found pleasingly musical, followed by a rendering by Bongaree, whose singing ability was, however, limited. The local singers then recommenced their song, and finding that their audience listened attentively, each selected one of the British and sang into his ear. Others appeared, joining in the songs and dances. Flinders provided a few gifts and there was an amusing exchange of names, each group struggling with the pronunciation of the other's language.

The *Norfolk* sailed from the bay on 31 July. By five o'clock in the afternoon the highest Glass House was a tiny peak to the southwest that soon disappeared from the view of those on deck.

A day and a half later they sighted Sandy Cape, the northern extremity of modern Fraser Island. As charted by Cook, however, the cape was the head of what he called Great Sandy Peninsula. The *Norfolk* passed over the far end of the tail of reefs Cook had named Breaksea Spit and against a southeast night wind beat into Hervey Bay.

Flinders explored the bay for five days, observing with his instruments, sounding, sketching the coastline and watching for a river or a second opening to the sea. The bay was extensive, the eastern shore sandy, with white bluffs and sand hills 'slightly covered with vegetation', the west side a low, wooded coast rising into hills. To one side Flinders was looking at a large island and to the other at the mainland.

Southward the bay narrowed into the strait that further separates Fraser Island from the mainland, but this waterway eluded the explorers. Repeated attempts to get around an island were blocked by shallows, and with the sun low in the west and no desire to remain in shoal water after dark, Flinders turned the *Norfolk* to the northwest. He then shaped his course for the northern end of Breaksea Spit, thus bypassing one of Hervey Bay's main rivers, the Burnett.

At nine o'clock in the evening of 7 August, with deep water under his keel and the vessel's latitude by the star Vega at 24°22'S agreeing with the log, Flinders believed he had passed the Spit. At half past ten he confirmed this with the sloop's position at 24°21'S by the star Altair and, soon after, a sounding of 13 fathoms. The next day the *Norfolk* was in the Pacific, steering for Port Jackson.

Flinders found that, contrary to Cook's observations, the southward current was strongest between six to twenty leagues from shore. He therefore remained barely within sight of land. At dusk on 20 August 1799 the *Norfolk* was in Sydney Cove, secured alongside the *Reliance*. Flinders wrote, 'I must acknowledge myself to have been disappointed in not being able to penetrate into the interior of New South Wales, by either of the openings examined in this expedition; but, however mortifying the conviction might be, it was then an ascertained fact, that no river of importance intersected the East Coast between the 24th and the 39th degrees of south latitude'.[13]

Yet all that he had seen deepened Flinders's fascination for this mysterious land. Years later he wrote: 'The vast interior of this new country was wrapped in total obscurity; and excited, perhaps on that very account, full as much curiosity as did the forms of its shores'. Regretfully, he added, 'This part of the subject, however, will scarcely be thought to belong to a naval expedition . . .'[14]

11

'If Adverse Fortune Does Not Oppose Me, I Will Succeed'

Why did Flinders and other navigators fail repeatedly to discover the outlets of Australian rivers? There were several reasons. English explorers expected rivers to flow into the sea by way of obvious estuaries, as did the Thames and other European rivers, and early river discoveries in Australia tended to support this idea. The Parramatta River emptied visibly into Port Jackson, the Hawkesbury into Broken Bay and, similarly, the Tamar and Derwent ran into large inlets. Flinders expected to see a river at the southern end of Moreton Bay, which had the appearance of an estuary, but failed to see the river mouths he actually passed.

The Australian shoreline, especially in the north, is typically screened by mud flats, sandbanks and mangrove-laced swamps, behind which a river, especially at its lowest stage, would disembogue almost unnoticeably. In fact, most rivers would eventually be discovered from the land side, not from the sea.

Furthermore, the British did not understand the effect of the seasons on these rivers. In the dry, cooler months of this essentially dry continent the flow of even major rivers shrinks dramatically. In August and September, for instance, several discharge less—and in some cases very much less—than ten per cent of the average annual discharge.[1] As exploration tended to be timed for the dry season, this would be the situation.

Flinders delivered the log of the voyage to Governor Hunter. His account contained some quite detailed observations on native people, and on plants and animals, but comments on his companions were few. He referred to Bongaree as 'an intelligent native of Port Jackson'[2] whose conduct was often the key to friendly relations with the people encountered. Trim, he later wrote, was responsible for guarding the *Norfolk*'s bread bags. Other than to state initially that Samuel Flinders was on board, Matthew made no mention of his brother. In later writings Flinders summarised the journey, explaining that the longer narrative was included in David Collins's history of the colony. The original log appears to have been lost.[3]

In a letter to Evan Nepean at the Admiralty on 15 August 1799, Governor Hunter discussed a replacement for the *Reliance*, which, as he wrote, was 'too weak and infirm to be longer employ'd here' but had been given 'such repairs as would enable her with safety to return home . . .'[4] Waterhouse had been told to be prepared to sail 'this season' for England by way of Cape Horn.

This was the letter in which Hunter reported the circumnavigation of Van Diemen's Land in late 1798 and early 1799, and included Flinders's manuscript chart of the island's coast. Put first into the hands of Alexander Dalrymple, the map was given for publication to the private cartographer, Aaron Arrowsmith of 24 Rathbone Place, London. It was entitled 'A Chart of Basses Strait between New South Wales and Van Diemen's Land Explored by Mattw. Flinders . . . by order of His Ex. Governor Hunter 1798–1799'. Flinders's name and work had again come before Britain's nautical authorities.

Matthew and Samuel Flinders were back on duty on the *Reliance* when, between August and December 1799, she made two trips to Norfolk Island, her return to Sydney on 24 December noted in the 'List of Ships and Vessels which Enter'd Inwards in the Port of Port Jackson . . .'[5]

Assisted by his brother, Flinders worked on the observations and narrative of the journey north, and on the northern manuscript chart, with revisions to the southern chart to make the two conform. The chart of the north coast was published in January 1800, under a title that gave full credit to Captain Cook's findings and the additions of other explorers, John Shortland, Captain Broughton of HMS *Providence*, the surveyor Charles Grimes, Captain Swain of the *Eliza* and the logbooks of the *Deptford*, 1797, 'collected and arranged by

Mattw. Flinders—2nd Lieut. of H.M.S. *Reliance*, Jan. 1800'. Thickened lines indicated parts of the coast drawn from Flinders's own survey.

The Flinders brothers also took a series of observations at Cattle Point, Sydney Cove's eastern headland, a grassy slope slanting down to a level rock ledge where the cattle of the First Fleet had been landed. Filled in with the construction of a sea wall in about 1850, Cattle Point became Bennelong Point, now occupied by the Sydney Opera House. Matthew and Samuel Flinders observed twelve meridian altitudes of the sun with sextants and artificial horizons and made 60 sets of lunar observations with four different sextants. They put the point's position at 33°52'02"S and 151°17'12"E. Their error was only 34" in latitude and 4'22" in longitude.

On 1 January 1800 Flinders acquired a grant of 300 acres at Botany Bay's Banks Town. The earlier grant of 100 acres was evidently cancelled, replaced by a similar one and the addition of two adjacent plots of 100 acres each, formerly owned by two marines.[6]

Flinders was fully aware of a persisting if limited official interest in the further examination of Australian coasts, deduced from the surveying missions on which he had been sent, and from official statements and informal conversations with Hunter and his fellow officers. In January 1800 Flinders wrote to a friend, Captain Pultney Malcolm of HMS *Suffolk*, that there was some word of one or two ships to be sent out by the government for this purpose, and that he would be given the command.[7] Joseph Banks's proposals on Australian exploration by Mungo Park had reached Hunter in July 1799, and it is likely that the governor implied something to his young officer. Flinders, then, would have believed there were ongoing possibilities for himself in the very area for which he knew he was better qualified than almost anyone else.

As repairs to the *Reliance* reached completion, Flinders's thoughts of a future in trade were shunted aside by the more immediate demands of preparations for the long voyage home. On 3 March 1800 the much repaired *Reliance* sailed for England by way of the Pacific and Cape Horn. In the months on board, Flinders's commercial aspirations clearly faded. Long-time ambitions revived. He weighed his future again in terms of his naval career, and its goals were once again exploration and discovery, and the fame and status that would come with great accomplishments in this field. These objectives and the ambition to achieve them became stronger, clearer and more specific than ever before.

The voyage was rough and difficult, the old ship making water at the rate of nine or ten inches per hour, so the pumps were kept going, a task at which two stowaway convicts were conveniently employed. Some 350 miles southeast of New Zealand, the men sighted a small, hitherto unknown island and several islets, barren and evidently inhabited only by seals. An eye-sketch survey, 'copied by S. Flinders', survives. Still uninhabited except by seals, the group now appears on maps of the Southern Ocean as the Antipodes Islands.

On 30 May the *Reliance* reached the mid-Atlantic island of St Helena, the precipitous cliffs of an extinct volcano rising from the ocean, discovered by the Portuguese in 1502 but held by the English East India Company since 1659. At Jamestown, its only settlement, the governor, Lieutenant-Colonel Robert Brooke, offered ready assistance to the sea-mauled *Reliance* and its exhausted men. The *Reliance* remained at Jamestown for three weeks. With Brooke, Flinders discussed Bass Strait as a possible route to China for the East India Company's ships, and on departure carried a letter from Brooke to the company in London, endorsing several suggestions.

HMS *Reliance* arrived at Plymouth on 27 August 1800 and subsequently at Portsmouth after an absence of five and a half years. Unhappy news from Donington awaited the Flinders brothers. Elizabeth, their best-loved sister, married and the mother of two young children, had died, as had Mary Franklin, who had been Matthew's 'dear little brother Molly' as they grew up.

During the passage home, Flinders had readied for publication three charts and an accompanying pamphlet of observations and sailing directions. He had also developed a plan for further exploration of Terra Australis that, if implemented and entrusted to him, would surely give him the advancement and eminence he wanted. Later he would write to Banks:

> I have too much ambition to rest in the unnoticed middle order of mankind. Since neither birth nor fortune have favoured me, my actions shall speak to the world. In the regular service of the Navy there are too many competitors for fame. I have therefore chosen a branch which,

> though less rewarded by rank and fortune, is yet little less in celebrity. In this the candidates are fewer, and in this, if adverse fortune does not oppose me, I will succeed; and although I cannot rival the immortalized name of Cook, yet if persevering industry, joined with what ability I may possess, can accomplish it, then will I secure the second place . . .[8]

The words, although written in 1804, express well what Flinders had evidently determined by the time he reached England in 1800. He was at a point in his life at which, he decided, he must either act towards these goals or content himself with the 'penury', as he had put it, of a lifetime as an undistinguished lieutenant. And he was, he believed, the obvious choice to lead the exploration that would yield this success. There were difficulties. At 26 years of age he was young for an important command. His seniority as a lieutenant amounted to less than two years. His background provided no useful connections, and he was once more without patronage.

Yet he had contacts and he intended to use them. And of these the most important was Sir Joseph Banks. On 6 September 1800, eleven days after his arrival in England, he wrote a letter to Banks at his London home in Soho Square. It was one of the sudden, impetuous acts that Matthew Flinders would sometimes commit. This one was marked for success.

Flinders's decision to approach Banks directly was both astute and logical. There were other possible sources of support for his plans: the Admiralty or the Home Office, then responsible for colonial matters. He also carried a letter from Robert Brooke to the London office of the powerful East India Company. But Banks, he knew, was regarded as the ultimate authority on Australia and the wielder of enormous influence in scientific and colonial affairs, and in countless other areas. In any decision related to New South Wales Banks was likely to be consulted. To go to him would be to go to the summit.

Flinders began his letter by referring to his charts of Van Diemen's Land and Bass Strait and summarising briefly the results of his work on the east coast of New South Wales. He then discussed the apparent lack of large rivers and the possibility of a strait separating New South Wales in the east from New Holland in the west. He stressed the importance of this exploration to geography and natural science and to the interests of Britain. He wrote:

> It cannot be doubted, but that a very great part of that still extensive country remains either totally unknown, or has been partially examined at a time when navigation was much less advanced than at present . . . a person or persons . . . should examine into the natural productions of this wonderful country . . . the mineralogical branch would probably not be the least interesting.[9]

These were themes that had long preoccupied Joseph Banks.

Since his arrival Flinders had learned that the brig *Lady Nelson* had been dispatched six months earlier for exploration and charting on the Australian coast, and saw the likelihood of his being ordered back to Sydney to take over those explorations in a vessel he considered too small to perform well in the waters he knew. Diplomatically, he continued: 'if Sir Joseph Banks will excuse me, I presume she must be very inadequate to the task, as perhaps would be any single vessel'. He then put forward a general plan for the country's circumnavigation, stressing the need for two vessels, at least one of which should be considerably larger than the *Lady Nelson.*

He went on: 'If his Majesty should be so far desirous to have the discovery of New Holland completed . . . and the late discoveries in that country should so far meet approbation as to induce the execution of it to be committed to me, I should enter upon it with that zeal which I hope has hitherto characterized my service'. He concluded with his intention to call upon Banks at his Soho Square residence and apologised for the informality of the letter, explaining this by his long employment abroad and an education among 'the unpolished inhabitants of the Lincolnshire fens . . .'

It was a sincere, yet very clever letter, and despite its conventional but appealing apologies, it was a startlingly bold move for a young and fairly junior lieutenant to approach uninvited this rich and famous Englishman. As it happened, Banks was not in London but at his estates in Derbyshire and later, apparently, at Revesby Abbey in Lincolnshire, and it would be November before he returned to the city. While the letter may have been forwarded to Banks, a silence of nearly two months followed, giving Flinders considerable cause for anxiety as he reflected on what could well be interpreted as unacceptable audacity on his part.

By late September the *Reliance* was at the Nore, the naval anchorage in the estuary of the Thames. Brown tides moved in and out, and by night there was the star-like gleam of the Nore Lightship in midstream, a glimmer on the water and sometimes a blurred beacon in the fog.

Flinders now wrote to Ann Chappelle. She had not answered his letter of March 1799, nor two he had written before that, and he now reproached her good-naturedly for this and wrote of his grief at the loss of his sister Elizabeth and of Mary Franklin. He continued: 'As you are one of those friends whom I consider it indispensibly necessary to see, I should be glad to have some little account of your movements, where you reside and with whom; that my motions may be regulated according . . .'[10]

As to those motions, he said, as soon as the ship was ordered to Woolwich or Deptford, he would be going to London to put into effect 'the business I have got to do' and, once paid off, would probably spend two months and more in the city to complete the work; 'But if the absence of people from London at this time, should oblige me to defer some part till they return, then I shall take that opportunity of coming into Lincolnshire, if so long a time as three weeks can be spared'. He went on:

> You see that I make everything subservient to business. Indeed my dearest friend, this time seems to be a very critical period of my life. I have long been absent,—have done services abroad that were not expected, but which seem to be thought a good deal of. I have more and greater friends than before, and this seems to be the moment that their exertions may be most serviceable to me. I may now perhaps make a bold dash forward, or may remain a poor lieutenant all my life.

He was, he assured his 'dear friend Annette', her 'most affectionate friend and brother, Matthew Flinders'.

He folded, refolded and sealed the letter and, picking up his quill, addressed it to Miss Chappelle at Barton, where she was visiting. Flinders wanted to maintain the relationship with Ann, but his future and what he must do to provide for it were foremost in his mind. It appears that Ann, too, had reservations but, her emotions perhaps heightened by the thought of seeing Matthew again, subsequent correspondence suggests that she answered, although the letter has not survived.

On 7 October the *Reliance* entered the harbour at Deptford. The ship's company were paid off and the vessel was dismantled and submitted to the dockyard carpenter. He found the old ship's masts and yards rotting, the bottom and main- and quarter-decks leaking and the 'whole of the hull . . . in a very disabled state'.[11]

Samuel Flinders journeyed to Donington. His father wrote, 'I find Saml. grown and improved equal to my most Sanguine Expectation. Mattw.'s affairs yet detain him in Town, but I hope to see him ere long . . .'[12] Samuel had, however, shown some disdain of his naval career, which disturbed his father, but at the time it was a minor point. On 6 November Samuel left Donington to join HMS *Almene*, 64 guns, an appointment largely arranged by Matthew. Having passed the necessary examination, Samuel was promoted to lieutenant on 1 March 1801 at the age of eighteen.

A month after the docking of the *Reliance* at Deptford, Flinders travelled to London and, paid off, took lodgings at 16 King Street in Soho, not far from Banks's town residence. Accommodation had been found for Trim in Deptford, where a forbearing landlady looked after a cat that had known no home but a ship. Flinders would then have gone to the Admiralty to put his charts before the authorities there, and probably was referred to Alexander Dalrymple.

Dalrymple, aged 63, had for the past five years been in the process of creating the Admiralty's Hydrographical Office, in small quarters and with a small staff to examine and organise more than a century's accumulation of hydrographic material, at the same time processing incoming documents. Not yet equipped for printing new charts, the Office passed many such surveys on to the private concern of Aaron Arrowsmith for engraving and publication.

Flinders saw two charts produced by Arrowsmith from his own surveys and was delighted with the exemplary styling and accuracy of the work, as well as the careful inclusion of his own notations and nomenclature. Now he presented Arrowsmith with an amended version of his Bass Strait chart and two new charts covering sections of the New South Wales coast and Van Diemen's Land. Flinders's work was not flawless. While headlands, shoals, islands and other navigational features were located with reasonable precision, long sections of the intervening coastlines were the sketchy result of rapid running surveys. Nevertheless, the 50-year-old chartmaker and the young navigator established a cordial working relationship that was to last for the rest of Flinders's life.

Flinders also arranged for the publication of his 42-page memoir, *Observations on the Coasts of Van Diemen's Land, on Bass's Strait and its Islands, and on Part of the Coasts of New South Wales; intended to accompany the Charts of the Late Discoveries in those Countries. By Matthew Flinders, Second Lieutenant of His Majesty's Ship Reliance.* Printing began in February the following year. Flinders had by then received from Joseph Banks permission to dedicate the pamphlet to him, and the dedication duly appeared with the customary adulatory praise.

Flinders now took advantage as well of the East India Company contact he had made at St Helena. In October he wrote to the Court of Directors, probably enclosing Robert Brooke's endorsements and possibly some summary of his own work. Almost certainly he pointed out advantages to the company in his discoveries and petitioned for some form of financial assistance.

Flinders's stay in London was filled with pleasure and excitement. His work on charts and sailing directions was being recognised by some of the most important men in the field, and he had access to England's centre of naval navigation and cartography. Here he would have asked questions, listened to the suggestions of experienced men, studied other people's maps and applied himself in every way to learn more about his craft. He saw the most recent surveying equipment at the establishment of the eminent instrument-maker Edward Troughton. Undoubtedly he spent time in bookshops, perhaps buying a few professional books and, it appears, one or two volumes of literature. He had never before had the opportunity to walk the cobbled city streets, to gaze at London's impressive public buildings, to see the squares with their trees now turning gold in the crisp autumn air.

Probably Flinders saw George Bass, although there is no record of their meeting. Bass had arrived in England in early August, three weeks before the *Reliance*, and plunged immediately into arrangements for a commercial voyage to Port Jackson with Charles Bishop. This involved the purchase of a ship and a cargo of goods that could be expected to sell profitably in Sydney. Henry Waterhouse learned of the scheme when he arrived with the *Reliance* and, a man always interested in a promising investment, was eager to participate in the enterprise. His father was similarly prepared to invest. With the help of additional speculators, including his mother and an aunt, Bass formed a company and bought the sturdily built *Venus*, 142 tons.

Bass had met Henry Waterhouse's sister Elizabeth before leaving England in 1795, and evidently now found himself very much in love with her. Elizabeth adored him and, accepting that she could not accompany him on the voyage to which he was committed, she was prepared to wait for his promised return. On 8 October 1800 Bass and Elizabeth Waterhouse were quietly married. Henry Waterhouse and his sister Mary were recorded as witnesses, but it is possible that Flinders was present. On 21 December 1800 Waterhouse, Elizabeth and their father watched the *Venus* spread its sails and move down the Thames.

In the middle of November Flinders received Joseph Banks's reply to his letter:

> Soho Square, Novr. 16 1800
>
> Sir
>
> Jos: Banks present his Compts. to Mr. Flinders he is sorry indeed to have been prevented by bad health from answering a Letter he Received some time ago from Mr Flinders will be happy to see him in Soho Square at any time he will be so good as to Call upon him.[13]

Flinders's relief must have been overwhelming. He promptly presented himself at the handsome townhouse at 32 Soho Square. Banks received him cordially, listened and approved all the main points of his plan. A week later the mechanism of bringing into reality a major voyage of exploration was fully in motion.

The remarkable speed with which this project came alive shows that despite limited government interest, some serious considerations of the faraway continent had been developing in the minds of certain influential men. Banks had discussed New South Wales at length in meetings as early as 1797 with Collins and Paterson, when they returned to

England, and particularly with Philip King. Letters between Banks and King on the colony's affairs go back to 1790, and during the two years he spent in England recovering his health, King had been in frequent contact with Banks.

Questions about the strange new land abounded. Was it a single landmass or two great islands? What lay in that mysterious centre? Surely there were potential harbour sites, mineral resources and a safer route through Torres Strait that needed only to be located. The security of Britain's faraway little settlement in a time of recurring war and international rivalry would have been an inevitable backdrop to their discussions.

Clearly Banks had been impressed by Flinders's letter of 6 September 1800. He had already considered Flinders qualified to command an exploration ship. Now he must have been further convinced of the young officer's ability and dedication. It seems likely that Banks received Flinders's letter while in Lincolnshire, and took some action in the weeks during which Flinders waited anxiously for a reply. Banks obtained the support of Earl Spencer, First Lord of the Admiralty, in what seems to have been a straightforward agreement between two powerful men with similar views, views probably reinforced by knowledge of a French expedition of discovery then under preparation. King George III gave his assent. And on 21 November, only five days after Banks had addressed an invitation to see him to Flinders, the Admiralty had selected a ship for the voyage and ordered the Navy Board to begin her refit at Sheerness.

Flinders had acquired more than a powerful patron; he had secured the solid backing of a man who was prepared to extend to him a kind of partnership in a common endeavour. Flinders assiduously cultivated Banks's support and friendship. Banks expected compliance from those he favoured, but he could reciprocate with very firm loyalty to friends and protégés.

As Flinders was aware, Britain's plans for discovery in 1800 already included the *Lady Nelson*, a vessel designed by Captain John Schanck, a commissioner of the Transport Board, and launched at Deptford in November 1798. A craft suitable for coastal exploration, especially in the search for Australia's elusive rivers, had been a matter of concern among the interested parties. This little ship seemed an answer to the problem. Fifty-two and a half feet long by 17½ feet beam and of 60 tons burden, she was flat-bottomed with three sliding keels or centre-boards, which, when raised, gave her a draught of about six feet. King found her under construction and reported the unusual craft to Banks, who promptly used his influence to tranfer the vessel from a reluctant Transport Board to the Colonial Department.

The *Lady Nelson* was completed as an armed surveying brig and readied for sea at Portsmouth. On arrival in Sydney she was to be taken over by Matthew Flinders for coastal exploration and surveys. Philip King sailed for New South Wales as governor-elect in November 1799. The *Lady Nelson* followed in March 1800 with Lieutenant James Grant in command. Arriving in Sydney in April 1800, King found that Flinders had left for England with the *Reliance* the previous month. By the time the *Lady Nelson* reached New South Wales in December an entirely different ship was being prepared in England for an expedition to be led by Flinders. A few months later the Admiralty decided that the *Lady Nelson* should be included in Flinders's expedition as a tender under his orders.

During a long stay at Cape Town on his way to Port Jackson, Grant had received instructions to survey the recently discovered Bass Strait. Grant sighted the Australian coast near the present border between Victoria and South Australia. An excellent seaman but not a qualified hydrographic surveyor, and extemely short of provisions and therefore time, Grant was able to produce only a rough eye-sketch of the Bass Strait area. The *Lady Nelson* had not been the ideal vessel for coastal work, beating to windward only with great difficulty and too readily kept weather-bound in port. Nevertheless, in 1801 and 1802 King sent her out for further exploration along the south coast of New South Wales, and her commanders, Grant and then Lieutenant John Murray, completed a number of charts.

12

Enlightenment and Exploration

Matthew Flinders's birth into England's middle class and the education and training he received gave him the background and outlook of a man who was heir to the accomplishments and beliefs of the scientific revolution of his own time and of the preceding 17th century. To a greater or lesser extent such persons shared in the European intellectual climate that regarded its ideas on God and man, reason and nature, as liberal, rational and enlightened beyond those of any preceding period in history, and as constituting an age, in fact, of Enlightenment.

The exploration of the planet was, in the view of 18th century England's educated classes, an extension of the philosophical concepts of the Enlightenment. Springing largely from the scientific achievements of the previous decades, most particularly from Newton's encapsulating the laws of planetary motion in a few mathematical equations, these concepts carried a strong belief in humanity's ultimate ability to achieve and understand Knowledge. Solutions to humanity's problems could be attained through the correct application of rational thinking. Thus the Enlightenment signified progress. As well, it conduced to first-hand observation and experience being the prime means of obtaining information. Such members of England's elite as Joseph Banks believed further that knowledge should then be used for the continued improvement of society, which could be a very widely defined notion. It could be seen as economic prosperity and the daily comforts this could bring, as better health, as political stability, as philanthropy, among many other interpretations.

Exploration fitted perfectly into such a scheme. It sought and acquired information of every kind, which was gained through the personal experience of the explorer, who brought home knowledge that could be of value to others. The explorer's methods of navigation and cartography were themselves derivations of and sometimes improvements upon the mathematical work done by previous navigators, surveyors, mathematicians and astronomers. In the course of his discoveries there unrolled before the explorer, and such scientific specialists who might accompany him, an entire new world of information on hitherto unknown or little known lands, to be documented in drawings, paintings, notes and journals and carried home.

A sense of gratification in sharing in the expansion of knowledge was a feature, too, of the Enlightenment. This was manifest in the widespread communication among scientists and in the collections, museum displays, botanical gardens and published atlases and journals that became available for both public viewing and serious study. The application of such information to what were perceived as useful projects could be endless, ranging from the introduction of beneficial new products to reducing the hazards of the sea, from unfolding commercial opportunities to political and territorial advantage. Joseph Banks's espousal of the transportation of breadfruit trees from Pacific islands to the West Indies was just such a useful result of exploration, the discovery by European investigators of a valuable food product and the subsequent transfer of this food source for the benefit of West Indian planters. Similarly, Banks directed his explorer–botanists to bring back rare and interesting specimens for the Royal Botanical Gardens at Kew, where the public could enjoyably share in new knowledge and derive satisfaction, even happiness, from being part of a progressive and enlightened society. For the little outlying colony of New South Wales, the Enlightenment's desire for information served a helpful purpose. Botanical and zoological collecting, observations of its exceptional geographical features and tentative anthropological studies all roused further interest in a distant land and eventually pointed to the ways in which it could be increasingly valuable to Britain.

The importance given by European society to the acquisition of knowledge transcended in some ways the barriers of political rivalry among nations. There was a complex combination of international scientific cooperation and international competition, particularly in relations between Britain and France, that led on occasion to the British government's preparedness to support further discovery even if it was not its own.

Internal conflicts and European wars had to a large extent curtailed French exploration in the 16th and 17th centuries. By the early 1700s, however, a strong, unified and centralised French state was prepared to join in searching the oceans for the planet's unknown places. The theories of scientists and other savants spurred these endeavours, for the mystery of a great legendary continent to the south remained unsolved, and existing knowledge of lands and islands to the east held many questions. A new literary genre centred upon discoveries, both real and hypothetical, was further popularising the idea of voyages of exploration. Thus in the later 18th century the European nations, but principally England and France, channelled considerable energy into the pursuit of worldwide geographical knowledge. Effective in the enhancement of science, this knowledge was also applied to commercial and strategic advantage.

The pressure in France of its mercantile interests was considerable. To add to existing French colonial holdings in North America and the West Indies, trading companies were established to secure, pursue and oversee commerce with east Africa, India and the East Indies. Seeking halfway stations for their ships on long voyages and new potentially lucrative trade opportunities, French navigators gradually claimed for France an expanding, largely insular empire. Thus in 1715 Guillaume Dufresne d'Arsel annexed Mauritius, which he renamed Ile de France; in 1739 Jean-Baptiste-Charles Bouvet de Lozier sighted the ice-bound little Indian Ocean island that is now Bouvetöya, and in 1769 Louis Antoine de Bougainville completed the first French circumnavigation of the globe, ushering in French claims to empire in the Pacific. Three years later Marc-Joseph Marion Dufresne followed Tasman's track to Tasmania and New Zealand, while Yves Joseph de Kerguélen-Trémarec discovered the subantarctic islands that bear his name. In 1772 François Alesno de Sainte-Allouarn sent a party ashore at Shark Bay in Western Australia to take possession in the name of King Louis XV of France.

In the late 18th century, however, the French expeditions of Jean-François de Galaup, Comte de la Pérouse, and Joseph-Antoine Raymond de Bruny d'Entrecasteaux ended abortively. Hence, in 1799 the Institut National de France, the scientific society that had succeeded the pre-revolutionary Académie des Sciences, set up a committee to examine a proposal to continue the work of these two explorers.

The proposal came principally from Nicolas Thomas Baudin, originally an officer in the French merchant service, but more recently the leader of two Austrian expeditions collecting rare botanical specimens for the palace gardens of Emperor Joseph II. While on a third voyage, Baudin learned that Austria and France were at war. He returned to France and later retrieved his extensive botanical collection, left in Trinidad, for the Muséum National in Paris. Baudin thereby won a reputation as an outstanding navigator with a special interest in natural history, and his proposal for a French scientific voyage in the track of D'Entrecasteaux came before a receptive committee. An original plan underwent revisions and in March 1800 Baudin and the committee approached Napoleon Bonaparte, who headed France's new government, the Consulate. Bonaparte approved the expedition. He was genuinely interested in science, and a successful voyage of exploration could only glorify the cultural image of a new, progressive French nation.

The revised plan for the scientific voyage centred largely on New Holland. It had been developed by members of two very highly respected scientific bodies, the Muséum and the Institut, and its purpose was specifically stated to be the pursuit of science.

There was no overt suggestion of territorial aggrandisement. Official instructions included no requirement to claim or recommend locations for settlement. The question nevertheless arises as to whether, in giving his approval, Napoleon Bonaparte had any military or political designs on the southern continent.

It seems unlikely that in 1800 Bonaparte was prepared to attempt a settlement on the other side of the world. His navy had suffered severely in Egypt while his armies were increasingly successful in Europe. By the Treaty of Amiens in 1802 Bonaparte conceivably could have demanded space in New Holland. He did not do so. His decision not to pursue an overseas empire is perhaps further suggested by the sale of the Louisiana Territory in 1803 to the United States. In 1800, then, British authorities were prepared to accept the Baudin expedition as a scientific enterprise, the official view being that the international benefits of a scientific voyage must be supported.

The French chose two corvettes, renamed and thoroughly outfitted for the expedition. They were the *Géographe*, about 400 tons burden, and the *Naturaliste*, a little less in tonnage, both well-built ships, although the *Géographe* was the better sailer. Baudin commanded the expedition and the *Géographe*. Jacques Felix Emmanuel Hamelin commanded the *Naturaliste* and was the expedition's second-in-command. Each ship carried a very large staff of officers. As well, twelve scientists boarded the *Géographe* and ten the *Naturaliste*—hydrographers, astronomers, zoologists, mineralogists, a botanist, as well as gardeners and artists. Baudin was given an ambitious itinerary with instructions to examine the D'Entrecasteaux Channel and reconnoitre Bass Strait and the continent's unknown south coast; to explore New Holland's southwest, west, northwest and north coasts, known and unknown, and to make a detailed investigation of the Gulf of Carpentaria and the south coast of New Guinea. At all times Baudin was to facilitate the work of the scientists. Both ships were lavishly equipped for their work, with an extensive library and a complete range of instruments and supplies for surveying, navigation, astronomy and other studies. Probably no scientific voyage had ever been so munificently prepared.

Although France and Britain were at war, communication among their scientific elite remained open. The French government now requested safe-conduct passports for the expedition, guaranteeing the safety of the vessels from British ships and in British ports. This was negotiated through Banks and granted by Earl Spencer. On 19 October 1800 the two ships sailed from Le Havre. Their first landfall was to be Ile de France, today's Mauritius, and their second the coast of New Holland.

Despite ready official cooperation with the French in the name of science, some British factions believed that there were serious commercial and political motives behind the search for new geographical knowledge. The East India Company, which held a very lucrative monopoly on Britain's trade, was interested in harbours on Australia's northwest coast and did not want promising locations occupied by the French. As well, the company saw the alarming possibility of the French discovering new sea lanes eastward and French privateers operating from bases in New Holland, as they were doing from their established haven in Mauritius. Scientific circles saw important French discoveries taking place where English geographers and naturalists should be bringing out new findings. For over half a century Britain had led in maritime exploration with the voyages of George Anson, Cook, Bligh and George Vancouver, and for many the possible surrender of this pre-eminence to France was unacceptable.

The intellectual force of the scientific revolution of the 17th and 18th centuries had its roots in the earlier period of the Renaissance. The great burgeoning of thought and talent that then took place in art, science, technology and so many other fields extended to a driving desire to investigate the world beyond Europe. Thus European expansion across the oceans began in the 15th century as Portuguese ships crept year by year down the coast of Africa, around its southernmost point and eastward, and Spanish vessels caught the northeast trade winds to cross the Atlantic Ocean to the islands and coasts of the Americas. The ships of other nations followed. By the mid-18th century attention focused on the Pacific Ocean, which, however, Spain considered to be its own. Claimed by Vasco Núñez de Balboa in 1513 and crossed by Ferdinand Magellan in 1521, its eastern rim was secured by Spanish colonies along the American littoral, while its principal sea lanes were anchored at either end by the trade emporiums of Manila in the Philippines and Acapulco in Mexico. The papal bulls of 1493 and the Treaty of Tordesillas of 1494 firmed the Spanish claim. From the Spanish point of view this was recognised by the Treaty of Utrecht signed by Britain and Spain in 1713 and by the treaty between the two nations concluded at Versailles in 1783. Thus throughout the 18th century Spain continued to regard the Pacific as its territory.

By the middle 1700s, however, other European powers were overshadowing Spain, and wars in Europe were providing the incentive to carry hostilities and the expectation of rich plunder into the Pacific.

In 1740–44 an English naval squadron under George Anson attacked Spain's Pacific ports and shipping, and despite appalling losses, stimulated British interest in possible commerce with Spain's American colonies and in hitherto undiscovered lands. Britain's protestations that its voyages were solely for purposes of discovery met with Spanish disbelief. Inevitably, the Spanish reasoned, discovery would be followed by possession.

Thus the British expedition of 1764 under Commodore John Byron sailed in secrecy, for Byron's instructions included taking possession of uninhabited lands or other 'suitable situations'. In the same year Britain sent into the Pacific a second expedition, two ships commanded by Captain Samuel Wallis and Lieutenant Philip Carteret. 'Trade and navigation' were their stated objectives, but both officers were instructed to find the legendary Great South Land, to purchase land for bases from its inhabitants, or if uninhabited, to take possession for Britain. In 1768 the French expedition under Louis Antoine de Bougainville entered the Pacific through the Strait of Magellan. Bougainville's instructions included taking possession for France of lands useful for commerce or navigation over which no other European nation had established claims. Spurred by the voyaging of other powers into its oceanic territory, Spain dispatched several expeditions into the Pacific during the 1770s.

A new element was now added to the agenda of European exploration. Expanding scientific interests concerned the organisers of these expeditions. Bougainville's voyage of 1766–69 was accompanied by a scientific staff that included the eminent naturalist Philibert Commerson. Less obvious, however, was the fact that scientific investigation was being merged with the geopolitical ambitions of the European powers. Science, held in such high regard, was being used as a camouflage for military and political reconnoitring.

Britain's maritime scientific investigations went back to the 1699–1701 explorations in Australian and New Guinea waters of William Dampier, and the astronomical studies conducted at sea by Edmond Halley between 1676 and 1700. Britain's greatest seagoing scientific effort, however, was the voyage of the renovated collier, *Endeavour*, under the command of Lieutenant James Cook. The expedition was organised by the Council of the Royal Society, with the cooperation of the Admiralty, for the purpose of observing the transit of the planet Venus across the face of the sun, and to the ship's complement were added well-equipped scientists, artists and assistants. The astronomical work at Tahiti completed, Cook went on to the second part of his instructions. This ordered a search for the great unknown south land. The political element of Cook's instructions, however, went beyond discovering the mythical continent. Britain's prosperity was built on commerce, and the vision of a great trading empire was an inextricable part of her explorations. Failing to find the elusive south land, Cook continued west and, in New Zealand and Australia, made official claims of possession for Britain.

In the Spanish view their territorial rights in the Pacific were being transgressed by France, Russia and most seriously by Britain. The assertion of British rights to Australia's 'adjacent' Pacific islands, even to the Australian east coast itself, could be construed as encroachments upon Spanish sovereignty as reaffirmed, if indirectly, in 1713 and 1783. Spanish authorities were also well aware that their colonies of Mexico, Peru and Chile were focal points of British attention, for here Spain's trade monopolies blocked the commerce coveted by Britain.

Any number of schemes for attacking Spain in the Americas were considered by the British government during the 18th century, schemes supposedly designed to free restive native peoples from Spanish oppression, whereupon Britain could receive preferential commercial treatment from independent 'Kingdoms'.[1] In fact, London's ignorance of conditions in these areas was considerable, and despite a number of appeals by individuals claiming to represent revolutionary cliques, it was almost twenty years before active independence movements awoke throughout Spanish America.

The idea of a British colony on the east coast of the Australian continent was taking shape during the early 1780s in the minds of certain Englishmen. Among them were Sir Joseph Banks and John Montagu, Earl of Sandwich and First Lord of the Admiralty. Also involved were James Matra, who, like Banks, had sailed with Cook in 1770, his patron and a Fellow of the Royal Society, Sir George Young, and Sir John Call, a member of the Royal Society and also a member of Parliament and its Committee on Transportation. These men developed several reasons for establishing such a colony. A suitable site for an overseas penal settlement was an accepted requirement, and Matra suggested that it would provide for resettlement of displaced American Loyalists. Behind these, however, lay significant political, commercial and military interests.

Cook's favourable reports on New Zealand and Australia together with a French presence in the Pacific roused serious concern that rival European powers would establish colonies in those locations. Britain's commercial expectations for the area were considerable: the production of cotton, tobacco and sugar in New South Wales and of flax, hemp and timber in New Zealand and Norfolk Island; fur trading with the Aleutian Islands and commerce with China, Korea, Japan and the Moluccas, now Indonesia's Maluku. Matra, Young and Call also pointed to the advantages of a New South Wales colony in the event of war with the Dutch in the East Indies or with Spain in Chile and Peru.

For Spain, English preparations for settlements at Botany Bay and Norfolk Island were an alarming signal of dangers to come—British territorial expansion into the Pacific, strangling commercial rivalry, contraband trade, privateers haunting her sea lanes, British-inspired revolts in her American colonies. France also was curious as to British activity in the Pacific, and her island colony of Ile de France in the Indian Ocean served as an advance base and listening post, a circumstance of which Britain was well aware. John Call had, in fact, visited the island in 1770 and returned home with a sixteen-page report and a manuscript plan of the harbour and surroundings of Port Louis.

Thus the settlement of New South Wales in 1788 added fuel to centuries of distrust among the imperial European nations. The response to this situation was a policy of secret observations and reports to be made by ship commanders visiting foreign ports under the aegis of peaceful scientific and navigational enquiry.

In 1785 there sailed from France two ships under the command of an experienced naval officer, Jean-François de Galaup, Comte de La Pérouse. Originally conceived as a commercial probe, the expedition had developed into a major voyage of scientific enquiry. La Pérouse was not to make territorial claims, but sweeping in great arcs through the Pacific, he was to observe and report on the trade, defences and political movements of the European communities at which he called, particularly to discover British colonial intent. This last point gained significance when at Petropavlovsk on Russia's Kamchatka peninsula, he received letters couriered from Paris to inform him that a British colony was being prepared for New South Wales.

On 26 January 1788 La Pérouse's two ships entered Botany Bay just as the men and vessels of Governor Arthur Phillip's First Fleet were being transferred to a new settlement site at Port Jackson. Nevertheless, there was contact between the two groups not 19 miles apart by boat and, typically, whatever the reservations of their superiors in Europe, there were cordial relations between Europeans meeting on the other side of the world. Six weeks later La Pérouse sailed from Botany Bay and vanished into the vastness of the Pacific. Ironically, his last surviving reports to France went by way of arrangements made by Arthur Phillip.

In 1791 France's new National Assembly sent out a second expedition, led by Joseph-Antoine Raymond de Bruny, Chevalier d'Entrecasteaux. Its dual purpose was a search for La Pérouse and the prosecution of scientific studies. Yet political and commercial concerns were included in the same directives as had been given to La Pérouse. D'Entrecasteaux found no trace of La Pérouse and made no calls at Port Jackson, but carried out surveys on the south and southwest coasts of Australia before his death, bitter rifts between royalist and republican factions on board and the detention of the ships in the East Indies by the Dutch ending the expedition.

Nor were France and Britain alone in their investigations of what other Europeans were doing in the Pacific. In mid-1789 a Swedish ship, *Gustaf III*, apparently masquerading as the English *Mercury* on a voyage of exploration, visited Tahiti, Hawaii, Tinian, the Aleutian Islands and Guangzhou.[2]

On 12 March 1793 two ships of the Spanish Royal Navy sailed into Port Jackson. They were the corvettes *Descubierta* and *Atrevida*, commanded by Alexandro Malaspina, on a survey of political conditions and natural resources in the Spanish colonies of South and North America, the Mariana Islands and the Philippines. Scientific studies had taken them to New Zealand and, together with a need for water and firewood, to Sydney. They were not unexpected. In 1790 Governor Phillip had been advised from London of the impending visit and a hospitable reception recommended; on Phillip's departure the information was passed to the acting governor, Major Francis Grose. From Port Jackson Malaspina wrote to the Spanish ambassador in London: 'there has been no attention nor generosity which we have not been favoured with . . .'[3] Socially the visitors and the long-isolated colonists enjoyed a happy interval of receptions and parties, and on their departure the Spaniards made their scientific findings available to the English.

Nevertheless, there was a secret purpose to the expedition. Malaspina and his officers were charged with compiling comprehensive reports on the political and expansionist activities of Russian settlements in the North Pacific and British colonies in New South Wales and the South Pacific. In Port Jackson Malaspina saw little to justify Britain's official reasons for establishing the colony—the relocation of convicts and acquisition of ships' timber and flax for cordage. Scant success in agriculture and the expense of maintaining the settlers seemed to suggest there were more compelling reasons. These had to be commercial: supplanting Russia in the Alaskan fur trade, monopolising trade with China, intruding into the Moluccan spice trade; and territorial: a British Pacific empire, enveloping a huge part of Terra Australis and reaching across the Pacific islands.

Malaspina saw as intensely menacing to Spain the convict settlement at Port Jackson, from which a two- or three-month sail 'could bring to our defenceless coasts [of South America] two or three thousand cast-away bandits to serve interpolated with an excellent body of regular Troops'.[4] Malaspina's extensive report on the British at Port Jackson was a harsh indictment of what he saw as aggressive anti-Spanish intentions. Beneath the benign cover of scientific work, espionage had functioned well.[5]

In October 1800 the French expedition under the command of Nicolas Baudin sailed for Terra Australis and from May 1801 until mid-1803 was mainly in Australian waters. To what extent, if any, was Baudin directed to carry out spying activities? His instructions, drafted by the Comte de Fleurieu, a Councillor of State and a noted geographer, did not include a visit to Port Jackson, which Fleurieu might have regarded as potentially provocative in wartime, possibly endangering the validity of the ships' passports. Political interest can, however, be read into Baudin's orders to give particular attention to Tasmania's Derwent River–D'Entrecasteaux Channel area, previously explored by the French.

Essentially Baudin's orders dealt only with scientific activities, yet how can navigational and cartographic information not serve either a commercial or strategic purpose? A remark in the journal of a nineteen-year-old sub-lieutenant, Jacques de Saint-Cricq, on the unsuitability for settlement of the entrance to the Swan River, could be interpreted as reflecting a political motive. The attractive drawings of the artist Charles Alexandre Lesueur are, in fact, visual records of the layout of Sydney, the port and countless details including gun placement.

There were events that suggest secret instructions. On 16 March 1801, the day after his arrival at Ile de France, Baudin addressed a letter to the island's administrators, informing them without explanation that there were political motives for the voyage. Alarmed, the governor reported the matter to Pierre Alexandre Forfait, Minister of Marine and the Colonies, assuring him that he had told no one of the letter.[6] Even more curious is an incident that took place a few months later. During the expedition's stay at Timor, Baudin became dangerously ill and, thinking that he might die, told his second-in-command, Captain Hamelin, where he would find a secret directive that he must obey implicitly or be personally responsible to his government and to posterity.[7] Baudin recovered, and there seems to be no further reference to the mysterious order.

Although Baudin was not instructed to take his ships into Port Jackson, the expedition, beset by storm damage and sickness, did come into the English port, where it spent five months undergoing repairs and recuperation.

Here the cover of scientific work was actively put to use by the zoologist, François Péron, in some extensive spying, with observations that he compiled into a lengthy although not always accurate report on conditions in the colony, the expansionist intentions of the British and recommendations for a French invasion. A young officer of the *Naturaliste,* Louis Claude de Saulces de Freycinet, gathered information on the harbour for use in landing troops. There is no direct evidence of Baudin's knowledge of these activities, but that he was as concerned as Péron with the progress made by the colony in the fourteen years of its existence is clear from a letter he wrote in May 1803 to Forfait: 'I should warn you that the colony of Port Jackson well merits the attention of the Government and even of the other European powers, especially Spain ... It seems to me that politics demands that we weigh by whatever means possible the preparations they are making for the future, which foreshadows some large projects'.[8]

France and Britain were at war throughout much of this period and the outlook of many officers and scientists could not be divorced from patriotic notions of political and military advantage. This is obvious in the activities of Péron and Freycinet. And Governor King had his suspicions. When the French ships left Port Jackson, the colonial surgeon James Thomson travelled to Europe on the *Naturaliste*, carrying a letter from King to Lord Hobart, Secretary of State for War and the Colonies. King wrote of Baudin's extensive natural history collections, adding:

> . . . yet I am inclined to think from his Geographical pursuits that collecting alone is not the principal object of his Mission, as it has very forcibly struck me that they have an intention of looking for a place proper to make a similar Establishment to this, on the W. or N.W. Coast, it has also occurred to me, that they may have some intention of laying claim to Van Diemen's Land, now it is known to be insulated from New Holland . . . [9]

On hearing a rumour shortly afterwards that the French did intend to found a settlement in Van Diemen's Land, King dispatched in great haste Acting Lieutenant Charles Robbins in the schooner *Cumberland* to find Baudin, observe events and deliver a letter on the rumour. Robbins was to mention that he was on his way to find a suitable British settlement site in southeast Van Diemen's Land, in King's words 'a blind', intended to emphasise British claims to that area. Baudin at once denied the idea of French intrusion, but King retained his suspicions. He wrote to Joseph Banks: 'What political object the French have in view of exploring this coast I do not know, but I suspect they have a settlement on the west coast in view'.[10]

The idea of French encroachment on New South Wales persisted. Some evidence appears to indicate that in 1810 Napoleon ordered a squadron to be prepared to take Sydney. In 1813 Earl Bathurst, Secretary of State for War and Colonies, wrote to Governor Lachlan Macquarie of 'a Plan said to be entertained by the Enemy of attacking the settlements under your Government'.[11] Clearly, nothing developed from either idea.

13

'A Ship Is Fitting Out for Me'

With the Admiralty's selection of a ship in November 1800 for a voyage of exploration, Matthew Flinders knew that he was returning to New South Wales. And in the exultation of this knowledge, there were some serious personal concerns. Perhaps with the prospect of more long years away from home, perhaps because of Bass's marriage, Flinders's thoughts of Ann Chappelle took on deeper significance.

Ann's father had been John Chappelle, a shipowner and master mariner of Hull. The descendant of a French Huguenot immigrant who had established a family shipping business engaged in Baltic Sea trade, he was an intelligent and cultivated man who suffered from acute headaches and died at sea at the age of forty. His widow, Anne, also from a Hull seafaring family, had lost two of her brothers to the sea. A short, stout, efficient woman, with a reputation for being strict but kind, she was left with a small daughter, Ann. Born on 21 November 1770, Ann was about four years old when her father died.

Through church activities her mother met the Reverend William Tyler who, as a curate in the village of Partney, had purchased a house there. They were married and, although Tyler became rector of Braytoft and had parochial duties elsewhere as well, the family settled in the thatch-roofed cottage near Partney's square-towered church of St Nicholas. At twelve Ann contracted smallpox. A blister erupting in her eye was lanced and she lost her sight in that eye. Two years later her mother bore another daughter, Isabella, and despite the difference in age, the half-sisters, growing up in a close and supportive family, were devoted friends all their lives.

The village of Spilsby was only a few miles south of Partney and probably Ann first came to know the Franklin family living there and through them the Flinders family. By the time Matthew Flinders sailed on the *Reliance* in 1794, Ann was one of the 'charming sisters' with whom he was exchanging letters.

Ann Chappelle was a small, slim young woman with dark curly hair, three and a half years older than Matthew Flinders. Intelligent and artistic, she drew flowers and wrote poetry. Educated as far as most young women could expect to be at the time, she combined a considerable emotional fragility with something of her mother's practical strength. She would have grown up amid reminders of the losses to the sea that she and her mother had sustained, and her hesitation in becoming too involved with a naval officer is evident. She did not answer Flinders's later letters from Port Jackson, and even as their relationship developed she was uncertain and sought reassurance from Matthew that they might remain together, and not be separated. In 1800 she was 30, perhaps already resigned to spinsterhood. Yet the image in her mind of the young officer from Donington would have been strong and precious, and the correspondence was resumed. Ann's letters to Matthew are not extant, but from Matthew's replies it is clear that they soon discussed marriage and the possibility of Ann's accompanying him to New South Wales.

Flinders now saw himself facing new expenses: continued residence in London, probably the purchase of some personal items for the voyage, and evidently the feasibility of marrying Ann. Flinders wrote to his father, asking for a loan of £200.

It was an unfortunate time to approach the frugal Dr Flinders for money. In his diary's summary of the events of the year Dr Flinders wrote:

> I am concerned to note that a combination of distressing circumstances have closed upon us with the year & yet continue sufficient to outweigh the satisfaction of my long absent Sons arrivals—what we have long feared, has arrived my very unfortunate Son John is returned upon my hands and in a state terrible to conceive—viz a deranged one, totally unfit for any species of Business—a burden of the first magnitude, grievous to be borne—and to add to my embarassment my Daughter Susan has arrived with Mattw with a demand of a considerable Sum to set her in Business. my Son Matthew has also requested me to

> advance him a considerable Sum. all these coming upon me in the midst of the dearest winter ever known in living Memory—with my Strength, Health and Spirits very much impaired, and consequently my capability of Business much abated, have almost proved too much for me... [with] regard to the greatest distress my unfortunate Son we are leaving no Stone unturned to find out a proper receptacle for him... I have put of Matts. demand for another year. he asked for £200, but I have promised but one...[1]

The father's distress did not end there. In November Flinders had written to his father very much in the role of the family's eldest son, discussing Samuel's future and describing his and Samuel's visit to Susanna at Dartford, where she was serving her apprenticeship in millinery. Matthew remarked that 'If she is to be a milliners journey woman...'[2] she could not be in a better situation. This followed soon after Samuel's visit home, when he remarked 'in several companies' that his career was a 'beggarly thing'. Dr Flinders now took Matthew's comment as criticism of his having put Susanna in an apprenticeship, which, even if in good circumstances, was below the family's social position, and as reflecting complaints from Susanna.

On a cold Sunday morning in late November 1800 Dr Flinders wrote to Matthew. He first discussed calmly his two naval sons' career prospects, and then abruptly launched into a bitter tirade defending his belief that young people should support themselves. He cited his own hard years of work and saving, and went on:

> ...it cannot be a hard task for a grown Person in Youth, Health and Strength, to obtain their own support. I know it is much harder for a weak infirm Father in the decline of life, to continue labouring for the whole, to the last hour of his earthly race... Why my Childn should expect that I am able to make them all great people must be owing to their mistaking the amount of my property, and supposing that I have much more than I really have.[3]

Lest they assume that he had done nothing for them as young adults, he listed the cash amounts he had provided each since his or her education was finished.

Matthew was shocked and wrote back to say that except for affection, his father should now consider that he had only four children. 'I shall want no further pecuniary assistance'.[4] He then wrote to Ann of the angry exchange, apologising unhappily for the fact that he had surrendered any chance of the financial assistance he would need to marry her. Letters between father and son soon resumed with their usual vein of loyalty and affection, but Matthew continued to feel the pain of the quarrel. In fact Dr Flinders's cantankerous outburst might indeed have been the expression of a sick man. He died seventeen months later after what his widow, in a shaky hand, recorded in his diary as 'a long and trying affliction I may say for more than these 12 months'.[5]

Events were moving quickly, and marriage to Ann now seemed impossible. With countless immediate demands, complicated long-range planning to be done and uncertainty as to his promotion, by mid-December Flinders had achieved a degree of resignation regarding Ann, steeling himself to the conclusion that he could not afford to marry her 'unless I was to marry thee and leave thee in thy father's house; and would not such a step bring five years of redoubled misery on us?'[6] That precisely that misery lay ahead, Matthew never imagined.

The letter, addressed to Ann at Hull, where apparently she was visiting relatives, continued:

> ... a ship is fitting out for me to go out to New South Wales in, She is to be ready, it is said, in the beginning of January. An astronomer and a naturalist are already engaged, and draftsmen are searching for. Everything seems to bespeak the utmost haste, but my appointment is not yet given out ... It seems, that promotion cannot accompany any appointment to the command of her; there are, however, some promises made on that head, to take place shortly ...
>
> No Annette, every present appearance dooms us to be two distinct people ...
>
> Let us then, my dear Annette, return to the 'sweet, calm delights of friendship'. Let us endeavour to return to that serenity of mind which thou possessed but lately. I must call ambition to my assistance since it must be so; and in a life of activity and danger put out of my mind

> but that we are friends. The search after knowledge . . . may, nay must prevent me from casting one thought on England—on my home.

He would dismiss dreams of returning to New South Wales with 'a partner of my love' and occupy his mind only with business. She also must occupy herself. With his own passion for knowledge, he wrote, 'Learn music, learn the French language, enlarge the subjects of thy pencil, study geography and astronomy and even metaphysics, sooner than leave they mind unoccupied. Soar, my dear Annette, —aspire to the heights of science. Write a great deal, work with thy needle a great deal, and read every book that comes in thy way, save trifling novels'.

They must, however, meet: 'By personal conferences we may able to come to a better and more final understanding than by letter. Let us meet as lovers, and part as friends my Annette . . . With the anxious hope of meeting thee, I am most affectionately thy Mattw F'.[7]

Matthew evidently spent Christmas and New Year's Day at Spilsby and Partney, as he did not come to Donington until 2 January and on the 13th returned to London. On seeing Ann he clearly lost the sense of detachment he had proposed in his letter. In mid-January he wrote, 'The love of thy head and heart—a philosophic love, which I had flattered myself that mine was, became reinforced by another; and between them, I had near been carried away beyond the bounds of reason and prudence. I do not mean to flatter thee Annette, but thy person does much exceed my expectation of it'.[8]

Ann had been distant. The day after his return to London he wrote despairingly, 'Thou seemed to wish no conversation upon the subject that I was so interested about'. He had not even been able to see the expression in her eyes, for 'I could so seldom meet them . . . *My* feelings are almost too powerful for me'. Heartbrokenly he asked her to let him know when she married and wished her happiness with someone who could give her what his circumstances could not, 'whilst I am tossed by winds and waves, on various coasts and in various climes . . . I am torn to pieces . . . It is seldom that I have written a letter in tears'.[9]

Ann was deeply moved by this overflow of feeling. She replied, asking whether there was any 'possibility' of their living together. He answered that the possibility was too remote. She must forget him. He had before him a Herculean task in which he would try to smother her memory. Otherwise there would be in his mind '... no other being in the world than Annette ... But remember Annette—remember that I am thy friend'.[10] These were confusing, anguishing messages for Ann. He recognised that he was fortunate to have his work to occupy his mind. Ann had no such recourse. In the quiet rectory at Partney she could only grieve and remember.

Flinders's work had indeed become pressing. One worrying fact was that the French expedition had sailed in October, and might be well into making discoveries in New Holland before he even sighted its shores. It was important, too, that he arrive in New South Wales at the beginning of the southern summer, so that exploration could commence at once; this meant he had to reach Port Jackson by early December 1801. He had, therefore, approximately one year in which to fit out and provision a ship and travel halfway around the globe. The task was enormous. However, the Admiralty, moving with unusual alacrity, had bypassed the normal correspondence with the Navy Board on the selection of a ship. On 10 December 1800 the Board was instructed to prepare for foreign service the armed ship *Xenophon*, which by naval commission was renamed *Investigator* in January 1801.

The ship chosen for a voyage of exploration had been built as a three-masted collier in 1795 and purchased by the Navy three years later. Flinders wrote that she was 'of three-hundred and thirty four tons; and, in form, nearly resembled the description of the vessel recommended by captain Cook as best calculated for voyages of discovery ... having been newly coppered and repaired, was considered to be the best vessel which could, at that time, be spared for the projected voyage to Terra Australis'.[11] The gundeck was 100 feet four inches long, the width 25 feet five inches, and draught about 13 feet. Refitted by the Navy as an armed ship for convoy duty in the Channel, she had large gunports cut in her sides, necessary for the 32-pound carronades but weakening to her structure. Nevertheless, she was described as in good condition, flat-bottomed so she would rest upright if stranded on the sea floor, and sufficiently roomy to carry the stores needed for a long period at sea. Who selected the ship is not known, nor is there any record of who chose her new name. Flinders wrote, 'On the 19th of

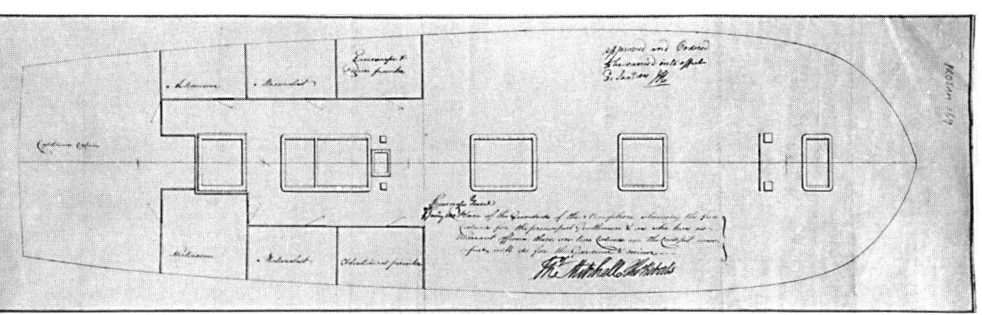

Plan of the main deck of HM armed ship Xenophon, *shortly to be renamed* Investigator, *showing the cabin arrangements for the captain, at left, and the senior members of the scientific staff. (GRG 56/81/169, State Records of South Australia)*

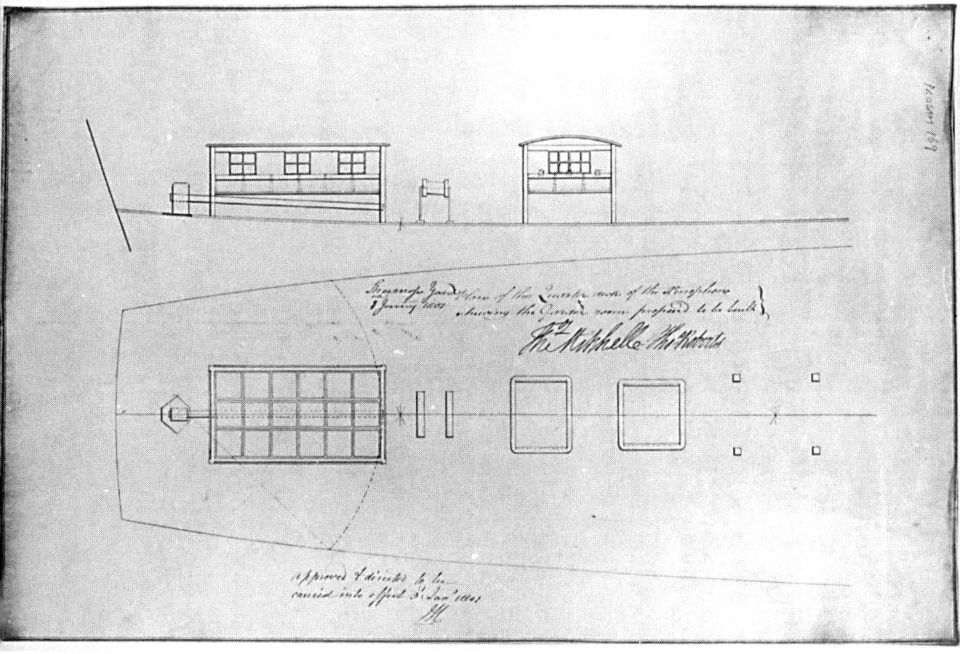

Plan and elevation drawing of the quarterdeck of the Investigator, *showing the plant cabin, probably designed by Joseph Banks, which was carried dismantled to Port Jackson and there assembled and installed on the quarterdeck. The height and size of the cabin were then somewhat reduced for greater safety. (GRG 56/81/169, State Records of South Australia)*

January 1801, a commission was signed at the Admiralty appointing me lieutenant of his Majesty's sloop *Investigator* . . .[12]

In the upper corner of the hoist the ship's white naval ensign bore the new Union Flag, adopted on 1 January to symbolise the union of Great Britain and Ireland.

On receiving the thick, carefully folded and heavily sealed document of his commission, Flinders immediately headed down the Thames for Sheerness where, on the 25th, he mustered the ship's company, read his commission and took over the vessel from Commander John Henry Martin. Then he inspected his ship, evidently for the first time. He was pleased with what he saw. It was, he wrote to Banks, 'a comfortable ship', his only criticism being that the space allotted to cabins could be better used. Besides a captain's cabin and stateroom, there were individual cabins for the scientists and artists. Some alterations in the arrangement would provide more space for stores and scientific specimens.

With the concurrence of the Navy Board and the assistance of Isaac Coffin, the resident naval commissioner, Flinders made additions to the ship's complement, its armament and the number and type of boats to be carried. A plan for a prefabricated plant cabin to be erected later on the quarterdeck, probably drawn up by Banks, was approved and work commenced. On Coffin's advice, Flinders had the hull coppered two streaks higher than it had been and took on board a spare rudder, which was taken apart and stored. He found that the ship's large gunports would almost always have to be kept closed when, deeply laden, the sloop was at sea. Flinders ordered scuttles cut into the gunport lids to admit light and air. Topmasts, spare sails, naval stores and the disassembled plant cabin were loaded. He returned provisions then on the ship and asked the victualling officer to order from the agent at Chatham the best casks and the newest and best available supplies for the voyage.

The ship's younger crew members who volunteered were retained, and other young, fit volunteers were sought from other ships with considerable success. Among the seamen was Samuel Smith, aged thirty. Although little educated, he would write with highly original spelling and grammar a journal of the voyage that vividly presents a seaman's view of events.

A frigate and other vessels in a fresh gale off Sheerness at the mouth of the Thames River, engraving by John Cleveley Junr. In the background appear some of the buildings of the Sheerness naval dockyard where HMS Investigator *was fitted for her voyage to Terra Australis. Here Flinders took command of the ship on 25 January 1801.*
(© National Maritime Museum, London)

Flinders received the new establishment, the roster specifying the number of men, with their ranks and ratings, allotted by the Admiralty, which set the ship's complement at 83, including 15 marines. The roster did not list a commander, the rank he very much wanted for himself. Writing to Banks, he brought up the need for a passport from the French government to assure the safety of the ship, a vessel engaged in purely scientific work, in any encounter with the French, with permission to seek help if needed. He then pressed tactfully for his own promotion.

A few days later Flinders received his commission as commander, dated 16 February. Immediately he wrote to thank Banks. Although a sloop generally called for a commander as its captain, Flinders had been arguably too junior for the promotion; on their early voyages Cook and Bligh had been lieutenants, although older than Flinders, who, in fact, had raised his age on the muster roll by a year. It is also possible that his independent hydrographic experience, which timewise had amounted to no more than some twelve months of surveying in the *Tom Thumbs*, *Francis* and *Norfolk*, was regarded as inadequate. Banks, however, had successfully brought his influence to bear. He wrote back, 'I give you sincere joy at the attainment of your wish in your appointment of Commander. I have long known that it was Certain, but I am glad it is now placed beyond the Reach of accident, or the change of administration'.[13]

To command the preparation of his own ship for the greatest voyage of his life was a heady experience. All around him at Sheerness there was the purposeful activity of a naval yard in wartime, vessels on the slips, workshops receiving and disgorging sails and rigging, steaming houses processing timber, men at the machines for masting and unmasting ships, and everywhere the salty, penetrating sea-smell of ships. Here the *Investigator* was being shaped into a tool for discovery, for acquiring new knowledge and for his own ambitions. Evidently it was at this time that Flinders had a miniature portrait of himself painted, showing his short, curling dark hair, large dark eyes and a strong chin, framed in the black neckcloth and gold-edged standing collar of his uniform, with a commander's single epaulette on the left shoulder.

Banks urged Flinders to come to London to oversee the selection of instruments for the voyage. Eager to do this, to see Arrowsmith about his charts and memoir and to meet with the East India Company's Committee of Shipping, Flinders obtained leave, and long discussions with Banks followed. Officers were one topic.

Robert Merrick Fowler, the *Xenophon*'s first lieutenant, was well recommended by his captain and wished to make the voyage. Twenty-three years old on the *Investigator*'s muster list, he was the son of a Lincolnshire man known to Joseph Banks. His portrait shows attractively even, clean-cut features and short dark hair falling loosely forward. He continued as first lieutenant. Flinders had once received from the First Lord, Earl St Vincent, an assurance that Samuel Flinders, having passed his examination, would be appointed the *Investigator*'s third lieutenant. When this position did not eventuate, Flinders suggested his brother as second lieutenant and, probably through Banks's influence, Samuel received the appointment soon after his promotion. On the ship's muster roll his age, like his brother's, was raised by a year. Flinders wrote to his father that taking young Samuel

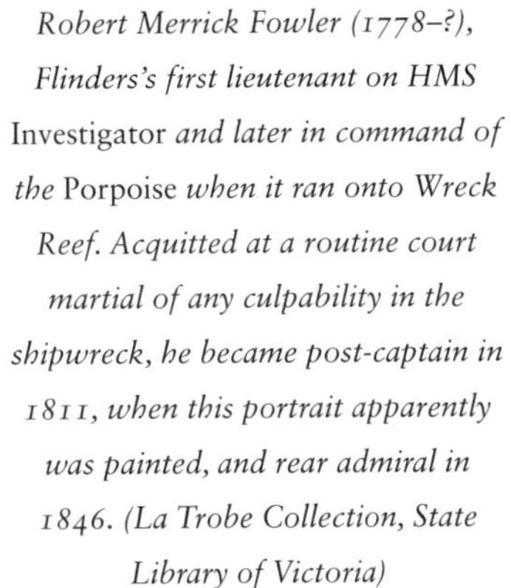

Robert Merrick Fowler (1778–?), Flinders's first lieutenant on HMS Investigator *and later in command of the* Porpoise *when it ran onto Wreck Reef. Acquitted at a routine court martial of any culpability in the shipwreck, he became post-captain in 1811, when this portrait apparently was painted, and rear admiral in 1846. (La Trobe Collection, State Library of Victoria)*

with him as an officer in the *Investigator* was the strongest possible proof of his devotion to the family: 'By his being promoted and appointed by my request, a considerable part of what may arise from his inattention or inexperience will be placed to my discredit. I have had one unpleasant instance of this already . . .'[14]

To complete the positions specified by the ship's establishment there remained to be signed on four midshipmen, three warrant officers—a boastswain, carpenter and gunner—and a clerk, sailmaker, armourer and surgeon. In July fourteen-year-old John Franklin of Spilsby, already a veteran of Nelson's battle of Copenhagen, joined as a midshipman. Enthusiastic and happy-natured, John was as yet very much a boy, but would become one of the most promising of the *Investigator*'s midshipmen. Sherrard Lound, midshipman, was a small, slight youngster, the son of one of Matthew's former teachers. Flinders's greatest concern, however, was that he had not yet filled the important position of master. The long voyage away from the likelihood of prize money discouraged many possible volunteers. In a spare moment Flinders retrieved from temporary lodgings in London his cat Trim, who now found himself once again comfortably ensconced in one of His Majesty's ships.

Surveying and navigational instruments were selected: chronometers by Earnshaw and Arnold in their sturdy wooden cases, Troughton's eight-inch reflecting sextant, quadrants, a telescope, quicksilver artificial horizons, compasses, theodolites, surveying chains, barometers and thermometers and many smaller items, together with drawing equipment, blank-paged books for journals and navigational work, three kinds of ink and 2000 quills. An assembly of charts covered the Pacific islands, the coasts of Terra Australis and Torres Strait.

Books included the third edition eighteen-volume *Encyclopaedia Britannica* presented by Banks, narratives of previous voyages to Terra Australis and the Pacific, technical texts on astronomy, timekeepers and marine surveying, tables and ephemerides. Among Flinders's own possessions was his copy of John Milton's poetry. Tents and camping gear were provided for shore excursions, with quantities of goods for barter or gifts for natives. Guns, ammunition and anchors—five bower, two stream and two kedge anchors—came on board. Everything had to be listed for submission to the Navy Board, the goods priced, bought, checked and delivered to the ship in almost continuous progression.

Victualling was a complicated process, the ship's needs projected months ahead and fitted into the vessel's limited space. As Port Jackson's food supply was barely adequate for its own population, arrangements were made to ship separately an additional twelve months' supply of provisions to Sydney specifically for the *Investigator*. Flinders's commission also designated him purser, so he was responsible for all food delivered and the relative accounts. The East India Company, in the meantime, expressed its interest in the expedition with a generous contribution of £600 table money—money for food and delicacies above normal issues—to be divided among Flinders, his officers and the scientists. The same amount was to be given again at the end of the voyage. The gardener and miner, who would not be messing at the officers' tables, each received £20 from Flinders's share.

On 1 March Flinders received the Admiralty's authorisation to take on board as supernumeraries a scientific staff of six with four servants to attend the naturalist, the astronomer and the two artists. Banks had assumed almost the entire responsibility for selecting the group. Salaries were to be paid by the Admiralty, but the financial arrangements, the written agreement on the requirements of their employment and, lastly, locating suitable men and persuading them to join the expedition were left with Banks.

Banks handled this delegated authority tactfully. He observed the Admiralty's normal procedures, and carefully sought the opinions of Secretary Evan Nepean and his staff even in matters that he knew would be his to decide. In a memorandum to the Admiralty dated 18 April 1801, Banks queried, 'Is my proposal for an alteration in the undertaking in the Investigator approved?' On the same piece of paper a reply in the hand of Nepean reads, 'Any proposal you will make will be approved. The whole is left entirely to your decision'.[15] Banks wrote privately to Governor King that he was never refused anything he asked for. The Admiralty had, in fact, adopted a very pragmatic attitude. No one knew more or cared more about the expedition's purpose or requirements than Joseph Banks, nor had anyone else the contacts and the understanding of the work to be able to select more judiciously.

Among the scientists the only choice not made by Banks was that of the astronomer, John Crosley. He was selected by the Admiralty, the Board of Longitude, of which Banks, however, was a member, and the Astronomer Royal, Nevil Maskelyne. Crosley had been on a surveying voyage in the North Pacific in 1795–97. The ship had been wrecked, and Crosley returned to England in poor health. Offered the position of astronomer on the *Investigator*, he accepted after some hesitation. Crosley came on board in March to set up his equipment in his cabin. In addition to some fine instruments of his own, he brought with him those supplied by the Board of Longitude, including two Earnshaw and two Arnold chronometers and an Arnold pocket watch to be used by boat parties on separate surveys.

The chief naturalist chosen by Banks was a short, lean 27-year-old Scot who was serving as an ensign and assistant surgeon in a Scottish regiment in Ireland. Despite having studied medicine, Robert Brown's great interest was botany, and he came to Banks's attention through

Robert Brown (1773–1858), c. 1840, engraving based on a portrait by H. W. Pickersgill. Brown, the naturalist on HMS Investigator, *amassed a collection of some 3900 Australian plant species, of which more than 2000 were new to science. His book,* Prodromus Florae Novae Hollandiae, *remains a landmark work in Australian botany. (ML Ref: P3/B, Mitchell Library, State Library of New South Wales)*

Banks's librarian, the botanist Jonas Dryander. Favourably impressed, Banks offered Brown the position of the expedition's naturalist. Brown accepted with enthusiasm and, exerting influence at high levels, Banks secured his release from his regiment despite wartime complications. His portrait shows a striking face with a high forehead and long, slender nose. Brown was an inspired choice, quiet and reserved, wrapped in his work, which he did with brilliance and devotion.

Ferdinand Lukas Bauer, a 40-year-old Austrian, accepted the position of botanical painter. Bauer, whose brother Franz was a botanical artist at the Royal Gardens in Kew, was a man of exceptional talent and industry. He was the oldest of the scientific staff, a gentle, courteous man liked by everyone.

Finding a landscape and figure painter was more of a problem. Two experienced artists declined. Eventually the offer was made to William Westall, younger brother of the well-known artist Richard Westall and a student at the Royal Academy School. Westall was nineteen and 300 guineas (£315) a year was an attractive salary for a young artist, in addition to which he could take with him a personal servant. Westall began the voyage with enthusiasm, his early work showing a zestful interest in his subjects. In a later self-portrait he is a fashionably dressed young man, pleasant looking, the expression a little eager, a little shy. His youth was reflected in a letter Flinders wrote to Ann, remarking of 'young Mr. Westall' that 'his foolish days are not yet passed'.[16] His task was principally to record for later navigators the appearance of new land, particularly the shoreline as seen from the sea.

Joseph Banks offered the post of gardener to Peter Good, a kitchen gardener at Wemyss Castle, Scotland, and previously a foreman at the Kew Royal Gardens. At that time Banks had engaged Good to assist the botanist Christopher Smith in transporting a shipment of English plants to the East India Company's garden at Calcutta, and Good had returned to England with a selection of plants for Kew. Good happily accepted the post, writing to William Aiton, head gardener at Kew, who had presented Banks's offer, 'it shall be the business of my life to merit so particular a distinction'.[17] He became Brown's very capable assistant, an indefatigable worker, 'a zealous, worthy man'.[18]

Plans for the scientific staff included a mineralogist, but Banks simply looked for a miner, and one John Allen was found. He apparently came from Derbyshire, probably located by William Milnes, Banks's estate steward at Overton Hall in Derbyshire, to whom Banks had evidently written rather imperiously to find 'a person who engages in the mineral line'.[19] Like Good, John Allen received a salary of £100 a year. Both men messed with the warrant officers and received their standard of accommodation.

The official document setting out the conditions of employment for the scientists was written by Banks and served extremely well. It stressed the need for obedience to the orders of the ship's commander and, repeatedly, the importance of propriety, courtesy and ready cooperation within the scientific team itself. At the end of the voyage, journals, sketches, collections and the like were to be surrendered as directed, but profits derived from information published by the Admiralty would be divided between the ship's commander and the scientists, and items no longer needed returned to their owners. This was signed by Brown,

Bauer, Westall, Good and Allen in the presence of Banks as official witness at Soho Square on 29 April 1801.

For the ship's surgeon Banks contacted Sir Gilbert Blane, the Navy's most noted physician, who appointed to the *Investigator* Hugh Bell, from HMS *Seagull*. Bell seemed pleased, writing to Blane of an interest in natural history, particularly botany. Banks, seeing the letter, was satisfied. During the voyage Bell sometimes accompanied the scientists on their excursions ashore, but he was an abrupt, blunt-spoken man who was not popular and did not get on particularly well with Flinders.

The berths and moorings of wartime Sheerness were in demand. Ships whose stores and major repairs had been completed were ordered out, with any remaining work to be done at the Nore. At seven in the morning of 27 March, Flinders ordered the gunshot signal for a pilot and at ten the *Investigator* unmoored and moved out of the dockyard. An hour later the ship dropped a bower anchor in 11 fathoms at the Nore. Landward lay the great sweeps of mud at the mouth of the Thames and midstream was the Nore light vessel some 41 miles below London Bridge.

Chief among Flinders's concerns now was the need for a French passport that would protect his scientific expedition from hostile interference. Perhaps preoccupied by the demands of the fighting ships, the Admiralty failed to ask the Foreign Office to apply for a passport until 20 March. The Foreign Secretary, Lord Hawkesbury, took no action until May, and with the normal enquiries from the French that followed, the passport did not arrive in London until 23 June.

14
A Possibility of Marriage

There appear to be no letters from Matthew Flinders to Ann Chappelle from February and March 1801, and he may have stopped writing. News of his promotion would, however, have reached Donington and spread rapidly among friends and family in the neighbouring villages. On 3 April he wrote a long letter, at once businesslike, affectionate and conciliatory, to his father. He was departing on a long, uncertain voyage, and like many other seamen, Flinders wanted to arrange his affairs should he not return. He had drawn up a will and appointed his father and his London agent as co-executors.

Marriage in his circumstances, and seemingly after a long silence between Ann and himself, was not feasible. He wrote: 'I have no present or future intention of marrying either her [Ann] or any person'. He was, however, concerned that 'her acquaintance with me, may have prevented her from forming other connexions',[1] and willed half his property to Ann if, at the time of his demise, she remained unmarried. He then specified how the remaining half should be divided within the family and listed the recipients of the customary mourning rings, among them Ann, family members, George Bass, Joseph Banks and James Wiles in Jamaica. Flinders told his father that he did not need the £100 his father had promised for the following year, and discussed how it could be applied instead to helping Samuel meet his expenses as a new lieutenant. Finding the £150 needed by Samuel was a serious problem for the family.

Flinders was increasingly aware of his position as the family's eldest son, an important feature of the social structure of the period, and, coupled with his father's outburst on money, was anxious to stress his financial independence. 'With respect to myself', he added in his letter, 'there will be no money transaction immediately between us; but I do not forget the sums you have advanced to me, and on my account, as stated in your letter of November 24th last'.[2]

Just three days later, there was a complete reversal of all his stated intentions. He wrote to Ann not only with a direct proposal of marriage but also with a plan by which this could be accomplished as quickly as possible. Without preamble, he referred back to her earlier letter on whether there was a 'possibility' of their marriage.

Investigator, at the Nore
April 6, 1801

My dearest friend,

Thou hast asked me if there is a *possibility* of our living together. I think I see a *probability* of living with a moderate share of comfort. Till now, I was not certain of being able to fit myself out clear of the world. I have now done it; and have accomodation on board the *Investigator*, in which as my wife, a woman may, with love to assist her, make herself happy. This prospect has recalled all the tenderness which I have so reluctantly endeavoured to banish. I am sent for to London, where I shall be from the 9th to the 19th or perhaps longer. If thou wilt meet me there, this hand shall be thine forever.

If thou hast sufficient love and courage, say to Mr and Mrs Tyler, that I require nothing more with thee than a sufficient stock of clothes, and a small sum to answer the increased expenses that will necessarily and immediately come upon me; as such for living on board, as providing for at Port Jackson; for whilst I am employed in the most dangerous part of my duty, thou shalt be placed under some friendly roof there. I will specify this sum to be £200, or if great inconvenience will result from advancing it, I will say £150; and I leave every thing future to the justice and generosity of thy parents and friends.

It is but a bad specimen of my stability to change in this manner, as appearances will bespeak I do; but it is no change. It is only just now that I see attendant comfort; the want of which only kept me back.

I need not, or at this time have I time to enter into a detail of my income and prospects; it will, I trust, be sufficient for me to say that I see a fortune growing under me, to meet increasing expenses. I only want to have a fair start, and my life for it we will do well, and be happy. I will write further tomorrow; but shall most anxiously expect thy answer at 86 Fleet St London on my arrival on Friday; and I trust thy presence immediately afterwards. Mr or perhaps Mrs Tyler will most probably accompany thee. I have only time to add, that most anxiously I am most sincerely thine

Mattw Flinders

It will be much better to keep this matter entirely secret. There are many reasons for it yet, and I have also a powerful one. I do not exactly know how my great friends might like it.[3]

What had happened?

The sudden, impetuous decision to marry Ann and to take her with him to New South Wales was one of the rash, emotion-charged decisions that Flinders sometimes made. His spacious cabin could accommodate Ann comfortably over the many months' journey. His improved financial situation—a commander's pay and a purser's income—enabled him to support a wife 'clear of the world'. These conditions, however, had existed for some months. To his cousin Henrietta Flinders, always a good friend, he wrote that in drawing up the will he was led 'to think a great deal more of her [Ann] . . . with such force, as to induce me to reconsider the question'.[4] Feeling overwhelmed the earlier, steadier decision.

Flinders firmly believed that his discoveries would bring him fame and fortune. Now the conviction was no doubt exultantly buoyed by the prospect of having Ann with him. And Ann, reading his letter, would have had no doubt but that Matthew, brave, determined and wonderfully competent, would successfully arrange all this to happen. Yet the postscript was a warning that Flinders himself, in his swift, ardent determination, had failed to consider seriously enough the ramifications of his decision. Naval wives rarely travelled in His Majesty's ships, although a few ship commanders had been allowed to transport their families to the colony and home again aboard their own vessels. Lieutenant William Kent, whom Flinders knew well, did so. No voyage of discovery, however, with all its uncertainties, had ever been accompanied by a woman. Although Flinders intended to leave Ann in Sydney while he carried out his principal explorations, he undoubtedly knew that the hazardous, demanding work of closely examining an uncharted shoreline would probably begin on reaching Australia's southern coast. Recognising that his 'great friends', Banks and the Lords Commissioners of the Admiralty, would very likely refuse him permission to bring a young wife on such a journey, he conceived the idea of taking her with him without their knowledge. It was a reckless decision. Keeping such a secret was scarcely possible, and he made a regrettable mistake in not consulting his patron, Joseph Banks.

Flinders secured leave to go to London, where he first attended to business in the Hydrographical Office and with Arrowsmith. Ann apparently felt it indelicate to travel to London to be married. Thus on 13 April Matthew wrote to her that he would exert every effort to come to Lincolnshire, urging haste and as little 'noise' about the wedding as possible. The next day he wrote to his father announcing his intention to marry Ann before leaving England, as his finances now permitted him to do so without calling upon the doctor for assistance. He mentioned selling his New South Wales property, and that the Reverend Mr Tyler had agreed to provide an additional sum as a dowry for Ann. He added, 'No person is acquainted with this business, yourself and Mr. Tylers family excepted; and I wish it to be kept as quiet as possible, for several reasons'.[5]

Flinders called on Banks to say that he would be going to Spalding, where Banks knew Flinders had relatives. Then he changed his mind and hurriedly wrote to Banks: he was going to Boston. The reason may have been to complete the sale of his New South Wales property to William Bowles, an old schoolmate and an attorney of Boston. Bowles bought Flinders's 300 acres for £300, less legal and conveyance fees. He made his first payment of £100 in April 1801 and the balance with interest in May 1802.[6] In telling Banks that he would be in Boston, Flinders was apparently not deceiving his patron but omitting the more important facts.

On 15 April Flinders requested from the Admiralty a week's extension of his leave, time, he said, he could spend more usefully in London than on the ship. That evening he boarded the coach for Lincolnshire and in the swaying carriage travelled the night and the next day through the green English countryside, reaching Spilsby that evening. With

St Nicholas Church, Partney, Lincolnshire, where Matthew Flinders and Ann Chappelle were married on a sunny spring day, 17 April 1801. A small ship model now surmounts the bell tower. (Photo by David Simpson, Boston, Lincolnshire)

Hannah Franklin, his stepmother's sister and mother of the young Franklins, he went to Partney. Here in the Tyler cottage he no doubt explained his financial prospects to Ann's parents, as was expected, and Mr Tyler reciprocated with the promise of a sum of money for Ann. Ann's flaxen-haired, rosy-cheeked half-sister, Isabella Tyler, was then sixteen, and years later wrote of the joyful excitement of the wedding, for which she had 'assisted with delight in preparing the home made brides-cake'.[7]

The marriage ceremony took place on Friday morning, 17 April 1801, in Partney's 600-year-old stone church on its small rise amid ancient trees. The register was signed in the little vestry:

> Matthew Flinders, Commander in His Majesty's Royal Navy and Ann Chappelle, of this parish, were Married in this Church by Licence this seventeenth Day of April in the Year One Thousand eight Hundred

The interior of St Nicholas Church, where Matthew Flinders and Ann Chappelle were married by Ann's stepfather, the Reverend William Tyler. The marriage certificate was probably signed in a small adjoining chamber, possibly at a desk that still stands there. (Photo by David Simpson, Boston, Lincolnshire)

> and onc By me Wm. Tyler, Rector of Bratoft. This Marriage was solemnized between Us Mattw Flinders, Ann Chappelle, in the presence of Hannah Franklin, Mary Hudson.

Isabella wrote:

> Never man more happy than poor Matthew & he determined to be so, in spite of the Lords of the Admiralty & Sir Joseph Banks.—Yes, of all the merry group none more merry than he . . . I can see him now, distributing his little gifts to the Bridesmaids,—mine was a little inkstand, . . . pretending to tell their fortunes by the lines in their palms, promising, of course, to all good husbands & soon . . . we were all fun and mirth.

As the wedding party evidently walked through the village, 'the sun shone brightly, & the bells rang merrily. Nevertheless I heard afterwards that there were tears, many and bitter—one wept at losing a friend and companion in the Bride.—& one wept at losing the Bridegroom—My heart was too full of joyful anticipation to admit a shade of sorrow, for my Sister was married and I was going to London!'[8]

For Ann there was the joy of marrying Matthew, but also the realisation that she would soon be parted, perhaps for the rest of her life, from home and family and all she knew. Later in the day she found time to write to her dearest friend, Elizabeth Franklin:

> April 17th 1801
>
> My beloved Betsy,
>
> Thou wilt be much surprised to hear of this sudden affair; indeed I scarce believe it myself, tho' I have this very morning given my hand at the altar to him I have ever highly esteemed, and it affords me no small pleasure that I am now part, tho' a distant one, of thy family, my Betsy. It grieves me much thou are so distant from me. Thy society would have greatly cheered me. Thou wilt today pardon me if I say but little. I am scarce able to coin one sentence or to write intelligibly—I shall leave with our dear Hannah a trifle, which I trust will serve to call my Image to thy recollection . . . It pains me to agony when I indulge the thought for a moment, that I must leave all I value on earth, save one, alas, perhaps for ever. Ah, my Betsy, but I dare not, must not, think. Therefore, farewell, farewell. may the great God of Heaven preserve thee and those thou lovest, oh, everlastingly—I cannot, cannot write as I wish—this is a miserable happiness, but fate wills it sho'd be so . . . Adieu, dear darling Girl; love as ever, though absent and far removed, from your poor
>
> Annette[9]

To Ann's letter Flinders added a short, affectionate note.

One account states that as they prepared to depart the next day, Mr Tyler handed Flinders the promised bank notes, which Flinders put 'in his boot as a place of safety'.[10]

Flinders later described the flying affair to his cousin Henrietta: 'I set off on Wednesday evening from town, arrived next evening from town at Spilsby, was married next morning which was Friday. On

Saturday we went to Donington, on Sunday reached Huntingdon, and on Monday were in town'.[11]

The arrival of the newly married couple at the Flinders house in Donington was something of a shock to the family, despite Flinders's earlier letter. Later, the doctor wrote: 'With concern note that my Son Mattw came upon us suddenly & unexpectedly with a Wife on Sat. April 18 & left us next day—it is a Miss Chapple of Partney. We had known of the acquaintance, but had no Idea of Marriage taking place until the completion of his ensuing Voyage. I wish he may not repent of his hasty step'.[12]

That Dr Flinders should say he 'had no Idea' of the marriage seems strange, unless Matthew's letter had not reached him. Whatever the case, he evidently made his disapprobation abundantly clear when the young couple called. In subsequent letters Matthew earnestly tried to soothe this parental disapproval, while Ann added a dutiful note to one of his letters. The doctor, however, had other unsettling griefs. Under the same date as his comments on Matthew's marriage, the unhappy father wrote that his son John had been placed in the York Lunatic Asylum. Six months later he wrote that he had no hopes of his son's recovery. John Flinders died in the asylum in March 1834, aged fifty-two.

Travelling in the post chaise, 'the cheapest for the three of us, and by far the pleasantest mode',[13] Ann, Matthew and Isabella arrived in London on Monday. '... Next morning I presented myself before Sir Joseph Banks with a grave face, as if nothing had happened, and then went on with my business as usual'.[14]

Banks would regard this behaviour as foolhardy deception.

Ann, Matthew and Isabella remained in London at the home of a sister of Ann's mother until the following Sunday, 'providing all my dear wifes necessaries for the voyage'.[15] The aunt assisted in buying Ann's new outfit, for, as Isabella wrote, 'the haste with which the marriage was got up gave no time for preparations. Many pretty dresses were chosen, one in particular suited to appear at the Governor's table [in Sydney]'.[16]

On Monday, Flinders's extended leave having expired, the young couple boarded the *Investigator* at the Nore, where they remained, making excursions into the city to shop for further necessities for Ann and, on one occasion, spending the day on the Essex side of the

Thames. No doubt Flinders showed Ann the sights of London, while on board the ship she saw for the first time something of her husband's way of life.

Preparations for the journey continued. Three tons of beer came on board satisfactorily, but fresh beef from the victualler in Chatham was short in weight. The special equipment arrived, instruments, charts and a large box of stationery. Peter Good and John Allen embarked, while news of a ship equipping for explorations brought interested visitors. There was, too, the normal daily routine—watches, cleaning, meals, punishments. There were delays and complaints. Seaman William Brown received twelve lashes for neglect of duty.

Isabella, meanwhile, had been joined in London by her father, who preached an annual sermon for the London Missionary Society. Before leaving for Lincolnshire the Reverend Tyler and Isabella came down to Sheerness to bid Ann and Matthew farewell. Watching from the inn window, Isabella was 'astonished & half frightened' at her first sight of port prostitutes. They were, however, quickly forgotten as Flinders came across the square with his firm, light step, happy and confident in a world that seemed to hold every promise: '... in his handsome uniform, his cocked hat put slightly over one eye—his sword by his side—did he not look handsome?'[17] Isabella also remembered the thrill of being taken out in a boat, and from alongside the hull of the *Investigator* being hoisted up in a chair, so 'I set my feet for the first time on the deck of a King's ship'. The officers dined festively with the guests, and afterwards Isabella happily walked the quarterdeck with Samuel Flinders and John Franklin, boys near her own age.

Continuous delays gave Flinders the chance to make another important change to the ship. The quantity of stores needed for the voyage had restricted the space for water in the holds to 50 tons. Flinders now proposed that ten of the twelve six-pounder long guns previously installed on the main deck be removed and carronades, light enough to be carried on the quarterdeck, substituted. This allowed the ship to carry 10 additional tons of water. This was approved. The sloop's final armament consisted of two 6-pounder long guns, two 18-pounder carronades, six 12-pounder carronades and two swivels.

With Banks Flinders maintained his usual discussions by letter of events and problems as they came up. As if to remind Banks of his dedication to the enterprise, he wrote, 'My greatest ambition is, to make such a minute investigation of this extensive and very interesting country [Australia], that no person shall have occasion to come after me to make further discoveries'.[18] It was an inspiring if unrealistic goal.

The non-arrival of the French passport was now of major concern to Flinders. The other principal matter to be concluded was providing a master for the ship. Flinders was anxious to have on board an experienced man with some knowledge of surveying. Having failed in his own efforts to find one, he applied to the Navy Board for a volunteer whose 'abilities and conduct will enable him to be an useful assistant to me in carrying on the services on which we are about to engage'.[19]

Inevitably word reached the Admiralty that Commander Flinders's wife was on board and that he intended to take her to New South Wales. A traditional story holds that John Jervis, Earl St Vincent and First Lord of the Admiralty, paid an unannounced visit to the *Investigator*. No one recognised or met him as he came on board, and he entered the captain's cabin to find Mrs Flinders sitting on her husband's knee, her bonnet removed as if she were at home. A variation of the story has a group of Admiralty officers making the same discovery. Whatever the truth, naval gossip would have relayed the information that Mrs Flinders was living on board. Nor was the marriage of Donington's young naval commander to Ann Chappelle of Partney a secret in Lincolnshire. A Lincoln paper published the news.

On 21 May an extremely upset and disappointed Joseph Banks sat down at his desk and wrote to Flinders:

> Dear Sir,
>
> I have but just time to tell you that the news of your marriage, which was published in the Lincoln paper, has reached [me]. The Lords of the Admiralty have heard also that Mrs. Flinders is on board the *Investigator*, and that you have some thoughts of carrying her to sea with you. This I am very sorry to hear, and if that is the case I beg to give you my advice, by no means to venture to measures so contrary to the regulations and the discipline of the Navy; for I am convinced, by the language I have heard, that their Lordships will, if they hear of her being in New South Wales, immediately order you to be super-

> seded, whatever may be the consequences, and in all likelihood order Mr. Grant to finish the survey.[20]

A day or two later the letter was carried on board the *Investigator*.

The shock of Banks's absolute disapproval and the threat to Flinders's command were devastating. The entire happy prospect that Flinders had constructed collapsed, and he was faced with a desperately painful ordeal. Ann's grief was probably even greater. That she would be accompanying Matthew on his voyage was part of the basis of their marriage, of her faith in her husband, the event for which she had said her farewells to all she knew. Flinders had therefore not only his own pain and fragmented hope to confront, but Ann's shattered trust and grief as well, and the necessity of explaining to her the choice he was going to make. For Flinders seems not to have hesitated. Command of the great voyage was the pinnacle of his career, on which he based his future in the navy, his expectations of fame and wealth. It meant the fulfilment of an ambition he could not surrender. That he loved Ann is beyond question, but without this opportunity his future was empty and, he reasoned, his future was also hers.

Nevertheless, he clung to some shred of hope and attempted an explanation. On 24 May, probably the very day Banks's letter arrived, he replied.

> *Investigator*, at the Nore,
> 24th May, 1801.
>
> I am much indebted to you, Sir Joseph, for the information contained in your letter of the 21st. It is true that I had an intention of taking Mrs. Flinders to Port Jackson, to remain there until I should have completed the purpose of the voyage, and to have then brought her home again in the ship, and I trust that the service would not have suffered in the least by such a step. The Admiralty have most probably conceived that I intended to keep her on board during the voyage, but this was far from my intention . . . If their Lordships understood this matter in its true light, I should hope that they would have shewn the same indulgence to me as to Lieut. Kent of the Buffalo, and many others . . .

> If their Lordships' sentiments should continue the same, whatever may be my disappointment, I shall give up the wife for the voyage of discovery; and I would beg of you, Sir Joseph, to be assured that even the circumstance will not damp the ardor I feel to accomplish the important purpose of the present voyage, and in a way that shall preclude the necessity of any one following after me to explore. It would be too much presumption in me to beg of Sir Joseph Banks to set this matter in its proper light, because by your letter I judge it meets with your disapprobation entirely; but I hope that this opinion has been formed upon the idea of Mrs. F.'s continuing on board the ship when engaged in real service.[21]

Flinders said what he could to save his and Ann's hopes, but the ultimate decision had been made. If necessary he would surrender 'the wife for the voyage . . .'[22]

Banks responded to Flinders's letter promptly, saying he would lay Flinders's explanations before the Admiralty. Banks wrote on 26 May, but the letter did not reach Flinders until 2 June, when the *Investigator* was at Spithead. In the interval events had occurred that convinced Matthew Flinders that he must indeed give up the hope of taking his wife with him. Just before the *Investigator* sailed from the Nore, three of her crew deserted. They were part of a working party of fifteen whom Flinders had been ordered to lend to another ship. On being recalled, the three had vanished.

Late on the moonlit night of 27 May, the *Investigator* moved out of the Nore to an anchorage at the Downs. The next day the pilot was discharged, and in the afternoon on a southeasterly breeze, the ship began working her way toward Spithead. Before six o'clock, moving at 2¾ knots in the soft daylight of a summer evening, she swung onto a leg toward Dymchurch on the coast between Folkestone and Dungeness. Flinders was below with Ann. At a quarter to six the leadsman sounded 15 fathoms and, unbeknown to the officer of the watch, Robert Fowler, the leadsman left the chains. No one relieved him.

At six Samuel Flinders relieved Fowler, unaware that no one was in place to call soundings. The offshore distance was reported to Flinders at two leagues. Flinders, in his cabin, 'intended to stand on for half an hour longer; but in ten minutes felt the ship lifting upon a bank'.[23] It was a stunning, horrifying moment. Flinders shot up to the quarter-deck. Sails were instantly thrown aback. Boats were hurriedly lowered to sound around the ship, which was found to be resting quietly on a sand ridge known as The Roar, which lay nearly parallel to the shore-line, with its 3-fathom outer edge about 1½ miles offshore. With a smooth sea and a rising tide, Flinders was able to float the vessel off the sand in less than two hours. Apparently the ship was undamaged. Had the tide been at ebb, the consequences would have been far more serious.

How could this have happened? Neither Fowler nor Samuel Flinders was familiar with the coast towards which the ship was directly headed, and there was no master on board. The captain was below. Slack discipline had made it possible for no one to be sounding.

In his own defence Flinders would maintain that where the ship was stranded 'the least possible distance from the nearest shore was, in the commander's estimation, 2½ miles; but it was guessed to be nearer 4 miles'.[24] The Roar appeared on at least two older charts (1797), but through some oversight Flinders had not been given these. The one he received did not show the bank. With reason, Flinders blamed his error on having received an incorrect chart. Nevertheless, had the captain been on deck to watch the pilotage, an accident by daylight on a calm sea might have been avoided. As well, with proper discipline, there would have been soundings within that critical half hour or so before the ship struck. Explaining this and to some extent de-emphasising the circumstance, Flinders wrote in the log, 'the supposed dist. of the land by the officer of the watch, being 6 miles, the lead had not been attended to minutely at the time . . .'[25] Finally, Flinders exaggerated, then and later, the distance of the reef from shore in order to clear himself. It was not an unusual practice.

Flinders sailed back to the Downs and anchored for the night. Here a lesser but nonetheless unfortunate incident took place. At the Nore Flinders had been asked to take on board a carpenter from HMS *Trent* for passage to Portsmouth. The man had been identified as a deserter, but did not come under guard. Flinders had refused him permission to go ashore, but on this brief return to the Downs, with only a midshipman on the quarterdeck, the man absconded in a departing boat. Flinders wrote to report the *Investigator*'s grounding to the Admiralty. He also reported the escape of the carpenter.

On the morning of 30 May the *Investigator* sailed from the Downs and on 2 June arrived at Spithead. Flinders reported his arrival to the Admiralty, mentioning also the desertion of his three crewmen. At Spithead he found HMS *Buffalo*, which had arrived from Port Jackson six days earlier, bringing home Governor Hunter. No doubt there was an enthusiastic exchange of news, the latest from Port Jackson and the exciting events of Flinders's own crowded year. Flinders also made the fortuitous discovery that on board the *Buffalo* as master's mate was John Thistle, previously of the *Reliance*, who as an able seaman had been with Bass on the whaleboat voyage into Bass Strait and with Flinders on both *Norfolk* expeditions, during which he had assisted with the surveys. Flinders regarded Thistle highly, and Thistle, eager to join a surveying expedition and to return to Sydney, was prepared to leave England again almost immediately after an absence of six years. His master's warrant was dated 3 June 1801 and he joined the *Investigator* eleven days afterwards.

On the three days' sail from the Downs to Spithead, Flinders had evidently considered again, probably over and over, the question of Ann's accompanying him to New South Wales. Very likely he anticipated something of the Admiralty's response to the grounding of his ship with his wife on board. His command could again be challenged. His credibility with Banks would be further shaken. Flinders's emotions would have been deeply torn. Ann's reaction to the misadventure is not recorded, but without doubt she was profoundly distressed for Matthew, possibly frightened by the accident and probably aware that without her on board, he would most likely have been in command on deck.

No one knows what passed between the two in those three days at sea or what explanations Flinders tried to give Ann, evidently seasick as rain and greyness swept about the ship. But the day after they anchored at Spithead, on 3 June, he wrote to Banks, from whom he had received on arrival the letter promising to relay to the Admiralty Flinders's explanations on taking his wife to the colony:

> I feel much obliged by your offer to lay the substance of my letter before the Admiralty, but I foresee that although I should, in the case of Mrs.

> F.'s going to Port Jackson, have been more particularly cautious of my stay there, yet their Lordships will conclude naturally enough that her presence would tend to increase the number of and to lengthen my visits. I am therefore afraid to risk their Lordships' ill opinion, and Mrs. F. will return to her friends immediately that our sailing orders arrive . . . I sincerely hope that the passport is now arrived, and that nothing will detain us more than one week here at most.[26]

Flinders said nothing of the grounding or other mishaps. Banks seems to have received this letter the next day, and immediately went to the Admiralty for news of the *Investigator*. He was appalled by what he heard. He was, he wrote to Flinders:

> . . . mortified to learn there that you had been on shore in Hythe Bay, and I was still more mortified to hear that several of your men had deserted, and that you had lost a prisoner entrusted to your charge . . .
>
> I heard with pain many severe remarks on these matters, and in defence I could only say that, as Capt. Flinders is a sensible man and a good seaman, such matters could only be attributed to the laxity of discipline which always takes place when the captain's wife is on board, and that such lax discipline could never again take place because you had wisely resolved to leave Mrs. Flinders with her relations.
>
> I really wish you had given me a detail of these circumstances in your letter of the 3rd . . . your character would have been better supported yesterday had I known from you what happened.[27]

Flinders replied with a long letter in which he restated the distance of the sandbank to have been 3–4 miles from shore, and pointed out that the deserters had left the ship to which they had been loaned, while the carpenter had not come to the *Investigator* as a prisoner. He also remarked that he could have omitted reporting these incidents to the Admiralty. Banks loyally assumed the burden of protecting Flinders, and with some success pleaded his case in a lengthy conversation with Evan Nepean. Two questions remained unanswered: why only a midshipman was on the quarterdeck when the carpenter escaped, and why the lead was not going when the ship ran aground. For these lapses Flinders had to accept responsibility.

On 10 June the *Investigator* was towed into Portsmouth harbour and warped into the dock. As the tide receded the bottom was carefully inspected. It was undamaged and the next day the ship returned to her Spithead anchorage. If there had been injury, Flinders's position would undoubtedly have been more difficult. Three days later Brown, Bauer and Westall joined the ship. Thus Ann met three more of the men who would be with her husband throughout the journey. The courteous Bauer was particularly kind to her and, as a talented painter of flowers herself, Ann viewed his work with admiration.

A week later the ship's company were paid up to 31 May plus an additional two months' pay in advance, with officers allowed to draw bills for three months' pay in advance. That afternoon Flinders received orders to come to London on Admiralty business. No doubt apprehensively, he boarded a post chaise the next morning. With him were Ann and her possessions. As it turned out, the Admiralty matter related to a court case in which Flinders was required as a witness. No formal charges were, in fact, brought against him for the incidents aboard the *Investigator*.

While in London for almost a week, he tried unsuccessfully to see Nepean. The Secretary was unwell, and his wartime waiting room was crowded with naval men wishing to see him. Whether Flinders's lack of welcome was due to anything other than the press of business remains a question. Flinders returned to Spithead while Ann was taken by friends to stay with them at Battersea until Mr Tyler could come from Lincolnshire to take her home. The family's bitter feeling appears in Isabella's reference, even years later, to 'these savage old Lords . . .'[28] Ann was utterly crushed with grief and disappointment and, while no specific cause is described, was physically ill. Gradually she recovered, writing to Flinders almost daily as he wrote steadily to her.

On the *Investigator* the waiting for final orders continued. The ship's livestock—goats, sheep, pigs and poultry—were already in pens and crates on the forward deck, as were the hunting dogs taken by the scientists to flush out wild animals. Brown and Bauer botanised on the Isle of Wight. John Thistle came on board as the master. There were disciplinary problems with a bored and restless crew, paid but not allowed to go ashore. Flinders's efforts 'to bring the ship's company under good order and government' received the cooperation of the majority, 'but some of the *heedless* occasionally fell under the lash',[29] some for attempted desertion.

To a certain extent the shore came to them, women and others flocking off boats during the men's off-duty hours, frequently smuggling in spirits, so drinking, carousing and fornication took over the messes. More sobering were the experiences of groups of sailors sent in boats to other ships to witness punishments, the hanging of a mutineer and the flogging around the fleet of four seamen.

Flinders wrote repeatedly to Ann, worrying over her health and her desperate unhappiness, and missing her profoundly. 'The philosophical calmness which I imposed on thee, is fled from myself; and I am just as awkward without thee, as one half of a pair of scissors without its fellow', he wrote. His own loneliness was all the more acute in his position of command: 'Here there is no one I can speak to upon the subject . . . I have a brother indeed, but the nature of our situations almost debars one from a close intimacy with him. I must sit independent and impregnable; must acknowledge no weakness, no distress, no fear'.[30]

He did have his career, his hopes and his ambitions, and a few days later he tried to have her share in them:

> Rest confident, my dear, of the ardent and unalterable affection of *thy own* MF; he *does* love thee beyond everything. I go, my beloved, to gather riches and laurels with which to adorn thee; rejoice at the opportunity which fortuitous circumstances give me to do it. Wilt thou not feel a pride in thy M? who will have gone through so much, and with whose labours, individuals in all parts of the world will be acquainted as an useful member of society?[31]

As her health improved and she wrote that she could again 'run up stairs', Flinders considered asking her to come to Portsmouth or Gosport, so they could see each other more frequently in the time that remained. Others, too, missed her presence. Bauer 'seldom forgets to add "and Mrs. Flinders' good health" after the cloth is withdrawn; and even the bluff Mr Bell does not forget you'.[32] But by mid-July Ann had been taken home to Lincolnshire by the Reverend Tyler.

Flinders now wrote to his father at length and with great affection, seeking to show himself a dutiful son and acknowledging his debt to his father, whose retirement he hoped, with typical confidence, to assist through his own success. He also wrote to his friend Thomas Franklin and to Joseph Banks. Banks had already written his farewell, 'with sincere good wishes for your future prosperity, and with a firm belief that you will in your future conduct do credit to yourself as an able navigator and to me as having recommended you . . .'[33]

On 17 July a packet arrived from the Admiralty. Flinders opened his sailing orders, the French passport and some accompanying documents.

15

The Voyage Out

The route and requirements of the *Investigator* had been laid out largely on the basis of suggestions by Banks, and possibly Dalrymple, and signed by the Lords of the Admiralty, John Jervis, Sir Thomas Troubridge and J. Markham. Flinders was instructed to call at Madeira Island and the Cape of Good Hope for water and supplies. Once on the New Holland coast he could, if necessary, put into King George the Third's Harbour, now King George Sound. He was then specifically to examine the section of the continent's south coast unknown to Europeans, which ran from 130°E longitude, approximately at the head of the Bight, to Bass Strait. This meant passing cursorily along the stretch between Cape Leeuwin and 130°E, a shoreline seen by earlier explorers. From the 130° mark, however, his 'best endeavours' were to be employed in searching for harbours or 'any creek or opening likely to lead to an inland sea or strait', which he could explore either then or later.[1]

When he found it necessary, he was to continue to Sydney to refit the ship, rest his people, confer with the governor and take under his command the brig *Lady Nelson* as tender. He was then to return to a very diligent exploration of the south coast from King George Sound to Bass Strait, repairing to Sydney when the weather became inclement and returning to the south coast survey as soon as possible.

His exploration was to be thorough, covering soil, products and the inhabitants, and fixing accurately the positions of headlands, bays and harbours. Again, rivers were of prime interest, to be investigated as far inland as possible. Exploration of the northwest coast of New Holland was to follow, again seeking harbours, and then the Gulf of Carpentaria, Torres Strait, where he was to execute 'a careful investigation and accurate survey', and 'the whole of the remainder of the north, west, and north-west coasts of New Holland', with emphasis on finding advantageous sea lanes for East India Company ships. Finally the east coast of the continent should be examined, stopping at his discretion at Fiji or other Pacific islands. Throughout, the naturalists and artists were to be given as much time as possible to gather their collections and complete their drawings. Detailed directions on the handling of plants and the plant cabin were included. All of this accomplished, Flinders was to lose no time in returning to England, where he would submit to the Admiralty all journals, logbooks, sketches and charts kept by officers and petty officers.

It is evident that the Lords Commissioners had little idea of the magnitude of what they were asking of the expedition. They had no real concept of the enormous distances involved, of the extraordinary length of the Australian coastline, of the number, size and intricacy of inlets and island groups. Much of this Flinders himself did not realise, and with characteristic enthusiasm, confidence and optimism he accepted that it could be done within three or four years. He did in fact accomplish much of it, although there were failures. He found no great rivers. He had to omit an examination of the northwest coast, the area of greatest interest to the East India Company. On his charts he not achieve the precision and thoroughness he wanted. What he did do was infinitely more important. For the world at large, he gave shape and significance to a continent.

The French passport was entirely in French, which Flinders did not understand. Later he wrote in his journal that he 'had had its general purport explained . . . by one of our gentlemen on board the *Investigator*, who understands the language a little'.[2] The translator may have been the naturalist, Robert Brown, whom Flinders would call upon during the voyage to act as interpreter. Now, however, he found it sufficient to know that the passport was made out for the protection of HMS *Investigator*, under the command of Captain Matthew Flinders. By his own admission he scarcely looked at it again. In view of the passport, he also received the Admiralty's instructions 'to act in all respects towards French ships as if the two countries were not at war'. Importantly, he was not to take on board 'letters or packets other than such as you may receive from this office, or the office of His Majesty's secretary of state'.[3] A memoir from Dalrymple on wind and weather on the south New Holland coast, an order to Governor King in Sydney to place the *Lady Nelson* under Flinders's command and to assist him in the prosecution of the voyage, and copies of various lists completed the contents of the packet.

Flinders now ordered from shore provisions to replace those consumed while the sloop waited at Spithead. These arrived the next morning. The boats were in place, the gig nested into the launch set on beams across the waist opening, the two cutters hung from davits on the ship's quarters. Final letters went ashore, and the ship slipped her moorings.

In the afternoon of 20 July 1801 the men of the *Investigator* saw the last of England as the mariners' long-time landmark of Start Point paled into nothingness. Under full sail in an easterly breeze the ship cut through the dark blue water at almost 4 knots, her bows pushing out white crests that swirled and danced alongside until they merged into the wake. No one knew that under her outer planking and new copper sheathing the *Investigator* was already the victim of an insidious and deadly menace.

On the second day out from Spithead Flinders issued his standing orders. These minutely detailed the duties of the officer of the watch and of the master's mates and midshipmen, and covered the issuing of stores, determining the ship's location each noon, and discipline in general, which Flinders expected to be strictly kept. There were exact directions on maintaining a clean ship. Decks were to be washed, sprinkled with vinegar and dried and aired with fire in the stoves, and on wet days cleaned without water. Hammocks and the contents of the men's bags and chests were to be set out regularly in fresh air. In all of this Flinders's orders were in direct line of descent from James Cook. On fine evenings there could be dancing on the forecastle to fife and drum, along with 'other playful amusements which might occasionally be more to the taste of sailors, and were not unseasonable', for such amusements were part of his program for maintaining both good health and spirits.[4]

Crews were to be mustered each Sunday and Thursday, clean, shaven and acceptably dressed. Apparently there were no prayer services, which Flinders evidently felt were not necessary for the good health and spirits of his men. His own religious beliefs seem to have been firm but simple, little given to abstract enquiry or moralising, possibly the teleological belief of many science-minded men of his time that creation had been designed with a purpose by a knowing God and as such could be accepted without much question.

The men's diet was that of the Royal Navy at the time. There was sweetened rice or oatmeal for breakfast, a drink of hot wort with onions and half a biscuit for lunch, salt meat or cheese with boiled pease for dinner. Scurvy was hopefully prevented with drinks of lime and sugar in hot weather and sweetened wort or sauerkraut and vinegar in the colder latitudes. Flinders conferred with the ship's surgeon, Hugh Bell, but there was little either could do to alter the basic fare. What could be done was to vary and augment the food through hunting and fishing later in the journey and the purchase of fresh fruit or vegetables where these were available. On the Australian coast these last items would be very scarce indeed.

As the crew settled into their routines, so the scientific staff became accustomed to the patterns of their shipboard lives and to each other. Crosley and Brown, as the senior men in the group, messed at Flinders's table, although Crosley, often ill, would have kept to his cabin much of the time. With the departure of Crosley at the Cape of Good Hope, Bauer and Westall joined the commander's table.

Robert Brown's medical training and military background provided a certain basis for rapport with the captain, a doctor's son with ten years of naval discipline behind him. For the most part, as Flinders expressed it, he and Brown worked together 'smoothly', evidently with mutual respect. Brown, however, had the same intense, single-minded devotion to his particular work as did Flinders, and there were differences. Brown wrote to C. F. Greville, a botanist and an associate of Banks, 'I have found C. Flinders upon all occasions ready to give me every opportunity of collecting, but I find considerable difficulty in procuring proper, or indeed any, boxes made for my collection, or a safe place to place it in'.[5] Carpenters were almost continuously engaged in the upkeep of wooden ships, and this, not plant boxes, was Flinders's first priority.

Brown was loyally supported in his work by Peter Good and Ferdinand Bauer. On many occasions when he remained on board to process his growing collections, the others undertook the botanising ashore. Good made many excursions on his own—'...a more active man...could hardly be met with', commented Brown. The naturalist was equally satisfied with Bauer. 'He has indeed been indefatigable, and has bestowed infinite pains on the dissections of the parts of frutification of the plants.'[6] Brown made no comment on Allen and Westall.

Of the supernumeraries, Flinders remarked that only one was an exception to harmony. Although unnamed, this was probably Hugh Bell, the surgeon.

Flinders initiated a series of observations and experiments involving himself and others. Air, surface sea water and deep-sea temperatures were taken and compared, and salinity measured. The rise and fall of the barometer was observed in relation to land and sea breezes. With John Thistle he experimented with the compass, seeking to explain deviation. Observations were taken with every compass on the ship, as they were taken to different locations on the deck, and changes were recorded from the ship's different headings and as the sloop neared the equator.

Much more distracting were faults beginning to show in the ship itself. The *Investigator* was scarcely out of the Channel before Flinders 'had the mortification to find the ship beginning to leak...in the last three days she admitted three inches of water per hour'.[7] In a calm sea he had a boat lowered and, with the carpenter, went around the ship to examine the seams and butts near the waterline. They 'seemed sufficiently bad...for the leak to be attributed to them...' and as most water came in when the ship heeled, 'I hoped the cause need not be sought lower down'.[8] Less important, but also frustrating, were rotted spars and defective rigging that had to be replaced.

Flinders later attributed to wartime exigencies the fact that he had received a flawed vessel. 'I was given to understand no better ship could be spared from the service; and my anxiety to complete the investigation of the coasts of Terra Australis did not admit of refusing the one offered'.[9] At the time he had, in fact, offered no criticism, in his eagerness possibly failing to notice defects that could have been made good at Sheerness and ignoring 'what I had been able to collect from the dock yard officers, [which] had given me an unfavourable opinion of her strength'.[10] Changes and improvements that he asked for were made. His own order to cut scuttles into the gunport lids evidently added to the weakness already caused by the gunports.

On the first of August they sighted some of the uninhabited islets of the Portuguese Madeiras archipelago. Two days later the *Investigator* neared the principal island. Becalmed, the ship was towed to anchor before the town of Funchal, where they found the island to have been occupied just nine days before by a British regiment, brought in by a naval squadron now lying in Funchal Road.

The *Investigator* remained at Madeira for four days. Flinders and Crosley took observations. The naturalists made overnight excursions. The *Investigator* was heeled and the carpenters caulked two seams above the copper all around the hull. Water, fresh provisions and wine at an 'enormous' price were taken on board. Both Flinders brothers sent letters home. It had been a swift and pleasant passage, Matthew wrote his father.

In variable winds, high temperatures and frequent rain, the *Investigator* ran south between Africa and the Canary and Cape Verde Islands. Eleven degrees north of the equator a steady southwest wind set in, with a heavy swell from the south. The *Investigator* rose and plunged, working the oakum out of the seams. Water was seeping in at five inches per hour. In a ship intended for uncertain, possibly perilous conditions, this was deeply disturbing. Flinders altered his heading and lightened and rearranged the ship's upper works. The two 18-pounder carronades, stern chasers, were struck into the afterhold. The spare rudder was shifted to a centre position and the six 12-pounder carronades on their carriages were run inboard as far as they would go. After this the shaking of the timbers with every blow of the sea diminished and the leaking lessened somewhat.

As the *Investigator* approached the equator on the evening of 7 September, Flinders gave permission for the traditional ceremonies of King Neptune's coming on board, and 'to conclude the day with merriment'.[11] For English crewmen the event was virtually a right, a rare opportunity to acceptably vent some of the frustrations of their very circumscribed lives.

Crossing of the Line practices descended from an earlier period when European sailors crossed the equator into an alarming antipodean world of contrary conditions. By tradition those who had crossed before were the knowledgeable ones, whatever their position on the ship. Anyone else was their victim. By the late 18th century the event had become a satirical shipboard play that could legitimately deride, even reverse, the role of authority.

Thus on the night of the seventh the ship was put under snug sail and the men received all the grog they wanted. Peter Good observed, 'Performed the usual Ceremony of Shaving for having Crossed the Equator and as usual too the Sailors got drunk and turbulent at night. Some were insolent to the officers'.[12] Seaman Samuel Smith noted with satisfaction that 'the greatest part of the Officers and Men was shaved'.[13]

The line was crossed in nearly 17°W about seven o'clock the next morning. There was, however, a disciplinary corollary to the night before. Good's journal entry reads:

> Wind and weather as yesterday Latitude Observed 0°.18 South Lon 17° West at 1 P.M. Turned the hands out and the Captain very handsomely and humanely admonished the Sailors respecting their conduct the proceeding evening and took the blame on himself for having permitted them to have so much liquor and that as they had abused that indulgence they must not expect any more leniency and so dismissed them very much to their satisfaction—[14]

Peter Good was clearly satisfied as well. In the context of early 19th century naval discipline, Flinders rarely failed to take the kind of action that seamen of the time could accept, even approve.

At eight o'clock on the morning of 16 October the high land of the Cape of Good Hope emerged on a hazy horizon. Flinders had decided not to go into Table Bay, where Cape Town lay below the great mass of Table Mountain, because heavy gales swept the sound late in the year. Instead, he took the *Investigator* around the Cape into False Bay. Steering into the bay's inner cove of Simon's Bay, they found at anchor a squadron of seven British warships. Flinders immediately reported to the commander-in-chief, Vice-Admiral Sir Roger Curtis. He showed his orders and explained the serious condition of the *Investigator*, and had the great satisfaction of reporting that he had no one on the sick list.

The *Investigator* remained in Simon's Bay for eighteen days and received every assistance possible from the squadron. Expert caulkers were recruited from other ships and, with the *Investigator*'s crew, caulked the sloop's sides inside and out. The ship was repainted and its sea-worn sails sent to the flagship HMS *Lancaster* for repair. Good fresh water was brought from north of the bay. Local naval stores could not supply biscuits, and vegetables were few, but fresh beef and mutton were plentiful, and oranges and lemons arrived from the naval hospital in Cape Town.

Flinders exchanged four crewmen for more suitable people from the flagship, and, as he wrote to Ann, Nathaniel Bell, one of two midshipmen brothers on board, 'left the ship by his own application, finding as he said that he was unfit for the service; and I have gotten a fine young Irishman Denis de Lacy of about 17 in his lieu, a red hot volunteer for the service'.[15] Thomas Bell remained on board. The brothers were not related to surgeon Hugh Bell.

The naturalists were almost constantly ashore. 'The plants for variety and beauty were beyond description', wrote Peter Good. Despite rain and fog he and Brown climbed to the top of Table Mountain. A fascinated Westall captured the impressiveness of the mountain as well as its picturesque detail.

Meanwhile, Flinders and Crosley set up their tents and observatory on the south shore of the bay. Samuel Flinders was put in charge of the camp, serving also as Crosley's assistant 'in making and calculating the observations, for which he was qualified'.[16] The rates of the *Investigator*'s timepieces were found to be satisfactory except in the case of the Arnold No. 82, which they stopped using.

Crosley, however, had been frequently ill and now wished to quit the expedition and return home. His loss was sharply felt by Flinders, who would miss the astronomer's professional skills; Flinders now had to assume responsibility for the observatory work himself. Of this, he wrote to Banks, he hoped he and Samuel had sufficient knowledge to carry on, and as no replacement astronomer could reach Port Jackson in fewer than twelve months or the ship in fewer than eighteen, he would not apply to the Board of Longitude for one. Remuneration for his brother and himself he entrusted to the Board's discretion.

Crosley left with Flinders a copy of his instructions and the instruments provided by the Board of Longitude, but took with him his own very excellent Earnshaw watch and Troughton reflecting circle, which

Flinders considered a serious loss. The Board did send out to New South Wales a replacement astronomer, James Inman, but as expected, he arrived in Sydney too late to join the expedition as it headed north.

With Matthew Flinders increasingly occupied as commander and surveyor, the work of the expedition's astronomer fell more and more to Samuel. He apparently enjoyed the complex mathematical computations; he learned and did well.

Flinders sent three yearning, passionate letters to Ann from the Cape, pleading for word from her. 'Write to me constantly, write me pages and volumes. Tell me the dress thou wearest, . . . tell me thy dreams,—anything: so do but talk to me, and of thyself'.[17] To his father he wrote with satisfaction of 'the great improvement' that had taken place in Samuel: 'Instead of being a burthen to me, I now have great hope of his proving himself a very useful assistant to me in the voyage; and I believe, that opportunities will not be wanting to enable me to bring him into some repute, which would open a door for him to fame, if not to fortune also'. He added, 'Long before our return I hope to hear of your having retired from business to a snug situation suited to your taste . . . I have great hope of being able to assist you in accomplishing this desirable purpose soon after our return, if your circumstances should not by that time have enabled you to do it'.[18]

On 3 November 1801 Flinders dismantled his observation site and sent on board the tents, observatory and instruments. The ship was ready for sea. The scientific team was not. They were entranced with their findings among the scenic hills and mountains of the Cape. With some amusement, Flinders remarked, 'though it were to proceed to the almost untrodden, and not less ample field of botany, New Holland, I had to engage with the counter wishes of my scientific associates . . .'[19]

Delayed by contrary winds and then by calms, the *Investigator* quitted False Bay two days later. Before the ship and her company lay the great, empty expanse of the South Indian Ocean. Flinders had made this passage of some 5000 miles three times before, and now chose the 37th parallel for his path across the sea as sufficiently south to catch a prevailing westerly while avoiding the gales of the higher latitudes beyond. It was a satisfactory choice. Winds and weather were mostly favourable and the *Investigator* moved along at an average daily run of 140 miles, an acceptable speed, Flinders thought, for a deeply laden collier-built vessel. The ship made no more than two inches of water per hour, which was well controlled by normal pumping. The usual routine of a ship at sea was re-established. As well, marines and seamen exercised with the large guns and small arms. Flinders continued his compass observations and other experiments. He had planned to land at mid-ocean Amsterdam Island to check his timekeepers and plotted a course accordingly. Fog, however, prevented any sighting.

When he could, Flinders dwelt upon his future and the distinction that he was certain he would attain. As the *Investigator* ploughed through the South Indian Ocean, he sat in his cabin and wrote to Willingham Franklin, young John's eldest brother, a long-time friend then at Oriel College, Oxford. With the success of his voyage, he said, he looked forward to being not 'unknown in the world; my acquaintance in Soho Square will introduce me to many of the first philosophers and literati in the kingdom . . .' He would then probably be in a position to give Willingham 'a lift into notice'.[20]

His voyage had to be written up and published and, he continued, 'I am now engaged in writing a rough account'. For the style and language required for the final copy, however, he needed the help of a literary man, and suggested that Willingham assist him. 'A little mathematical knowledge will strengthen your style . . . Study the writings of different authors both for the subjects and the manner in which they are treated'. Thus to someone with whom there were no barriers of rank, Flinders wrote with the confidence and quiet self-importance that were part of him. By the time Flinders returned to England, Willingham Franklin had forged his own successful career. He advised Flinders on legal matters and later became a judge of the Supreme Court in Madras, India, where he and his wife and daughter died of cholera in 1824.

16

Terra Australis

In the evening twilight of 6 December 1801, after a passage of 32 days, land came into view straight ahead at 'the supposed distance of ten leagues', about 30 miles. 'Landt van der Leeuwin' had appeared on a Dutch map of 1627, named for the ship from which Europeans had received their first known sighting of Australia's southwest coast. Flinders stood for the coast until eleven that night, then veered to the southwest. At five in the morning, he saw from aloft the largest of what, nine years before, D'Entrecasteaux had named the Iles St Allouarn, but realising that it was, in fact, part of the mainland, Flinders renamed it Cape Leeuwin. It was the continent's southwesternmost point, a sloping, apparently lightly wooded promontory, backed by green hills. As the day brightened, Westall drew the cape from a distance of four or five leagues, noting that the drawing was 'taken at 7.30 A.M. 7 Dec. 1801'. Actually, he would have finished it over a period of time, but its purpose was to serve as a navigational aid accompanying the chart, and he wished to show the land as it looked from a certain distance at a certain time of day.

Flinders shaped the course of the *Investigator* eastward. He was watching a shoreline previously witnessed by only three other recorded navigators: in 1627 by the Dutch Pieter Nuyts, who had followed a mysterious coast for some 1000 miles to the Nuyts Archipelago; in 1791 by George Vancouver to approximately today's Esperance Bay, and a year later by D'Entrecasteaux, to just beyond the top of the Great Australian Bight.

Farther to the east lay a great length of shoreline within the region claimed for Britain by Cook, but which no known navigator had seen. Flinders's orders were to examine closely this unknown coast from

130°E longitude to Bass Strait, and then, having proceeded to Port Jackson for rest and refit, to return to explore thoroughly the long, partially charted stretch from Cape Leeuwin east.

Flinders, however, had already decided to begin his careful survey at Cape Leeuwin. He argued, 'The difference of sailing along the coast at a distance, or in keeping near it and making a running survey was likely to be so little, that I judged it advisable to do all that circumstances would allow whilst the opportunity offered'.[1] There were also the practical considerations of time spent and wear on the ship should he continue first to Port Jackson and then double back for the survey, factors that he believed the Lords Commissioners of the Admiralty would accept. Flinders's decision, however, was complicated by the knowledge that somewhere on the vast continental littoral of Terra Australis, the French expedition under Nicolas Baudin could be making discoveries ahead of him, a prospect that had greatly concerned him in England.

Now, however, the attraction of making a complete survey was irresistible. Flinders's instructions emphasised locating harbours and any opening on the coastline 'likely to lead to an inland sea or strait'.[2] He himself believed that 'it was scarcely credible that, if this vast country were one connected mass of land, it should not contain some large rivers'.

He added, 'The apparent want of rivers had induced some persons to think, that Terra Australis might be composed of two or more islands . . . whilst others, believing in the continuity of the shore, thought this want might arise from the interior being principally occupied by a mediterranean sea'.[3] Openings to such a strait or sea were thought to be on the unexplored south coast. Yet Flinders believed that 'something remained to be done upon the parts already seen . . . an investigation of a coast so extensive, would not fail to produce much useful information'.[4]

Flinders later said that on board the *Investigator* the French expedition was frequently a topic of conversation, but judging from his writings, he now relegated the problem to the back of his mind and was concentrating on a thorough investigation of the continent's southern rim. Before making this search, however, he needed a sheltered anchorage where the *Investigator*'s masts could be stripped, her sails put in order, and the rigging extensively renewed. King George the Third's Harbour, the magnificent roadstead that Vancouver had discovered, charted and named ten years earlier and that the Admiralty had suggested for refreshment and watering, was clearly the place for this.

The *Investigator* approached King George Sound in the evening of 8 December. By eight o'clock it was dark, but Flinders confidently took the ship around the headland and into the entrance. The night was fine and 'I did not hesitate to work up by the guidance of captain Vancouver's chart'.[5] Typically sure of himself, he steered the sloop into the darkness of the bay and, at eleven o'clock, dropped anchor just southeast of Seal Island. In midnight stillness the men looked out over the water, saw the dim outline of a new land and breathed the scents of strange vegetation.

Work and exploration began the next morning, and excitement ran high as the scientific staff and their dogs landed to make their first Australian investigations. Flinders and John Thistle, meanwhile, began searching the bay for a suitable anchorage for the *Investigator*.

King George Sound opens through narrow entrances into two inner coves, Oyster Harbour in the north and Princess Royal Harbour in the west, where the city of Albany now stands, both harbours named by Vancouver. Several small islands and protruding rocks lie in the Sound itself.

On the 12th the *Investigator* was run into Princess Royal Harbour and moored about a third of a mile from the north shore and its highest hill, now Mt Clarence. In the evening the tents were pitched on land under a guard of marines. The next morning the observatory and instruments were landed in the care of Samuel Flinders.

In the days that followed, the *Investigator*'s topmasts and upper spars and rigging were brought down for repair, fresh water was hauled to the ship, trees felled and firewood brought on board. The scientists spread into the surrounding country, examining rocks and soil and collecting new varieties of plants and seeds. There were benefits. Good fishing provided snapper and mullet, seals and birds were shot for fresh meat and Oyster Harbour yielded such a harvest of oysters that the entire company was fed on them. Two very large nests, built on the ground, intrigued the Europeans, 'the branches of trees and other matter, of which each nest was composed, being enough to fill a small cart'.[6]

Searching for items reportedly left by Vancouver in 1791, Flinders landed on the weathered burl of granite that is Seal Island. There was no sign of natives having been there, yet the staff, cairn and a bottle containing a parchment were not to be found. The mystery grew when on one shore the men found trees felled with axe and saw. Then on the eastern side of the bay they found a small plot of ground 'trimmed like a garden'[7] and on it a piece of sheet copper inscribed 'August 27, 1800, Chr. Dixson ship Elligood'. The following year the *Cape Town Gazette* noted the return of the whaler *Elligood* after fourteen months and the deaths of her captain, 'Dickson', and nine men from scurvy.

There were at first brief encounters with very shy Aborigines, who did their best to sign that the newcomers should go away, but within days a few had come up to the tents looking for gifts, of which the favourites were handkerchiefs and red night caps. Many objects they accepted were later found thrown away on the beach. Their language was entirely different from that of the Eora people of Port Jackson. Flinders wrote, 'We found their pronunciation difficult to be imitated; more so, indeed, than our language was to them. Several English words they pronounced perfectly'.[8] The sex of the apparently beardless visitors puzzled them, and they were much gratified when enlightened.

Flinders's main preoccupation was a survey of the Sound and its harbours, for while carefully crediting Vancouver's work as far as it went, he soon came to recognise its limitations and began his own trigonometrical survey. This triangulation method entailed using a surveyor's chain, possibly multiples of the Gunter's chain of 66 feet, to lay down a base line running in a recorded compass direction, which at King George Sound was initially done on a long sandy beach. The position of one end of the base line was established, and the angle measured from there to a suitable natural feature seen inland, such as a hill. The process was then repeated at the opposite end of the base line, establishing a triangle with its apex, in this case, at the hill.

With the length of one side of the triangle and the size of two of its angles known, the remaining lengths and angle could be computed. Using the same base line, sightings were made on other features and further triangles developed. Additional base lines, contiguous to the original or separate, and further observations to and from islands and mainland elevations provided a framework of triangles that extended over the bay, the two inner harbours and beyond. Intersecting points derived from these were plotted on a rough chart and detailed with sketching to indicate heights, wooded areas, rivers and the like.

Flinders also surveyed from the ship, moving the *Investigator* among the islands and along the mainland shore. Here a measured base line was formed by the track of the ship as she moved forward. Bearings were taken to prominent features ashore and the resulting triangle solved trigonometrically to give the necessary distances. Soundings and various notations and descriptive comments were added. Here and elsewhere, Westall sometimes accompanied the surveying team, climbing to high points to draw panoramic views associated with the surveys.

At the observatory Flinders, Samuel and several midshipmen made numerous and repeated observations, recorded temperature and barometric readings and kept a register of tidal variations. At times cloud and rain prevented observations and one heavy gale blew away the top covering of the observatory, so the instruments were drenched.

Assisted by the marines, the botanists prepared their plant boxes and their live specimens. The boxes were then brought on board and secured in the breadroom, for the disassembled plant cabin would remain in the hold until Sydney. Brown noted in his letter to Banks that in 24 days at the Sound, he had collected nearly 500 species of plants, of which about 300 were entirely new.

Christmas Day began with the usual Sunday muster. The officers and scientific staff then 'had the pleasure', wrote Peter Good, 'of eating a Christmas Dinner with the Captain [while] the Sailors had a holliday & were more regular and orderly than usual on such occasions however several got compleatly drunk'.[9]

On the 30th the *Investigator* was ready for sea. Seeing a number of Aborigines still at the abandoned tent site, Flinders ordered the fifteen marines ashore to execute a musket drill for them. The red jackets and white cross belts astonished the audience, all the more because they themselves were decorated with red ochre and white clay crosses, and even more amazing to them were the drum and especially the fife, which some attempted to snatch. 'But when they saw these beautiful red-and-white men, with their bright muskets, drawn up in a line, they absolutely screamed with delight'.[10]

They watched the drill with intense and silent attention, several moving their hands with the motions of the marines, while one old man placed himself at the end of the line and, with a short staff, mimicked the shouldering, presenting and grounding of the muskets. Before the firing of the guns the Aborigines were warned, so the volleys produced only a sudden start that, as Seaman Smith observed, 'caused them to Dance and hollow unmercifully'.[11] It was a satisfying event for all concerned. One native was sufficiently confident to allow Brown and Bell to measure him and to name the parts of his body for their notes on vocabulary.

The study of language was a serious pursuit of some 18th and 19th century scholars. Classification systems originating in other disciplines were adapted to language, and different languages compared in terms of vocabulary, grammar and phonology to discover origins and relationships. On James Cook's first voyage Banks and others compiled vocabularies of Pacific languages, and on Cook's second journey the linguists Johann and Georg Forster, father and son, did extensive work. Brown and Bell were not language scholars but shared in the popular interest, and it was from the contributions of many such travellers that specialists drew information not otherwise accessible to them.

A strong adverse wind held the *Investigator* in Princess Royal Harbour until 3 January. In the Sound Flinders zigzagged the sloop, pulling a trawl and dredge to bring up a variety of small fish, shells, coral and seaweed for the naturalists. A bottle with a parchment stating the arrival and departure times of the *Investigator* was left on Seal Island. On the fifth a strong, wet westerly took the *Investigator* into the Southern Ocean.

For three days the *Investigator* followed a low, sandy shore, Flinders attempting to keep close enough to see from the deck the breaking surf and any sign of a river, without endangering the ship. When this was not possible, he was at the masthead with his telescope. He often took bearings from aloft, clinging there in sun and wind for long hours, with Thistle, Samuel or a reliable midshipman on the deck noting his figures as he called them down. With the land still in sight to allow immediate corrections, he fixed the position of land features and recorded the ship's position by the timekeepers or astronomical observations. The course was then drawn on a rough chart. An unbroken line on the chart marked the ship's track by day, a pecked line her movement by night. Flinders named few coastal features. Most were identified by numbers, upper and lower case letters or combinations of them, or with Greek letters. The same numbers and letters were used in his log. Other symbols and notations indicated the *Investigator*'s noon position and heading, amplitude and azimuth bearings, currents, wind strength and direction. Brief comments described weather and the appearance of the land.

Each evening at dusk the ship was hauled off from the coast to ride through the night under easy sail. In his cabin before he retired, Flinders laid out his information and, in the swaying yellow light of the lantern, completed the rough chart to the point that had been reached and wrote into his journal the day's astronomical observations, bearings and remarks. At dawn the sloop returned to where the survey had ended the day before. In port or when being out to sea provided the time, Flinders set all of these records before him and compiled new, corrected and more accurate charts. He wrote, 'This plan, to see and lay down every thing myself, required constant attention and much labour, but was absolutely necessary to obtaining that accuracy of which I was desirous'.[12] It was a meticulous method, demanding on himself and often excluding others from tasks they might have considered their prerogative.

Inevitably, reactions among his officers varied. Fowler, the first lieutenant, had been with the ship when she was the *Xenophon* and evidently had some ideas of his own about her handling that he only gradually relinquished. On reaching Port Jackson after an association of almost ten months, Flinders wrote to Ann, 'Mr. Fowler agrees better with me than he did earlier in our acquaintance; he does not find it so difficult a task to please me, as he once thought; and I believe he now has the inclination to do it'.[13]

It was less simple with Samuel Flinders, both the second lieutenant and the captain's younger brother. Early in the voyage Matthew had acknowledged that their positions on board necessarily imposed distance between them. Samuel, however, was bright and had shown considerable ability in chart-making even as a youthful midshipman;

Samuel Ward Flinders (1782–1842), Matthew's younger brother, who sailed with him as midshipman and subsequently as second lieutenant on HMS Investigator. *Samuel Flinders lived his later years in or near Donington on half-pay from the Navy. The photograph is of a miniature by an unknown artist. (La Trobe Collection, State Library of Victoria)*

faced with the departure of John Crosley at the Cape of Good Hope, Matthew apparently had little hesitation in assuming that he and his brother could take on the responsibilities left by the astronomer. These, as time went on, devolved mainly upon Samuel. The situation probably became more acute as the *Investigator* made her way through the many navigational hazards and extreme summer heat along the south coast. Samuel was relieved of his watch on deck in order to work at the complex astronomical computations in the hot, airless cabin below. Apparently at one point, Samuel objected. Matthew's disciplinary response was immediate. Samuel was ordered to keep his normal watch during the night. Then, 'from a stimulus of pride', he proceeded to keep his watch by day as well, while producing the same amount of astronomical work as before.

Samuel Flinders was now eighteen. A faded photograph of a miniature of years later shows dark eyes, a rather pointed nose and smallish chin, and a thick thatch of seemingly light brown hair. Since the age of twelve he had been subordinate to his older brother, of whom he had heard much even before that time. Matthew had been instrumental in obtaining his naval appointments and in regulating his financial affairs. In the later months of this long voyage perhaps many factors fostered flashes of rebellion against a demanding captain-brother who, indefatigable himself, expected the same from his sibling.

At the journey's end Matthew gave Samuel full credit for his duties as astronomer. However, in commenting to Ann on Fowler's apparent wish to please his captain, Flinders added, 'I wish so much could be said of my brother; the distance between us has widened considerably. He is satisfied with being as much inferior to the other officers as I would have him superior to them'.[14]

The westernmost island of the Archipelago of the Recherche came into view shortly before sunset on 8 January. The island group named for D'Entrecasteaux's ship stretches some 94 miles, hundreds of granitic islands, islets and rocks, some rising nearly 600 feet and topped with vegetation, others visible only as the sea breaks upon them. Some of this navigational nightmare was charted by the notable hydrographer Charles François Beautemps-Beaupré as, in 1792, he sailed with D'Entrecasteaux along the archipelago. No one had penetrated the maze. This, if weather permitted, Flinders decided to do.

Throughout the following day the *Investigator* threaded its way into the midst of the islands, with rocks and islets protruding from the water ahead and off both bows like indiscriminately laid giant's stepping stones. By early evening Flinders at the masthead saw breakers and rocky outcrops studding the sea on every side. There was no space of open water in which the ship could stand off and on for the night, nor any island that could provide shelter. However, looking shoreward between the islands, he saw a beach. Flinders conferred with Thistle, and with his agreement, steered directly before the wind through the narrow passage between rocks and islets towards the mainland. At seven that evening the *Investigator* entered a small sheltered inlet and dropped anchor in 7 fathoms.

At the scientists' request the ship remained for four days at the inlet, which Flinders appropriately named Lucky Bay. The surrounding country was arid but the botanical gentlemen, as Flinders called them, gathered an impressive harvest of shrubs and small plants. From a hilltop Flinders took angles and, in the haze, counted 56 islands and islets, excluding the submerged rocks seen only as breakers. Later he reduced the number to 45, acknowledging that many more were out of sight. There were minor but interesting discoveries— a huge bird's nest similar to one that had mystified everyone at King George Sound, three monstrous sharks, one of which was caught and brought aboard, and zamia palms, with juicy seeds that a number of people ate, becoming sick for the rest of the day.

There were no meetings with indigenous people, but the air was heavy with smoke; at one time nine different fires were counted. Some sailor added another, setting ablaze one of the brush-covered islands. Peter Good complained that 'the smoak from so many [fires] darkened the air so that we could not see much of the country'.[15] A continuing worry was differences in the readings of a compass set at the binnacle and elsewhere on the ship, and with changes in the ship's heading. The area around the binnacle was searched for marlin spikes, sail needles or other loose iron objects, and Flinders sent down into the hold the two carronades standing closest to it. There was little change.

There were anxious moments as the *Investigator* left Lucky Bay. Thirty fathoms under the keel shoaled to ten, then swiftly to three, 'when', Flinders noted, 'the bottom was distinctly seen under the ship'.[16] Peter Good was more forthcoming: 'instantly the Ship touched—but fortunately suffered no damage'.[17] A later examination did show, as Seaman Samuel Smith wrote, 'her copper loosened being the only damadge done'.[18]

Another safe anchorage was found at Middle Island, the largest in the archipelago. For two days the scientists explored the island while Flinders climbed its stony northwestern height, observing a mainland promontory that he later called Cape Pasley for his early patron. Thistle discovered a small lake with salt-saturated, rose-coloured water and great quantities of fine, crystallised salt on its margins. Rare little tammar wallabies were seen, on one island small blue penguins and, on nearby Goose Island, great numbers of geese that provided some generous meals. There was, however, no fresh water.

The Recherche Islands sank into the haze as on 17 January the *Investigator* continued eastward. The shoreline changed, rising into cliffs some 300 feet above the sea,[19] a perpendicular wall of white limestone with an upper strata of darker sandstone cutting across the sky so that nothing beyond could be seen, even from the masthead. Dwarfed, the *Investigator* slipped along below, as had Pieter Nuyts's little *Gulden Zeepaert* almost 175 years before. For a time the cliff wall lowered and fell back, leaving a sandy shore. Then it closed in on the coast and rose again, its high upper edge 'almost as level as the horizon of the sea'.[20]

Watching the cliff wall slide past, Flinders speculated on its origins, attempting to form 'some conjecture of what may be within it; which cannot, as I judge in such a case, be other than flat, sandy plains or water. The bank may even be a narrow barrier between an interior and exterior sea . . .'[21] Later he added, 'much do I regret the not having formed an idea of this probability at the time; for notwithstanding the great difficulty and risk, I should certainly have attempted a landing upon some part of the coast, to ascertain a fact of so much importance'.

If Flinders had succeeded in such a landing, he would have largely ended half a century's debate on Australia's interior, for behind these cliffs the near-desert wastes of the Nullabor Plain stretched for hundreds of miles. Flinders's comments touched upon the truth, but they contributed also to the fantasy of a great inland sea. As it was, Flinders simply labelled the blank space behind the cliffs 'Part of New Holland—Discovered by Peter Nuyts 1627'.

In the early evening of the 26th the *Investigator* crossed the 130° meridian where, according to Flinders's instructions from the Admiralty, his serious surveying should have started. Now, having commenced the survey almost two months before, he was about five weeks later at this point than he would have been otherwise. The next day the cliffs ended, and the coast became a sand strip backed by a barren-looking ridge. Just beyond the head of what Flinders would later call the Great Australian Bight, he wrote, 'The examination of Admiral D'Entrecasteaux terminates at the place of our situation this afternoon', adding with some satisfaction, 'and these breakers were not seen by him'.[22] A day or two later he was in an area last traversed by European navigators, Pieter Nuyts and the *Gulden Zeepaert*'s men and captain, François Thijssen.

For the first nine days of February 1802 the *Investigator* explored the offshore island group Flinders called the Nuyts Archipelago. The ship plunged heavily in a strong head swell, making 3 inches of water per hour. Flinders, however, believed the leaks to be in the upper works of the ship, and when the deep pitching ceased, so would the leakage.

The landwind was hot and sultry, and again thick haze made observations difficult. One day at noon Flinders and his officers arrived separately at six or seven different latitudes. On his chart he marked parts of the shoreline as a broken line, 'seen through the haze'. Surprisingly, there was smoke rising from a number of places.

Shore parties explored an island that Flinders recorded as St Francis, assuming it to be the island so named by Nuyts. The heat was stifling. In the shade of a rock Peter Good's thermometer registered 100°F, and in the sun rose to 130°; '...almost intolerable', commented Robert Brown.[23] As well, huge flocks of sooty petrels lived on the island, and their burrows, everywhere in the hot sand, had the explorers sinking into them and falling over. However, enough petrels were caught so every man on the ship was served four birds. There was no water, nor any wood beyond some sun-seared shrubs. Closer to the mainland the *Investigator* came upon a larger uninhabited island, which Flinders, again using Nuyts's nomenclature, set down as St Peter.

Expectations that they had found a river mouth rose in Denial Bay. 'The numerous smokes in the neighbourhood, the insects which usually frequent rivers and lakes of fresh water, the birds, and the grass and other refuse in the water, all tended to excite hope'.[24] But testing the water, Flinders found it as saline as the sea.

Briefly Flinders returned to St Francis Island to recalculate his position, achieving figures that he accepted, but that were still very much in error.

The *Investigator* now followed an exposed lee shore with strong prevailing westerly winds and seemingly no safe harbours, water or wood. Then, as the ship rounded a point later called Cape Catastrophe, they saw before them what appeared to be a strait running northeast with no land in sight in that direction. As well, the outgoing tide was remarkably strong. This combination, as Flinders wrote, 'did not fail to excite many conjectures. Large rivers, deep inlets, inland seas, and passages into the Gulph of Carpentaria, were terms frequently used in our conversations of this evening; and the prospect of making an interesting discovery, seemed to have infused new life and vigour into every man in the ship'.[25]

On his chart, following his habit of using numbers and letters rather than names, Flinders labelled the opening No 12 Inlet.

17

Tragedy at No 12 Inlet

Early in the morning of 21 February, in an eager and cheerful frame of mind, Flinders and Thistle carried their surveying instruments onto land bordering the inlet to the east, uncertain as to whether it was an island or part of the mainland. On their way up into wooded hills they came upon a speckled yellow carpet snake asleep on the ground. It was a prize for Brown to examine, and Flinders held it down at the neck with the butt of a musket while Thistle sewed up its mouth with needle and twine. A little farther two white eagles swooped threateningly on the men: 'it seemed evident that they took us for kanguroos . . .'[1]

From a rise Flinders could see that the inlet continued to run north, open water dotted with islands. Apparently they stood on an island, which for the moment he called Uncertain Island. They looked in vain for fresh water, and after a time returned to the ship.

Flinders had intended to weigh after midday, but on comparing his observations for longitude with those Samuel had just taken on board, he found differences. Flinders returned to the island for new sightings. By the time he again boarded, it was too late to sail. Fresh water, moreover, was needed, and after dinner he sent Thistle to search the mainland shore for water and a suitable achorage. Thistle pushed off in the cutter with a midshipman and six able seamen, while Fowler took the second cutter on a separate errand to Uncertain Island. Just after sunset the lug sails of Thistle's returning boat were seen about halfway between the ship and the mainland, probably a little over three miles away. A stiff breeze was blowing from the southeast and the tide was running strongly from the north, but as Good wrote, 'not the least danger was apprehended—I was on Deck and frequently looked at her to observe the effect of the Current—I had not taken my eyes 5 minutes from the boat when I looked again and could not see it... I immediately said I had lost sight of the Boat, Mr. Evans who had the watch on Deck made the same observation, a general look took place'.[2]

The cutter had disappeared.

Fowler now returned and in the deepening dusk, Flinders immediately sent him to the spot where the cutter had last been seen. Despite what was soon complete darkness, Fowler and his crew, holding a lantern, rowed and sailed in every direction where they thought the boat might be found, while on the *Investigator* the men called and fired muskets. By eleven o'clock Flinders, now anxious for Fowler's safety, had a gun fired for his return. The first lieutenant came aboard to say that while he had seen nothing of the cutter, his own boat had been nearly swamped in about the same place in a 'strong rippling' of the tide.

The search resumed at daylight. Flinders moved the *Investigator* into a small cove closer to where Thistle had disappeared, and observed the strong rush of the tide where islands narrowed its passage. A man with a telescope was stationed on a headland to watch for anything that might be carried seaward. Fowler continued the search in the boat, and Flinders with one group and Brown with another walked the shore. On a little beach they saw footprints where the men evidently had looked for water before their disappearance. Fowler returned, towing the wreck of the cutter, bottom up and stove-in as if she had been dashed on the rocks. There was no sign of the men. Yet, as Seaman Samuel Smith expressed it, 'there was A Possibility of them swimming on shore if they cou'd escape the ravinous shirks which was very Numerous'.[3]

The search continued for three more days. Flinders sent Fowler to the small islands in the southern part of the inlet and himself took a boat some 10 miles along the windings of the shore to the north. The cutter's undamaged compass and binnacle were found, as were a small cask belonging to Thistle, some fragments of the boat and an oar. Days later a boat's sail was seen floating in the bay. As to what had happened, they could only conjecture: the cutter swamped in opposing wind and tide, men trapped under the lug sails and swept out to sea. Only two of the men could swim well.

On the shore of the cove where the *Investigator* was anchored, Flinders had a stout pole driven into the ground and nailed to it a copper sheet with an engraved inscription commemorating the loss of John Thistle, master, William Taylor, midshipman, and six able seamen. On his manuscript chart of the area Flinders recorded the names Memory Cove and Cape Catastrophe, and later named the uncertain island for Thistle and a nearby island for each of the other drowned men.

Westall sketched Thistle Island, depicting a dry, sparse landscape with the inlet beyond. He also drew and tinted a brown and yellow snake, perhaps the one that Flinders and Thistle had brought on board for Brown.

Flinders was deeply stricken by the loss of the men. In his account of the voyage written years later he included tributes to them, citing Thistle's career from before the mast to midshipman and to master: 'truly a valuable man, as a seaman, an officer, and a good member of society . . .' And of the others: 'Mr. William Taylor, the midshipman of the boat, was a young officer who promised fair to become an ornament to the service, as he was to society by the amiability of his manners and temper. The six seamen had all volunteered for the voyage. They were active and useful young men'.[4]

Confident as Flinders normally was of his decisions, he might now have questioned his own response to events. Had he acted as quickly as he should have when the cutter disappeared? He had waited for Fowler to return from Uncertain Island. Should he have summoned him at once with a gunshot? Should he have immediately sent out another officer in the launch or the gig? These were doubts that a commanding officer discussed with no one. Months later he wrote to Ann, 'It will grieve thee, as it has me, to understand that poor Thistle was lost upon the south coast. Thou knowest how I valued him; he is however gone . . .'[5]

The need for fresh water had become urgent and waiting for the bodies of the men to surface would now probably be in vain, considering the number of sharks in the bay. On 25 February the *Investigator* steered north and in the mid-afternoon entered a large, natural harbour that Flinders was to call Port Lincoln, 'in honour of my native province.'[6] The temperature was pleasant and the men not 'incommoded by noxious insects'.[7]

The next day, still searching for water, the *Investigator* was moved to the southwest corner of the harbour. Here they found water some 100 yards from the shore by digging about a yard down through a layer of white clay. Although whitish, it tasted sweet. The water casks were rafted from the ship to the beach, rolled into place and filled, the working party chopping firewood whenever the pit needed time to replenish itself. Then there was the slow, heavy labour of rafting the casks back to the ship, hoisting them on board and stowing them in the hold. Samuel Flinders brought ashore the tents and observatory instruments and began making his observations.

Meanwhile the science men tramped into the countryside with their dogs, between excursions working on board to describe and preserve their specimens. Westall drew views of the harbour with the headlands, inlets, boulders, sparsely leaved trees and a round native hut of bent branches.

After a few days Fowler was sent back to Memory Cove and its neighbouring islands to search again for the bodies of the lost men. He found none.

Flinders had begun his survey. Unable to find a convenient beach on which to measure a base line for his triangles, he left orders on board to fire three large guns in sequence at given times and went to an island at the harbour entrance with a pendulum consisting of a musket ball slung with twine and made to swing half seconds. From the instant the flash of each gun was seen to the time he heard the report, Flinders counted the swings of the pendulum and from this data established his distance from the ship and thus a base line.[8]

With this start, Flinders's triangulation covered the southern section of the Port Lincoln area. He merely sketched by eye the northern part, which he later named Boston Bay. To make the network of triangles work, a correctly established position was necessary. The site of the expedition's encampment was therefore carefully if laboriously determined, its latitude of 34°48'25"S 'from the mean of four meridian observations of the sun taken from an artificial horizon' and its longitude of 135°44'51" 'from thirty sets of distances of the sun and stars from the moon'.[9]

Only two Aborigines were glimpsed in the vicinity of the tents, and others were heard calling, but that they frequented the area was obvious from many bark huts and some deeply trodden paths. Flinders was certain that the ship and camp were being watched, natural behaviour, he thought, in anyone witnessing the unheralded arrival of utterly strange creatures. From past experience he believed that had he waited a few more days, they would have overcome their shyness and approached. 'Such seems to have been the conduct of these Australians',[10] he wrote later in *A Voyage to Terra Australis*. It was one of the earliest references to the natives of the land as Australians. The peaceful pursuits of his people would, he hoped, help to create a friendly reception for the next visitor.

By 4 March the watering was complete. The *Investigator* had her full capacity of 60 tons. The day began with cloud and rain, but as it cleared towards noon, the ship's company witnessed an almost complete eclipse of the sun.

The sloop was prepared for departure, the camp was struck and on the 6th the *Investigator* quitted Port Lincoln and stood to the north. During the afternoon, according to naval custom, the clothing and general belongings of the lost boat crew were sold at the mast, the buyers' wages debited in the ship's books to the amount of the purchase. Thistle's effects were sold the next morning. Only small personal items were retained for the men's families.

For three days the ship followed a low-lying coast stretching north and northeast, their hopes of finding a waterway now 'considerably damped by the want of boldness in the shore, and the shallowness of the water; neither of which seemed to belong to a channel capable of leading us into the Gulph of Carpentaria, nor yet to any very great distance inland'.[11]

There was no evidence of fresh water, and Flinders's disappointment mounted as the sides of the inlet contracted to less than 4 miles in width, and farther ahead seemed to close except for small channels among the banks. The western shore remained low, but to the east a ridge of mountains ran closely parallel to the coast.

Brown led a party onto the eastern shore, wading over a mile in mud and seaweed before reaching dry land. As they began the ascent of a mountain Flinders had simply designated as X, Brown's and Westall's servants were overcome by heat and fatigue and were left behind. The others continued through stiff, spiny grass and scattered eucalypts, casuarina and grass trees, to reach the summit at sunset.

Here in golden sunlight they had a view that Good described as 'probably the most extensive ever had in New Holland, being elevated 3000 feet above the level of the sea and it may be said 100 miles in the heart of the Country'.[12] They stood on a ravined and gullied ridge, seeing in all directions a vast level plain. Darkness overtook them on the way down and they spent a chill, thirsty night on stony ground before rejoining their servants at the bottom of the mountain the next day. These two had found fresh water and, with a good fire going, had been relatively comfortable through the night. Flinders later named the peak they had climbed Mt Brown. Although at times handicapped by 'sore legs', as he wrote his friend C. F. Greville, Robert Brown never spared himself.

Meanwhile, Flinders, accompanied in the cutter by Hugh Bell, had explored northward into the narrowing head of the inlet. In mid-channel the water was relatively deep, but shoals extended over a mile from the shore on either side until they reached a broad, flat-topped hill, which Flinders climbed to take bearings. To the north he saw the inlet meandering between mudflats and mangrove-covered banks. They followed it through the day, camping that night among the mangroves. In the morning the pursuit of black swans for fresh food set the boat's crew rowing up the inlet 'with all their might'. But 'at ten o'clock our oars touched mud on each side, and it was not possible to proceed further'.[13] The water was almost as salty as it was where the ship lay at anchor.

Flinders compared his findings with Brown's and considered the results discouraging. Brown described the general view from Mount X as 'dead, uninteresting, flat country', while Flinders's own exploration had ended the hope of any major waterway penetrating the continent from No 12 Inlet. The city of Port Augusta, on the coast of what Flinders would later call Spencer's Gulph, lay very much in the future, and the rugged ridge of mountains to the east was yet to be named Flinders Ranges by another explorer. Both Flinders and Brown had seen smoke and other evidence of local inhabitants, but no one appeared.

Early the next morning the *Investigator* began sailing down the gulf, along the low shore of what is today South Australia's Yorke Peninsula.

While Flinders was deeply disappointed with the results of his exploration of No 12 Inlet, he was satisfied with the survey itself. He gave the width of the entrance to the gulf as 48 miles and its length as 185 miles 'into the interior of the country'. He continued, 'For the general exactness of its form in the chart, I can answer with tolerable confidence; having seen all that is laid down and, as usual, taken every angle which enters into the construction'.[14]

On 20 March Flinders considered his work in the gulf finished. From the southwestern tip of today's Yorke Peninsula land was dimly visible through haze to the south, so he turned the *Investigator* in that direction. At noon the wind became variable and the barometer fell. By midnight a heavy sea was running and a full gale surging in from the southwest. Under straining, treble-reefed topsails the wave-swept ship climbed, dropped, wallowed and climbed again as she struggled southward. By daylight land ahead extended east and west as far as the eye could see. They saw neither smoke nor any other indication that it was connected to the mainland.

In strong squalls they followed the coast eastward, and by early evening came to anchor in quiet water within a mile of what is today Kangaroo Island's Kangaroo Head. Along the rail every telescope was focused on this new land. There were dark shapes, like rocks, which some of the midshipmen believed were moving. Teasing messmates asked if they were seeing elephants.

At eight o'clock in the morning an armed party went ashore. Numbers of large, heavy, dark brown kangaroos were feeding on the grass, undisturbed by the men's arrival. So unafraid were they that 'the poor animals suffered themselves to be shot in the eyes with small shot, and in some cases to be knocked on the head with sticks'.[15] As a result 31 were shot, ten of them by Flinders with a double-barrelled gun. Flinders wrote: 'I ordered that 50 or 60 lbs. should be stewed into soup each day in the ship's coppers; and that as much meat besides, should be served to the messes as they could eat'.[16] All hands turned to skinning and cleaning kangaroo, and for days they consumed all the soup and steaks they could eat, an ongoing feast after months of salted fare. Of the skins, the men made themselves caps. Flinders added, 'In gratitude for so seasonable a supply [of food], I named this southern land Kanguroo Island'.[17]

Leaving the scene of what he termed 'this butchery', Flinders scrambled through brush and over fallen trees to find higher ground for his observations, a vain effort, for densely growing trees cut off any view. Instead he took bearings the next day from a small headland near the ship. He was, however, convinced that this was an island. There were no signs whatever of human occupation, and the tameness of the animals also suggested that this was so.

The scientific staff explored with enthusiasm. They examined rocks, the reasonably good soil, varieties of trees and types of kangaroos, seals and birds. The large number of fallen trees puzzled everyone. Traces of fire suggested a conflagration some 10–20 years earlier, and Flinders raised a possibility that he himself thought unlikely: that the island had been visited by the vanished La Pérouse. Brown thought the trees had simply fallen because of age. Westall's pencil sketches depict the large flat rocks, seals and tall, spare-looking trees, as well as one of the expedition's hunting parties, three men resting among boulders.

Three days later the *Investigator* sailed. Gale-damaged sails and topmasts had been repaired and the sloop, reprovisioned with kangaroo meat, crossed the 25-mile strait separating the island from the 'heel' of the mainland's Yorke Peninsula. To the east of this point open water ran north. Another large inlet? Or the mouth of a waterway inland?

Flinders returned briefly to Kangaroo Island to make a necessary connection with his running survey. He then steered back across the strait and crossed the inlet opening to approach its eastern side, where those on deck at night saw fires. With daylight the land emerged as low and sandy, rising into a wooded ridge running north, with a peak Flinders would call Mt Lofty. An unobstructed body of water lay ahead.

For three days the *Investigator* moved slowly north in light breezes and occasional calms, following the coast of a bay that on his manuscript chart Flinders labelled No 14 Great Inlet, and years later named the Gulph of St Vincent. Again, and perhaps a little tentatively, hopes rose. Could this be the coveted channel or the estuary of a great river?

The ship anchored near the head of the bay. Here Flinders and Brown manoeuvred the cutter between mudbanks and, beaching the boat, pushed through mangrove thickets to find flat, sandy land rising gently into low, grassy hills. There was no seaway and no river. Later Flinders summarised his exploration of the area: 'Our examination of the gulph of St. Vincent was now finished; and the country round it had appeared to be generally superior to that on the borders of Spencer's Gulph. Yorke's Peninsula between them, is singular in its form, bearing some resemblance to a very ill-shaped leg and foot'.[18]

The *Investigator* was approaching the eastern limit of the unknown coast, and the vision of a great waterway north was dissolving. Flinders had, it seemed, so far proven what there was not.

18

Encounter Bay

A final section of the unknown south coast remained to be seen. First, however, Flinders wanted to check the rates of his timekeepers and also to give his men a few more meals of fresh meat. The *Investigator* returned to Kangaroo Island, coming to anchor in quiet darkness at midnight on 1 April. The next day Samuel Flinders began making observations. In the nine days since the chronometers were last rated on the island, the error of the timekeepers was equivalent to an error of 2'10" longitude, and a proportional adjustment was made to the longitudes recorded since then. The next morning the *Investigator* sailed.

Very shortly it was discovered that the chronometers had stopped. Someone had forgotten to wind them at noon the day before. This was not an unusual oversight, but it was frustrating and inconvenient. For exactness the complex procedure of re-establishing the rates needed to be done on shore and could be severely hampered by the absence of a clear sky. The timekeepers were Samuel Flinders's responsibility, but he might have delegated this routine duty to a senior midshipman, possibly John Franklin. The *Investigator* returned yet again to Kangaroo Island.

To use the enforced time on the island to some advantage, officers and crew were immediately set to the usual onshore tasks, while the science men left on their investigations. Flinders and Brown took a boat up a narrow channel running inland, seeking a sandy height visible from the shore that would give them a view into the interior of the island. At some distance from the coast they entered a lagoon where small islands were covered with pelican rookeries, immense numbers of both young and mature birds and countless skeletons that evidenced the birds' long use of the site. Flinders was very moved. He wrote, 'There could be no more undisturbed place than these islets in a hidden lagoon of an uninhabited island, situate upon an unknown coast near the antipodes of Europe; nor can anything be more consonant to the feelings, if pelicans have any, than quietly to resign their breath, whilst surrounded by their progeny, and in the same spot where they first drew it'.[1]

The two men also reached and climbed the sandy hill that was their objective, and in astonishment found themselves looking out at the sea. At this point Kangaroo Island narrows to just over 2 miles, with a south coast of low cliffs swept by wind and waves. Unable to reach the ship before dark, the men spent a cold night in a tent trying to sleep, as Brown recorded, on 'a bed of shells'.[2]

At dusk the hunting and fishing parties returned to the ship, having had little success. One of the boat crew was in considerable pain. Richard Stanley (or Staley) had, as Flinders put it, 'been simple enough to attack a large seal with a small stick'.[3] The seal had reared up and bitten him deeply in the leg. Flinders felt little compassion. As the man had attacked the animal for no useful purpose, 'he was not undeserving of some punishment . . . he has paid severely, for it is probable that he will allways be more or less lame from it'. Flinders was not mistaken.

Flinders would have found it difficult to ignore the opportunity to investigate Kangaroo Island's south shore. However, four days had been lost, winter storms were not far away, provisions were dwindling. And an unknown coast still lay ahead. In the early morning of 6 April, the ship was unmoored and the topgallant yards sent up. At nine o'clock the *Investigator* weighed and in a light breeze headed east.

Opposing winds and tides made their progress exasperatingly slow. By the morning of 8 April, however, they were in a large open bay with the mainland, low, sand-edged and today part of Coorong National Park, some 5 miles away.

At four o'clock in the afternoon the man aloft called down that he had sighted a white, pyramid-shaped rock ahead. Shortly—and startlingly—it took shape as a ship. Every glass on board was focused upon it, every man watching, as it came on towards them, the first sail they had seen in five months. Flinders's immediate thought was that she might be an English whaler or sealer, but as she continued to approach, a heavy-looking ship with no topgallant masts up, he gave the order to beat to quarters and clear the ship for action. *Investigator*'s pennant and Union Jack were hoisted, and aboard the strange vessel French ensigns fluttered up at the main- and foremastheads, followed by an English jack forward. Flinders raised a white flag of truce.

By sundown, an hour and a half after the sighting, the French ship was passing the *Investigator* to leeward. Flinders hove to and hailed but, taking no chances, veered the *Investigator* so as to keep her broadside to the newcomer. In a brief exchange he learned that this was the *Géographe*, under Captain Nicolas Baudin, of the French scientific expedition. It was stunning news. That the two ships should meet on this long coast and empty sea seemed almost unbelievable. The French, it turned out, had at first thought the approaching *Investigator* to be its separated consort, the *Naturaliste*.

Flinders brought his ship again into the wind and, as the French ship hove to as well, had a boat lowered. At this time Flinders knew no French. He therefore asked Robert Brown, who did, to come with him. The two men were rowed across and boarded the *Géographe*. An officer met them and pointed out Baudin, who courteously conducted them to his cabin. Flinders asked for Baudin's passport from the Admiralty, 'and when it was found and I had perused it, offered mine from the French marine minister'.[4] Baudin handed it back without looking at it.

The meeting was an even greater surprise to the French commander than to Flinders, for while the British had been uncomfortably aware of the earlier sailing of the French expedition, Baudin had no knowledge of Flinders's sailing or his passport, signed in Paris a month after his own departure from Le Havre.

A number of discrepancies occur in the accounts of this interview. Flinders records 'No person was present at our conversations except Mr. Brown; and they were mostly carried on in English, which the captain spoke so as to be understood'.[5] In his journal Brown confirms his presence: 'I accompanied C. Flinders on board her & remained with C. Baudin about ¾ of an hour . . . From the extreme badness of his English I could not well comprehend . . .'[6]

Baudin, however, was to claim that he and Flinders were alone in their discussions, mentioning only that Flinders had come aboard with another person. He told Flinders that he had spent some time on the south and east coasts of Van Diemen's Land, and here his largest boat with a crew of eight had disappeared, presumed lost. In a heavy gale in Bass Strait the *Géographe* was separated from its consort, the *Naturaliste*, but in the fine weather and fair winds that followed, Baudin had explored the mainland's south coast from Western Port to where he met the *Investigator*. He had not, he said, discovered any river or harbour suitable for anchorage.

Displaying an 'imperfect copy' of Flinders's chart of Bass Strait, published in 1800, he criticised sharply the representation of its north side, until Flinders pointed to a note on the chart explaining that this coast had been seen by Bass from an open boat, with no chance of accurately fixing either latitude or longitude. Baudin seemed surprised. Flinders then promised, if the ships remained together overnight, to bring to him updated charts of the area, and a copy of his own *Observations*, his memorandum for navigators in Van Diemen's Land and Bass Strait waters.

Flinders asked about a large island said to lie in the Strait's western entrance, later called King Island, but Baudin had not seen it and seemed to doubt that it existed. Baudin's impression was that Flinders was pleased with this information, as it would give him the chance to make the discovery. Flinders, however, was surprised that Baudin was asking no questions about his explorations.

It was agreed that the two ships would remain together until morning, and in the evening twilight, Flinders and Brown returned to their vessel. While their captains had conferred, Flinders's boat crew and the French sailors had been talking, exchanging information as best they could. In Samuel Smith's words, 'we found her poorly Mann'd, having lost A Boat & Crew & several that run away—her acct was, that they had parted compy with the Naturalizer French ship on investigation, in a gale of wind, have been from France 18 months'.[7] Peter Good added in his journal that a number of men had died during Baudin's earlier stop at Timor.

In return, the British sailors had described their own voyage. Although neither Flinders nor Smith mentioned it, they would hardly have missed the signs of scurvy in the French. The topgallant masts had, in fact, been struck to reduce work for a weakened and depleted crew.

About six o'clock the next morning Flinders and Brown 'again went on board Le Geographe'.[8] Baudin later stated that he and Flinders breakfasted together, but neither Flinders nor Brown mentioned this. According to Flinders, Baudin was now much more inquisitive as to the activities of the British. Evidently, some of his officers had picked up from the crew that the *Investigator*'s purpose was discovery. On hearing the considerable extent of their survey along the New Holland coast, he seemed, Flinders thought, 'somewhat mortified'.

Flinders told him in general of his findings—the two gulfs, the location of fresh water and the abundance of fresh meat to be had at Kangaroo Island, pointing out the kangaroo skin caps worn by his boat crew. Baudin, in turn, gave Flinders the location of a dangerously submerged rock on the track eastward. Flinders, according to Baudin, was 'much less reserved' than he had been the day before.

The French commander said later that he told Flinders that, having examined the unexplored section of the coast, he would put into Port Jackson and, on leaving, Flinders encouraged him to do so. Baudin's instructions were, in effect, to avoid Port Jackson, and he evidently reached this decision on his own, a decision he would later explain somewhat defensively to the French Minister of Marine, citing scurvy, firewood and water shortages, and spoiled provisions.

According to Brown, the meeting lasted about an hour, but from the times given by Flinders—leaving the French ship at eight—it ran somewhat longer. As they parted Baudin asked Flinders to assist the men of his lost boat, if he should find them and, should he meet the *Naturaliste*, to tell the captain that he was to go to Port Jackson when bad weather set in. Flinders asked the name of the captain, whereupon, oddly, according to Flinders, Baudin asked the English commander his name; realising it was the name on the chart he had criticised, he apologised handsomely.

That Baudin did not know the name of his visitor seems extraordinary. Baudin, in his journal and in his letter to the Minister of Marine, stated that he learned Flinders's name at the start of their first meeting. It seems hardly credible that Flinders would not have given his name as they met, but that the foreign word was not clear to Baudin is entirely possible. By the time of their second meeting, he should perhaps have learned the name from those of his officers who had spoken to the crew, some of whom had talked to the English sailors. In a fractured conversation among untutored men, a strange word could easily have been misunderstood. In asking Flinders his name, Baudin may simply have been confirming that he had heard it correctly. It was not a detail he would have mentioned in his journal or in his letter to the Minister.

There remains, of course, the simple explanation that Flinders entirely misunderstood Baudin, although in speaking to Brown afterwards, he must have had some confirmation or denial that his interpretation of events was correct. Further, Baudin made no mention of Robert Brown's presence as the voyages were discussed, stating, in fact, that he and Flinders were alone—'nous trouvant seul'.[9] Here it is possible that as the interview was conducted 'mostly' in English, Brown's role was minor, and that Baudin dismissed him as merely an interpreter who was not needed, an unimportant onlooker. There is also the question of how well Brown spoke French. When, during preparations for the voyage, Flinders first received his French passport, he had turned for a translation to 'one of our gentlemen on board the Investigator, who understood the language a little'.[10] If this was Brown, Baudin may have had cause to consider him of little use in a three-way conversation. That there were considerable language difficulties is evident from Baudin's writing later that Flinders told him he had been separated from his companion ship and had lost a boat and eight men at Kangaroo Island. The French expedition's zoologist, François Péron, also mentioned the disappearance of the *Investigator*'s non-existent consort.

At this time there were pressures on Nicolas Baudin, now aged 52, of which Flinders was unaware. There were serious enmities within the expedition, some officers denigrating their commander, and he expressing at times considerable disdain of the scientists on board, which François Péron reciprocated with something akin to outright hatred. Although an experienced merchant marine officer, Baudin made mistakes in his handling of a naval command and in navigation. Dissensions were serious enough to bring about the earlier discharge of twenty officers and scientists and the desertion of 40 seamen at Mauritius.

Numerous delays had plagued the expedition. Held up in Le Havre at the start of the voyage by bad weather and by the grounding of the *Naturaliste*, the ships had encountered calms and adverse winds as they travelled south in the Atlantic, problems in provisioning at Tenerife, and unseasonably contrary winds between the Cape of Good Hope and Mauritius, then Ile de France. Here disputes with the local administration, quarrels among the expedition's officers and scientists, dissatisfaction among the crew, all handled tactlessly by Baudin—resulted in a stay of 40 days rather than the fourteen days allotted by Baudin's instructions. On reaching Cape Leeuwin in May 1801, Baudin chose to sail north up the Australian west coast to Timor, where he spent 56 days before heading south again to Van Diemen's Land. Here the expedition remained from January to March 1802 before entering Bass Strait and following the mainland's south coast to the point of encounter with Flinders and the *Investigator*.

What extent of the unknown coast had the French expedition explored? On 3 April the *Géographe*, heading west, had been off the present border between Victoria and South Australia. Shortly, they passed Cape Banks. Unknown to Baudin, the south coast that then lay behind him had been explored and partially surveyed by James Grant and John Murray successively in 1800, 1801 and 1802 in the *Lady Nelson*. The brigs *Harbinger* and *Margaret*, with Captains John Black and John Buyers, had also been in the area, as is known from their track charts.

However, between Cape Banks and the point at which he met the *Investigator,* a stretch of some 175 miles, Baudin was the first known navigator to see and record the Australian shoreline. On his completed chart of Terra Australis, 1814, Flinders labelled this region 'Coast Discovered by Capt. Nicolas Baudin, 1802', and preserved the names given by the French to coastal features, although with some mistakes as he never actually saw the French charts.

A group of hazardous rocks off the coast between Cape Jaffa and Cape Lannes he named the Géographe's Rocks in his logbooks, but later changed to Baudin's Rocks, a personal tribute to the warning given to him by Baudin. Flinders was, however, in error, as the actual 'rock' seen by Baudin was today's Margaret Brock Reef, about 10 miles off Cape Jaffa, which Flinders passed unseen during the night.

The Southern Ocean bight in which the French and British ships met, Flinders named Encounter Bay. Approximately 30 miles to the north of the meeting place the greatest river in the continent ends its 1606-mile journey across southeastern Australia and empties into a huge lagoon, today's Lake Alexandrina, and the 62-mile saltwater strip of the Coorong, running along the coast behind the giant sand dunes of Younghusband Peninsula. A narrow gap at the north end of this sand barrier is the river's only direct exit to the sea, an opening that Flinders had no opportunity to see as he had sailed and encountered the *Géographe* well to the south.

At eight-thirty in the morning after the final meeting with Baudin, Flinders and Brown were back on board the *Investigator*, 'and we then separated from Le Géographe; captain Baudin's course being directed to the north-west, and ours to the southward'.[11]

Flinders was no longer on an unknown coast; it had been seen and charted by the French. Watching the dune-lined shore, Flinders must have reflected on time spent on his survey earlier in the voyage that, if used simply to press on, would have given him this section of the coast as well. It was, however, a coast without rivers or harbours, according to Baudin, and if the French had pre-empted him here, he had done much else, including settling—most likely—the question of a seaway splitting the continent of Terra Australis in two. Solving that geographical riddle had been part of Baudin's orders as well. Further, the coast east of Cape Banks had already been observed by the men of the *Lady Nelson*. Baudin, however, did not know this. Nor did Flinders. Now he hurried. The need to survey closely a coast already seen by the French was less, and time was eluding him.

Steering south and southeast, the sloop worked against adverse currents and winds, spray flying across her deck. At other times the ship was virtually becalmed, while a heavy swell running north slowed her further. The barometer fell. Heavy squalls with rain and hail obscured the cliff-bound coast they were following.

On 20 April, in thick darkness, they were frighteningly unsure of how the land trended. Suddenly the rain lifted for a few moments and moonlight shone upon a gleaming, heaving sea, and to their horror a high headland loomed just three to six miles away. With additional sails set the *Investigator* was forced away from the land. The storm intensified and with huge seas bludgeoning the rising and plummeting ship, men clutching at spars and rigging fought to take in sails. At some point during the night they passed Cape Otway, and in the first grey light of day found themselves safely out of sight of land. The wind moderated, the sky cleared and the barometer rose. Flinders's survey of this coast was sketchy and inadequate, but he planned to improve upon it on a return voyage.

The *Investigator* was now entering Bass Strait. With the subsidence of the sea Flinders suspected the protective presence of a large island, of which he had spoken to Baudin. He remembered that in 1799 Captain William Reid of the schooner *Martha* had reported his visit the year before to the south coast of such an island. In fact, King Island had been seen and named in January 1801 by John Black in the brig *Harbinger*, and even more recently charted by John Murray in the *Lady Nelson* and William Campbell in the brig *Harrington*. Of these events, however, Flinders knew nothing when he decided to confirm the existence of the island.

Land was sighted on the morning of 22 April, and in the afternoon of the next day the *Investigator* anchored off the island's northeast end where, beyond the beaches, great ridges of sand were backed by dense brushwood. The expedition's visit was brief, Flinders and the botanical team pursuing their usual activities while several animals were shot for fresh meat. Two days later the *Investigator* was again off the mainland coast.

The land was high and wooded, then low and sandy, with a bluff promontory ahead. Rounding the point and closing in, Flinders saw a band of breakers across a narrow opening to a large expanse of water. Intrigued, he ordered 'every man ready for tacking at a moment's notice', and on the strong inflowing tide steered the ship over the breaking water into a huge bay stretching into the distance. Flinders had come upon Port Phillip Bay on the coast of the present state of Victoria, reaching some 30 miles inland, today with the city of Melbourne at its head. The narrow opening, just 1.75 miles wide, still confines the flow of the tides to a single channel, so they rush through with great force. This Flinders quickly discovered. As the *Investigator* emerged from the entrance, the depth suddenly diminished and before the sloop could come around, the powerful 'flood tide set her upon a mud bank, and she stuck fast'.[12]

With a kedge anchor and wind in the sails, the ship was drawn off into deeper water where, as it was now dark, the anchor was dropped. This had been Flinders's third grounding since the *Investigator* had left the Nore. Again, he was lucky that she had touched, undamaged, on a soft bottom.

Flinders's first thought was that he had come into Western Port, explored by Bass three years earlier, but the next morning he realised that this was not Bass's inlet. Nor had it been seen by Baudin, who had found no harbours on this coast. Exultantly Flinders concluded that he had made a new and important discovery, and despite the ship's food shortages, he was determined to give several days to as close a survey of the bay as he could manage. Even from aloft he could not see where it ended to the north. Unknown to him, the bay had been investigated just over three months earlier by John Murray in the *Lady Nelson*.

On the southeastern side of the bay a hill rose just over 1000 feet above wooded country. With Brown, Westall, Franklin and others, Flinders took the cutter to a beach at the foot of the rise, which he called Bluff Mount, not knowing that Murray had already named it Arthur's Seat for a hill in Edinburgh. To everyone's surprise, the limits of the bay could not be seen even from the summit. Flinders took numerous bearings and, with the others, walked along the ridge, looking out on forested hills and valleys and to the east another bay, which was, Flinders was sure, Bass's Western Port.

Brown recorded the excursion light-heartedly. The ascent was neither 'distant nor difficult', and the group later dined 'on oysters found at high water mark on the beach'.[13] Meanwhile Bauer, Allen and Good were landed on the southern beach and walked across the narrow, gently rolling peninsula to the windy, sea-exposed shore on its opposite side. Good was delighted with this neck of land, which reminded him of 'a Gentlemans Park in England, being covered with fine Green grass and Numerous Trees and bushes in pleasing irregularity'.[14]

In the early evening all parties returned to the ship. There was general pleasure and satisfaction with the day's findings—a green, attractive country, soil that was probably the best they had seen so far, a wealth of new plant and animal specimens, oysters and other shellfish, and great numbers of black swans, pelicans and other birds. There were many signs of inhabitants—deserted fireplaces, piles of oyster shells, a burnt-off area, and rising smoke—but they saw no one.

Flinders's hopes rose, although with caution. Was it possible that this splendid harbour held a passage, perhaps a river, into the interior? Only a circuit of the bay would answer the question. An attempt to use the *Investigator* for this purpose proved too time consuming, and Flinders resorted to the cutter. With his surveying instruments, provisions for three days and a boat crew that included the enthusiastic young redhead, Midshipman Lacy, he followed the long beaches of the southeast coast, watching the shoreline curve northwest until it faded from sight. Then they rowed west to windward across the harbour towards what Flinders called Indented Head, the Bellarine Peninsula today, a distance of approximately 17 miles, sounding as they went.

The weary men reached the shore and set up their main camp at nine o'clock that night. Flinders continued his survey from here, sailing and rowing west. With three of the boat's crew he climbed an 1100-foot hill, now called Flinders Peak, and from the panoramic view before him, eye-sketched the shoreline, estimating the size of the bay to be at least 30 miles from north to south. Under a small cairn he left a scroll of paper with a brief record of the ship's visit. By mid-afternoon the group had rejoined Lacy and the others at the boat, 'much fatigued, having walked more than twenty miles without finding a drop of water . . .'[15] In the evening they rowed back to the main camp on Indented Head.

They had encountered few Aborigines. Seemingly shy but unafraid, three had followed along on the beach abreast of the cutter. They unhesitatingly accepted birds Flinders had shot and eventually were confident enough to join the surveyors at a noonday meal. Others were seen but did not approach. Their apparent understanding of what guns could do Flinders attributed to their having watched him, unobserved, soon after his arrival. But in this he was mistaken, the men of the *Lady Nelson* having preceded him. The Europeans took care to leave the huts they found undisturbed, and in one left strips of the usually coveted red cloth.

At the end of the fourth day Flinders and his party returned to the *Investigator,* which again had run onto a mud shoal, but once more without damage. Flinders could afford no further expenditure of either time or provisions. His survey was inadequate. He had not been able to establish a measured base line, and simply depended on bearings.

The far side of the bay remained unseen, an incomplete line on his rough chart. Only by returning could he discover what lay there.

At daybreak on 3 May, the *Investigator* weighed on the outgoing tide and cleared the narrow opening to the sea. From five miles out Westall made his profile drawing of the entrance, with its rocky promontory and white-edged breakers. Following the coast through Bass Strait, Flinders checked and corrected the longitude of islands and shoreline features recorded by Bass from the whaleboat and by himself in the *Norfolk* and the *Francis*.

The *Investigator* rounded Cape Howe in rain and heavy cloud and steered directly north. At four o'clock in the afternoon of Saturday, 8 May 1802, the twin heads of Port Jackson came into view. Out of the evening twilight, British colours emerged on South Head, and the *Investigator* hoisted a white flag, its private signal.

Flinders eagerly attempted to beat into the familiar harbour during the night, but the opposing wind was too strong. He entered the heads at one o'clock the following afternoon, and the pilot boarded. 'There was not a single individual on board who was not upon deck working the ship into harbour . . .'[16] he wrote with justifiable pride in the good health of his men, although to the Admiralty he admitted that four men were not well. Presumably they had not been too sick to do their work.

Shortly after three, the *Investigator* dropped anchor at the entrance to Sydney Cove. The men crowded the rails, those who remembered and recognised the town and those to whom it was a strange little settlement clinging to a foreign shore. They had reached their destination in just under ten months—295 days from Spithead to Sydney. Immediately a boat was lowered and Flinders rowed to the Governor's Wharf. He stepped ashore and walked up the hill to wait on Philip Gidley King, Governor of New South Wales.

In his months off the south coast of Australia, Matthew Flinders had not found the hoped-for seaway into Terra Australis or any great rivers. Yet he had effectively traced the entire southern shoreline of the continent and for the first time established its outline and its extent. Even more significantly, he had shown that the great southern continent was not split north to south into island-like segments, but was one great land, extending from the Indian Ocean to the Pacific.

19

Sydney—1802

Sydney had grown since Flinders last saw it from the deck of the departing *Reliance* in early March 1800. The cove seemed full of ships—the naval vessels *Lady Nelson* and *Porpoise*, the *Naturaliste* of Baudin's expedition, a whaler and a privateer. The town had spread over the slopes facing the cove. The tall, restored tower of the unfinished St Phillip's church and the windmill stood against the sky. A new wharf and warehouse ran along the western waterfront. Government House was longer by a single-storey extension at its eastern end. Peter Good observed: 'though there is nothing grand or magnificent in the Construction of any of the Buildings of the Town yet there is a degree of neatness and regularity which had a fine effect. Several of the principal houses are built with Brik and white washed others with wood painted, they are all covered with wood cut in the form of Tiles'.[1]

Samuel Smith noted the town as '... Built in the form of a Cresent, the streets in A regular form; altho not paved, the Houses are Built in Regular lines',[2] while in a letter to his sister in Lincolnshire young Franklin declared Sydney to be 'near the size of Spalding'.

The day after the arrival of the *Investigator* the whaler *Venus* came in, bringing from the Cape of Good Hope the news that a peace had been signed between Britain and France the previous October.

Philip Gidley King had returned to New South Wales in April 1800, and had assumed government at the end of September on the departure of John Hunter. King was 42, stocky, round-faced and balding. He had been extremely anxious to take over the administration and its powers from Hunter but, having done so, found himself confronting the same deeply entrenched cliques and practices that had defeated his predecessor. His attempts to control the importation and sale of spirits brought him into almost continuous conflict with the military, in which his response, sometimes vacillating, sometimes autocratic, even vindictive, was not earning him the respect he desperately wanted as governor. The arrival of Flinders and a naval ship were a welcome source of support and an area in which his authority was undisputed.

King had received from the Admiralty directions to put the *Lady Nelson* under Flinders's orders during his survey and 'to give Captain Flinders every information and assistance which may be in your power, to enable him to carry on the said survey'.[3] On a more personal level, King and Flinders shared an important mutual friend in Joseph Banks and a contact that went back to King's command at Norfolk Island and the calls made there by the *Reliance*.

Flinders was warmly received by the governor. Having presented his orders and delivered the letters he carried, he would have sat in the Government House drawing room, engaged in long conversations with the governor and Mrs King—relating the story of the voyage, news from England, the circumstances of his marriage, with many questions of his own on conditions in Sydney. King would have required a detailed explanation of the loss of Thistle and his boat crew and, a seaman himself, probably asked some pertinent questions on the search for the cutter. Evidently he was satisfied with Flinders's response, for no official enquiry was made.

Flinders learned of the south coast explorations of Grant and Murray in the *Lady Nelson*, and Murray's discovery of Port Phillip Bay. With Flinders's wish to proceed with his explorations as quickly as possible, the governor concurred fully, Flinders hoping that all preparations could be made within two months. King was unfailingly helpful. Flinders told Banks, 'In Governor King I find everything that can be expected'.[4]

The day after their arrival the *Investigator*'s company were immersed in preparations for the next stage of the voyage. The ship was warped to a mooring near Cattle Point and tents and a marquee erected on the promontory's level ground. Here the armourer set up his forge, the cooper began repairing empty casks and sailmakers started work on torn and battered canvas. The next day the observatory was established with the chronometers and astronomical instruments in the care of Samuel Flinders and John Franklin, the two officers to generally supervise the activities around them as well. A small detachment of marines guarded the camp.

On board the ship work was also in progress. All stores were taken up on deck for inspection. Topmasts and topgallant masts were struck and new-rigged as necessary. Flinders asked for one major alteration. 'I had found the barricade of the quarter deck to stand so high, as to be not only an obstacle to beating to windward, but a great inconvenience in surveying the coast',[5] for when the wind was on the land side Flinders, with his short stature, could not see over the bulwark to take bearings except by the somewhat undignified expedient of standing on top of the binnacle. King had a committee ensure that no injury would be done to the ship by lowering the bulwark. Four convict carpenters were then borrowed from the dockyard and, with the *Investigator*'s own carpenters, brought down the height of the barrier. Flinders also asked for a boat to replace the cutter lost with Thistle. This was constructed of banksia and cedar wood under the supervision of the colony's master builder, Thomas Moore, successor to Daniel Paine.

Another job was the erection on the quarterdeck of the prefabricated plant cabin, which the *Investigator* had carried from England. Flinders believed that once filled with boxes of earth the cabin, as designed, would badly strain the deck, and in foul weather might have to be jettisoned. With Robert Brown's consent, it was reduced to two-thirds of its original size and its legs shortened, this in turn requiring alterations to the tiller and the main braces to create as little inconvenience as possible to the working of the ship.

It had been a source of great relief to Flinders that on the entire passage from the Cape of Good Hope the ship had not made more than three inches of water in an hour. Hence, very little caulking was deemed necessary.

The science people were occupied with their own priorities. Four days after their arrival Brown and Good found comfortable lodgings on shore where they could collect, dry and otherwise prepare their specimens away from the damp and confining quarters aboard, and without waiting for boats to take them to and from land. The live plant collection was sent to the Government House garden in Parramatta and, despite heavy downpours of rain, excursions were made into the surrounding countryside, on one occasion together with the botanist from the *Naturaliste*.

Flinders's own principal task was the preparation of his manuscript charts to be forwarded as quickly as possible to the Admiralty, and the writing of the reports and letters to accompany them. The whaler *Speedy* was preparing to sail for England, and this material was to go with her. In completing and copying the charts, the heavy burden of the comprehensive and meticulous work fell mainly on Flinders himself.

Wearing out a series of quills, he wrote for the Admiralty a long summary of the passage from the Cape of Good Hope to Sydney, with a list of the positions of the principal places where the *Investigator* anchored. He reported the loss of the cutter and its eight men and the *Investigator*'s arrival in Sydney with 'officers and crew—four men excepted—in good health'.[6] In a separate letter to Evan Nepean he asked for a supply of boatswain's stores and provisions to be sent to Port Jackson for the sole use of the *Investigator* and her people in 1803 and 1804, as neither naval stores nor salt provisions were available. There was a note, too, for Alexander Dalrymple on certain innovations on his charts, and to the Astronomer Royal he sent back the Arnold timekeepers Nos 82 and 176, which had stopped.

To Joseph Banks he wrote that he was happy to announce the success so far of the voyage, 'and scarcely less so' in having examined the 'most interesting part of New Holland' before meeting the French, although 'we were not happy enough to have completed the whole of the unknown part'.[7] Nevertheless, he considered it fortunate that instead of 'passing along the coast cursorily', he had 'made a very strict and minute examination of it'. When Banks received his charts he would be able to judge 'how far the task has been well performed . . .' In a postscript Flinders noted that 'a flying report' of peace with France had reached Sydney. He added, 'I hope that the difficulty in obtaining promotion which usually follows a peace will not extend to the Investigator'.

Interpreting his orders in his own way, Flinders had left approximately 175 miles of the south coast for the French to discover. He could only hope the Admiralty lords would see the logic of his actions. Writing to others, as to Banks's associate C. F. Greville, he referred only to long delays in England as the reason for the French having reached that section of coast first.

Flinders failed to complete the numerous and extensive charts in time, and the *Speedy* sailed with only his letters. In disregarding the Admiralty's specific orders to first survey closely the southern shoreline from 130°E to Bass's Strait, he failed to provide with his letters the more limited charts of the unknown coast that the Admiralty saw as the most necessary part of his report.

King's concern for the safety of Flinders's charts created further delay, for he was unwilling to send them by any but an English vessel. HMS *Glatton*, under Captain James Colnett, arrived in Sydney on 11 March 1803 and sailed again on 17–18 May, with Lieutenant John Murray in command. Flinders's charts were delivered by Murray to the Hydrographical Office in December, a year after they had been expected.

Arriving in London in November 1802, Flinders's letters were regarded as of little value without the charts, which were needed for plans then in progress for a settlement at Port Phillip Bay. Banks was therefore faced with another embarrassment on behalf of his protégé. His reply to Flinders's letter expressed his 'infinite satisfaction' in learning of the success of the first part of the enterprise and the 'gallantry' with which it had been carried out. But he then went on to deliver a sharp reproach for the failure of the maps to arrive. This had reflected poorly on Flinders, he said, and Banks could have defended him better if he had had even a 'Few Sketches'.

Banks also wrote to King on the non-arrival of the maps, a 'great misfortune to the voyage'.[8] Flinders's friends would have been better impressed with his success had the charts arrived, while 'his enemies suspect idleness on his part, or some other bad reason, for omitting to send them'. Consideration was even given to assigning some of the east coast exploration to another officer. Neither letter reached Sydney until after Flinders's return from the circumnavigation of the continent in 1803.

Flinders conferred with King on the next step of the explorations. His instructions called for a return to the south coast. Time, however, had run away, and the southern winter would arrive shortly. Flinders pointed out that to a large extent he had already covered the south coast. He proposed, therefore, to proceed northward, examining Torres Strait and the Gulf of Carpentaria before the northwest monsoon set in with winds that could trap him in the gulf. This was expected in November, and having hopefully completed his work in the gulf and reached the north and northwest coasts by then, he would have to deal with it as he could. The Admiralty accepted departures from their instructions owing to weather conditions. In their initial journeys to the Pacific both Cook and Bligh received discretional orders with regard to rounding either Cape Horn or the Cape of Good Hope during the southern winter, and in charting North American coasts Cook and Vancouver selected specific routes and timing according to their own judgement.

King agreed with Flinders on his proposals for the voyage, and Flinders planned accordingly. Included in his arrangements was the 60-ton brig *Lady Nelson*, which was to accompany the *Investigator*. While Flinders had disparaged the *Lady Nelson* as too small for extensive exploration on her own, he appreciated the added safety and advantage of having two vessels on a voyage of discovery. He believed her sliding keels would be 'peculiarly adapted for going up rivers, or other shallow places',[9] and evidently was prepared to accept the vessel's shortcomings.

The brig was commanded by Acting-Lieutenant John Murray, aged about 25, who had arrived in New South Wales in November 1800 and had been in the navy for eleven years. He had served under James Grant on HMV *Lady Nelson* and on Grant's resignation took over the brig and the ambitious program of exploration and surveying on the south coast ordered by Governor King.

With stormy weather, the *Lady Nelson*'s difficulty in beating to windward and apparently, at times, his own dilatoriness, Murray implemented fewer than half of King's instructions. Discipline among his crew of 'trustworthy' convicts had to be maintained with floggings, disratings and putting some men in irons. Nor was Murray an experienced surveyor. His charts contained serious defects in orientation and distances. Evidently he and Flinders had not met before embarking on the northward journey together.

With reservations as to Murray's hydrographic skills, Flinders sent on board with him Midshipman Denis Lacy, who had acquired some experience under Flinders. Murray's first mate was the sailor and game hunter, Henry Hacking, whose description of an inland river had inspired the second *Tom Thumb* journey. As his second mate Murray had on board a man who called himself John Johnson, but who was actually a Danish adventurer, Jørgen Jørgenson.

No letter from Ann awaited Flinders. He learned later that she had been ill on her return to Lincolnshire, emotionally exhausted and with an eye inflammation, probably exacerbated by weeping, that had required a sight-saving operation. He wrote to her lovingly and at length. He was safe and well, but 'alas, my dearest love, I am all in the dark concerning thee, I know not what to fear or what to hope . . . June 1st. a ship is now off the heads of the harbour, but I am afraid to hope; the sensation however will rise, in spight of me, and until I know I will endeavour to intertain thee . . .'[10]

He described the voyage, the disappointment of finding no sea passage inland and the loss of Thistle and his crew, adding such details as he thought would interest her. A ship that had sailed from Spithead while she was aboard the *Investigator* had brought to Sydney the news that Ann would be accompanying him, and there were now many enquiries about her 'and much abuse of me for not bringing them so valuable an addition to their society'. She would have been as comfortably settled in Sydney as he had assured her she would be, with Mrs King and Mrs Paterson her 'choicest friends, and for visiting acquaintances there are five or six other ladies, very agreeable for short periods, and perhaps longer. When I see this and feel the warmest wishes constantly rising for thy presence, I accuse fortune of great unkindness, and think ill of those who, except in this, are my most valuable friends'.

Yet, thinking of the alarms and discomforts that she would have experienced on the voyage so far, 'and more especially, if what thou fearest had taken place', he sometimes thought it best that 'it should be as it is'. As was 'proper', he informed her of his financial affairs, handled by his agent in London, and said that he believed the voyage would make him £1500 richer. He wrote of the distance between himself and his brother, and that John Franklin was 'worthy of notice . . . capable to learning every thing that we can show him, and but for a little carelessness, I would not wish to have a son otherwise than he is. Young Lound also turns out to be a fine lad, but does not grow'. Trim was well and John Elder, his servant, good and faithful.

To Banks he wrote of Brown and Bauer as 'two men of assiduity and abilities . . . their application is beyond what I have been accustomed to see'.[11] Another duty was to report the death of John Thistle to the navy agent, James Sykes, and to send him Thistle's books and papers, to be forwarded to the master's mother.

Brown's letters to Banks and to the botanists Dryander and Greville reflected his somewhat pessimistic outlook. Of the 750 plant specimens observed on the south coast, he estimated only 300 to be entirely new species, and in transporting the plants the lack of a garden on board had been a serious drawback. Insufficient time had prevented much work with animals, and as for mineralogy, only surface specimens had been gathered, Brown forgetting, perhaps, that this was the extent of John Allen's assignment. The time spent at anchor and thus at botanising amounted to two months, he wrote, but scarcely more than half was 'as a season, favourable to botany'.[12]

In Sydney there arose again the contentious problem of the ship's carpenters not being given time to build plant boxes while the refit of the vessel was in progress. To mollify all parties, Governor King arranged to have settlement workers construct them, but Brown found them 'miserable'. It was, however, by then too late to do anything but accept them.

In addition to the refit, Flinders had many concerns. The colony, suffering food shortages, was on reduced rations. To provision the *Investigator* for the journey to come, he managed to contract for the necessary 30 000 pounds of bread and biscuits, 8000 pounds of flour and 156 pounds of kiln-dried wheat, and, from two American ships, sufficient rum and tobacco for the journey. Feeding his men during the stay in Sydney was also difficult, with fresh meat at an exorbitant price and vegetables available solely from the governor's garden. Only on the king's birthday was Flinders able to provide a quarter of fresh beef for his people. The men were also given money to seek their own food. On 13 June, to his great relief, the convict ship *Coromandel* arrived with most of the twelve months' supplies that he had ordered while at Spithead, and he cancelled some of the Sydney arrangements. As livestock on board, he purchased sheep, pigs, geese and other fowl. Together with firewood and the filled water casks, all of this was ferried out to the ship in the launch.

With a deficit of four crew when she left England and the loss of eight men on the south coast, the *Investigator* was short-handed. As well, two men were discharged as invalids, a marine and the seaman Richard Stanley (or Staley), who had been lamed on Kangaroo Island. Five replacements were found and, with the assistance of King, Flinders received in addition nine convict volunteers, some seamen, who were promised conditional emancipations or absolute pardons at the end of the voyage at Flinders's discretion, on the basis of good behaviour.

As master Flinders was able to engage John Aken, chief mate of the ship *Hercules*, which had arrived from Ireland. Aken was to prove himself a 'plain man but a good one', easy-natured and a competent navigator and master.

Remembering the helpfulness of the Aborigine Bongaree on his voyage north in 1799, Flinders applied to the governor for permission to take on board as supernumeraries two 'natives of this country . . . if two proper persons (volunteers) can be found'. King gave his authorisation and Flinders engaged the 'worthy and brave' Bongaree, who 'now volunteered again', and Nanbaree, a 'good-natured lad'.[13]

With the *Investigator*'s crewmen from England there were difficulties. Flinders's determination to sail again within two months of his arrival meant immediately setting to work on the ship's refit and other tasks. Except on Sundays, when one watch at a time was allowed ashore, the crew were denied any time for recreation, and resentment built into drunkenness and mutinous language, for which several men were flogged. Nothing interfered, however, with the customary arrival of local women on board after the working day.

Very much a presence in Sydney were the two French exploration vessels and their men. The *Naturaliste* had been in the harbour when the *Investigator* arrived, courteously received by Governor King under the conditions of the passport it carried from the British government, and Flinders immediately conveyed to Captain Hamelin Baudin's message that with the onset of bad weather he should go to Port Jackson. The *Géographe*'s lost boat and its crew, picked up in Bass Strait by the brig *Harrington,* were safely on the French ship. Hamelin now chose not to remain in port any longer, and on 17 May, after a stay of 23 days, sailed for Ile de France. Three days later the *Géographe* dropped anchor, apparently just inside the heads at Port Jackson. The

Sydney pilot who met the ship found her company so crippled with dysentery and scurvy that they were unable to work the vessel into the harbour.

King ordered the harbour master to the assistance of the corvette, and several boats, including one from the *Investigator*, towed the vessel at least partway against the wind to anchor in Neutral Bay. Despite the colony's serious shortages, the governor had oxen slaughtered and fresh meat sent aboard the French ship, while 23 sick were admitted to the military hospital.

After the encounter with the *Investigator*, Baudin had followed the south coast as far as the Nuyts Archipelago, before heading for south-east Van Diemen's Land and, with navigational difficulties and a growing sick list, north to Port Jackson.

Flinders and Baudin exchanged shipboard visits, and Flinders showed Baudin his manuscript map on which the explorations of the *Lady Nelson* and the extent of the French discoveries were marked. Baudin 'found his portion to be smaller than he had supposed',[14] but made no objection.

Baudin was unable to show Flinders any recent charts, explaining that the cartographic information was transmitted to Paris and the charts constructed there. 'This mode appeared to me extraordinary',[15] commented Flinders. It later appeared, however, that Baudin was not a trained hydrographer, and the expedition's expert, Charles Boullanger, was at the time with the *Naturaliste*.

The *Naturaliste*, meanwhile, had attempted the southern route westward around Van Diemen's Land but, unable to make headway against gale-force winter westerlies, returned to Port Jackson. The ship came through the heads on 26 June, but was wind-bound for eight days before joining the *Géographe* in Neutral Bay. King's treatment of his foreign guests was extremely generous. To allow the French astronomer to make his observations, he gave Baudin permission to erect tents and land instruments at Cattle Point, not far from the *Investigator*'s camp. The *Géographe*'s copper bottom needed cleaning and repair, and she was careened on the beach on the western side of Cattle Point. The French expedition's artist, Charles Alexandre Lesueur, drew the busy scene—men at work around the tents, the *Géographe* on the foreshore, the *Investigator* and the hulk *Supply* at anchor, and a group of

Aborigines tending a small fire in the foreground. Largely to prevent attempted escapes by convicts, restrictions were placed on the movements of the French boats, unauthorised persons were not allowed to board the French ships and curfews were imposed on certain activities. However, French officers in uniform received the same courtesies as British officers.

The colonists at every level welcomed the social novelty of their French visitors, and the atmosphere became quite festive with the knowledge that there was peace in Europe. It was a peace that Banks would call 'no more than a turbulent and quarrelsome truce', but for the moment there was peace. Baudin and King enjoyed a very cordial personal relationship. With both the governor and his secretary, William Neale Chapman, speaking French fluently, the visiting captain was regularly at Government House.

There was a certain bond between King and the French navigators. When at Botany Bay in 1788 the British had met the arriving expedition of La Pérouse, it was the French-speaking Lieutenant Philip King who talked to the explorer. After the First Fleet had encamped at Sydney Cove, King returned to Botany Bay to discuss charts and exploration with La Pérouse, on whose ship he then spent the night. King was thus the last known person to speak at length with the French navigator before he disappeared at sea.

By July the refit of the *Investigator* was apparently far enough along for Flinders to add to the sociability encouraged by news of peace. King, greeted with a thundering 17-gun salute and all the honours due to his position, dined on board. Then the lieutenant governor, Colonel Paterson, was joined on Flinders's ship by the two French captains, some of their officers and François Péron, the expedition's zoologist. They were received with an 11-gun salute and the gathering was, in Flinders's words, 'particularly agreeable'.

Péron later described the extensive hospitality he received. As a naturalist he displayed an interest in many aspects of the colony, and his hosts accorded him opportunities to gather information that would not have been extended to a naval or military officer. He took full advantage of this. A personable man of 26, his portrait shows him with short, thick dark hair, a firmly rounded chin, aquiline nose and heavy eyebrows. Joining the French army in 1792, he had been blinded in one eye in combat a year later. Evidently a young man of some charm, he was welcomed at Government House and treated with particular warmth by Colonel Paterson, 'a very distinguished *savant*', in whose home he was received, in his own words, 'as a son'.[16] The surgeon, James Thomson, Charles Grimes the surveyor, John Palmer the commissary, and Samuel Marsden of Parramatta were friendly sources of information, and with Paterson he journeyed inland, observing the countryside and the smaller settlements.

From all of this Péron compiled a copiously detailed report on Sydney and other locations, describing opportunities in New South Wales and New Zealand as promising immense future prosperity. He reported on the number of British troops in the colony, the inadequate defences, and a likely uprising by the Irish population. His final remark was a recommendation that the flourishing colony 'should be destroyed as soon as possible'.[17] On the return trip to France, the *Géographe* stopped at Mauritius. Here Péron provided the governor with a copy of his report, and on reaching France wrote similarly to the Minister of Marine. Péron was not alone in turning hospitality at Port Jackson into an opportunity for espionage. Ostensibly examining the bay for navigational purposes, Lieutenant Louis Claude de Saulces de Freycinet explored the harbour and its entrance for suitable landing sites for an invading army and produced a chart that recorded extensive soundings.

The extent to which the efforts of Péron and Freycinet were dictated by personal inclination or by orders from any of their superiors is difficult to gauge. Clandestine reconnaissance of the territories of rival nations was a frequent part of exploration at the time, nor can the patriotic motivation and underlying hostility of individuals be discounted. Péron's report seems not to have had any immediate effect on France's plans or policies, but in the hands of the governor of Ile de France it would contribute to the crushing fate of Matthew Flinders.

In the midst of the turmoil of preparations for the continued exploration, Flinders found brief intervals for his friends in Sydney. He was received hospitably at Government House not only by the governor but also by Mrs King, and seems to have won the regard of their five-year-old daughter, 'little Elizabeth'. He also re-estabished his friendship with the Patersons. 'Two better or more agreeable women than Mrs King and Mrs Paterson are not easily found',[18] he wrote to Ann.

He did not mention Elizabeth Macarthur. Dissension between the governor and John Macarthur had escalated into a rancorous quarrel that eventually drew William Paterson into the fracas. In September 1801, this had culminated in a duel between Paterson and Macarthur. The lieutenant governor was seriously wounded and Macarthur, ordered to stand trial in England, sailed from the colony in November, leaving his wife to deal with his business and farm at Parramatta and to care for their young family. There appears to be no surviving record of Flinders's contact with her in 1802, but in view of the friendship demonstrated in a letter written when he returned to Sydney a year later, it seems unlikely he remained entirely out of touch. Yet it might have seemed necessary to Flinders at this time to maintain a show of his loyalty to the Kings.

Did Flinders renew any possible female contacts from his earlier, unwed days in Sydney? Probably not. Flinders's sense of duty and obligation was very strong, and he very much loved and missed his wife. It was with overflowing feeling that he wrote, 'think on me, and how much I love thee; and believe me, as *indeed* I am, thine with the utmost constancy and affection'. He described to Ann the events of the king's birthday, which was celebrated 'with due magnificence. The ship is covered with colours and every man is about to put on his best apparel, and to make himself merry. We go through the form of waiting upon His Excellency the governor at his levee, to pay our compliments to him as the representative of Majesty; after which, a dinner and a ball are given to the colony, at which not less than 52 ladies and gentlemen will be present'. He added, 'Amidst all of this, how much preferable is such a right hand and left as we have had at Spilsby, with those we love, than that which we shall go through this evening'.

Nevertheless, in this small society Flinders could not but be conscious of his own growing importance, something he found very gratifying and again wanted to share with Ann: '—my situation makes me of some consequence in the eye of the world, and this should extend to thee, and have its influence in regulating thy appearance and mode of conduct'.[19]

The quiet life of a young married woman at the rectory in Partney and the extent to which Ann's small funds would go to improve her appearance were evidently far from Matthew's comprehension at the time. She received through Matthew's London agent, W. A. Standert, an allowance of £40 a year, but, as he wrote, if she desired comforts or necessities not covered by this sum, she could draw an additional amount. Regardless, Ann's circumstances left little opportunity to display an enhanced appearance or to conduct herself other than as a respectable young wife left without her husband. Flinders was certain that news of the *Investigator* and its discoveries would appear in English papers. He therefore asked Ann to record in her journal what 'is said of the *Investigator* & of me . . .'[20]

Letters from Ann reached Matthew before he sailed. They were sad, fretful, almost petulant letters. She had been so distraught on Matthew's departure that she had not written to him for three months, and then waited two months before writing a second letter. She did not believe he loved her, as he had chosen to go on his voyage instead of leaving the navy to be with her. Deeply distressed, he wrote back tenderly, reminding her that it had been the assurance of this employment that had enabled him to undertake her support as well as his own:

> Dost thou know, my beloved, that we could barely have existed in England? That both thou and me must have been debarred of even necessaries; unless we had given up our independence to have procured them from perhaps unwilling friends.
>
> . . . Heaven knows with what sincerity and warmth of affection I have loved thee,—how anxiously I look forward to the time when I may return to thee, and how earnestly I labour that the delight of our meeting may be no more clouded with the fear of a long parting . . . look my dear Ann to the happy side. See me engaged, successfully thus far, in the cause of science and followed by the good wishes and approbation of the world'.[21]

It is doubtful that Flinders understood the humiliation and perhaps the sense of betrayal Ann must have felt returning to Partney alone after the farewells and the good wishes for a new life on the other side of the world that had followed the wedding. Financial independence and the cause of science probably meant very little to Ann as she returned to her parents' house.

Meanwhile, rain, inefficiencies and other problems hampered the work on the *Investigator*, and it was almost three months before she was ready to sail. Then, however, she looked in excellent condition, hull, spars and mastheads handsomely repainted in black, her new rigging tarred to dark brown. Flinders had finally completed his charts and left two copies of the set with Governor King, one to be held in Sydney until Flinders's return, the second to be forwarded to England at the first opportunity.

On the morning of 22 July 1802 the *Investigator* made sail in a fresh breeze and, with the brig *Lady Nelson* under Lieutenant John Murray, passed between the heads into the Pacific. The French expedition sailed four months later. The ships having passed through Bass Strait, the *Naturaliste* would head for Europe, carrying much of the expedition's natural history collections, the remaining sick and some of the scientists. King had obtained permission from Baudin to send with her the surgeon James Thomson and his family, who wished to return to England. The *Géographe*, meanwhile, was to continue her explorations, and to provide her with a tender in the absence of the *Naturaliste*, King allowed Baudin's purchase of a 20-ton colonial-built schooner, which the French commander named the *Casuarina* for the wood of which she was constructed.

The day before his departure Baudin sent an effusive letter of thanks to King for the hospitality he and his people had received. To Mrs King he sent a donation of £50 for her home for colonial orphans, perhaps a kind of token compensation to the colony for taking with him as his mistress a young convict girl, Mary Beckwith. He also gave money to a boys' school on the Hawkesbury. In addition, he left with King the original and twelve copies of a letter addressed to the administrators of Ile de France and Ile de Réunion, describing Governor King's generosity to his expedition and recommending the British ship and commander carrying one of the letters. Blank spaces were left for King to fill in with the name of the particular captain and ship. King no doubt received these with appreciation, set them aside and apparently forgot about them.

20

The Circumnavigation Begins

The *Investigator* followed the coast of New South Wales northward with little incident. This was a coast surveyed by Cook in 1770, and as far as Hervey Bay by Flinders in 1799, and no significant new findings could be expected. Flinders checked recorded positions, made corrections and refinements. A day out of Port Jackson the *Lady Nelson* fell behind. It was to be a recurring event, the *Investigator* lying to as she waited or going on to a prearranged rendezvous location.

On 28 July the *Investigator* reached Breaksea Spit, continued north until she was able to pass over its tail and entered Hervey Bay. Two days later she was joined off Sandy Cape by the *Lady Nelson*. Unwilling to follow a strange coast closely, John Murray had kept land barely in sight and so had encountered a strong current running south. This confirmed for Flinders his previous observations on these coastal currents, but he was also convinced now of the 'indifferent' sailing qualities of the *Lady Nelson*.

The expedition remained off Sandy Cape the the next day to allow the naturalists to go ashore on the great, paradoxically well-wooded sand island, today's Fraser Island: '. . . it is astonishing to see what Vegetation is produced from Sand',[1] wrote Peter Good. Murray led a wooding party and, with four sailors, Flinders and Bongaree headed for the point of the cape.

Suddenly there appeared before Flinders's group several Aborigines aggressively waving tree branches, clearly telling them to go back. Bongaree laid down his spear, stripped off his clothes and attempted to talk to them first in his own language and then in broken English. Obviously neither was understood, but tensions relaxed. Gifts were exchanged and soon about twenty natives returned with the visitors to the boats to feast on the blubber of two porpoises, brought on shore for them. Bongaree demonstrated the use of his womera, hurling a spear a great distance. This was evidently something entirely new to the local people, and the man who attempted to replicate the feat threw both spear and throwing stick.

The ships crossed Hervey Bay towards the western shore where Flinders's 1799 survey had ended. Here the Burnett River empties into the bay, but no one on either ship identified the 'shallow inlets' they saw as a river mouth. Flinders's measurement of the width of Hervey Bay at 43 miles differed notably from the 59 miles given on Cook's charts. Discrepancies continued to emerge between the calculations of the two navigators, a result, as Flinders carefully pointed out, of Cook's lack of a chronometer. Cook had calculated longitude by the complicated lunar method, often with error.

The ships ran north easily and on 5 August Flinders began the exploration of a long, sheltered inlet that he labelled No 1 Port, but later named Port Curtis. Attempting a shore excursion, Brown and his companions were met by Aborigines hurling stones, hiding and attacking again. No one was injured and with musket shots fired into the air, their assailants disappeared. There were other setbacks. The *Lady Nelson* grounded and lost her main sliding keel, and on weighing for departure three days later, the *Investigator* lost an anchor fluke, a buoy and buoy rope. Nevertheless, they sailed on a fair wind that in the course of the day carried them across the Tropic of Capricorn into the Australian tropics.

The afternoon brought the ships into Cook's Keppel Bay, which extended finger-like inlets into the coast. Shallows limited the use of even the *Lady Nelson*, and for eight days Flinders explored the bay mainly in the whaleboat. About 4 miles up the westernmost inlet he climbed what he later called West-arm Hill, marking on his chart a higher hill from which, had he climbed it, he would have seen the 300-mile Fitzroy River.

He explored the easternmost inlet with Brown, following its branches past swamps and mangrove islets. At dusk they slashed their way through the trees to establish a camp on slightly higher ground. For most it was not a restful night: '. . . swarms of mosquitoes and sandflies made sleeping impossible to all except one of the boat's crew, who was so enviably constituted, that these insects either did not attack him, or could not penetrate his skin'.[2]

Continuing up the channel, which had turned south, they were astonished to find themselves entering the Port Curtis inlet. The channel was actually a shallow strait connecting Port Curtis—or No 1 Port—with Keppel Bay. Returning at low tide, they found a 2-mile stretch dry or almost dry, over which they had to manhandle the boat. Exploring a second channel, they were caught at nightfall in shallow water among the trees. With nowhere to land, they waited in the boat for the rising tide, when they rowed and pushed their way back into the bay to reach the *Investigator* before midnight.

Further probes into the mangrove-walled channels produced little result. Flinders commented wryly, 'It would perhaps have been easier to climb up the trees, and scramble from one to another upon the vines, than to have penetrated through the intricate net work in the darkness underneath'.[3]

On Sunday a part of the ship's company was allowed on shore. One group sighted some emus and, with guns and dogs, went in pursuit. They were abruptly stopped by a number of armed and initially menacing Aborigines, but after a time the spears were laid aside and some twenty of the natives good-naturedly accompanied the sailors back to the boat. It was then discovered that a seaman and the master's mate, Thomas Evans, were missing. Darkness fell. A boat and crew remained on the beach until eight or nine o'clock and a musket was frequently fired. The men did not appear. At daybreak a cannon was fired. The crack of a musket responded from the swamps, and the cannon was fired again. Fowler went in the direction of the musket shot and Flinders took a boat around to Cape Keppel at the bay's entrance.

No further shots were heard, and Fowler was readying a well-armed search party when the two sailors were seen coming along the beach with a small crowd of Aborigines. The two had strayed, become lost in the swamp and spent the greater part of the night wading in mud and trying to fight off clouds of ravenous mosquitos. In the morning they found themselves surrounded by about 25 Aborigines, one of whom approached them 'with the bough of a tree making Signals' for them to leave. Then apparently another made 'a signal of peace'.[4]

From Peter Good's imprecise account of the lost men's probably garbled story, it is difficult to understand exactly what happened. Nor is it clear whether the Aborigines acted entirely out of sympathy for the terrified, exhausted and mud-covered strangers or with the realisation that escorting them to their companions would bring some reward. Their actions, however, were kindness itself, taking them to a fire, feeding them on roasted fish and duck, and then leading them to the beach. The two sailors were 'a ludicruous figure . . . their cloaths all rags without Shoes or Stockings having all Stuck in the mud',[5] wrote Peter Good. Samuel Smith added that, with everyone delighted with the rescue, 'a boat was sent on shore with Drum, Fife & Fiddle, likewise presents'.[6]

The rescuers, however, did not appreciate the musical reception. According to John Murray, 'they signified their displeasure and some of them ran off but on our ceasing returned'.[7] They accepted hatchets, red night caps and mirrors and went back into the woods. Good commented on their confusion when they looked into the mirrors: they 'started suddenly on perceiving the reflexion of themselves & could not be brought to look at it steadily . . . They were the strongest made Native we had Seen in New Holland . . . some were thought upwards of 6 feet high'.[8]

The ships now moved north inside the Great Barrier Reef. Repeatedly the *Lady Nelson* fell behind, usually catching up with the anchored *Investigator* the next day. By 21 August the expedition was off a bold, rocky shore where a cove offered an exceptional anchorage, with excellent fresh water, quantities of fish and pine wood, which the carpenters began to cut for a new main sliding keel for the *Lady Nelson*. An unimpressive sailer at best, she was especially unsafe on a lee shore without the keel. Initially calling the harbour No 2 Port, Flinders later named it Port Bowen, for Captain James Bowen, RN. Westall's drawing of the port's north shore displayed vividly the poetic beauty of cliffs rising from the sea and ravines filled with evergreen forest. Westall regularly produced the required coastal profiles and some botanical drawings, but the sameness of many Australian landscapes bored him, and some of his scenes were only superficially finished. No sketches of shipboard life seem to exist. Apparently he took little interest in the ship or his companions.

Two days later the ships were again on their way and from late August until 28 September 1802 they explored approximately 60 miles of the Australian coast, investigating and charting a series of inlets.

Shoalwater Bay was entered on a strong, swift tide running between a mainland bluff and Cook's Townshand Island. Anchoring in mid-channel, Flinders had gone ashore with the science team. Returning to the *Investigator* at dusk, he saw at once that two of the boats were missing. Fowler explained that as the cutter was being hoisted from the fast-running tide, it had been swamped and the boatman flung into the water. He was caught by the men in the *Lady Nelson*'s boat, but the cutter was carried away. Two men in the gig quickly went after it. Night fell. Early in the morning the gig returned, the men safe despite an anxious night on little understood waters. The cutter had not been seen. Noting that the tide in the channel ran at least five miles an hour, Flinders named it Strong-tide Passage and did not recommend it as a safe entry to Shoalwater Bay.

Flinders explored the bay for a week, difficult and generally frustrating work. Shallows and sandbanks kept the *Investigator* in the middle of the bay, miles away from the mangrove-covered shore. Alternating between the brig and the whaleboat, Flinders investigated southward, while Brown and his party were taken to the west side of the inlet. Some Aborigines fled on their approach, but shortly afterwards a well-armed but friendly group of men and boys appeared; they accepted gifts and joined the botanists for a time.

The ship's company was now suffering from extreme fatigue. The constant moving about of the ship in restricted space, the work ashore and the continued search for the cutter, all in high, humid heat, seriously frayed tempers. There was drunkenness and a fight: the boatswain, Charles Douglas, was suspended from duty, and the seaman, William Job, was lectured on the serious transgression of striking an officer and given twelve lashes. Scurvy and diarrhoea were probably incipient. Flinders had intended to climb a hill some two miles inland but, sick and exhausted yet, refusing to entrust the task to anyone else, took bearings instead from a small island he later named for John Aken.

The expedition quitted Shoalwater Bay at noon on 4 September and the next morning entered Thirsty Sound, where Cook had made his third landing on the Australian east coast. Flinders went on to Pier

Portrait of an Aborigine of Shoalwater Bay, Queensland, by William Westall. Flinders spent a week exploring this large, shallow bay, with its muddy, mangrove-covered banks. Aborigines encountering the explorers were at first alarmed, but later spent time amicably with them. (R4333, by permission of the National Library of Australia)

Head, a round, barren hill on an island, from which Cook had taken bearings. Cook had found anomalies in his compass of approximately 30 degrees, which he attributed to iron ore in the surrounding hills. From the same position Flinders made his observations with particular care, using the theodolite and dipping needle, an instrument consisting of a magnetised needle with a counter arm to control its sensitivity. The variations found by Flinders were very much smaller than those noted by Cook, which Flinders ascribed mainly to the positioning of his instruments. He concluded that the general stone mass of Pier Head caused the variations.

Wind and tide embayed the ships the next day and, to employ the time constructively, Flinders, in the whaleboat with Westall, sailed across to the nearest of the offshore Northumberland Isles to look for turtle and take bearings, returning the next day despite heavy weather. In the interval the *Investigator*'s carpenters finished a sliding keel for the *Lady Nelson* from logs cut at Port Bowen, and sent it on board the brig.

The chronometers, which had not been rated since Port Jackson, were losing time, and fresh observations were essential before heading for the Gulf of Carpentaria. Flinders took the vessels into Cook's Broad Sound and, with tents, provisions and a marine guard, the instruments were sent ashore with Samuel.

For twenty days the expedition explored the Sound's shoaly waters and mangrove-covered shore. Briefly the *Investigator* grounded on sand. Four days later, much more alarmingly, the ship was caught on a bank of quicksand and, swinging around, was struck broadside by the force of the tide. She heeled frighteningly. Sails were struck and the best bower anchor let go. Then she righted, swinging to the tide. The *Lady Nelson* had also struck ground and now lost part of her after sliding keel, which floated away. Bauer, Westall and Good headed for the highest visible hills, from where they had 'a fine prospect'. Far below the *Lady Nelson* lay at low tide, 'Dry mud all around her'.[9]

On a rising tide Flinders left the camp with the brig and the whaleboat. Again the *Lady Nelson* grounded, but without damage. Then, anchoring at high water but expecting to be left dry by the ebb, they raised the fore and after keels. The new main keel could not be lifted, immersion having swollen the fresh pine wood. As the tide fell and the vessel touched ground, she swung violently. The keel cracked in two and the well was damaged. After another grounding, Flinders took to the whaleboat, but repeatedly shallows and mangroves formed impenetrable barriers to landing.

In extraordinary tidal variations the appearance of relatively deep water vanished as the tide ebbed and left grey sand and mud exposed. Flinders measured the variation at 32 feet and thought it could go higher by another 3 feet during spring tides. From a rare landing site Flinders's group walked across flat, grassy country to some low hills from which Flinders could take a number of useful bearings.

After four days Flinders returned to the camp to find that the timekeepers had been allowed to run down and the week-long process of obtaining new rates would have to be restarted. The *Lady Nelson*, meanwhile, was found to have lost two sheets of copper from her bottom and large sections of her keels. Apparently with little comment but no doubt with strong feelings of frustration, Flinders left Samuel to re-establish the rates and John Murray to careen his vessel and effect repairs as best he could. Flinders sailed with the *Investigator* in search of water and to examine nearby Long Island.

Yet another search was, as he wrote, 'always present in my mind'.[10] It had been fourteen years since the French explorer La Pérouse had sailed from Botany Bay, never to be seen again. It was thought that he had probably been wrecked in the vicinity of New Caledonia and, 'if so', Flinders continued, 'the remains of his ships were likely to be brought upon this coast by the trade winds, and might indicate the situation of the reef or island which had proved fatal to him'. After so many years survivors could hardly be expected, yet the hope and the possibility existed. Walking along the various beaches, especially north of Cape Capricorn, Flinders regularly examined the debris left by the tides for some telltale piece of ship's timber.

On his return to the camp Flinders found that the timekeepers had again been let down. Preoccupied with taking numerous sets of angular distances between the sun and moon, Samuel Flinders had forgotten to wind them. It had become an exasperating situation. Good rates were imperative for all the longitudes yet to be calculated; at the same time, the approach of the monsoon season made a prompt departure from Broad Sound equally important. Flinders compromised.

'On comparing the last day's rates with those of the four days previously obtained, the letting down did not appear to have produced any material alteration; I therefore determined to combine the whole together, and to sail immediately'.[11] In his journal he referred more bluntly to the rates they achieved as the best 'we could scrape together'.

Flinders's most pressing concern now was to reach the Gulf of Carpentaria before the onset of the monsoon, and this meant bringing his coasting to an end and, after a rapid examination of the Northumberland Islands, finding a passage to open sea and hopefully a fast cruise north to Torres Strait.[12]

Flinders was aware of a number of reef formations in the area. Cook's charts showed the location of the *Endeavour*'s strike upon a coral reef in 1770 and the ship's subsequent track among the reefs and islets the explorer called the Labyrinth. In 1797 reefs had been encountered by the *Deptford*, commanded by Captain William Campbell, roughly 95 miles northeast of Broad Sound, and in 1798 by Captain Swain's *Eliza*, even farther offshore from approximately Shoalwater Bay. Flinders himself had seen the formations lying before the entry to Torres Strait. Were any of these connected? He debated the possibility, but had no concept whatsoever of the magnitude of the barrier that lay in his path.

The Great Barrier Reef extends more than 1250 miles or 2000 kilometres from Queensland's Breaksea Spit at Hervey Bay to the coast of Papua New Guinea, and consists of several thousand reefs, shoals and islets of coral and coral sand, many of them mysterious blue-green shapes forever below the surface, others barely submerged or even dry at low tide, still others fringing small green-crested islands. Long white lines of breakers form and reform endlessly as the Pacific rolls in upon the reef's seaward edge, while along its inner rim it shelters long corridors of quiet water. Unbreachable rampart that it might seem, there are openings, deep, narrow channels of dark blue water between the coral formations.

On 28 September 1802, in light breezes and fine but hazy weather, the *Investigator* and the *Lady Nelson* left the coast and by early evening reached the Northumberland group where the expedition spent five days at a cluster of small wooded islands. A little cove, at high water 'one of the prettiest places imaginable', provided fresh water, wood, fish and soil for the ship's garden. However, servants of the science staff somehow set fire to a part of the island, which hampered some activities and burned, candescent in the night sky, like 'a large town on a dark night well lighted up',[13] according to Murray. Flinders later called the cluster the Percy Isles and mentioned the cavorting whales as someting of interest for visitors.

The vessels sailed at dawn on 4 October. Reefs were sighted from the masthead a little before noon. Flinders wrote, 'These reefs were not exactly those seen by Mr Campbell; but they . . . probably . . . form part of the same barrier'.[14] As one was passed, another came in sight. Two days later, 'at nine a reef was passed on either beam; and at noon . . . there were five others.[15]

It was a pattern that would continue for eleven more perilous days as Flinders searched for a way through the coral barrier. Channels between the reefs turned into torrents with the rush of incoming and outgoing tides. Huge breakers to the east, exploding in high-flung foam, raised their hopes of nearing the reef's edge, for 'nothing less than the unobstructed waves of the ocean could produce them'.[16] Then they would find themselves on water so smooth that there was no doubt there were, after all, many more reefs between them and the open sea. At dusk they anchored in these quiet passages, usually safely enough in 30–35 fathoms of glassy blue water above a sea floor of sand and broken coral. In the soft, warm darkness of the night, sky and stars seemed laced into the network of the rigging. The weather held good. In the light airs and occasional calms of the day there were delays but no serious danger.

On the afternoon of the 9th they found themselves surrounded by coral reefs on every side except the west, from where they had come. Flinders decided to wait until low water, when many reefs would be dry and channels between them more visible. With Brown and his party, he descended to an exposed reef, dry for almost a mile around them. He marvelled at the shapes of the corals:

> We had wheat sheaves, mushrooms, stag horns, cabbage leaves, and a variety of other forms, glowing under water with vivid tints of every shade betwixt green, purple, brown, and white; equalling in beauty and excelling in grandeur the most favourite *parterre* of the curious florist . . . [But] whilst contemplating the richness of the scene, we could not long forget with what destruction it was pregnant.[17]

The tide was rising as they returned to the ship. In a light breeze there was no option but to steer west and southwest, a boat sounding ahead as best it could, but spun about from time to time in whirlpools. At six o'clock they anchored and the next day resumed their search for a passage. The dangers of this maze had impressed themselves anew upon Flinders, and he now issued further, more detailed orders on keeping lookouts from the forecastle and from the masthead.

The ships suffered irreparable losses. In one of the narrow channels where the tide ran with 'extraordinary violence', the *Investigator* lost an anchor and had another damaged. A last medium-sized stream anchor was brought up from the hold. Murray in the *Lady Nelson* had previously lost one anchor and now raised another to find it broken. With only one large anchor left, he applied to Flinders for another.

Having none to spare, Flinders sent over two grapnels. Murray backed them together and they held the brig.

Flinders realised that the narrow channels he was following presented too great a risk:

> My anxious desire to get out to sea, and reach the North Coast before the unfavourable monsoon should set in, had led me to persevere amongst these intricate passages beyond what prudence could approve; for had the wind come to blow strong, no anchors, in such deep water and upon loose sand, could have held the ship; a rocky bottom cut the cables; and to have been under sail in the night was certain destruction.[18]

It was a rare admission of fault on his own part. He abandoned the endless little winding waterways and steered north in the smooth water inside the larger reefs, watching for a sufficiently wide opening to the sea.

Alarms were yet to come. On the night of 12 October they were at their eleventh anchorage among the reefs in 32 fathoms of clear water on a bottom of sand and shells. Dry reefs lay 2½ and 1½ miles away; others had been visible from aloft. Coming on deck at daybreak the next morning, Flinders was shocked to see that the ship had drifted. From the soundings marked every hour on the log board it was clear that between four and five o'clock that morning the anchor had been lifted or dragged by the tide, the ship drifting 2 miles to the northeast into shallower water among the reefs. Here the anchor had caught. No one had noticed the movement, and as it had taken place during a change of the watch, it was, as he wrote, difficult to assign blame. The ship's log related briefly the change in position. His journal entry, written later, elaborated: 'This [the movement of the ship] had not been perceived by the watch, a neglect that might have proved fatal to us, and which I am determined not to pardon a second time. The officer of the middle watch is the person to whom I attribute the blame'.[19]

The journal indicates further that Robert Fowler had the first watch and Samuel Flinders the middle watch. As well, a distance of 2 miles covered by a drifting ship would, presumably, have taken longer than the few minutes required for the changing of the watch. Someone had failed, but evidently Flinders let the incident go without further comment.

For two more days the vessels threaded their way among the reefs, coming to anchor off one of the Cumberland Islands charted by Cook, and Flinders's sightings added several more to the map. The expedition sailed at daylight on 17 October. By noon no reefs were in sight, and as they steered generally northeast through the afternoon, the masthead lookout saw only clear and open sea.

Flinders had obviously entered the Barrier Reef with every intention of proceeding north with the *Lady Nelson* in company. Now he reconsidered the question. The little brig had lagged behind regularly, her difficulty in beating to windward exacerbated by the loss of her main keel and part of her after keel, which had been switched forward and the forward keel set aft. Of her three anchors one had been lost and another damaged, and the *Investigator*'s own loss of three anchors made her unable to supply replacements. Other equipment wanted by the brig was similarly in short supply aboard the ship. While the brig was useful in exploring shallow waters, a boat could perform the same task, sometimes more efficiently. Finally, although a second vessel would be essential in case of the loss of the *Investigator*, Flinders now felt that the ship was more likely to be the rescuer than was the brig.

Flinders conferred with Fowler but not, it would seem, with John Murray. Although in his letter of explanation to Governor King he wrote of consulting both men, Murray's log entry reads otherwise:

> At 6 P. M. she [the *Investigator*] anchored within half a mile of us... Saw a boat lowered and in half an hour Lieutenant Fowler came on board and informed me that Captain Flinders meant to part company in the morning with the brig and therefore to get all ready for that purpose. At daylight hoisted out our long boat and sent her on board the Investigator. I received from Captain Flinders orders to proceed to Port Jackson as fast as circumstances would allow.[20]

This was clearly one of the fairly drastic decisions Flinders made to preserve and advance his mission. It was the decision of a commanding officer, made in his view for good reason and for which he need make no explanation to his subordinate. An explanation to Governor King was, however, another matter. Flinders drew up a list of the advantages and disadvantages of retaining the *Lady Nelson*, and in a letter to the governor he summarised these points and stated his decision to send the brig back to Sydney. But he looked forward to using her, he said, once she was repaired, in a future expedition. In *A Voyage to Terra Australis* he wrote: 'Lieutenant Murray was not much acquainted with the kind of service in which we were engaged; but the zeal he had shown to make himself and his vessel of use to the voyage, made me sorry to deprive him of the advantage of continuing with us; and increased my regret at the necessity of parting from our little consort'.[21]

A number of changes were made. A seaman from the *Investigator* was exchanged for two from the brig. Nanbaree, the young Aborigine aboard the *Investigator*, wanted to go home and so transferred to the brig, while Midshipman Denis Lacy, loaned to the *Lady Nelson* at the start of the voyage, returned to duty on the *Investigator*. Stores for the voyage supplied to the smaller vessel were sent to the ship. The brig's launch was left with the sloop in place of the lost cutter.

Flinders wrote two long letters to Governor King, both dated 18 October 1802. In addition to an explation of his resolve to order the *Lady Nelson* back to Sydney, he sent an *Abstract of the Investigator's Proceedings since leaving Port Jackson, 20th July, 1802*, a concise summary of the coasts examined and discoveries made, from which he asked King to forward to the Admiralty the information he judged material. In the second letter he wrote that he did not expect to be back at Port Jackson until June 1803 and possibly later. He requested King to acquaint Joseph Banks with the main events of the voyage so far, as the necessities of charting and of handling the ship did not allow him time to write. However, Flinders dispatched letters to William Paterson, his friend William Kent and Captain E. H. Palmer of the merchant ship *Bridgewater*. Perhaps some feeling of culpability kept him from writing to Banks. Contrary to his instructions from the Admiralty, he had put a resurvey of a coast already examined by Cook ahead of exploring the north coast. He well knew that in his absence an explanation for his actions, reported by King or by himself, would devolve upon Sir Joseph, the man most responsible for his being where he was.

He wrote a short note to Ann. He told her the journey was advancing well and that amid all his many and constant occupations she was 'not one day forgotten . . . Be happy, my beloved, rest assured of my faith, and trust that I will return safely to sooth thy distress, and repay thee for all thy anxieties concerning me'.[22]

Others also seized the opportunity to write, including Good, who 'sent some letters for England', Bauer, writing to his brother at the Gardens in Kew, and Robert Brown, who wrote to Banks. He listed the places at which the ships had anchored, adding, 'In most of these places I have had excellent opportunities of collecting had the season been more favourable. A very considerable proportion of the plants observ'd, were destitute of both flower and fruit . . . A very small proportion are new . . . In zoology our acquisitions are by no means great . . .'[23]

The two vessels were under sail by nine o'clock in the morning of 18 October, and, showing their colours in farewell salutes, parted. John Murray's personal reaction to the abrupt order to return to Port Jackson seems to be unrecorded. Flinders's earlier appraisal of Murray as a surveyor was unenthusiastic, with some justification. However, the reasons Flinders now listed for sending back the *Lady Nelson* related only to the inadequacies of the brig herself.

Lieutenant Murray's journey back to Sydney was a minor epic in itself. With broken anchors, no main keel and a damaged after keel now set forward, the *Lady Nelson*, struggling against the wind and at times relying on her sweeps, took nine days to reach Shoalwater Bay. Here, losing one of her two defective anchors and unable to hold the brig with the other, Murray cross-bound two brass swivel guns to form a kind of anchor and then found an ironbark tree which, in a week of laborious effort, the carpenter shaped into a 20-foot wooden anchor, almost a third of the length of the brig itself. When waterlogged and with two swivel guns tied to it, this anchor held. With this huge creation lashed to her side the *Lady Nelson* continued south and, at mid-morning on 22 November, reached Sydney Cove. The great wooden anchor was let go but, having dried out on the journey south, in final ignominy it floated. The surviving light bower anchor was dropped and the little vessel at last secured abreast of the governor's wharf. In May 1803 Murray returned to England on HMS *Glatton*, carrying with him Flinders's manuscript charts of the south coast for delivery to the Admiralty.

Governor King would have read Flinders's letters and his report with considerable surprise and possibly with some displeasure. While it had been agreed that, owing to winter conditions in the south, Flinders should sail north, the object had been to reach Torres Strait and the Gulf of Carpentaria as quickly as possible, and King had already advised the Admiralty in those terms. He was fully aware that Flinders's orders put an examination of the north coast second only to the exploration of the south coast. A resurvey of the east coast already charted by James Cook was last in the sequence of undertakings proposed to Flinders.

What was Matthew Flinders's thinking, as in effect he reversed the priorities he had been given? There was an element of practicality in his decision. He was following a coast that Cook, without chronometers, did not survey without error. As he passed, why not survey it more correctly? Before sailing from England in 1801 Flinders had written to Banks of his ambition to examine the Australian coast so minutely that no one should 'have occasion to come after me to make further discoveries'.[24] Perhaps even in the wake of the revered Cook, this unattainable but irresistible desire possessed him.

Flinders had no intention of charting the east coast instead of closely surveying the north coast. He would do both. As he had done in the south, he took on a task greater than what was required, and in time found himself confronted by difficulties. Flinders knew that the Lords Commissioners of the Admiralty, many of them navy men, could look leniently on digressions from their instructions by a commander thousands of miles away, particularly when he was exploring in virtually unknown conditions. His orders contained many phrases allowing for the use of his own judgement. Clearly Flinders believed in the rightness of his undertaking and that success would obviate censure.

For the *Investigator* there was to be yet another hazardous escape from the reefs. The east wind freshened, raising a short swell that 'tried the ship more than anything we had encountered from the time of leaving Port Jackson',[25] and to his great concern the ship began taking water at 5 inches per hour. They were again among reefs, but the sight of the sea breaking with high surf on a row of small coral ridges raised their hopes of an opening, and they pressed ahead.

Flinders wrote happily, 'We were successful. At four, the depth was 43 fathoms, and no reefs in sight; at six, a heavy swell from the eastward and a depth of 66 fathoms were strong assurances that we had at length gained the open sea'.[26] Reefs were seen for another two days, but were entirely out of sight by dusk on 21 October. They had been among the reefs for fourteen days and had sailed more than 500 miles in their search for an exit. The *Investigator* had come through what is now known as Flinders Passage at 18°46'S, 148°00'E. Addressing any future commander who proposed to enter the reef area, he later wrote, 'if he do not feel his nerves strong enough to thread the needle, as it is called, amongst the reefs, while he directs steerage from the masthead, I would strongly recommend him not to approach this part of New South Wales'.[27]

On his *General Chart of Terra Australis or Australia Showing the Parts Explored Between 1798 and 1803 by M. Flinders Commr. of H.M.S. Investigator* he labelled the known reef area The Great Barrier Reefs. It was the first time the name was formally attached to this vast coral build-up. While he depicted on his chart only the reefs specifically known to him, his thinking went further: 'I therefore assume it as a great probability, that . . . our Barrier Reefs are connected with the Labyrinth of captain Cook; and that they reach to Torres' Strait and to New Guinea, in 9° south; or through 14° of latitude and 9° of longitude; which is not to be equalled in any other known part of the world'.[28]

With the hydrographic surveys that followed, Flinders's term eventually came to include the entire 1250-mile length of the world's greatest coral reef formation.

21

The Strait and the Gulf

For six days the *Investigator* bore mainly northeast by day, lying to under reduced sail at night. Anticipating possible attacks while among the Torres Strait islands, the marines and crew drilled with small arms, the swivels and the larger guns. An evening squall with rain, thunder and lightning seemed a precursor, as Flinders thought uneasily, of the oncoming monsoon, but the next day the skies cleared. Heading northwest, they sighted a cluster of reefs that Flinders named the Eastern Fields, and skirted to the north. Then, steering west, he approached the strait that had been penetrated for the first time by a European navigator, Luis Baéz de Torres, 196 years before. At noon on 28 October the *Investigator* was at the entrance taken by Captain Edward Edwards of the *Pandora* in 1791, which Flinders had chosen in preference to the more northerly track steered by Bligh in 1792. The *Providence* and the *Assistant* had spent nineteen days traversing the strait. Flinders intended to find a much quicker and easier route.

Steering west and then south-southwest, the *Investigator* neared Flinders's immediate objective, today's Maer, the largest of the Murray Islands. A number of poles rising from the water worried him at first, looking as they did like the masts of a fleet of canoes, but coming closer, he saw that they were piles fixed on the reefs, probably in connection with fishing. Along the beach numerous huts were enclosed by palisades seemingly of bamboo. Flinders later estimated the island's population at about seven hundred. Two smaller, steep-sided islands appeared uninhabited.

Aside from the fierce assault made by the warriors of these islands on the *Providence* and the *Assistant*, Flinders knew also of the killing in 1793 of at least five men from the merchant ship *Hormuzear* (also

Hormuzier or *Hormuzeer*), captained by Matthew Wright Bampton, and the whaler *Chesterfield* under Matthew Bowles Alt, when the two ships, sailing for Timor, had followed the south coast of New Guinea. Of a small group landed on an island to find water, searchers later found little more than severed, fire-blackened hands and additions to piles of human skulls. Now, as Flinders neared the Murray Islands, he had the marines under arms, the carronades clear and matches burning.

As the *Investigator* dropped anchor a few miles from the main island, three canoes approached carrying some 40 to 50 men with bows and arrows visible in each boat. However, there was no sign of belligerence. Remaining at a short distance, the islanders held up barter goods—coconuts, plantains, bamboo sections filled with water, bows and arrows, baskets—loudly calling out their word for iron, *toree, toree*. Flinders described them as active, muscular men, dark brown in colour and of medium height, naked, some with shell or plaited hair or fibre ornaments around the waist, neck or ankles or, as Good observed, 'pieces of a kind of pearl shell neatly cut and fixed in the ears'.[1] Flinders was impressed, as he had been ten years before, with their canoes, sturdy, decorated and extremely fast: '. . . how these long canoes keep the wind, and make such good way as they do, without any after sail, I am at loss to know'.[2]

A lively bartering session ensued. A seaman would hold up a hatchet, nail, knife or other piece of iron. In response an islander offered a bunch of plantains, a coconut or other item he thought commensurate with its value. When he received a sign of agreement, he leaped into the sea, swam to the ship and made his exchange with the sailor, who had climbed down the side to meet him. At sunset the trading was over. Two canoes paddled swiftly to the island. The third raised a single narrow, rectangular sail between its two masts and headed northwest.

In the first grey light of the next morning, there appeared the long, dark shapes of seven canoes, each carrying ten to twenty men. As the sky brightened, the canoes gathered around the ship and some fifteen or twenty men climbed on board, offering pearl oyster shells, cowrie shell necklaces and bows and arrows in exchange for pieces of iron. Bongaree understood nothing of their language and they virtually ignored him. Flinders permitted the busy trading in the hope of securing the islanders' friendship for future vessels passing through. To make a

The Murray Islands of Torres Strait, painted by William Westall, with the principal island, Maer, and two lesser islands, which Flinders believed to be uninhabited. Seven native canoes with fifteen to twenty men in each approached the Investigator, *and a lively bartering session took place on deck. Oyster shells, cowrie shell necklaces and bows and arrows were traded for pieces of iron. (R10986, by permission of the National Library of Australia)*

special gift, he selected the oldest man in the group, gave him a handsaw, hammer and nails and tried to show him how they were used. He had little success, however, as the old man became agitated at being singled out. Curiously, one man traded a bow with a piece of blue-striped, apparently European-made cotton cloth tied to it. It was the first of several puzzling finds the *Investigator*'s company were to make on the north coast.

Westall produced his view of the Murray Islands, and a variety of scenes and portraits. It was not thought safe, however, for the *Investigator*'s botanists to land. As the ship prepared to get under way at about eight o'clock, the men who had come on board at first seemed unwilling to leave, but when the seamen began climbing aloft and loosening sails, 'they went hastily down the stern ladder and the ship's sides, and shoved off; ... without our good understanding having suffered any interruption'.[3]

Keeping to the south of the route taken by the *Providence*, the *Investigator* followed a chain of reefs running west-southwest, anchoring in the afternoon at an island, 'little better than a bank of sand, upon a basis of coral rock; yet ... covered with shrubs and trees'.[4] With Brown, Bauer and Westall, Flinders explored the island, and in his later account discussed the process by which coral islands are formed, as he had observed them.

The next day heavy winds swept through the channel, foam-crested seas ramming the ship. The *Investigator* found shelter in the lee of a large island, which Flinders eventually identified as Wednesday Island, named by Bligh. An attempt to take some of the science staff ashore was abandoned when the boat was nearly swamped in high surf.

The Flinders brothers established the ship's position, and deduced that of the more westerly Booby Island, which, coincidentally, had received the same name from both Cook and Bligh. But in attempting to reconcile the longitude laid down by Cook for the island with their own, and to relate their surroundings to the features on Cook's chart, they were 'altogether at a loss to know what these islands were, under which we had anchored'.[5] The land they could see to the south should have been Australia's northernmost point, Cape York, but no islands such as those that surrounded them now were marked to the north of the cape by Cook.

Confused and uneasy, Flinders studied a sketch made by Bligh while traversing the strait in the launch, which indicated a different arrangement of islands. A hazy sky made observations impossible at first, but eventually he and Samuel were able to conclude that 'our anchorage was under the southern group of the Prince of Wales' Islands, the longitude of which, by captain Cook, is 1°12' west of what I make it'.[6] Specifically, they were in the lee of Bligh's Wednesday Island, and Cook's error meant a serious difference of 77 miles. No observations for longitude were recorded here by Cook, and presumably an unclear sky had prevented the astronomer, Charles Green, from taking lunar measurements. The alternative of dead reckoning, calculating the position of the ship from its course and rate of travel through the water, would not have produced accurate data among shoals and islands.

Flinders's later charts of Torres Strait were compiled from information derived from the records of Cook, Bligh, Bampton and Alt, as well as his own, with the tracks of all of the vessels involved.

The worry of not knowing their location had been underlaid in Flinders's mind by a fear that ran much deeper. The carpenter, Russel Mart, had reported several times during the passage through Torres Strait that when running with a fresh side wind, the ship had been leaking at the rate of 10–14 inches per hour. The range of difficulties, the outright peril, that this suggested was horrifying. However, as at those particular times the ship had generally been heeling to starboard, Flinders believed that the weakness was in the planks of the starboard bow, and hopefully could be remedied by caulking. For the moment there was nothing he could do. The ship needed to be careened for an inspection of her hull, and among the islands there was no suitable place for that.

The wind moderated. In a final landing in the area, Brown, Westall, Bell and Fowler were set ashore on a small island, and Flinders followed in the afternoon with Bauer and Good. They saw at first hand the tall, conical, pale brown constructions that had puzzled them when seen from the ship on other islands. They were termite hills, hard-packed mounds of pinkish earth, some rising to 8 feet or more in peaks like Gothic spires. It was a pleasurable excursion except for 'excessively numerous' black flies, 'almost as troublesome as Dampier describes them to be on the North-west Coast'.[7] Flinders later named the island for Peter Good, whose name it retains on modern charts.

The *Investigator* now turned her bows to the southwest and, on 3 November 1802, made her exit from the Prince of Wales Channel, the principal western entrance for modern shipping through Torres Strait.

Matthew Flinders had taken the *Investigator* through the Strait in six days, and he believed that this 'may be accomplished *in three days*'.[8] The passage was dangerous but feasible, and would take five or six weeks off the time required to sail from the Pacific to the Indian Ocean by the usual route to the north of the island of New Guinea. It was gratifying, too, that despite the late time of year there had been no sign of monsoon weather. However, Flinders's work in the Strait was not what it was intended to be. His instructions from the Admiralty were to execute 'a careful investigation and accurate survey' of Torres Strait, and in his haste his survey was superficial. This he intended to rectify. Acknowledging the difficulties that remained unknown in the channel, he wrote, 'I had great hope of obviating many of them, and even of finding a more direct passage by the south of Murray's Islands in the following year, when I should have the assistance of the Lady Nelson in making a survey of the Strait'.[9]

The Gulf of Carpentaria, 300 miles wide at its entrance, extends 375 miles south from the Arafura Sea in a huge indentation cutting deeply into the low, level plain of the Australian north. Its shorelines are fronted by tidal flats, rimmed with mud banks, mangrove swamps and occasional sand beaches, and laced from the far interior by some twenty rivers making their way in great serpentine loops to the coast. Under a relentless sun it lies still and blue, with shores receding into invisible distance. In the northwesterly gales of the monsoon its waters can pile in churning crests against the shore, flooding into the swamps and across the flat, low-lying country. Cyclones also strike the gulf and its coast, ripping at land and water with appalling force.

In 1606 the Dutch navigator Willem Jansz sailed some 125 miles down the eastern side of the Gulf as far as Cape Keer-weer, where he turned his little ship, the *Duyfken*, and retraced his track for some distance up the coast before heading back to the Dutch East India Company's base in the Banda Islands. In the course of the succeeding 150 years, Dutch expeditions sporadically followed and charted the Gulf coasts. Jan Carstensz made landings in 1623. Two ships under Jean Etienne Gonzal explored in 1756. Despite Gonzal's modestly favourable report on farming possibilities on Cape York peninsula, the voyage was considered a failure. Concluding that there existed in the region neither natural resources of value nor commercial opportunities to be gained from its inhabitants, the Dutch East India Company sent out no more ships.

Matthew Flinders's entry into the Gulf in 1802 was the first attempt at its exploration in 46 years. As he wrote later, 'the real form of this gulph remained in as great doubt with geographers' as that of Torres Strait.[10] There was a lingering hope that somewhere at the head of the huge inlet a substantial waterway led into Australia's interior.

The *Investigator* steered for the east coast of the Gulf of Carpentaria on a southwesterly sea breeze, and shortly after three o'clock in the afternoon of 4 November, land was sighted. By five the ship was following the coast at a distance of 4 miles. 'It was sandy and low... indifferently covered with shrubs and small trees, but totally destitute of any thing like a hill; fires bespoke it to be inhabited'.[11] Robert Brown wrote to Banks, 'It is in reality one vast sandy beach'.[12]

Flinders had been supplied by Dalrymple with an 'old Dutch chart', evidently a copy of Melchisédec Thévenot's 1663 map, on which the French cartographer had incorporated the discoveries of Tasman and other Dutch explorers. From this Flinders tried to identify the land features, particularly the rivers, indicated by the Netherlanders. Two days into the Gulf he sighted a large opening at a latitude that nearly agreed with that given by the Dutch for a Batavia River. Shoals kept the ship at a distance of 6 miles and on his chart he wrote tentatively, 'Opening, probably the *Batavia* R. of the old charts',[13] but identified it more positively in his narrative of the voyage. The inlet is now Port Musgrave, into which flow the Wenlock and Ducie Rivers, each of which has been identified as the Dutch Batavia.

The next morning the breeze died. An anchor was dropped about 3 miles offshore, and with the botanical group anxious to examine the vegetation, Flinders had the whaleboat lowered and, with Bongaree and the boat crew, accompanied Brown and Bauer to the beach of a small inlet.

It was a difficult approach, the channels among the shoals narrow and winding. When several spear-carrying Aborigines appeared on the north side of the inlet, Bongaree, naked and unarmed, went ashore and towards them, but they quickly retreated. Further efforts to make friendly contact failed, and Flinders decided the location was not safe for the botanists. They returned to the boat and rowed a mile farther into the inlet and up a creek to land at a green-wooded point.

While Brown and Bauer proceeded with their botanising, Flinders set off to shoot birds, but hearing voices in the woods, he returned and sent his party to the boat. They waited but no one appeared. They then rowed back to the entrance, which was sandy and open except for a few pandanus and casuarina trees. Guards were posted on the hillocks while Brown and Bauer made their collections. Preparing to leave, Flinders had a hatchet fastened to the branch of a tree. They had just shoved off when sixteen spear-armed men appeared, calling out, but when the whaleboat was turned back toward the beach, they fled. On the opposite side of the entrance four others also ran off. Flinders left a second hatchet. He identified the opening as that of the Coen River of the Dutch maps, but coincidentally the landing had been made at the mouth of the Pennefeather River, the site of Willem Jansz's first landing on Australian soil in 1606.

The following day the *Investigator* sailed with a sea breeze into a large, shallow bay, the wide entry held pincer-like between two points, which Flinders named for the ships of Dutch explorers, Duyfhen—more correctly Duyfken—Point, and Pera Head for Jan Carstensz's vessel. Pera Head, he noted, was 'remarkable for having some reddish cliffs'.[14] He gave no name to the bay. Now it is Albatross Bay, where the port and mining community of Weipa are located, the reddish cliffs part of the area's bauxite-laden earth

On 10 November the *Investigator* reached the latitude given by Jansz for Cape Keer-weer, where he turned his little craft around. Flinders wrote, 'I could see nothing like a cape here; but the southern extreme of the land, seen from the mast head, projects a little; and from respect to antiquity, the Dutch name is there preserved'.[15]

The *Investigator* continued south, in light and variable winds and occasional squalls. Shallows extending from the shore sometimes forced the ship so far out that land was scarcely visible from the deck, and Flinders probably guessed that the waters of the Gulf were not very deep. Its maximum depth is, in fact, only 230 feet. The coast was 'lower than before; not a single hill had yet been seen; and the tops of the trees on the highest land, had scarcely exceeded the height of the ship's mast head'.[16] They saw a fire, grey smudges of smoke and small groups of Aborigines, sometimes watching the ship from sandy knolls.

With little success, Flinders continued trying to locate the rivers marked by the Dutch. Navigators of that time calculated latitude with such simple devices as the cross-staff or astrolabe; longitude they frequently did not even attempt. Their recorded positions, therefore, were often very much in error. On the other hand, their small, shallow-draught vessels could usually come in for much closer observation of the coast than a ship like the *Investigator*; undoubtedly they saw details that were missed from the larger vessel. As well, in early November, at the end of the north's dry season, many rivers would have been at their lowest, some probably no longer flowing. Where the Dutch had indicated the mouth of the Nassau River, Flinders saw only a beach and a lagoon. He did not see the river itself where it empties about a mile to the south. Nor did others on the *Investigator* show any aptitude for distinguishing river entrances. Robert Brown commented to Banks, 'The rivers laid down in the Dutch charts are probably nothing more than creeks or lagoons'.[17] Thus Flinders not only failed to find most of those on the old map, but currently known rivers as well, among them the Archer, Holroyd, Edward, Mitchell and Gilbert on the east side of the Gulf alone.

At 17°3'15"S latitude and 141°0'E longitude the shoreline trended westward, much as it did on the old charts, which, as Flinders wrote, began to 'disappoint the hopes formed of a strait or passage leading out at some other part of Terra Australis'.[18] Then the coastline swung to the northwest. Another vision of discovery had closed in the face of a more stark reality.

A low hill, 'the highest land we had seen in Carpentaria',[19] appeared two days later, about two miles off the mainland, and thinking that the open water between it and the coast might be some kind of opening in the land, the explorers' expectations rose. A landing, however, showed the hill to be on an island, which Flinders named Sweers Island, for Cornelius Sweers, in 1644 a member of the Dutch council in Batavia, now Jakarta, and a signatory to Abel Tasman's orders. From the top of the rise, which Flinders called Inspection Hill, the island stretched to the northeast like a flung-down robe of tufted green, with the blueness of the Gulf on either side.

The leaking of the ship while in Torres Strait could now be investigated. Over two days the carpenters examined the *Investigator*'s hull, and on the port side found two planks and the timber underneath to be rotten. A sheltered anchorage was needed where the ship could be further inspected and caulked, where fresh water could be obtained and the 'botanical gentlemen', as well as Flinders, could do useful work. The largest of the surrounding islands, which Flinders later called Bentinck Island, lay across a narrow strait from Sweers. Lesser islands, one of which Flinders would name for the miner John Allen, and numbers of tiny, low, brushy islets clustered mainly to the west. Much of the mainland, also very low, was visible only from aloft. Perhaps it was during some of these quiet evenings at anchor, after the lanterns had been lit, that Flinders stretched out on his couch to read from his small store of personal books, among them Milton's *Paradise Lost*.

On one small island three Aboriginal men were seen dragging through the shallows six small rafts of tied-together mangrove branches. Flinders and his party brought their boat on shore and walked after them. Apparently deciding that the Europeans could not be avoided, the Aborigines came onto the beach with their spears and waited. Three others, whom Flinders took to be women, were sitting on some rocks at a distance. A degree of friendliness was established and gifts were exchanged. Flinders was impressed by two of the men, who were 'advanced in years' and looked like brothers. They were the tallest Aborigines Flinders had seen, 'being from three to four inches higher than my coxswain, who measured five feet eleven'.[20] The Aborigines signed that they should all walk back to the Englishmen's boat. They did so, hand in hand, but stopped halfway. Flinders then realised that this was a ruse to draw the strangers away from the women, who were quietly picking oysters. Not wishing to annoy anyone, Flinders took his party off in another direction.

The best anchorage for the needs of the expedition was found in the channel between Sweers and Bentinck Islands, a well-sheltered passage that Flinders later called Investigator's Road. Clear, fairly fast-flowing water was found 10–11 feet down under sand and clay just behind a long white beach.

The ship was moved as close as possible to the beach. With the seamen and marines Fowler established a camp and work parties set off. The gunner brought the powder ashore and spread it in the sun to dry. Samuel Flinders returned to Inspection Hill for further observations, while Aken and the carpenters began their checking and caulking of the ship's sides. The weather held fine, with no more than light breezes and occasional thunder and flickers of lightning in the north-east. At some point someone carved on the trunk of a tree (*Celtis paniculata*) near the beach a name and date: 'Investigator 1802'. Neither Flinders's journal nor any other diary kept on board mentions the incident, but later visitors to the island saw it and some carved additional names.[21]

The Battle of the First of June 1794, *oil painting by Philippe Loutherbourg. Two days of sightings and minor clashes between French and English warships climaxed in a major battle on 1 June in the Atlantic some 450 miles (about 720 km) west of Brest. Flinders, aboard HMS* Bellerophon, *took an active part. (© National Maritime Museum, London)*

The Glass House Mountains of Queensland, seen by James Cook in 1770 and visited by Matthew Flinders in 1799. With a small group Flinders walked from Pumicestone Passage to the nearest of the peaks, which are volcanic plugs 25 million to 30 million years old. (Courtesy of Tourism Queensland)

Matthew Flinders (1774–1814), c. 1800, miniature portrait painted on ivory. The portrait was evidently painted soon after Flinders, newly in command of HMS Investigator, *received his promotion to commander in February 1801. Later engravings were made from this portrait. (ML Ref: MIN 52, Mitchell Library, State Library of New South Wales)*

Model of HMS Investigator, *made by Roland Michel Laroche, 1980. Originally a three-masted collier, the ship had been purchased by the Navy in 1798 and three years later was fitted for Flinders's voyage of exploration. (Photo by Marinco Kojdanowski, © Powerhouse Museum, Sydney, 2000. Courtesy of the Powerhouse Museum Collection, B2371)*

William Westall (1781–1850), self-portrait from about 1820. Westall joined the Investigator *expedition as landscape and figure painter in 1801 at age 19. He was not impressed by the arid Australian landscape. Commissioned by the Admiralty to provide illustrations for Flinders's* A Voyage to Terra Australis, *he produced oil paintings and engravings by others of idealised scenes. (R10986, by permission of the National Library of Australia)*

Views of the South Coast of Australia *by William Westall, 1801. To assist navigators in determining their location, these drawings were intended to show specific features of the coastline as they appeared from the sea at a given time of the day. Cape Leeuwin, the continent's southwesternmost point, was Flinders's first Australian landfall on the journey from England in 1801. (R4385, by permission of the National Library of Australia)*

King George Sound as seen from the northwest by William Westall. The Investigator *entered the sound during the night of 8 December 1801, and here the expedition made its first landing in Australia, exploring the bay and its coves and islands until 5 January. (R4263, by permission of the National Library of Australia)*

Lucky Bay by William Westall. Amid the islands and rocks of the Recherche Archipelago, the Investigator *found a safe anchorage in an inlet on the mainland which Flinders named Lucky Bay. Although very dry, the surrounding country provided the botanists with many interesting plants. (R4268, by permission of the National Library of Australia)*

Grevillea banksii *by the botanical artist Ferdinand Lukas Bauer, one of over 2000 drawings of plants he made during the* Investigator's *circumnavigation of Australia and in the two years that followed. His work was published in his* Illustrationes Florae Novae Hollandiae. *(The Natural History Museum, London)*

Two platypuses, drawing by Ferdinand Lukas Bauer. Accompanying HMS Investigator *on her voyage around Australia, Bauer produced almost 200 drawings of animals in addition to his drawings of plants. After the voyage Bauer continued his work in New South Wales and on Norfolk Island. (The Natural History Museum, London)*

Sydney, c. 1803, seen from the west side of the cove, watercolour, unsigned. An open space and the colony's three long hospital buildings occupy the foreground. Across the cove is Government Wharf with Government House on the rise above it. At far left, the Tank Stream empties through mudflats into the cove. (ML Ref: XV1/1803/1, Mitchell Library, State Library of New South Wales)

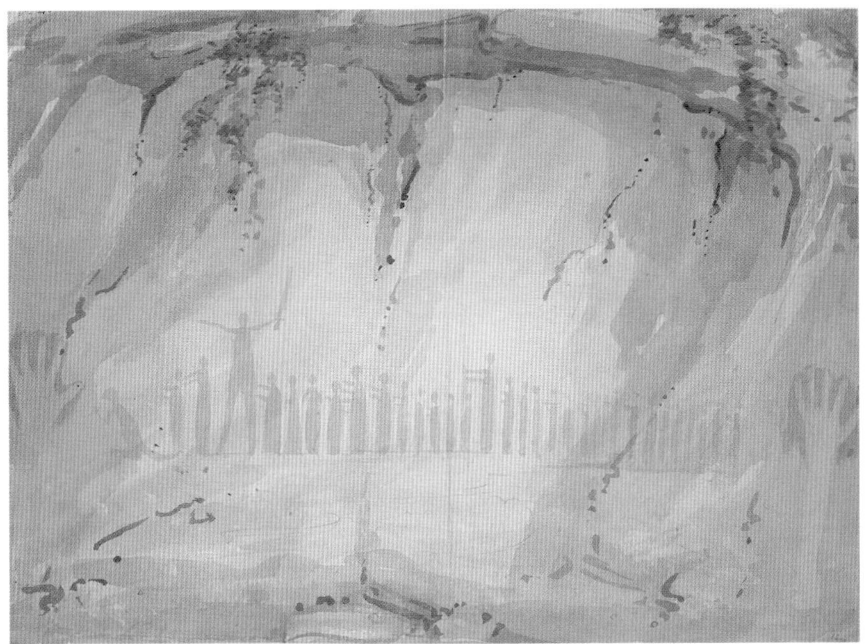

Aboriginal rock wall painting at Chasm Island in the Gulf of Carpentaria copied by William Westall. A file of 32 persons, the third notably larger than the rest, intrigued both Flinders and Westall. Flinders speculated that the taller figure with his upraised stick represented someone in authority. (R4356, by permission of the National Library of Australia)

Portrait of Captain-General Charles Mathieu Isidore Decaen, governor of Ile de France, now the Republic of Mauritius, 1803–1810. A dedicated soldier and Bonapartist, Decaen took command of Mauritius in August 1803. In September he learnt that France was again at war with Britain. His association with Matthew Flinders, who arrived in December, was largely one of confrontation, despite the two having met only once. Decaen left the island in December 1810, after its capture by British forces. (Courtesy of the Mauritius Institute, Port Louis, Mauritius)

Portrait of Sir Joseph Banks (1743–1820), c. 1808, by Thomas Phillips. Banks was 65 years old in 1808, President of the Royal Society for 30 years, holder of countless other offices and honours, and a victim of chronic gout. This would have been Banks as Flinders, returning from his detention in 1810, again met him at his Soho Square residence in London. (ML Ref: DG 25, Dixson Galleries, State Library of New South Wales)

Ann Flinders, in black, her sister Isabella Tyler on the left and daughter, Anne, centre, in later years. In 1815 the family, joined by Ann's mother, left London and over the years lived in various towns in south England. (Courtesy of Lisette Flinders Petrie, Arlington, Polegate, E. Sussex, England)

Robert Brown and his people pursued their own activities on various islands. They gathered a reasonable assemblage of plants and examined with astonishment the stumps of several casuarina trees that had been neatly cut with sharp-edged tools. Obviously outsiders other than themselves had been here. Who? Between their excursions they worked on board at preserving their collections, which in warm, humid weather required considerable attention.

The sharply cut tree stumps were among several strange findings. Flinders came upon similarly hewn trees, a piece of teak wood and a broken earthen jar. More unsettling was the discovery by a fishing party of six or seven human skeletons near extinguished fires, some of the bones, in the opinion of Peter Good and others, appearing to have been in the fire. To Flinders these findings seemed to point to the wrecking of a ship, probably from the East Indies, and the killing of part of the crew by the Aborigines. If survivors had escaped to the mainland, possibly on rafts, they could still be in distress, if not danger. There was, however, little he could do except to be alert to further clues, especially later when they explored the mainland. A more urgent matter was now pressing upon him.

The carpenters had continued with their caulking, but as they moved along, their reports to Flinders grew more and more alarming. Rotten places were 'found in different parts of the ship,—in the planks, bends, timbers, tree-nails, &c'.[22] Shocked, Flinders ordered Aken and Mart to make a thorough examination and submit to him an official report, together with their considered answers to specific questions on the safety of the ship under various conditions. The hold was cleared as far down as possible to provide access and, together with the oldest carpenter's mate on board, Aken and Mart began their inspection.

Their report, two days later, was devastating. Of the ten top timbers forward on the port side, four were sound, one partly rotted and five entirely rotten. On the port quarter the examiners saw one timber that was entirely rotten. On the starboard bow, close to the stem, they found three timbers that were completely decayed. Metal bolts had started as the wood had rotted under them. Boring into timbers in the main hold and other parts of the ship, they found some to be sound, others badly decayed. Treenails were generally rotted. From what they had seen of other areas, they expected to find more rot, fore and aft.

Their opinion was that in a strong gale with much sea running, the ship would hardly escape foundering and if she grounded, unless briefly on a soft bottom and in smooth water, 'she would immediately go to pieces'.[23] Nor would the vessel bear the strain of heaving down without starting or loosening her copper and butt ends. The two men concluded, 'it is our joint opinion that in from eight to twelve months there will scarcely be a sound timber in her; but that if she remain in fine weather and happens no accident, she may run six months longer without much risk'.[24]

Flinders wrote, 'I cannot express the surprise and sorrow which this statement gave me'.[25]

> From the above dreadful state of the ship, I find the complete examination of this country, which is one of the nearest objects to my heart, to be greatly impeded, if not destroyed. I have hitherto considered that my business is to make so accurate an examination of New Holland that there shall be no necessity for any further navigator to come after me . . . with the blessing of God, I would not have left anything of import to be discovered hereafter upon any of the shores of this great country . . .[26]

Shock and fear pervaded the ship: '. . . we Dispair'd of ever Arriving safe into any port, espesially if we met with Boisterous Weather',[27] Samuel Smith wrote.

It was clear that to safeguard the lives of the men on board and to preserve the charts and other work already accomplished, the *Investigator* should return immediately to Port Jackson. Yet the audacious, unrealistic goal that he had set himself many months before still held Flinders, and to give it up was to succumb to despair. Even in the formal account of the voyage he published twelve years later, he wrote:

> I had ever endeavoured to follow the land so closely, that the washing of the surf upon it should be visible, and no opening, nor any thing of interest escape notice . . . and with the blessing of God, nothing of importance should have been left for future discoverers . . . [but] with a ship incapable of encountering bad weather,—which could not be repaired . . . —which . . . could not run more than six months;—with such a ship I knew not how to accomplish this task.[28]

With Aken and Mart, Flinders raised the question of why, if the ship was in such grave condition, no sign of it had been seen at the dock in Sheerness, or when she was extensively caulked at the Cape of Good Hope, or when the quarterdeck barricade was lowered at Port Jackson. Their belief was that 'two years back when the ship underwent repair in the dock, she could not be a quarter part so bad as she now is',[29] nor, most likely, had the shipwrights examined the vessel except for the usual shorter voyages near home; when she was caulked at the Cape the work had been merely routine caulking with no suspicion of any serious problem; and in removing the barricade, the carpenters at Port Jackson had laid bare only relatively new wood, as the barricade was a recent naval addition. Aken had seen similar situations and had found that such rot could spread very quickly. But that the *Investigator* had carried these flaws from the start of the voyage was abundantly clear.

Even an immediate decision to return to Port Jackson was not a simple solution. To do so by steering west meant sailing directly into the northwesterly monsoon with a ship 'that in a strong gale, . . . would hardly escape foundering'.[30] To retrace their route to the east meant a smiliar hazard amid the reefs and islands of Torres Strait and the Great Barrier Reef. There remained the alternative of continuing the survey of the Gulf of Carpentaria by sailing north in the shelter of its western shore while monsoon weather prevailed, and when the southeast trade winds returned in about April 1803, to proceed to Port Jackson by steering west. That Flinders resolved to continue the survey in this way—probably in any way he could—is obvious. On the same day as he received the terrible report, he wrote in his journal, 'For the present, however, I determined to go on in the examination of this gulph, if the NW monsoon does not prove too great a hindrance; and afterwards to act as circumstances shall most require'.[31]

In his published account he added that if, in heading west, the ship should prove too weak to meet winter weather on the south coast, they would 'make for the nearest port in the East Indies'. Probably this was in his mind the final consideration, one he scarcely wanted to think about. He also recorded in his book that Aken and Mart had given the ship twelve months before there would no longer be a sound timber in her. He omitted the mention of eight months.

By 28 November the carpenters had made what repairs they could to the deteriorating parts of the ship, and the *Investigator* sailed the next morning. For nine days Flinders explored the group he later called the Wellesley Islands, of which Sweers and Bentinck were a part. He discovered the much larger Isle Mornington, as he named it, and a number of very small islands.

Coming ashore late in the afternoon on one of the islets, the men found turtle tracks and their hunger for fresh food took over. Turtles had been seen in the water and their remains on shore, but here there were live ones coming onto the beach. Some were taken at once. Then Fowler and a group stayed on the beach all night turning over the animals as they came in. It took nearly the entire following day to get their catch on board, stowing them in every available space. Forty-six turtles averaging 300 pounds each were taken, as well as hatfuls of eggs, and a swarm of tiny hatchlings that Flinders 'found crawling in every part of the boat'.[32]

Seaman Samuel Smith wrote with satisfaction, 'they was made into soup for the Ships company, which was an excelent refreshment',[33] while Flinders named the site of their feast Bountiful Island. In addition, seven large tiger sharks were hooked alongside the ship. Less pleasant was the experience of Brown, Bauer and Good, who had found some cycad palms, and, as Good wrote ruefully, 'the fruit being both pleasant to the taste and sight I eat some as also Mr Brown & Bawer. on coming on board Mr Bawer and I were taken with a violent reaching . . . the greater part of the night it had an unpleasant effect with Mr Brown'.[34] Others, too, had succumbed to the fruit.

A north-northeast wind filled the *Investigator*'s sails as, on 5 December, she quitted Bountiful Island and, in sea breezes by day and a land breeze at night, followed the 'tedious uniformity' of the low, wooded mainland. Rain began to fall out of a darkened sky rent with lightning and rumbling with thunder. A water spout with gushing rain and a brief, strong wind created some excitement. The monsoon, it seemed, had arrived.

The danger of sailing uncharted waters in a fragile ship struck everyone with renewed force a few days later. Evidently tempted to make a little more headway before anchoring for the night, Flinders had the *Investigator* moving forward in the darkness just before eight o'clock. Suddenly the depth diminished to 2½ fathoms. Before the helm could be put down, the ship touched a rock and hung there. With full sails it got free but in five minutes was horrifyingly hung upon another rock. Flinders managed to swing her off, reversed his course and, despite one more 'slight touch', got into deeper water. With palpable relief, Flinders noted, '. . . it could not be perceived that any injury had been sustained'.[35] There was no one on board who did not recognise a very lucky escape.

Before dawn, with the vessel quietly at anchor in still water, Flinders was on deck to take altitudes of the star Rigel to ascertain their longitude. To his extreme annoyance he found that the timekeepers had stopped, 'my assistant having forgotten to wind them up at noon',[36] the assistant obviously being Samuel Flinders. The chronometers were set forward and, with a combination of previous and succeeding observations and information from the log, the longitudinal position of their anchorage was established at 137°37'18"E. It was Sunday, and the ship's company were mustered and 'seen clean'.

At sunset the masthead lookout sighted land that was noticeably higher than any seen so far in the gulf, probably the rise that appeared on the Thévenot map as Cape Vander Lin. Flinders had come upon the islands he later called the Sir Edward Pellew Group.

The Pellew Islands are moderately high, with sandy soil and a cover of coarse grass, shrubs and trees. Flinders spent a fortnight tacking back and forth, exploring the principal island, which he named Vanderlin, four smaller ones and numerous rocks and islets. There were repeated landings in spite of frequent thunderstorms and intervals between them that were suffocatingly hot, steamy and alive with pestilent black flies. The botanists discovered a wild nutmeg. Some small cabbage palms were new to botany, and Brown classified and named them *Livistona inermis*, now *Livistona humiles*, while the seamen dried the young leaves and wove hats for themselves.

Aborigines were seen, at one time a group of some thirty or more watching the ship from the beach, but after that there were only glimpses of them. The explorers were much puzzled by two roughly cylindrical stones, about 18 inches high, set on the ground inside a small bark hut. Encircling black stripes and oval black or dark brown spots, together with stuck-on white bird down and feathers, marked them as something special, but gave no clue as to their meaning.

The men found more of the clearly foreign objects that they had seen elsewhere—broken earthen jars, a wooden anchor, three boats' rudders, remnants of bamboo lattice work, a Chinese-style hat of palm leaves sewn with cotton thread, a remnant of blue cotton trousers. Most puzzling were low, rough stone walls, with dividers on one side to create numerous compartments. Charcoal, firewood and cut-down mangroves were all around. Flinders abandoned his earlier theory of a shipwreck. These remains had been left by visiting Asians, but who they were and what they sought on these islands, other than just possibly the nutmegs, remained a mystery.

The botanists had also come upon a skeleton in a cave, tied into a roll of bark, which to them appeared to be that of a European. 'There was some hair upon the skull', wrote Peter Good, 'of a brown colour, which as well as the scull & skeleton agreed perfectly with the European'.[37] It was perhaps a precipitant conclusion, but here there seemed to be another of the mysteries of the Gulf.

Wild storms swept in, particularly in the evenings, as Flinders, Westall and a boat crew pursued a four-day excursion in the whaleboat among islands mainly to the west and south. Securing their tent in high wind to the loose, sandy ground was a struggle, and on the second night lightning speared out of the sky so close that they were afraid to pitch the tent near trees, and remained relatively exposed in torrential rain. Each morning the weather cleared somewhat and, although at times battling contrary winds, they continued their investigation of the smaller islands. They returned to the ship on the afternoon of Christmas Day. There was little to set the day apart from any other. The ship's remaining provisions would now have been mainly the usual salt fare, and there is no reference to extra rations of grog.

On Flinders's chart the mainland here appears as a broken line labelled 'These parts of this low coast seen very indistinctly'.[38] Thus he missed the mouth of the 150-mile McArthur River, although the entrance would probably have been indistinguishable from the rest of the marshy coastline. From the first day of 1803, however, he began following the shore as closely as the shoals would permit, usually 6–7 miles off.

The sea bottom became irregular, and the whaleboat was sent ahead to sound. When a stiff northeast wind set in and the sea rose, the boat was called back. Veering to get astern of the *Investigator*, the whaleboat filled and came adrift. The two boatsmen were thrown into the water and disappeared. Another boat was immediately lowered. Flinders ran the ship to leeward and dropped an anchor. William Job reappeared, grabbed hold of the whaleboat and was pulled in unhurt. William Murray did not reappear. Here accounts of the story diverge. Flinders commented, 'William Murray, captain of the foretop, being unable to swim, was unfortunately lost'.[39] Peter Good wrote, 'The men were both swimmers . . . one soon appeared again . . . the other was never seen'.[40] Samuel Smith added, 'the Boat was pickt up but much Damaged'.[41]

On Flinders's 'old chart' a large, roughly circular island lay off the coast almost 100 miles north of the Pellew Islands. It carried Tasman's name of Groote Eylandt and Flinders decided to circumnavigate it. To accommodate the botanists, a landing was first made on the mainland. Brown and his party ranged through woods and marshes, coming upon some freshwater lakes and a native burial ground. Human skeletons were found in hollowed tree trunks set upright, some fallen with time. No one was seen.

The next day the ship stood to the east for Groote Eylandt, with its forested central hill, jutting headlands and groups of offshore rocks and islets. Anchoring the ship near one of the steep-sided islets, Flinders landed with the botanists and set off to take bearings from the uppermost cliffs. He found the higher parts of the island deeply scored with chasms that would have made a climb to the top far more time-consuming than he intended. Instead, he took a few bearings from a lower point and joined the botanists. They came upon an apple-sized fruit, acidulous, but not disagreeable. There were large numbers of nutmegs, but not, Flinders thought, of a taste to rival those of the Moluccas.

In the walls of the chasms they found caves and, on shadowy surfaces under the overhangs, pictures

> . . . made with charcoal and something like red paint upon the white ground of the rock. These drawings represented porpoises, turtle,

> kanguroos, and a human hand; and Mr. Westall, who went afterwards to see them, found the representation of a kanguroo, with a file of thirty-two persons following after it. The third person of the band held in his hand something resembling the *whaddie*, or wooden sword of the natives of Port Jackson . . . [42]

The 'whaddie', Flinders assumed, was a badge of authority, also indicated by the image of the individual drawn on a larger scale. He theorised: 'They could not, as with us, indicate superiority by clothing or ornament, since they wear none of any kind; and therefore, with the addition of a weapon, similar to the ancients, they seem to have made superiority [greater size] of person the principal emblem of superior power'.[43]

Westall made a watercolour copy of the scene. His portraits of Aborigines at Port Jackson were executed with both directness and sensitivity, despite his classical styling, and this first look at native cave art obviously intrigued him. Evidently it was a moment of interest in what he increasingly regarded as a tedious and unrewarding journey.

22

Diverse Encounters

Flinders completed his survey around Groote Eylandt on 17 January and resumed charting the mainland coast. In a large, shallow bight that Flinders called Blue-Mud Bay, the *Investigator* anchored off a small, wooded island, with the mainland visible to the west and a long, narrow island Flinders named Isle Woodah to the east. The explorers saw fresh footprints in the sand, but no one appeared.

Wooding and fishing parties came ashore the next morning, as well as Westall, the botanists and a group with Flinders. All were armed as no one had any knowledge of the local people.

Flinders made his observations from the far side of the island, then walked through entangling brush to return to the boat and the wooding party. Westall, sketching at some distance from the woodcutters, saw six Aborigines arrive in a canoe from Isle Woodah. As they pulled up on the beach and started walking briskly towards him, he and his servant thought it best to move closer to the sailors, who were about to approach the new arrivals in a friendly manner. At that point Flinders and his group appeared, and the six native men ran off, stopping some distance away. Satisfied that everyone was safe, Flinders and the botanists rowed back to the ship for dinner. They had scarcely reached the side of the vessel when the sharp cracking of musket fire came from the beach. Flinders saw the seamen waving and supporting someone to the boat. Immediately he dispatched Aken with two armed boats, one carrying the surgeon. Flinders was sure that his own men had been the aggressors, and Aken's orders were to make peace, and under no circumstances to pursue the natives into the trees. If the natives had been the aggressors, he was to seize their canoe.

John Whitewood, the master's mate, was brought on board with four spear wounds in his body. It appeared that the two groups had confronted each other with their weapons ready. Whitewood, carrying his gun, and John Allen, unarmed, came forward. According to a somewhat chaotic account by Good:

> ...the Natives divided themselves 3 to each. those nearest Mr. Allen had laid down their spears & had exchanged a green bough with him [while] that next to Mr Whitwood (who still kept his musket) held out a Spear which Mr Whitwood held out his hand to take hold of when he run it into his breast he then attempted to fire his musket but it missed fire Mr Allen seeing this run down the hill & Spears flying past him but was fortunate enough to escape them. Mr whitwood also run as fast as he could but several spears having hit him and one hanging in his Side he now presented his Musket which now went off... [1]

His companions attempted to fire, apparently fumbled and finally got off two shots. Half-carrying him, they got Whitewood to the boat. Unhurt, the attackers fled, one of them snatching up a sailor's dropped straw hat as he went.

Aken now reached the island and took his boat around the beach to get the canoe. Against orders he sent Midshipman Lacy into the bush to head off the warriors, three of whom nevertheless reached the canoe first and pushed off. Lacy's men opened fire, one Aborigine fell into the canoe, the two others dived and swam away. The seaman who claimed to have fired the killing shot waded out to retrieve the boat, the body and what he recognised as his hat, but upset the fragile craft, tipping the body into the sea.

The next day Flinders sent men to retrieve the canoe and the body. Westall made a raw and poignant drawing of the dead man stretched on his back. Although the wound was in the back, Westall made it visible by showing it to be in the chest. The body was further examined by the naturalist and the surgeon. Their dissection showed scant respect for the dead, but would have been very much the kind of anatomical investigation that Hugh Bell would have made many times in becoming a surgeon and probably at various times since, examining conditions that were new or interesting to him.

In the midst of the excitement, almost half-forgotten, Thomas Morgan, marine, died. Having worked ashore almost all day hatless, he apparently collapsed from sunstroke and was taken off the beach together with Whitewood. Carried aboard unconscious, he went into convulsions 'and died in a state of frenzy, that same night'. The next day Thomas Morgan, also known as 'Benjamin', was 'committed to the deep . . . the island was named after him, Morgan's Island'.[2] Whitewood, meanwhile, gradually recovered from his wounds.

Flinders was extremely displeased with Aken and distressed by the turn of events. He did conclude that the attack was intentional and wondered if this aggressiveness did not stem from encounters with other intruders on these people's territory. But, as he wrote, 'the mischief was done'.

A slow, difficult examination of Blue-mud Bay continued for two more days against strong winds with frequent rain, thunder and lightning. Flinders decided that no stream of any size entered this shallow bight, but the fine blue mud of the bottom, he thought, might be useful in manufacturing earthenware.

The *Investigator* resumed the journey in recurring rain. Landings were made to accommodate the science staff and to look for water. At one such landing Robert Brown went inland alone except for a seaman to carry his specimen box. When at dusk they had not returned to the boat that waited for them, anxiety mounted. At ten o'clock a gun was fired. Soon after daybreak, however, the two men arrived. Without a compass in thick woods they had become confused, and at twilight reached the wrong beach, where they remained for the night. The report of the gun having provided direction, they found their way without difficulty in the morning.

As the ship approached today's Caledon Bay, several unarmed Aborigines appeared on the beach and, on Fowler's coming ashore in the boat, met him with immediate friendliness, which became even more enthusiastic with the appearance of Bongaree. When the ship's fishing party began work, two of the natives joined in hauling the seine, for which they received a portion of the catch. Their familiarity with strangers was evident in their awareness of guns and the use of an axe. Bongaree found their language unintelligible, but Brown and Bell compiled a vocabulary of about 50 words.

As soon as camp was established, the botanists and their attendants headed into the woods, each European with an Aborigine walking beside him arm in arm. When one native suddenly snatched a hatchet from a servant, the botanists did not respond, but when a second man grabbed a musket, a gun was fired, at which the natives fled into the trees. The botanists returned to the tents. However, several Aborigines continued to hover about the camp, and two of them were told that a hatchet would be given on the return of the musket.

The musket arrived; the stock was broken and the ramrod missing but the hatchet was paid. The next day, however, a wooding axe, an essential tool, was stolen, and Flinders resorted to capturing a man and a lad of about fourteen. The man was promptly released, having been made to understand that on the return of the axe, the boy would be freed. There was no response.

In the evening Flinders attempted negotiations by taking the boy, Woga, in the boat and rowing to a place where the people were gathered. Flinders demanded the axe and was told, in effect, that the thief had been beaten and run away. Two men then carried forward a young girl, by signs offering her to Bongaree if he would come on shore. The offer was declined, and with no axe appearing, Flinders returned to the ship with a strongly protesting Woga. On board, as Flinders wrote, the lad 'ate heartily, laughed, sometimes cried, and noticed everything; frequently expressing admiration for what he saw, and especially at the sheep, hogs, and cats'.[3]

When Brown and his people landed the next day, they were approached by armed Aborigines. They began retreating towards the boat, but were surrounded, the warriors closing in with poised spears. When pointing a musket had no effect, the botanists fired with buckshot at the two nearest men, whereupon the entire group took flight. Very unsure of their safety, the botanists returned to the ship.

By evening it seemed evident that no axe would appear in exchange for Woga. For the sake of explorers yet to come—and he believed Baudin could be expected at any time—Flinders did not want to create antagonisms. And while the lad could have been a source of valuable information, there was, as he wrote, no justice in keeping him. He therefore took the boy ashore, gave him clothing and other presents, while Woga promised earnestly to bring back the axe, and let him go.

'As far as two hundred yards, he walked away lieusurely; but then, looking first behind him, took to his heels with all his might, leaving us no faith in the fulfilment of his pathetic promises'.[4]

The next morning the final observations were made, the tents struck and the equipment embarked. The botanists made a last, undisturbed excursion ashore, and with wood and water complete in the hold, the ship was made ready for sea.

Flinders described the easternmost point of Arnhem Land as 'a smooth, grassy projection ... no where of much elevation',[5] as on 11 February 1803 the *Investigator* sailed past. The first known sighting of Arnhem Land by a European navigator was in 1623, when Willem Joosten van Colster brought his ship *Arnhem* along its coast, which he took for a series of islands. On the Dutch chart the point bore no name, so Flinders called it Cape Arnhem. From here the Australian continent trends steadily to the west. Cape Arnhem therefore marks the western entrance, or exit, of the Gulf of Carpentaria, although Flinders considered his exploration of the gulf finished some 40 miles farther to the northwest, at what he was to call Point Wilberforce.

First, however, he rounded today's Gove Peninsula and entered Melville Bay, 'the best harbour we found in the Gulph of Carpentaria'.[6] Its entrance was wide and free from danger, the bottom of mud or sand a good holding ground with sufficient depth that 'four or five sail might swing there in perfect security'. Flinders and the botanists examined the area, where they found mosquitos and sandflies 'numerous and fierce'. Worse were the small green ants that made their nests in the bushes: 'In forcing our way amongst the underwood, we sometimes got our hair and clothes filled with them; and as their bite is very sharp, and their vengeance never satisfied, there was no other resource than stripping as expeditiously as possible'.[7]

Mineral deposits of commercial value were of great interest to the British government and to Banks personally, and Robert Brown examined the rocks on the north side of the bay, finding granitic stone mixed with quartz, mica and coarse garnets. Traces of iron were discovered elsewhere, but the enormous wealth of bauxite in this ground was neither suspected nor understood.

The *Investigator* headed north for Cape Wilberforce on 17 February, and in heavy rain and with endless tacking under double-reefed top- and mainsails against a strong west-northwesterly wind, rounded the cape and sailed southwest along the coast; '. . . thus', Flinders wrote, 'was the examination of the Gulph of Carpentaria finished, after employing one hundred and five days in coasting along its shores and exploring its bays and islands'.[8]

Flinders now had to consider seriously what action he would take next with his decaying ship and exhausted men. Before he could come to any decision, however, a startling sight appeared. The *Investigator* was steering through a narrow strait between a mangrove-covered foreshore and a nearly parallel chain of moderately high islands. Near the closest island they saw first a canoe full of men, and then at the south end of the same island, 'six vessels covered over like hulks, as if laid up for the bad season'[9] with, as Good noted, 'some Canoes paddling about them'.[10]

Obviously these were the people whose traces of all kinds the *Investigator*'s men had so often come across, but who were they? Conjecture ran through the ship. Flinders had thought that they might be Chinese fishermen. Now the covered-up vessels made him think with real apprehension that they were pirates, hiding here among the islands to emerge when the weather permitted or some prey appeared. The *Investigator* worked up closer. The men were at quarters and the ship's pennant and ensign were run up. In response, each of the strange craft hung out a small white flag. As the *Investigator* came to anchor within musket shot, the whaleboat was lowered and, with an armed crew, Samuel Flinders approached the vessels.

The *Investigator*'s company watched every movement on the whaleboat and on the vessel that she came alongside. The meeting seemed peaceable. Samuel stepped back into his boat and returned to the ship. The vessels, he said, were 'prows', that is, praus, from Macassar, now Makasar, on the Indonesian island of Sulawesi. Promptly afterwards the six captains of the praus came across in a canoe and boarded the *Investigator*. Through sheer coincidence, Flinders's cook, Abraham Williams, was, in Matthew's word, a Malay, and able to interpret. The chief of the six praus was a short, elderly man called Pobassoo. His squadron of six vessels was part of a fleet of sixty with some 1000 men, belonging to the Rajah of Boni and commanded by one Salloo, which were then on the coast diving for trepang, or *bêches-de-mer*.

Portrait of Probasso or Pobassoo, Macassan chief, by William Westall. Pobassoo's squadron of six praus was part of a fleet of some 60 boats and 1000 men that came annually to the Australian north coast for trepang or bêches-de-mer. *(R4366, by permission of the National Library of Australia)*

Dried, smoked and sailed at the end of the season to an Indonesian meeting place, the trepang was sold to merchants arriving yearly in junks from China, where it was prized as medicine and an aphrodisiac.

The fishing fleet had been coming to these shores for twenty years, said Pobassoo, who, one of the first, was now on his sixth or seventh voyage. He had never seen a ship here before, nor did he know of a European settlement in the country. Westall, intrigued by the novelty of the meeting, made sketches of the praus and their crews and drew Pobassoo's portrait, depicting the calm dignity of his broad, weathered face.

The captains were taken through the *Investigator*, in which they showed much interest despite, being Muslims, their horror at the hogs kept in the ship's launch. They did, however, accept a drink of port wine and requested another bottle on their departure at sunset. The night was windy and wet, but the *Investigator* was kept in readiness for possible attack with the carronades manned.

In the morning Flinders boarded Pobassoo's vessel with 'two of the gentlemen', presumably Brown and Bauer, and his cook-interpreter Williams, and afterwards the six captains again visited the *Investigator*, while their men gathered in canoes around the ship to barter. Just before noon five more praus sailed into the roadstead and additional canoes crowded about the *Investigator.* This particular anchorage was the trepangers' first stop on the coast, where they filled their bamboo sections with fresh water before entering the Gulf of Carpentaria.

Flinders was eager to learn all he could about their activities and Pobassoo answered his numerous questions patiently, even delaying his squadron's departure by a day. The fleet, he said, travelled with the monsoonal winds, their only navigational instrument, as Flinders discovered, a small Dutch compass. Nor was the work without its hazards. One of their vessels had been lost the year before, and on being shown a rudder that the *Investigator*'s people had picked up, the captains recognised it. There were also skirmishes with the Gulf's inhabitants. Pobassoo had once been speared in the knee and on this voyage one man had been slightly wounded. Pobassoo's vessel carried two small brass cannon, but the others had only muskets, and at the captains' request the *Investigator*'s gun crew fired a carronade.

In return for their courtesies, Pobassoo and his captains were given coveted iron tools and, on the chief's asking for one, an 'English jack, which he afterwards carried at the head of his squadron'.[11] He also asked for a letter, presumably describing their friendly meeting, to show any other ship that he might encounter, and Flinders therefore wrote a letter for Pobassoo to give to Baudin, who could be expected in the Gulf shortly.

At daybreak the next morning there was considerable commotion among the praus as they raised their tall, rectangular sails and headed up the channel on the track that the *Investigator* had just left. Despite the interesting diversion of the encounter, Flinders was glad not to be surrounded by large numbers of armed men. Commemorating the meeting, however, he named that section of the channel Malay Road and the island in the lee of which the trepangers had sheltered, Pobassoo's Island. From a position on the island Westall drew the sweep of the channel, the louring sky and the low mainland shore, which he eventually developed into an evocative painting. A spot of colour on the foreground shore depicts one of Pobassoo's men with his red wrap blowing in the wind.

For two weeks the *Investigator* remained in the principal channels of the island chain Flinders eventually called the English Company Islands in recognition of the financial assistance he had received from the East India Company. With the *Investigator* frequently at anchor, Flinders, variously accompanied by Westall, Bauer and Bell, took the whaleboat to explore shores and islands. They worked despite heavy downpours of rain, spent disagreeable nights wet and ferociously attacked by humming clouds of famished mosquitos, and on one occasion would have gone entirely without food except for Bongaree's spearing of fish. There was a frightening interval when the *Investigator* grounded on a soft shoal in opaque brown water but she got off without apparent injury. It is obvious that no one realised their great good fortune in not encountering one of the fiercely destructive cyclones that are often part of the monsoonal season in northern Australia. Of this feature of the Australian weather pattern they were probably entirely unaware.

On 5 March the *Investigator* quitted Arnhem Bay and the English Company Islands and headed north. Thirty miles on they passed through another chain of islands, later named Wessel's Islands by Flinders, without further investigation.

23
The Journey Back

The weather was changing. Grey rain clouds had lifted and a steady east wind was blowing. It appeared that the northwest monsoon was finished and the southeasterly trades had commenced. Conditions for the continued survey of the north were excellent, the land itself had become much more varied and interesting and this was a coast that Flinders was specifically instructed to survey, seeking harbours and sea lanes for the East India Company. This, above all, was what he wanted to do. Deferring the journey south would also mean avoiding an arrival on the southern coast in June with its rough winter seas, dangerous indeed for a ship in the *Investigator*'s state.

Much, however, was against this. Three months had passed since Aken and the carpenter had delivered their opinion 'that in from eight to twelve months there will scarcely be a sound timber in her', and reaching Port Jackson would require an additional two or three months. His crew were exhausted and many were unwell. Knowing that the leaky state of the *Investigator* might require even greater exertion from everyone, Flinders asked the surgeon to report on the fitness of the ship's company.

Bell found 22 men with symptoms of scurvy—spongy gums and livid sores on the legs, although only four or five were actually ill. Bell recommended a course of lime juice. On bringing up the cases, however, they found many of the bottles broken and, as no quantity of citrus fruit could be expected in Port Jackson as a replacement, Flinders, his future charting always on his mind, decided to keep what was left of his principal anti-scorbutic because the 'next expedition, if we should be able to get another ship, would probably be much longer than the present one'.[1] He had not relinquished his plans.

For some three months many of the ship's company had also been suffering from diarrhoea, which Bell attributed to hot, wet and humid weather. As well, the men were simply worn out. The effort demanded by close surveying was considerable and almost continuous. Flinders himself had serious problems. In his first direct mention of scurvy on board, he wrote that scorbutic ulcers on his feet were making it impossible for him to climb to the masthead, even to get in and out of a boat. He continued, 'as the whole of the surveying department rested upon me, our further stay was without one of its principal objects'.[2] Characteristically, he would not delegate; he could not accept that anyone else's effort could equal his own.

In his journal Flinders's regret in not completing the survey is heavy with self-censure, for despite his hopes, there was, he acknowledged, 'a possibility, nay perhaps a probability, that I may never again return to accomplish it', and in abandoning his explorations now he would show little of 'that genuine spirit of discovery'. He could not boast, he said, of possessing 'a single spark of that ethereal fire with which the souls of Columbus and Cook were wont to burn!',[3] despite having pursued discovery since reading *Robinson Crusoe* as a boy. Clearly, Cook's achievement remained the frame of reference against which Flinders measured his own accomplishments. Yet there was an important difference in the way these two men had acquired their commissions and in their approach to their tasks. Cook had been selected to command the *Endeavour*; he accepted the appointment and his success in handling the expedition made him the natural choice for the subsequent voyages. Flinders selected himself. He formulated a plan for exploration, brashly made the necessary contact and laid his own proposal before a receptive patron. In this, despite the differences wrought by the passage of three centuries, Matthew Flinders bore a likeness to a Columbus, a Magellan or a Pedro Fernández de Quiros, all of whom fought to win the support of kings, councils and even the Pope for extraordinary plans they themselves had conceived.

If by 'ethereal fire' Flinders meant a passionately desired goal pursued with an unrelenting drive, disregarding even the cost in lives, he was not without it. At this point he had not yet conceded defeat. For the moment, however, there was no alternative but to head for Kupang, the Dutch settlement on the island of Timor.

In the late afternoon of 31 March 1803 Matthew Flinders entered Kupang Roads for the second time, ten and a half years after his first arrival as a midshipman on HMS *Providence*. From an American and a Dutch vessel lying outside the port he received assurance that, as far as they knew, the Peace of Amiens still held; the Netherlands was not at war with Britain. The *Investigator* moved into the harbour. Samuel disembarked to pay his captain's respects to the governor, to make known the ship's needs and to arrange for mutual salutes. He was courteously received and shortly ship and fort each fired the appropriate thirteen guns. By evening a boatload of foodstuffs had arrived. The next day Flinders and three of his officers waited upon Governor Johannes Geisler, with Captain Johnson of the Dutch brig acting as interpreter.

On sailing for Timor Flinders had been stubbornly devising plans by which he could complete his northern survey. He hoped to find in Kupang a ship on which Robert Fowler might sail to England to request from the Admiralty a vessel suitable for finishing the survey, which he would bring to Port Jackson as quickly as possible. In the meantime the *Investigator* would remain at work on the north and northwest coasts through the oncoming period of good weather. She would then return to Sydney in time to meet Fowler and the new exploration vessel. The scheme was precariously dependent on numerous factors, including the state of the *Investigator*. Yet Flinders was encouraged by the fact that the ship had leaked very little since the repairs and caulking at Sweers Island. Further, the carpenter, now directed to bore again into some of the timbers inspected at the time, reported little change. With enough provisions on board, the survey could be resumed.

On arrival, however, Flinders found that an England-bound ship had left Kupang only ten days earlier, and there was no opportunity to send Fowler home. Captain Johnson was willing to take letters to Batavia to be forwarded from there, and Flinders wrote at length to the Admiralty, describing the work and findings of the voyage so far, together with Aken and Mart's report on the condition of the ship and information on the trepang industry. He wrote to Banks, to his agent in London and at length to his friend Christopher Smith, to whom he expressed, as he did to Banks, his hope of getting another ship for the survey. In his letter to Smith he also discussed his prospects of promotion. He was not, he said, looking beyond the rank of post captain whatever the credit he might receive for the execution of the voyage, but added, 'Think not however my good friend, that I have lost my ambition—no, truly, for if to covet honour may be a sin, my spirit is indeed a wicked one'.[4]

He wrote also to his cousin Henrietta Flinders, to Thomas Franklin and to Ann. The mood of these letters was subdued. With Henrietta he dwelt on repaying 'some part of the kindnesses done me in my childhood' by Henrietta and her parents, for it was Henrietta who had brought him to the attention of Captain Thomas Pasley. He went on, 'My brother and myself are in tolerable health, and as far as we can see into futurity, have fair prospects of some little share of eminence. It is now our harvest, and the labour is both heavy and tedious, we hope the fruits will be adequate . . . in two months I expect to be again at Port Jackson, not without the hope of receiving one or more letters from you'.[5]

His letter to Ann was begun while still in the Gulf, loving, rambling, troubled, his feelings laid bare. He wrote much as he had years before, to 'a friend who can feel'. He told her, 'In the evenings I oft take a book, reclining on my little couch, and running o'er some pleasant tale or sentiment, perhaps of love, my mind retraces with delight, our joys, our conversation, our looks, our everything of love'.[6] He had found such a 'tale or sentiment' in Milton's *Paradise Lost*, which with 'delight I last perused . . . But', he added, 'in thee I have more faith than Adam had in Eve . . . how much dearer art thou here than our first mother!' For Ann had not sought their separation as Eve had separated herself from Adam by eating the apple of knowledge. Ann was as a vine whose twining arms had been torn away, to 'lie prostrate, broken; —life scarcely left enough to keep the withered leaf from falling off . . .' The painful, rhapsodical image filled his thoughts, but realities intruded.

He concluded the letter in Kupang, explaining the many transfers it would undergo before it reached her, if it did. He added, 'write to my father saying generally how we proceed, for at this time I am not going to do it . . . Good bye, my love, for two months, until we reach Port Jackson. Pray offer my affectionate regards to Mr. Tyler, thy mother, *my* sister Belle! and to Mrs. Mallison [Ann's grandmother]; and rest assured of the sincere love of thy Mattw Flinders'. He could not bring himself to write to his father, with whom he still felt some estrangement, of anything but success, but a touch of humour remained for young Isabella.

Robert Brown wrote a long letter to Joseph Banks, describing in some detail the voyage, landings, people and the trepang fishing. With his botanical and other scientific endeavours he was again disappointed:

> Our acquisitions in botany are much fewer than I had hop'd for in a country so completely new, the number of species in addition to those we had already observ'd ... scarce amounting to 400, and of these ... the number of absolutely new species hardly amounting to 200 ... In zoology we have not done much ... Our additions in ornithology are exceedingly few ... Minerology continues as barren a field as ever.[7]

Brown was a man to whom the natural sciences, especially botany, were virtually the sum of existence, and with apparently little private life of his own, he would go on to become one of the outstanding botanists of his time. His high expectations of the voyage on the *Investigator* were never fulfilled and his letters always carried the underlying inference that the opportunities allowed for his research were never enough.

The *Investigator* remained at anchor at Kupang until 8 April. Local boats ferried out water and food supplies. But there were no salt provisions, the essential fare of a long voyage. No extended explorations on the north coast could be considered without them.

The social niceties, however, were observed. Flinders entertained the governor and others on board and, with his principal officers and the botanical gentlemen, dined ashore with the governor, 13-gun salutes booming across the harbour on both occasions. With the governor's permission the botanists and the artists ranged short distances into the countryside.

On the final day, with work on the *Investigator* finished, part of the ship's company went ashore. By evening Abraham Williams the cook and Mortlake, a lad from Port Jackson, had failed to return. The town was searched without result, and Fowler made a second fruitless attempt in the morning. The *Investigator* stretched out of Kupang Bay without her deserters.

Flinders's instructions from the Admiralty had included directions 'to examine as particularly as circumstances would allow, the bank which extends itself from the Trial Rocks to Timor'. The Trial Rocks derived their name from the English ship *Trial*, which had been wrecked on them in 1622, but their location was unknown, appearing differently on different charts. Flinders thought the bank could have been confused with the great Sahul Shoal between Timor and Australia. Nevertheless, he sailed southwest from Timor, sounding every two hours but finding no bottom with 100–240 fathoms of line.

Then, accepting the position of the Trial Rocks to be 20°40'S and 104°30'E as laid down on a chart published by Arrowsmith, he steered for that location. For five days the *Investigator* sailed back and forth, with no soundings even at considerable depths and no sightings that suggested an outcrop of land. After a final all-day search on 27 April, Flinders laid his course to the south-southwest. He had spent twelve days in the search.[8]

With the *Investigator*'s departure from Kupang, the weather had deteriorated. Rain enveloped the ship. Thunder and lightning raced through dark and heavy skies. The men were falling sick. By 21 April ten crewmen were down with fever and diarrhoea and many others were ill although less seriously affected. Six days later so many officers were stricken that Flinders tried to ease everyone's burden by dividing the crew into three watches and the officers into four. Every effort was made to keep the ship dry and well-aired, and the sick clean and as comfortable as possible in their hammocks. Still the disease took more victims. Flinders thought that the cause lay in the change of diet—fresh meat, vegetables and fruit procured at Timor to combat that other dreaded sickness, scurvy. Then the water obtained at Kupang, their only water, became suspect.

For eight days the *Investigator* ran steadily southwest, heading across the Indian Ocean hundreds of miles from the Australian coast. Then, in rain and a southwesterly, the course was altered for the southeast and Cape Leeuwin. As day broke on 14 May, Flinders saw once more the southwesternmost point of Terra Australis. He steered along the coast at a distance of something over 20 miles, sighting remembered landmarks when the haze thinned.

On 17 May Peter Good wrote in his journal, 'past noon departed this life Charles Douglas Boatswain of a Dysentery with which he had laboured since the middle of Aprile—Self and several of the Crew labouring under the Same disorder'.[9] Charles Douglas was the ship's first loss to sickness. Peter Good, clinging to life, made no more entries.

In traversing once more the sea off the continent's south coast, Flinders saw a precious opportunity to fill in sections of his charts that had been left incomplete in 1801–02. The first of these was along the outer islands of the Archipelago of the Recherche, where he could also stop at Middle Island, and its adjacent little Goose Island, to obtain geese as fresh food for the sick, seal oil for lamps and, from the lake on Middle Island, some casks of salt.

The *Investigator* began her cautious passage among the rocks and islands of the archipelago on the morning of 17 May, Flinders confirming or correcting positions he had previously charted. As noted by Good, Charles Douglas died; Flinders gave his name to the islets they were passing. By six in the evening the ship was anchored in Middle Island's Goose Island Bay. Douglas was buried in Middle Island's sandy earth and the ship's company dispersed across the island and, despite heavy surf, onto nearby islets on their various tasks. Seals were killed and boiled down, but the geese were few, while the salt in the lake had been largely dissolved, probably by recent rains. A hole dug to find fresh water to replace the water from Timor yielded only brine.

There was further difficulty. As the ship weighed to depart at daylight on the 21st, she was caught by a sudden, fresh northwest breeze and dragged towards some rocks. In the frantic effort to control her, two bower anchors were lost before jib and staysails could be run up and the rocks cleared by a few fathoms. During the day William Hillier, quartermaster, a 'quiet, good man', died of fever and dysentery.

Flinders shaped his course generally towards the southeast and Bass Strait. There were, however, several surveys, unfinished the year before, that he wanted to make on the way. He had seen from a hilltop but had not explored the south side of Kangaroo Island. He had not charted the mainland from Cape Northumberland to Cape Otway, passed during a storm. Useful surveying could also be done at Hunter's Isles in Bass Strait and in the Furneaux group, where there were rocks and islands laid down on the charts with questionable accuracy by various captains, including some he himself had positioned incorrectly from the *Norfolk*. The weather held good and the *Investigator* was at no time leaking more than 5 inches an hour, 'but', as he wrote in his officially published book, 'the sickly state of my people from dysentery and fever, as also of myself, did not admit of doing any thing to cause delay in our arrival at Port Jackson'.[10] His decision, however, was not as straightforward as this.

On 26 May he had noted, 'This day James Greenhalgh, serjeant of marines, died of the dysentery; a man whom I sincerely regretted, from the zeal and fidelity with which he had constantly fulfilled the duties of his situation'.[11] There were then fifteen who were very ill and many others simply unwell.

Flinders's wish to extend his survey would have been discussed by the officers. There is no record of their reactions except in the case of Surgeon Bell, and Bell's reaction was explosive. Hugh Bell was not a popular man, apparently brusque and ungracious. He was regarded by Flinders, even at the outset of the voyage, as the only exception to an otherwise congenial group. Nevertheless, Bell was evidently a conscientious ship's surgeon. He had conferred with Flinders on several occasions in their joint effort to maintain the health of the crew, and only days earlier had made, as Flinders said, the 'well-judged' suggestion that cables kept coiled between decks could be moved to provide more sleeping and messing space for the men. Accordingly, Flinders had the cables put in the hold with the many now empty casks. Through the cooperation of the two men the decks were washed almost every morning with boiling water and sprinkled with vinegar, and with outside temperatures dropping, stoves were kept going night and day to dry and warm the air for the sick.

Now Bell began a daily correspondence with Flinders that immediately became a bitterly acrimonious exchange. Bell's five letters are not extant, but their content can be surmised from Flinders's four replies, in which he quoted Bell. The surgeon began by telling Flinders that he should proceed to Port Jackson without any delay whatsoever. The sickly state of the ship's company had not affected, and did not seem likely 'to influence your speed'. Evidently the tone of the letter was imperious and rude.

Flinders was very angry. He wrote back to Bell that while the surgeon's concern for his patients was 'very laudable and would have received my warmest approbation', Bell had taken upon himself not only 'to be judge' of what Flinders ought to do, but also 'of the proper mode of doing it'.[12] This was a trespass upon the captain's authority, an infringement upon his rule of the quarterdeck and the decisions made there. The extent and the aloneness of his responsibility for this tiny, solitary world on an empty ocean demanded and was compensated for by deference to his judgement. The surgeon had no part in his decisions, he wrote Bell. The decision to go directly to Port Jackson had already been made and did not require the surgeon's views. In all this, Matthew Flinders was at one with probably every other ship commander in the Royal Navy or, in fact, on any other seagoing vessel. An accusation of failure in his duty to his ship and her people also involved that very crucial element of a naval officer's make-up, his honour, which was challenged. As well, it disputed Flinders's own view of himself as a humane and considerate officer. Bell seemed to want 'to raise yourself a character of Humanity, by putting a malignant stigma upon mine'.[13]

There was a divergence in the duty of a surgeon and a commander, which Flinders pointed out:

> Your duty must necessarily coincide with humanity towards the ship's company in all cases, whereas that of a Commander may be either diametrically opposite in the case of exposing them to great danger; or it may be so in part, such as at the present time to sacrifice a few days to accomplish a particular object in order to prevent the necessity of a future expedition. Had the health of the people been the great object of my duty as it is yours, and I had been permitted to follow my own plan for their preservation, I should certainly have left them on shore in their native country, and not have exposed them to the danger of the seas and enemies and to pernicious changes of climate, to all of which the execution of my orders makes it necessary.[14]

Evidently Bell's reply only roused Flinders's ire further, and spurred an answer similar to the first. It seems possible that others were drawn into both sides of the quarrel. In his final letter Flinders wrote, 'I wish to preserve a good understanding with the officers and gentlemen on board, as well as to see them friendly with each other, and am very sorry to see you disinclined to co-operate with me'.[15]

The *Investigator* was now entering Bass Strait and beginning to pass the islands that Flinders wanted to resurvey, but whether from the pressure of Hugh Bell's bitter criticism or the fact that the sick list had acquired yet more names, Flinders did not stop. It was not an easy decision to make. Even for public scrutiny he later wrote:

> It was a great mortification to be thus obliged to pass Hunter's Isles and the north coast of Van Diemen's Land, without correcting their positions in longitude from the errors which the want of a time keeper in the Norfolk had made unavoidable... but when I contemplated eighteen of my men below, several of whom were stretched in their hammocks almost without hope, and reflected that the lives of the rest depended upon our speedy arrival in port, every other consideration vanished; and I carried all possible sail, day and night, making such observations only as could be done without causing delay.[16]

The Kent's Group came in sight, close enough so that the growling of the seals could be heard. 'A set of bearings here would have been essentially useful in fixing the relative positions of these lands, which remained in some degree doubtful; but I dared not lose an hour's fair wind to obtain them'.[17]

On 2 June John Draper, also quartermaster, 'and one of the most orderly men in the ship', died and was committed to sea. Samuel Smith wrote, 'every Day, more distress came upon us in the loss of Men carried off by the Flux'.[18]

The wind veered to the northeast and, under a cloudy sky and sometimes rain, the *Investigator* beat towards Cape Howe. Again the wind turned and the ship ran due north as familiar landmarks began to appear. A day later the ship was once more working slowly against a north wind, as Thomas Smith, a convict seaman, died; 'had the wind continued long in the same quarter', Flinders wrote, 'many others must have followed. Happily it veered to the southward'.[19] At daybreak on 9 June the *Investigator* tacked between the Sydney Heads and at noon came to anchor off Garden Island.

One hundred and sixty years before the conclusion of Matthew Flinders's voyage, Abel Janszoon Tasman had circumnavigated the

Australian continent in a great encircling arc that at times put him thousands of miles from its coast. He saw no part of it other than a section of Tasmania. A close and deliberately planned circumnavigation had now been completed, and hundreds of miles of observed south coast, blank on previous maps, had made the charted shoreline of the continent a virtually continuous line. And the question of a great waterway dividing Terra Australis in two had been answered: it did not exist.

24
The Porpoise

Flinders stepped ashore at the Governor's Wharf and made his slow way on ulcerated feet up the familiar hill to Government House to officially inform King of the return of the *Investigator* and her company. Despite the disappointments of the voyage, King's reception of Flinders was warm and his response to Flinders's requests for assistance was prompt and cooperative. Two topics dominated their conversation: the state of the *Investigator* and arrangements for the sick.

Eleven men were taken off the ship the following day and placed in the colonial hospital under Sydney's principal surgeon, Thomas Jamison. Vegetables and fresh meat, fortunately available at the time, were contracted for regular delivery to those still on board. A daily pint of wine was provided for all those whose health the surgeon felt required it.

Peter Good was too ill to be moved and died on 12 June 1802. The *Sydney Gazette and New South Wales Advertiser* noted that 'a party of marines fired three vollies over the grave'.[1] Flinders asked Brown to take charge of Good's papers and supervise the sale of his books and clothing to the ship's company. His plant specimens were incorporated into Brown's collections. Within a few days Oloff Wastream and John Simmonds, seamen, and Robert Chapman, marine, had also died. Midshipman Thomas Evans, master's mate, was dangerously ill.

For the rest of the *Investigator*'s company the return to Sydney was a subdued affair but one of infinite relief. Bongaree greeted his family with exuberance. Flinders found waiting for him James Inman, the astronomer sent by the Board of Longitude to take the place of John Crosley, who had left the *Investigator* at the Cape of Good Hope almost twenty months earlier. Inman had arrived in Port Jackson well after the *Investigator* had sailed in July 1802, but now joined the ship, took over the timekeepers and principal astronomical instruments and, on Cattle Point, began work with Samuel Flinders to correct recent errors in longitude resulting from different rates in the timekeepers. Neither chronometer was performing dependably.

Sydney Cove seemed crowded with ships—HM armed vessel *Porpoise*, the East India Company Indiaman *Bridgewater*, the merchant ships *Rolla* from Ireland and *Cato* from London, the whaler *Alexander*, the brig *Nautilus* with a cargo of pork from Tahiti, and the *Lady Nelson*, to Flinders's relief, safe and now newly returned from the fledgling Derwent River settlement in Van Diemen's Land. He learned that the French ships, the *Géographe*, the *Naturaliste* and the colonial-built schooner that Baudin had bought and named *Casuarina*, had sailed from Port Jackson on 17 November 1802, four months after his own departure in the *Investigator*.

He would also have learned that within hours of their sailing, Governor King had dispatched Acting Lieutenant Charles Robbins in pursuit of Baudin in the colonial schooner *Cumberland* with a letter concerning the rumour of an intended French settlement in Van Dieman's Land.

Robbins had found the French at King Island, delivered King's missive and, in an excess of zeal, raised the British flag among the tents of the French. Baudin was annoyed, but took no action except to write King courteous public and private letters denying any intention to establish a settlement. The French expedition had remained at King Island into December, the *Naturaliste* sailing for Europe on the eighth and Baudin with the *Géographe* and the *Casuarina* heading for Australia's north at the end of the month.

The ramifications of this affair were considerable. King was convinced of French plans to establish a colony in Van Diemen's Land, and took steps to pre-empt such a move. In September 1803 the governor sent a group to settle at Risdon Cove on the Derwent River. In October 450 marines and convicts arrived at Port Phillip from England under David Collins, and a year later King sent a second party to settle Port Dalrymple, today's Launceston. There were some shifts in the location of the communities, but by the end of 1804 Britain had secure possession of Bass Strait and the southeastern coasts of Australia.

Flinders gave King the survey report on the condition of the *Investigator* drawn up by Aken and Mart in the Gulf of Carpentaria, and requested an immediate additional inspection of the ship. King issued the order at once. The ripping off of a plank just above the waterline around the ship began on 11 June, while appropriate officers were selected and organised for a survey three days later.

Letters from England awaited Flinders, among them one addressed to him in his stepmother's unsteady hand. The letter's announcement of his father's death was a terrible shock. He believed that the rift between them, which had come about over his request for money before his marriage and was aggravated by his father's disapproval of the sudden marriage, had not yet been fully healed. He wrote to Bass, 'to my great regret our good understanding was not complete'.[2] Guilt overlaid grief. He wrote to his stepmother:

> My dearest mother,
>
> ... the joy which some letters occasioned is dreadfully embittered by what you my good and kind mother had occasion to communicate. The death of so kind a father and who was so excellent a man is a heavy blow ... I had laid such a plan of comfort for him as would have tended to make his latter days the most delightful of his life ... Oh, my dearest, kindest father, how much I loved and reverenced you, you cannot now know.[3]

He resumed the letter the next day with assurances of his devotion to her. It was a letter more calculated to comfort and reassure the bereaved than it was truthful:

> As for Samuel and me, we are going on very well laying a sure foundation, I trust, for future fame and fortune. Our voyage has gone prosperously, my credit with the great friends who have pushed me forward seems to increase, and I am getting richer every year. At this time I consider our business to be nearly half done; therefore, as we left England in July, 1801, we ought to arrive again about the same time in 1805; but ... it would be better not to expect us before the end of the year.

Despite the loss of his father, they would 'still be a family, and still be respectable'. In Flinders's mind the responsibility for this unity now lay with him, the eldest son, as required by conventions of the time. His stepmother had evidently written that he inherited from his father £600, and he asked that, until he returned home, the interest of this be applied to the education of his two young half-sisters. The ties of family must, however, include his wife, whose reception in the home at Donington just after their marriage had probably been less than warm: 'That you will cultivate a good understanding with my dear wife I cannot doubt. Those who love or care for me, will love my wife, who is the dearest half of me; for I cannot have any friend who is not a friend to her'.

Flinders then set the letter aside, for no ship was then sailing for England. He finished it fourteen months later and sent it home from Mauritius.

Six letters from Ann, written between December 1801 and September 1802, some containing enclosures from her parents, awaited him in Sydney. It was almost a fortnight after his arrival before Flinders felt able to write in reply, for to her he related something of the sorry tale of death and disappointment, and expressed his own grief.

> Port Jackson, June 25 1803
>
> Grateful for thy recovered health, my dearest love, and grateful to thee for thy many, and long and most dear remembrances of me, which I have received on our arrival here some days since, how shall I express the anguish of my heart at the dreadful havock that death is making all around. How dear is the name of father to an affectionate son . . . how much I loved him, how dreadful is the blow . . . alas, I have lately had too much experience of death's power . . .[4]

He described the condition of his ship: 'it was the unanimous opinion of the surveying officers that had we met a severe gale of wind in the passage from Timor that she must have been crushed like an egg and gone down'. Of himself he wrote, 'I have been lame about four months and was much debilitated in health . . . but am now recovering and shall soon be altogether well'. He went on to write of the men with whom he had shared the journey. Flinders wrote the first draft of his letters in his private letter book, crossing out what he decided to omit in the finished missive. Here the crossed-out sections are in square brackets.

> Mr. Fowler is tolerably well [and is a good-natured fellow and suits me very well,] my brother is also well, becoming steady, and is more friendly and affectionate with me since his knowledge of our mutual loss. Mr. Brown is recovered from ill health and lameness [we are not altogether cordial, but our mutual anxiety to forward the complete success of the voyage is a bond of union; he is a man of abilities and knowledge, but wants feeling kindness.] Mr. Bauer, your favourite, is still polite and gentle [and is so to a considerable depth, but I fear there is a dreadful disposition at the bottom].
>
> Mr. Westall wants prudence, but is good natured; the last two are well and have always remained upon good terms with me. Mr. Bell is misanthropic, and pleases nobody [he may possibly leave us]. Elder continues to be faithful and attentive as before. I like him and apparently he likes me. ... Trim, like his master, is becoming grey. He is at present fat and frisky, and takes meat from our forks with his former dexterity; he is commonly my bedfellow. The master we have in poor Thistle's place, is an easy good-natured man [whom you do not know].
>
> ... I shall be better able in a few weeks to say how the voyage will be prosecuted, and how soon we may probably return ...

Flinders never explained his changed opinion of Bauer.

There were paragraphs expressing his gratitude for Ann's love:

> Thou has shewn me how very ill I have requited they tender love in several cases. I cannot excuse myself now but will plead for respite until my return, when in they dear arms I will beg for pardon and if thou canst forgive me all, will have it sealed with ten thousand kisses. If I could laugh at the effusions of they tenderness, it would be to me the idolatrous language thou frequently usest to me. Thou makest an idol, and then worshippest it ... Thinkest thou not my dearest love that I shall be spoiled by thy endearing flatteries?

As she had done before, Ann accused him of allowing ambition to separate them. He replied, 'so soon as I can ensure for us a moderate portion of the comforts of life, thou wilt see whether love or ambition have the greatest power over me. [In the meantime believe me, oh truly believe me that I pursue discovery only to avoid the future necessity of parting from thee.]' Did Flinders question his own honesty when he struck out that last sentence? Perhaps with more basic truth, he reminded her, 'Before thou was mine, I had engaged in this voyage . . .' and added, 'without it we could not live'.

This letter too he put aside. It also accompanied him to Mauritius and with a long postscript was finally sent to Ann in 1804.

On 14 June Flinders accompanied the officers appointed by King to conduct the survey of the *Investigator*, Acting Lieutenant William Scott, commander of the *Porpoise*, E. H. Palmer, captain of the *Bridgewater*, and Thomas Moore, master builder of the colony. Flinders was appalled at the extent of the decay in the uncovered timbers. 'In the starboard bow there were thirteen close together, through any one of which a cane might have been thrust'.[5] In the southerly breezes along the south coast the *Investigator* had heeled to port, keeping the starboard bow out of water, so the leaks were minimal. Had the wind come from the north, the pumps were not likely to have been able to keep up with the inflow. In a hard gale the ship would have gone to the bottom. The surveyors' report unequivocally condemned the ship. The three men were 'unanimously of opinion that she is not worth repairing in any country, and that it is impossible in this country to put her in a state fit for going to sea'.[6]

Flinders then wrote officially to King, requesting a vessel for the completion of the coastal survey. The governor, too, had been shocked by the extent of the rot in the *Investigator*, and long discussions followed at Government House on how Flinders's work could be completed, for there remained to be fully charted certain islands in Bass Strait, the Cumberland Islands on the east coast, Torres Strait and the extensive north, northwest and west coasts. The ships available in the colony were considered, all of those under his authority generously offered by King, if they met Flinders's needs.

The roomy, 462-ton *Buffalo*, which possibly would have been Flinders's first choice, was, however, on a voyage to the Moluccas, Penang and Calcutta to purchase cattle and horses, and was not expected to return until January 1804. In fact, she did not return until June of that year.

In the harbour was the privately owned *Rolla*, for which her captain quoted the exorbitant purchase price of £11 500, and it was estimated that refitting her for a survey voyage would take some six months. Further, the *Rolla* had run aground in England with a full cargo, and could have developed undetected weaknesses. The price was more than King felt he could authorise, and the delay was precisely what Flinders wanted to avoid.

A combination of the *Lady Nelson* and the schooner *Francis* was another possibility, but both were small and would need frequent reprovisioning on the north coast, with numerous time-consuming trips to Timor. And the *Francis* was believed to require extensive repairs. There remained the armed vessel *Porpoise*, 308 tons burden and once a Spanish prize. Although only a little smaller than the *Investigator*, her interior construction was such that the space was insufficient for all Flinders's people. This, however, could be compensated for by having the *Lady Nelson* in company, manned by members of the *Investigator*'s crew. At the time both vessels were either away or just departing on colonial business, and while no final decision could be made until their return, Flinders apparently felt that a possible solution had been found.

With preparations for the voyage deferred, in late June Flinders went to the Hawkesbury settlement for some days of rest. As he wrote, 'the fresh air there, with a vegetable diet and medical care soon made a great alteration in the scorbutic sores which had disabled me for four months'.[7] No further details on this visit seem to exist. At the beginning of July he returned to Sydney, nearly recovered.

On 4 July the *Porpoise* returned from Van Diemen's Land. Flinders promptly wrote to the governor formally accepting for his continued explorations the offer of the *Porpoise* and a colonial vessel, most likely the *Lady Nelson*, as tender. He also asked that the *Porpoise* be surveyed to ascertain that she could in a short time be made sound enough to take the weather at sea for the two and a half years he estimated the voyage would require. King immediately issued the order for the survey to John Aken, Russell Mart and Thomas Moore. Three days later their findings were presented in writing to King. The report shattered Flinders's hopes. The repairs needed to make the *Porpoise* fit to take the risks of weather at sea for two and a half years would take no less than twelve months to complete. In addition, her copper, irreplaceable in Port Jackson, was partly gone.

King repeated the other options, none of them suitable or available in any time frame that Flinders could accept. King added that if Flinders rejected the *Porpoise*, he intended to send her to England, a journey which it was judged she could accomplish without renovation. If Flinders wished, he could travel with her to England to apply to the Admiralty for another ship to complete the survey. This proposal Flinders accepted. He would travel as a passenger, requesting only that the journey be made by way of Torres Strait and that he be given the full cooperation of the commanding officer in completing the survey of the route he had found. Without the responsibility of command he would also be able to work on his charts and reports during the long trip home.

Meanwhile the decommissioning of the *Investigator* progressed. Rigging was removed and stowed below, topmasts and topgallant masts were struck, main and mizzen tops lowered and stowed. The ship's general upkeep continued, and each Sunday the crew were mustered and inspected for cleanliness and parties sent ashore to attend church. Flinders had not conducted Sunday services on board, but apparently at this point thought it appropriate to send the men to worship. Of the *Investigator*'s sick, a few had returned to duty, some were convalescing, two were still very ill. There was another death when a marine sentry at the gangway fell asleep, tumbled overboard and drowned.

Flinders sought out his acquaintances in Sydney. To his profound disappointment George Bass had sailed from Port Jackson the previous February. Bass, however, had left two letters for Flinders with a sick and 'wholly dispirited' Charles Bishop, who remained in Sydney. The trading venture in which Bass, Bishop and their associates had made a very major investment had not met with success. On arriving from England in the *Venus*, Bass and Bishop found Sydney to be, unusually, glutted with the very goods they had brought. Seeking to meet their considerable financial obligations, Bass had obtained from Governor King a contract to import salt pork from the Pacific Islands, and, with his merchandise in government storage, had sailed for Tahiti and the Hawaiian islands.

His initial voyage was profitable. He sold his salt pork, 10 000 pounds of it going to Baudin's expedition then in port. In addition to further pork importation, the energetic Bass arranged several new speculative schemes, ranging from establishing a fishery in New Zealand to the purchase of the hull of the brig *Norfolk,* wrecked at Tahiti, which Bass thought could be rebuilt for his pork trade.

Bass had also received from King a certificate addressed to the Spanish commander of any South American port, authorising Bass to purchase for the colony of New South Wales food and livestock for breeding purposes. This, as King explained in a dispatch to Lord Hobart of the Colonial Office, meant 'guanacoes from the coast of Peru', animals which were hoped to become a food source in New South Wales. These were the stated objectives of the voyage, but evidently there was more in Bass's mind. On 1 January 1803 he wrote to his friend and brother-in-law, Henry Waterhouse, 'The voyage before me is not altogether for pork. I mean to cross the South Pacific upon a venture; with the prospect that if a failure happens there, the original pork voyage to the Sandwich Isle, are again before me'.[8]

On 5 January he wrote to Waterhouse with more detail. He hoped to buy guanacos and 'pacos', perhaps alpacas, or cattle, but if he could find no Spanish governor who would permit this, he would resort to another cargo of pork from the Pacific Islands. 'That is the worst prospect', he wrote. Then he added in Spanish words to the effect that depending on how long he remained in the ports of New Spain, he would not be idle with respect to 'commercio secreto', for which he was prepared and ready.[9] It was a curious addition to a letter otherwise written in English.

Spanish authorities in South America permitted the purchase of food by British ships, but the importation and sale of foreign goods were illegal and severely punishable. Governor King had described to Lord Hobart the experience of the little brig *Harrington*, captained by William Campbell, when it carried a quantity of goods to the 'coast of Peru and Chili, . . . he was chased by an armed vessel, which took his ship's boat and thirteen men'.[10] Although the *Harrington* returned to Sydney after Bass had sailed, it was common knowledge that merchandise brought into South America was considered contraband.

Bass, it seems, had decided to take the risk. Apparently carrying items of his unsold trade goods, he sailed in command of the *Venus* on 5 February 1803. Flinders, arriving in Sydney four months later, received his friend's letters and wrote in reply, commenting on Bass's enterprise and describing his own voyage and its further prosecution, his hopes for advancement despite peace in Europe and the possible non-completion of his survey. He remarked on Henry Waterhouse, who was succumbing to drink: '. . . his sun seems to have passed the meridian, if they say true'.[11] Flinders also expressed his continued disappointment in his brother Samuel, who, he wrote, 'I hope may be something above the common-run of his class; he is however yet below it in some points'. On his departure two months later, Flinders left with Governor King this last letter to his friend, which Bass, vanishing into the Pacific, would never claim. In spite of rumours and speculation, serious enquiries made over many years, most persistently by Bass's father-in-law, William Waterhouse, yielded no substantiated explanation for his disappearance.

Warmly entertained by the Kings, Flinders also saw the Patersons and Elizabeth Macarthur, whose husband was in England. Of the vindictive quarrels among members of these families he wrote regretfully to William Kent's wife, Eliza, who maintained a busy correspondence with their friends. He felt great uneasiness, he said, 'that the Colonel and Mrs. P___ should be upon terms of disagreement with [the Kings]. There is now Mrs. K___, Mrs. P___ and Mrs. M___, for all of whom I have the greatest regard, who can scarcely speak to each other; it is really a miserable thing to split a small society into such small parts: why do you ladies meddle with politics? but I do not mean *you*'.[12]

On 6 July he wrote a short letter to Elizabeth Macarthur. She had apparently asked him to obtain information on legal procedures relative to the sale of some cattle. Flinders consulted the *Encyclopaedia Britannica*, contributed by Banks to the *Investigator*'s library, and from this and 'what I can hear' offered his advice. A fortnight later he wrote again, expressing his regret that the governor's illness and his own business were preventing his visit to Parramatta. The *Porpoise* would sail shortly and he was going home with the promise of 'fortune's smiles, and with the delightful prospect of enfolding one to whom my return will be a return of happiness'.[13] For his 'dear friend' he wished the

Almighty Power to impart the fortitude she needed to carry alone the responsibilities of a large family, and that she would soon hear the 'glad salutes' of her returning husband and children.

Two members of the expedition now wrote letters expressing dissatisfaction with the journey on the *Investigator*. To Joseph Banks Brown wrote, 'I confess I am upon the whole disappointed'.[14] Neither high mountains nor navigable rivers had been seen. On shore, he added, 'very frequently my time has been so much limited that but little could be done'. He raised again Flinders's failure to meet his requests for better storage facilities for his botanical specimens, adding, however, that 'I am inclin'd to impute his conduct . . . more to his total inexperience in these matters . . .'

Brown's comments on his associates were typically astringent. Mr Allen was 'really of very little use'. With Mr Westall he had nothing to do professionally, adding that the artist was bringing home a small collection of plants that Banks would see 'if you think proper . . . I suppose . . . there is nothing that I have not got'. Even the invaluable Peter Good 'was in the habit of collecting everything which had the least appearance of being ripe, and from an examination of several I am convinced he was often mistaken'.

William Westall was particularly displeased. On 31 January 1804 he wrote to Banks. The voyage to New Holland had not met with his expectations, although they had not been high. But he would have been fully recompensed for the long period spent 'on that barren coast, by the richness of the South Sea Islands which on leaving England I had reason to suppose we should have winter'd at instead of Port Jackson. I was not aware the voyage was confined to New Holland only had I known this I most certainly would not have engaged in a hazardous voyage where I could have little opportunity of employing my pencil with any advantage to myself or my employers'.[15]

Actually, Westall did apply his pencil satisfactorily to the coastline scenes that were a principal part of his assignment. The quality of his other sketches apparently depended on his interest in the subject, and in his figures and portraits his classical draughtsmanship sometimes conflicted with reality. Visiting the Pacific islands was, in Flinders's instructions, a final option, merely a possibility, but apparently one that young Westall had taken to heart.

On 7 July the *Investigator* was warped into Sydney Cove to lay down a pair of chain moorings. Here she was secured. The *Porpoise* was moored alongside to allow the easy transfer of men and stores. William Scott, commander of the *Porpoise*, and some of his men had chosen to be discharged in Sydney. Governor King then appointed Robert Fowler to the command of the *Porpoise* and necessary officers and crew were selected and transferred from the *Investigator*. On the eighth Flinders went aboard. With him as passengers went 21 other men from the *Investigator*, including Samuel Flinders, John Aken, John Allen, William Westall, Flinders's servant John Elder and the midshipmen, except for Thomas Evans, who remained in hospital. Flinders's cat Trim, carried aboard, quickly found his niche in yet another king's ship.

Robert Brown and Ferdinand Bauer asked to remain in New South Wales to pursue their work until Flinders's return with another ship or the arrival of new instructions within eighteen months of the *Porpoise*'s departure. Their servants remained with them. Initially John Allen, too, had decided to stay, but changed his mind. As Hugh Bell, in King's words to Flinders, 'is recommended by you for a Passage to England in the Bridgewater',[16] the surgeon was discharged from the *Investigator* into the merchant ship. Of the nine convict volunteers taken aboard the *Investigator* as crew the year before, one had died and another had behaved so poorly that Flinders could not recommend him to the governor. The other seven were given their liberty, and four now joined the *Porpoise*. Their rehabilitation, however, had not been entirely successful. Flinders later wrote, 'the subsequent behaviour of two was different to what it had been when their liberty was at stake, and... a third was condemned to the hulks not very long after he reached England'.[17] A few other seamen of the *Investigator* decided to remain in Sydney.

Through the later part of July, with several days of rain finally clearing, stores, furniture and the men's bedding and chests were transferred from the *Investigator* to the *Porpoise*. Some equipment was left on the *Investigator* in the care of Robert Colpitts, the gunner, who remained in Sydney. Other items were to be taken to the commissariat store for reissue to other ships. Meanwhile fresh provisions were delivered to the *Porpoise*. Westall's drawings went on board, as did Flinders's charts and journals, placed in a cabin that was built for Flinders on the upper deck.

Flinders entrusted copies of his charts to the governor and in March 1804 these left Sydney in the hands of King's secretary, William Chapman, travelling to England in HMS *Calcutta*. They were duly delivered to the Admiralty's Hydrographical Office in London, where Alexander Dalrymple set them aside with other maps by Flinders. As was his habit, Flinders had identified most geographical features with numbers and letters, evidently assuming that the Admiralty would provide the nomenclature. The Hydrographical Office, however, considered the explorer's input necessary for the task of naming.

The *Investigator*'s greenhouse was reconstructed on the *Porpoise*'s quarterdeck for the living plants, with a man from Port Jackson hired to care for them, while boxes of seeds and a puncheon packed with dried specimens went into the hold. Brown, typically, had serious misgivings as to the safety of his specimens.

A scrap of news from the outside world reached Sydney when, on 16 July, the snow *Adele* arrived from Mauritius with the information that the British had evacuated the Cape of Good Hope, returning it to the Dutch. That this important stopover site on the route from England to Australia was no longer in British hands was not welcome news.

As dusk gathered over Sydney Cove on 22 July 1803 Flinders concluded his final entry in the logbook of the *Investigator*: 'and into the Porpoise for a passage to England, the Commander & remaining officers & people . . . At sunset, hauld down the pendant'.[18] The hulk *Investigator* was now a storeship permanently moored in Sydney Cove. However, a final chapter in her extraordinary story was yet to come.

At the beginning of August E. M. Palmer, captain of the Indiaman *Bridgewater*, about 750 tons, and John Park, captain of the ship *Cato*, about 450 tons, indicated that they wished their ships to accompany the *Porpoise* through Torres Strait on their way to Batavia. Flinders wrote, 'The company of these ships gave me pleasure; for if we should be able to make a safe and expeditious passage through the strait with them, of which I had but little doubt, it would be a manifest proof of the advantage of the route discovered in the Investigator, and tend to bring it into general use'.[19]

25
Shipwreck

There was a holiday atmosphere on 10 August when the governor and his party boarded the *Porpoise* to accompany her as far as the Sydney Heads. The ship weighed and made sail down the harbour, where she was joined by the *Bridgewater* and *Cato*, the little convoy enthusiastically escorted by many of the colony's small boats. Just before the heads the *Porpoise* hove to. Flinders wrote, 'I took leave of my respected friend the governor of New South Wales, and received his dispatches for England . . .'[1] The governor then left the *Porpoise* amid cheers from the men on the three ships, 'and lieutenant Fowler having received a small code of signals to the Bridgewater and Cato, we sailed out of Port Jackson together'.

Light breezes gave way to steady favourable winds, and by noon on 17 August, with the *Porpoise* leading, the ships had crossed the Tropic of Capricorn and were approximately 320 miles east of Keppel Bay. Soon after two o'clock the *Cato*, some distance off the *Porpoise*'s port quarter, made the signal for land. The *Porpoise*, the faster sailer, signalled for the others to go on and hauled up to look more closely at a small, dry sandbank. Soundings around it found no bottom at 80 fathoms and there was no indication of other reefs. The *Porpoise* resumed her station at the head of the little fleet.

The appearance of the sandbank aroused some concern for the oncoming night, but it seemed an isolated feature at considerable distance from the dangers of the Great Barrier Reef. By evening the ships were 35 miles north of it and no other threat had been seen. There was a fresh southeast breeze under a cloudy sky, and as Flinders later wrote, 'It did not therefore seem necessary to lose a good night's run by heaving to; and I agreed with lieutenant Fowler, that it would be sufficient to make the signal for the ships to run under easy, working sail during the night,—to take our usual station a-head,—and to charge one of the *Investigator*'s warrant officers with the lookout on the fore castle'.[2]

The signals were made and the *Porpoise*'s topsails were double-reefed. At eight o'clock the lead was cast but no bottom found at 35 fathoms. Russell Mart, the *Investigator*'s carpenter, took his place on the forecastle and the master, John Aken, was on the quarterdeck. Flinders, a passenger, was below in the gun room, conversing with some of the officers. The *Porpoise* moved on through the night at 8 knots. At half past nine the *Cato* was a mile away on the port quarter, the *Bridgewater* half a mile on the starboard quarter.

Suddenly there was a cry. Almost at the same instant Aken and Mart had seen the pale glimmer of breakers in the darkness ahead. Instantly the helm was put down, but with only double-reefed topsails set, the *Porpoise* could not come around. Fowler rushed up to the deck. Flinders, thinking it was a fairly commonplace problem with the tiller rope and having no orders to give, remained in the gun room with the others for some minutes. Then, realising it was something more serious, he ran up and saw the sails shaking against the sky, the ship swinging away from the wind and to leeward huge breakers hurling themselves into the darkness.

Helpless, the ship was swept in among the breakers and struck violently. She heeled over on her side, her bottom stove in, surf flying over her. The heave of the ocean raised and dropped her with terrible force, and with the second or third shock the foremast broke away. Through curtains of spray the *Cato* and the *Bridgewater* could be seen at no more than a cable's length (200 yards). Unable in the avalanche of spray across the tilted deck to fire a gun or bring up a light, the *Porpoise*'s people shouted frantically. The other two ships were tacking towards each other. There was deathly silence on the *Porpoise* as the men watched, shocked, scarcely breathing, waiting for a horrendous crash. Then the space between the oncoming ships opened a little and they slid past each other without touching. The *Cato* steered to the northeast, the *Bridgewater* to the south. Exultation swept the *Porpoise* and then horror. Two cables' length away the *Cato* crashed onto the reef. She rolled on her broadside, her masts disappeared into the water, and at that distance in the darkness nothing more could be seen.

Now everyone looked to the *Bridgewater*, for a light burning at the masthead showed that she had cleared the reef. There could be no doubt but that she would tack at once and send her boats to the stricken ships. Then came the realisation that, for the *Bridgewater*'s own safety she could not possibly approach the reef by night and in a fresh wind, nor send boats in among the breakers in the dark.

The men on the *Porpoise* turned their attention to their own perilous position. The ship had heeled towards the coral reef, so the surge of the breakers struck her bottom, surf and spray flying over her without washing heavily across the decks. Clearly she was bilged, and how long the damaged vessel would hold together no one knew. The depth of water on the reef was found to be only a few feet, and to lighten the ship so she might be pushed by the surf higher onto the coral, Fowler ordered the main and mizzen masts and the starboard anchor cut away. Flinders concurred, then reminded him that with the next high tide the ship might slide over the top of the reef into deeper water on the other side. This had occurred with the *Pandora*. Fowler stopped any further lightening.

Under the ship's lee the water was seen to be smooth. Beyond this there was the moving shimmer of breakers but seemingly a quiet surface on the other side. It occurred to Flinders that if the *Bridgewater* was aware that her boats could approach from that side, a rescue might be mounted more quickly. He had no specific responsibility on the *Porpoise* and thought that his influence with Captain Palmer might be greater than anyone else's. He had on occasion written to Palmer; there was obviously an acquaintanceship. Flinders had another reason for wishing to reach the *Bridgewater*. In his account of the wreck that was forwarded by Governor King to the Admiralty, he wrote: 'At this time I spoke to Lieutenant Fowler, the commander of the ship, and told him of my intention to get my charts and log-books of the Investigator's voyage into the small boat and get on board the Bridgewater, and with her boats get the people out of the ship as soon as possible. To this he assented'.[3]

The gig, safely lowered, was lying a short distance from the wreck. Flinders jumped into the water and swam to her. That he got his materials into the gig is clear, but how he kept them dry, or mostly dry, he does not explain. In the little boat he found six men, three who could row and three—the armourer, a cook and a marine—who could not, together with two mismatched oars. The non-rowers bailed frantically with hats and shoes as the gig was run—and nearly swamped—through the breakers into the quiet water beyond. Then, clumsily in the overloaded craft, they began rowing towards the *Bridgewater*'s light.

Very soon, however, they realised that the Indiaman was maintaining her course and speed, and unless she tacked there was no chance of reaching her. They headed back towards the *Porpoise,* meeting eight or nine men in the cutter, which had been holed but the leak partly stopped. Rather than risk another plunge through the surf, the two boats remained rowing gently in the lee of the breakers. Should the *Porpoise* break apart, they would be there to pick up what men they could.

Slowly the long night passed, the men in the boats, all in wet clothing, shivering in a fresh, chill wind. On the reef every rush of the sea violently jarred and drenched the stricken body of the *Porpoise*. Samuel Smith wrote, 'in this mizerable situation we spent the Night, every heart fill'd with Horor, continual Seas dashing over us . . .'[4] Several blue lights were burned. There was no response. At two o'clock in the morning the *Bridgewater*'s light disappeared.

In the greyness of dawn the scene of the shipwreck emerged. The tide was ebbing and the *Porpoise* lay quietly in shallow water on the coral reef. Flinders waded across and, using the fallen masts, climbed on board. That the boats were safe cheered everyone on the ship. Through the night Fowler had had the men build a raft of yards and topmasts, with short ropes all around it, to which people might cling. A cask of water, a chest of provisions, the *Investigator*'s logbooks and a sextant were lashed upon it. With her bottom to the waves, however, the *Porpoise*'s hatches, with their stores and provisions, had remained closed and relatively whole, while her upper deck was deluged but left fairly intact.

Farther along on the reef they could see what remained of the *Cato*, which in striking the coral had heeled so that her upper works, tilted and open, faced the sea, which had surged into her, breaking up decks and bulkheads and washing away everything inside. Only her forecastle and bowsprit were above water, with heavy surf rushing and sucking around them, and here her terrified people were clinging, waving and calling. There were, however, two cheering sights. In the distance the sails of the *Bridgewater* were visible on the horizon. And not more than half a mile away there was a large dry sandbank. It appeared to be about a mile in width and, as they later discovered, it was part of a chain of sand cays and coral reefs stretching farther east and west than could be seen from the *Porpoise*. On subsequent charts they were collectively named Wreck Reef.

Flinders took the gig to the sandbank, where a number of seabird eggs showed that it stood above the high water mark. Sending the gig back to inform Fowler, he fastened two handkerchiefs to a tall oar, which he set up in the sand to attract the notice of the *Bridgewater*. At about ten o'clock, however, the ship apparently went on another tack and was seen no more that day. She had been sighted from both the *Porpoise* and the *Cato*, but whether she had seen the low-lying reef and the wrecks, they did not know.

Fowler, meanwhile, had sent a boat to the wreckage of the *Cato*. With the water now lower around them, Captain Park and his men jumped into the sea and, clinging to planks and spars, swam through the surf to the boat, which carried them to the *Porpoise*. Flinders wrote:

> Several were bruised against the coral rocks, and three young lads were drowned. One of these poor boys, who, in the three or four voyages he had made to sea, had each time been shipwrecked, had bewailed himself through the night as the persecuted Jonah who carried misfortune wherever he went. He launched himself upon a broken spar with his captain; but having lost his hold in the breakers, was not seen afterwards.[5]

Low water came at one o'clock. The reef on which the *Porpoise* lay was dry at a very short distance from the ship, and stores, provisions and clothing were brought up on deck and, despite squalls, transferred to the reef, in Samuel Smith's words, 'with great hardship and Difficulty'.[6] They were then loaded into the boats and rowed to the sandbank. In the midst of it all someone picked up Trim and brought him to the bank. Everyone worked and, before dark, five half hogsheads of water and four or five casks of flour, rice, salt meat and spirits had been landed, together with the sheep and pigs that had survived. Those who

View of the sandbank at Wreck Reef during low water, by William Westall. In August 1803 the vessels Porpoise *and* Cato, *on their way to England, were wrecked on one of the reefs now collectively known as Wreck Reef off the Queensland east coast. Camp was set up on a nearby sandbank, the flag flown upside down as a signal of distress. Flinders later commented that corals shown in the foreground were never actually that much above water. (R1992, by permission of the National Library of Australia)*

had clothing shared with those who did not, Fowler dressing four or five in lieutenants' uniforms, instant 'promotions' that occasioned a good many humorous remarks, as Flinders was glad to see.

At dusk a fire was lit and heaped with pieces of wreckage to warm them through the night. Several times someone thought he saw the *Bridgewater*, but it was evidently only hope and imagination. Finally, under shared blankets and greatcoats, the exhausted men slept on the sand. The two cutters and the gig saved from the *Porpoise* had been drawn up on the sand on the lee side of the bank, but during the night the little gig, not properly secured, was floated off by a tide that came in higher than expected, 'to our great loss'.

In the morning it was clear that the *Porpoise*, although still on the reef, was beyond retrieval, while the remnant of the *Cato* had shattered and all but disappeared. On the sandbank there were 94 men from the two ships, and Flinders, as senior officer present, decided it was both advisable and appropriate that he take command of the entire group. There could not be two communities under two separate commanders on this small place of safety. Fowler and Park agreed without hesitation.

Flinders assembled both ships' companies and informed the *Cato*'s seamen, some of whom had grumbled about working, that as they expected to share in the provisions saved from the *Porpoise*, they would work exactly as did the men of the king's ship and be subject to the same punishments if deviating from obedience and good behaviour. They were then distributed through the *Porpoise*'s messes in the proportion of one to three and Fowler, who was in charge of provisions, was instructed to victual all equally. The surgeon of the *Porpoise* examined the injured and provided a list of seven or eight who, badly cut or bruised on the coral, were unable to work.

Working parties then went off in the two cutters to the *Porpoise* and in the next four days extracted from the wreckage of the ship and ferried to the sandbank all of the vessel's water supply and enough food, together with 225 gallons of spirits, 113 gallons of wine and 60 gallons of porter, to sustain 94 men at full allowance for almost three months. Salvaged stores included a new suit of sails, spars, canvas, iron work, the armourer's forge, a kedge anchor and many smaller items. One chronometer appeared to have been unaffected by the violent motion of the ship as it crashed. Another had stopped and the Arnold No 1736 watch was spoiled by salt water. They also brought onto the cay two swivel guns and several muskets and pistols, with powder, ball and flints, and eventually landed the carronades. Easing their work, the wind moderated and the weather became fine.

On the sandbank a row of tents sprang up, water and provisions securely stored in one large tent made of spars and sails, where Trim was established to guard against such vermin as had come ashore with the goods, and a separate tent raised for each mess of officers and men. On the highest part of the bank a topsail yard was erected as a flagstaff with a large blue ensign hoisted to the peak, union down in a signal of distress. Westall depicted the scene in one of his drawings. One man, a liberated convict, became disorderly. The articles of war were publicly read and he 'was punished at the flagstaff'. There were no further breaches. According to Flinders, 'the men worked cordially together, and in all respects we preserved the same discipline and order as on board His Majesty' ship'.[7]

The *Bridgewater* did not appear, and criticism of Captain Palmer became bitter. Initially Flinders saw Palmer's actions in terms of preserving the safety of his ship. The *Bridgewater* was a large vessel with a draught of about 20 feet, confronted with an uncharted reef. In his first report on the shipwreck, Flinders wrote, 'I was inclined to attribute it to his apprehension of danger which prevented him from thinking reasonably upon the subject; for fear might over-persuade his reason that every one of us had perished . . .'[8]

However, as he reconsidered the circumstances, Flinders's condemnation of Palmer grew. It should be noted, however, that although blue lights had burned on the *Porpoise* during the first night, with daylight no sign that there were survivors had been made other than Flinders's oar with handkerchiefs at the top. Preoccupied with rescuing the *Cato*'s men, with saving stores and provisions and, in Flinders's case, also with preserving his logs and charts, it appears that no one thought of building up the night's fire or perhaps erecting some kind of sail. The upside-down ensign was evidently hoisted a day or two later.

What had transpired on board the *Bridgewater*? After the wreck Palmer abandoned his intended passage through Torres Strait and took his ship north of New Guinea to Batavia and then to Tellicherry in southwest India. Here, months after the event, he filed a report to the Admiralty on the total loss of the *Cato* and *Porpoise* and their people. In *The Orphan*, a Calcutta newspaper, he stated that on the morning after the disaster he sighted the two wrecks but, unable to weather the reef, concluded 'that it was too late had it been in our power to give any assistance'.[9] He saw the wrecks again in the afternoon, but believed all had perished. Surgeon Hugh Bell, also on the *Bridgewater*, wrote to Joseph Banks from Bombay, now Mumbai, and mentioned the deaths of 'all' the *Investigator*'s company, except for himself and those in Sydney.

Palmer sent his report ashore with his third mate, Williams, whose journal takes a different view. He recorded that the morning after the wreck, 'The ships were very distinctly seen . . . I was convinced that the crews of those ships were on the reefs'.[10]

Oddly, both accounts claim that the two wrecks were visible, whereas very little of the *Cato* remained to be seen by morning. Williams then left at Tellicherry his own 'contrary account' and later abruptly quitted the ship, forfeiting wages and personal belongings. The *Bridgewater*'s first officer and several others also left the ship, but their reasons are unknown. Hugh Bell remained in India as well.

Palmer sailed for England. He and the *Bridgewater* were never heard from again.

By the evening of 23 August the *Porpoise* had been emptied of almost everything essential to the survival of the community on the sandbank. Various personal effects had also been rescued. Flinders's most valued possessions had suffered some loss and damage. The falling mizzen mast, cut down to lighten the ship, had ripped off the roof of his upper deck cabin, so sea water swirled in, carrying away loose papers and other objects, including some books, part of his collection of shells and rocks, and the charts of the Gulf of Carpentaria's west side and of the north coast on which he had been working during the afternoon before the wreck. However, other charts, his logs, bearing books and astronomical observations remained, although water-damaged. Westall's work also suffered; a few of his drawings were destroyed and quite a number left wet but retrievable. They incurred further damage, it seems, when on the reef young Franklin let the sheep run across them as they lay drying on the sand. The flourishing contents of the greenhouse were, as Flinders wrote, 'totally destroyed by the salt water; as were the dried specimens of plants'. Fortunately, Brown and Bauer 'had put on board only a small part of their collection'.[11] Brown's boxes of seeds, packed into sturdy cases, were landed safely.

Gathering wood to make a fire for their first night on the sandbank, someone had found a worm-eaten piece of timber that Aken judged 'to be part of the stern post of a ship of about 400 tons'. Flinders, in his continuous search for evidence of La Pérouse's vanished ships, 'thought it might not improbably, have belonged to *La Boussole* or *L'Astrolabe*',[12] carried by currents from somewhere southwest of New Caledonia, a destination the French navigator had indicated when in Botany Bay. Several known coral formations and undoubtedly many unknown lay on La Pérouse's intended course. 'This space', Flinders remarked, 'might be very appropriately called the Corallian Sea'.[13]

By 22 August the prospect of help from the *Bridgewater* seemed increasingly remote, and Flinders called a council of officers to discuss means of effecting their own rescue. Several decisions were made. The largest of the two six-oared cutters would be lightly decked over and Park, Flinders and a boat crew would proceed to Port Jackson to either hire or obtain from Governor King enough vessels to carry everyone back to Sydney or to India, from where passage to Europe might be found. Flinders believed that he could bring back assistance within two months. However, lest there should be an accident to the cutter, a small vessel should be laid down immediately, to be built from parts of the wreck. It should be large enough to carry all the men on the bank except for one officer and one boat crew. In two months' time, or as soon after that as it was ready, the reef-built boat was to be boarded and headed for Port Jackson. The *Investigator*'s carpenter, Russell Mart, suggested that two smaller boats could be built more easily and would be sufficient to carry the people. This was approved.

The smaller, remaining cutter, together with one officer, a boat crew and provisions, would stay a few weeks longer, and should no vessel arrive by then, they too should proceed to Port Jackson. With them Flinders left his charts and books. In his journal Flinders noted that one reason for not taking his most valuable papers with him was to increase the confidence of those on the bank that he would certainly return. His papers would 'be my pledge'.[14]

As the last officer to remain on the bank Flinders had intended to designate his brother, but Fowler claimed it 'as the post of honour' and, respecting this, Flinders acceded. The *Porpoise* had been Fowler's command. To be in charge of the two new boats, then, were Samuel Flinders and John Aken, each with a master's mate capable of continuing the journey should illness or accident happen to either officer. In his own cutter Flinders had John Park as his second, the *Cato's* second mate, Flinders's own boatswain Charrington and ten seamen. In his journal Flinders wrote:

> On Friday, August 26, the cutter, which was now called the *Hope*, was ready for sea ... and notwithstanding the day, which in the seamans

> calandar, is the most unfortunate to sail upon of the whole week, we embarked to the number of fourteen, with three weeks provisions and two small casks of water, so that the boat was rather too deeply laden ... we took leave of our shipmates on the bank. After pushing off the boat, they saluted us with three cheers ... [15]

The cheers were answered from the boat and a seaman on the beach, receiving permission, ran to the flagstaff, hauled down the ensign with its union downwards and raised it again with the union uppermost. Flinders wrote, 'I cannot express the pleasure this little incident gave me'.[16]

With the southerly breeze in their sails they steered westward in the lee of Wreck Reef, as numerous humpback whales played around them. When the wind died at midday, they stopped at one of the cays to cook their dinner, consisting mainly of noddies that Flinders had shot from the boat.

Now they faced open sea, across which Flinders laid a southwesterly course for Sandy Cape at the entrance of the mainland's Hervey Bay. The whales left them and at sunset they were alone on the water. Sea and sky were still. They rowed through the night, twelve men taking watch on watch at the oars, Flinders and Park at the helm. By daybreak they were moving at 4 knots and had covered 90 miles. In the afternoon the wind freshened and in a cross sea with jumbled waves the cutter was plunging dangerously. She was lightened. One of the water casks was emptied, and the stones for their fireplace, firewood, a bag of pease and a few other items went overboard. The boat became easier and before dark the sea quietened. Two days later they saw the purple-blue mainland against a sunset sky. The perils of open sea were over and through a fine, clear night with a fair wind they ran south parallel to the coast.

Water became a necessity. They tacked in closer to the shore and anchored under Point Lookout on today's North Stradbroke Island. Some twenty Aborigines on a hill first surprised the Englishmen with 'dances in imitation of the kanguroo',[17] but understanding their signs for water pointed to a small stream falling into the sea. Two of the seamen stripped and swam ashore with the empty cask. The natives fell back, watching with quiet interest while the sailors filled the cask and chopped a bundle of wood. From the boat, however, the men had seen a shark follow the swimmers towards the beach. Anxiously, they hauled up the anchor and moved in as close as the surf allowed, and men, water and wood were safely brought on board.

For eight days they continued coasting south in changeable winds. On the eleventh night, in squally rain, they slept for the first time on the beach, huddled under the sails. By the late morning the weather cleared. With their water cask refilled and some cakes baked in the ashes of their fire, they stood out again. Through the following night they rowed hard against a southeast wind, but by noon of the next day, abreast of Broken Bay, a breeze set in from the east-northeast. Now, 'we crowded all sail for Port Jackson, and soon after two o'clock had the happiness to see ourselves between the heads of the harbour. Never do I recall experiencing sensations of joy greater than those with which my breast was animated at this time'.[18]

The men were jubilant, exhausted but physically well except for one with dysentery. They had safely covered some 750 miles in twelve and a half days in an open boat and could bring rescue to those still stranded on the reef.

Flinders and Park walked up to Government House 'to wait upon His Excellency governor King, whom we found at dinner with his family'. The Kings were stunned to see before them two men whom they supposed to be hundreds of miles away at sea. Nor was the men's appearance anything but astounding, 'for though we were not very ragged, a razor had not passed over our faces from the time of the shipwreck'.[19] Their reception, however, was 'most affectionate', with 'an involuntary tear'.

As soon as Flinders and his companions had been accommodated, the governor turned to the rescue of the men on Wreck Reef. In the harbour almost ready for sea was the merchant ship *Rolla*, bound for Guangzhou, and King and Flinders immediately contacted her captain, Robert Cummings. Wreck Reef was on Cummings's route northward, and he was willing to stop at the sandbank and embark all who wished to go to China. Already among his passengers was John Inman, the astronomer, now joined by John Park and his second mate. King quickly concluded an agreement with Cummings on provisions, salvage and payment. He then ordered the colonial schooners *Francis* and *Cumberland* to accompany the *Rolla* and to bring back to Sydney those who asked to return, together with the *Porpoise*'s carronades and remaining stores.

The news of the shipwreck roused the entire community and private gifts of wine, vegetables and livestock were sent on board the *Rolla* for the men on the reef. A detailed account of the event was published in the *Sydney Gazette*, while a distressed Robert Brown wrote to Banks of his losses, a letter he gave to Flinders to carry to England.

Flinders had vital decisions to make. The proper survey of Torres Strait had been an important part of his plans for his voyage on the *Porpoise*. As well, he saw as imperative his getting back to England as speedily as possible, in order to petition for a new ship and to arrange for the completion of his Australian surveys. Travelling with the *Rolla* meant bypassing Torres Strait, and finding transportation from China to England could add months to the journey. It was a prospect he could not accept. King offered Flinders the schooner *Cumberland,* built in Port Jackson the year before. The *Cumberland* was small, of just 29 tons burden. More objectionable than her lack of size were 'the quickness of her motion and the want of convenience, which would prevent the charts and journals of my voyage being prepared on the passage . . . time lost to this important object'.[20]

Yet the *Cumberland* would provide the opportunity for Flinders to survey Torres Strait and be in England for the soonest possible procurement of another ship. It was important also 'to put an early stop to the account which captain Palmer would probably give of our total loss'. And all this, Flinders admitted, was 'joined to some ambition of being the first to undertake so long a voyage in such a small vessel . . .'[21]

There were delays. The *Cumberland* was up the Hawkesbury River on colonial errands; the *Francis* lay on shore and could not be got off until the spring tides; the *Rolla* was not yet fitted for sea. It was thirteen days before all three were ready to sail, while Flinders worried incessantly that the people on Wreck Reef would embark on some unsuccessful attempt to save themselves; 'every day seemed to be a week until I got out of the harbour with the three vessels'.[22]

The *Cumberland* finally arrived in Port Jackson, and Flinders assembled a crew of Charrington and ten seamen. Governor King ordered Flinders to assume command of the schooner and proceed to England, and Flinders specifically agreed that the *Cumberland* was capable of making the long voyage. Its small size, however, would make necessary several stops on the way for provisions and water. Flinders suggested Kupang on Timor, Ile de France, the Cape of Good Hope, St Helena and an island off west Africa.

King objected to Ile de France as he did not wish to encourage traffic with the French colony and had been told, as well, that cyclones occurred in its vicinity at the time of year when the *Cumberland* would be there. King himself had put into Mauritius in 1790 when, travelling to England, he had found passage from Batavia on a Dutch ship on which, within days of sailing, almost the entire company were sick or dying of 'putrid fever'. King had brought the stricken ship into Ile de France.

The final decision on stopping at Ile de France King, however, left to Flinders, giving him two letters to deliver or forward to the governor of the French island colony, General François Louis, Comte de Magallon de la Molière. These concerned the arrival of the snow *Adele* with spirits for sale in the colony, which King had accepted, but now informed the governor that any further such cargoes would be turned away.

Neither King nor Flinders was aware that peace in Europe had failed and that Britain and France had been at war since May 1803. Word of renewed hostilities reached Sydney in November, two months after Flinders had sailed. The peace had lasted fourteen months. Flinders believed firmly that the Admiralty intended that he continue his survey, virtually forgetting, it seems, the possibility of war and a change in naval priorities. What mattered was to secure a ship without delay and return to his survey.

The *Cumberland*, the *Rolla* and the *Francis* left Sydney on 20 September 1803. The voyage to Wreck Reef took seventeen days, during which Flinders learned some unwelcome facts about the *Cumberland*. From sea he wrote to Governor King:

> From her want of breadth the Cumberland is exceedingly crank . . . She had also been very leaky, and in one hour and a half's cessation from pumping the water washes the cabin floor . . . I am now sitting on the lee locker with my knees up to my chin for a table to write on, and in

> momentary expectation of the sea coming down the companion and sky light, for they have broken me two panes out of the four already.[23]

Three days later he added:

> We lose much time from inability to carry sail . . . [I] dislike still more the loss of time to writing and chart-drawing from hence to England . . . Writing here is like writing on horseback in a rainy day . . . [The *Cumberland* was] a good property, but of all the little things I ever saw, this schooner, for bugs, lice, fleas, weavels, mosquitos, cockroaches (large and small), and mice, rises superior to them all. We have almost got the better of the fleas, lice, and mosquitos, but in spite of boiling water and daily destruction amongst them, the bugs still keep their ground . . . I have . . . usually slept upon the lee locker with my clothes on, notwithstanding which I have at least a hundred lumps upon my body and arms; and before this vile bug-like smell will leave me, must, I believe, as well as my clothes, undergo a good boiling in the large kettle. I shall set my old friend Trim to work upon the mice.

There was then a curious paragraph of self-analysis that began with assurances of Flinders's gratitude to the governor and his wife for their many kindnesses. Flinders wrote:

> It is a part of my disposition to avoid receiving obligations as much as possible; but when . . . brought under the yoke, . . . few are more desirous of making returns. To balance this, I am but little given to conferring kindnesses . . . I am more guided by justice than generosity, for an act of the latter never escapes me from natural impulse; it is upon mature deliberation if I am ever generous. This is saying but little for myself, but I wish to be known by the few whom I would have for my friends.

It was a self-portrait that does not match well with Flinders's circumstances and his actions. His career depended on patronage, which inescapably placed him under obligations to such men as Banks and King. He was a loyal friend who readily exerted himself to assist those who needed him, and to his family was fond, kind and generous, without acting, it would seem, upon 'mature deliberation'. It appears that at this time of adversity Flinders wanted to be seen as a man guided by cool intellect, little subject to impulse and emotion.

Wreck Reef was sighted from the *Rolla*'s masthead six weeks to the day from Flinders's departure from the sandbank. By four o'clock in the afternoon of 7 October the three vessels were anchored under the lee of the reef and, Flinders recorded, 'a salute of eleven guns, well charged, was immediately fired from the bank . . . I landed immediately, and was greeted with three hearty cheers and the utmost joy'. His own happiness in returning 'cannot be described'.[24]

There was one exception to the excitement. In his journal Matthew Flinders wrote, 'Lieutenant Flinders was in his tent calculating some lunar distances, when one of the young midshipmen ran to him, exclaiming, Mr. Flinders! Sir! Sir!! There is a ship and two schooners in sight! After a little consideration, Mr. Flinders said he was glad of it; he supposed it was his brother come back'.[25] Calmly, Samuel then asked to be informed when the vessels came to anchor. When told that the vessels were anchoring, Samuel, commanding officer on the bank, ordered the salute to be fired and joined the welcoming crowd.

The little community on the sandbank had been orderly and active in Flinders's absence. The men had explored the neighbouring reefs and sand cays, fished, hunted for turtle, birds and birds' eggs, planted a garden and manufactured charcoal for the forge.The principal focus of everyone's attention, however, had been the boat they were building. With a 32-foot keel, it was being tested just off shore when the rescuers arrived. The keel for a second boat had been laid.

The division of men, provisions and stores into the ship and the schooners went quickly. The *Rolla* took on board those wishing to travel home by way of China, among them Robert Fowler, Samuel Flinders, John Franklin and William Westall, together with substantial amounts of salvaged stores and provisions. Fowler was charged with delivering to the Admiralty the officers' logs and journals that had survived the wreck, together with copies of four of Flinders's charts of parts of the east and north coasts. Denis Lacy, who wanted to return to Sydney, was put in command of the new boat and, with James Aikin commanding the *Francis*, took all those desiring to go back to the colony, along with what equipment the boats could handle. Lacy carried Flinders's letter to Governor King and was to report to him on the condition of the *Porpoise* and any stores left on Wreck Reef.

Flinders chose ten officers and men for the *Cumberland* and gave them a day to decide whether or not they wished to make the long journey to England in that small craft. Only his clerk declined. Thus the little *Cumberland* received on board John Aken, master, Edward Charrington, boatswain, John Elder, Flinders's servant, and seven good seamen. Flinders gave James Inman the instruments belonging to the Board of Longitude, keeping only a telescope and a timekeeper, which Samuel Flinders rated, also working out compass variations for Matthew. A few additional stores and a full supply of water were loaded. Into the schooner as well went Flinders's trunks and chests of papers, charts, books, a box containing letters from Colonel Paterson and Governor King's dispatches to London, a cask with some of Matthew's collection of shells and rock samples, and Trim.

By now Flinders knew the *Cumberland* well, but, he wrote, 'notwithstanding what had been discovered of the bad qualities of the schooner, I determined to proceed, at least so far as to reach some port where a passage might be procured in a better vessel without losing time'.[26] Flinders's complete self-confidence and his overwhelming desire for a new ship to complete his explorations—and perhaps something of that challenge 'of being the first to undertake so long a voyage in such a small vessel'[27]—edged out any doubts as to the wisdom of his decision.

The *Cumberland* spent her last day at Wreck Reef off an islet where the men made a final hunt for turtle and seabirds' eggs. The *Rolla* joined her the next day, and Flinders went on board to say goodbye to his brother and his companions of the past three years. At noon on 11 October 1803 the ships parted company with cheers, the *Rolla* setting her sails for the north-northeast and China, the *Cumberland* steering for Torres Strait.

For eight days the *Cumberland* ran northwest towards the reefs at the entrance to Torres Strait. Having skirted them to the north in the *Investigator*, Flinders now entered the strait to the south, by today's Pandora Passage. The principal Murray Island was sighted and on the beach a large number of men and canoes. The *Cumberland* was too small and her complement too few to take any risks, and Flinders steered around the island. Then, on a southwesterly course, he ran past Cape York, to come in among the Prince of Wales Islands by a new channel, later named Flinders Passage. Here, however, the water shoaled and he turned north into the Prince of Wales Channel.

Three days after he had entered Torres Strait, Flinders anchored at the western end of Booby Island. His new route, however, was intricate and shallow, unsuited for shipping. In the wet, crank little schooner, with getting to England foremost in his mind, Flinders recorded his normal observations but attempted no surveying. A thorough charting remained to be done under better circumstances.

The high land of Timor came distantly into view on 6 November, and in the early evening four days later the *Cumberland* dropped anchor abreast of the fort in Kupang Bay. Johannes Geisler, the governor of Flinders's previous visit, had died, but a Mr Viertzen, serving in his place, offered every possible assistance, providing Flinders with a house near the fort where he could bring his chronometer and other instruments to ascertain a new rate. Flinders learned that Baudin had reached Kupang almost a month after the *Investigator*'s departure and that on encountering calms, contrary winds and sickness on board in the Gulf of Carpentaria, the French commander had abandoned his explorations and sailed for Europe by way of Mauritius.

The *Cumberland*'s condition had worsened. The schooner leaked badly whenever the wind had her lying over on the side, and the port-side pump was failing. Kupang had no facilities for repairing the pumps, nor pitch to pay the schooner's seams after they were caulked. Nothing was achieved by delay and the *Cumberland* sailed in the evening of the fourth day.

Flinders laid his course across the Indian Ocean for the Cape of Good Hope, 6663 miles from Kupang. If they were too much impeded by contrary winds or the schooner's difficulties, he would steer for Batavia or some other island port for repairs. A few days out of Kupang he was faced with precisely that possibility; the wind veered to west of south, the ocean built into heavy swells and lightning repeatedly split a dark northwestern sky. The crew prepared for a run towards Java, erecting a boarding net against pirate attack, reportedly frequent in the waters between Timor and the bigger island. Then the wind changed. A steady southeast trade wind set in and, despite swells, frequent rain and occasional thunder and lightning, the *Cumberland* ran west-southwest under all the sail she could safely carry, sometimes making 7 knots.

Drenched in rain and spray but exultant, the men began to feel that they were indeed headed for the Cape.

The leaks increased. On 4 December a following sea came in from the east to meet the southwest ground swell, 'and the jumble caused by these different movements made the vessel labour exceedingly ... the starboard pump, which was alone effective, was obliged to be worked almost continually, day and night; and had the wind been on the starboard side, it is doubtful whether the schooner could have been kept above water'.[28]

Passage around the Cape of Good Hope could mean even larger seas and the possibility that the overused pump would fail. Unless the boat was caulked and the pumps rebored and fitted, the danger was too great. As well, Flinders was having second thoughts about going all the way to England in a boat as small as the *Cumberland*. Batavia was now too far off their track to consider. On the evening of 6 December Flinders altered their course half a point for the island of Mauritius. Everyone on board was relieved.

Governor King had left a stop at Mauritius to Flinders's discretion, but Flinders knew that, in the case of accident to the schooner, having acted against the preference of a superior officer could be grounds for a court martial. Against this possibility, Flinders now enumerated in his journal the reasons for his action. The necessity of caulking the schooner and refitting the pumps was the primary reason. The second was to reprovision the boat with wood and water and to purchase a small supply of spirits; the boat's company had been on short allowance as only 22 gallons had been available at Timor. Thirdly, there was the possibility of finding a homebound ship on which he could obtain a more 'expeditious and convenient passage to Europe than can be expected in so small a vessel as the *Cumberland*; for her greatest rate of sailing ... is only seven knots ... it is impossible to go on in completing my charts and accounts of New Holland while on board here ... it is only in the finest weather that I can do more than write the daily log'.[29]

The schooner might then be sold or freighted back to Port Jackson. He listed a number of lesser reasons for stopping at the island:

> Delivering governor King's letters to General Magallon, the governor, which were otherwise to be sent from the Cape.

> Learning some further intelligence of the *Géographe* and the *Naturaliste*.
>
> Acquiring a knowledge of the periodical winds and weather there:—of the port, and the present state of the French colony; and how far it or its dependencies in Madagascar may be useful to Port Jackson; as also whether it may not be a convenient place for me to touch at during some part of my future expected voyage.
>
> The possibility of another war having taken place, in which case by touching at the French colony, for which I have a passport, the necessity of stopping at the Dutch settlement at the Cape, for which I have no passport, could be avoided; for I could take in a sufficiency at Mauritius to carry us on to St Helena.[30]

These were, Flinders felt, entirely rational and uncontentious reasons for stopping at Île-de-France, where, in any case, he had the protection of a French passport.

An additional factor mentioned in the journal was that he and two others had been affected by 'a bilious remitting fever, such as is usually thought to be generated by the miasma of marshes or swamps . . .'[31]; it was probably a type of malaria contracted at Timor. What caused malaria would not be understood for almost another century, and Flinders attributed it to wet and sultry conditions on board and the impossibility of keeping their crowded living space sufficiently clean and well aired.

Strong winds and heavy rain came and went as the *Cumberland* laboured on. A ship was seen but the chance to communicate was lost as night fell. Flinders had no chart of Mauritius and little knowledge, but he learned from the *Encyclopaedia Britannica* that the principal town, Port Louis, was on the northwest side of the island and seemingly could be approached by going around the island either to the north or to the south.

26 Mauritius

The humped outline of the island of Mauritius emerged from the early semi-darkness of 15 December 1803. The wind was east by south and Flinders hauled to the north, but sighting a distant promontory that the schooner could not clear in a high-running sea and with a current setting to leeward, he turned to round the south end of the island instead.

Five hundred miles east of Madagascar and almost another 600 miles from the African continent, the island rises steeply out of the Indian Ocean, one of a group of three tropical islands known collectively as the Mascarenes. Volcanic in origin, its white, beach-rimmed shoreline is almost encircled by coral reefs that create lagoons of green, crystalline water. In the interior a northern plain and a central plateau are bordered by small mountains that may be the remnants of the rim of an ancient volcano.

With its island neighbours, Réunion and Rodrigues, an uninhabited Mauritius was probably known to Arab seafarers at least from the 10th century. It was visited in the early 1500s by Portuguese navigators but no claims of possession were made until 1598, when a Dutch fleet arrived at today's Grand Port and the island was named Mauritius, for Prince Maurice of Orange and Nassau, stadholder of the United Provinces of the Netherlands. For the next 60 years European ships visited Mauritius for food and water and to log its ebony forests.

In 1638 the Dutch East India Company established a settlement, but abandoned it after twenty years. A second colonisation attempt was made soon after, but in 1710 the Dutch again departed and the island became a haven for pirates. At some unknown date during these years the large flightless bird, the *Raphus cucullatus* or dodo, today featured on the island republic's crest, became extinct.

In 1715 France claimed the island, and six years later the French East India Company, finding it deserted, occupied and renamed it Ile de France. In 1767 Mauritius and Réunion passed to the control of the French government of Louis XV. There was now a growing population, flourishing businesses and plantations, and a fortified naval base at Port Louis.

For some 75 years Mauritius played an important role in the colonial conflicts of the 18th and early 19th century wars fought by European powers. It was a principal station for French troops and supplies sent into the campaigns against the British in India. It was a base for French exploration in the Indian and Pacific Oceans, for elements of the French navy operating in the East and for privateers, largely well-armed locally owned merchant ships that harassed British maritime trade on sea lanes to India and Southeast Asia. The profits could be huge. To a great extent cut off from both commerce and support from France, the economy of Ile de France thrived on this plunder.

At the island's considerable distance from Paris, the impact of changes wrought by the French Revolution was slight at first. Royalist place names were altered, Port Louis becoming Port Nord Ouest. A local Colonial Assembly was formed to assist the governor in his duties, which gave the colonists greater control of their own administrative affairs. In 1794 the National Convention in Paris abolished slavery, which the Ile de France community saw as an economic blow and, in view of there being 63 000 African slaves as opposed to approximately 6500 Europeans and under 1000 Free Blacks, a danger.[1] The delegates from France were sent home and slavery remained. In a bid to win back the alienated colonists in May 1802, the government of the First Consul, Napoleon Bonaparte, legalised slavery, which was thus preserved on Mauritius for another 33 years. The same decree ordered the dissolution of the colony's local governing bodies in preparation for tighter control from Paris. However, when no further instructions arrived, the Colonial Assembly continued in its usual role.

In August 1803 General Charles Mathieu Isidore Decaen landed at Port Nord Ouest. Accompanied by his troops and ignoring the authority of the Colonial Assembly, he took possession of the colony's military headquarters. He was there to await additional forces from France for an invasion of India the following year, designed to retrieve for France the possessions it had lost to Britain and for which Decaen had prepared the ground through alliances with Indian princes. Aged 34 and a general since he was 31, he was an experienced and very capable soldier, passionately patriotic, a devoted admirer of Bonaparte and an avowed enemy of England. Brusque, quick-tempered, ambitious and bluntly authoritarian, he put an end at once to any attempt by the colonists to establish cooperative relations.

On 25 September the corvette *Berceau* arrived in Port Nord Ouest with the news that France and Britain had been at war since the previous May. Plans for an invasion of India were shelved; French ships and soldiers were needed elsewhere. Decaen was appointed Captain-General of Ile de France and Réunion and took over the powers of government from the governor, General Magallon, whom he sent to administer the subordinate island of Réunion. On Ile de France he dissolved the Colonial Assembly and other governmental bodies and set up new institutions that left little or no authority in the hands of the residents. The island was divided into easily policed *quartiers* under military commanders whom he appointed.

Decaen's control of the colony was unchallenged. Ile de France was to be transformed into an island fortress from which, under his command and to his glory, French forces would destroy British power in the Indian Ocean region. On 15 December 1803, unaware of any of this, Matthew Flinders sighted the island of Mauritius and in the schooner *Cumberland* approached the south coast.

Soon after eight o'clock that morning, the *Cumberland* doubled the southeastern point of the island, and Flinders steered west along the coast looking for a vessel that could provide information on reaching Port Louis. When a flag was seen on one of the hills, 'our colours were then hoisted, and afterwards a French jack at the fore-top-mast-head, as a signal for a pilot'.[2] At noon a small seaside town came in sight. A schooner emerged from the harbour and Flinders manoeuvred to speak with her. The schooner immediately headed back in among several other boats and, assuming he was to follow, Flinders steered through a narrow opening in the reef into a river estuary forming a little harbour ringed with stony bluffs that ended in a small promontory. The island schooner dropped her anchor and, to the Englishmen's amazement, its crew hurriedly launched a canoe 'and without furling the sails they went hastily on shore [and] up a steep hill . . . They were met by a person who, from the plume in his hat, appeared to be an officer, and presently we saw several men with muskets on the top of the hill'.[3]

Watching uneasily, Flinders began to suspect that war had broken out once more. Then, thinking of his passport and the hospitality extended at Port Jackson to Baudin's expedition, he felt reassured. His reception here could be no different. 'I pleased myself with the idea of the honourable reception we should meet with after so many risks and fatigues.'[4]

To encourage someone to come aboard, he held up the letters he had for General Magallon. No one seemed to move. He then hoisted out the *Cumberland*'s small, leaky boat and sent Aken ashore with the letters and the passport. Presently the master returned with the officer and two men armed with swords and pistols.

The officer was Marie Claude Antoine Marrier, Baron d'Unienville, a handsome man of about 38, major of the district, at whose estate in the hills above the estuary a messenger on horseback had arrived to report that at about two o'clock that afternoon a vessel flying the British flag was seen chasing a local schooner into the harbour, 'an occurrence all the more alarming as a British frigate was said to be cruising between the islands'.[5] The panicked crew of the schooner believed that their vessel was surely lost, as the British, they reported, had landed 40 men.

The excitement and activity, recorded by a descendant of D'Unienville, was considerable. D'Unienville immediately sent the information to the signal station at Citronniers Hill from which, by way of flags, the news 'would fly from one mountain top to the other until it would reach Headquarters in Port Louis'.[6] He then contacted the neighbouring estates for reinforcements, ordered women and children inland and cattle driven into the woods. Mustering five or six national guardsmen and his own twelve male slaves, he rushed down to the shoreside promontory to oppose any landing. From here 'he could observe the tiny Cumberland peacefully at anchor, with scarcely a soul on deck'. D'Unienville hailed in French. There was no answer. 'He tried in English, caused some stir, was able to summon a boat [the *Cumberland*'s boat with Aken] and was taken on board.'[7]

Now, Flinders wrote, 'I learned to my great regret that war was actually declared . . . Dunienville . . . spoke a little English; he asked if I was the captain Flinders mentioned in the passport,—whether we had been shipwrecked, and he demanded to see my commission. After perusing it, he appeared to be satisfied, and politely offered to perform any service for us, or supply us with what we immediately wanted, and invited me to go ashore to dine with him . . .'[8]

Flinders explained that he wished to go directly to Port Louis, but needed a pilot. He also requested fresh water. A pilot was promised for the next day, and D'Unienville ordered the crew of the local schooner to fill the *Cumberland*'s empty water casks and the schooner's master to guide the *Cumberland* to a safe mooring.

As soon as the officer had left, Flinders studied his passport. It was entirely in French, which he did not understand. Now, with rising concern, he examined it very carefully. As far as he could determine, it referred solely to the *Investigator*. Yet Flinders wrote in his journal, 'The intention of the passport was doubtless to protect the voyage of discovery, whether it was wholly executed in the Investigator, or whether accident might oblige me to take another vessel . . .'[9]

There was no such provision or even inference in the passport. He continued, 'I saw that if the governor should adhere to the letter, rather than to the intention of the passport, the Cumberland was certainly not mentioned in it, and might, therefore, be seized as a prize. I was not without apprehensions upon this subject: the idea of being detained, even a week more than necessary, was intolerable'.

An hour after he had left, D'Unienville returned aboard the schooner with his superior, the district commandant, Thomas Estienne Bolgerd, and a man who spoke English 'intelligibly'. Bolgerd, an estate owner and shipbuilder, was abrupt and ungracious. With the help of the interpreter, he examined Flinders's passport and commission, and Flinders, watching, was disturbed to see a sullen, distrustful expression on his face. Bolgerd pointed out that the passport was not made out for the *Cumberland*, and Flinders again explained the loss of the *Investigator*, the shipwreck and his presence in the *Cumberland*. He was told that the papers would be sent to the governor in Port Nord Ouest while he waited with the *Cumberland*. Flinders objected; his papers were his only protection, particularly now in time of war. It was then agreed that he should travel overland with his papers to Port Nord Ouest, while Aken followed in the *Cumberland*.

Flinders was taken to D'Unienville's home on his estate, Montrose, a mile back from the coast, in order to be ready for an early departure on horseback the next day. On the way to the house he learned from the interpreter that General Magallon was at Réunion, having been superseded on Ile de France by General Decaen, 'an officer of the French revolution'. Flinders's host, D'Unienville, had been a lieutenant in the navy under the old government, but was now a major in charge of the *quartier* of Savanne in the island's southwest, under General Decaen's appointee, Bolgerd. At the large, gracious country residence of Montrose, Flinders was courteously received by D'Unienville's wife and, according to the family record, was entertained at dinner among the ladies and gentlemen who earlier that day had taken to the hills and to their weapons.

After breakfast the next morning Flinders and D'Unienville waited for orders from Bolgerd. When there was no word by ten o'clock, Flinders impatiently went down to the harbour, which he now knew as Baie du Cap, determined to sail with or without a pilot. The wind, however, was against getting out of the bay and would not turn, he was told, until four o'clock in the afternoon. Pressed by D'Unienville to return to the house for dinner, Flinders did so. Before the meal was over, however, an order arrived allowing Flinders to depart for Port Nord Ouest in the *Cumberland*. Accompanied by some of the other guests, who sent on board gifts of fresh fruit, Flinders and D'Unienville returned to the harbour. A squall coming off the island allowed the *Cumberland* to depart; 'at five o'clock, the pilot being on board, we stood out from the reefs ...'[10]

Flinders asked the pilot who held the Cape of Good Hope. He was almost determined, if the Cape were again British, to somehow make a run for it, even with the *Cumberland* in her precarious state. He was told that the Cape was in the hands of the Dutch.

As the *Cumberland* sailed north through the night, Flinders turned over and over in his mind the position in which he found himself. The unfriendly behaviour of the commandant at Baie du Cap was cause for anxiety. Yet, he assured himself, 'the intention of the passport to protect the persons employed in the expedition, with their charts and journals, must be evident'.[11] Further, Bonaparte 'was a professed patron of science' and a governor appointed by him could hardly be less obliging than other French governors had been to other explorers. There was reassurance, too, in that D'Unienville had told him the *Géographe* had arrived at Port Nord Ouest in early August and was evidently remaining in the harbour for some time. Flinders learned that Baudin had died a little over a month after his arrival from a pulmonary disease, described variously as cancer or tuberculosis, and that the ship was presently commanded by Pierre Bernard Milius, formerly lieutenant on the *Naturaliste*, who had shared in the hospitable reception of the French ships at Port Jackson.

Unknown to Flinders, the *Cumberland* was being followed through the darkness by a corvette, guarding against any attempt to escape.

At eight o'clock in the morning the mastheads of the ships in the harbour at Port Nord Ouest came in sight, the tallest of which Flinders hoped was that of the *Géographe*. Against an opposing wind it was four in the afternoon before the *Cumberland* came to anchor at the entrance of the port near the largest ship. She was the frigate *Atalante*. The *Géographe* had sailed for France the day before.

27
Detention

With the renewal of war between Britain and France, a passport that specified protection only for a lost ship, and the departure of Milius with the *Géographe*, Flinders began to realise the gravity of his anomalous position. To meet and explain the situation immediately to the governor and to ask for his permission to obtain the necessary repairs to the *Cumberland* as quickly as possible seemed the proper thing to do. He put on his frock uniform with hat and sword. Within the hour a health officer came on board, asked some questions in English, and took Flinders ashore. Here a port officer and an interpreter conducted him to the large white-pillared government house. An aide-de-camp informed them that the governor was at dinner and they should return in an hour or two.

They retreated into the shade of some trees where the officers seemed to congregate. Some spoke English and asked a number of questions. Had Flinders really come from Botany Bay in such a small boat? Had he seen the corvette that had followed him during the night? They asked about the colony at Port Jackson and Baudin's conduct there. And they asked if Flinders knew of the voyage of Monsieur Flinedare. Failing to understand, he replied that he did not. This clearly surprised the French officers, and it was not until later that Flinders realised that the mispronounced name was his own.

After two hours he was taken back to the governor's residence. The group of officers preceded him, and it was an additional half hour before the interpreter escorted him into another room. Here two officers were standing at a table. One was an aide-de-camp, a quiet, 'genteel-looking man', as Flinders later wrote, 'whose blood seemed to circulate more tranquilly'.[1] The other was the Captain-General Decaen, short, stocky, in a laced round jacket, who stared sternly at Flinders and, without greeting or preamble, brusquely demanded to see his passport and commission. Antagonism apparently flared instantly between the two.

Flinders, fatigued from a sleepless night and worrisome days, perhaps still feeling the effects of his bout with malaria, was angered and alarmed by the long wait and now by the lack of welcome. Whatever his difficulties at sea, Flinders had invariably received ashore the attention and respect, even the acclaim, of a man involved in an important scientific endeavour, an eminent explorer, courtesies well beyond those normally due to a naval officer still of junior rank. The warmth of welcome extended to the French in Port Jackson, who had received fresh food denied to his own men, contrasted acutely with his reception here.

The general saw before him a short, slight British commander in a crumpled, sea-stained, ill-smelling uniform, who had not bothered to remove his hat. Decaen had been briefed on the inapplicable passport, a boat unreasonably small for the journey claimed for it, and no doubt also the denial of this man that he knew anything of Monsieur Flinedare. Decaen was not only a seasoned soldier, but also one whose interest and experience encompassed many aspects of geopolitical strategy.

One of the responsibilities of his position was to gather information on British activities east of the Cape of Good Hope. He had organised extensive espionage against the British in India. From a comment by François Péron it appears that Decaen asked the zoologist for a report on Port Jackson. Undoubtedly he knew of the clumsy spying effort of an officer called Robbins, who had pursued Baudin's expedition in a little vessel called the *Cumberland*. He had also received Bolgerd's report of the suspicious behaviour of this man, who had chased an island schooner into the harbour. He would have been fully aware that scientific expeditions, however extensive their academic activities, almost invariably cloaked the surreptitious preparation of political reports on the regions they visited.

From Decaen's point of view the intruder was almost certainly a spy claiming the neutrality of a scientist. Probably above all, Decaen, the dedicated and patriotic Bonapartist, saw before him a brazen and

Government House, Port Louis, Mauritius, where Flinders met and was interrogated by the French Governor, General Charles Mathieu Isidore Decaen. The second floor was added to the original building by Decaen. (Courtesy of Mauritius Tourism Promotion Authority)

highly suspect representative of the enemy, Britain. Their nations were at war. He had every right to hold this man.

He glanced through the documents and peremptorily wanted to know Flinders's reason for coming to Ile de France in the small schooner *Cumberland* with a passport for the ship *Investigator*. Briefly Flinders explained the loss of the *Investigator* and his coming to the island for repairs and provisions. The governor then demanded to see Flinders's orders for embarking in the *Cumberland* and for stopping at the island. Flinders replied that the former was on board the schooner and he had no orders for calling at Ile de France.

At this Decaen lost patience. Gesticulating and raising his voice, he exploded, '*Vous m'en imposez, monsieur*! [You are imposing on me, sir!]' It was a statement of disbelief. It was not possible, he said, that the governor of New South Wales should ' "send away the commander of an expedition on discovery in so small a vessel!—" He then gave back my passport and commission'.[2] Sharply, Decaen gave orders that Flinders did not understand, adding something in a softer tone, and Flinders was led back to the wharf and on board the schooner. It was dark now, and by lantern light in the small, littered cabins of the *Cumberland* all charts, papers and journals pertaining to the voyage, and all letters and packets from Sydney, including boxes of documents from King and Paterson, were gathered by the officers and packed into a trunk that was lashed up and sealed, Flinders signing his own statement to the effect that they had been taken.

The French officials were polite and, encouraged by this, Flinders gave vent to his anger, adding that 'the captain-general's conduct must alter very much before I should pay him a second visit, or even set my foot on shore again'.[3] The interpreter replied gently that he hoped Flinders would come ashore, as he and the accompanying officers had orders to bring him to lodgings in town. Flinders was shocked. 'What! I am then a prisoner!' he exclaimed.[4]

Matthew Flinders had taken his expedition to sea with the single specified purpose of geographic exploration and scientific research. No visits to foreign settlements or territory other than Tenerife, and consequently no undercover agenda of a political or military nature, had been written into his instructions. Until his detention in Mauritius, Flinders's own writings show no interest in political methods or manoeuvrings, or in anything he might have known of intrigue related to other expeditions. Single-mindedly he pursued his purpose which, as he saw it, perhaps naively, related only to his ship, to discovery and hydrographic research, and to recording the results for scientific study. The complex framework of Decaen's thinking, incorporating as it did the military and diplomatic issues of the international scene, was virtually alien to Flinders's experience. The course taken by the governor's reasoning was beyond his comprehension, and the conclusion Decaen had reached seemed unbelievable.

Yet the officials with him acknowledged that he was, in fact, a prisoner, but added that they hoped it would only be for a few days while his papers were examined. In the meantime John Aken was to accompany him on land, and together the two men, still incredulous, laid a few clothes into another trunk. Flinders put an anxious Charrington in charge of the crew and the schooner, which, with guards on board, was presently warped farther into the port.

At one o'clock in the morning Flinders and Aken were escorted through the sleeping community 'to a large house in the middle of the town, and through a long, dark entry, up a dirty stair case, into the room destined for us; the aide-de-camp and interpreter then wished us a good night, and we afterwards heard nothing save the measured steps of a sentinel, walking in the gallery before our door'.[5]

The room contained latticed windows, two little truckle beds, a small table, two rush-bottomed chairs and a mirror in a faded gilt frame. The two men stripped and went to bed, but kept awake by 'mosketoes above and bugs below', along with the events of the day, neither slept until nearly daybreak.

Flinders awoke suddenly at six o'clock in the morning and stared in disbelief as two armed genadiers entered the room. One spoke to the other and left. The other began walking back and forth between the beds, paying little attention to the men in them. Flinders quickly decided he could not sleep 'in such company', and woke Aken, whose startled reaction on finding a French soldier pacing by his bed would, as Flinders said, have been funny at any other time.

At eight o'clock an excellent breakfast of fresh bread, meat, vegetables and fruit—rare and delicious treats—was brought to them and a similarly lavish dinner appeared at twelve. They were housed, they learned, in what was reputedly the town's best tavern, the shabby Café Marengo in the Rue Nationale. At one o'clock the aide-de-camp, whom Flinders now knew as Lieutenant Colonel Louis Auguste Fulcher de Monistrol, appeared and conducted him to an office where a German secretary speaking some English interrogated him at length from a written list of questions similar to those that had been put to him the day before. They covered his journey from Port Jackson to Ile de France, the reasons for his actions, why he did not have with him any of the scientists assigned to the voyage, whether he knew of the contents of the two boxes of official correspondence that he carried. This time Flinders's answers were written down and, together with his instructions from Governor King relating to the *Cumberland*, were taken to Decaen.

Flinders began to feel that his situation was easing a little. At five o'clock he was invited to join the governor at dinner. A later notation by Decaen indicated that the invitation came from his wife, but it is possible that Flinders did not understand this. In his journal written at the time, he recorded simply that he received an invitation from the general to go to dinner which he declined. Later Flinders explained that at first he could not believe the invitation was serious; he answered that he had already dined. This was patently impossible and, pressed to accept, evidently by Monistrol, he seems to have veered from confusion to arrogance.

In his published account he said that he believed his identity as a British naval commander was being tested, that after such gross insults only an impostor would acquiesce to dining with the governor; as a British officer he could not debase his position by accepting the invitation. He went on to say to Monistrol that when he was set at liberty he would accept such an invitation with pleasure. Monistrol carried the message to Decaen, who replied only that Flinders would be invited when he was set at liberty.

Flinders had slammed the door upon an opportunity to meet the governor on a social level. Such a meeting might not have altered the events that followed, yet it could have alleviated some of their grimness. Decaen had made a gesture. Hubristically, and in doubt and anger, Flinders cast it aside.

The interrogation continued. Questions and answers in either language were translated into the other, so as to be understood by both parties. It was now growing dark but in the office the day's heat was still stifling. After six hours of questioning Flinders was very tired. Finding that a number of questions could be answered by entries in the third volume of his rough log, Flinders pointed out the relevant sections to the secretary and suggested he make such extracts as would provide the information he needed.

He went on to ask that the sentry be taken out of his room at the inn and that Aken be allowed to return to the *Cumberland* to keep order. It was too late to make arrangements, he was told; His Excellency would see him in the morning. With the exception of the third volume of his log, Flinders's books and papers were returned to the trunk and between seven and eight o'clock in the evening Flinders was taken back to his room. He never again saw the third volume of his log.

For the next two days Flinders waited to see Governor Decaen. The sentry in his room was removed to the hall outside and his and Aken's general treatment improved. They were given permission to use the tavern's billiard room. Aken was allowed on the *Cumberland* to bring away the timekeeper and Flinders's sextant and artificial horizon, and the two began a series of observations in preparation for sailing. Apparently at this time little black and white Trim was brought ashore to share his master's confinement and the company of the playful and affectionate cat eased the men's captivity a little.

The next day Edward Charrington came from the *Cumberland* to report general misbehaviour by the schooner's crew, and Flinders decided to take the opportunity to write a formal letter to Decaen, which, he hoped, would bring the impasse to an end. He wrote:

> To the captain general and governor in chief over the French settlements to the east of the Cape of Good Hope
>
> Sir
>
> If you have found reason to believe that I was actually the Commander of His Britannic Majesty's ship *Investigator* for which a passport was given by the first consul of France, and that I am now in prosecution of the service on whose account that passport was given, I beg Your Excellency's attention to the following circumstances.
>
> My officer and myself being taken out of my vessel, all subordination and regularity amongst my seamen have ceased, they are permitted to go into my cabin and take spirits, they commit disorders and are even permitted to go on shore. To correct these and for the preservation of the vessel's stores, I have to request that my officer may be permitted to remain on board.
>
> The principal objects for which I put in at this port were to get the upper works of my vessel caulked, and the pumps fresh bored and fitted; and if Your Excellency sees reason to accord with the first paragraph, I request that these works may be begun upon, that I may be able to sail as soon as possible after you shall be pleased to liberate me from my present state of purgatory.

With all due respect, I am,
Your Excellency's obedient servant,
Mattw. Flinders
From my confinement—Decr. 20th. 1803[6]

If the letter related in a businesslike manner to his men and his ship, it was essentially a bid for freedom, and as such the final remark was extraordinarily tactless. Indubitably Flinders assumed that the hydrographic work he did in the interest of science gave him the status of a neutral, that his passport gave him complete immunity from the fact that war existed between his nation and that of Decaen. To Decaen, who had no particular interest in the pursuit of science, this was a false premise, and the groundless insistence and impudence of his prisoner were intolerable irritants.

There were now in the harbour two neutral American merchant ships, the *Hunter*, which had been at Kupang with the *Investigator* in April, and the *Fanny*, known to Flinders from Port Jackson in July 1802. While briefly aboard the *Cumberland*, Aken had been visited by the mate of the *Hunter*, seeking additional crew. Convinced that he would soon be freed, Flinders wrote to the master of the *Hunter* on his and his men's joining the vessel, and in the afternoon of 20 December the *Hunter*'s mate and the captain of the *Fanny* called at the inn to discuss possibilities.

In the evening the interpreter, Joseph Hyppolyte Théophile Bonnefoy, arrived to inform Flinders that the corporal of the guard on the *Cumberland* had been punished for allowing disorder, and the most recalcitrant member of the crew had been put in the guard house. An answer to the rest of Flinders's note would come in the morning.

Flinders received his answer as promised. At about eleven o'clock Monistrol and Bonnefoy arrived with a copy in French of the governor's orders, which they translated for him. Flinders had transgressed the purpose of his passport and violated his neutrality by his unauthorised stop at Ile de France in order to gain knowledge, as he himself had written in his journal, of the 'periodical winds in this neighbourhood, of the port, and of the present state of the French colony, &c'. Monistrol was therefore directed to board the *Cumberland* with Flinders and, in his presence, to collect into one or more trunks all remaining papers that might add to the proofs of misconduct already in the governor's possession. Flinders was then to be again confined, his crew transferred to a prison ship, an inventory taken of everything on the *Cumberland* and all stores put under seal and guard.

Flinders could not believe that this was the response to his letter and an actual interpretation of the reasons he had carefully listed for stopping at the island. He was considered a spy.

The governor's orders were carried out immediately. Flinders, Aken, Monistrol and Bonnefoy boarded the schooner, all remaining books and papers, including personal letters received over several years, were packed into a chest and a cask, secured and sealed. Flinders and Aken were permitted to take only their clothes. Through all of this, however, the French officers remained both courteous and apologetic, Monistrol saying that undoubtedly the governor was somehow mistaken and that he would approach him on the matter.

There were, however, factors relating to his detention of which Flinders was unaware. On his recent departure from Ile de France on the *Géographe*, the naturalist François Péron had left with Decaen a copy of his detailed report on the British colony in New South Wales, which concluded with the advice that this flourishing arm of Britain be promptly 'destroyed'.[7]

Péron's lavish description of the colony's prosperity or even its threat to Spanish America would not have moved General Decaen towards any thought of destroying Sydney. The part of the British empire he wanted demolished was in India, and Péron's paper probably interested him mainly insofar as it showed that Britain's expanding hold on Australia would contribute economically and perhaps militarily to Britain's position in India. Nevertheless, Péron's claims would not have disposed Decaen to any sympathy for Matthew Flinders.

In addition, there was among Flinders's papers something much more inflammatory. Flinders's professed mission, and in consequence his passport, were based on the premise of his carrying out strictly neutral scientific activities. Anything that could be interpreted as hostile to the French Republic or its allies nullified the protection extended by the passport, and Flinders had therefore received explicit instructions from the Admiralty not to take on board 'letters or packets other than such as you may receive from this office, or the office of His Majesty's secretary of state'.[8]

Against these orders, Flinders had carried Governor King's dispatches to Lord Hobart, Secretary of State for War and the Colonies. Discussing briefly Flinders's explorations in the *Investigator*, King commented to Hobart on the great advantage to navigation of a safe passage through Torres Strait, and how it would facilitate Port Jackson's contact with India, Timor and other islands. He mentioned the possibility of 'a settlement being made to the northward'.[9]

These were natural considerations for a governor of New South Wales, but Decaen would have felt distinctly uneasy to read of this acceleration of British commercial interests. British trade in the East largely financed the prosecution of the war in Europe, and Decaen saw it as his duty to obstruct that trade in any way he could. Withholding from the British the information in Flinders's third logbook, which described the Torres Strait passage, would contribute to that. As well, any new, quicker route to India from any direction could reduce the advantage held by his mid-ocean bastion in guarding and facilitating French naval and military activity in the region.

Much more serious, however, was another part of King's letter to Hobart:

> I consider it my duty most respectfully submitting to your Lordship's consideration the possibility in any future war of the Government of the Isle of France annoying this colony, as the voyage from thence may be done in less than seven weeks; and on the same idea this colony may hereafter annoy the trade of the Spanish settlements on the opposite coasts. But to defend this colony against the one and annoy the other, it would be necessary that some regard should be had to the military and naval defences. The defences of the port may be made as strong as the defences of any port I know of.[10]

King went on to discuss the placement of batteries at Port Jackson and to say that 'a small establishment of artillery officers and men are wanted to work these guns effectually in case of necessity'. He recommended that the colony's present defences 'be increased also by six more twelve-pounders, if the above artillery officers and men are sent'.

To Decaen the fact that Flinders had risked making the journey to England in so small a boat pointed to the urgency of bringing King's letter to the British government. Flinders's putting in at Ile de France in order to observe conditions added further substance to a growing picture of hostility. Decaen was fully aware of the weaknesses of his small, isolated command, and the importance of keeping the details of those weaknesses from the enemy. He was also aware of the extent of damage being done to British shipping by French ships operating out of Ile de France. Flinders would later form a partial estimate of £1 948 000 in losses to British commerce inflicted by ships from Ile de France in the first sixteen months of the war. Decaen would have had a more accurate and undoubtedly higher figure.

That King should have given such a letter or, for that matter, any official letter to Flinders while he was under the protection of a French passport is difficult to understand. And Flinders, who would maintain that he did not know what the dispatch box contained, was certainly aware of its official character. Having accepted it in Port Jackson, he should have flung it into the sea during the final night when he was sailing for Port Nord Ouest, for he knew by then that war had been renewed. Directions to 'prepare of sinking' and throw overboard official papers under threat of capture by an enemy were virtually standard.

As it was, the letter was entirely in opposition to the purpose of Flinders's passport and his professed function, and his possession of it could hardly have failed to arouse further Decaen's ire and perhaps confirm to some extent the warnings of Péron and the likelihood that Flinders was indeed a subversive agent. Flinders had violated the neutrality of the passport he had received from France. There was, however, considerable irony in the fact that on sailing from Ile de France that December, the *Géographe*, protected by an English passport as a ship of science, had carried dispatches from Decaen to Bonaparte, with a detailed scheme for the overthrow of British power in India.

Increasingly conscious of his helplessness before a powerful and obdurate opponent, Flinders seems now to have tried to ignore the facts of his situation, and resorted instead to an emotional appeal to the governor based on the abstractions of justice and scientific progress. He cited the instructions received by La Pérouse to observe conditions in all the ports he visited and the freedom of Baudin and Hamelin to comment upon Port Jackson and its features, although war was in progress on Hamelin's arrival. He again described the purpose of his own voyage and the sequence of misfortunes that had brought him to Ile de France. He continued:

> Now, Sir, I would beg to ask you whether it becomes the French nation, independently of all passport, to stop the progress of such a voyage, and of which the whole maritime world are to receive the benefit? . . . I sought protection and assistance in your port, and I have found a prison! . . .
>
> Judge for me as a British officer employed in a neutral occupation,—
>
> Judge for me as a zealous philanthropist, what I must feel as being thus treated.[11]

Obviously Decaen saw Flinders in neither of these categories, and there was no reply. However, a final request, that his servant, John Elder, might attend him at the inn, was granted. Elder was brought from the prison ship the next day.

Summer in Port Nord Ouest was oppressively hot and humid. Cut off from the trade winds to the east and south by the serrated peaks of its surrounding hills, the town lay in breathless heat under a tropical sun. Heavy rains brought brief respites, followed by high, unrelieved humidity lying like a cloak over the town. Those who could left the coast for the higher altitudes of the interior.

In the confined space of their rooms at the Café Marengo the prisoners found conditions almost insupportable. Within the latticed windows the air was still, heavy and hot, and after the three previous months on the cramped and crowded decks of the little *Cumberland*, they ached for physical activity. Even worse were the bugs and mosquitos that besieged them in their beds at night. Bites on bodies still on the edge of scurvy were inflamed and painful, and Flinders's ulcers broke out again on his legs and feet. Once more he was barely able to walk.

On 23 December Flinders wrote to Decaen, this time only requesting the attention of a surgeon and asking under what conditions he might write to the Admiralty and to friends and family in Britain. The response was prompt. He might write to whom he wished, but the letters were to be sent open to the town major, evidently the senior military commander of Port Nord Ouest, who would forward them. That evening and on the following two days the surgeon called, dressed the sores and prescribed lemonade, fruit and vegetables.

On the 25th Flinders noted in his diary that Christmas Day was not observed at Ile de France; shops were open and people were at work. The day passed without incident, with no word from the governor. Exasperated, Flinders wrote again, much as before, but remarking on the governor's early accusation of being imposed upon and his actions, which showed that Decaen had intended before even seeing Flinders to stop the *Cumberland*.

This time the general's reply came within hours. Flinders's hopes rose, and with a French dictionary he sat down eagerly to try to decipher the message. The letter was brief. There was no purpose in commencing a debate on the detention of the *Cumberland*. While the general was willing to attribute Flinders's 'unreserved tone' to his present situation, his voyage in the *Cumberland* was 'proof of an officious zeal, more for the private interests of Great Britain than for what had induced the French government to give you a passport'. Further, Flinders's last letter, 'overstepping all the bounds of civility', left Decaen with no alternative: all correspondence 'tending to demonstrate the justice of your cause' was to cease, 'since you know so little of how to preserve the rules of decorum'.[12]

The next day Flinders confirmed his rough translation with the interpreter. Extremely angry and bitterly disappointed, he determined not to plead for his release, at least for a time. Instead he requested his printed books, private letters and papers and some charts and manuscript books for completion of his chart of the Gulf of Carpentaria. He also passed on complaints from his men of scanty food and hot, closed-up quarters at night. He was told that his people would receive the same treatment as French seamen in service and, if this was not the case, the situation would be rectified.

Monistrol and Bonnefoy arrived at the inn the next day and Flinders's trunk from the *Cumberland* was brought in. Monistrol's manner was gentle, but he made it clear that he personally regretted the tone of Flinders's letters to the governor. He believed that it would tend to protract rather than shorten the time of his detention. Flinders defended himself. He had sought justice, not favours; hence no adulatory style was required. Politely, the two Frenchmen did not disagree, but again they said that a different manner of writing would have served him better. Flinders was unmoved. Later he wrote: 'So soon as the two gentlemen were gone, I took out my naval signal book from the trunk and tore it to pieces; the private signals had been lost in the shipwreck, so that my mind was now freed from apprehensions which had given much inquietude'.[13]

Flinders's dealings with authority on Isle de France would be conducted mainly through Colonel Monistrol, whose life to this point had run remarkably parallel to his own. Monistrol was born at Lorient in Britanny in the same year as Flinders, and entered the army in 1789, when young Matthew's name had appeared on the muster role of HMS *Alert*. By 1801 Monistrol had attained the rank of *chef de bataillon* or major, and as aide-de-camp to General Decaen had landed at Ile de France in February 1803. Flinders would regard him with some resentment as an extension of Decaen, but he could entertain no real criticism of this courteous and essentially very considerate young French officer.

In the final days of 1803 Flinders was allowed to take from his trunk at the government house additional letters, journals of bearings and astronomical observations, logbooks and charts. The third volume of his log was missing, as were the dispatch boxes from Sydney; they were, he was told, with the governor. On the last day of the year he sent to the town major an unsealed letter to the Admiralty, briefly recounting events since his sailing from Port Jackson in the *Porpoise*, and two personal letters, one to Ann's father, the Reverend Mr Tyler. None of these reached their destinations.

28

The Garden Prison

Flinders began the year 1804 with serious work on his records and charts of Torres Strait and the Gulf of Carpentaria. Many of the originals had been lost or damaged in the seas that had overwhelmed the *Porpoise* on Wreck Reef. He was handicapped by the lack of the third volume of his logbook, which contained his most recent observations in the area, but compensated to a large extent with Aken's very similar journal, a fact he did not reveal to the French.

On 26 February he wrote in his diary: 'My employment lately has been to complete the accounts of the time-keepers and write up the logbook intended for the Admiralty'.[1] Aken was making a copy of Flinders's bearing book and Elder was working on a copy of the log to replace the one spoiled in the shipwreck: '. . . our time is not in vain'.

The Englishmen's living conditions improved a little. They were given an additional room and mosquito nets for their beds. At Flinders's request, the cask of printed books left on the *Cumberland* was delivered to the inn. The surgeon, M. Chapotin, and the interpreter called regularly. As Flinders's ulcers improved, the surgeon recommended outdoor exercise, but this was refused. In fact, their supervision had become more strict. Chapotin and Bonnefoy were required to show written orders when they called, and as Flinders's sores began to heal, they came less frequently.

The master of the ship *Hunter* was questioned by Decaen on his contact with Flinders and he and the master of the *Fanny* were told to accept no letters to be forwarded on Flinders's behalf. Earlier a resident Swiss, a Dutchman and a Norwegian had also called, but no one came a second time. Only the Swiss, Johann Boand, managed an occasional surreptitious greeting. No one wanted to risk the suspicions of the captain-general. For Flinders and Aken their principal link with the outside world was Elder, who was permitted to go to the market and to visit the *Cumberland*'s men in the prison ship.

Flinders now faced a financial problem. While meals at the inn were provided, Flinders and Aken had to meet personal expenses for such things as laundry, fruit and items of clothing, many of these necessary replacements for clothes lost in the shipwreck. Flinders's few dollars[2] were quickly spent and there was no facility for cashing his English bills. With Decaen's permission, Bonnefoy enlisted the help of the Danish consul, who offered to cash Flinders's draft on the British Navy Board. A brief uproar occurred when the guard at Flinders's rooms saw him handing to Bonnefoy the necessary papers and, not understanding what was being said, seized and arrested the shocked interpreter. The matter was cleared up and Bonnefoy returned in the evening with 264 dollars, representing Flinders's back pay from the navy up to 30 October 1803. Later the French provided Flinders with an allowance of 60 dollars per month, with an additional 20 dollars for Elder. Aken received 40 dollars a month. Every month Flinders had Elder purchase a large basket of fruit and vegetables, which he was allowed to deliver to the *Cumberland*'s people. The battered schooner, meanwhile, had been laid up and, like her stores and provisions in the commissariat, was steadily deteriorating.

Flinders again requested a meeting with Decaen. There was no reply, and when he pressed Monistrol for an answer, he was told flatly that there was none. Apparently, Decaen told Monistrol that any conversation between Flinders and himself would be such as to oblige the governor to send Flinders 'to the tower'.[3] Any response to Flinders's letters and messages was now made verbally through Monistrol or Bonnefoy, often to the effect that the general would consider the matter when the press of other business subsided. Simple requests might be complied with without comment. At other times there was only silence. Flinders was never again to see the governor. His first meeting on the day of his arrival at Port Nord Ouest was also his last.

In mid-January 1804 Decaen directed to Denis Dècres, the French Minister of Marine and the Colonies, a complete report on what had occurred regarding his English prisoner and referring to the third volume of Flinders's log and to King's dispatches to Lord Hobart, he cited the political considerations that had motivated his actions and Flinders's role, as he saw it, in events. Decaen had excerpts from King's dispatches translated into French, 48 pages that he signed and forwarded to the ministry.[4]

In a letter dated 30 July 1804 Dècres replied that he had passed the Flinders matter on to the Council of State, which had approved Decaen's measures and through a sentiment of generosity—'*par un pur sentiment de générosité*'[5]—was pleased to grant Captain Flinders his freedom and the restitution of his vessel, pending the approval of Bonaparte. Although he did not know it, Flinders was at this point just a step away from liberty.

Decaen would have received Dècres's letter about the end of October 1804 and probably was satisfied with the reply. He had placed the problem of Matthew Flinders in other hands. In doing this there were ramifications. Decaen could no longer act independently on liberating Flinders as or when he wished to do so. If at first Decaen had intended to hold Flinders for a time, and having punished him sufficiently, set him free, he now had to await an official decision from Paris. This was something Flinders did not understand, which added to his frustration and sense of hopelessness.

A month after dispatching his letter on Flinders, Decaen sent to Dècres a plan for an invasion of India. The minister's reply assured him that the project would be considered when, as events developed, it merited the attention of Bonaparte. Together with the case of Matthew Flinders, the plan for India was set aside in the rush of much greater events. French troops were being massed at Boulogne, apparently in preparation for an invasion of Britain. As well, the process of transforming Bonaparte's consulate into a hereditary empire was in progress.

Again denied an interview, Flinders wrote the general a letter outlining three propositions: to be allowed to leave Ile de France with his vessel and papers, pledging his honour not to reveal for a specified time any information on the colony; to be sent to France; or to allow Aken and the crew to depart on the *Cumberland*. In view of all that had transpired, Flinders was remarkably naive to believe that the governor would negotiate with him on any of these premises. Perhaps they were the product of desperation, thrown out with no real expectation of success. Flinders later commented, 'of no part of this letter was any notice taken'.[6] Flinders was, in fact, advised by Bonnefoy that the correct procedure in contacting the general was to write to Monistrol, as aide-de-camp, who would pass on the message. Flinders replied that this was not his method. He wrote again to Decaen, confining himself, however, to a request for certain of his charts. It was a short letter, which he concluded, as was now his habit, 'Your Excellency's prisoner, Matthew Flinders'. There was no answer.

In early February 1804 Flinders received a visit from a man whose friendship would help to create important changes in the conditions of his internment. The man was Captain Jacques Bergeret of the French navy, who had used the independent authority of a naval officer to override the objections of Decaen in his handling of English prisoners. In 1795 Bergeret had been captured by the British at the end of a long and courageous sea battle, and had become a personal friend of the notable naval officer Sir Edward Pellew. Two years later he was sent on parole to Paris to negotiate the liberation of Admiral Sydney Smith, then a prisoner of the French. Failing to secure Smith's release, Bergeret returned to London, and when the admiral later escaped, was freed in recognition of his honourable conduct during the negotiations.

By 1803 he had left the navy and purchased the merchant ship *Psyche*, arriving at Ile de France just after the outbreak of war. Resuming naval service, he raided British shipping in the Indian Ocean, and in early 1804 returned with three prizes, the merchantmen *Superb*, *Alfred* and *Admiral Alpin*. On board the *Admiral Alpin* there were several army officers and four of their wives. Once ashore, Bergeret arranged for the women to remain together with their husbands. The couples were housed at a tavern in the town, the single men at a residence in the country. Bergeret then visited Flinders. He expressed sympathy for his situation, saying that he regretted not having been ashore when Flinders arrived, as he may have been of help in preventing what occurred. He avoided any explanation of Flinders's confinement, but seemed to want to improve conditions for him and offered money if needed.

Cheered by the thought of a group of English men and women nearby, Flinders sent Elder to the tavern where they were held. Elder returned with magazines, newspapers and a Steele's list of naval events up to mid-August 1803, which 'after so long an ignorance of what was passing in England, were highly acceptable'.[7] Possibly heartened by this, Flinders bluntly asked Bonnefoy what he thought was likely to be done with him and Aken. 'He replied that we should probably be kept prisoners *so long as the war lasted...*'[8]

Flinders was appalled. Bonnefoy had to be wrong. The interpreter's opinion was surely 'that of a man unacquainted with the nature of a voyage of discovery, and the interest it excites in every nation of the civilised world, and not least in France'.[9] He could scarcely believe that there were people who thought so little of 'a voyage for the investigation of new countries' that they would put 'a stop to it... [with]... no more consideration than if it were a common voyage. To be kept a prisoner so long as the war should last, did not therefore enter into my conception as within the bounds of probability'.[10]

And in this much later account he added what must have reflected a kind of sad acceptance, achieved perhaps hours, days or even years later: 'it is the failing of men of all professions to over-rate the importance of that which they themselves adopted, and into this error it will probably be thought I had fallen with respect to voyages of discovery'.[11]

Some days later he concluded that even if he should shortly be set at liberty, it was too late in the season to attempt a passage around the Cape of Good Hope in the *Cumberland* and, in another year's time, the ship would probably be too rotten to undertake the voyage. He therefore asked for the governor's permission to sell the schooner and repeated his latest request for his charts and books. The reply was to 'have a little patience'. Flinders was coming more and more to think that his situation had been referred to Paris and that, despite Bonnefoy's opinion, freedom would soon come from there.

In early March Captain Bergeret called again. He did not think that anything could be done at the time to secure Flinders's release, but said he would speak to the governor about allowing Flinders and his companions to live in the country. About a week later he did so, but no decision was forthcoming. On 23 March Charrington and the crew of the *Cumberland* were brought ashore to be transferred to a prison in the district of Flacq, some 20 miles from Port Nord Ouest on the east side of the island. Flinders was permitted to speak to the boatswain in the presence of a French officer, and he urged that no attempt be made to escape, as he believed they would be set at liberty by the French government in six to eight months. Meanwhile Charrington must do what he could to keep the men clean and well behaved. The crewman who had created serious difficulties earlier had, with the consent of the French, joined a Spanish frigate.

Increasingly convinced that relief must come from outside the island, Flinders began considering ways of sending letters to England other than through the town major's office. He did not know whether those letters were actually forwarded, and obviously they had to be written with restraint. The Admiralty needed to know the facts before steps could be taken from Britain to secure his liberty and, as he soon discovered, clandestine means of getting letters out of Ile de France were not difficult to find. Fellow officers, foreign captains and travellers and eventually some French friends were willing to carry his letters when they left the island.

He therefore addressed to the secretary of the Admiralty a complete account of his arrival and treatment on Ile de France, enclosing copies of relevant letters, but being careful to say nothing that could be taken as an infringement of the conditions of his passport. All of this he enclosed in a letter to a friend in London, and sent with a willing carrier by way of the United States. He learned later that the letter arrived in England in the middle of August and was reported in *The London Chronicle* of 18–21 August 1804. He also wrote to Banks, and the letter apparently reached Sir Joseph at the same time.

Flinders's letter received prompt attention from the Colonial Office and the Admiralty. An abstract of his case was to be transmitted to the French government, and the Minister of Marine requested to provide British authorities with duplicates of dispatches regarding Flinders. His speedy release was generally anticipated, largely because of the hospitality extended to Baudin's expedition at Port Jackson. Little, however, seems to have eventuated from these initial plans.

The war had by now severed almost all official communication between the British and French governments, and events in the early months of 1804 had intensified the suspicions and antagonism between the two countries. Reports of royalist plots to overthrow Bonaparte circulated in France, while the First Consul seized from outside the French border a Bourbon prince, the Duc d'Enghien, whom he summarily executed. The Grande Armée was in camp at Boulogne.

Nearly 2000 ships, certainly an invasion fleet, were gathered between Brest and Antwerp.

Almost immediately after he received Flinders's letter, Joseph Banks initiated a private and unofficial application for Flinders's release by writing on 22 August 1804 as President of the Royal Society to its French counterpart, the Institut National de France, of which he was a member. Tactfully, he recounted the events that put Flinders on Ile de France and, 'in consequence of some misunderstanding of the Governor', his having been accused of being a spy.[12] He went on to mention the French government's favourable treatment of Cook and the generous reception in Port Jackson of Baudin's expedition. To Governor King he wrote:

> Poor Flinders, you know, I suppose, put into Isle de France for water, and was detained as a prisoner, and treated as a spy. Our Government have no communication with the French; but I have some with their literary men, and have written . . . and have sent in my letter a copy of the very handsome one M. Baudin left with you. If this should effect Flinders's liberation, which I think it will, we shall both rejoice.[13]

Banks also wrote to Robert Brown, still in New South Wales, with the news of Flinders's detention, adding that 'as the French are great favourers of science, and as the ship has a passport', Flinders's release would in time be effected.[14] Banks did not realise that the passport issued to the *Investigator* was invalid for the *Cumberland*. Nor did he know of the dispatches from King to Lord Hobart that Flinders had carried. Apparently no one in London was aware of these circumstances, and as the war drew on, successive Lords of the Admiralty showed diminishing interest in seeking the return of the hydrographer who had charted the coasts of distant Terra Australis. Such requests were mainly reserved in wartime for ranking naval officers with battle experience. The confident assumption that the importance of Flinders's scientific work would set him free was about to be engulfed in the minutiae of military and political priorities.

By 1804 there had developed in the Indian Ocean area a cartel system that provided for the exchange of prisoners of war between Britain and France. Officers, crew and passengers on ships captured by French privateers and naval vessels were brought to Ile de France.

Growing numbers and the expense of providing for them made it expedient to ship them out in exchange for French captives taken by the British. At various times a British ship would approach the island under a flag of truce, discharge a number of French prisoners and take on board a like number of English captives of similar rank.

Several English officers hopefully awaiting exchange were housed at the edge of Port Nord Ouest in the Maison Despeaux, a large, old, stone-built residence also known as the Garden Prison. With no immediate prospect of being relocated in the country, and 'being most heartily weary of close confinement',[15] Flinders now asked to be taken to this place. His request was approved.

A surgeon by the name of Despeaux had built the spacious, two-storey plantation house now hired by the government as an open prison for British officers. It stood on fairly high ground about a mile north-east of town, surrounded by a large garden of tropical fruit trees enclosed by a dry-stone wall. Flinders later quoted the area of the garden as two and a half acres, but an existing plan shows it to be about twice that size. To the east lay a green valley and wooded hills; to the west the harbour and the open sea. It had a colourful history, having once been a gambling establishment and a popular seamen's gathering place, and later accommodation for the envoys of Tippu Sahib, Sultan of Mysore, when he was engaged in anti-British negotiations with revolutionary France. On each floor several small bedrooms opened to a large central room.[16] An adjoining guard house and sentinels at the gate made the residence a place of internment, but within its garden walls several British officers lived with a reasonable degree of freedom.

At seven in the morning of 31 March Colonel Monistrol and another officer arrived at the Café Marengo and walked with Flinders to the house to choose rooms for himself, Aken and Elder. On the upper floor, they 'took up one end of one storey of the house'. The wide grounds were knee-deep in grass, but the site was 'very airy and agreeable' and the 'fresh air, which in comparison with our place of confinement, made me think it a paradise'.[17] The mile walk, however, demonstrated Flinders's weakness. He would not have made the distance, he said, without the support of Monistrol. In the evening carts transported the

Englishmen's belongings to the house, and they enthusiastically 'took possession of our new prison'.

There were eight other men at Maison Despeaux, two who had been caught on Ile de France by the outbreak of war, four from the Indian army, taken on the *Admiral Alpin*, and two midshipmen captured on a prize ship retaken by the French. Apparently, whenever numbers increased much beyond this, some were moved to the prison facility at Flacq.

Trim, too, was taken to the Garden Prison. However, 'fear of some clandestine proceedings on the part of the soldiers of the guard', as Flinders wrote, persuaded him to accept the offer of a French woman to take Trim as a companion for her little daughter, and only a fortnight later, the little black cat, veteran of so many seagoing adventures, disappeared. 'All research and offers of recompense were in vain, poor Trim was effectively lost', all too probably stewed and eaten, as Flinders wrote, by some hungry slave. 'Thus perished my faithful intelligent Trim! The sporting, affectionate and useful companion during four years . . .'[18]

Maison Despeaux offered simple pleasures that were sheer delight to the three men from the Café Marengo. With the grass cut and paths cleared, the extensive garden presented the opportunity to walk, the many trees providing shade in the heat of the day. At least a part of the roof of the house was flat and could be reached by a stairway and a door. Here, in the cool of early evening, the detainees enjoyed the sight of the sea and through their telescopes watched the movement of ships in the harbour. In one of the building's large central rooms meals were served at two tables, Flinders and Aken sharing one with the two young midshipmen, Seymour and Dale, and Walter Robertson, surgeon of the Bengal Establishment, who had been visiting in Mauritius for his health when caught on the island by the renewal of war. There was the diversion, too, of visits by French friends and neighbours, who often brought gifts of food together with local news and gossip.

Flinders himself was the object of some interest. While many regarded his situation with sympathy, there were also speculations as to whether he was who he claimed to be, with reports of his having chased a French vessel on shore and of soundings and surveys of the island's coast found upon him. It is evident, however, that the personal qualities that won Flinders friends in Sydney did so on Mauritius as well. The surgeon of an American ship wrote to his wife of having 'dined with Captain Flinders . . . I have seen him but three times but conceive the highest opinion of him.'[19]

The Garden Prison provided Flinders with the opportunity and the space he needed for work on his books and charts, and the relief of some diversions:

> Before breakfast my time is devoted to the Latin language, to bring up what I formerly learned. After breakfast I am employed making out a fair copy of the Investigators log in lieu of my own which was spoiled at the shipwreck. When tired of writing, I apply to music, and when my fingers are tired with the flute, I write again until dinner. After dinner we amuse ourselves with billiards until tea, and afterwards walk in the garden till dusk. From then till supper I make one at Pleyels quartettes; afterwards walk half an hour and then sleep soundly till day light when I get up and bathe . . . my time does not pass wearily or uselessly . . .[20]

The works of Ignaz Josef Pleyel, an Austro-French composer, were popular throughout Europe, particularly his quartets and *symphonies concertantes*. He also published sheet music, which apparently was available on Ile de France. There was a fullness of melody, 'a grand stile' and then sweet plaintiveness, as Flinders observed even in his simpler pieces. Flinders did not mention any early training on the flute, but obviously he was proficient enough to participate in a group. He also arranged for a French teacher, but the lessons were forbidden by Decaen. He wrote in his diary, 'Blessed is he that expects nothing, for he shall not be disappointed'.[21]

The Garden Prison allowed callers. Permission to visit was required from the town major, but rarely denied to 'persons of respectability'. Bonnefoy came, always considerate and helpful. He arranged for the return to Flinders of some of his personal belongings stored in the commissariat, had the first of three promised tables delivered and obtained permanent permission for Elder to pass the sentinel at the gate in order to deliver messages or make small purchases in the town. Flinders bought writing paper in some quantity, an item probably landed by American ships. At one point he had to set aside his work because paper was temporarily unavailable.

When not at sea, Jacques Bergeret visited. His proposal to Decaen that Flinders be sent to France was turned down, but he persisted in asking that Flinders and Aken be removed to live in the country. A Captain Halgan of the French corvette *Berceau* called several times, offered money if needed, and, as Flinders wrote somewhat cynically, appeared to be concerned for him. On being ordered to France, Halgan applied for Flinders to be sent with him. As expected, this was denied.

One evening two other French naval officers appeared at the Maison Despeaux, one of them an astronomer with whom Flinders had an interesting conversation. The astronomer promised to request that more of Flinders's books and papers be sent to him; the other man offered money. An element of what very simply might be called a brotherhood of the sea had settled about Flinders. There was a firm bond among men who knew the fragility and isolation of their fragment of wood and sail passing over a seemingly endless, empty, watery plain. Injustice had ensnared one of their own and they came to help.

It was undoubtedly in his awareness of this sense of fraternity that, in April 1804, Flinders wrote to the French naval commander in the Indian Ocean area, Rear-Admiral Charles Alexandre Léon, Comte Durand de Linois, then at Ile de France. In February Linois's ships had encountered the extremely valuable British China Fleet, sixteen big East Indiamen and twelve other vessels, sailing for England from Guangzhou. Most of the *Investigator*'s old company were with the Fleet, and on the advice of Robert Fowler, the commodore reinforced the complements of three Indiamen with experienced naval men who brought the merchant vessels as close as possible to the fighting standard of 64-gun king's ships. Linois took the three Indiamen for British ships-of-the-line and, after a brief exchange of fire, drew off. The China Fleet reached England safely in August. Robert Fowler and Samuel Flinders were recognised for their performance in the battle.

Linois returned to Ile de France on 1 April 1804. Some news of the battle must have filtered through to the inmates of the Garden Prison, but it was a year before Flinders read a full account of the event. In 1804, however, what interested him most was a rumour that the admiral's flagship, the *Marengo*, was being prepared for passage to France.

In his letter to the admiral Flinders wrote a complete account of his work and difficulties. He would willingly undergo, he said, an examination by the captains of the French squadron to determine whether or not he had performed 'any act of hostility against the French nation'.[22] If he could not be set at liberty, he asked to be taken to France where his case could be submitted directly to the French government for a decision.

Linois replied at once, saying in effect that as he had not been on the island at the time of Flinders's arrival, the Englishman was subject to Decaen's authority. He would, however, speak to the governor. Unfortunately, Linois's failure with the China Fleet had brought stormy recriminations from Decaen, and his intercession on Flinders's behalf was met with the usual rebuff.

In June Linois sailed not to France but on another cruise, and on his return to Ile de France on 31 October 1804, he wrote to the eminent geographer, Councillor of State Charles Pierre Claret, Comte de Fleurieu, entreating him to secure the liberation of Flinders. No action was taken. In May 1805 Linois and his squadron sailed again and thereafter did not return to Ile de France.

In the meantime Flinders had also written to Richard Wellesley, Marquess Wellesley, Governor-General of Bengal. Wellesley responded promptly with a letter to Decaen, which the governor ignored.

While he wrote various letters seeking his release, Flinders could scarcely bring himself to write at any length to his family. Less than a fortnight after his arrival on the island, Flinders had written a short note to the Reverend Tyler, which he gave to the town major. Much later he told Ann that he had written her father briefly on 14 April 1804 as well, a letter he also handed to the authorities. Apparently Mr Tyler received neither message. In late April Flinders wrote again, a letter he evidently sent out by private means:

> To the Rev. W. Tyler Partney near Spilsby Lincolnshire
>
> Isle of France April 26 1804
>
> My dear Sir
>
> Lest my letter of Dec. 31 last from this place should not have reached you, I again write, that I am a prisoner in this island with very little

> prospect of being soon set at liberty. I beg you will inform my friends of the circumstance, and especially that *dear* friend under your protection to whom I cannot write in my present unhappy situation. Add, if you please, that I am recovered from the scorbutic state in which I last wrote, and at this time am in very good health.
>
> Believe me, my dear Sir, to be, with the greatest regard your sincere friend and humble servant
>
> Mattw. Flinders

Then, abandoning restraint, he added, '"*The pleasures of memory*". "*Forget me not*"! Oh never'.[23]

This was possibly the family's first word from Matthew, with its few facts and sad, emotional postscript. In May Flinders wrote again, asking Mr Tyler to let his stepmother know that before leaving Port Jackson he had received her letter on his father's death: 'I had hoped by this time to have been with her to have made such arrangements as would have been most for her comfort, but I am debarred from all those who are dear to me: I am wrung with anguish. When my family are the subject of my meditation, my bonds enter deep into my soul'.[24]

He did not write to the family again for three months.

Petty restrictions regularly reminded the men at Maison Despeaux that they were prisoners. On 1 June the guards' commander, Captain Neufville, demanded that all spyglasses, the small telescopes owned by the officers, be turned in. Each would be returned to the owner on his receiving permission to leave the island, but, as Flinders recorded, 'to the best of my knowledge not one of them could obtain their own'.[25] Flinders lost two, his own and one probably belonging to the Board of Longitude. Soon after, the door to the flat roof was nailed shut. As the prisoners were forbidden to walk in the grounds after sunset, the loss of the evening walk on the roof was much resented. Flinders wrote, 'It being afterward suspected, and not without reason, that some of the gentlemen had forced the door, we were officially informed that the sentinels had received orders to shoot any one who might be seen on the roof; this produced greater circumspection, but the pleasure of the walk and having a view of the sea was such, that it did not wholly remedy the evil'.[26] Whether he was one of those exercising 'greater circumspection' Flinders did not say, but he remarked that sometimes he climbed a tall almond tree to look at the harbour.

The day after walking on the roof was forbidden, the resident sergeant demanded all swords and other arms possessed by the prisoners. Flinders sent a note to the governor: he would surrender his sword only to an officer of equal rank to himself. A week later Captain Neufville called to apologise for the mistake. Swords were taken only from prisoners, and the captain-general had no intention of making Flinders a prisoner until ordered to do so. This puzzling explanation Flinders pursued when Neufville came next to the house, and was assured that he was not a prisoner. He was merely 'under *surveillance* for a short period'.[27] Three months later, however, an officer politely requested the sword by order of the governor. Although the officer was of inferior rank to himself, Flinders delivered the weapon. Not to do so could have meant 'further degradation'. No one asked whether either Flinders or Aken, whose sword was also taken, had any other weapon.

A source of resentment, too, was Decaen's order that the English officers were not to step outside the garden gate. Thus, 'the convenience of buying poultry and other provisions at the gate will most likely be prevented'.[28]

A more calculated insult occurred on the birthday of King George III, when the flagship *Marengo* flew French colours above the British ensign, which was turned union down. Flinders considered this: 'Such an action . . . would be deserving of contempt, were it not from the reflection that such things tend to keep alive national animosity, and the flames of war'.[29]

Their limited finances were always a worry to the detainees. At the Café Marengo food and accommodation were paid for by the government. At the Garden Prison rent had to be paid out of the prisoners' allowances. This, Flinders commented, 'is perhaps the first instance of men being charged for the accomodation of a prison'.[30]

A day or two after the Marengo incident Flinders was startled by the appearance of a seaman from the *Cumberland* and another inmate from Flacq behind the wall of the Garden Prison. Desperate with hunger, they had come to complain of the single meal per day they were receiving, consisting only of bread and a very small portion of fish or meat. The promise of French seamen's rations had apparently been forgotten, and an appeal to the officer in charge had brought no result. Alarmed lest they be captured as escapees, Flinders gave them money and sent them with Elder to Bonnefoy, asking that he take them to the town major's office. They were put on board the prison ship and kept in irons for several weeks. Through Bonnefoy, however, Flinders was able to secure for the boatswain, Charrington, the allowance and limited freedom granted to the mates of merchant ships, and when he could, sent tea and a little money to the crew.

A rumour reached Flinders that his trunk of books and papers still at the government house had been opened and copies of his charts made to forward to France. Few things could have been more upsetting. In the meantime, however, Bergeret had obtained permission for Flinders to take from the trunk the remaining charts and related material, and in early July Bonnefoy conducted Matthew to the office of the secretary at the government house, where he anxiously inspected the bindings and seal on the chest. Inside he found his belongings exactly as he had left them. He lifted out the charts, papers and books that needed work or were necessary to complete other documents, the fragmented purser's accounts of the *Investigator*'s stores, and his passport, commission, letters and letter book. Flinders asked for the third volume of his logbook but again this was refused. The trunk was then lashed up and resealed.

For the remainder of the day with Bonnefoy, Flinders had the happiness of being free. Together they called on several of Flinders's new acquaintances, among them the Danish consul, the Chevalier Charles de Pelgrom, who invited them to dinner, and in the quiet tropical evening they walked peacefully back to the Garden Prison.

Flinders's own assessment of Decaen had by now taken shape and in his diary he wrote:

> It seems that all description of people here are as much afraid of the captain-general as if he were the almighty holding destruction in his right hand and salvation in his left. The truth I believe is that the violence of his passions outstrip his judgement and reason and do not allow them to operate, for he is instantaneous in his movements and should he do injustice still he must pursue it because it would lower his dignity to retract. His antipathy moreover is so great to Englishmen

> ...that immediately the name of one is mentioned, he is directly in a rage... With all this, he has the credit of having a good heart at the bottom.[31]

It was, perhaps, a reasonably fair assessment of a man who had done Flinders so much harm and whom he had met face to face only once.

29 Letters

At about this time Flinders was shown some correspondence regarding his internment that had appeared in the French newspaper, *Le Moniteur*. Incensed by some of the statements, Flinders wrote to the Admiralty describing the occurrences and protesting the comments, and on 11 March 1805 wrote with similar protests to the Comte de Fleurieu. This letter ran to fifteen foolscap pages, with which he enclosed copies of five items of supporting correspondence. He sent a copy of the letter to the Admiralty.

In the years of his detention Matthew Flinders would write countless letters to innumerable persons. Invariably this correspondence repeated the story of his harsh and unjust treatment. That he had been engaged in purely non-combatant scientific endeavours had not been enough to win his freedom, and the theme of the injustice done to him became paramount. There were, however, things he never mentioned in these letters: the fact that his passport covered only the *Invesigator* and was invalid for the *Cumberland*; the manner in which his own behaviour had angered Decaen; the folly of his having carried Governor King's official dispatches. These facts he kept to himself.

The result of this correspondence was not always to Flinders's advantage. Recipients who were in a position to complain on Flinders's behalf officially or even personally to Decaen sometimes did so, which angered the governor. Apparently, too, such letters added to the perceived importance of his captive. Evidently Decaen never ceased to suspect Flinders of being a spy, and there could have been political implications for his own career that he had no desire to risk.

In August 1804 Flinders was able to send a letter to Governor King in Sydney through Robert Campbell of the merchant firm of Campbell,

Clarke & Company in Calcutta, by then also trading in Port Jackson. Among the letters retrieved from Flinders's trunk was the first part of a letter to King written from Kupang in November 1803, with the account of the voyage of the *Cumberland* from Wreck Reef to Timor.

Now Flinders described events since. His protests to the French governor had no effect, he said, for 'a military tyrant knows no law or principle but what appears to him for the immediate interest of his Government, or the gratification of his own private caprices'.[1] Added to the loss of 'promotion, peace of mind, fortune, fame, and everything that a man holds dear', the shipwreck and its subsequent risks had created 'no very common portion of suffering'. In a postscript he added, 'Lord Hobart's dispatches, and I believe Col'l Paterson's box, have been opened, but all other letters remain untouched'.

The letter drew an immediate response from Governor King. Philip King and his wife were sincere friends of Matthew Flinders, and the impact of this very emotional message would have been considerable. Learning that his dispatch box had been opened, King would have realised with pain the damaging effect of its contents upon Flinders's situation, while the thought of a Frenchman reading his dispatches no doubt added to his displeasure. There was also an oversight he probably remembered. King had failed to give Flinders a copy of Baudin's letter to the administrators of Ile de France and Réunion, recommending any British ship and commander bearing one of the letters.

On 30 April 1805, evidently within days of having received Flinders's letter, King addressed a very formal and official letter of remonstrance to 'The Governor of the Isles of France and Réunion'. On the same day he wrote to Lord Camden, Secretary of State for War and the Colonies, and to Secretary Marsden of the Admiralty, enclosing copies of Flinders's letter and his own reply to Decaen. Evidently King considered hiring a vessel to demand Flinders's release, but decided that Flinders would have been set free before this could be arranged.

Seemingly with King's approval, Flinders's letter was published in part in the *The Sydney Gazette*. In October the following year it was reprinted in England in *The Times* and *The London Chronicle*, and some six months later in a Madras newspaper.

Flinders had written several times to Joseph Banks, but so far had evidently received no reply. Thus on 12 July 1804 he wrote a long and impassioned appeal to Banks. Cut off from the normal contacts of his career, he was filled with desperate worry about the loss of opportunity for promotion, and for the lessening of Banks's interest and patronage. He had been seven months in prison and believed it would be another five before orders regarding him could arrive from France. He added, 'and probably the vessels carrying the dispatches will be taken [by British ships] and the letters thrown overboard... My dependence, therefore, is on the Admiralty demanding me to be given up, by virtue of the French passport'.[2]

The charts that he had sent to England had been completed as well as possible despite reaching the north coast late in the season 'and the early rotteness of the Investigator'. Flinders did not know that these charts lay untouched at the Hydrographic Office and that Banks himself had not taken time to inspect them. Flinders went on:

> No part of the unfortunate circumstances that have since occurred, can, I believe, be attributed to my neglects or mistakes; and therefore I am not without hope, that when the Admiralty know I am suffering an unjust imprisonment, they will think me worthy to be put upon the post-captains' list... It is to you only, Sir Joseph, that I can address myself upon this subject. I have ample testimonies of your power...

This was a vain plea. As Flinders knew very well, prisoners of war were not promoted, and despite his efforts to show himself as an exceptional case, not having been designated as a prisoner of war by Decaen, the Admiralty remained unimpressed. Passionately, Flinders continued:

> If I do not prove myself worthy of your patronage, Sir Joseph, let me be thrown out of the society of all good men. I have too much ambition to rest in the unnoticed middle order of mankind. Since neither birth nor fortune have favoured me, my actions shall speak to the world... although I cannot rival the immortalized name of Cook, yet if persevering industry, joined with what ability I may possess, can accomplish it, then will I secure the second place if you, Sir Joseph, as my guardian genius will but conduct me into the place of probation. The hitherto obscure name of Flinders may thus become a light by which even the illustrious character of Sir Joseph Banks may one day receive an additional ray of glory.

Then he returned to reality:

'But this is visionary, for I am so fast in prison that I cannot get forth; the thought is bitterness. When I recollect where and what I am, and compare it with where and how I ought to be employed, it is misery'. He ended abruptly, 'Excuse me, Sir Joseph, I am your most obliged and obedient servant. Mattw. Flinders'.

Banks's reply, dated 18 June 1805, was blunt and practical. 'From the moment that I heard of your detention, I have used every effort in my power towards effecting your release.'[3] He explained the impossibility of communication between the French and British governments and his own efforts through the National Institute of France. Flinders received the letter in October 1805.

Flinders's fellow prisoner Surgeon Walter Robertson had received parole and permission to return to England by way of the United States. He was scheduled to leave the island in August 1804 and offered to take with him Flinders's charts and letters. Flinders now felt that he could face writing to his family.

Thus on 13 July 1804 he laid on his table the letter to Ann that he had begun in Sydney on 25 June 1803. 'Curious have been the turns of fortune, my dearest wife, since the former part of this letter was addressed to thee',[4] he wrote. As his brother, arriving in England before Matthew's letter, could tell the first part of the story since leaving Port Jackson in the *Porpoise*, he would write of events after parting from Samuel on Wreck Reef. Ann could justly complain that he had not written, but 'in this confinement, watched and suspected, my sighs must be smothered, and the effusions of my love must be given to the winds in some secret corner'. His health was restored and he hoped to be removed to the country; his case had been referred to the French government, but he relied more on the Admiralty's demand for his freedom. In a few months after she had received the letter, he would return to her arms and 'the memory of this misery shall be buried, as a frightful dream'. To various members of his family he sent his 'best love and remembrance . . . How much I do want to see every body, but above all, *thee* . . .'

When Robertson's sailing was delayed, Flinders continued his letter.

> Yesterday I enjoyed a delicious piece of misery in reading over thy dear letters, my beloved Ann. Shall I tell thee that I have never before done it since I have been shut up in this prison. The first day of January I dedicated to 'the pleasures of memory' and was violently tempted to go farther, but I rushed into something else and escaped a further addition to the misery of recollection.

Now he wondered if she could be happy joining him in his prison. He was not without friends among the French, he said, but had one powerful enemy, and again expressed his indignation at the injustice meted out to him 'contrary to the express orders of my passport'. Worrying about Ann's health, he urged her to 'buy a little horse . . . and take the air so often as thou canst, I am sure it will do thee good'.

His last paragraph, teasing and good-humoured, was written for Isabella. She had not written him 'one line for these livelong three years'. It was therefore unlikely that he would bring her any of the exotic souvenirs she would surely love to have: 'a speckled piece out of the coral reef upon which we were shipwrecked . . . or a stump shell brought up by the lead from the bottom of the sea 200 fathoms deep or a little sea horse . . . or perhaps a set of Trim's finger nails which he shed in the Gulph of Carpentaria . . .' He enclosed a bill addressed to his agent on which Ann could draw twenty pounds.

Flinders also resumed the letter to his stepmother that he had started in Sydney on receiving the news of his father's death. 'What has been written above has been lying by me a very long time', he wrote. 'I little expected to finish the letter in a prison'.[5] Again he described the injustice of his detention, the sympathy of even the French on the island and, when Robertson's departure was postponed, he wrote of family members. He was concerned for his aging uncle and aunt in Spalding, his father's always impecunious brother and his wife. If his stepmother had on hand any money of his, 'I would be glad if you would make them a present of ten or twenty pounds . . .'

He wrote to Samuel. Word had reached him that Robert Fowler and Samuel Flinders 'had an active share in driving off the French Admiral Linois. I hope it will prove correct information, for next to my own honours and advancement yours will be the most gratifying to me'.[6] Of his detention he wrote:

> They formed erroneous opinions of me on my arrival,—they imprisoned me,—I remonstrated,—they were enraged that a prisoner should accuse them of injustice, and determined to punish me; I was too obstinate to sacrifice one tittle either of the honour of my country or of myself, and therefore prepared myself to suffer . . . there is but one man here who I believe is my enemy. The governor both hates and fears me . . . Upon a review of probabilities I think we shall be at liberty in December and in England 4 months afterwards.

He urged Samuel to get himself into 'the best style of naval service', to observe and endeavour to excel 'what the most deserving officers do'. With his reading, writing and chartmaking, he was himself 'almost as busy in prison as ever you knew me'. It was very much the letter of an older brother and a naval officer.

Flinders also redated and continued a letter to Joseph Banks, which he sent together with a general chart of Australia that he entitled 'Chart shewing such parts of Terra Australis and its vicinity, as were discovered or examined by the following vessels: Schooner *Francis* of 60 tons burthen in 1798, Sloop *Norfolk* of 25 tons, in the years 1798 and 9, Schooner *Cumberland* of 29 tons burthen in 1803, and by His Majesty's Ship *Investigator* in 1801, 2 and 3, by M. Flinders, Commander'. In the letter he discussed the name he thought applicable to the entire southern continent, which his explorations had shown to be one body of land:

> The propriety of the name Australia or Terra Australis, which I have applied to the whole body of what has generally been called New Holland must be submitted to the approbation of the Admiralty and the learned in geography . . . as it is required that the whole body should have one general name, since it is now known . . . that it is certainly all one land, so I judge that one more acceptable to all parties and on all accounts cannot be found there than that now applied.[7]

Flinders was not the first to use the name Australia. He may have known it from a 1799 chart of the navigator James Wilson, possibly from a 1622 account of the voyage of Willem Schouten and Jacob Lemaire, or some other source. His use of the name, however, eventually helped to make it better known to a public accustomed to Terra

Australis. Flinders had also written and now included a paper entitled 'Concerning the Differences in the Magnetic Needle on Board the *Investigator*, arising from an Alteration in the Direction of the Ship's Head', which he thought Sir Joseph might wish to present to the Royal Society, but asked that it first be examined by an expert on magnetism.

On 27 August, two days after Flinders had written his letter to Samuel, a British naval squadron under Commodore John Osborn appeared off Ile de France. Two 74-gun ships-of-the-line and several frigates took up blockading positions with the intention of intercepting Admiral Linois and his group on their return from a cruise. The sighting of the ships threw the island into near panic. A few days later the *Cumberland*'s boatswain, Edward Charrington, and six merchant ship officers in the Flacq prison made a daring escape in a boat and reached one of the British ships.

According to Flinders, Decaen flew into 'a paroxysm of rage'.[8] The French commanding officer at Flacq was dismissed and the inmates rushed off to a more secure prison. Every Englishman on Ile de France was closely confined. Paroles and permissions of every kind were cancelled and few visitors were admitted to Maison Despeaux. No ship left the harbour. Surgeon Robertson was returned to the Garden Prison, his departure indefinitely postponed.

Among the English, however, hopes rose for an exchange of prisoners. For three days in September one of the British frigates lay off the port flying a flag of truce, while boats passed repeatedly between the ship and the shore, anxiously watched by the prisoners. With their swords having been taken from them, Flinders and Aken began to hope that they had fallen into the classification of prisoners of war.

They learned that Captain Cockburne of HMS *Phaeton* had come into the port to negotiate an exchange, particularly that of Flinders. He had been met, blindfolded and taken aboard the regular prison ship. However, no officer appeared to treat with him and he was informed he would not be seeing the governor. Flinders, he was told, was not a prisoner of war and therefore could not be exchanged. Disgusted, Cockburne returned to his ship. No prisoners were exchanged.

During the months of September and October 1804 Matthew Flinders was, in fact, recorded in a roll of prisoners now in the Mauritius Archives as *Prisonnier d'Etat*. In November this was suddenly changed; he was recorded as *Prisonnier de Guerre*.[9] Meanwhile, the six remaining *Cumberland* prisoners from Flacq were in greater misery in their new prison than before. Hurried off after the escape of Charrington, they and others had left behind their clothes and were now virtually naked. Letters from Flinders, first to Decaen and then to the town major, resulted many weeks later in their being given some clothing.

The blockade failed. With his ships and three prizes, Linois reached Grand Port on the island's southeast coast on 31 October, and the same evening Commodore Osborn and his squadron sailed for India. Restrictions on the island's prisoners were lifted. Robertson's parole was restored, and Flinders redated his letters to 4 November 1804. On the 14th Robertson, bearing Flinders's chart, papers and letters, sailed from Ile de France on the American ship *Bellisarius*. He left with Flinders his young black servant, Toussaint, bought as a slave, whom he had been unable to take with him.

The departure of friends from the Garden Prison was always difficult for those left behind. Flinders wrote, 'I suffer the loss of an agreeable companion in him [Robertson], and of a well-informed good man, but rejoice sincerely in his liberty'.[10]

Robertson reached England in March, saw to the delivery of the letters, called on Sir Joseph Banks, and collected correspondence for Matthew from his friends and family, which he arranged to send safely back to Flinders at Ile de France.

John Aken had fallen seriously ill and in September was taken to the hospital. Flinders gave no explanation for his illness, which perhaps was not understood. After six weeks Aken asked to be returned to the Garden Prison, where, although he was no better, he felt more comfortably accommodated and more adequately fed. Through Bergeret it was arranged for George Adler, a seaman from the *Cumberland* and once carpenter's mate on the *Investigator*, to attend him as his servant. The two young midshipmen at the prison, Seymour and Dale, obligingly stepped in to assist Flinders for the next several months with his charts and records, Alfred Dale, a senior midshipman, in particular having some skill in cartography. Flinders in turn lent them books and enjoyed helping them with the studies required of midshipmen.

The month of December brought the depressing realisation that, after a year of imprisonment, there was no imminent sign of freedom. On the 17th Flinders sat at his table, writing a letter to the governor to remind him of the year that had elapsed, pointing out again his irretrievable loss of time, advancement and much else, and once more requesting to be sent to France. It was a difficult letter to write, as he noted in his diary: to urge the governor's compliance, and yet not to sacrifice his own or his country's honour, not to give up 'one tittle' of the justice of his cause and yet not to injure the general's pride, to beg yet not lower his dignity. He wrote and rewrote the letter four times. There was no reply. At the end of a week Flinders wrote again. There was no answer.

Flinders was profoundly discouraged. As well, he suffered a return of his 'constitutional gravelly complaint', a painful urinary problem that had him passing gravel-like crystals, and a 'bilious disorder' such as he had not experienced for months. Glands in his neck became swollen and, most alarmingly, his eyes became extremely weak, their vision fading. The years of close work on charts, so often in the weak, wavering light of a swinging lantern, and of looking into bright skies with his instruments seemed to be taking their toll.

On the last day of 1804 Flinders wrote to Ann. He reflected upon himself and the effects that the long, sad year may have had. He wrote:

> I shall learn patience in this island, which will perhaps counteract the insolence acquired by having had unlimited command over my fellowmen. You know, my dearest, that I always dreaded the effect that the possession of great authority would have upon my temper and disposition. I hope they are neither of them naturally bad, but when we see such vast difference between men dependent and men in power, every man who has any share of impartiality must fear for himself...
>
> My brother will tell you that I am proud, unindulgent, and hasty to take offence; but I doubt whether John Franklin will confirm it although there is more truth in the charge than I wish there was.[11]

These were rare revelations of thought and feeling normally restrained by dignity and pride. Then, still with a sense of humour, he wrote that his health was much better than expected, 'and my appetite is so great that I believe it has an intention of revenging me on the governor by occasioning a famine in the island. Falstaff says "confound this grief it makes a man so thirsty. Give me another cup of sack." Instead of thirsty, read hungry; and for a cup of sack, read mutton chop; and the words would fit me very well'. It would seem that Flinders's little store of books included a volume of Shakespeare.

The island's hottest months drew on, with torrential rains and sudorific humidity. Flinders, unwell and deeply despondent, abandoned his charting. The principal physician of the island's medical staff visited and recommended that the three *Cumberland* men be transferred to the country. He provided a certificate to this effect, which Flinders passed on to the governor through Colonel Monistrol, now town major, Port Nord Ouest's senior military commander. There was no response, but Flinders heard later that Dr Laborde had been reprimanded for interfering in matters that did not concern him.

Finally, almost as if in defiance of the governor, Flinders collected himself. He planned a demanding regimen of activity, rising very early in the morning to exercise in the garden before the day grew warm, then applying himself with energy to his charts and writing. Too busy and too determined to think of his ills, he felt better and, more importantly, he 'acquired a tranquil state of mind, and had even the happiness of forgetting De Caen, sometimes for days together'.[12] Aken could not join him. Weakened and very sick, he returned to the hospital.

With the departure of the British squadron the coming and going of people at Maison Despeaux resumed. Flinders renewed his acquaintance with the Baron d'Unienville, the officer who had met him on his first landing at Cap de Baie. He was also coming to know well a French merchant, Charles Thomi Pitot de la Beaujardière, an educated, English-speaking man of twenty-six. 'To him', Flinders wrote, 'I am principally indebted for having passed some agreeable days in prison . . . nor am I the sole English prisoner who will mention the name of Thomas Pitot with eulogium'.[13]

Members of the old French nobility, Thomi Pitot and his brother Edouard had lost their property in France in the Revolution and for a time were imprisoned in the Bastille. In 1793 the brothers returned to Ile de France, where they had been born, and at the time of their meeting with Flinders, headed a flourishing trading company. Pitot was the secretary and an influential member of the island's society of arts and sciences, and on its behalf wrote regarding Flinders to the famous navigator and councillor of state, Louis Antoine de Bougainville; the astronomer Joseph Jérome de la Lande; the scholar and councillor of state Charles François Dupuis and the minister of interior, Jean Antoine Claude Chaptal. In his portrait a hint of a smile and a gentle, kindly expression light up a round, pleasant face with a receded hairline. He acted with honesty as well as consideration towards his English friends. When Flinders showed him copies of his letters to Decaen, Pitot in effect shook his head. He told Flinders—to Flinders's great surprise—that he was doing himself no favour by his attitude.

Flinders reciprocated some of Pitot's kindness by writing to Lord William Bentinck, governor at Madras, on behalf of two relations of the Pitots held prisoner there. Bentinck set the two men free.

However, Flinders had lost his contact with the invariably helpful interpreter Bonnefoy. When two American newspapers fell into his hands, Bonnefoy had taken one to the governor but given the other to friends. Decaen dismissed him. Afraid to further anger the governor, Bonnefoy would not ask for permission to visit Maison Despeaux again.

Flinders also lost the company of John Aken. In April and May 1805 permissions were being granted to additional prisoners to leave the island in American ships. Flinders urged Aken, who was still in hospital, to apply for reasons of long ill-health, making no mention of his association with Flinders. On 7 May Aken arrived happily at the Garden Prison with the surprising news that he was free to depart, having given his parole 'not to serve against France or its allies, until after having been legally exchanged'.[14] Thinking that some recent directive from France had made this possible, Flinders sent 'as humble a letter as I could bring myself to write',[15] petitioning the governor for his own departure on parole. There was no answer.

With Aken's assistance Flinders quickly made up packets of material for the master to take with him, the originals or copies of everything he had that related to the *Investigator* or the voyage itself. Sixteen charts with an explanatory memoir and a copy of his logbook up to March 1803 were addressed to Banks, together with a long, humble and eulogistic letter.

He wrote to Ann, to his stepmother, to Thomas Franklin and to Samuel. He begged his brother for news of their family and former shipmates, asking whether he had seen Banks, Dalrymple or Maskelyne, and of 'what the talk is of me'.[16] The timekeeper and the other mathematical and nautical instruments belonging to the Navy Board that were still in his possession also went with Aken.

The captain of the American ship *James*, bound for New York, provided free passage for Aken and George Adler, and on 20 May 1805 the *James* sailed out of Port Nord Ouest, 'to my great satisfaction', said Flinders. Of the ten men who had been with Flinders in the little *Cumberland*, only four remained on the island. Elder, who had refused repatriation, was with Flinders at the Garden Prison, 'determined to stay by me until we shall weather this storm of adversity', as Flinders wrote to Ann.[17] William Smith, seaman, was in hospital with a broken leg, two others were in prison. A month later, however, these two were able to sail as crew on American ships.

In October 1804 Jacques Bergeret had sailed from Ile de France in his ship *Psyche* for a raiding cruise in the Indian Ocean. In February, after a murderous battle, Bergeret was forced to surrender to the British *San Fiorenzo*. The *Psyche* was taken to Trincomalee in India as a prize and Bergeret was turned over to his long-time friend, Rear-Admiral Sir Edward Pellew, now commander-in-chief of the British fleet in the Indian Ocean. On 23 June 1805 the ship *Thetis* arrived at Ile de France from Bengal under cartel colours. On board were Bergeret and those of his men who had survived the action with the *San Fiorenzo*.

It appears that an effort to secure Flinders's release was in progress. Richard Wellesley, Governor-General of Bengal, wrote to Decaen and seems to have inferred that Bergeret could be exchanged for Flinders. The reply was apparently that Flinders's case had been referred to Paris. Thus there was no exchange for Bergeret but, on his giving his parole not to engage in further hostilities against Britain, the English nevertheless released him.

Arrangements made a month later for an exchange of all British prisoners on the island contained a stipulation that Flinders believed was made with reference to himself, and probably instigated by Decaen. The exchange did not include naval commanders and post captains and their army equivalents. The only English officer on Mauritius in this bracket at the time was Flinders.

At the Garden Prison, however, there were at this point almost no restrictions on visitors. Officers from the British cartels in the harbour called frequently, as did some French officers. M. Reigier of Monistrol's staff, assuring Flinders that he was authorised to do so, escorted him to the theatre. The performance consisted mostly of comedy, with witticisms that Flinders did not understand, and his attention was mainly caught by the sight of 'so many handsomely dressed women'.[18] Bright, beautiful and expensive gowns exposed arms, necks, shoulders and 'nearly half the breasts', and while he found the older women to be generally overweight, some of the younger ones were very pretty, and he saw one who 'might be very well called a beauty'. Such a display in an English theatre would have caused an uproar. Much amused by the thought, Flinders wrote in his diary, 'The modest would be offended, the prudes would break their fans, the aged would cry, shame! the libertines would exult and clap, and the old lechers would apply for their opera glasses'.

The cartels sailed in the evening of 19 August. Midshipmen Dale and Seymour went with them. At the Garden Prison there remained only Flinders, Elder, who again had refused to leave, and William Smith, seaman, recovering from a broken leg, the sole English prisoners on the island. The rooms of the residence were suddenly very large and empty. At his table with his diary, Flinders's mind meandered:

> Took three pinches of snuff . . . Mm. must not take so much snuff when I return, for it makes me spit about the rooms . . . Took up my flute . . . Must have Pleyels musick when I return to England . . . and Mozarts and Haydns and some of Hoffmusters and Duriennes . . . musick is so very dear in England . . .
>
> Returned upstairs, washed and sat down to dinner at two o'clock . . . Determine to have a court-martial upon the loss of the schooner, as it will give me an opportunity of making known my treatment in this island in an official manner . . . Find my headache better after dinner.[19]

He considered the advantages to the East India Company and to the British navy of a settlement and naval station on Australia's northwest coast.

> Would I go out as governor of a settlement there, should it be proposed to me? I can't tell, it would depend on many circumstances. Wish to finish the examination of the whole coasts of Australia before I do anything else . . . it would be desirable to explore by land from the head of the great inlet on the southeast [Spencer Gulf], and from Port Phillip. The asses of this island would be very useful in these excursions. To propose to Sir Joseph to touch here, when I go out again, to take in six asses, and some fruit trees . . . Find myself a little sleepy.
>
> Five. Waked . . . Went down to the gate and sat down in the sentry box, looking at the people who passed by . . . French soldiers talk much more than English soldiers do . . . At sunset returned up stairs . . . Necessary to read over again the article Meteorology in the Encyclopaedia Britannica.
>
> Went to bed at half past nine. Lay considering for some time upon the causes of the trade and of the westwardly winds, especially upon the earth's revolution round its axis. Think they are certainly owing in some part to this cause, as well as to the rarefaction of the air under the vertical sun. Must have some kind of trap set for that rat which comes disturbing me every night . . .
>
> Waked about one by the noise of the soldiers in the guard house, who are playing about and running after each other like children. Wish that loud fellow had taken a dose of opium. Fell asleep again. Dreamed that general De Caen was setting a lion upon me to devour me . . . Got up soon after six, much agitated, with a more violent headache than usual, and with bilious sensations in my stomach.

The next day a letter arrived from Colonel Monistrol. The governor had given his permission for Flinders, accompanied by John Elder and William Smith as his servants, to reside in the interior of the island. Thomi Pitot had received for Flinders several offers of accommodation, and together they chose the plantation of a widow, Madame D'Arifat, at Wilhems Plains, in the southern interior of the island. At some distance from the sea, it seemed the location least likely to arouse any objections, and Flinders had written to express his choice. This was now granted. Furthermore, he was free to spend two or three days in Port Nord Ouest before leaving for the country.

30 Wilhems Plains

On 20 August 1805, after sixteen months behind the garden walls of the Maison Despeaux, Flinders took his leave of 'the old serjeant, who had behaved kindly to all the prisoners', and walked out through the iron gate; '. . . even a prison one has long inhabited is not quitted without some sentiment of regret, unless it be to receive liberty'. Of himself he added, 'my strength and appearance were so changed, that I felt to be scarcely recognisable for the same person who had supported so much fatigue in exploring the coast of Terra Australis'.[1]

It is possible, however, that he felt more altered than he actually was. Matthew Flinders could drive himself to the very edge of endurance, almost totally ignoring sickness and fatigue, but with the pressure relaxed, he was very conscious of his state of health. Months of inactivity, awareness of precious time sliding away and a recurrence of his 'gravely complaint' no doubt heightened this tendency.

Flinders's first act was to call gratefully on Jacques Bergeret, who had been chiefly responsible for obtaining this change for him. The next morning Bergeret accompanied him to the office of the town major to give his parole. Colonel Monistrol was satisfied to take it verbally, but Flinders chose to make it in writing. This was arranged and he signed it two days later:[2]

> His Excellency the captain-general DeCaen having given me permission to reside at Wilhems Plains, at the habitation of Madame D'Arifat, I do hereby promise, upon my parole of honour, not to go more than the distance of two leagues from the said habitation, without His Excellency's permission; and to conduct myself with that proper degree

> of reserve, becoming an officer residing in a country with which his nation is at war.
>
> I will also answer for the proper conduct of my two servants.
>
> Town of Port North-west,
> Matthew Flinders.
> August 23, 1805

Flinders was well aware that in signing this parole he was surrendering any honourable possibility of escape. He was almost certain, however, that an order for his liberty would arrive in another few months. As well, he held a quiet hope that British forces would soon occupy the island to put an end to the losses being suffered by English shipping from Mauritius-based French ships. Of this he said nothing to anyone. He did note in his journal Monistrol's offers at this time to be of service to him. The colonel had never been other than polite and, insofar as he could, helpful. Yet there may now have been additional incentives: the precarious position of Ile de France as British squadrons repeatedly circled, and the seeming importance of the prisoner, Matthew Flinders.

During the four days of his stay in Port Nord Ouest, Matthew Flinders was a guest at the home of Thomi Pitot and under no restrictions of any kind. Bergeret and the Pitots took him on a highly sociable round of breakfasts, dinners and suppers with friends and numerous relatives. One evening he attended a musical gathering 'where some pieces were performed by superior players'. The following evening there was a large supper party at the home of a Monsieur Deglos, a relation of Thomi Pitot. The honour of conducting to table the lady of the house was assigned to Flinders, 'which as I understood so little French and spoke less, and have moreover been little accustomed to female society, embarrassed me not a little'.[3] However, any failure on his part was politely ignored. Whatever feelings against Britain the French may have felt, they unfailingly extended a very amiable courtesy to Flinders.

He also climbed Le Pouce, a nearby mountain of 'about 2400 French feet (2661 feet)'. Despite heavy rain, Flinders and Edouard Pitot pursued their way under umbrellas for some time but, with no view to be seen through veils of rain, finally descended.

At a party at the Pitot residence later that day, Flinders met Toussaint Antoine de Chazal de Chamarel, 'an intelligent and respectable man' just four years older than himself, whose country house was situated near the D'Arifat plantation. Toussaint Chazal had spent two years in England during the French Revolution and spoke good English. He promised to see that Flinders's trunks and furniture were transported to Wilhems Plains. In the evening the group attended a performance consisting of several very short plays. In one piece there appeared an 'English lord' who supposedly spoke very bad French. Flinders understood little and 'did not like to inquire of my neighbours, fearing the piece was more satyrical than it was'.[4] Briefly he returned to Maison Despeaux to complete some letters and a paper on the marine barometer that was read to the Royal Society in London in March 1806.

After another musical evening, Flinders was taken to call upon Madame D'Arifat, at whose country home he would be staying. With her three young daughters and two youngest sons she would be moving to the country with the onset of the hot season. His last evening in town was spent with the extended Pitot family, gathered for supper and to play *bouilloté*. 'This game', Flinders remarked, 'seems to be quite the rage . . . '[5]

Flinders took his leave of some of his new acquaintances in Port Nord Ouest on 24 August. He wrote, 'About 4 I set off for the country, accompanying nearly the whole of Pitot's family. At sunset we reached his country house' near the deep chasm of the Grande Riviere, about five miles from the town. Set among trees with windowed wings on either side of a wide, pillared entrance porch, it had an appearance of welcoming, shaded coolness. 'Here we remained all night, the evening being passed at boulliоté as usual; and into which they initiated me'.[6] Although 'initiated', Flinders commented later that he did not enjoy the game.

An early morning hunt for hares followed. Dogs sent into the woods were heard in full cry while the men waited, but without result.

Finally, with the large party riding donkeys, Flinders's journey was resumed on rough dirt roads winding southward through partially wooded country. Four or five miles from the Pitot house the group stopped for dinner under a huge banyan tree on the grounds of Le Réduit, the white-pillared government country house. Here Pitot and his friend, Antoine Bayard, a judge in the court of appeal, parted from their families to continue the journey with Flinders.

Flinders was anxious to reach the D'Arifat plantation, but the men detoured to visit a friend of the judge, a former officer in the Mahratta service in India. They walked over some of his 400 acres to see his coffee and clove trees, orchards, vegetable gardens and fish ponds, and spent the evening at his billiard table. The journey was resumed the next afternoon, the men riding through fields of sugar cane, coffee, maize, manioc and sweet potato. Then the rainforest closed in; 'we found ourselves surrounded on all sides by wood,—the road had diminished to a foot path,—it was dark,—and began to rain'.[7] With no idea of where they were, they turned back towards a point of light showing from a house they had passed earlier. Here they found a resident Irishman, Thomas Druse, who conducted them to the nearby D'Arifat house.

On finding that Elder, Smith and the baggage had not arrived at the plantation, Flinders and his companions continued with a guide the additional mile and a half to the Chazal residence. Here they found Elder and the lame Smith, with all their equipment. Supper was provided 'and beds, to which we gladly retired soon afterwards'.[8]

Wilhems Plains—or Plaines Wilhems—was named for a hermit known only as Wilhem who, according to legend, had once lived in the district. The region is a plateau at a general elevation of about 1000 feet, subject to heavy rainfall and temperatures normally several degrees lower than on the coast. Part of the area was occupied by largely self-sufficient plantations. Supplies that the plantations did not provide for themselves were brought up from Port Nord Ouest, some nine miles directly north, while farm produce, usually carried on the heads of slaves, was sent down to the town market on winding trails that considerably lengthened the distance to be travelled. In Flinders's time extensive forests sheltering monkeys, deer and wild hogs covered parts of Wilhems Plains and an elevated area known as Vacoas, for the nearby Mare aux Vacoas, a lake ringed by swampland, with pandanus trees or *vacoas* growing on its margins.

With rugged mountains to the west, two rivers cut across Wilhems Plains. The D'Arifat residence stood near one of these: the main house, two small buildings referred to by Flinders as pavilions, a separate cook- or storehouse and, at a short distance, a double row of cottages for the slaves. The plantation was called Le Refuge, appropriately named, as Flinders remarked, for his purpose.

In the morning the Chazals' overseer, Peter Salomon, sent slaves with Flinders's baggage to Le Refuge. There Alain, the D'Arifats' man in charge, had instructions to accommodate Flinders in the main residence, but Flinders chose instead to establish himself in one of the two small pavilions, with Elder and Smith in the other. Flinders wrote, 'The good black overseer, according to his orders, was desirous of accomodating me with everything, and some things I was under the necessity of receiving, but as I was desirous of laying myself under as little obligation as possible, I took only some provisions for the present day, and two or three articles of furniture'.[9]

Flinders's new servant, the lad Toussaint, apparently arrived at Le Refuge at some point and most likely became part of the D'Arifat household staff.

Arrangements were made for a supply of poultry, vegetables and other produce from the nearby farm of a free black planter. While Smith and Elder arranged the pavilions for occupation, Pitot took Flinders to call upon a 'Madame Cove', actually, Couve de Murville, whose plantation bordered the D'Arifat land. The lady and two daughters in their mid-teens were among the few who lived mainly on their plantation, the husband coming up from town at intervals. Flinders was invited to visit informally at any time, the invitation 'not less agreeable for that the two young ladies were musicians and had good voices'.[10] Again Flinders, depending on Pitot for translation, found himself acutely embarrassed by his inability to understand or to respond properly in French.

After dinner in the early afternoon, Pitot and Bayard left for Port Nord Ouest. There they would arrange for bread, meat and other items not available at Wilhems Plains to be bought at the market for Flinders, for the plantation maintained daily contact with the town. Flinders turned to setting up his bed and putting in order his personal belongings and such books and papers as had not been sent away with John Aken.

In the following weeks Flinders explored the surrounding countryside and made the acquaintance of those of his neighbours who happened to be at their plantations at this chilly and rainy time of year.

The area to which he was restricted by his parole, within a radius of two leagues from the D'Arifat home, was sufficiently large for many long walks, and the wild, green beauty of the area's rainforests, swift-running streams and mountains rising into spectacularly pointed peaks were a continuous delight. Roads were usually muddy tracks, which the inhabitants travelled on foot or on donkeys or horses, the women sometimes carried in palanquins. Lifetime habits of careful observation and recording of what he saw returned and, in the published account of his voyages years later, Flinders included pages of information on the part of Mauritius that he came to know.

He was determined to learn French and, alone on his walks, he went over the French phrases and grammar he was teaching himself. He paid frequent visits to Madame Cove's plantation, where he found a Monsieur Murat, a former merchant marine captain. Murat knew no English, but this and his seagoing background made him for Flinders the ideal person on whom to practise speaking French.

Early in September they walked the five miles to the home of the commandant of the *quartier*, 'M. Giblot', evidently Félix Giblot Ducray, so that Flinders could officially report his presence in Wilhems Plains. They found the commandant to be an elderly, bedridden man who had not been advised of Flinders's arrival in his district, which Flinders found gratifying, as 'it showed I was not an object of suspicion in the eye of the government'.[11]

Toussaint Chazal visited his country house and received Flinders there 'with his usual plain goodness'. He showed Flinders something of the plantation where, aside from the usual crops, he cultivated exotic plants and reared silkworms. Flinders stayed the night and after breakfast the next day Chazal took him to an elevated area on the west side of his extensive property from which they looked out at the sea. Chazal apparently had no kindly feelings towards England. His friendship was reserved for the individual Matthew Flinders and, understanding this, Flinders was careful to avoid speaking of the war or anything related to it.

To Samuel he later wrote, speaking of himself in the third person, 'he is, besides, amongst foreigners, and although personally friendly to him, yet dislike his countrymen as a nation and their government. The dissimilarity of manners is also considerable and with much affection towards these friends he does not find himself altogether at home amongst them'.[12]

On their part, his friends were clearly not blind to Flinders's sometimes unwise behaviour. As Bonnefoy, Monistrol and later Pitot had let him know, they considered him partly to blame for his predicament. This did not, however, stand in the way of their evidently sincere affection for him.

Flinders also visited the Irishman, Thomas Druse, a carpenter who had lived on the island for some twenty years. Speaking English was a pleasure for both men. Flinders found that at least one of the island's signal hills and its pole were visible from Le Refuge, and he learned to watch for the red flag that meant the presence around the island of British cruisers. It was a small contact with his former life.

He was determined to regain his physical strength. Although the mountain weather was colder than he had expected, at times 12–15 degrees Fahrenheit cooler than on the coast, he bathed early each morning in the stream behind the house. He then walked for two hours or more on visits, or exploring the different roads. He ate solidly of fresh foods and slept early. For a few days he felt unwell 'from a cold or from an approaching fit of the gravel', but this passed.

Many days, however, were wet and blustery, and for warmth against the chilly wind that pierced his little house, he borrowed from the main residence an iron pot of glowing charcoal. He used his time writing up the second volume of his logbook, playing his flute, reading French and keeping up a regular correspondence with Pitot and Bergeret. Pitot's frequent letters brought news of the town, of shipping and sightings of English warships, of rumours that he knew would interest Flinders. In early October Bergeret arrived for a day's visit. He brought word of the expected arrival from France of an officer with dispatches possibly containing orders for Flinders's release. In his diary Flinders wrote:

> I have, however, been so often deceived in my expectations, of this kind, that I no longer rest confidence in this kind of hopes . . .
>
> I cannot say that, at present, I am very unhappy. Time has softened my disappointments. I have my books, am making acquisitions in knowledge, enjoy good health, and innocent amusements for which I

> have still a relish, and look forward to the hope of overcoming all objections and difficulties with honour to myself . . . [13]

The dispatches from France contained nothing relating to Flinders.

On 9 October 1805 Madame D'Arifat arrived with her three daughters and two of her sons to take up residence in their country home. 'The morning was rainy, and they were all wet', Flinders remarked.[14]

Madame Louise Geneviève Labauve D'Arifat was the daughter of an official at Ile de France, and the widow of a captain of the royal regiment stationed on the island in 1777. He was the son of a French noble family, with heraldic arms conferred by Henry III, and a castle near Castres in southern France, in which his parents were living at the time of his marriage. The couple's eldest son, Paul David Labauve D'Arifat, referred to by Flinders as Labauve, was 27 years old when Flinders met him. A second son of 26, Marc André, had married the previous year and lived in the district of Flacq, but during his frequent visits to Le Refuge Flinders came to know him as well as his wife, Anne Marie Jeanne, and later a small daughter. A third son, Pierre Henry, of whom Flinders makes little mention, would have been twenty-four. The eldest daughter was Delphine Louise Antoinette Marie, whom Flinders described as being 21, but by existing records she would have passed her 22nd birthday when he met her late in 1805. Petronille Louise Sophie, known as Sophie, was 17 and, like Delphine, evidently knew a little English. Louise Sophie, called Lise, turned 13 a month after the family arrived at Le Refuge, and there were two boys, Marc and Aristide, whose ages Flinders gave as 'between 10 and 7'. It was a family that Flinders later described as large, but not rich.

The day after her arrival Madame D'Arifat sent a note to Flinders, inviting him to live in the main house without expense to himself, which Flinders declined. Indebtedness to the D'Arifats was inevitable, but he would try to make it as little as possible. A fortnight later, however, the pleasure of the family's company had become more than he could resist. He wrote a note, proposing 'to bring myself and forty piastres per month to her table', which the lady accepted and, as he recorded, 'Accordingly, I dined with the family today . . . I find the family so very agreeable and interesting, that I am become desirous of being as much with them as possible'.[15] Madame D'Arifat thereafter accepted Flinders's monthly stipend without comment, and he remained in possession of his pavilion for sleep and work. The arrangement gave him privacy, yet the companionship of the widow and her children.

Almost immediately Flinders had found that the two older daughters were as eager to improve their English as he was to improve his French and, two days after the family's arrival, he wrote that he had commenced 'what is to be a regular course of study. Writing and reading French under the correction of the two eldest young ladies, whilst they do the same in English to me. I find we are pretty nearly equal in our acquaintance with each others language'.[16]

As well, he undertook to teach the younger boys mathematics and some principles of navigation. In his published account of his years with the D'Arifat family, he later wrote, '. . . in a short time I had the happiness to enumerate amongst my friends one of the most worthy families on the island'.[17] The initial feelings of the family were no doubt sympathy, even pity, and evidently curiosity, for a lonely man stranded in their midst. But it soon went beyond that. He wrote in his diary, 'Madame and her amiable daughters . . . seemed to take it upon themselves to dissipate my chagrin, by engaging me in innocent amusement and agreeable conversation. I cannot enough be grateful to them for such kindness . . .'[18]

Other 'habitants', families who lived in town residences during winter and returned to their country estates in summer, were arriving at Wilhems Plains. Flinders began to accompany the D'Arifat family on visits to their neighbours, joined their social gatherings at Le Refuge and sometimes arranged picnics and fishing excursions for the group. On one occasion, observing the D'Arifat girls together with the two daughters of Madame Cove, he wrote: 'It struck me what an acquisition it would be to our colony at Port Jackson, to have these five healthy and agreeable young ladies transported there. They would not remain long unmarried; whilst in this island they will scarcely obtain husbands. Young women are much more abundant than young men here'.[19]

Flinders was at first reticent in speaking of his own situation. His diary entry for the day continued: 'After our return in the evening, Madame was a little inquisitive concerning my voyages, the cause of my imprisonment here, my shipwreck, and finally my family in England; in all of which she seemed to take much interest'. Flinders gave the necessary answers and showed Madame D'Arifat such of his papers as offered the best explanations but, as he noted, 'I did not say that . . . I had a beloved wife in England who was expecting my return in sickness and in tears; because I saw that the scene would become too interesting, and oblige me to retire'.[20] It was less than a fortnight, however, before he shared much more of his past life and its concerns with the D'Arifat women.

Believing that physical exercise was necessary to his health, Flinders continued his walks and sometimes longer excursions with Monsieur Murat. On one overnight expedition they visited the Grand Bassin, a lake at some altitude five or six miles south of Le Refuge that appeared to Flinders to be the deep, steep-sided caldera of an ancient volcano. Several streams were said to originate from the lake, and Flinders searched for their source, perhaps remembering the fenland explorations of his boyhood. From a nearby hill he looked across an expanse of forest to the sea. The sense of being confined, barred from the freedom of the oceans he knew so well, must have been intense.

Two days later he and Edouard Pitot walked with guns and dogs to the 100-foot cataracts of the Tamarind River. Edouard Pitot had some artistic talent, and sketched while Flinders explored. The waterfalls intrigued Flinders. He climbed around the cascading water and found a cave-like hollow under the fall. Theorising on the creation of the rocks, he thought they would undergo changes that eventually would reduce the height of the fall, a levelling process that he related to human society. 'The greater the inequalities are (the higher the mountains are above the valley, or that kings are above other men) the more is a sudden fall or revolution to be apprehended'.[21] He also reflected upon the vicissitudes of his own life, his growing up in a countryside flat and devoid of hills:

> [and having] visited a great variety of countries, made three times the tour of the world, find my name known in more kingdoms than that where I was born . . . and this moment a prisoner in a moutainous island in the Indian Ocean, lying under a cascade in a situation very romantic and interior, meditating upon the progress which nature is continually making toward a moderate degree of equality in the physical and moral

worlds; and in company with a foreigner, a Frenchman, whom I call, and believe to be, my friend.

As a naval officer and explorer, Flinders had rarely paused for such reflections.

The next day Flinders had the almost unbelievable joy of receiving a packet of letters from England, the first direct communications he had had in three years. He had been spending the evening with the Chazals, when Elder appeared. The packet, sent by Walter Robertson, had arrived in the port that morning with an American brig from London, and Thomi Pitot, to whom it was addressed, had sent it immediately to Le Refuge. Flinders made his excuses and hurried to the privacy of his pavilion. There were letters from Ann, from his cousin Henrietta and half-sister Hannah jointly, from Sir Joseph Banks and from Robertson, the latest dated 20 July 1805, only three months before. Having read his letters and unable to contain his joy, Flinders joined the D'Arifat family 'as usual' and now made the explanations he had withheld earlier. Delightedly, he wrote in his diary, 'They congratulated me very sincerely upon my happiness'.[22]

Ann's letters brought welcome news of her own good health and less happy news as well: the bankruptcy of Matthew's cousin William, the serious difficulties of the Franklins, and the death of Matthew's uncle, Samuel Ward, who had named Flinders his executor and left a legacy of £200 each to Matthew and Samuel. Flinders replied, 'I think all my relations are becoming unfortunate in their concerns: they are all miserably poor. Notwithstanding my misfortunes I seem to be luckiest of the whole; my father was the principal support of the name and it seems as if I was destined to take his place.[23] To be unable to discharge his responsibilities as head of the family was, to Matthew, one more grievance against Decaen.

He described to Ann his amiable relationship with the D'Arifat family, their studies and other activities. They discussed many subjects, even politics, he said, and despite differences of opinion, could do so good-naturedly. He had particularly attached himself to the eldest son and daughter, he wrote, and, as if to reassure Ann, told her that the young D'Arifats talked of visiting England when peace should come 'to see and be acquainted with thee'. He went on, '. . . to love thee more than I have done, and now do, I think cannot be, thou hast the sole undivided possession of my heart'.

He wrote, too, of achieving a financial position whereby 'we shall be able to sit down quietly without further occasion of voyages of discovery'.[24] There is no doubt that for Flinders this was a very real dream for the future but, even as he comforted Ann, there were tasks that he wanted to complete first. 'Before thou was mine, I had engaged in this voyage . . .'[25] he had written to her two years before, and the fact remained.

Banks's letter of 18 June was relatively short and to the point. As there could be no exchange of any kind between the governments of France and England, he had written to the National Institute of France, through which he had already obtained the release of five other captives. Unfortunately, his letters had been delayed for some months in Holland, while the Emperor, whose approval was necessary, remained in Italy; '. . . I entertain sanguine hopes of a favourable answer when he shall return to Paris, from the marked and laudable attention His Imperial Majesty has always shown to scientific men'.[26] Flinders, the letter suggested, could now hope for an order from France that would soon set him free. Past disappointments, however, made Flinders 'almost afraid now to permit myself to expect with much anxiety'.[27]

Banks wrote that he had heard many times from Mrs Flinders and had done his 'utmost to quiet her mind and sooth her apprehensions'.[28] Of prospects for discovery he had no news. The recent succession of First Lords of the Admiralty had included no one who was interested in exploration, 'and none less than the present Lord Barham . . . 84 years old'. Banks added, 'Capt. Bligh has lately been nominated Governor of New South Wales'. Only an unfinished rough draft of Banks's letter survives, but it is evident from Flinders's remarks to Ann that in the letter that he received, his friend and patron was critical of his handling of his situation in Mauritius. Flinders wrote, 'I did not find the letter of Sir J. B. so kind as I could have wished. I see that he is not satisfied with the conduct I have observed towards the French government here. I have rather considered the justice of my cause than policy, and therefore, in his estimation, treated them with too much haughtyness, and by that means have lengthened, or perhaps caused, my imprisonment'. To Ann, Flinders defended his behaviour as that of a man deserving of good treatment and meeting with ill, and so was justified in his unbending indignation. 'Should the same circumstance happen to me again', he wrote, 'I fear I should follow nearly the same steps'.[29]

In the second of her letters Ann had tentatively suggested that she join him in Mauritius. It was a wonderful thought, but an impractical one. It would necessitate her travelling first to the United States and from there to Ile de France. There was the long sea voyage to consider, her sometimes uncertain health and, above all, the need for an entirely reliable male escort. Nor did Flinders know if he would be given permission to bring a wife onto the island. For the moment he set aside the thought and said nothing about it in his reply to her letter.

He also wrote affectionately to his stepmother, expressing his interest in the education of his half-sisters and his hope to have one of them live with him and Ann on his return to encourage, by his own example, her desire to study.

Of his daily life in the later months of 1805 Flinders wrote in his diary:

> I rise every morning with the sun and go out to bathe in the river, which is tolerably cool work; afterwards I dress, and either accompany the ladies in a walk round the plantation . . . or read till half past seven . . . After breakfast, I retire to my pavilion to read and write for two or three hours; after which I . . . translate French into English, and English into French and read French under the correction of Mademoiselles Delphine and Sophie; and they do the same in English to me; these last until or very near dinner time, which is at two o'clock. After dinner I read and write, or sometimes walk and sometimes sleep . . . about 5 o'clock . . . I join the ladies again . . . After tea . . . at half past six, we retire to the parlour for the evening, which is passed in reading French and English, in conversation or sometimes singing and flute playing, or sometimes at cards. At nine we sup, and at ten retire to bed . . . [30]

Time was also spent with his hospitable neighbours, the Chazals, actually a family of two men, Chazal and Chevreau, married to sisters. Madame Chazal was a fine musician and owned an excellent English harpsichord, taken in a prize ship, for which she had paid the considerable sum of 1000 piastres. She was also 'one of the most agreeable women' Flinders had ever met. He would arrive with his flute in his pocket and, with Madame Chazal at her harpsichord and Flinders and sometimes a third person on the bass beside her, the duets and trios were enjoyed by everyone. There were also games of tric-trac, similar to backgammon, and much interesting conversation. The ladies of Ile de France, Flinders found, were avid readers of Voltaire.

In early December he joined the eldest D'Arifat son and some of his friends in a deer hunt in the wooded high country around Grand Bassin; despite heavy rains the chase continued for three days, although with little success. To Flinders it was an interesting opportunity to observe a group of young Frenchmen in a relaxed, purely masculine environment, as in the evenings their conversation turned upon past hunts, 'intermixed with that of their amours, but as I understood nothing of the one subject, and I never make the other a topick of conversation, and besides spoke French very badly, I remained silent, lying down upon my mat'. The young Frenchmen were, he thought, 'more brotherly with each other, more kind in their language', than a comparable group of young Englishmen, 'speaking to the other in the second person singular . . .' They were, however, 'more free in their language', with liberal use of profanity, and tended 'to avow circumstances which an Englishman generally thinks it better to keep secret'.[31]

One evening at the Chazals, with several neighbourhood families gathered, there was dancing, French contra-dances and waltzes, which Flinders had never seen before. He observed, 'Having been accustomed to our close modest English step, the high vaulting manner of dancing used by the French, did not appear so graceful or so decent as I should perhaps have otherwise thought it'.[32]

A fortnight later at another home, evening tea was followed by 'a little ball': 'I adventured to waltze for the first time, with my two fair instructresses [Delphine and Sophie D'Arifat]. The [dances] continued till midnight, when a good supper was prepared, and after another dance, we broke up at two o'clock'. That Flinders enjoyed himself is evident. He observed good-humouredly, 'As in England, the ladies here are much more fond of dancing than the men. Our three ladies have been sick more or less for the last week, and Miss D. had even taken medicine on the very morning. Nevertheless not one of them missed joining in every dance . . .'[33]

The next day the harder realities of Flinders's position re-emerged when Captain Bergeret arrived. He had spoken to Decaen on obtaining for Flinders more of his books and papers from the trunk still in the governor's possession. These Flinders could have by returning those he had previously taken. The exception was, however, the third logbook, 'the very book I want'. Bergeret learned from Decaen that he had never opened Flinders's last letter, written in August, lest it contain something that would anger him. He did not 'wish to use any more severity' against the Englishman.

The year 1805 was sliding away. The first of December was the anniversary of the coronation of Emperor Napoleon, and Flinders noted only that it 'was to be celebrated with great pomp at the port'. The 17th marked the end of the second year of his detention on Mauritius, but he made no comment in his diary. On 25 December Flinders merely noted that in the evening 'Our family paid a visit . . . I accompanied them'.

The next day there was something that evidently touched him more closely. He wrote, 'This afternoon Mademoiselle Delphine D'Arifat departed upon a visit to Flacq on the other side of the island, to see her brother; by which I lose my best instructress for a month.'[34] Matthew Flinders was apparently losing something more than merely lessons from his best instructress. From the first weeks of his acquaintance with the D'Arifats he had been especially impressed with Delphine. In early November 1805 he wrote in his diary:

> The family, particularly Mademoiselle D. become daily more interesting. She is indeed an extraordinary young lady, possessing a strength of mind, a resolution, and a degree of penetration which few men can boast of, and to these are joined activity, industry and a desire for information. 'Tis pity she had not been born a man, and in a more extensive field than the Isle of France.[35]

Flinders admired strength and intelligence in a woman. At the time when he had felt marriage with Ann was not feasible, he had urged her to 'soar', to study, to write, to read, to 'aspire to the heights of science'.[36] He admired Elizabeth Macarthur, who dealt successfully with the responsibilities of farm and family in her husband's absence, and his own very capable cousin Henrietta. With his own passion for knowledge, Flinders would have found Delphine's 'desire for information' extremely attractive. No portrait of Delphine seems to exist nor any written description of her other than Flinders's reference to his 'fair instructress', and to what extent this was gallantry is hard to determine. Yet at 22 she would have had the physical attractiveness of youth, she was well-bred and evidently sweet-natured. No doubt with considerable and perhaps obvious admiration, she turned to Flinders for the knowledge he was eager to impart. Flinders was 31 and, after several years of almost no contact with young women, he was spending many hours a day with this profoundly attractive girl. Despite his undoubted devotion to his wife, there was clearly in Matthew Flinders an emotional attachment to Delphine D'Arifat.

On the first of January 1806, alone in his pavilion, he wrote her a long letter.

> My pavilion at the Refuge Jan. 1 1806
>
> My dear Miss D'Arifat
>
> Permit me on the opening of the new year to present you with my respectful compliments, and best wishes for your happiness during its continuance, and at the same time do me the favour to accept of a little fan, similar to two others your Mama has permitted me to present to your sisters; the smallness of its price is by no means a measure of my regard, but will demonstrate the sense I entertain of your delicacy and my fear lest you should refuse to accept of a present that was of any value; for to have the little overflowings of friendship and esteem refused by those whom we admire and respect is a severe punishment... you will not for a very trifle inflict it upon one you have ever honoured with the appelation of *friend*.[37]

He wished her happiness and amusement with her friends at Flacq, but hoped that in thinking of her mother, sisters and brothers, she would remember that 'there is a certain unfortunate Englishman at the Refuge scarcely less anxious for a place in your recollection...' She might remember at various times of the day what he and her family would be doing, and '...when you see the moon, it might remind you that I am taking a solitary walk beneath its beams, thinking sometimes of my beloved friends in England...' Flinders then slipped into a recitation of the injustices he had received and his gratitude to the D'Arifat family, of which she was 'so bright an ornament; excellent qualities of the head and heart... Your beauty—but this is the affair of your lovers, and therefore no concern of mine'.

Flinders never sent this letter. It survives only as a rough draft in his private letter book, with many words and phrases crossed out, together with a notation saying that he sent instead 'a complimentary note' for the new year. Perhaps caution and conscience prevailed, and he kept his evidently confused feelings to himself.

We know even less of Delphine's feelings. No diary or letter survives. She can only be glimpsed within the sheltering framework of her life, following its pleasant daily routine, like her sisters going nowhere without her mother, as Flinders observed, with little intellectual challenge and limited contact even with young men of her class and age group, so many having left the island for business or wartime service.

There is no evidence to suggest that Delphine D'Arifat ever left the strict confines of propriety, but that she was moved by this stranger is certainly very likely. Was the month's visit to Flacq motivated by anything other than a desire, perhaps, for a change of scene or her brother's company? Was there an awareness on her part, or perhaps on her mother's, that a period of distance between her and the Englishman was advisable? There is no way of knowing. Delphine returned to Le Refuge, probably in late January, and the regular course of Flinders's life with the family continued.

In late February 1806 a cyclone struck. The fields were flooded, bridges collapsed into roaring streams and the huts of slaves, storehouses and even larger buildings were unroofed or blown over. In the port vessels were driven aground or blown out to sea. No English cruisers were in the area, as Flinders learned with relief. Soon after, however, he made his way across the ravaged countryside to watch with fascination the wild torrent of the Tamarind River, 'a magnificent prospect', he wrote.

Eighteen days later the island reeled under a second cyclone. With a seaman's interest, Flinders recorded the swinging of the wind around the compass, driving grey walls of rain before it, at the same time struggling to protect his papers from water spraying and seeping into his pavilion. Buildings under repair were again bludgeoned, debris of every kind hurtled across the ground, roads dissolved into undefined mires, while the booming of huge waves upon the shore could be heard for miles.

Throughout November and December 1805 and the first weeks of 1806 Flinders, encouraged by the knowledge of Banks's appeal to the National Institute of France, waited for dispatches from Paris that could bring him freedom. In February an aide-de-camp of General Decaen arrived with letters for the governor. None mentioned Flinders.

At the end of the month Decaen's brother arrived from France with further communications. His great news was of Napoleon's fresh triumphs—victory at Ulm in October 1805, entry into Vienna in November, a great victory at Austerlitz on 2 December. The governor ordered dazzling celebrations, balls, receptions and other festivities. News of the British victory in the naval battle off Cape Trafalgar was also received but passed over in silence. Again, there was no word on Matthew Flinders. Despairingly Matthew wrote to Samuel, 'my hopes are, therefore, now more feeble than ever . . . it appearing that amidst the great events with which the French ministers are occupied, they have forgotten or have not time to think of me here. It is now a great problem whether I shall obtain my liberty during the war'.[38]

He wrote again to Decaen, pleading to be sent to France for a speedy resolution of his case, whether found innocent or guilty. Bergeret delivered the letter to the governor and supported its message. The reply was a verbal promise that Decaen would repeat Flinders's request to the ministers in Paris.

Letters by Flinders or on his behalf continued to emanate from Ile de France. Deciding to reach out to authorities above and beyond Decaen, Flinders wrote to Denis Dècres, the French Minister of Marine and the Colonies. He begged that he be released or sent to France and concluded the letter in a relatively humble manner. Similarly, he wrote again to the geographer, the Comte de Fleurieu. These letters, sent by complicated undercover routes, probably did not reach their recipients until the following year. By then there had been other developments in the matter of his internment.

A letter was sent to the Institut National de France from the literary, philosophical and scientific society of Ile de France, the Société d'Emulation or Society of Emulation, organised in 1802 by scientists from the Baudin expedition. The society's appeal set forth Flinders's situation and asked for the Institut's influence on his behalf. Again, there seemed to be no response.

In early April there was a change in Flinders's own household. Seaman William Smith, his leg fully healed, was sent home. Monistrol arranged for his passage to Boston, Massachusetts, in the United States, from where he would have to find means of reaching England. John Elder, offered the same opportunity, again refused to leave.

Flinders, meanwhile, made a disturbing discovery. Through one of his friends, possibly Bergeret, he learned something of the contents of the dispatches that he had carried on the *Cumberland* and surrendered on his arrival at Port Nord Ouest. He wrote to Banks:

> I have learnt privately that in the dispatches with which I was charged by Governor King, and which were taken from me by the French General, a demand was made for troops to be sent to Port Jackson for the purpose of annoying Spanish America in the event of another war, and that this is considered to be a breach of my passport. 'Tis a pity that Governor King should have mentioned anything that could involve me in the event of war . . . or that . . . he did not make me acquainted in a general way with the circumstance, in which case I should have thrown them overboard on learning war was declared.[39]

Having left Port Jackson in a time of peace, he said, he did not suspect that the documents contained references to war. However, he did not attach blame to King. Hindsight, he wrote, always made clear what should have been done.

Soon after, he learned of the publication of parts of his letter of August 1804 to King in the *Sydney Gazette* and subsequently that it had appeared in London newspapers. The article, Flinders heard later, did not please Decaen, whose displeasure was compounded when, probably in May 1806, he received Governor Philip King's letter of 30 April 1805. It was a censorious letter. King contrasted the generous care received by the distressed *Géographe* in Port Jackson with Flinders's having been 'treated in every respect as a spy, except in not being executed as one', despite his 'commission, passport, the recital of his distressed sufferings, the unquestionable documents he possessed, and finally the recent cause of his putting into the Isle of France'. King continued, 'This undeserved, unprecedented, and I may add (conceiving his and Captain Baudin's relative situations) ungrateful treatment... must be a subject of concern to every man of science and of humanity'. It was a duty incumbent upon him 'to require' the release of Flinders together 'with every document connected with his voyage of discovery'.[40] He enclosed a copy of Flinders's letter of August 1804, which described his reception on Ile de France in highly uncomplimentary terms.

The general's temper exploded. Not only were both the content and the language of King's letter offensive, but it was evident to Decaen that Flinders had not fully represented the events of his arrival, with no mention of the behaviour that Decaen saw as arrogant and insubordinate. Nor did Decaen have any intention of accepting interference from the Governor of New South Wales, whose dispatches had contained remarks and assumptions hostile to France. Possibly, too, the repeated recitations of the hospitality extended in Sydney to Baudin, whom Decaen had apparently disliked, were becoming tiresome and irritating.

Flinders himself wrote a long letter to King and told him how the contents of the dispatches were said to have invalidated his passport. He added:

> General Decaen has very lately received from you a letter of remonstrance... This has irritated the General somewhat more against me, and prevented me from obtaining permission to visit some friendly families in another part of this island than this where I am placed. These little privations, however, are more than counterbalanced by the pleasure I have to know that you espouse my cause with such friendly concern.[41]

Flinders was being polite. Some of those who had seen Decaen's reaction considered that it was 'a great act of forebearance that he did not order me to be closely confined in the tower'.[42]

With Monistrol's consent Flinders was, in fact, spending several days in town with the Pitots, and had received a favourable answer to a request that his remaining books and papers be returned to him. He had also been given permission to visit friends living outside the limits of his parole. To his surprise, both privileges were abruptly denied and his stay in Port Nord Ouest shortened. Decaen had just received King's letter.

Flinders, although puzzled, nevertheless enjoyed his stay in town. Aside from Bergeret and the Pitots' friends and families, he saw D'Unienville and Johann Boand, the Swiss who had befriended him at the Café Marengo in 1804. He could not resist a visit to the Garden Prison. The familiar grounds were deserted. The big house was almost empty, its only occupant the old sergeant, with whom Flinders now would have spoken in fairly comprehensible French.

31

'They Have Forgotten Me'

Having received no word on his future in the recent dispatches from France, Flinders felt that he would probably remain interned until the war ended, and the thought of Ann's joining him became deeply desirable. Yet there were difficulties, not least the fact that although 'the conduct of a woman on board a ship without her husband, be ever so prudent and circumspect, the tongue of slander will certainly find occasion, or it will create one, to embitter the future peace of her husband and family'.[1]

Nevertheless, to provide for the possibility of her travelling with some respectable party, he sent Ann's father drafts on his London agent, W. A. Standert, for £800. Thomi Pitot arranged with his agent in France for a 300-dollar letter of credit for Ann, should unforeseen circumstances bring her there. To Banks Flinders wrote that Mrs Flinders had written of joining him on the island but that he had left the decision to her. He asked Banks to give her any relevant information and his opinion on her undertaking the journey. To his stepmother he wrote that with promotion to post captain and Ann beside him, he could 'even be happy'.

A month later he wrote to Aken, suggesting that he might be willing to escort Ann to Ile de France. Flinders would pay all expenses and more and, if Aken was still under parole and in effect a non-combatant, the Admiralty might wish to have him carry letters to Flinders. It was an extraordinary request to make of a man who had never met Ann and for whom Ile de France was probably one of the last places on earth to which he would want to return. By December Flinders was writing to Banks that he had news of Aken's arrival in England with the charts and papers entrusted to him. There is, however, no record of Aken's having received or answered Flinders's letter regarding Ann. In any case, the difficulties of safely bringing Ann to Ile de France seemed increasingly insurmountable, and evidently Ann did not press further to attempt the trip.

Flinders's restless curiosity did much to provide distractions that took up his time and attention and gave him the satisfaction of adding to his knowledge. He speculated on the origin of a huge circular indentation in the ground, some 200 feet deep and by his estimate four or five acres in area at the bottom. At the Baie du Tamarind, the sandy inlet into which the Tamarind and Rempart Rivers empty—in a painting by Edouard Pitot, a curve of yellow sand, a few huts and palm trees and the Indian Ocean—Flinders investigated the depth of the bay and the extent of the coral reef.

Elsewhere he examined a series of caves, seeking their geological origins. There was a sanguineous tale about the caves. Some 30 years earlier they had been inhabited by a group of black outlaws, whose murders and depredations spread terror throughout the area. Their hideout was unknown until a man they had left for dead saw them enter the caves and managed to alert the authorities. Soldiers shot the lookout, who had fallen asleep at his post in a tree, and rushed the cave. Flinders recorded that on his visit, sleeping places outlined with stones were still to be seen. He added, 'The skull of their captain, who was said to be possessed of much cunning and audacity, was at this time lying upon a stone at the entrance of the cavern . . .'[2]

A part of La Ménil, the plantation of a Monsieur Airolles, had once been the home of the explorer La Pérouse. Flinders walked thoughtfully about the garden the navigator had laid out, with its still-blooming roses and the ruins of the house, and arranged with Airolles to set up a simple stone monument. The following year Flinders sent the island's Society of Emulation a ten-page paper on Wreck Reef and his related ideas on the disappearance of La Pérouse. Together with a paper on magnetic compass deviations, the Wreck Reef article was sent on to the Institut in Paris.

A reminder of happier days was a visit from a young French officer, Charles Baudin—unrelated to Nicolas Baudin—who had been a midshipman on the *Géographe* during her Australian voyage. Now serving on the frigate *Piémontaise*, Charles Baudin was at Le Refuge for several days and described to an immensely interested Flinders the explorations of the *Géographe* and the *Casuarina* after they sailed from Port Jackson in November 1802.

Despite these distractions, Flinders's mind was circling more and more obsessively upon his detention. His disillusion with the French government was now partnered by disappointment in his own, which had made no public appeal for his liberty and had halted, as he later wrote, 'the advancement I had been led to expect in consequence of the voyage ... This could not be from inattention, and therefore probably arose either from a want of information, or from some misconceived opinions at the Admiralty'.[3] He would rectify this by a new account of the circumstances of his imprisonment, accompanied by copies of all pertinent correspondence.

By the end of May the wet season had come to the island's highland interior, with continuous rain and relatively low temperatures, a time when many plantation families left for homes on the coast. These were weather conditions that Flinders heartily disliked, and as the Garden Prison was unoccupied, he wrote to Monistrol asking if he could spend the season in the old building. He received permission to do so, but understood from friends that there would be tight restrictions on his movements and on visitors. Borrowing a horse, he rode into Port Nord Ouest to personally ask for a more relaxed parole, but was told that it was unlikely that the governor would permit this. Flinders returned to Le Refuge.

With grey rains sweeping about his pavilion, he went to work on a document that he entitled 'A Narrative of the causes that prevented His Majesty's ship the Investigator from completing the examination and discovery of the Coasts of Australia &c'. Despite the title, it merely summarised the *Investigator*'s voyage and concentrated at length on the circumstances of his detention. That the Admiralty was fully aware of this unhappy story and could not effectively act in the midst of a war, Flinders refused to accept. He fully expected the account to rouse the Admiralty into taking decisive steps on his behalf. An accompanying letter to William Marsden, First Secretary of the Admiralty, also stressed the misfortunes of his captivity. The narrative, with extensive appendices, was entrusted to a Captain Larkins, captured with an East India Company ship, who was being returned to England.

There was certainly some justification in Flinders's feeling that no decisive step had been taken on his behalf by either the Admiralty or the British government. Besides the initial notification of Flinders's case sent to France in 1804 and a request for duplicates of dispatches to Ile de France regarding Flinders, there had been no action, no application for his release. Banks's work through his personal connections had constituted the principal effort to liberate him, thus a rumour that Joseph Banks had died was a serious shock to Flinders. He found it to be mere gossip, but it was a depressing reminder of the weakness of his position. He wrote to Banks on 28 July 1806, 'I sometimes fear—and it is a sickening thought—that I may be kept here until my patron, my conductor in the road to fame, shall be no more. Where, Sir Joseph, shall I find another disinterested friend . . . ? Without fortune, rank, or connexions, what can I hope for?'[4]

In mounting desperation, Flinders also turned to Bergeret who, in August 1806, was preparing to sail for France. Flinders wrote him a letter emotively pleading with him to explain to France's most eminent men of science the misery and bitterness of his plight. It was a magnificently eloquent letter, which Flinders included in *A Voyage to Terra Australis* as evidence of his despairing state of mind at the time.

In August, too, Thomi Pitot had left Ile de France for Réunion, and Flinders's emotional state declined rapidly in the absence of these two friends. In late August his diary also noted that Delphine had gone to town in the company of her brother to spend a few days with a friend. Although this was perhaps a minor factor, it may have added to his profoundly low mood. He began keeping to himself in his pavilion. By late September he had decided to withdraw entirely from all company. He made arrangements for a solitary dwelling away from the D'Arifats, and at noon on the 26th sent a letter to Madame D'Arifat to tell her of his intentions. In his diary he wrote, 'The afternoon and evening passed in a depression of spirits inconceivable, and before supper I received an answer from Madame D'Arifat in which she requested to know what reason she was to give to the world for my abrupt departure'.

Flinders replied that she should tell the truth, that 'I cannot resist the attacks of melancholy and desire of being alone . . . If this does not appear to be a sufficient answer, say that I am an hypochondriac . . .'[5]

That Madame D'Arifat had seemed displeased disturbed Flinders greatly 'and I retired to my couch in a fever', wishing simply to die. The unexpected arrival of letters from England roused him. The next day he wrote, 'I mustered spirits enough to go to breakfast with our good family and communicated the happy intelligence I had received, and which with the soothing consolations and reasonings of Madame D'Arifat induced me to abandon my ill-omened project . . .'[6] Of this same episode he wrote years later that he had suffered 'a dejection of spirits which might have proved fatal, . . . [but] such an end to my detention would have given too much pleasure to the captain-general'.[7]

Once again he strove to occupy his mind with work, reconstructing some of his charts on a larger scale, writing an explanatory memoir, studying French and reading. By the beginning of October he was able to write, 'Find my spirits much composed within these few days', and he slipped back into the pleasant social world of Wilhems Plains. Nevertheless, later that month his letter to Thomi Pitot on Réunion was unhappy and self-absorbed; 'This long absence of yours tires me . . . Indeed my friend I have need of your friendly consolation to keep up my spirits . . .'[8]

In November 1806 Flinders acquired a copy of *Steel's List of the Royal Navy* of December 1805, and with amazement saw an entry for a brig named the *Investigator*, lying at Plymouth. In a state of tremendous excitement, he wrote to Ann, 'a new Investigator! What is the meaning of it? Is she coming here to me to finish my voyage of discovery? Or is it some other officer to reap the harvest of my labours whilst I am let to remain in prison? I know not what to think . . .'[9] It was some four month later that, on meeting the supercargo of an American ship that had been at Port Jackson the previous year, Flinders learned something about the transformation of his old ship and her final journey home. It was a tale in itself.

In May 1804 Governor King had inspected the *Investigator*, lying as she had been left by Flinders, a hulk moored in Sydney Cove. King found the bottom and copper still sound, despite the rottenness of her upper works, and ordered an official survey, which stated that by 'Cutting off her Upper Deck and Topsides' and making additional repairs, she would 'prove a Serviceable Vessel for Four or Five Years Or more'.[10]

King intended to use her for colonial business between Port Jackson and other settlements, and in January 1805 a cut-down, brig-rigged *Investigator* sailed for Norfolk Island under Lieutenant John Houston, returning a month later. King then decided that she should be sent to England with dispatches. He placed in command William Kent, an exceptional navigator and seaman. After an additional inspection and some further alterations, Kent accepted the vessel and, on 24 May 1805, the brig *Investigator* sailed for home by way of Cape Horn. Among the vessel's passengers were Kent's wife and three children, Robert Brown and Ferdinand Bauer. Brown had been working at Port Phillip, several locations in Van Diemen's Land and islands in Bass Strait and Bauer had spent eight months on Norfolk Island.

The botanists did not find the appearance of the cut-down *Investigator* encouraging, but from both King and Kent they received full cooperation in preparing their collections for what promised to be a wet and difficult voyage. Among the vessel's papers was a copy of Baudin's letter to French authorities, which King had neglected to give to Flinders. King also included a letter to the commander of any French port at which the *Investigator* might stop, asking in the name of science for particular protection for Brown and Bauer and their collections.

The *Investigator*'s journey was harrowing. The ship doubled Cape Horn in mid-winter, her low single deck almost constantly under water. In Brown's words, she was 'not only a crazy but absolutely a defenceless ship'.[11] Kent's remark was not much different: 'A more deplorable crazy vessel than the Investigator is perhaps not to be seen'.[12] Nevertheless, Kent brought her through. On their arrival in Liverpool on 14 October, the Admiralty ordered Kent take the ship on to Plymouth despite bad weather. Six men deserted. Brown begged not to risk his collections any further, and requested that they finish the journey to London on land. Battered by storm winds, the shattered ship was forced to put in at Falmouth before struggling on to Plymouth.

What Flinders heard of the *Investigator*'s voyage was fragmentary, and he remained confused and distressed. The *Investigator*, condemned while under his command, had just over three years later successfully completed the journey from New South Wales to England under another commander. This, he believed, reflected badly upon himself and, as he wrote to Ann, would give his enemies further unjust grounds for suspicions against him. That neither Ann nor Samuel had informed him of the vessel's arrival was additionally upsetting. He did not know that Governor King had written to Banks to defend Flinders from any criticism of the kind that Flinders feared, and that Kent, offered the task of completing Flinders's survey of New Holland, was interested only if Flinders had neither wish nor opportunity to do so.

Another cause for concern was William Bligh's nomination to succeed the ailing Philip King as governor of New South Wales, which Flinders understood from a remark in Banks's letter of 18 June 1805. Late in 1806 he read in the *Asiatic Mirror* that Bligh had reached the Cape of Good Hope, retaken by the British in January that year. With continuing his survey of the Australian coast never far from his mind, Flinders wrote to Banks, 'I should indeed desire not to be placed under his immediate orders, since the credit, if any [which] should be due to my labours, would be in danger of being monopolised'.[13] It had been thirteen years since Flinders had parted from Bligh, but, in his profoundly discouraging and stressful circumstances, the disquiet and insecurity of the young midshipman evidently returned.

In the same letter Flinders repeated his concern for promotion. He searched Steele's List 'continually', hoping to find that the Admiralty was sufficiently satisfied with his work and 'penetrated with the injustice' done him, 'to have given me that step which is the great object to young naval officers. I need not say that disappointment has hitherto been the result'. Still, he had a 'latent hope' that 'our gracious Monarch', informed of the circumstances, would order his name inserted in the 'list of post-captains from the commencement of my captivity'. He had hoped, too, that 'a new Investigator' was to have been sent out for him at Ile de France for the completion of his explorations. Twelve months later 'this hope is nearly dissipated'.[14]

By December 1806 Flinders evidently felt emotionally secure enough to write letters to several members of his family. He wrote many pages to Samuel, whose letter, written in February and containing considerable family news, had arrived in September. Flinders's reply contained a bitter outpouring of indignation at the failure of the British government to 'claim' him, his vessel, books and papers, and a description of his 'depression of mind from seeing myself so long neglected'. He confessed that he had quit his work and studies and given himself up to 'what the French call *dissipation*, and we pleasure...'[15] He asked Samuel to press his case on such persons as William Marsden, Dr Nevil Maskelyne, Alexander Dalrymple and other notables.

Samuel had apparently written that he was unwell and not on a ship while he awaited Matthew's return. Matthew sympathised, but told Samuel that his return was very problematical indeed, and continued at length on the importance of his brother's pushing on with his career and improving himself at all times. He asked many questions about friends and associates, financial matters, Bligh's appointment and the new *Investigator*.

To his stepmother he wrote more lightly, encouraging a musical education for his young half-sisters, and to Isabella Tyler, his demi-sister, as he called her, he wrote with waggish humour. He had had no letter from her, he said, but there was 'a report amongst the whales in the Indian Ocean, that a scrap of a letter did pass by for Port Jackson, and a flying fish in the Pacific even said he saw it, but there is no believing these travellers'.[16]

A few days later he wrote to Ann, discussing financial matters, including compensation to her father for her upkeep. He wrote of the despair he had recently felt, and added:

> should no important change take place before the end of May next, I must and will attempt something; great risks must be run and sacrifices made, but my honour shall remain unstained. No captain in His Majesty's navy shall have to blush in calling me a brother officer. But enough of this, and perhaps too much to thee; depend upon my resolution and foresight and leave the rest to Providence.[17]

Only by private arrangements could Flinders have sent out a letter such as this and not suffer at least some consequences. Yet Decaen and Monistrol knew what he was doing. They had seen references to—even copies of—Flinders's letters in correspondence they received. For reasons of their own, they did not interfere.

Despite the positive outlook expressed in his letters, Flinders did not entirely escape his bouts of despondency before the end of 1806. His diary entry of 20 December is deeply low-spirited:

> there is a weight of sadness at the bottom of my heart, that presses down and enfeebles my mind. Everything with respect to myself is viewed on the darkest side. The little knowledge I have is not reckoned or is unappreciated; that which I have not is exaggerated: the errors or faults I have committed are exaggerated, whilst those of my actions which might bear the name of good, are depreciated. In society I have no confidence nor scarcely presence of mind; . . . I am satisfied nowhere . . . Sometimes, when I forget myself in my occupation, I cease to be miserable; but this is not often . . . I may truly say, that I have no pleasure in life . . . Miserable state! . . . the energy of my mind is I fear lost for ever; or is not to be recalled except by some great change of situation.[18]

He had written what a modern psychiatric evaluation would most likely find a good description of a major depressive illness.

Nevertheless, Flinders remained part of the social activities at Wilhems Plains—a hunting expedition, dinners and suppers with neighbours, an evening of music. Chazal, a competent artist, had decided to paint Flinders's portrait, and on several occasions Flinders spent the day at the Chazal home, posing for the picture. During the last two days of 1806 and on the first of the new year he was in Port Nord Ouest, obtaining money for bills of exchange drawn on his naval pay and procured for him by Johann Boand. He sent out letters with an English naval surgeon being repatriated by way of Hamburg, Germany, and purchased small New Year's gifts for the D'Arifats:

> a pocket housewife of morocco, containing various little instruments; to the young ladies three fashionable hats, with sweetmeats, to which a pretty needle case for the eldest was added; to Mr. L. [Labauve] a box of pastels with drawing paper, and to the little boys, pocket knives with sweetmeats, amounting in the whole to 52 dollars, with which I had the gratification to find them well pleased.[19]

Chazal finished his portrait of Matthew Flinders in January. It shows a young man in a black, gold-trimmed uniform, with short, curling hair and a thin, clear-featured face. The nose is long, the mouth small and tight, the brown eyes alert, direct, almost wary. Executed in oil on canvas, it is the only known full-scale portrait of Matthew Flinders painted from life.

At some point Flinders wrote a little book, which he called 'A Biographical Tribute to the Memory of Trim'. It was the story of his black and white cat, written with all the sense of fun, humour and affection of his letters to Isabella, and which delighted children in his company. In February 1807 he noted that he was translating it into French, probably to entertain the young D'Arifats. He took the manuscript with him to England but never attempted its publication.

Unknown to Flinders, a very slow effort towards his liberation had been grinding on. On 30 December 1806 Secretary Marsden of the Admiralty wrote to Sir Edward Pellew, commander of the British fleet in the Indian Ocean, headquartered in India. The letter was accompanied by a document from the French Council of State that directed the release of Matthew Flinders from detention on Ile de France. The directive had been issued on 14 July 1804. It was ratified by Napoleon on 11 March 1806.

Any explanation for the long delay is speculative. However, to be seen as pre-eminent in science contributed considerably to a nation's prestige. It was therefore to France's advantage if François Péron, the Baudin expedition's naturalist, could complete the first volume of his *Voyage de Decouvertes aux Terres Australes,* before Flinders returned to England and published his account of Australian explorations. The National Institute of France as a body had responded promptly and with sympathy to Banks's request for assistance in freeing Flinders as a man of science, but there would have been individuals not at all opposed to postponing any action. And certain councillors of state might have felt similarly.

By early 1806, however, the pressure of appeals for Flinders's liberation had begun to build. Aside from Banks's communications, there were Flinders's letters to Fleurieu and other letters from Ile de France to several of France's most respected scholars and scientists. The Council of State's 1804 directive on Flinders's release was finally ratified and three copies sent to Ile de France in three separate ships. Two of the ships were intercepted by the British and their dispatches flung into the sea. The third copy evidently reached the island in August 1807. A fourth copy had been sent to England and in December 1806 was forwarded by Marsden to Pellew with the recommendation that it be taken to Ile de France on a British warship under a flag of truce. Thus on 19 June 1807, Pellew ordered the frigate *Greyhound* to sea to carry the order for Flinders's release to Port Nord Ouest.

On 11 December 1806 Flinders had written to Ann, telling her that should no important change take place before the end of May in the coming year, he would 'attempt something', even at great risk. Thus he began the year 1807 with certain determinations and, as a result, a sense of renewed strength. Looking forward to the restitution of his career, he reconsidered his comments on William Bligh, now governor of New South Wales, and on 23 March he began a long, courteous letter to Bligh, much of it on a topic of mutual interest: the surveying and charting of Torres Strait. He discussed the charts of James Cook, acknowledging that, like many others, he, Flinders, had been so dazzled by the reputation of Cook that he had assumed all his charts to be absolutely accurate, without considering Cook's lack of a chronometer. Flinders then compared his own and Bligh's results, carefully praising Bligh's cartographic skill, especially the results he achieved in 1789 in an open boat. It was a detailed and technical discussion.

At the end of his letter Flinders touched upon their past personal relationship. He had gained his first knowledge of nautical science, he wrote, from Bligh, who had learned from the 'great master himself', and 'the unfortunate antipathy you took against me in the latter part of our voyage in the Providence', would never prevent him from acknowledging the governor's rare navigational ability and his contributions to science.[20]

Flinders enclosed a short paper entitled 'Manner of preparing maize for the table in the Isle of France', which, as he wrote to Banks, could 'be useful to his colonists'. It was the result of one of his many investigations into the agricultural methods and economy of the island. He added, 'I hope the letter will convince His Excellency of the respect I entertain for his talents and services in nautical science; and perhaps he will see the injustice of considering me with an unfavourable eye'.[21]

Flinders sent his letter to Bligh through Campbell, Clarke & Company in Calcutta and Sydney. While it may have reached Bligh towards the end of the year, the governor, embroiled by the following

January in a tumultuous contest with the New South Wales Corps, would probably have had little inclination or opportunity to answer.

In this better frame of mind, Flinders was considering other possibilities for the development of his naval career. During a solitary walk late on a moonlit night he reflected on how a short period in the regular navy would help him to 'recall and improve my knowledge of the service and good discipline',[22] before embarking again on his explorations.

By the last day of May, however, he had taken no steps towards achieving freedom on his own. He wrote to Ann, 'Oh my dearest love, the six months of which I spoke in my last letter to thee of Dec. 11, 1806 are elapsed and yet no change, no better prospect . . .' Nevertheless, he enjoyed 'good health, and . . . the sadness that took possession of me some time is much abated'.[23] Flinders had visited friends in town to join in welcoming Thomi Pitot back to the island. Pitot's return would have been a joy to Flinders, and the whirl of festive gatherings that greeted his friend provided enjoyable distractions.

John Elder's situation was very different. While Flinders had been imprisoned at the Café Marengo and the Maison Despeaux, Elder's duties had taken him regularly into the town to the shops and marketplace, and from time to time to visit the *Cumberland*'s incarcerated crew. As well, he sometimes met and talked to English sailors on parole. This was an important aspect of his life, as Elder did not speak French—despite Flinders's attempts to teach him—and typically had no special liking for the French. He was involved, too, in Flinders's work. In a good, clear hand he copied documents and made a fair copy of the *Investigator*'s official logbook from material damaged in the shipwreck.

In the country, however, his activities were much curtailed. The copying of the books and papers in Flinders's possession was finished, and only occasionally was it necessary for Elder to make the long walk into town. With the black slaves around him, even the overseers, all French-speaking, he had little in common.

His friend and companion, fortunately, was Seaman William Smith, who shared his pavilion. In April 1806, however, a kind of final isolation closed about Elder when Smith left Ile de France. Flinders spent much of his time with his hosts and friends, in reading and writing, and for some months was withdrawn into his own depressive state. A physically healthy man of 27, accustomed to activity, John Elder had little to do and almost no one to talk to. As intensely as Flinders, he would have dwelt on his hopes for freedom, and apparently had come to count strongly on an audience with Decaen that Flinders had planned for April 1807. Flinders may have told him that he intended 'to use all the reasonings and persuasions' in his power to obtain their freedom. The interview was refused and the impact of this and the collapse of the hopes attached to it hit John Elder acutely. Flinders's letter to Ann continued:

> Since the refusal of the general, my poor Elder, the faithful servant and companion of all my dangers and misfortunes for six years past, has fallen into such a state of melancholy and dispair, that I have been made apprehensive for his intellect and even for his life. He has taken it into his head, that everybody about us and even the whole of the island are more or less our enemies, and are laying plots against us . . . there is not a book, or newspaper that he reads which does not furnish him with imaginary proofs of their conspiracies. If he sees two people talking together, he thinks it must be about him; if they laugh, it is in ridicule of him, and all the reasonings and proofs I give him to the contrary cannot eradicate his ridiculous suspicions.[24]

Elder had evidently succumbed to a psychotic illness. In his book Flinders added, 'finding no other means of cure than persuading him to return to England, where he might still render me a service, permission for his departure was requested'.[25]

Two days later Elder's return to England by way of the United States was approved. There remained, however, the wait for a ship, while Elder's irrationality persisted. Towards the end of June, however, he became convinced that he was really leaving, and his condition eased. Flinders, who earlier had doubted that Elder could be trusted to carry letters or parcels, now began packing a trunk to be delivered by Elder to Flinders's London agent. A mass of papers went into the trunk—charts, logs, letters, receipts, books, including Banks's journal from the *Endeavour* voyage, which he had loaned to Flinders, packets of letters from people on Ile de France, 'four table and five tea spoons' and, in the remaining space, a package of clothing and household linen. All of these parcels were numbered and their contents itemised on a list carried by Elder.

There were letters to Marsden and Dalrymple, and private letters for Joseph Banks, Samuel and Ann, for whom there was also a little box containing some silver Indian coins and a necklace made for her by the D'Arifat girls. For Elder himself there were careful instructions as to how to proceed in his journey and on the deposition of the trunk and letters and, with his official certificates of discharge, a long and very complimentary letter of recommendation and the sizeable sum of 100 dollars.

On 6 July 1807 Flinders was allowed to visit Port Nord Ouest to arrange Elder's passage on the *Phoebe*, a 150-ton American brig sailing for Baltimore, Maryland. Flinders had intended to pay for Elder's passage, but Elder chose to join the ship as a member of the crew. He arrived in town the following day and boarded the *Phoebe*, which sailed on the ninth. Flinders noted, 'Elder is therefore now relieved from his inquietude, and I from much care'.[26] As his servant Flinders now took the black youth, Toussaint, formerly the slave of Walter Robertson. Elder arrived in London on 31 January 1808. He delivered Flinders's trunk to Standert, forwarded the letters and on 3 February wrote to Ann; in reply to her many questions, he wrote a second letter, assuring her of Flinders's good health, despite not looking by far as well as he had in the past, his dark hair having turned 'very white'.

In shipping out more of his work, Flinders had relieved himself of another serious concern. Were he to attempt an escape, he would have to leave behind almost all of his possessions, including some results of years of navigational and hydrographic labour. This had been a major deterrent to plans for flight. Now he wrote to Ann that if no word on his release came on either of two expected ships from France, 'I must have recourse to other means, and I am preparing for it. Pray Heaven my project may succeed'.[27]

The same letter contained a reference to a disagreement between Ann and Samuel. Anxious to smooth any difference between his wife and his brother, he wrote gently, 'Samuel mentioned to me, as thou hadst foreseen, something of a tiff between thee and him, but he gave thee all the merit of being right, except that of too freely communicating to thy female correspondent his pecuniary affairs'.[28] He thanked Ann for letting him know of the matter and went on to chide her mildly for the three months that had elapsed between her two most recent letters.

Disagreements were not confined to Flinders's family in England. On 19 July he wrote in his diary: 'A little quarrel with my friend D. [Delphine] which has now kept us at some distance for five or six weeks still continues and gives me uneasiness. I was the party that had a right to be offended at what was said to me, but wished to pass it over; for which I am punished by opposition and neglect as if the case were the reverse'.[29]

Flinders never explained the cause of the original spat. His avowed reticence to speak of anything of a romantic nature suggests that there may have been some misunderstanding or dissension of this kind. Flinders's statement in his diary that he was the party with the right to be offended and his apparently unwavering devotion to Ann would seem to suggest that there might have been some hope or expectation on Delphine's part that met with a painful rebuff.

32
Intimations of Freedom

On 18 July flags whipping in a cold, wet wind on Signal Hill announced the arrival of several vessels at Port Nord Ouest. One of them was the East India Company *Marquis Wellesley*, a cartel with French prisoners from Madras. On the twentieth Flinders commented, 'This morning the red flag was hoisted, for an English ship being in sight'.[1] The next day the red flag was down, but Flinders learned that the vessel had been the frigate HMS *Greyhound*, commanded by Captain Troubridge, which had put into the harbour but was ordered out the next day. Troubridge had delivered to Decaen the fourth copy of the document from the French government directing the release of Matthew Flinders.

Four days later a packet from Monistrol brought Flinders the letters and enclosures from Admiral Sir Edward Pellew in Madras that had come with the *Marquis Wellesley*, which remained in the harbour. Pellew wrote that he had received a letter from Marsden at the Admiralty, together with a document 'transmitting instructions for your release under the authority of the French minister of marine, to the captain-general of the French establishments'.[2] Pellew enclosed an extract of the document and suggested that Flinders depart Ile de France on the *Greyhound*, congratulating him on 'this long protracted event'. A second letter from the Admiral offered Flinders accommodation at his house in Madras until passage to England could be arranged. A note from Captain Troubridge welcomed Flinders to his ship, which, of course, had sailed days before.

Flinders was filled with amazement, indignation and hope. Subduing his excitement, he wrote to Monistrol asking for confirmation of the order from Dècres to Decaen. Seven days later he received a short letter from Monistrol, which confirmed that the governor had received a dispatch from the Minister of Marine and the Colonies of France relative to Flinders. A copy of the dispatch was included. Monistrol added that he was to inform Flinders 'that so soon as circumstances permit, you will fully enjoy the favour which had been granted you by his Majesty the Emperor and King'.[3]

Flinders now understood that almost precisely three years earlier, in July 1804, the French Council of State had made a decision on his case. They had approved the action taken by Captain-General Decaen and magnanimously granted Flinders his liberty and the restitution of the *Cumberland*. It had then taken until March 1806 to obtain the approval of Napoleon, and although sent in triplicate by French ships, the fourth copy had arrived at Ile de France in July 1807 on an English frigate under a flag of truce. Now he was told to await the 'circumstances' that would permit the execution of the council's order. When would that be?

With some confidence he wrote to Ann on 12 August: 'At length orders have arrived here to set me at liberty, and to restore to me my vessel . . . I think it probable that I shall be sent to India in a cartel now lying here, and that the time of our departure will probably be one month hence. In this case I hope to be in England about April or May'.[4]

The last of his trunks in the government office was now returned to him intact, except for letters and papers wholly or partly eaten by rats that had gnawed their way in. He was refused the return of the third volume of his logbook and the two boxes of dispatches and letters from Governor King and Colonel Paterson. He was told that the former was still required for extracts, despite having been in Decaen's possession for three and a half years, and the latter had been long disposed of, Monistrol indicating that something in their contents had contributed to Flinders's imprisonment.

His sword and telescopes would be restored to him on his departure and he would receive compensation for the *Cumberland* and her stores as they had been valued on his arrival. Flinders asked if he could depart on the *Marquis Wellesley*. He was told that the international situation made this an unsuitable time to apply for his departure. More or less anticipating this reply, Flinders had unpacked the trunk and sorted out what had survived the rats—monthly muster books, dead tickets for the *Investigator*'s lost men, and letters that he had carried from Port Jackson. These, together with letters to the Admiralty and to Marsden, describing recent events, he arranged to go with the *Marquis Wellesley* to Admiral Pellew.

With a mixture of anger and new-found confidence, Flinders also wrote to the Minister of the French Marine. There was little probability, he said, of Decaen executing the order he had received, in view of his personal enmity, which went back to Flinders's refusal to dine with him. Now, he said, he intended to recall his parole and would probably be 'closely shut up in the tower'. He sent this with a French ship that was captured by the British, the letter probably—and perhaps fortunately—thrown into the sea. There was no reply.

Nonetheless, Flinders continued to hope for a sudden call to sail with the *Marquis Wellesley*. On 10 October he wrote to Charles André Panon Desbassayns, a settler from Réunion and a particular friend who had become engaged to marry Lise, the youngest D'Arifat daughter, 'I know not when I may be permitted to quit the island, but lest *by hazard* it should be very soon, . . . I write to you now . . .' Failing this, 'I do not intend to remain upon my parole'.[5] Clearly Flinders's thoughts of escape were no secret among his French friends.

He then changed the subject to news of the D'Arifat family, of great interest to Desbassayns:

> Madame D. is as she has always been; neither sick not yet enjoying strong health. Her godlike disposition is also, and ever will be, the same. The three young ladies are in good health, but the eldest has not recovered from the state of sadness in which you left her: I believe she sheds many tears in secret . . . I no longer possess any place in her friendship, and my regret is proportionate to my loss: it has been one of the bitterest bitter ingredients in my chalice.

A happier picture followed, with particular attention to the maturing young Lise, not quite fifteen:

> The second [sister] is good, kind, sensible, and friendly; but it is of the third that I shall say most. Nature develops itself every day with her: her person is embellished, her manners gain in amiability, and her mind in sentiment . . . You are to be envied, my dear Sir . . . Mark and Aristide

> are at work with me; and they now and then enjoy the satisfaction of firing off your crackers: they are good boys, but do not always work as I could wish.

Flinders later commented to Ann that the Desbassayns family, which included Charles and three brothers, was one of the wealthiest in the two islands. His own confidence in Charles was such that he invested $1000 in his plantation on Réunion.

The *Marquis Wellesley* sailed in October 1807, after three months in port without any British sailors in exchange for the French prisoners she had brought. A number had been prepared for departure, but at the last minute Decaen countermanded his own orders for reasons unknown. Just before the sailing, A. Stock, the commissary for the exchange of prisoners, officially requested that Flinders embark with him. The reply reiterated that Captain Flinders would be set at liberty when circumstances permitted and, more surprisingly, that he would be sent to London. What this meant, neither Flinders nor his friends could imagine. One interpretation was that his freedom would only come with peace, unless, Flinders remarked wryly, Decaen would dispatch a cartel to England 'expressly with me . . .'

A curious event took place just after the *Marquis Wellesley* sailed. A year earlier Flinders had contrived to send to the Admiralty by a Captain Larkins a summary of the *Investigator*'s voyage followed by a lengthy description of his detention. Flinders had continued working on this narrative and in mid-1807 completed an up-to-date copy. He entrusted this, together with letters, to Johann Boand, who was to leave the island on the *Marquis Wellesley*; at the last moment, however, he was ordered not to board. Days later, Boand received permission to depart on the Danish ship *Waldemar*. He visited Flinders at Le Refuge and, as he was to see the governor the next day, promised to bring up Flinders's situation. Boand found Decaen extraordinarily good-humoured,[6] even with 'a sort of gaiety' when he mentioned Flinders. Still, the governor referred to the 'insolence' displayed by Flinders at their first interview, his 'haughtiness' and the deterioration of the international climate since the order for his release was approved in France.

Boand boarded the *Waldemar*, but late that evening, in Flinders's words, 'the officers of the police presented themselves, searched the trunks of Mr. Boand, took away eleven letters, and then told him he was at liberty to sail, they had got what they wanted'.

Flinders's bitterness was intense. They could only have wanted his letters, proof of Decaen's personal vendetta against him. Not wishing to send his police aboard a cartel, the governor had Boand embark on the *Waldemar* and then struck. 'He had no doubt hoped to find that I had given some information that might be injurious to the Isle of France . . . [and] contrary to my passport'.[7]

In fact, Boand had separated Flinders's correspondence and hidden it elsewhere; it was delivered to Pellew and sent on to England, as Flinders learned some months later.

In his indignation, however, Matthew Flinders ignored the fact that these letters, like countless others, were being sent out by means contrary to regulations. Decaen and Monistrol had long been aware of his clandestine correspondence. Why then this sudden and fairly drastic interference?

A month after he had received by the *Greyhound* the order relating to Flinders's release and just after the arrival of the French ship carrying the third copy of the same order, Decaen wrote to Minister Decrès. He acknowledged the directives and explained that the officer in question was 'dangerous', and he was therefore waiting for a more suitable time to carry out the emperor's instructions.

Early 1806 had, in fact, offered the prospect of a let-up in the war. The Treaty of Pressburg, which crushed the power of Austria, had been signed in December 1805. In February 1806 Napoleon imposed a treaty upon Prussia and during the succeeding first months of the year Britain's government, under Charles Fox, was making some tentative moves towards appeasement. By late 1807, however, conditions had changed. In November 1806 Napoleon issued the Berlin Decree, which declared Britain to be in a state of blockade, all commerce with it forbidden and all goods coming from the British Isles or its colonies to be seized. In mid-1807 a massive defeat of the Russian army by the French led to the Treaty of Tilsit between the two nations. At the end of 1807 the Napoleonic empire stood at the summit of its power.

At the far edge of this international scene there remained Decaen and his little island fortress. French military and diplomatic triumphs in Europe had not altered the vulnerability of Ile de France. The substantial naval and military support that he had repeatedly requested had never arrived. His plan for the invasion of India lay in abeyance. The island was subject to frequent and sometimes serious food shortages until, during some brief absence of the British cruisers, ships could slip in from Madagascar, Batavia and Réunion with rice and corn.

Decaen, however, was encouraged by reports of French negotiations with Turkey and Persia. In September 1807 he sent his brother René Decaen to Paris to impress on the emperor the feasibility of an attack on India jointly from Persia and Ile de France. There would have been no doubt in Decaen's mind that his long-time English prisoner had absorbed a very thorough knowledge of the island and its weaknesses. If the time finally came for the attack on India, an enemy who knew the island so well could certainly be dangerous if returned to his countrymen. Rumour added to the picture: Flinders had been seen, some said, taking soundings around the island at night. It is possible that Decaen reasoned that a search of Flinders's letters to England might prove that the man was indeed dangerous and justify the governor's decision not to release him despite instructions to do so.

A few days after the *Marquis Wellesley* had sailed, Flinders wrote to Monistrol asking to be informed when the liberty accorded by the emperor would be granted by the captain-general. He was ready, he said, 'to embrace *any means*, or *any route*,—in the Cumberland even',[8] if it was the soonest possible means of departure. The reply, delivered eight days later, assured him that as soon as a convenient opportunity for his departure presented itself, he would be informed.

'What measure was I now to adopt?' Flinders asked himself.[9] To escape was contrary to both his conscience and his honour. To retract his parole could mean incarceration in the worst sense of the word. His French friends were strongly and apparently unanimously against Matthew's abrogating his parole and attempting a reckless escape. An unnamed friend wrote, 'you will only rivet the chains by which you are bound'.[10] Should he then simply wait until Decaen found it necessary to withdraw 'his sanguinary talons'?[11]

Flinders was also debating the continued legality of his parole. Decaen represented the French government, and 'that government had ordered me to be set at liberty', requiring only a convenient time to do so. The captain-general having ignored so many opportunities, 'had I not then a right to seek that opportunity for myself?'[12] He reached no decision.

January 1808 brought the marriage of Lise D'Arifat to Charles Desbassayns. The wedding was celebrated with the ritual of the Roman Catholic Church, followed by a civil ceremony. As a member of the family, Flinders signed both certificates. Desbassayns had promised Flinders that if his first child were a boy, he would be named for him. Flinders, in turn, pledged that if the lad were sent to England, he would supervise his education there. In February the young couple departed for Desbassayns's property on Réunion, and the family at Le Refuge settled again into its normal routine, with Flinders starting Marc and Aristide on algebra.

But he could not let go the idea of escape. He wrote to Banks that if he were not freed to sail with the *Semillante*, a French frigate then in harbour, 'I am determined to embrace the first opportunity of getting to India or to America . . .'[13]

The *Semillante* sailed at the end of January without Flinders. Nevertheless, thinking that he could suddenly be summoned to board a neutral ship, Flinders packed whatever he did not need into trunks and hired five of the D'Arifat slaves to carry them into town to Thomi Pitot's residence.

The effects of the British blockade were being felt increasingly on Ile de France. Except for the few American vessels that got through the British cordon, foreign shipping had stopped almost entirely. There were frequent shortages of imported goods and those that were available rose sharply in price, the inflated price of quill pens and candles being of some concern to Flinders, who often wrote late into the night, alone in his pavilion. Shortages of naval stores were critical, for damaged ships could not be repaired, while the harbour itself was deteriorating. The economy was in serious difficulties. Bills of exchange issued by the administration were not honoured in France. Local businesses, distrusting the government's credit, refused loans.

The island's principal source of revenue lay with the privateers and the prize ships and cargoes they brought home. Changes in the political and military scene in Europe had set Spain and Portugal against France, and their ships were now prey along with British vessels. Privateers and their prizes waited at Réunion or Rodrigues island for intervals when the British blockade was lifted, or slipped through into the smaller, less guarded ports of Ile de France. Cargoes of grain or naval stores were in immediate demand, and there were occasional captures of specie or bullion. Other captured goods were sold to local buyers or to neutral traders, such as the Americans. In the last six months of 1808 French naval ships and privateers captured and sent to Ile de France 22 British ships, a total of 9112 tons. The sale of these prizes brought the island government 6 600 000 francs.[14]

In January 1808 the British blockade extended its patrols from the northwest coast near Port Nord Ouest, now Port Napoleon, to the island's southwest section. Here the savannah-like Black River plain, with its broad sugar cane fields, ran from angular mountains in the east to the Baie du Tamarind and farther south the Baie de la Grande Riviere Noire, sandy bights fronting the sea. Labauve and his friend Antoine Curtat, a lawyer and businessman, owned a large property facing Tamarind Bay, and in early March Flinders began receiving reports from them of British warships sighted offshore.

Flinders's mind leapt to the possibility that the ships were there to facilitate his escape. He sent luggage containing clothes to Labauve's Tamarind Bay plantation house and, one evening after dark, rode surreptitiously into Port Napoleon to arrange his affairs with Pitot, on whom he conferred his power of attorney. Leaving before dawn the next morning, he rode to Labauve's house, Les Tamarinds, a popular gathering place for Labauve's brothers and friends, which Flinders knew well.

Early on the morning of 16 March 1808, Flinders's 34th birthday, it suddenly seemed that his hopes were a reality. Before daybreak Flinders had gone down to the beach to fish, and saw a ship at anchor about two miles off. A canoe followed by three boats with six or seven men in each was steering for the opening in the surrounding reef. Flinders raced along the beach towards them but, as the sky brightened and the boats came nearer, he saw that the rowers were black. His heart plummeted. He watched despairingly as the ship weighed and headed for the Black River estuary. She was the *Perle*, a government vessel from Réunion.

He began planning a more organised escape. He returned to Le Refuge and, with paper, quills and inkwell lined up on his table, began a letter 'To the Captain or Commander of any H. M. ship of the Indian or Cape of Good Hope squadron'. He introduced himself, cited the circumstances of his detention and detailed a plan for his rescue. The ship must cruise off the island for several days, and on the third evening after having observed red signal flags on the hills, should be off the coast at Tamarind Bay. He wrote, 'At the first break of the morning a six-oared cutter should approach the bay . . . she may land at the inner end of a long white beach without difficulty. I will be there . . . with my trunk and one black man . . . '[15]

Should the rendezvous fail, the ship was to make sail at once and after two days return to repeat the operation. He dated the letter 20 March 1808. It now had to be put into the hands of someone on a neutral ship who would pass it on to a British naval officer, and Flinders knew that time and patience were required before this was likely to occur. As it happened, the opportunity never presented itself.

Nevertheless, satisfied for the moment that he had put an escape plan in motion, Flinders returned to the routine of Le Refuge. His lessons with young Marc and Aristide continued, good work sometimes rewarded with firecrackers. Once they measured 'a rectangular fish pond in the garden to show my young scholars how to find the quantity of water contained therein'.[16] Flinders kept the boys' interest in almost daily lessons for over four years. By mid-1809 he had them started on spherical trigonometry.

At Easter Flinders accompanied Madame D'Arifat to the Church of Saint Pierre in the neighbouring district of Moka. The D'Unienville family history records that as Flinders, in full uniform, entered, the district commandant escorted him into the chancel to a prie-dieu normally reserved, presumably, for the local troop commander. To an enemy national and a non-Catholic, this was a remarkable gesture of respect and friendship.[17] A number of Flinders's friends on Ile de France were Freemasons, whom he mentioned hosting to madeira wine at his pavilion. In July 1807 he wrote of attending a masonic feast and of Labauve's initiation into the organisation the next day. The extent of his own interest in the order is not clear; his contact seems to have been mainly social.

Inevitably, there were times when he felt alone among the French. He recorded in his diary, 'Persecuted a little upon the subject of politics and national character— ... [some] Frenchmen ... take a great pleasure in deprecating the English character; ... this is done by pleasantries generally, which it is best to answer ... in the same way'.[18]

He wrote to Ann. He had not had a word from her or from any member of his family since her letters of June and October 1806, which he received in May and June 1807. This drought of letters, a 'long and cruel silence', was to continue for at least two more years.

Why did Ann not write? One reason was probably the tightening of the British blockade, with few ships—to which any willing carrier would have had access—departing for Ile de France, and even fewer finding their way through the cordon. Another reason may have been the fact that in March 1808 Ann had received Flinders's letter of 12 August 1807, saying that he hoped to be in England 'about April or May'.[19] It seems, however, that even when it had become obvious that he would not be freed as he had hoped, she did not write.

These were difficult years for Ann and her family. The Reverend Tyler, aged 59, died on 14 July 1808 and his daughter Isabella wrote, 'as is too often the case on the death of a clergyman his family is broken up & dispersed, so it was with us.—Altho' we did not inhabit a parsonage the house was our own, but we were advised to sell it and we left dear Partney & another took our place'.[20]

The displacement of the three women from their home of many years clearly brought on a sad, painful and undoubtedly humiliating time. Ann lived with a series of friends. Isabella remained with their ailing mother, going, as Isabella wrote, from 'place to place for a change of scene & air', before the women eventually came together again in a small house at Bearsley.

The question has been raised as to why, during these years of relative inactivity, Flinders did not begin work on the full narrative of the *Investigator*'s voyage, which he knew eventually would be required. Flinders questioned his ability to write sufficiently well for publication, and in 1805 and 1807 had sent away with Aken and Elder many charts and records. Yet it seems likely that enough material remained for at least a first draft, which he certainly would have been capable of writing.

Ile de France brought him under influences very different from those of his naval life. After August 1805, when the last of his fellow British officers left Maison Despeaux, he virtually lost contact with the men, conditions and language of his past existence. He lived by a gentler, slower rhythm of life, in the midst of a large, close family, much of the time among its women. He spoke a new language, indulged in music, read books and developed interests very different from his previous concerns. Time and circumstance allowed, even encouraged, philosophical ponderings. He worked regularly on his charts and navigational data, but year by year there was less to do and the voyage itself slipped further into the past. Was the prospect of resurrecting the journey and confronting all its circumstances almost too difficult?

In April the French frigate *Semillante* returned to Port Napoleon. In a close battle with the British frigate *Terpsichore* Flinders's young friend, Ensign Charles Baudin, had been wounded. His right arm, shattered by a cannonball, was amputated. Flinders was permitted to visit him, bringing a welcome gift of 53 oranges. Three months later young Baudin attempted his first letter written with his left hand, which he addressed to Flinders.

Flinders, at Les Tamarinds with Labauve, replied immediately. He regretted that Baudin had been drawn by circumstance from his early career in discovery and science into war service and expressed at length the wish that their nations would together follow a mutually beneficial course in developing the arts and sciences. Young Baudin, he hoped, would take Newton and Cook for his models rather than Nelson; 'the labours of Newton and Cook were beneficial, whilst those of Alexander and Caesar desolated mankind'.[21]

The words encapsulated Flinders's own ideals of science and exploration, to the exclusion of political and military affairs. There was clearly a pacific slant to his thinking that perhaps lay to some extent behind his choice of exploration above front-line naval service. Despite the loss of his arm, Baudin returned to active service and the two men exchanged letters until Flinders's death. Charles Baudin enjoyed a successful naval career, rising to the rank of admiral and command of the French Mediterranean fleet.

In August 1808, when Flinders learned that three friends were sailing for France, he decided to write again to the French Minister of Marine and the Colonies, Denis Dècres, and began 'a memorial containing the circumstances previous to and attending my imprisonment . . . with authenticating papers annexed . . . in this I explained the late conduct of the captain-general'.[22] Numerous letters from distinguished friends on the island to persons in the French government and Institute were to accompany the document.

The memorial ran to eleven pages of closely written script. Flinders pointed out that while Decaen believed that he, Flinders, was too well informed on the island's defences to be released, others had observed conditions on Ile de France much more extensively and had been liberated. Now, with the minister's order for his release, he considered himself free of his parole. Essentially, however, the letter was a repetition of what Flinders had written many times before. One copy, with the many accompanying letters, was taken by Charles Baudin, and additional copies by two of Charles Desbassayns's brothers. High hopes were centred on the memorial by Flinders and his supporters. A favourable reaction was almost certain; Decaen would surely receive an order to set Flinders free.

Not long afterwards Flinders learned of Decaen's letter to Decrès on suspending the execution of the emperor's directive on Flinders until a more propitious time. Flinders accepted this latest shock with reasonable equanimity, commenting to Ann that fortunately he had paid less attention to the governor's words than to his actions.

There was no response to the memorial. In Flinders's words, 'week after week passed as before, without any intimation of this so much desired event'. Nor was there any reply to another impassioned appeal to the Admiralty. Perhaps worse still was the continued silence from Lincolnshire.

Flinders eventually had to accept that his plan for rescue by a British warship could not be implemented. Its weakness was the virtual impossibility of getting his instructions to an English officer. Still, in early September at Les Tamarinds, he began 'cutting a road in the wood toward a point from where I shall have a view of the sea to leeward'.[23]

For three days on his own and aided one day by two workers lent him by the Chazal overseer, he cut through thick vegetation to reach and create a lookout on an 1800-foot mountain on the south side of the Baie du Tamarind. Now called the Tourelle du Tamarind, the slope provides a magnificent view of the west coast of Mauritius, 'to the breakers on the coral reefs which skirt the shore, and to the sea expanded to a very distant horizon'.[24] Flinders wrote no explanation for the days of hot, strenuous work, but clearly the tie to the sea was there.

33

'Six Years, Five Months and Twenty-Seven Days'

On 1 January 1809 Flinders wrote, 'Fine weather for the slaves, who have this day entirely to themselves and receive gifts from their masters. Their dancing began yesterday at sunset . . . An English cruizer came before the port . . .'[1]

In his pavilion, having acquired from his friends considerable information on Madagascar, he began work on a chart of the northern part of that large island. Ports on the east coast, particularly a French settlement at Tamatave, were important sources of cattle and other provisions for the Mascarene islands. The map work was part of the 'constant occupation' that was his 'resource to beguile the time'.[2] Did he also hope to put it into English hands? Whatever his thoughts on this, references show that it was not until 1813 that it was in the possession of the British government.

He also began drawing a map of Ile de France, recalculating correctly, he said, the longitude of Port Napoleon. Had Decaen known of this, it would certainly have confirmed further his suspicions of his prisoner's subversive activity. In addition, Flinders continued his research into the magnetism of ships.

Upsetting news came in early January 1809. The excellent natural history collections of the Baudin expedition had greatly impressed the Institute and, subsequently, Napoleon. The Institute was authorised to publish at government expense the narrative of the voyage, with François Péron to write the record of the journey and its findings in natural history and ethnography, and Louis Freycinet to handle the hydrographic, geographic and navigational aspects. The handsome first volume, *Voyage de Découvertes aux Terres Australes, éxecuté par ordre de Sa Majesté l'Empereur et Roi, Sur les Corvettes Le Géographe, Le Naturaliste, et la Goelette Le Casuarina, Pendant les Années 1800, 1801, 1803 et 1804*, was issued in 1807. On 7 January 1809 Flinders, shocked and indignant, wrote in his diary: 'In a Moniteur of July 1808, I read a letter of M. Henri Freycinet [brother of Louis Freycinet]; by which it appears that that part of the South coast of Australia discovered by me, as well as that first seen by Lt. Grant and M. Baudin is to be called *Terre Napoleon*...'[3] He wrote to Banks:

> This is an injustice to our nation in general, and to Lieut. Grant and to me in particular... The two gulphs discovered by me have been named at Paris, Golphe Bonaparte and Golphe Joséphine; and my Kangaroo Island... is transformed into l'Ile Decrés; even my discovery of the north coast of Van Diemen's Land in 1798 is represented... to be a new discovery of the Géographe. Thus, whilst General De Caen keeps me prisoner here, they search at Paris to deprive me of the little honour with the scientific world which my labours might have procured me.

Flinders could not believe that either Freycinet or Péron could be the authors 'of these piracies... it must be the French Government, or at least some of its members... I have much scruple to believe that my imprisonment is connected with this invasion of the maritime reputation of England'.[4]

Flinders may not have been entirely wrong. There was, however, the fact that Flinders had named very few of the geographical features he charted; it would be 1814 before they were published with names. In the interval, any narrator or cartographer of the voyage would of necessity have to provide a nomenclature. However, with the exception of Baie du Géographe, Péron also replaced the names assigned by Nicolas Baudin, often with politically slanted terms. Péron's published narrative was similarly biased, its details at times exaggerated, even fictitious, and it was full of his undisguised detestation of Baudin, whom he not once referred to by name, merely as the commander.

In March, someone else from Flinders's happier year of 1802 arrived at Ile de France. The French frigate *Vénus* anchored at Port Napoleon, with Captain Jacques Felix Emanuel Hamelin replacing Rear-Admiral

Linois as commander in the Indian Ocean. Flinders knew Hamelin, then commander of the *Naturaliste*, from their many sociable meetings in Port Jackson, and he would have looked forward to word from him. Later, however, Flinders noted dryly, 'His affairs, or some other cause, prevented him from seeing or writing to me . . .' The Pitots averred that Hamelin wished to see him, but feared to displease the governor and that, according to Hamelin, several officers of the *Géographe* and the *Naturaliste* had applied to the Minister of Marine for Flinders's freedom, to be told that an order for his release had been sent. There is no way to verify this claim.

Further, Hamelin reputedly said that territory on the Australian coast discovered by Flinders had been marked as such on the French maps with 'scrupulous justice'. This was simply not true. At the time these assurances brought relief and pleasure to Flinders, but learning that all the officers of the French expedition had received promotions, he wrote, 'no one of my officers had been advanced on their arrival, and in addition to so many years of imprisonment my own promotion was suspended . . . the extreme difference made between the two voyages could not but add to the bitterness of my situation'.[6]

Flinders could not abandon the thought that some new order regarding himself had reached Decaen. Certain that there would be no reply to a direct enquiry, he probed indirectly. He wrote to the governor asking if his wife would be granted permission to remain with him if she arrived at Port Napoleon. Flinders had no intention of asking Ann to join him. It was the reply to his query that interested him. For this he waited six weeks. The answer was that his wife's residence on the island would not be opposed if she had made the necessary applications to the British and French governments. To Flinders, this clearly signalled that there had been no word for his release.

Commodore Hamelin put to sea in May 1809 with a small but well-armed squadron and returned to Ile de France at the end of the year with several large prizes and smaller craft. The inadequacy of the British blockade was obvious to the Admiralty, as was the underlying problem: ships could not maintain themselves indefinitely at sea and the British harbours to which they returned were hundreds of miles from the Mascarenes. A naval support base nearer to the French colony was necessary. Thus, in May 1809 a small British expeditionary force seized

Rodrigues, the smallest Mascarene island. Naval activity increased. In August a moonlight raid captured two small French vessels in the Rivière Noire. In September an amphibious operation against St Paul on Réunion destroyed the shore batteries and took three ships. In the course of the raid black slaves rose in rebellion, committing a number of atrocities before being brought to order by the British.

Decaen prepared for the expected attack. Males between 16 and 60 belonging to the free populations had been under arms since December 1803. Under his direct command he had about 1600 troops. In August 1809, against the protests of their owners, he began mobilising slaves, but the uprising on Réunion put an immediate stop to this. Decaen faced the doubtful loyalty of some of the island's population. Among the colonists there were royalists. There were republicans resentful of Napoleon's suppression of their early liberties. There was bitterness even among Bonapartists, who had suffered materially during the war from the neglect of their islands by the metropolitan government. And there was the unpredictability of the slaves.

In September 1809 all British prisoners were deprived of their paroles and ordered into close confinement, Flinders restricted to the D'Arifat plantation. He kept busy, writing a corrected copy of his journal in the undisturbed hours to midnight. And there were always letters to write, a special one in July, congratulating André d'Artifat and his wife on the birth of a daughter.

From the month of August an English ship had waited at Port Napoleon for a break in the blockade to carry exchanged prisoners to the Cape of Good Hope. To an officer scheduled for departure, Flinders entrusted a letter for Vice-Admiral Albemarle Bertie, British naval commander-in-chief at the Cape, and there has been speculation but no evidence that Flinders sent Bertie his map of Ile de France. Finally, with the beginning of the cyclone season in January 1810, the British cruisers left. The cartel prepared to sail. With irrepressible hope that he might be ordered to the ship, Flinders had removed from their storage with the Pitots his trunks, which departing friends took on board. At the end of January the cartel sailed with 200 freed British captives. No order had come for Flinders to join them.

On 12 December 1809 another British cartel, the *Harriet*, had arrived at Port Napoleon, allowed through the British blockade on

Decaen's assurance that an exchange of prisoners would definitely take place. The commissary in charge of the exchange was Hugh Hope, who had been very specifically instructed to secure Flinders's freedom by Gilbert Elliot-Murray-Kynynmound, Lord Minto, Governor-General of India. A few days after his arrival, Hope obtained from Flinders copies of all correspondence between him and Monistrol concerning his imprisonment. Towards the end of the month the commissary informed Flinders that the question of his liberation had been received favourably by the governor and he had some expectations 'of final success'.

Flinders's experience with Decaen, however, dampened any faith in this latest attempt at his rescue. His diary entry for 1 January was matter-of-fact: 'I learn from various quarters that Mr. Hope proposed to make every effort to obtain my liberty and that he had hopes of succeeding'.[7] In a letter to Banks on 18 January he made no mention of the negotiations.

Remarkably, Hugh Hope was making progress. On 13 March a letter from Hope arrived at Le Refuge with the information that he had obtained the captain-general's promise for Flinders's liberty and his departure from Ile de France on the *Harriet*. Flinders did not believe it. Nevertheless, he enquired generally whether anything was known to have transpired within the island government to precipitate such a change. Seeking to soften the very likely blow of disappointment, his friends argued that it was not possible that Decaen would let him go at this time, when an attack was expected on the island.

Then, on the 28th, a hurried messenger arrived from Pitot with a letter from Colonel Monistrol:

> His Excellency the captain-general charges me to have the honour of informing you, that he authorises you to return to your country in the cartel Harriet, on condition of not serving in a hostile manner against France or its allies during the course of the present war.
>
> Receive, I pray you, Sir, the assurance of the pleasure I have in making you this communication . . .
>
> P. S. The cartel is to sail on Saturday next (31st.)[8]

In a tumultuous state Flinders began taking leave of his friends. He visited all who were nearby and until past midnight was at his table writing letters by candlelight to those he could not reach. His servant Toussaint and two of the D'Arifat slaves were sent into town with his luggage, and after dinner Flinders took leave of the family who had sheltered him for four and a half years. It would have been a difficult farewell.

Turning his back on the plantation of Le Refuge, he set off down the winding road into Port Napoleon, stopping only to call on the Chazals. At Thomi Pitot's house he was met by Hope and the *Harriet*'s Captain Ramsden, 'neither of whom knew any other reason for setting me at liberty than that the captain-general had granted it to Mr. Hope's solicitations'.[9]

The discussions between Hope and Decaen had been strictly private and Hope offered no details on his 'solicitations', nor has any record of the talks come to light since. Flinders learned only that Hope was instructed by Minto to press for his release by every possible means and, finally, was content to let the cause of his release remain 'involved in mystery'. Questions can be raised. Why, at so critical a time, did Decaen free a man whose knowledge of the island he firmly regarded as dangerous? Flinders remarked that 'unless he [Decaen] had received a new and positive order, he could not with any degree of consistency set me at liberty'.[10] Decaen later stated that no such order had been involved. Thus the question remains: why, through Hugh Hope, did Lord Minto succeed when so many others had failed?

Decaen knew that, regardless of the defence he might put up, his islands would be taken by the British. Thus it is possible that in liberating Flinders he negotiated some advantage for the surrender or even for his own freedom and safety.[11] After the capitulation to the British on 3 December 1810, Decaen and his suite were allowed to sail for France on the transport *Emma*. This would have been expected conduct on the part of the British, but would Decaen have been sure of it? Another consideration might have been the thought that if Flinders remained on the island to be freed by British forces, the governor could have been confronted by a determined opponent with legitimate grievances that could complicate his own repatriation.

As well, Decaen had been bound for seven years to France's little ocean outpost with meagre support and recognition from Paris, while in Europe his contemporaries were winning glory on Napoleon's battlefields and emerging, as Flinders observed, as 'counts, dukes and marshals of the empire'.[12] Freeing himself of the islands and rejoining an army in the field had to be a welcome prospect. Flinders theorised that Decaen looked forward to an attack. Success in repulsing the British would bring prestige. Surrendering, he would be returned to France. Freeing Flinders, who knew the island's lacks, might advance the British attack. This, to Flinders, was 'the sole motive which, upon a review of the general's conduct, I can assign for being set at liberty so unexpectedly'.[13]

Decaen's thoughts on Flinders are known exclusively from the first and only meeting between the two men, through official correspondence and from the comments of others. Decaen's memoirs were unfinished at the time of his death in 1832 and, 38 years later in the Franco-Prussian War, many of his personal papers were destroyed when his home in Montmorency, north of Paris, was ransacked by German troops.

Beyond all the conjecture as to why Flinders was set free, one thing is obvious. His freedom was secured as an element in political manoeuvring, an adjunct to imperial designs. It had not been won in the interests of science.

Once in town, Flinders and Commissary Hope met with Monistrol to discuss the disposition of the *Cumberland* and to request again the third volume of Flinders's logbook. Monistrol consulted the governor and returned with his reply. As Flinders's release had not been ordered from Paris, Decaen could not return either the *Cumberland* or the third volume of the logbook. Flinders's request to make a copy of the book was refused. Hope was told that the matter now lay between the French and British governments.

Blockading British warships outside the port delayed the sailing of the *Harriet* for five weeks. For Flinders it was a happy time, with many convivial gatherings at the homes of friends. The president of the Society of Emulation gave a lavish party in Flinders's honour. Other British prisoners scheduled to sail were present, and while Flinders thoroughly enjoyed the occasion, he had the somewhat distracting experience of having difficulty in 'speaking English after a cessation of four years'.[14]

Flinders was allowed to spend 24 hours at the Pitot country residence, where there were to be festivities that included some of the

English. Curtat loaned Flinders a horse and he joined 'a great cavalcade of chaises, palanquins and horses' up the five miles to the house at Grande Rivière. The gathering was highly congenial: 'some appropriate songs were sung, in on[e] of which was a verse complimentary to the English . . . and a wish that before a year the two nations might be as united as we were at that time . . . Dancing went on till two in the morning when we supped, and the dancing afterwards continued till daybreak'.[15]

Flinders was not again permitted to visit friends in the country, but the D'Arifat family came to town to see him. From André D'Arifat at Flacq, there had been a fond letter of farewell, concluding, 'My wife sends her most affectionate compliments and your little girl—for in my absence she has adopted you as her papa—sends her love'.[16] With the D'Arifats remained young Toussaint, Walter Robertson's and then Flinders's servant. William Herman, seaman, took Toussaint's place in attending Flinders.

While the *Harriet* waited, Thomas Estienne Bolgerd, who had so brusquely received Flinders six and a half years earlier, was captured in a British raid on the south coast. Flinders noted that Bolgerd and a fort commander were exchanged for twenty soldiers of the British 69th Regiment. Another source, however, maintains that 'most local historians agreed that Mr. Bolger was exchanged for a dozen pigs, goats and fowls'.[17]

On 8 May the British to be repatriated were ordered on board. Visitors were forbidden, but 'Some of our lady friends having come to row around the cartel, the serjeant permitted them to come on board, and my friend Pitot with them'.[18] Some days later Labauve, too, managed to reach Flinders. His parting gift was a set for the game of tric-trac.

To pass the time constructively, Flinders borrowed a dictionary and began learning Malay, which 'may be useful to me in exploring the islands between Timor and New guinea, which I propose to do in my future voyage'.[19] Meanwhile, a parole document was brought on board for Finders to sign, and he promised on his word of honour 'not to act in any service which might be considered as directly or indirectly hostile to France or its allies, during the course of the present war'.[20]

At daybreak on 13 June the pilot boarded. Flinders's sword was delivered, but there was no sign of his two telescopes. By three in the afternoon the *Harriet* had weighed. The ship touched ground and hung there while her passengers watched in alarm as a packet flying a flag of truce came in from the British squadron and a boat from shore approached one coming from the packet. At that point the *Harriet* lifted and moved out of the harbour, eluding any possible interference. At sunset 'the French pilot left us, . . . and after a captivity of six years, five months and twenty-seven days, I at length had the inexpressible pleasure of being out of the reach of general De Caen'.[21]

The scent and sight of the open sea around him would have been happiness itself for Matthew Flinders. However, the *Harriet* was bound for India, and Flinders faced a longer route home than a run by way of the Cape of Good Hope. Opportunely, he discovered that the *Otter* sloop of war, part of the blockading squadron, was sailing shortly for the Cape. Arrangements were made with the commodore, Josias Rowley, and the next day, to the sound of cheers from the *Harriet*, Flinders was rowed across to the flagship *Boadicea*, and in the evening transferred to the *Otter*.

Africa's southernmost tip, Cape Agulhas, was sighted on 10 July and at eleven o'clock the next night, the *Otter* came to anchor in False Bay. The following day a telegraphic signal from Vice-Admiral Bertie summoned Flinders to Cape Town. Learning that a packet then at Table Bay was sailing for England, he 'thought it possible that admiral Bertie wished to send me in her . . .' With a dragoon as guide and relays of horses, Flinders covered the approximately 23 miles in three and a half hours. He 'arrived at half past four, alighting at the admiral's door. The ship sailing for England was just then going out of the bay'.[22] No other ship would sail for England for more than six weeks.

It was soon obvious that Vice-Admiral Bertie's interest was not to get Flinders to England but to obtain information on Ile de France. Bertie read Flinders's parole and decided 'that I was under no obligation to refuse any information, that might be required of me relative to that colony and Bourbon [Réunion] . . .'[23] Bertie was preparing plans for the invasion of the French island and wanted all the intelligence he could get. He was a busy man, ill and 'so little polite' that Flinders scarcely dared to ask about passage to England. Bertie was not a man to brook objections from a mere commander, and Flinders, desperate to resume his career on the best possible terms, was confronted for the first time in years with the demands of a very senior officer. He offered no argument. Flinders compiled four quarto pages of questions and answers on Ile de France, prepared charts of suitable landing places and a plan of Port Napoleon and, using his journal, drew up a list of shipping in the port between January and June 1810.

Generally, Flinders's stay at Cape Town was enjoyable. He obtained comfortable lodgings for Seaman Herman and himself with a Mrs Pieterson, and received numerous invitations from the colony's highest civil and military officials, including the governor, Lord Caledon. Full dress was required at many events, and reluctantly Flinders outfitted himself at Cape Town's exorbitant prices. Some gatherings were heavy-drinking affairs, and he was relieved to dine with 'commissioner Shields . . . his wife and daughter, forming a regular, sober, *English* family'.[24] He read the newspapers available up to March, and from *Steele's List* saw with pleasure that John Franklin had been promoted to lieutenant and, distressingly, that Samuel Flinders had lost three years in seniority, which he assumed resulted from a court martial.

In late August two officers arrived from Commodore Rowley's squadron with the news that the island of Réunion had been taken by the British. A cutter was ordered to take the two men to England and, with Admiral Bertie's probably surly consent, Flinders was allowed to sail with them.

On 24 October 1810 the *Olympia* dropped anchor at Spithead. Flinders went ashore at Portsmouth, on English soil for the first time in nine years and three months.

34 The Return

News of Flinders's release had reached England a month before with the ship that had left Table Bay as Flinders arrived in Cape Town. The day after Joseph Banks received word, he wrote to Ann Flinders.

> Revesby Abbey. Sept 25 1810
>
> Madam
>
> I have infinite satisfaction in informing you that Capt Flinders has at last obtained his release and is expected in England in a few weeks, and that on his arrival he will be immediately made a Post Captain.
>
> I am Madam your most faithful servant
>
> Jos. Banks[1]

Three days later, fearing that his first letter had not reached her, Banks wrote again and at greater length, but evidently Ann, her sister Isabella and their mother had already received their first news of Matthew's being on his way. Isabella wrote: 'One evening we were preparing to go to church,—the post came,—it was only a newspaper, it would keep till we returned.—I was first ready, & while I waited I took up the despised paper,—I read in the ship news from the Cape—that a ship had arrived there, having on board *Capt'n Flinders* as a passenger'. The excitement of the three women was beyond description. 'We read it again & again, could it be true?'[2] With Banks's letters of confirmation, there was no doubt.

At Portsmouth Flinders called immediately on Vice-Admiral Sir Roger Curtis, whom he knew from the *Investigator*'s stop at the Cape of Good Hope almost exactly nine years before. Finding that there was no transport for London until evening, he spent the rest of the day at the dockyard with a welcoming James Park, the master-attendant, a friend from the days of readying the *Investigator* for her voyage.

The mail coach travelled through the night and arrived in London at seven in the morning on 25 October. Flinders went directly to his friend Charles Bonner, and learned from him that Ann was in town; he had had no word from Ann for nearly four and a half years. He took lodgings at the Norfolk Hotel and went to the Admiralty. The massive building stood as he remembered, with its columned entrance and tall upper storey windows. He was received with 'flattering attention' by the First and Second Secretaries, John Wilson Croker and John Barrow, and learned that his promotion had taken place on 24 September, the day it was known that he had arrived at the Cape of Good Hope.

'At noon my Mrs. F. came to me . . .' Thus, laconically, Flinders described their meeting. Ann saw a white-haired man who looked much older than his 36 years. She was almost forty, and had been through years of sickness and grief. Yet it seems that time fell away and emotion overwhelmed them. John Franklin, who was there, left abruptly. A few days later he wrote apologetically to Flinders, 'I felt so sensibly the affecting scene of your meeting Mrs Flinders that I would not have remained any longer in the room under any consideration; nor could I be persuaded to call a second time that day'.[3]

Ann, however, had with her Mrs Penelope Proctor, a Flinders relative, and Flinders had to call upon Charles Philip Yorke, First Lord of the Admiralty. He returned to the Admiralty and sent up his card. Waiting, he sat with a long-time acquaintance, William Pearce, an old hand at the Admiralty who 'let me a little into circumstances and characters. When sent up for, Mr. Yorke received me with urbanity and appeared to appreciate my suffering in the Isle of France'.[4]

Yorke told Flinders that his commission as post captain would be dated back to his embarkation in the cartel, which was the earliest that the patent of the existing Board of Admiralty would allow without an order of the King in Council. Flinders was, further, appointed to HMS *Ramillies*, 74 guns, which was, however, out of commission.

Flinders left with Yorke a petition for an earlier date on his commission. When he left England, he had understood from Earl Spencer, First

Lord, that on his return, expected to be in 1804, he would receive his promotion to post captain. A commission retrospective to that year would give him a very significant six years of additional seniority, and Flinders argued that the useful results of his voyage, the unusual circumstances of his detention and his continued work on charts and other navigational matters made his situation exceptional.

Now he put numerous letters into the post and headed back to the Norfolk Hotel. On the street he met Ferdinand Bauer. It was a heartily cordial meeting, with much news to exchange. The artist, returning to England on the *Investigator* in 1805, had brought with him more than 2000 botanical drawings, from which he was preparing a selection for publication.

In the evening Robert Brown called. Since his return to England Brown had been working with the huge botanical collection he had amassed in Australia, eventually publishing some of his results in his classic *Prodromus Florae Novae Hollandiae*. In 1811 Brown became Joseph Banks's librarian, and later did important pioneering work in the microscopical study of plants. He often visited Flinders. The tension that had sometimes existed between the two men during the voyage was gone, and there remained their strong mutual respect and the relaxed pleasure of many shared experiences.

That evening, also, Flinders wrote to Banks, still in Lincolnshire. He 'had the happiness', he wrote, of announcing his return, described his meeting with Yorke, discussed the further antedating of his promotion and noted that William Bligh, removed from his governorship of New South Wales, was on his way home. Brown having departed and Flinders's obligations discharged, Ann and Matthew Flinders could begin to pick up the threads of a marriage held in abeyance for more than nine years.

For the next month Flinders was immersed in the many problems and accumulated responsibilities incurred by his long absence. A proper appearance was necessary. He had his hair cut and was measured for new clothes, undoubtedly taking particular pride in the captain's jacket with gold lace trim and a gold-fringed epaulette on the right shoulder. He visited the Transport Office to learn the whereabouts of French prisoners of war from Ile de France, for whom he had letters and money, and at the office of the Secretary of State for the Colonies submitted an official letter and some relative documents on the loss of the *Cumberland*. At the hotel he wrote letters and added postscripts to letters to friends and family that Ann would have spent the day writing. On 26 October a letter from the Admiralty confirmed his promotion from 7 May. The next day he delivered to the Admiralty copies of papers relating to the French order for his liberation and later spoke at length with Secretary John Barrow on backdating his promotion further and also on the writing and publication of his account of the voyage.

Barrow was one of the two secretaries who supervised the regular business of the Admiralty Board. Important and influential, they attended the boardroom meetings of the Lords Commissioners, and made many decisions, including financial ones. John Croker, the First Secretary, was a parliamentarian whose principal interest was his political career. John Barrow, however, was a civil servant who, from 1807, would serve as Second Secretary for 38 years. Barrow had a quiet passion for exploration, and from his desk at the Admiralty he set in motion over the years numerous expeditions into distant regions of the globe. Barrow considered Flinders's circumnavigation of Australia a great achievement, and when he became responsible for handling costs for the publication of Flinders's narrative of the voyage, there was frequent and cordial contact between the two.

Flinders remarked that Barrow, himself an author, 'paid me the compliment to say, that the writing of it [the narrative] could not be in better hands than mine'.[5] This was a matter to consider. The Admiralty's instructions had not specified that an account of the journey was to be written by Flinders. However, Banks's directions to the scientists, approved by the Admiralty, had stated that sufficiently important information from the voyage would be 'published in the form of a narrative, drawn up by the Commander . . .'[6] There were also the precedents set by Cook and Vancouver, who had produced written accounts for publication.

Flinders's own financial affairs required visits to his agent, to banks and to the Navy Office. He began proceedings to transfer to his name the legacy of £600 from his father, together with an additional sum of £500 mainly in interest on the inheritance that had accrued since his father's death in 1802. Despite charges, this added up to a substantial £1050.

He wrote to First Secretary Croker asking for approval of full pay as commander of the *Investigator* from 20 July 1803, the date of his discharge from the ship, to 25 October 1810, when he reported to the Admiralty on his return to London. This was granted, less such sums as he had drawn by bills at Port Jackson and Ile de France. Credit balances for accounts kept in connection with the *Investigator* and expenses such as tax payments and Standert's commissions eventually produced a modest balance in his favour, which was paid to him on 13 May 1811.

A further request to the Admiralty was for compensation for the servants to whom he was entitled, four on the *Investigator* and one on Ile de France. Flinders wrote to Croker a very long recitation of his adversities since leaving the *Investigator*, and detailed the hydrographical and other navigational work he accomplished on Ile de France. In this last he included as his own the contributions of Aken, Elder and Midshipman Dale, as captains customarily did. Evidently Flinders had hoped to receive compensation for four servants even after leaving the *Investigator*, but the Admiralty rejected this. He received instead a single substantial payment of £500 for expenses after leaving his ship; he left this sum with Standert, with directions for investment. Flinders's handling of his finances was not unlike that of his father; he took assiduous care to collect what was due to him, and was cautious in investment and willingly, if carefully, generous to friends or family in need.

Flinders saw numerous personal friends. He found Henry Waterhouse, his captain on the *Reliance,* 'in a very bad state of health' owing to his heavy drinking. They would have spoken of many things, among them their mutual friend George Bass and his widow, Elizabeth, Waterhouse's sister, who refused to believe that Bass would not return.

Flinders also met Elizabeth Paterson, who had welcomed the young Flinders to her home in Sydney. She and her husband had sailed from the colony in May 1810, and William Paterson, a very sick man, had died on the way to England. He had accumulated no assets, and his widow was denied a pension.

Another old friend, Captain William Kent, then in Lisbon, wrote supportively, Flinders's difficulties being 'melancholy proof of our devoted Service being in the hands of a set of *Borough-Mongers*'. Kent enquired whether Waterhouse was still living 'or has pernicious Grog washed him to death?'[7] Kent's much-loved wife, Eliza, had died, and he asked that Flinders visit her monument in a church at Paddington Green.

On the street Flinders ran into John Hunter, who had once approved the adventurous explorations of the young Bass and Flinders. Hunter was in good health, at 73 white-haired and ruddy-faced, and a newly promoted vice-admiral, who called on Flinders the next day. Flinders visited Anna Josepha King, widow of the former governor of New South Wales. King had lived less than a year after returning to England, and Mrs King and their three daughters, the youngest Flinders's 'little Elizabeth', lived in London on a small pension. King's two older sons and young Phillip Parker were in the navy and at sea. Flinders also contacted the parents of Midshipman Alfred Dale, a young friend from the Garden Prison.

One Sunday Ann and Matthew travelled by coach to Hackney to visit Ann's relatives, the Hippius family. There must have been a special joy for Ann in appearing before this family with her husband beside her, for it had been Aunt Hippius who, nine years earlier, had helped to choose the 'pretty dresses' Ann was to take with her to New South Wales.

There were invitations to dinner, most importantly from the First Lord, Charles Yorke. Callers were frequent, among them a Mr Gold from the *Naval Chronicle* and Charles Bonner with a newspaper article that mentioned Flinders. Willingham Franklin came, often accompanying Flinders on his errands. In London's naval circles Flinders was someone new and interesting, and clearly he very much enjoyed the attention he received.

Banks was not in London. Only days before receiving Flinders's letter, his librarian and friend, the Swedish botanist Jonas Dryander, had unexpectedly died. Responding to Flinders's complaint on his promotion, Banks wrote Barrow somewhat grimly that extending the date to 7 May 1810 was being very generous.

Meanwhile, Ann and Matthew had started their new life together. They went shopping and dined quietly in their rooms at the Norfolk Hotel. The weather turned dull and chilly, and some days Flinders remained at home, writing letters, in the evenings reading Chateaubriand's romantic novel *Atala* to Ann.

The novel *Atala* was part of the awakening Romantic movement in literature that was displacing the minute and rational analysis of people and society that, shaped by the strictures of the age of reason, characterised earlier 18th century writing. Here instead was a simple yet richly imaginative tale, an exotic natural setting, a glorification of religion, pastoral life and passionate love. As he had in reading *The Mysteries of Udolpho*, Flinders seems to have set aside the considerations of reason and science to immerse himself in the feeling and fantasy of a profoundly romantic story.

On Friday 2 November Ann and Matthew inspected accommodations near the Banks residence in Soho Square. On the 5th they 'took . . . [themselves] and luggage by coach to 16 King Street Soho to our new lodgings at Mrs Major's'.[8] In the house where Flinders had lived briefly as a lieutenant on the *Reliance*, they shared a home for the first time.

Samuel was one of Flinders's concerns. On their return to England in 1804 Samuel, Robert Fowler and other officers of the *Porpoise* had undergone the necessary court martial and were exonerated for the loss of the vessel on Wreck Reef. Samuel had then served on a series of ships and in June 1806 received command of the *Bloodhound*, a 12-gun brig. In August 1808 the commander-in-chief at Sheerness, Rear-Admiral John Wells, brought Samuel to court martial on charges of disobedience to orders and falsifying logbook entries. The charges were apparently spurious, but Samuel chose to defend himself, apparently in a manner that the court found offensive. As well, a young midshipman testifying in Samuel's defence broke down under questioning and false statements were allowed to stand. Samuel was declared guilty and discharged from his ship, his seniority as a lieutenant degraded by three years. Disgusted and unwell, he retired on half pay, took a cottage at Jump in Devonshire and neglected even to keep his name on the Navy List.

Matthew learned of Samuel's situation from Willingham Franklin, and soon afterwards received from his brother a letter and a packet of letter books and other papers. Samuel arrived in the evening of 5 November, and the brothers spent a day going over his affairs. Matthew then wrote to Captain Edward William Campbell Rich Owen, who had commanded Samuel's squadron, describing his brother's usefulness on the *Investigator* voyage and remarking on the severity of what had befallen him since. Samuel's name was restored to the Navy List the following year, but as he was unwilling to go to sea except in command or as a first lieutenant, he needed promotion. Samuel had found lodgings elsewhere, but frequently breakfasted, dined or spent the entire day with Matthew and Ann.

Also of immediate concern to Flinders were French prisoners of war for whom he had letters and money from families on Ile de France. In November he travelled to Odiham in Hampshire, where the men were held, distributed the items he carried and made financial arrangements for a recently captured nephew of the Curtats. Flinders wrote, 'in a few months, through the indulgence of the Admiralty and of the earl of Liverpool, secretary of state for the colonies, I had the gratification of sending five young men back to the island, to families who had shown kindness to English prisoners'.[9]

Flinders continued to work through the Office of Transport and by other means to assist the French from Ile de France who, mainly as prisoners of war, arrived in England. He also undertook the cause of a group who had been harshly treated on a British cartel. This brought him appeals from others who had felt themselves ill-treated and numerous requests from prisoners he could not help, but invariably he replied.

On the evening of 7 November Flinders dined at the City of London Tavern with the chairman and directors of the East India Company from whom 'I received the same obliging attention as I have every where found since my arrival'.[10] Further, he was assured that the Company would pay the second £600 instalment of the table money promised at the beginning of the voyage to the *Investigator*'s scientists and officers.

The money was paid two months later and, on Banks's advice, was apportioned as the first £600 had been, Flinders, as the expedition's commander, receiving £300, the three scientists splitting £150, and the four officers dividing another £150. Surgeon Hugh Bell having died, his share was divided between his heir, whom Flinders had to trace, and Robert Purdie, the surgeon's mate. Flinders invited the recipients who were in town to dinner to celebrate. Aken, captain of a merchant ship, was away, but on his return Matthew and Ann met him and his wife for a festive meal.

Joseph Banks arrived in London on 7 November. The next morning, despite rain, Flinders called at 32 Soho Square. The four-storey building of red-brown brick stood in the southwest corner of the square, its narrow frontage with columns and high windows overlooking the street and the square's now almost leafless trees. Inside Flinders would have remembered the large entrance hall, the great staircase of Portland stone rising to the upper levels, and the rooms and courtyard that ran back to Dean Street. Flinders was welcomed warmly by Sir Joseph, but as he wrote in his diary, 'There were too many people there for him to enter much into the subject of my voyage and situation, but he appointed me tomorrow morning'.[11]

Flinders joined Sir Joseph at breakfast. Banks was now 67, a big, ponderous man, with a habitually stern expression on his face; he was in almost constant pain from gout. Flinders evidently spoke mainly on the writing of the account of his voyage and the antedating of his commission to 1804. Banks listened with interest and seemed to concur with Flinders's views. There was also the matter of recompense to Flinders for the writing, which it now seemed he would be required to do, and there were decisions to be made on charts and illustrations, fees to the artists, payment for the actual publication, and much else. As to Flinders's desire for an earlier date for his commission as post captain, it was apparently agreed that he should make his request formally in a memorial to be presented to the King in Council.

Some ten days later Flinders received from Banks 'the skeleton of a Memorial . . . which he had got for me at the Council Office, Whitehall'. Flinders noted that on this occasion 'Gov. Bligh was there and talked much of his late arrest in New So. Wales'.[12] Bligh was Banks's friend, and Sir Joseph undertook to deal with his difficulties as he did Flinders's. Flinders later wrote to James Wiles: 'Our old friend Bligh . . . I believe he is proud to have had me for his disciple in surveying and nautical astronomy'.[13] At home that evening Flinders began writing a rough draft of the memorial.

Flinders now pursued the matter of a retrospective date for his post captain's commission with the same intensity he had shown in trying to obtain his release from Ile de France. The account of his deprivations became an implement in his effort to win recompense from his government, as he had previously used it in attempting to extract his freedom from the French.

What he stood to gain was six years of seniority, putting him ahead of the many captains whose seniority was dated later than 1804, and the advantage that this would provide if he was thinking 20 or 30 years into the future to flag rank. However, Flinders recorded no such considerations. The rank of post captain in itself lifted a man into a senior position. Antedating his commission to 1804 was an acknowledgement of the importance of his service despite the years of detention on Mauritius, a matter of receiving in full the professional recognition he felt he had earned. It meant the honouring of a promise he believed had been made to him by the Admiralty through Lord Spencer and an additional £300 or so in accumulated pay.

Flinders wrote and rewrote the memorial three times, frequently consulting Joseph Banks. Finally, through Banks and Barrow, the paper went to the First Lord for his approval before bringing it to the Council Office at Whitehall.

The very next day Banks told Flinders that there could be difficulties with the memorial. Anxiously Flinders went straight to the Admiralty, sent up his card and, after waiting in a crowd of other naval officers, was admitted. Yorke said that he looked upon the memorial favourably, 'but that he had not yet made his mind up upon it, and wished me not to flatter myself too much'.[14] This was alarming, and Flinders was prepared to make concessions. If the year 1804 was rejected for the backdating of his promotion, Flinders would accept a later date, 'perhaps the date of the [French] marine minister's order to set me at liberty'. The order had been ratified by Napoleon on 11 March 1806, and presumably this was the date Flinders meant, which would at least give him four years' added seniority over 7 May 1810. He assured Yorke that neither he nor Banks would carry the matter any further without the Lord's entire approval, 'and that I should receive with gratitude any accession of rank, which might accord with his ideas'.[15] For the moment the matter went no further.

Flinders had business in Lincolnshire and he and Ann were both eager to see their country friends and families. He booked places on the Cambridge coach for Friday 23 November 1810.

The journey was pleasant. The day was fine, the coach was not crowded and the horses covered the 51 miles in good time, Matthew and Ann alighting at the Blue Boar Tavern at half past four. Over the next two days, at times in rain, they travelled to Wisbech and Tydd St Mary to visit Flinders's relatives, the Hursthouses.

Matthew's father had made the senior Hursthouse the executor of his will, and on his death his son Charles had assumed the task. Thus, assisted by Charles Hursthouse, Flinders completed the transfer of his legacy of £600 and its accrued interest to his own name.

Ann and Matthew continued to Spalding, the scene of many boyhood visits. Charles's open, two-wheeled curricle travelled lightly over the fenland roads on which the night's rain was drying. The air was cold and clean, touched with the scent of the sea.

With Flinders's 73-year-old uncle, his father's brother John, they continued by post chaise to Donington. The little market town seemed unchanged, although the Flinders home on the town square had been let and Flinders's stepmother lived elsewhere with her youngest daughter, Matthew's half-sister Henrietta.

Ann and Matthew stayed a week with the family in Donington. The days and evenings were crowded with the visits of friends and relatives—his half-sister Hannah and her husband Joseph Dodd, his sister Susanna and her husband George Pearson from Boston, the Reverend John Shinglar, whose grammar school Matthew had attended at twelve, numerous relatives and friends from Donington and other towns, among them the children of his sister Elizabeth, who had died in 1799. Flinders later wrote to urge their father to send the children 'to a good school'. John Harvey seems not to have answered.

Captain Matthew Flinders was the focus of great interest, and the stories of his adventures and his long detention and sufferings on the French island were told over and over to fascinated listeners, while Ann no doubt watched with overflowing pride and happiness. A shadow was cast by the recent death of Hannah Franklin, Flinders's stepmother's sister and mother of the large Franklin clan, although grief was almost lost in the excitement of Flinders's return.

Assuming the long-postponed responsibilities of the family's eldest son, Flinders examined the accounts of his father's estate. Receipts for money owed to the doctor exceeded debts by £1/3. All assets had been left to the widow, to be divided among the children after her death. The old house was let to a John Hood Large from Leicestershire, who had bought Dr Flinders's practice for £100. Matthew and his stepmother inspected the house and, finding it in poor condition, Flinders proposed that it be sold and the proceeds invested to give Mrs Flinders an annual income slightly above what she was getting in rent. In the next several years, however, there were continuous problems of title and with the evidently wily Mr Large, and despite mentioning the attempted sale many times, Flinders never recorded the fate of the house.

On 3 December Flinders wrote in his diary, 'Went with my uncle to the Rev. Mr. Wilson for the purpose of getting extracts from the parish register relating to my great grandfather, etc. who came and settled here from Ruddington near Nottingham, about the beginning of the last century'.[16] Flinders's interest in his descent evidently awoke on this return to his old home. Undoubtedly he visited the graves of his forebears among the gravestones outside Donington's church of St Mary and the Holy Rood. Probably he entered the church where he and his siblings had been baptised, and under the high, pointed arches, had perhaps looked at an empty section of wall near the altar, where he visualised a group of white marble plaques commemorating himself and members of his family. He mentioned none of this at the time, but the plaques were detailed in his will. There is recent evidence that the Reverend John Wilson who assisted Flinders was the author of an account of Flinders's life by a hitherto unidentified writer.[17]

The next day Flinders set off at noon with Ann and his uncle in a post chaise for Boston. 'At 2 got out at my sister Pearsons, where we passed the rest of the day and evening, except that we accompanied her to her meeting house to hear Mr. Stevens, a Calvinistic preacher, who seemed to be a man of good sense and sound understanding.'[18]

Susanna's marriage to George Pearson had angered her father. She had married without his consent and, more seriously, had turned from the established church to Pearson's non-conformist faith. At the time Flinders had disapproved of the marriage of a young woman of 22 without the counsel of family or friends, but religion seems to have been a lesser issue. Whether Flinders was specifically influenced by the secularising tendencies of the Enlightenment is not clear, but it is evident that religion was an area of belief and abstractions that Flinders generally avoided. Staying with friends or family who went to church on Sundays, he usually, but not always, accompanied them, and he now seems to have accepted easily enough his sister's Calvinism. Susanna was an efficient young woman, her busy life divided between her growing family, of which there were already six children, and a serious interest in theological matters that was encouraged by Mr Stevens.

In Boston, with its great, dominating church tower and the boat-crowded Witham River, the names of friends, acquaintances and relatives filled the daily paragraphs of Flinders's diary. John Allen, the *Investigator*'s miner, came to see him. At an uncle's home there 'were several people desirous of seeing and talking with me about my voyages and imprisonment'. He met with William Bowles, to whom he had sold his property in New South Wales, and another former schoolfellow, William Pattison, now a merchant, from whom he purchased a tea urn 'and made a present of it to my sister Susanna, and gave sweetmeats to the children'.[19]

On Saturday 8 December '[we] packed up our trunks . . . We arrived at Mr. Franklins at 4 o'clock, and found there Willingham'. The Franklins now lived in Enderby, but on Monday Matthew and Willingham walked through new-fallen snow to Spilsby to deal with the will of Flinders's uncle Samuel Ward, from whom Flinders received an inheritance of £200. 'Called on Mr. Job. Lound my old schoolmaster, to hear news of his son Sherrard [midshipman on the *Investigator*] whom I wished to get promoted . . . We dined with the Rev. Mr. Walls of Spilsby . . . Walked home in the evening at dusk though the snow'. Flinders added with satisfaction, 'I do not feel the cold weather more than the others appear to do'.[20]

Ann, however, had one of her violent headaches, pains that attacked her 'now and then but seldom last more than one day', and kept to her room. With Ann's recovery, they spent two days with her friends at Partney. Flinders wrote, 'I went with Mrs. Flinders about Partney to visit her old friends, nurses, servants etc. to all of whom she wished to show her lion, and to give some trifle'.[21] In Ann's happiness now, perhaps the hurt and humiliation of the past were healing. By the afternoon they were on their way to Louth to see Flinders's aunt, his own mother's sister.

Flinders's diary entries from Tuesday 18 December to Thursday 27 December 1810—covering his first Christmas at home—are missing. When the entries resume on Friday 28 December, he and Ann are in Hull, with Matthew's favourite cousin, Henrietta, and her husband, John Newbald. Ann's sister Isabella was there and quite surely at some point Matthew and Ann saw Ann's mother, who appears to have been living in Beverly, a few miles north of Hull.

While missing pages from Flinders's diary may suggest that someone wanted an event or circumstance forgotten, subsequent entries seem to indicate that the stay in Hull was both pleasant and interesting. One afternoon Flinders walked out to the edge of town to see a curious new device, 'the steam engine, made by Watt', which was part of the town's water supply system.

Early on 1 January 1811 Ann and Matthew took the passage boat across the Humber River to Barton. The London coach called for them at noon the next day, and they travelled straight through, stopping only for meals: 34 hours in the swaying coach. They reached their lodgings about 10 o'clock on the night of 3 January after an absence of six weeks.

The next morning was frosty and windy. Overhead signs swung and creaked and rubbish swirled along the cobbled streets. Flinders made his way to Soho Square to learn from Banks that no decisions had been made on the narrative of the voyage. Of great interest, however, was the loan from Banks of a copy of Péron's account of the Baudin expedition, the first volume of which was published in 1807.

Flinders was incensed as he read it. To Charles Desbassayns he wrote, 'possession is taken of all my discoveries on the south coast of Australia, as having been made by them; . . . although it was I who gave them information of the principal points, when we met on the south coast'. He added, 'No charts of their voyage have been yet published, and some people here think, that they wait to see mine first, that after robbing me of the honour of a first discoverer, they may also pilfer me of the details'.[22] The Admiralty, he told Charles, had applied to the French government to exonerate him from the parole he had given on

Ile de France and to get back the third volume of his logbook, but no answer had been received 'and possibly none will'. However, a little over a year later the French government officially released Flinders from his parole. The logbook did not appear.

Nor did a retrospective date for Flinders's post captain's commission seem any more likely than the return of the logbook. An interview with Yorke was put off almost from day to day for a week. Yorke then told Flinders that arrangements for writing and publishing the account of the *Investigator*'s voyage would be referred to a committee of Banks, Barrow and Flinders himself. 'Upon the subject of my memorial for antedating my post rank', Flinders wrote, 'Mr. Yorke seems to have much cooled, and gives me very little hopes . . .'[23]

In the second week of February 1811 news reached England that Ile de France had fallen to British forces on 3 December 1810. Naval action around the island climaxed at the end of August when a British squadron was soundly beaten by the French off Grand Port. In late November, however, British troops landed and, after a brief defence of Port Napoleon, Decaen capitulated. Three weeks later the captain-general and his suite sailed for France.

Flinders had followed the invasion's progress in the newspapers and, in addition to his great pleasure at the thought that Decaen had been removed from the island, he hoped that now the third volume of his *Cumberland* log would be retrieved. It was not. No demand was made for it at the time of the surrender, and when a later search was ordered by Vice-Admiral Bertie, it was not found. Decaen carried the log's third volume with him to France and, despite both private and official requests from his own government, he kept it for three years before, seriously pressured by Decrès, he relinquished it. It then remained obscurely stored in the French hydrographic office, the Dépôt de la Marine, for another eleven years. In early 1825 the logbook was given to the Minister of Marine and Colonies, but not before someone in the hydrographic office had transcribed several pages in the original English for retention at the Dépôt. In June the volume was received by the British ambassador in Paris, forwarded to the foreign office in London,[24] passed on to the Admiralty, and eventually stored in the archives of the Public Record Office.

With the British occupation, letters from Flinders's friends on Ile de France came more frequently, Madame D'Arifat informing him of the weddings of Delphine and Labauve and the birth of Lise and Charles Desbassayns's second child, a boy whom they named Henry Flinders, 'your boy', as Charles wrote to Flinders. In London Flinders exchanged visits with Charles's brother Henry and his wife, who had stopped in England on their way from France to the island.

The British capture of Ile de France was, however, only an incident in the ongoing war. Fighting continued in Spain and Portugal and by 1811 new dark shadows were gathering on the continent, where the Franco-Russian detente was crumbling and Napoleon had begun immense preparations for an invasion of Russia.

Personal affairs also crowded Flinders's day. One evening in early March he concluded his diary entry for the day with a terse 'We dined today, stupidly, with Mrs. Major and a small party of Goths'.[25] Evidently there was a quarrel with guests Flinders considered barbarians, for the next morning Matthew and Ann moved to 'more commodius lodgings at No. 7 Nassau St. Soho'.

Flinders's trunks from Ile de France had been unloaded at the Woolwich dockyard and, visiting the yard, he made arrangements for their delivery to Nassau Street. In addition to being the *Investigator*'s commander, Flinders had been her purser, and settling the ship's pursery accounts was difficult as many of the papers had been lost on Wreck Reef. Pursuing these tasks took time, involving long walks or catching a hackney coach in order to see someone, sometimes only to find that person unavailable.

Another responsibility felt by Flinders was the promotions due to the officers who had sailed with him on the *Investigator*. Some had died. Midshipman William Taylor had drowned at Memory Cove in 1802, Denis Lacy had been lost at sea in 1804 and Kennet Sinclair, since a lieutenant, was also dead. The fact that Flinders had not returned to England with his officers in 1803 had meant that the survivors received no recommendations for promotion from their commander. Nevertheless, some had achieved higher rank. Robert Fowler had been made commander in 1806 and would go on to flag rank; several of the midshipmen were lieutenants. Soon after his return to England, Flinders had sought information on John Elder, who, he was pleased to find, was serving as master-at-arms aboard HMS *George*, a line-of-battle ship, 110 guns. In September Elder, still with the *George*, was in London and called on Flinders, who found him 'going on well'. Flinders also assisted some seamen who had not been paid after leaving the *Investigator*.

Two young men for whom Flinders now attempted to secure promotions were Sherrard Lound, of whom Flinders had once written with concern that he 'does not grow', and Samuel Flinders. Letters to the Admiralty and appeals to Yorke secured Lound's promotion to lieutenant in May 1811. Samuel's promotion, however, was snagged upon the fact of his court martial, although Yorke was willing to review the case. Matthew and Samuel went over all relevant letters and papers in their possession and delivered them as requested to the Admiralty.

As to the antedating of his own promotion, it now seemed clear that the Admiralty had rejected the idea of submitting his memorial to the King in Council. George III had lapsed into the last terrible years of his illness, and Parliament enacted the regency of the Prince of Wales. Yorke seemed to be avoiding further interviews with Flinders, and Banks apparently considered the issue closed. Commodore Josias Rowley had spoken on Flinders's behalf to the Admiralty secretaries, both of whom 'advised that I should say no more upon the subject'.[26]

Nevertheless, the Prince Regent's assumption of royal power seemed to open another possibility. Flinders spoke to First Secretary Croker on being introduced to the Prince, without result. Yet a month later he received other encouragement: 'Called upon the Rev. S. Clark at Knightsbridge (Librarian to the Prince) . . . He advised me by no means to give up my rank, but to endeavour at an audience with the Prince Regent'.[27] The prince, however, was not interested in meeting Flinders.

Unexpectedly, there appeared a different approach to the question. John Newbald, husband of Matthew's cousin Henrietta, had written of Flinders's situation to William Wilberforce, Member of Parliament for Hull and a well-known reformer. Wilberforce was interested, and Henrietta immediately sent his reply to Matthew. On 21 May Flinders wrote, 'Rec'd a polite note from Mr. Wilberforce to meet him this morning, and I went almost immediately. He requested to see my narrative, that he might better plead my cause with the ministers upon the subject of obtaining my back rank'.[28]

Flinders delivered the manuscript to Wilberforce. Three weeks later another note arrived. Wilberforce had been to see Yorke and found him, as Flinders recorded, 'strongly bent against antedating my rank; but that he had not convinced him [Wilberforce] of the impropriety of its being done. He now proposes to bring the affair before the house of commons, and requests me to seek for precedents of commissions antedated or given, by order of the king in council'.[29]

Flinders did not express his feelings on this proposal, but his response was cautious, even reluctant. Wilberforce was a noted political figure who had achieved prominence working for reform in areas ranging from Roman Catholic political emancipation to abolition of the slave trade in the British West Indies. One of his aims was to show that Admiralty procedures needed change. Flinders had never involved himself in any aspect of politics. To be drawn into the complex political world of Wilberforce and to have his difficulties within the navy, within the only career he had ever known, used to score points in public attacks on the government would have been an appalling prospect. And the long-term effect on his career of such a move could hardly be other than negative.

Flinders met Wilberforce and gave him the requested information, but a day later he was writing to his knowledgeable friend Pearce, at the Admiralty. Then, too worried to wait for a letter in reply, he went to see Pearce, 'to know his opinion upon the expediency of bringing the case of my rank before the House of Commons: he advised against it; and this corresponding with my own sentiments, I wrote to Mr. Wilberforce declining his offer for the present'.[30]

Wilberforce agreed with Flinders's decision. The antedating of Flinders's promotion was never granted, and Flinders never ceased to look upon the affair as a betrayal by the Admiralty. On his chart of Australia's north coast he named the cape that he considered the exit point from Melville Bay for 'William Wilberforce, Esq., the worthy representative of Yorkshire'.[31]

At 7 Nassau Street Flinders was trying to begin writing the narrative of his voyage, despite other demands on his time. There were also seemingly endless visits from relatives, friends and associates, as well as invitations that could not be declined. Particularly gratifying was Banks's request that he attend meetings of the Royal Society as a guest and that he regularly join Sir Joseph's Sunday evening gatherings.

35

A Voyage to Terra Australis

Writing and publishing the account of his voyage were now Flinders's foremost concerns. Yorke had assigned the arrangements to Banks, Barrow and himself. At the group's first meeting in mid-January 1811 it was agreed that the Admiralty would pay for the costs of reducing and engraving the charts, landscape and natural history illustrations, while the artists' fees, paper, printing and binding of the book and any related expenses would be paid from profits derived from sales of the narrative. Flinders's own remuneration would come from remaining profits, although it appears that no specific financial agreement was made. While this was normal procedure for Admiralty-published narratives, Flinders would be living on half pay throughout the process of writing and producing the book. And necessarily, he would be living in London at greater expense than if he were living in the country. He wrote, 'I ask[ed] if, during the time I was employed writing the voyage, I could not be put on full pay . . . but Mr. B. [Barrow] thought the Admiralty would object from the want of a precedent. Thus in all appearances, my time and labour must be given in,—it will cost me £500 or 600, and I cannot be employed during the time in any way that might be advantageous to my fortune'.[1] Although the arrangement was disappointing and worrisome, Flinders apparently did not press for any greater advantage for himself.

Preparations for producing the book moved quickly. Banks wrote to Barrow to offer his services in supervising the necessary transactions with draughtsmen, engravers and the like, as he had done for the publication of Cook's third voyage account. Three days later he informed Flinders that he had received the Admiralty's authorisation to superintend the work as he had proposed and to make payments as needed.

Flinders then received from Barrow an order addressed to the Hydrographer of the Navy, Captain Thomas Hurd, requesting that he return to Flinders all his charts, journals and other papers then in the Navy's Hydrographic Office.

By late January 1811 arrangements had been made for the expert cartographer Aaron Arrowsmith and the equally skilled younger John Arrowsmith[2] to reduce and engrave the charts from the voyage for reproduction in the atlas that would accompany the written narrative. It was Flinders's task to determine scales and the number of copper plates necessary, while Arrowsmith planned the chart limits, that is the size of the sheets on which the charts would be fitted, the placement on coastal charts of inserted harbour plans and other technicalities. William Bligh was present at a meeting with Arrowsmith, and Flinders was exceedingly pleased by the extent to which both Banks, who had never before examined the charts, and Bligh were impressed by his work. Flinders obtained and studied the work of other surveyors, including some French charts, and met with Charles Grimes, the former New South Wales surveyor.

At one of Banks's breakfast gatherings, Flinders spoke with George Nicol, bookseller to the king, who would publish his work. There were meetings with the *Investigator*'s two artists in order to eventually select 37 coastal views and landscapes from Westall's collection and 10 plates on botanical subjects from Bauer's, conferences with John Pye, who was to engrave Westall's views, and many meetings with those concerned to arrive at costs for the work.

Serious problems had emerged in the astronomical observations that had been made on board the *Investigator*: errors in the lunar tables published for 1801, 1802 and 1803, which had been used, and Flinders's own uncertainty as to the accuracy of his magnetic bearings. Flinders travelled to Greenwich, hoping to discuss these matters with Nevil Maskelyne, but reached little understanding 'upon anything' with the aged astronomer. Maskelyne died a fortnight later, and Flinders's concerns had to wait for the appointment of another Astronomer Royal.

In early March 1811 Flinders proposed to the Board of Longitude that all astronomical observations made on the voyage be recalculated under the Board's direction and at its expense, as had been done with observations made during Cook's expeditions. The record books containing the rough data would be made available to the recalculators, and Flinders suggested that Samuel, who had done much of the original work, might be considered as one of them. The Board favoured Flinders's proposal and referred it to the Hydrographer, Hurd, and the Astronomer Royal, a position filled a month later by the astronomer John Pond. By April it was understood, although not officially confirmed, that John Crosley, the astronomer who had been with the *Investigator* in 1801, would be doing the recalculation together with Samuel Flinders. Samuel gave up his Devonshire cottage and moved permanently to London.

Flinders prepared for the chart work. In some maps, the results of other surveyors had to be incorporated. For detail on the interior of New South Wales, he examined papers that had belonged to Philip King and William Paterson, now lent him by their widows, and consulted John Hunter and George Caley, a colonial government gardener and plant collector who had explored inland areas.

Geographical names had to be selected to replace Flinders's number and letter system. Apparently Flinders selected the names, which were then approved by Banks, Barrow and Hurd. In this Flinders honoured those who had assisted him at various times in his life—thus, the Gulph of St Vincent, Spencer's Gulf and the Sir Edward Pellew Group—and naval friends and others, as with Lacy's Isle, Point Brown, Cape Bauer and the Kent Isles. Several locations were already named for Joseph Banks, and Flinders added the Sir Joseph Banks Group of Islands, with the individual islands named for villages in Lincolnshire, among them Partney and Revesby. Another task was the titling of Westall's coastal views.

At home Ann and Matthew Flinders lived quietly. Generally he worked on his charts or pursued his business in town in the mornings and, following dinner in the early afternoon, would walk with Ann to make purchases, call on friends or stroll under the trees in Soho Square. After evening tea they often played chess. Ann, however, frequently suffered from headaches so severe that they kept her in bed, and Flinders sometimes entertained guests on his own.

In April Flinders's young sister Henrietta 'arrived early from the country', her unexpected arrival evidently dislocating the household so that Flinders, 'not being able to work in my writing room',[3] was thoroughly annoyed and left the house. However, he quickly recovered his good nature. He hired a pianoforte for Henrietta and in the spring evenings walked with Samuel and the two women, on one occasion visiting St Paul's Cathedral.

Isabella Tyler arrived from Yorkshire soon after. Flinders took the family to see the sights of the city, including William Westall's picture gallery, plants at Kew grown from seeds collected on the *Investigator*'s voyage and, on 4 June, 'the few illuminations made for the poor King's birthday'.[4] On Sunday evenings they attended church, after which Flinders would usually join Joseph Banks's gatherings.

Samuel assisted in entertaining the women, from time to time escorting his sister. Earlier hopes within the family that he and Isabella would be attracted to each other were fading. Flinders wrote to Madame d'Arifat, 'she is a very decisive lady, and seems to have taken a dislike to him'.[5]

At the beginning of May Flinders decided that he would set aside his chart work, for errors in the lunar tables he had used required entire reconstructions. 'I determined to wait awhile and begin writing the introduction of my voyage. Went out after dinner and bought paper and quills . . .'[6]

For Flinders it soon became a desperately busy time. He wrote to John Franklin: 'Miss Tyler and Henrietta are still with us . . . I endeavour to amuse them as well as my time will allow, but I am really so occupied, what with my own and other people's affairs, both public and private, beside writing the account of my voyage, that I scarcely know which way to turn myself'.[7]

For Ann the young women's presence would have been a welcome diversion. Matthew's work, and to a good measure his social life, was in a world of men. He attended meetings, made calls, dined and visited apart from Ann. Their guests were mainly his male associates, with the occasional appearance of wives or women relatives, and the conversations around her were often of people and on topics of which Ann had only partial knowledge. Of all this Ann seems to have been entirely accepting, writing after his death that her 'greatest earthly happiness' had been centred on Matthew. Isabella later wrote, 'we were all very happy'.

The presence of Henrietta and Isabella also brought visits by Ann's female Hippius relations and an occasional day spent at Hackney with that family. On one such trip Flinders joined a crowd of thousands watching the great novelty of a balloon carrying two men as it rose 'in good stile, about 3 o'clock, and went away gently to the E.S.E... in returning to town at nine, we met a coach with the balloon and car on the top of it'.[8] By the end of July Henrietta and Isabella had left.

Friends called or wrote to Flinders with requests, from time to time fathers who wanted their sons sent to sea under his care. Among these was James Wiles, once botanist on the *Providence,* who for the past eighteen years had been settled in Jamaica. His letter briefly mentioned the death of their mutual friend Christopher Smith, who had remained in the East, but his main purpose was to put his fourteen-year-old son Henry in the navy, and for this he was relying on Flinders.

Young Henry Wiles arrived in August and Flinders enrolled him in Dr William Burney's Naval Academy at Gosport, near Portsmouth, together with the son of Ann's relative, Alderman Andrew Hollingworth of Hull. Two months later the boys ran away, appearing at Flinders's door. Henry wanted to go immediately to sea, and a berth was arranged for him on HMS *Bedford*, 74 guns, on which John Franklin was third lieutenant. Henry's enthusiasm for the sea was short-lived. Three months later Flinders was writing to him sternly on his wish to quit the sea. Little else is known of Henry Wiles. Meanwhile, Andrew Hollingworth wrote to Flinders about taking on the care of a second son, but it appears that Flinders, privately exasperated, managed to avoid this.

The career of John Franklin was, however, a source of continuing satisfaction. In 1805 Franklin fought in the battle of Trafalgar and he was now engaged in patrol work on the Channel. Flinders would not live to know of his participation in naval actions against the United States in 1814 and 1815, of his remarkable Arctic journeys in the years from 1818 to 1827, or of his return to Australia ten years later as lieutenant-governor of Tasmania. Almost 40 years after the *Investigator* had sailed into Spencer Gulf, John Franklin erected a monument to the ship and her commander on a summit overlooking Matthew's No 12 Inlet.[9]

Despite obligations to his young women guests, Flinders had begun writing his narrative of the *Investigator* voyage in May 1811. The plan of the book included, first, a historical introduction that covered the early European explorations of the Australian coast, to which he added his and George Bass's discoveries; and, second, the narrative itself, covering the voyage of the *Investigator*, the shipwreck of the *Porpoise* and the journey of the *Cumberland*, ending with a full account of his detention on Mauritius. Three appendices followed, one on coastal longitudes, another a discussion of compass errors arising from magnetism, the third a dissertation on Australian botany by Robert Brown. The illustrations consisted of nine engravings of Westall's Australian scenes.

Some aspects of Westall's illustrations disturbed Flinders. Of the engraved view of Wreck Reef and its encampment, Flinders felt he had to write an explanation: 'Mr. Westall has represented the corals above water, to give a better notion of their forms and the way they are seen on the reef; but in reality, the tide never leaves any considerable part of them uncovered'.[10] Westall idealised the Australian landscape, creating lush, idyllic scenes that had none of the stark realism of the original sketches, nor did they bear out the factual style of Flinders's text. The romanticised imagery, however, was popular, and was probably felt to enhance the appeal of the book.

The book's accompanying atlas comprised sixteen of Flinders's charts, together with numerous views of the coast as seen from the sea by Westall and ten plates of plants from different parts of the country, which were Bauer's work.

In preparation, Flinders had a carpenter build a bookcase and spent several days cleaning and arranging his books, taking some damaged in the shipwreck to be rebound, buying others and exchanging still others.

His first project was the Introduction, 204 quarto pages with 80 000 words. For this he drew material from his own books and from texts borrowed from Banks's immense library. Authorisation from Banks gave him access to important books and charts in the British Museum, and through Banks also he was able to get at least one translation of a work not originally in English. At the Admiralty he consulted Cook's logbook and obtained his own *Providence* journals, sent to the

Admiralty by Bligh in 1793. For his and Bass's voyaging he had Bass's journal, brought to him by John Hunter, and his own records.

The writing went smoothly. However, reconstructing his chart work on the Furneaux Islands and Van Diemen's Land became a necessary but frustrating interruption. The original surveys had been made from the *Francis* and the *Norfolk* without a timekeeper and now gave him 'an infinity of trouble'.[11]

His financial situation also worried him. In July, writing to James Wiles, he discussed his pecuniary affairs. Interest on the invested legacies from his father and uncle was approximately £120 per year, which, added to his half pay, gave him about £250, his entire annual income. Living 'economically but decently' in London would cost twice that, and writing the *Investigator* narrative would necessitate remaining in the city for about two years. His request to the Admiralty for the allowance of a marine surveyor had been denied. Somewhat bitterly he remarked to Wiles that Banks, who could obtain additional funds for him from the Admiralty, evidently wished to keep him 'poor' to assure his continued service. A month later a diary entry further reflected his disappointment: 'Thursday 8. Writing the whole day at the Norfolk's Bearings; and meditating upon the general conduct of Sir J. B. towards me; in which I find many things not easy to be explained'.[12]

On 18 November, however, there was an unexpected letter from the Admiralty's Secretary Barrow: 'I am commanded to acquaint you that their Lordships have given an order to the Navy Board for impresting to you the sum of two hundred pounds, which is to be carried to the debit of the work and included in the expenses thereof'.[13]

Flinders's feelings were mixed. 'I had applied for the allowance of a marine surveyor (a guinea per day) instead of which the board *lends* me £200'.[14] In effect it was an advance, which Flinders did not entirely appreciate. Nevertheless, after speaking with Banks, he added with some relief, 'when that sum is expended, should more be wanted, he [Banks] expects it will be given; and that there can be no idea of my being called upon to repay the £200'.[15] As the money would enable him to cover the expenses of the year to come, Flinders was satisfied and, on writing again to Wiles, mentioned Sir J. B.'s 'kind interference'.

Flinders did have other funds. There was the £300 in table money from the East India Company, which may have covered what his income did not the following year, when he neither requested nor received a further imprest from the Admiralty. He also had an investment in the hands of Charles Desbassayns in Réunion, and another in cattle raising on Mauritius, an industry in which he had encouraged Labauve.[16] Both businesses appear to have been doing well at this time and he was reinvesting the profits in the islands at Desbassayns's discretion. There was also the option of withdrawing monies from his quite reasonable capital, but this he obviously did not want to do.

At the end of September Ann and Matthew shifted lodgings to 7 Mary Street-Brook Street at £90 per year, which was £19 less than what they were paying in Nassau Street. They made six moves between 1810 and 1814, but evidently not because of financial hardship. The move from King Street was made impulsively after a quarrel with the landlady and her guests; the rent in Nassau Street was the same. At Mary Street, Flinders appreciated the lower tariff, but he did not mention this as a reason for the move. There seems to have been another motivation. Mary Street, in the general area of Hampstead Road, was at what was then the edge of town. Flinders wrote, 'Here we shall be situated as near to the country, being close to the fields looking to Highgate and Hampstead, as we can be to live in London, to which I am obliged by my employment... Our new lodgings we find cleaner and better arranged'.[17]

Ann had suffered frequent and sometimes unusually persistent headaches in Nassau Street, on one occasion for four days, when a doctor was called. Sea or country air was generally believed to be beneficial to health, and this may have been a factor in their desire to move. A few days after settling into their new home, Flinders wrote that he had 'walked for an hour with Mrs. F. in the fields at the back of the street',[18] and many other walks in the fields were to come. Ann was now pregnant, which would have added weight to this consideration.

While the central locations of their lodgings in Soho had been convenient for Matthew, they were convenient also for time-consuming callers. Frequently, citing who had come for the evening, Flinders would conclude his diary entry for the day with the remark that he could do nothing afterwards. Mary Street was quieter.

All of Ann and Matthew's moves were to furnished accommodation, evidently in the narrow brick terrace houses typical of Georgian

London, which fronted the street with an entrance door and usually two tall windows to one side and the windows of two or three upper floors above. Other than personal effects, several trunks, some household goods, books, papers and Matthew's new bookcase, they owned very little.

On a dull, partly rainy day in early October, he noted that the troublesome chart of Van Diemen's Land, 'thank God! is nearly done'.[19] A week later he returned to writing the rough draft of his introduction to the *Investigator* narrative, some of which he read aloud to Ann.

There was another task to which he devoted an October day. This was the drafting of a will, which, however, he laid aside and did not take to a solicitor until July 1812, after the birth of his child. He was thinking, too, of a return to his music; he took his 'old flute' in for repair and bought some sheet music. Presumably, he sometimes found time to play, but there is no mention of being joined by anyone. Ann, who had been unwell for several days after their move, was better and, in the fine but chilly evening of their second Sunday in their new lodgings, Flinders accompanied her to the nearby St James Chapel in Hampstead Road.

Flinders was now quite often able to work whole days and evenings without interruption, although there were certain regular visitors. Samuel was frequently there, staying for dinner and sometimes accompanying Flinders on his calls. Robert Brown came from time to time. A Captain Farquharson Stuart arrived each Monday evening, and among Flinders's French callers were acquaintances and relatives of his friends on Ile de France or of those he had recently assisted. Occasionally there were visitors from the country, or gifts from Lincolnshire of turkey, goose, game or fruit. Just before Christmas Flinders sent back a present of three barrels of oysters.

As Flinders completed sections of his introduction he sent them to those whose critical opinion he valued: the historian and geographer Captain James Burney, George Nicol, William Bligh and Lord Liverpool. At Banks's Sunday evening 'conversations' he had the opportunity to discuss his work and related topics with knowledgeable men. On one occasion he brought with him twenty-year-old Phillip Parker King, and presented the young midshipman, already commended for gallantry in action, to Banks, to the navy's hydrographer Hurd and to Bligh, now a rear-admiral.

By the end of November Flinders was writing the fair copy of his introduction. A few days later he met with Banks and Bligh to apply names to the Torres Strait islands discovered by the admiral. Westall, Nicol and an engraver joined Banks and Flinders to discuss reproducing Westall's coastal views. In the meantime Banks returned to Flinders with his approval of the first quire of the fair copy of the introduction.

In the opening pages of the introduction Flinders recounted the history of names for the Australian continent and discussed choosing one for general use in his narrative. Preference for the terms New Holland and New South Wales had come from those who, like Brown and Arrowsmith, had published under those headings, but after considerable persuasion Banks agreed to accept Terra Australis as a collective name for the entire continent. Flinders wrote, 'I have, with the concurrence of opinions entitled to deference, ventured upon the re-adoption of the *original* Terra Australis; and of this term I shall hereafter make use, when speaking of New Holland and New South Wales . . . and . . . the adjacent isles, including that of Van Diemen'. In a footnote he added, 'Had I permitted myself any innovation upon the original term, it would have been to convert it into Australia; as being more agreeable to the ear, and an assimilation to the names of the other great portions of the earth'.[20]

Although Bligh expressed a liking for it, the little-known term was not seriously discussed. Terra Australis was a name familiar to the public, and the book was therefore titled *A Voyage to Terra Australis*. Only gradually over the next ten years did 'Australia' come into both common and official use.

The recalculation of the astronomical observations made on the *Investigator* was essential to the accurate reconstruction of Flinders's charts, but the Board of Longitude seemed incapable of formally appointing the recalculators. Suddenly, on 16 July, the Board confirmed John Crosley as employed for the task. Samuel was shocked. He was not mentioned, despite having assisted Crosley since April, providing information from the *Investigator*'s astronomical observation books in his possession. Against Matthew's advice and once without his knowledge, Samuel wrote several incensed letters to the Board of Longitude.

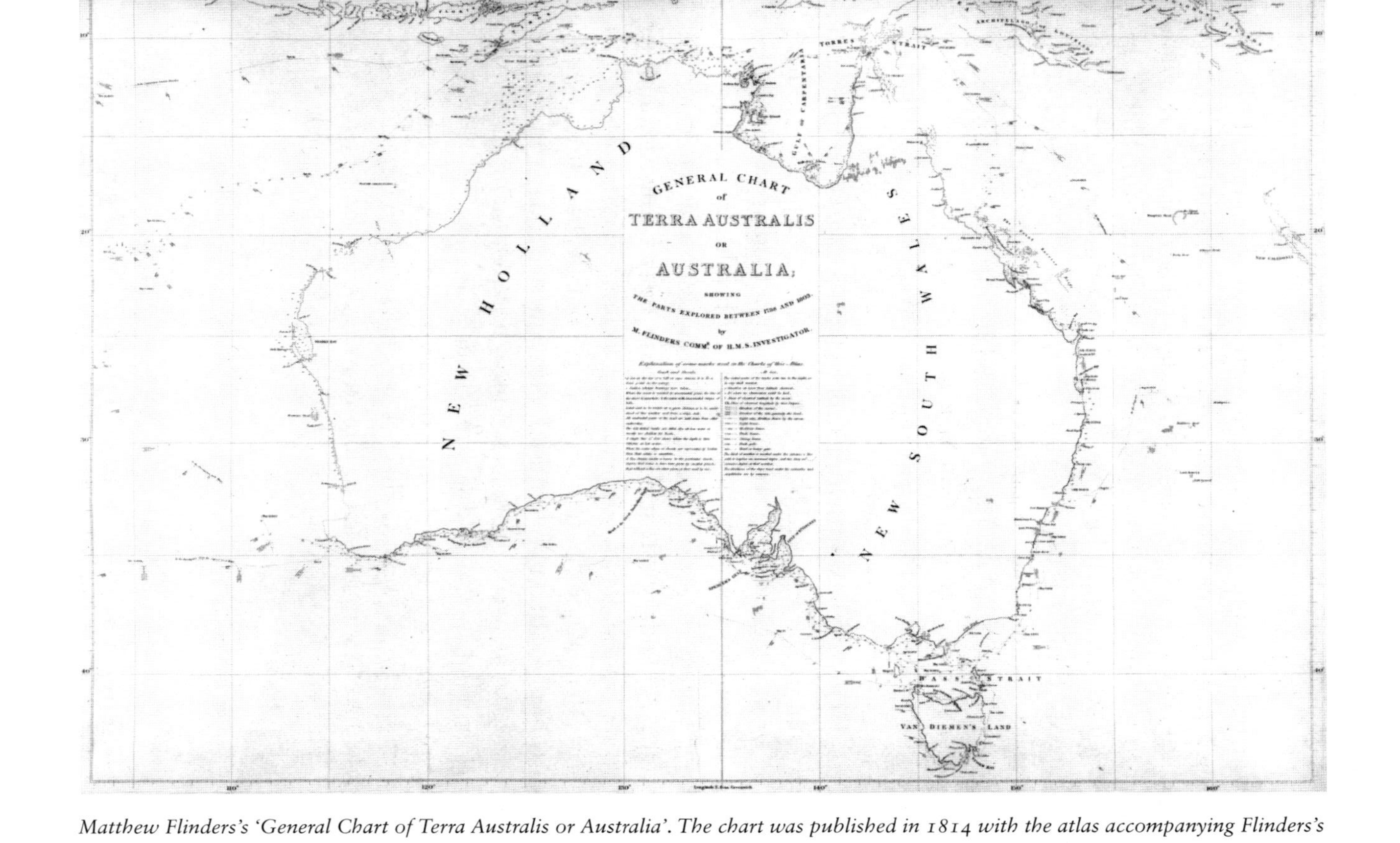

Matthew Flinders's 'General Chart of Terra Australis or Australia'. The chart was published in 1814 with the atlas accompanying Flinders's two-volume work, A Voyage to Terra Australis. *On the chart Flinders added his preferred name for the continent, Australia. (By permission of the National Library of Australia, Canberra)*

One letter that came into his hands Banks refused to pass on to the Board until it was put into a more presentable form.

On 14 December Flinders was summoned to Soho Square in consequence of one of Samuel's letters, and arrived to find an irate Banks 'indisposed to take any farther steps into the business of my brother being employed as a recalculator'.[21] Flinders relayed Banks's reaction to his brother and gave him 'the sketch of a letter' for Pond, the Astronomer Royal, which he hoped would smooth over the situation. The next day Samuel returned with the letter to Pond, 'so altered', according to Matthew, 'as to produce, in my opinion, a bad, instead of a good effect; but he will not be guided by my advice, nor is it an easy matter to pursuade him from his opinion'.[22]

Instead, Samuel wrote to the Astronomer Royal withdrawing himself and his and Flinders's navigational record books from the recalculation. This, Flinders felt, was detrimental to both Samuel's position and the recording of the voyage. Nevertheless, he rallied to his brother's side. He wrote to Crosley 'to bring all the books that we might see how far he could go on without those of my brother'.[23] But Samuel's next move shifted the quarrel to himself and Matthew. He came for dinner and, as Flinders noted, 'On his going away I requested him to deliver to me all the books not belonging to himself; when I found to my surprise, that he laid claim to such of *my* books as had either wholly or in part, been written in by himself. He requested a day to consider, before giving an answer'.[24] Samuel seems to have felt that if Banks had access to the books, he would ignore Samuel's interests.

The next evening a letter from Samuel confirmed his decision. He would not give up the books. Flinders was upset and extremely angry. The books had 'been confided to him to be used for the benefit of my voyage. This strange conduct in a brother, affected me much'.[25] He wrote to Samuel.

> Mary Street Dec. 27. 1811
>
> Sir
>
> The shock you have given me by your letter of this evening is more than I can express . . . The books in question were not originally yours; they did not become yours by your writing in them, for you did it

> voluntarily, without condition; they did not become so when delivered to you in April, for they were only *confided* to you, to be used for the benefit of the voyage.

The Board of Longitude would not suffer by this action, Matthew said. The damage would be done to him and to the record of the voyage, none of which was preventing the

> baneful influence of the passions that possess you; justice, confidence, gratitude are all trampled under foot. After having disobliged all the other of your relations by your pride, intolerance, and want of feeling; you now scruple not to injure the protector of your youth, and best remaining friend.
>
> You say you suspect Sir J. B. wants to make use of the books, and cast you aside. This is a most uncharitable sentiment; but will you for a *suspicion*, commit an act which every honest man must abhor? . . .
>
> Without the books are returned there can be no farther communication between us.
>
> Fare you well. Mattw. Flinders[26]

That this was a most difficult letter to write is obvious from the many lines written and then crossed out in the rough copy in Flinders's letter book. The letter broke Samuel's resolve. He wrote back offering to give up the books as a favour to Matthew, while still 'refusing them as a matter of right'.[27] This was not what Matthew wanted and, with Crosley, he went to Banks. Withholding the books, he was told, could result in legal prosecution against Samuel by the Board of Longitude, permanent loss of Samuel's future naval advancement and probably his removal from the list of lieutenants.

Flinders decided to accept the books on Samuel's terms and on his way home stopped at his brother's lodgings to tell him so. Flinders noted, 'he promised to proceed. He was, however, hurt that I did not chuse to shake hands with him, at parting'.[28] Samuel followed this with a letter of explanation to Matthew, which no longer exists, but in which he evidently assured his brother that he had not wished to injure him personally, and this, replying on the last day of the year, Flinders accepted, reminding his brother, however, that he was acting 'as I described myself to be, your best remaining friend'. The letter concluded, 'in fine, Samuel, I shake hands with you, and remain your affectionate brother'.[29]

A few days later Matthew, Samuel and Crosley agreed upon a list of the data from the observation books that was needed for the recalculation. In March 1812 the Board advanced Samuel £50, and in the ensuing months Samuel completed fair copies of the *Investigator*'s astronomical and other data. In January 1813 he evidently completed his work, in March receiving final compensation, which totalled £250 for his services. Matthew's letter to his brother reveals something of the feelings of the family for the difficult Samuel. Despite his moments of anger, however, Matthew remained firmly loyal to the brother who from the age of twelve had been in many ways his charge.

In fact, this had not been Samuel's first disappointing contact with the Board of Longitude. In 1806 he had written to the Board citing in detail his work as the astronomer of HMS *Investigator* after the departure at Cape Town of John Crosley, and with verifying documents from Brown, Bauer and Fowler, Samuel had submitted a request for 'such part of the Salary of the Astronomer as they shall think proper from the time of the Investigator quitting the Cape of Good Hope in Novr 1801 to the time of Mr. [John] Inman joining in June 1803'.[30]

The Board decided that some recompense was due to the Flinders brothers, and the then Astronomer Royal, Nevil Maskelyne, wrote to Matthew Flinders on Mauritius, asking for his opinion on the division of such funds. Matthew wrote back that the entire sum should go to Samuel, as he had been 'to all intents' the *Investigator*'s astronomer. In 1808 the Board agreed to pay £200 to Samuel Flinders. This, in payment for a year and seven months' service, was less than half of Crosley's annual salary on board the *Investigator*. In a letter to the Board Samuel acknowledged the payment but made clear his disappointment. There is no record of any further compensation to Samuel.

Despite the painful matter of the recalculation of astronomical data from the *Investigator*, Samuel and Matthew continued their effort to obtain Samuel's reinstatement to the naval position he occupied before the court martial and to secure his promotion. In August 1811, however, the Admiralty's First Lord bluntly informed Samuel that his court martial prevented any advancement. Despite Matthew's further enquiries, Samuel never obtained his promotion.

Flinders had received from Bligh a note to the effect that the king's brother, the Duke of Clarence, wanted to see Flinders's general chart of Australia. Rumour had it that the duke was likely to succeed Charles Yorke at the Admiralty, which would have been of keen interest to Flinders. The meeting took place on Saturday, 8 February 1812, and Flinders managed to bring up the subject of his post captain's commission. The duke, Flinders thought, showed 'a desire' to assist.

As well, Flinders's friend Joseph Whidbey, master-attendant at the Woolwich shipyard, 'judged' that Clarence would succeed Yorke as First Lord, 'which', Flinders commented, 'I think probable from the Duke's conversation to me'.[31] It was a failed hope. Yorke, resigning in 1812, was succeeded by Robert Saunders Dundas, Viscount Melville, who held office for fifteen years. Clarence became Lord High Admiral and First Lord of the Admiralty in 1827.

In mid-January 1812 Flinders wrote, 'Writing my introduction all the day and evening, and to my great satisfaction, finished it; a revision only being necessary'.[32] And on the 23rd: 'Began upon the Investigator's voyage'.[33] Thus, rising early and when not interrupted working into the night, Flinders began the 744 pages that would constitute the principal part of his book.

Flinders found time to write his sixth letter to Madame d'Arifat since his return to England. It was full of news of his family and of those, like Elder, whom she knew. Of Ann he wrote that she was fast approaching the delivery of their child and had been remarkably well. He added with typical good humour, 'Her sister Isabella comes next week, to take upon herself the office of regent of my domestic affairs, till Mrs. F. is able to re-assume the reins of government'.[34]

Isabella arrived on 13 March and enthusiastically took charge in anticipation of the baby that, as she remarked, the family had nicknamed 'Timothy'. Flinders's diary mentions a servant, which would have been usual for people in their position, and the household evidently was running smoothly. No doubt happily, Flinders retreated into his work, now correcting the rough draft of the first book of the voyage. A brief notation in his diary at this time, a matter also mentioned in a letter to his stepmother, concerned his collection of £18 on the tax paid on the annuity of his brother John, who in 1801 had been placed by their father in the York Lunatic Asylum. Months later

Flinders made another small collection, the money again credited to John's account. Flinders had once joined the family in seeking a suitable shelter for John. Now in his diary he repeatedly blotted out the brother's name, in one instance reinserting it in faint, minute letters. He carried out his duty as head of the family, but this brother's name was not one he wanted anyone to see.

Later that month Flinders received an order to attend a meeting of a Committee on Transportation at the House of Commons, where he met Hunter, Waterhouse and Sydney's first chaplain, the Reverend Richard Johnson, all there to answer the committee's questions on the areas of New South Wales that were fit for colonisation. Bligh, Robert Campbell and others had been similarly interviewed.

Asked which region he would recommend for development, Flinders expressed his preference for the Derwent River area in Van Diemen's Land, where settlements had, in fact, been made in 1803 and 1804. In July 1812 the committee published its findings in a 112-page paper.

Probably drawn by their interest in the expected baby, visitors seemed to flood the house—the Hippius family, Elizabeth Paterson, Anna King and her family, the Proctors and others. Ann, expecting her first child at nearly 42 years of age, was in considerable fear of not surviving the ordeal. She wrote what is the only known existing letter from her to her husband. It was a sad and prayerful missive meant to be read after her death. In the intensely emotional style of the period it enjoined Matthew to find happiness with someone else, but to protect their child, should it live, to remember her and to read scripture and pray. It is obvious from Ann's earnest request that Matthew pray, a word she underlined, and from her assurance that prayers were both heard and answered, that she was aware of her husband's fairly casual attitude to religion. Her love and adoration of him were similarly manifest. The letter, fortunately, was never read as intended.

On 1 April 1812, a day of thick fog over London, Flinders wrote in his diary: 'This afternoon Mrs. Flinders was happily delivered of a daughter; to her great joy and to mine'.[35] Isabella's comment was more exuberant. Mindful of the date as Matthew suddenly came into her room and 'desired me to get up immediately for Timothy was coming,—I said "Nonsense, you will not make an April fool out of me."—However the dear babe did arrive on that ominous day'.[36]

The next day Flinders wrote to his stepmother: 'Mrs. Flinders was happily relieved of her burthen, yesterday afternoon. She bore the trial with heroic fortitude, and thus far is doing remarkably well ... The child is a little black-eyed girl, without blemish, neither fat nor lean, and has a decent appearance enough; so that I hope you will have no occasion to be ashamed of your grand daughter'.[37]

To both Madame D'Arifat and Charles Desbassayns he wrote that Ann and their 'lively little girl' had brought him very near to perfect happiness, shadowed only by concern over expenses that exceeded his income. On 7 May in the tall-spired century-old church of St Giles-in-the-Fields the child was christened Anne, in line with tradition in Ann's family, every other generation adding the final *e* to the name. 'Dear little Anne', Isabella wrote later, 'how we used to dress her, & laugh at her, & toss her about & she soon began to crow and laugh & enjoy it all amazingly'.[38]

Nevertheless, Anne was placed, as was customary, with a nurse and for her first fifteen months lived apart from her parents. In his diary Flinders commented on his wife's remarkable recovery from the birth, but on 4 and 5 April noted his own 'attack of the gravel', which left him painfully unwell. He continued working and the difficulty passed.

The reconstruction of his charts evidently led to Flinders's reflecting again upon the effect of a ship's magnetism on the compass bearings he was now re-recording. Flinders had several times attempted a systematic study of the problem. On the *Investigator* he had cleared the area around the binnacle of iron objects and moved the ship's compasses to different positions. He had observed deviations as the ship changed direction and as she approached the equator.

On 13 April 1812 he wrote to First Secretary Croker at the Admiralty suggesting that magnetic experiments be made on board vessels lying in port. He outlined the procedures he proposed and included a table for recording the observations. The Admiralty approved the experiments for Sheerness, requiring that Flinders supervise them. He happily accepted. This was a project he had had in mind for years.

At noon on 19 April he boarded the coach for Chatham, and the next day at Sheerness met with the commander-in-chief, Rear-Admiral Sir Thomas Williams, who arranged for Captain Thomas New of

HMS *Raisonable*, 64 guns, and the dockyard's master-attendant, Mr. Douglas, to assist with the project. Early the following morning they sailed out to the Little Nore and boarded the brig *Starling*, commanded by Lieutenant Charles Napier. Unfortunately, no preparations had been made, and in the face of several difficulties, they resorted to the brig's steering compass, taking bearings by hand according to the mean of the findings of the four men, although with wind and tide against them, these could only be taken with the vessel's head at north, northwest, west by north and east ½ north. The procedure was 'rough and inconclusive', but an eight degree difference was noted between bearings taken with the brig's head at the various directions. Flinders and Douglas then boarded the frigate *Helder*, 36 guns, captained by John Serrell, for more but equally inconclusive work.

Flinders and Douglas continued their efforts aboard the *Helder* the next day, again with unsatisfactory results. On the third day they chose three compasses, which were found to agree closely, and returned to the *Raisonable*. Compasses were fixed at different locations and bearings taken as the ship's head was swung from west ½ north to northeast. The differences were found to be small, but 'the same way as before'. The wind rose and operations were suspended until the next day when, despite a fresh northerly and passing squalls, the *Raisonable* was warped through the full circle of the compass. Although the experiment had not been done with the thoroughness Flinders would have liked, it was, under the circumstances, acceptable.

Flinders delivered his completed report to the Admiralty, and Hydrographer Hurd, pleased and impressed by the work so far, informed him that further experimentation would be held at Portsmouth. Flinders was again asked to direct the operation.

Flinders arrived in Portsmouth on 15 May, presented his orders to the naval commander-in-chief, Admiral Sir Richard Bickerton, and checked with his friend James Park, master-attendant at the dockyard, on the preparations. An old French frigate, the *Loire*, was readied. Flinders spent two days with the astronomer James Inman, testing and adjusting azimuth compasses and taking compass and theodolite bearings from the cupola of the Royal Navy College.

With a pause in the work on Sunday, Flinders crossed the harbour to Gosport, to visit Nathaniel Portlock, who had commanded the brig

Assistant on the Tahiti voyage of 1791–92, and Dr Burney at the Naval Academy. Flinders subsequently wrote a paper on magnetism to be included in a nautical dictionary, which Burney was bringing up to date.

Flinders, Inman and Park's assistant, Payne, worked steadily aboard the *Loire*, each man taking bearings as the ship was swung around. During the second week the experiments were shifted to nearby Stokes Bay on board the bomb *Devastation*, a small, shallow draught vessel built to carry mortars. Over two days the vessel's head was swung through all the points of the compass and bearings taken from all stations. Then additional observations were made from the *Loire* and from Port-down Hill at Porchester. An interested observer was Captain Peter Heywood, a marine surveyor, once a midshipman on the *Bounty,* pardoned for his part in the mutiny. Robert Fowler appeared, also interested in the progress of the experiments. After dinner on board each day, Flinders returned to his lodgings to make up tables of the bearings and to write to Ann, sending 'kind love to Bell [Isabella] and little Nanny'.

Flinders and Payne sailed across the Solent to Ryde on the Isle of Wight on Thursday, 28 May, and from the tower on Ashedown took back bearings on the *Devastation* and other points. On Friday morning Flinders joined Fowler and others in a barouche and four for a satisfyingly fast trip back to London.

Flinders called on Hurd the next day to discuss a full report on all the experiments. On Sunday evening, having attended church with Ann and Isabella, he went to Sir Joseph's gathering: 'Sir J. expressed much pleasure at the successs of my experiments at Portsmouth and considered that I ought to go through with the account, although that of my voyage should be stopped for a while'.[39] Flinders then provided Secretary Croker with a detailed account of the proceedings and expressed his willingness to produce a report connecting all the experiments and the deductions drawn from them. Just over a week later he received the Admiralty's instructions to proceed.

Thus, at the beginning of July Flinders sent to Crocker a 45-page report entitled 'An Account of some experiments to ascertain the effects produced on the Compass, by the attractive power in ships; with the modes by which the errors may be obviated. To which is added, Observations of the present state of the compasses used in His Majesty's

Navy, and a proposal for improving the same'. Banks recommended it for printing. The Admiralty objected; it was too long and too technical for the average naval officer to read and understand. Flinders was asked to condense the report into a few pages and to include instructions to officers to make additional observations of magnetism on ships. Flinders did as requested, but wrote privately to Barrow that it was impossible to fully explain the cause of compass errors on ships in such an abbreviated form. Nevertheless, the navy was satisfied.

The short version, simply entitled *Magnetism of Ships*, was promptly printed and circulated to all British naval captains, commanders and commanding officers. Not all navigators were impressed, feeling that the error caused by a ship's iron was not great enough to be of concern, particularly in areas of high variation caused by the earth's magnetism, as were the seas around Britain. Flinders reconsidered the question and produced a detailed twenty-page discussion that became an appendix to the narrative of his voyage. Here he briefly referred to methods by which the problem of error could be avoided, which included balancing the attraction around the compass by 'one or more staunchions or bars of iron'.[40]

It was not, however, until several years after Flinders's early death that further scientific investigation was made into the question of a ship's magnetism. With the advent of more and more iron in ships, the matter gained importance, and by the later part of the 19th century the term Flinders Bar was applied to a bar of soft unmagnetised iron in a brass container placed in a vertical position near a magnetic compass to counteract deviation caused by iron in the ship itself.

Flinders settled back into the routine of writing his *Voyage*, and in June returned to his charts. The new values produced by Crosley and Samuel for the astronomical observations made on the voyage together with his findings in compass deviation were making possible more accurate adjustments to the bearings used in his surveys. The work, however, was slow. The occasional error in Crosley's calculations had to be rectified. Flinders's own tables of longitude had to be corrected. He bought a new parallel ruler and at his table made the most of the summer's long hours of daylight.

36

The Final Years

At the beginning of July 1812, when Anne was three months old, Flinders had a solicitor draft the will he had outlined before his daughter's birth. Flinders signed it on 6 July. It was witnessed by Isabella Tyler and the surgeon Joseph Hayes. Ann, Charles Hursthouse of Tydd St Mary and John Newbald of Hull were the executors. It was a long and extremely detailed document, with legacies specified in the case of his death first without issue and second with, and provisions for contingencies occurring a generation ahead. It also dispensed liberally to friends and family members Flinders's somewhat limited estate. In fact, in playing the part of a beneficent head of family, he greatly reduced what was left for his wife and child.

An initial bequest of £1200 to Ann was altered in the second part of the will to a lifetime annuity of £55, in addition to which she received all household goods, personal effects, books and papers, from which last items she was to give Samuel all those that related to the voyage of the *Investigator*, with the exception of letters. There was an annuity of £10 per year for his stepmother, while sums ranging from £100 pounds to £50 and £20 were left to his sister Susanna and to Samuel, to his half-sisters Hannah and Henrietta, to the children of his deceased sister Elizabeth, and to other relatives. One hundred pounds were to be set aside for separate white marble plaques or, as he termed them, slabs, inscribed to the memory of his great-grandfather, grandfather, father and himself, to be mounted on a wall space that he specified in Donington's parish church. Mourning rings to the value of two guineas each, inscribed with his initials, were to be provided for Joseph Banks, Labauve, Pitot and Charles Desbassayns, Isabella Tyler, his cousin Henrietta Newbald and several others. With these bequests and arrangements carried out, remaining monies were to go to his child or children. This included his investments on Mauritius and Réunion. Should his child or children die before the age of 21, the inheritance was to go to Matthew's nieces and nephews and Samuel.

It was a curious will for a man as aware as Flinders was of the deficiencies of his income and, by the time he signed it, with a wife and young child. At the time, of course, Flinders expected to live many more years. Since his return to England he had been untroubled by any physical problem except for an attack of 'the gravel', which he had experienced occasionally for many years, a rare cold and short-sightedness, for which he wore spectacles 'when in the street'. However, he could not have believed he was going to amass any great fortune.

What expectations did Flinders have at this time for his future? In July 1811 he had written to Wiles of the difficulty of meeting the expense of living in London. He added:

> After my task is completed, if nothing better turns up, I intend to purchase a small place house, with a garden in the country, and there retire with my books to live upon my little income . . . Should I sail out again, this little place would be a retreat for my wife during my absence . . . Such, my friend, are the plans I now make, but they may be subverted by my being called to act upon the theatre of life. But I go no more to sea, unless it is upon discovery; and therefore if a situation is not given me in the civil department of the navy, I shall retire and render my happiness independent of the will of others.[1]

Recognising now the restraints war imposed on naval resources, Flinders knew the chance for another voyage was slight. The hope lingered, but in subsequent months he investigated the possibilities of other employment. Hearing in January 1813 that the lieutenant-governor of the Royal Naval College in Portsmouth was to retire, Flinders wrote to the new First Lord, Lord Melville, to express his interest in the situation. Melville's reply, however, told him that there was no probability of the lieutenant-governor's retirement at the time. Apparently Flinders also considered teaching, applying to two nautical schools for a position, neither of which came about. Nor did a position in the navy's civil department materialise.

By early December 1812 Flinders was writing the fair copy of his narrative's Book I, which took the story to the *Investigator*'s first arrival in Port Jackson. This writing occupied his evenings and the rough draft of Book II his days. On the 10th he noted that Samuel 'has now finished for the B. of Longitude, of which I am glad'.[2] In mid-January Samuel left London for Lincolnshire, but a few months later was back in the city and resumed his visits to Matthew.

On 1 January 1813 Flinders made up his year's expenses, which amounted to £422/3, £156/19 in excess of his income. Apparently it was the additional £200 of the imprest from the Admiralty that had made possible the careful yet reasonably comfortable standard of life he and Ann maintained. Flinders also had funds enough to make minor investments, as he recorded visits to the Stock Exchange and banks to buy and sell stock, which, like his father, he seems to have enjoyed.

Considerable time was still taken up with the affairs of friends, particularly those connected with his stay on Ile de France, now renamed Mauritius, and invariably there were callers, especially in the evening, which meant he had to stop writing. Still, there were weeks when he could write almost all day and until late, switching between the fair and rough copies of Books I and II. On Sunday 17 January, however, he wrote, 'Mrs. F taken very unwell this evening; being threatened with a miscarriage'.[3] Five days later he noted that Ann was 'not yet recovered from her accident'.

Flinders started writing the rough draft of his narrative's final section, Book III, at the beginning of February. This began with his departure from Port Jackson in the *Porpoise* and went on to the shipwreck, the passage through Torres Strait in the *Cumberland* and his arrival at Baie du Cap in Mauritius. Then, from the beginning of Chapter IV to the end of the narrative, 137 pages, it was the story of his detention. It contained no navigational, hydrographical or new geographical information. As a practical guide for the navigator, as was much of the rest of the work, it served no purpose. Personal feelings had previously been handled with restraint. Now his many disappointments were detailed.

Flinders could not set aside his bitterness at what he felt to be the injustice of what had occurred on Mauritius and its aftermath in his dealings with the Admiralty. His inability to accept perceived unfairness to himself had been evident in the eighteen-year-old midshipman. Now his misfortunes on Mauritius echoed repeatedly in his conversation and his letters. In *A Voyage to Terra Australis* he could not resist telling his tale once again, more officially and more publicly than ever before.

This part of the work was written rapidly. He had his private journal as his principal source and no need for technical tables or explanations. Through the often windy and foggy days of March, he recorded repeatedly that he was 'writing rough Book III all day and evening'.

His work, however, was interrupted when he and Ann made yet another move, 'the conduct of the hostess here, and some of her lodgers being what we cannot approve'.[4] On 30 March 1813 they occupied the 'first and second floors with kitchen' at 45 Upper John Street. The rooms were larger and 'rather handsomely fitted up'. The annual rent was £5 higher than what he had paid at their previous lodgings.

A fortnight later Flinders received a letter from Labauve in Mauritius informing him of the death of Madame D'Arifat. Flinders read this with shock and sorrow, 'as if I had lost my own mother', he wrote to Labauve.

Ann and Matthew's residence in Upper John Street lasted only two months. An entry in Flinders's diary hints vaguely at an explanation: 'There having been many people calling at this house for money . . .'[5] They found new accommodation at 7 Upper Fitzroy Street, 'and having agreed for six months at £100 a year, hired carts for the morrow, and packed up'.[6]

The later part of July was rainy, with squalls and heavy cloud. On the 27th Flinders wrote, 'Our little Anne was taken home today, from nurse, where she had been fifteen months. She runs stoutly, and though able to say very few words makes herself understood'.[7] The little girl was a small, bright and lively child with curly black hair, whose running about transformed the quiet household. Less than a week later Flinders wrote, 'An operation was performed today upon my little girl, in whom a part was discovered to be closed which ought not'.[8] He did not elaborate, and the child apparently recovered satisfactorily.

A short time later Flinders's hurried pace was again complicated by illness at home. Ann and the child were both unwell, but as Ann recovered, the little girl's condition worsened. 'My little Anne very ill these three days', Flinders wrote in his diary, and then, 'My poor little child still continues unwell, since Sunday'. Finally, three days later, he could write as his first entry for the day, 'My little Anne better this morning'.[9] All Flinders's warm regard for children was now focused with overwhelming tenderness upon the little girl. In mid-September he recorded himself as 'not very well', but apparently recovered.

The hope of having his promotion backdated clearly had not died. In mid-May Flinders entertained at dinner a small group including the Reverend James Stanier Clarke, the Prince Regent's librarian, who had previously encouraged Flinders to approach the prince. Three days after the dinner party Flinders wrote Clarke a letter 'containing the heads of my voyage, for him to communicate to the Prince Regent', which, with four pictures from the journey, Flinders delivered personally in 'heavy rain and hail'.[10] The deeds of a naval explorer, however, failed to interest the prince.

Momentum for the publication of the book was gathering. Westall arrived at Upper Fitzroy Street with the last picture intended for it, one of Wreck Reef with its row of tents and defiant if inverted flag beneath a wide cloud-swept sky, the exposed coral in the foreground. The publisher, Nicol, and the printer, William Bulmer, agreed that printing should commence almost immediately, so Flinders took a part of his Introduction to Bulmer for him to print a specimen sheet. Meanwhile the younger Arrowsmith was reducing Flinders's original charts to the condition necessary for engraving. Flinders then had to compare the written text with the charts so there was no discrepancy between the two.

All of this had to be discussed with Sir Joseph, who was at Spring Grove, his retreat on the rural edge of London. Brown and Flinders travelled together to Islesworth, upriver from Kew, where on some 50 acres Sir Joseph carried on field studies in horticulture and botany and at times resided. The visitors walked in the gardens, dined and returned to town at 10 o'clock. A few days later Flinders received the first print sheet, had further discussions with Bulmer and talks with the manufacturer of the paper to be used.

Flinders then received an unpleasant shock, a note from Banks, 'in which, after I had used the term Terra Australis with his approbation and that of others, he disapproves of it . . .'[11] The name to be used for the continent was now New Holland, a change brought about, Flinders thought, 'by the reasoning of Mr. Brown'. Flinders protested. He had already changed his preferred name Australia to Terra Australis, which now occurred throughout his narrative and on his charts.

Two days later Banks agreed once more to 'Terra Australis'.

Proof sheets were coming in regularly to be examined and corrected. The engraving of the charts was in progress, and to have the work exactly as he required, he inspected each part minutely. He wanted nothing short of perfection in this ultimate evidence of his long years of effort, the work on which much of his reputation would stand, and paid repeated visits to Arrowsmith's, questioning the engravers on countless points until he was satisfied.

Flinders was now working by day on his charts of Torres Strait and, following that, the Gulf of Carpentaria; as daylight faded, he turned to mathematical work and checking proof sheets by lamplight. By 2 October the entire Introduction was sent to the printer. Quire by quire the first part of the narrative of the voyage itself followed, as Flinders set to work as well on the last of his charts, *Timor and some neighbouring Islands*. In mid-December Arrowsmith called to show him the first engravings of the charts.

Flinders's numerous business calls and the round of errands for French friends continued as December snows began to fill the streets and dense grey fog all but obliterated the outlines of the buildings. The callers were fewer. Farquharson Stuart had been politely asked by letter to discontinue his Monday evening visits, which each week had taken time from Flinders's work. There was a surprise visitor. 'M. Etienne Bolger Jun. called to solicit my advice. This is the son of the commandant of La Savanne, to whose misinterpretations I partly attribute my imprisonment in Mauritius'.[12] Young Bolgerd delivered two letters from French friends, but what advice he sought, Flinders did not explain.

The European winter of 1813–14 was excessively cold. The spires and rooftops of London were draped in white and icy winds funnelled through the streets. Hundreds of miles to the east Napoleon's army was being destroyed in the deep snows of winter on the plains of Russia.

At 7 Upper Fitzroy Street the wood fire burned. Flinders began each day's diary entry with 'More snow' and for several days worked indoors. By 22 January, however, he was out again on his errands, on the 28th calling on Arrowsmith, Brown, Bulmer and Nicol to 'forward the printing and engraving'.[13] On the 31st he added, 'the reductions by J Arrowsmith going on too slowly'.[14]

Why this sense of urgency? His diary offered no explanation at the time, but a fortnight later he remarked that not only was Ann unwell, but so was he. Ann took to her bed. Flinders continued working and in the afternoon was able to have Samuel dine with him. Three days later Flinders noted that the surgeon, Hayes, had called, but did not explain. That his old 'gravelly complaint' had reappeared is, however, obvious. And he had no time to be ill.

His obligations mounted. The Timor chart was finished and taken to Arrowsmith's. He wrote the fair copies of the later chapters of Book III. He ordered a harp requested by the Pitots. As well, Thomi Pitot had a legal case against the British government apparently involving a prize ship, possibly two, and Flinders tried to attend the sessions before the Lords of Appeal at the Treasury, sometimes waiting for as much as three hours, only to have the matter fail to come on.

On 9 February, he and Ann inspected new lodgings at 14 London Street, Fitzeroy Square, and on the 26th Flinders noted that he was packing his books. The next day the entry in his diary was very different: 'Communicated to Mr. Hayes our surgeon all the symptons of the complaint which alone ever troubles me, and which appears to be either a stone or gravel in the bladder. It is troubled me more within some months and become painful'.[15] Flinders did not record Mr. Hayes's opinion, and the move to London Street was made the following day. Their new home was again a furnished apartment, occupying two floors in a narrow stone and brick building directly fronting the street. Flinders gave no reason for the change.

Again snow fell on London. On 9 March Flinders made his way along the dirty, slushy streets to the Court of Appeal for the fourth time to attend Pitot's case, which once more 'did not come on'. He continued to the Admiralty, and called at Nicol's and on Robert Brown before going home to write 'fair Book III... Suffering much pain all today'.

On 16 March he noted that he had completed his 40th year. The next day he 'passed some rough pieces of gravel, which appear to have separated from a stone in the bladder'.[16] The day after it was 'gravelly sand'. Hayes, who was calling almost daily, recommended an hour's walk, and Flinders went out, but 'was obliged to move very snail-like'.[17] A consulting Dr Marcet expressed the opinion that there was not one large stone in the bladder but several small calculi or concretions, and advised discontinuing the citric acid in favour of muriatic acid. Dr Dale, father of Alfred Dale, provided a prescription 'consisting principally of the sirup of white poppies'.[18]

Flinders's interest in his condition was characteristic. He observed and recorded the symptoms in detail, and discussed them with Dr Hayes and others who took a scientific interest. There were mucous-like emissions, blood in the urine and crystals that were passed. The surgeon employed a bougie, but this produced no positive results and was discontinued for the irritation it caused. Other remedies were tried—calcined magnesia, which was later determined to be harmful, drops of citric and muriatic acid, onion water, leek water, and other liquids. An easing of the pain led to hope for improvement, but a few hours later the distress returned. Flinders's nights were difficult; he had to rise in despairing attempts to pass urine as many as fourteen times in nine hours and eventually more frequently. He called often upon the servant to bring him cups of hot tea.

The demands of the book multiplied. Proofs of the charts, plates from the engravers and proof sheets for the narrative arrived steadily to be examined, corrected and returned. A continuous supply of quires had to be prepared and sent to the printers. By the end of the month the fair copy of Book III was finished and in mid-April Flinders began working out the book's title and preface, and wrote to Banks for advice on the dedication. The book was named *A Voyage to Terra Australis; Undertaken for the Purpose of Completing the Discovery of That Vast Country, and Prosecuted in the Years 1801, 1802, and 1803, in his Majesty's Ship the Investigator, and Subsequently in the Armed Vessel Porpoise and Cumberland Schooner. With an Account of the Shipwreck of the Porpoise, Arrival of the Cumberland at Mauritius, and Imprisonment of the Commander during Six Years and a Half in That Island*, the words arranged on the page in two sizes of capital letters in a simple Roman typeface. The length and detail were typical of Flinders's titles. He wrote the preface as seven pages of explanations on the book and the accompanying atlas. The dedication was suitably made to the four successive First Lords Commissioners of the Admiralty who had held that position from the inception of the *Investigator*'s voyage to the time of the completion of the book itself: Spencer, St Vincent, Yorke and Melville. The title and title page for the atlas followed, again in a simple typeface, and here Flinders exercised a little leeway, inserting his own preferred name for the continent. He entitled the overall map of the continent *General Chart of Terra Australis or Australia*. The need to advertise the book now arose and Nicol arrived to discuss the matter.

With the improved weather of early spring visitors from the country arrived: his sister Henrietta, now Mrs Chambers, her husband, her cousin Henrietta Franklin and, evidently, her mother-in-law. With these and other callers, including Brown, Fowler and Samuel, Flinders struggled to contain his pain and, between guests, to pursue his work and also keep up with his letter writing, which, however, he could do little more than half an hour at a time. For the sake of convenience he now moved to a downstairs bedroom.

In May a few days of feeling better gave way to greater pain, weakness, a dry mouth and disturbed nights. Only cups of hot black tea and lying down seemed to provide any relief. Deeply worrying was his inability to sit at his table with his papers except for short periods, at times on a special cushion. Sometimes the work was, as he said, 'ill done'. He believed that a strong, persistent east wind aggravated his condition.

Robert Brown was a frequent and solicitous caller, content to sit and talk while Flinders rested on the sofa. On Sunday 26 June Flinders had spent most of the day in bed. He wrote, 'Mr. Brown called in the evening to say that he had obtained from Mr. Nicol a copy of the voyage and atlas to put on Sir Jos. Banks table this evening, which is the last meeting [of the conversation group] for some time'.[19] The comment is significant. The book and the atlas had been printed while Flinders was still receiving visitors.

By this stage Ann was desperate with fear and worry. Matthew was fevered, without appetite, increasingly weak, often sleepless and in agonising pain. As well, two-year-old Anne was sick. Ann wrote to her sister and Isabella recorded:

> my sister begged me to go to be with her... He was not in the room when I arrived, but soon entered. Could that be he?—wrapped in a long flannel Gown, with grey hair, and sunken cheeks—He said but little—his pleasant cheerful manner was gone. He laid down on the sofa.—after resting awhile in that position he would sit up, have a cup of tea, & sit again & write till wearied he would lie down again then rise, take tea & write, & so on.[20]

To Flinders's friend Thomi Pitot Ann wrote, 'so dreadfully was he altered, he looked full 70 years of age, & was worn to a skeliton'.[21] Flinders's own comment on Isabella was brief: 'Miss Tyler arrived to assist Mrs. F in nursing me, and little Anne who has got the meazles'.[22] Yet the presence of the devoted, cheerful, practical Isabella was encouraging. The next day Matthew wrote, 'Passed a tranquil night, rose before noon, and shaved and dressed, feeling somewhat better. Mr. Arrowsmith brought me a set of proof of all the charts of the Atlas, and I gave him a note to Sir Joseph expressing my approbation of the engraving. Mr. W. Franklin called on his arrival from Lincolnshire'.[23]

Thus Flinders saw on thick, white sheets of paper the Arrowsmiths' impeccable reproductions of the creations of his own strenuous years. Apparently soon after, the Hippius family rallied to him and Ann, offering their home, which they would vacate, as a more comfortable venue for Matthew's recovery. Isabella wrote that this 'seemed to animate him.—he felt better, talked cheerfully, promised what he would do when he was well & so forth'.[24] It did not last: 'from that night he did not leave his bed'. The family remained at 14 London Street.

Ann's later comments to Thomi Pitot confirmed that about this time Flinders saw his completed book. 'He just lived to know, the work over which his life had been *spent* was laid before the World, for he left this earthly scene of things, a few days after its publication.'[25] The *Naval Chronicle of 1814* also noted that he 'survived a few days the finishing of the printing of the account of his voyage'.[26] Despite the traditional belief that the completed book was delivered to 14 London Street the day a comatose Flinders died, it is obvious that he saw the finished volumes.

From this point on Flinders's diary devotes itself almost entirely to his illness. Willingham Franklin brought to the bedside a Dr Bailey, whom Flinders did not mention. Only briefly he noted that Samuel took his half-pay affidavit to the Navy Office to be effected. There were other callers, but the dying man's attention was concentrated almost to the exclusion of anything else upon his suffering and the incomprehensible behaviour of his failing body. The memory of a boy's delight in reading *Robinson Crusoe* distracted him briefly. When the *Naval Chronicle* announced a forthcoming new edition of the book, Flinders wrote to request that his name be inserted on the list of subscribers.

On Sunday, 10 July 1814 Flinders wrote in his diary, 'Did not rise before two, being, I think, weaker than before.'[27] He wrote no more. Thus the last nine days of Matthew Flinders's life were not chronicled. Samuel evidently came. An anonymous sketch of Matthew's life describes what became their final parting, Flinders stoically aware that he was dying: 'the last time his brother saw him alive he simply shook him by the hand and said, "Good-bye, Samuel," just as he frequently did when in health, the only difference being the tenderly affectionate look which accompanied the action'.[28]

Another unnamed writer professed to have been at the bedside, and perpetuates one of several legends about Flinders's last moments.[29] There were no known dying words from Flinders. Isabella Tyler wrote that Ann had been persuaded to go to her room upstairs and lie down. Isabella followed and both 'got a little sleep'. She continued:

> I was awake by my Sister arising,—she was going to the sick room. I begged her to let me go *first*—The sun shone brightly on me as I went down the stairs,—All seemed so still! What could it mean?—I entered the drawing room—his bedroom opened into it, the door was ajar, I went in—there lay the corpse—the spirit had flown, the countenance placid & at rest. Dear Matthew—I stood at the foot of the bed contemplating the scene for a few moments, then rushed up stairs to my Sister.—She was soon in the room of death & pressed his cold lips to hers—it was a heart breaking effort. All was now over.[30]

It was 19 July 1814.

Isabella made the arrangements for the funeral. Samuel, George Nicols, probably Willingham Franklin and, as Isabella recalled, 'another gentleman' walked in the little cortege to the burial ground of St James

14 Maple Street, Fitzroy Square, London, c. 1937, the house where Matthew Flinders died in 1814, when the address was 14 London Street. Flinders and his family lived here from February 1814 to his death on 19 July. Ann, with her mother, sister and child left the house and London the following year. The house was demolished in 1937. (ML Ref: SPF - Flinders, Matthew, Mitchell Library, State Library of New South Wales)

Chapel in Hampstead Road. The grave no longer exists. Some 40 years after the interment Isabella Tyler visited the cemetery, to find it re-arranged, with the older stones and remains removed.

Matthew Flinders died, insofar as a modern diagnosis can be made, from renal failure, of which the fever, dehydration and extreme weakness were symptomatic, and an autopsy revealed a disease-ravaged bladder. He would have suffered from chronic nephritis, that is, inflammation of the kidneys, and cystitis, inflammation of the bladder, the first indications of which appeared when he was about twenty-two. Long periods of having little water to drink and possibly the effects of scurvy, conditions that recurred several times during his life, would have been contributing factors.

Ann, in grief and ignorance, believed that his illness derived from his confinement on Mauritius, and that it recurred in England through his unremitting and necessarily sedentary work. In fact, nothing in his detention on Ille de France can be blamed for his illness, nor is it likely that his early venereal infections had any direct bearing on it. The ineffectual medical treatment of the time simply failed to stem its progress.

Isabella described the desolation in the household in London Street. Of little Anne she wrote, 'the poor child felt that something very dreadful had happened, but did not know what'[31] and begged her mother not to cry. There would have been some comfort in the arrival of Ann and Isabella's mother, the sturdy, practical Anne Tyler, who now joined her daughters. Henceforth the three women and the child lived together.

Despite shock and grief, Ann Flinders took up the multiple responsibilities and problems left by her husband. The will was read on 26 August 1814, and the division of Flinders's property would have been in progress by December. That Ann found it distressing is clear. On 28 December she wrote to Charles Hursthouse:

> Had my dear Captain F. seen his danger, he would never have left me in such a situation . . . His attention was particularly bent to concluding the voyage, without ever reverting to his own concerns, otherwise he would have provided for our comfort without leaving so much to others, out of his little property, and as his friends [i.e., relatives] will come in for the whole should anything happen to the child, before she is of age, I cannot see it at all necessary to lay a few pounds yearly to benefit them.[32]

The will evidently created a further rift between Ann and Samuel. Ann's comments survive in letters; there are none from Samuel. It is apparent, however, that Ann believed that Samuel resented not being named one of the executors, which may indeed have been so, and a cautionary remark to Thomi Pitot suggests that she thought her brother-in-law might seek to establish some right over the Mauritian investments. In its first paragraphs the will did, in fact, provide for Samuel's inheritance of this investment, but in the later section, written for the event of Matthew's being survived by a child, this was altered. Samuel, however, could have felt dispossessed. The will stipulated that Ann was to give books and papers relating to the voyage of the *Investigator* to Samuel, but this seems not to have been done. Ann kept the books and papers.

Funds received from the sale of Flinders's English investments amounted to the very reasonable sum of £3498/16/1, of which, however, nearly one-third went to the immediate expenses of probate, the funeral, debts that became due on Flinders's death, the many legacies, annuity payments and the memorials Flinders had wanted. Ann arranged and paid just over £101 for the commemorative plaques set on the chancel wall of the Donington church and over £14 for mourning rings.

There were many painful letters to write to friends and relatives. On 10 October 1814 she wrote to Thomi Pitot with the news of Flinders's death, describing his illness and her own great grief. She wrote that she was sorting out as well as she could Flinders's financial involvements with Pitot. She added, 'Your commission for harp strings & Music, shall be executed to the best of my ability . . . I have paid £1.12.6 for 3 months of the Times newspapers; . . . but my dr Sir, I must charge you with the whole expense, being now too poor to take a part'.[33]

With the mourning rings, she would send copies of *A Voyage to Terra Australis* to Pitot, Labauve and Charles Desbassayns. She was also sending 26 additional copies of the book, hopefully for sale on Mauritius.

A Voyage to Terra Australis was not a financial success. One thousand copies were printed in a standard edition of two volumes with a folio atlas, priced at eight guineas. A larger-sized edition of 150 copies, also in two volumes with a folio atlas, was priced at 12 guineas. Even at discounted prices it sold desultorily over many years. It was a very large, cumbersome book. Navigators found it interesting and even useful; the general public had no interest in its navigational detail and technical tables. The copies sent to Mauritius were stored by Thomi Pitot while he made arrangements for their sale, but before this was accomplished, the house in which they were kept was destroyed by fire, including all but a very few of Flinders's books. It was a loss deeply felt by Ann.

Ann's income consisted of the £55 annuity left her by Flinders and the annual £90 of her naval widow's pension. Over the years she received a total of £190 in royalties, all of which provided a modest living for her and her family. Ann, however, was aware that James Cook's widow, still living in England, received an annual pension of

£300. With Banks's support and later through William Wilberforce, she applied for an increase in her own pension. Both petitions were rejected. An application to the East India Company for assistance also failed.

Retrieving funds from Matthew's Mauritius and Réunion investments was a lengthy and difficult affair. From the sale of the surviving copies of Flinders's *Voyage* she received in 1818 a bill of exchange for £65 from Thomi Pitot.[34] Efforts to obtain payment for Matthew's investments with Labauve and Desbassayns continued into the 1830s, the Pitot brothers' firm apparently eventually recovering at least some hundreds of pounds on her behalf.

Before the end of 1815 Ann, her mother, sister and little daughter left London for Southampton, the first of many moves to various towns in southern England over the next 37 years. Ann died in Woolwich on 10 February 1852. The following year news reached the family that the colonial governments of New South Wales and Victoria had each granted the widow an annual pension of £100. This devolved upon her daughter, then Anne Flinders Petrie, who in her letter of appreciation said she would use it towards the education of her infant son, who in time became the eminent archaeologist and Egyptologist, William Matthew Flinders Petrie.

37

Matthew Flinders—Conclusion

From about the age of fifteen Matthew Flinders was convinced that his life lay in maritime exploration. This was not a surprising aspiration. Flinders grew up at a time when the horizons of English exploration were illumined by the far-reaching navigational achievements of James Cook, crowning a decade of British ocean discovery. Matthew Flinders was also the product of an age of intense scientific curiosity, only a generation or two separated from the revolutionary changes set upon civilisation by Newton, Laplace, Leibniz, Halley and so many others, the great minds of Europe's scientific renaissance. Flinders came to interweave his youthful dreams of discovery with a serious interest in the sciences linked to navigation and in passing on to others the evidence of his findings, charts so precise, as he thought, that they would make unnecessary any future voyage of investigation in the regions he had explored.

To this inspired purpose he gave a determination that verged on the obsessive, an ambition that burned very brightly indeed, a passion that brooked few obstacles. In an age when advancement required patronage, Flinders selected his patrons with care and discernment—Pasley, Hunter, King and Banks—cultivated them and also inspired them with his vision. He had flashes of sudden, reckless behaviour, giving way to strongly emotional responses, as when, having decided that marriage was not compatible with his goals, he nevertheless married. Yet within two months he had bent this relationship to the exigencies of his purpose. And he pursued that purpose with relentless dedication, with courage, disregard for personal pain and great skill. A portrait painted of him on Mauritius shows a thin-faced man of 32. The eyes are attentive and steady, the expression determined.

There was in Flinders a vein of self-importance amounting at times to arrogance. He was a naval officer of his time, a time when this was an attitude virtually intrinsic to naval or military rank, a time also of class consciousness and distinctions. Imperious when his rightful authority was challenged, he knew his place in his particular world. Of modest social background, he lifted himself into the company of some of the nation's great, a circumstance he clearly enjoyed, but always with the necessary degree of respect. He took great pleasure in Banks's invitation to be a guest of the Royal Society, before whom papers he wrote had been read. He was, however, never elected a Fellow of the Society as Cook and Bligh had been, and if Flinders expected or hoped for this honour, he never mentioned it. Among friends and family, particularly on his final return to England, he thoroughly enjoyed being the centre of attention.

He was also a man of strong affections and loyalties. He loved his wife with, on the evidence, absolute devotion. He was a considerate son and, despite differences in character, an affectionate and supportive brother. In a relaxed atmosphere he was genial and warm, with a whimsical sense of humour that expressed itself in the fond 'biographical tribute' he wrote on his cat, Trim, and in funny, imaginative letters to his young sister-in-law. Serious and professional as was his cartography, a touch of the same mischievous humour sometimes slipped through. Troubridge Shoal in the Bay of St Vincent was named for Admiral Thomas Troubridge, who had run his ship onto a shoal during the Battle of the Nile.

Flinders's dedication to his work required a mental discipline guided by reason and bound by scientific interpretations. In his working life there was little time for thought outside of these parameters, but there was a subdued flame of imagination, of emotional response to the exotic, of sheer enjoyment in the expression of feeling. It was there when he viewed the pelican rookery on Kangaroo Island, in his reading of Milton, in the pleasure he found in a romantic novel. It had burned very brightly in the boy who wished to emulate Robinson Crusoe, and even—although perhaps only tentatively—in the sick man who wanted to share once more the adventures of that castaway.

Flinders won lasting friendships at all stages of his life, which he reciprocated with kindnesses well beyond the usual, after his return to

England in 1810 spending ill-afforded time and money to assist the prisoner of war relatives of his Mauritian friends. A trespass upon his determined purpose in life, however, or a perceived injustice was not easily forgiven. His resentment of what he considered unfair treatment from William Bligh took many years to abate and for what he saw as the terrible injustice of his long detention on Mauritius by Decaen, there never was anything but bitterness and anger.

Flinders's concerns with justice or the lack of it were always within his personal experience. In New South Wales he put considerable effort into the legal defence of Isaac Nichols, but never involved himself in the wider rights or wrongs of conditions in the colony. He had little interest in abstractions, as is also evident in his fairly casual attitude towards religion. He conducted no regular services aboard his ship. His calm acceptance of his sister Susanna's non-conformist church was expressed in his comment that the preacher appeared to be a man 'of good sense'. What, then, were Flinders's religious beliefs? Perhaps, like many of the period's men of science, he believed in a universe created by God for a purpose, without caring to probe very far into that purpose. He never wrote on the subject. Evidently he did not feel religious discussions were any more necessary than debates on other abstractions.

Flinders avoided the restive political life of New South Wales largely, it seems, out of lack of interest but also, perhaps, in order to maintain the equilibrium of his own position. It was his absolute belief in the paramount importance of his work, a scientific pursuit that set it apart even from the political considerations of wartime, that in large measure brought him into conflict with Governor Decaen on Ille de France. He would make no concession to circumstance and in this arrogant righteousness inevitably clashed with a man equally convinced of the correctness of his position. Essentially, Flinders was, as he considered himself, a man of honour, an important factor in the life of contemporary military men. This did not, however, prevent minor infringements upon rules that restricted him from what he considered his due, and for which he found justification. On Mauritius he repeatedly broke regulations governing letters sent from the island and, towards the end, feeling that his parole no longer applied, seriously considered breaking it in order to escape.

The six and a half years on Mauritius, in many ways the great tragedy of his life, had, nevertheless, a certain ameliorating effect on this ambitious, driven man. 'I shall learn patience in this island', he wrote to his wife, and he thoughtfully contemplated the effect that the power of command might have had upon himself. This was an introspection that he would not have attempted before. Culturally he acquired a great deal. He learned French, played music, read important books, all things for which he would not otherwise have had time. He polished his own literary style through his writing of journals, memoirs and countless letters. He worked on navigational problems and the effects of magnetism in ships, which he was later able to present as serious and useful papers.

And despite what he considered the vindictiveness of Decaen, he learned much about the friendship and generosity of others. Here, away from the demands of his work, he could be overtaken by feeling—his warm regard for Pitot, reminiscent of his youthful devotion to Bass, his cautious affection for Delphine, the depression to which he succumbed. There was more space for the romantic and emotional aspects of his nature—solitary walks in the moonlight, a fascination with waterfalls, a lookout to the sea on a jungle-covered mountainside. The Flinders that returned to England was a gentler, wiser man. The burning fire of ambition, too, was banked. He would never refuse an opportunity for a further voyage of discovery but, failing such a chance, he at least believed himself content to retire to a cottage in the country.

What did Matthew Flinders accomplish in terms of the exploration that he made the central consideration of his life? In 1798 Flinders and George Bass proved that Tasmania was an island and gave the young colony of New South Wales a shorter, safer route between the Pacific and Indian Oceans. His greater voyage of 1801–03 established that the continent of Australia was a single great landmass, that no seaway separated it into lesser bodies of land. It was a discovery that gave to the continent the geographical unity that was essential to its political unity. There were, too, the innumerable geographical features that he charted and described to add to knowledge of the continent. In time his charts were superseded by the work of others, as is the nature of cartography, but necessarily much of this was built on what he had found and recorded first. Flinders had the avid scientific curiosity that was part of the intellectual life of his time. Thus his persevering work with the magnetic compass 200 years ago eventually solved a significant problem in modern navigation with the invention of the Flinders Bar.

Flinders's voyage, his methods and his accomplishment stood between the navigational achievements of James Cook, some 30-odd years earlier, and those of Robert Fitzroy in the *Beagle*, 30 years later. Cook's great oceanic sweeps dramatically changed the map of the world. He set new standards in the application of science to navigation and hydrography, and to the care of seamen. Intrinsic to Fitzroy's work was the meticulous collection of complex and extensive data, gathered from coastlines across the globe. Each of these two men worked superlatively within the technical limits and capacities of his times; as did Flinders, whose work was transitional, making wide, general explorations of uncharted coasts and also carefully accumulating much detailed information. In that sequence of accretions to the nautical sciences and to maritime discoveries, Flinders's charts, observations and studies held a very useful and historically important place.

Ultimately, Flinders's achievement rested upon his ability as a navigator and a leader of men. He was composed and controlled under stress, certain in his decisions and had the capacity to ignore his own suffering, as well as having exceptional skill in handling a vessel. As with any determined achiever, Flinders went further than what was necessary. Almost inevitably he sacrificed others to his goal. There was hardness, even a ruthlessness in his demands of his men, but no less of himself. His ability as a seaman was obvious to every man on his ship. He probably communicated something of his own dedication to those around him, for repeatedly men volunteered to follow him.

Those who wrote of him soon after his death immersed his memory in laudatory prose that was at times misleading, if the man was to be understood, and quite unnecessary. The legacy that he left Australia is clear cut and his contributions to hydrography and other aspects of science are easily discerned. Beyond that, despite his shortcomings, he earned much loyalty and devotion from those who knew him, and clearly—whether on his quarterdeck or at his chart table—as a determinedly contributive individual, who gave a substantial measure of talent and achievement to his world and to subsequent history.

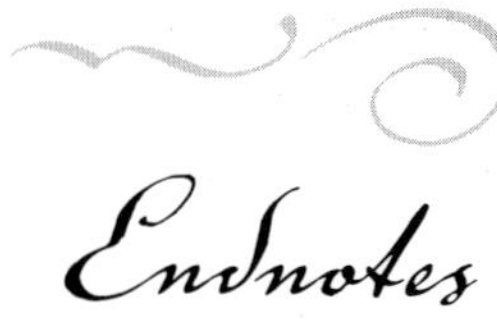

Endnotes

Abbreviations

ADM Admiralty Records
HRA *Historical Records of Australia*
HRNSW *Historical Records of New South Wales*
LA Lincolnshire Archives, Lincoln, UK
LTC La Trobe Collections, State Library of Victoria
ML Mitchell Library, State Library of New South Wales
NMM National Maritime Museum, Greenwich
PRO Public Records Office

Note: Spelling and punctuation in all quotations are as they were written at the time. Ellipses within quotations indicate the omission by the author of some of the original text.

Chapter 1 From the Fens to the Sea

1 Matthew Flinders, Sr, *Diary and Account Book*, 24 August 1786, Flinders 2/fol. 15v, by kind permission of Robert Perry, Ursula Perry and LA
2 ibid., 2 January 1787, Flinders 2/fol. 29
3 ibid., 27 April 1789, Flinders 2/fol. 36v
4 ibid., 30 December 1780, Flinders 1/fol. 49v
5 'Biographical Memoir of Captain Matthew Flinders, RN', *The Naval Chronicle for 1814, General and Biographical History of the Royal Navy of the United Kingdom, with a variety of Original papers on Nautical subjects,* vol. xxxii, Joyce Gould, London, note, p. 178
6 Muster Book, HMS *Alert*, ADM 36/10793, PRO
7 Flinders, Sr, *Diary and Account Book*, 31 May 1790, Flinders 2/fol. 43, LA
8 ibid., 3 September 1790, Flinders 2/fol. 45, LA

CHAPTER 2 THE VOYAGE WITH BLIGH

1 ibid., 20 May 1791, Flinders 2/fol. 48v, LA
2 Thomas Pasley to Matthew Flinders, 3 June 1791, Flinders Papers, 60/017, FLI/1 NMM
3 There is a discrepancy between the figure of 420 tons burden given by Bligh and the 406 tons burden given on the Admiralty's draught plan, quoted here from Geoffrey Ingleton, *Matthew Flinders: Navigator and Chartmaker*, Genesis Publications in association with Hedley Australia, Guildford, England, and Alphington, Victoria, 1986, note 2, p. 18
4 The human body requires between 30mg and 70mg of vitamin C per day; below a 10mg intake scurvy occurs. Ivan M. Sharman, 'Vitamin Requirements of the Human Body', in J. Watt et al. eds, *Starving Sailors*, NMM, Greenwich, 1981, p. 28
5 Matthew Flinders to Thomas Pasley, Flinders Papers, Manuscript Collection, 546/7, LTC. The dollar was probably the Spanish peseta or peso, international currency at the time, known by English-speaking people as the dollar.
6 Matthew Flinders, *Log kept on board H.M.S. Providence, Feb. 24 1792 to Feb. 10 1793*, 25 March 1792, ADM 55, PRO
7 Flinders, Sr, *Diary and Account Book*, 29 January 1792, Flinders 2/fol. 51v, LA
8 George Hamilton, *A Voyage Round the World in His Majesty's Frigate Pandora*, Hordern House, Sydney, 1998, pp. 66, 79
9 Flinders, *Log kept on HMS Providence*, 25 March 1792
10 William Bligh, *The Log of HMS* Providence *1791–1793*, 11 May 1791, Genesis Publications, Guildford, England, 1976
11 Matthew Flinders, quoted in Geoffrey Rawson, *Bligh of the 'Bounty'*, Philip Allan, London, 1932, p. 96
12 Matthew Flinders, *A Voyage to Terra Australis, Undertaken for the Purpose of Completing the Discovery of that Vast Country, and Prosecuted in the Years 1801, 1802, and 1803, in His Majesty's Ship the Investigator, and Subsequently in the armed Vessel Porpoise and Cumberland Schooner, with an Account of the Shipwreck of the Porpoise, Arrival of the Cumberland at Mauritius, and Imprisonment of the Commander during Six Years and a Half in that Island*, G. and W. Nicol, London, 1814, Australiana Facsimile Editions No. 37, Libraries Board of South Australia, Adelaide, 1966, vol. I, p. xxiii
13 ibid., p. xxi
14 Flinders, *Log kept on HMS Providence*, 6 September 1792
15 Flinders, *A Voyage*, vol. I, p. xxiii
16 Flinders, *Log kept on HMS Providence*, 11 September 1792
17 ibid.
18 Flinders, *A Voyage*, vol. I, p. xxix
19 Matthew Flinders's certificate for lieutenancy, January 1797, Flinders Papers, 60/017, FLI/5 NMM
20 Flinders, *Log kept on HMS Providence*, 2 September 1792
21 Francis Godolphin Bond to Thomas Bond, n.d., from St Helena, in George Mackaness, 'Fresh Light on Bligh: Some Unpublished Correspondence', *Australian Historical Monographs*, vol. V, Review Publications, 1949, p. 69
22 William Henry Smyth, 'A Brief Memoir of Captain Matthew Flinders', RN, Box 81/3(d) (No MS number), LTC. No author's name is given with the La Trobe copy, but the document is identified as Smyth's in Flinders Papers, 60/017, FLI/105, NMM
23 Flinders, *Log kept on HMS Providence*, 5 February 1793
24 ibid.
25 A captured vessel, or prize, was normally sold and the proceeds divided according to a formula among the victorious ship's company
26 Flinders, Sr, *Diary and Account Book*, 3 October 1793, Flinders 2/fol. 63

Chapter 3 War

1 Steve Pope, *Hornblower's Navy: Life at Sea in the Age of Nelson*, Orion Media, London, 1998, p. 21
2 Pasley to Flinders, 7 August 1793, 60/07, FLI/1, NMM
3 Matthew Flinders, 'Journal on *Bellerophon*', in Ernest Scott, *The Life of Captain Matthew Flinders, RN*, Angus & Robertson, Sydney, 1914, p. 48
4 James Wiles to Joseph Banks, 16 March 1793, Banks Papers Series 52.14, ML
5 Matthew Flinders, *Log of HMS Bellerophon*, 18 November 1793 Flinders Papers, 60/017, FLI/8b, NMM
6 ibid., 28 May 1794
7 ibid., 30 May 1794
8 ibid.
9 ibid., 31 May 1794
10 ibid., 1 June 1794
11 ibid.
12 Henry Waterhouse, 'Account of the Battle of the 1st of June 1794', Bass/Waterhouse Letters, CY 3970, ML
13 Flinders, *Log of HMS Bellerophon*, 1 June 1794
14 Flinders, Sr, *Diary and Account Book*, 10 June 1794, Flinders 2/fol. 66v

Chapter 4 The Colony of New South Wales

1 Flinders, *A Voyage*, vol. I, p. xcvi
2 Flinders, Sr, *Diary and Account Book*, 25 September 1794, Flinders 2/fol. 68v, LA
3 ibid.
4 Matthew Flinders to Mary Franklin, 23 January 1795, Flinders Papers, 60/017, FLI/4, NMM
5 Matthew Flinders to Ann Chappelle and Mary Franklin, 10 March 1795, 60/017, FLI/4, NMM; copy by W. M. F. Petrie in Flinders Papers, LTC
6 Henry Waterhouse to Arthur Phillip, 24 October 1795, Banks Papers Series 37.28, ML
7 Christopher Smith to Matthew Flinders, 30 June 1799, Flinders Papers 60/017, FLI/1, NMM
8 John Hunter to the Navy Board, 19 March 1794, ADM 106/1353, PRO
9 John Hunter to Under Secretary King, 1 May 1794, *HRNSW,* vol. II, p. 214
10 Daniel Paine, *The Journal of Daniel Paine 1794–1797*, eds R. J. B. Knight and Alan Frost, Library of Australian History, Sydney, and NMM, Greenwich, 1983, p. 1
11 Hunter to King, 25 January 1795, *HRNSW,* vol. II, p. 281
12 Watkin Tench, *1788*, ed. Tim Flannery, Text Publishing Company, Melbourne, 1996, p. 118
13 John Hunter to Secretary Evan Nepean, 3 September 1798, *HRA,* vol. II, p. 220
14 Flinders, *A Voyage,* vol. I, p. xcvii
15 Waterhouse to Phillip, 24 October 1795, Banks Papers Series 37.28, ML
16 Arthur Phillip to Lord Sydney, 15 May 1788, *HRNSW,* vol. I, Part 2, p. 122
17 Governor Hunter's Commisssion, *HRA*, vol. I, p. 513
18 John Hunter, 'State of the Settlements', 25 October 1795, Enclosure No. 3 in a letter to Portland, *HRNSW,* vol. II, p. 334
19 David Collins, *An Account of the English Colony in New South Wales,* ed. Brian H. Fletcher, A.H. & A. W. Reed, Sydney, vol. I, p. 359
20 Hunter to Portland, 11 September 1795, *HRA*, vol. I, p. 528

Chapter 5 The Tom Thumb Adventures

1 Flinders, *A Voyage,* vol. I, pp. xcvi–xcvii
2 Matthew Flinders, *Matthew Flinders' Narrative of Tom Thumb's Cruize to Canoe Rivulet*, ed. Keith Bowden, South Eastern Historical Association, Brighton, Victoria, 1985, p. 2
3 Flinders, *A Voyage,* vol. I, p. cxvii
4 Flinders, *Matthew Flinders' Narrative*, p. 2
5 Chapman, Frederik Henrik as, *Architectura Navalis Mercatoria*, Coles, London, 1971. Selected parts of the 19th century translation by the Rev. James Inman of the (author's) *Tractat Om Skepps-Byggieret*, originally published as *Architectura Navalis Mercatoria*, Holmiae, 1768
6 'Condition of Norfolk Island', *HRNSW,* vol. III, p. 146
7 Flinders, *Matthew Flinders' Narrative*, p. 2
8 Paine, *The Journal*, p. 1. On Canoe Rivulet four Aborigines 'jumped in', briefly making seven people in the boat. Chapman's encyclopaedia depicts contemporary 'Boats for the use of ships' as typically twelve feet or just under in length, and Paine, who had worked for years at England's Deptford dockyard, evidently built accordingly. Perhaps forgetfully, Flinders years later mentioned lengths of eight and nine feet for the *Tom Thumb*s.
9 Government and General Orders, 9 October 1797, *HRA,* vol. II, pp. 203–204
10 Flinders, *Matthew Flinders' Narrative*, p. 4
11 ibid., p. 9
12 ibid., p. 10
13 Flinders, *A Voyage*, vol. I, p. ci
14 Flinders, *Matthew Flinders' Narrative,* p. 16

Chapter 6 'No Ship Ever Went to Sea So Much Lumber'd'

1 Hunter to Nepean, 31 August 1796, *HRNSW*, vol. III, p. 91
2 Waterhouse to his father, 20 August 1797, *HRNSW*, vol. III, p. 287
3 William Kent to John Hunter, 16 May 1797, HRNSW, vol. III, p. 286
4 Hunter to Portland, 25 June 1797, *HRA,* vol. II, p. 32
5 Survey of the Supply, 2 June 1797, *HRNSW*, vol. II, p. 280
6 Waterhouse to his father, 20 August 1797
7 ibid.
8 ibid.
9 Waterhouse, 'Memorandum on the Timber of New South Wales', c. March 1802, in Paine, *The Journal,* p. 79
10 Hunter to Portland, 1 March 1798, HRNSW, vol. III, p. 363

Chapter 7 Van Diemen's Land—An Island?

1 Flinders, *A Voyage*, vol. I, pp. cxix–cxx
2 George Bass, 'Bass's Journal of the Whaleboat Voyage', in Matthew Flinders, *Matthew Flinders' Narrative of his Voyage in the Schooner Francis: 1798, Preceded and Followed by Notes on Flinders, Bass, the Wreck of the Sydney Cove, &C, by Geoffrey Rawson*, ed. Geoffrey Rawson, Golden Cockerel Press, London, 1946, p. 33

3 The group had escaped in a settler's boat, but found the boat too small for fourteen men. Seven were left on the island as they slept. The others reached Broken Bay, seized another boat, and went north. From Hunter to Portland, 1 March 1799, in *HRA*, vol. II, p. 133
4 Flinders, *A Voyage*, vol. I, p. cxix
5 Matthew Flinders, 'Flinders' Narrative', in *Matthew Flinders' Narrative of his Voyage in the Schooner Francis: 1798*, p. 70
6 Hunter to Portland, 1 March 1798, *HRA*, vol. II, p. 134
7 Flinders, *A Voyage*, vol. I, p. cxxviii
8 ibid., p. cxxxv
9 ibid.
10 ibid., p. cxxvi
11 Hunter to Joseph Banks, 12 March 1798, in Ingleton, *Matthew Flinders, Navigator and Chartmaker*, p. 32
12 Hunter to Nepean, 3 September 1798, *HRA*, vol. II, p. 221
13 Flinders, *A Voyage*, vol. I, p. cxxxviii
14 ibid., pp. cxxxix–cxl
15 ibid., pp. cxl–cxli
16 Matthew Flinders, 'Narrative of an Expedition in the Colonial sloop Norfolk, from Port Jackson, through the Strait which separates Van Diemen's Land from New Holland, and from thence round the South Cape back to Port Jackson, completing the circumnavigation of the former Island, with some remarks on the coasts and harbours, by Matthew Flinders, 2nd l't, H.M.S. Reliance,' *HRNSW*, vol. III, Appendix B, p. 786
17 Flinders, *A Voyage*, vol. I, p. clxix
18 ibid., p. clxxi
19 Flinders, 'Narrative of an Expedition in the Colonial sloop Norfolk', p. 801
20 Matthew Flinders, *Observations on the Coasts of Van Diemen's Land, on Bass's Strait and its Islands, and on Part of the Coasts of New South Wales: intended to accompany the Charts of the Late Discoveries in those Countries*, London, John Nichols, 1801; Australiana Facsimile Editions No. 66, Adelaide, Libraries Board of South Australia, 1965, pp. 1–2
21 Flinders, 'Narrative of an Expedition in the Colonial sloop Norfolk', p. 800
22 ibid., p. 802
23 Flinders, *A Voyage*, vol. I, p. clxxxvii
24 Flinders, *Observations*, Preface
25 Flinders, 'Narrative of an Expedition in the Colonial sloop Norfolk', p. 816
26 Hunter to Nepean, 15 August 1799, *HRA*, vol. II, p. 381

Chapter 8 Colonial Affairs

1 Hunter to Portland, 1 May 1799, *HRA*, vol. II, p. 356
2 Hunter to Portland, 21 February 1799, *HRA*, vol. II, pp. 247–9
3 Joseph Banks to John Hunter, 1 February 1799, *HRNSW*, vol. III, p. 532
4 'The King against the said Isaac Nichols', *HRA*, vol. II, p. 284
5 Matthew Flinders, report to Governor Hunter, 30 April 1799, *HRA*, vol.II, p. 333

Chapter 9 'Sea, I Am Thy Servant'

1 Matthew Flinders to Ann Chappelle, 16–19 March 1799, Flinders Papers, 60/017, FLI/25, NMM

2 ibid.
3 Christopher Smith to Matthew Flinders, 30 June 1799, Flinders Papers, 60/017, FLI/1, NMM
4 Matthew Flinders to Christopher Smith, 14 February 1800, Flinders Papers, 60/017, FLI/4, NMM
5 Matthew Flinders to George Bass, 15–21 February 1800, private collection, Australia; copy MSB 447, Flinders Papers, LTC
6 Michael Roe, 'New Light on George Bass, Entrepreneur and Intellectual', *Journal of the Royal Australian Historical Society*, vol. 72, Part 5, 1987, pp. 251–65
7 ibid.
8 ibid.
9 J. S. Cumpston, *Shipping Arrivals & Departures Sydney, 1788–1825*, Roebuck Society Publication, Canberra, 1977, pp. 36–7
10 Elizabeth Bass, note on letter from Flinders to Bass, 15–21 February 1800, private collection, Australia
11 Flinders to Bass, June 1803, in K. M. Bowden, *George Bass: 1771–1803*, Oxford University Press, Melbourne, 1952, p.127

CHAPTER 10 NORTH ON THE EAST COAST, 1799

1 Joseph Banks to Under Secretary King, 15 May 1798, Banks Papers, *HRNSW*, vol. III, pp. 382–3. Also in *HRA*, vol. II, p. 231
2 James Cook, *Captain Cook in Australia*, ed. A.W. Reed, A. H. & A. W. Reed, Wellington, 1969, p. 57
3 Flinders, *A Voyage*, vol. I, p. cxciii
4 ibid., p. cxciv
5 ibid.
6 Matthew Flinders, *Chart of Terra Australis by M. Flinders, Commr. of H. M. Sloop* Investigator. *1802*, *East Coast*, Sheet II, *Atlas*, *A Voyage to Terra Australis*
7 Flinders, *A Voyage*, vol. I, pp. cxciv–cxcv
8 Collins, *An Account*, vol. II, p. 164
9 Flinders, *A Voyage*, vol. I, p. cxcix
10 ibid., p. cxcvii
11 Collins, *An Account*, vol. II, p. 176
12 ibid., p. 177
13 Flinders, *A Voyage*, vol. I, p. ccii
14 ibid., p. cciv

CHAPTER 11 'IF ADVERSE FORTUNE DOES NOT OPPOSE ME, I WILL SUCCEED'

1 T. M. Perry, 'Seasons for Exploration', *Proceedings of the Royal Geographical Society of Australasia, Southern Australian Branch (Incorporated)*, vol. 76, December 1975, p. 55
2 Matthew Flinders, *A Biographical Tribute to the Memory of Trim*, John Ferguson–Halstead Press, Sydney, 1985, p. 27
3 A manuscript titled *A Journal in the Norfolk sloop by Flinders* is part of ML MSS C211. In his *Account of the English Colony in New South Wales*, vol. II, pp. 225–63, Collins

described the journey, including incidents not appearing in the C211 document. Flinders's own brief record appears in *A Voyage to Terra Australis*, vol. I, pp. cxciv–cciv
4 Hunter to Nepean, 15 August 1799, *HRA*, vol. II, p. 378
5 'List of Ships and Vessels which Enter'd Inwards in the Port of Port Jackson, in His Majesty's Colony of New South Wales, between the 3rd day of November, 1799, and the 13th day of May, 1800 . . .', *HRA*, vol. II, p. 571. An error puts the *Reliance*'s entry date in October.
6 Michael Murphy and Stephen Gilbert. Exactly how Flinders secured this land is not clear, whether by purchase or, more likely, as additional grants.
7 Matthew Flinders to Pultney Malcolm, 17 January 1800, Flinders Papers, LTC
8 Matthew Flinders to Joseph Banks, 12 July 1804, *HRNSW*, vol. V, pp. 397–8
9 Flinders to Banks, 6 September 1800, Banks Papers, Series 65.01 ML
10 Flinders to Chappelle, 25 September 1800, Flinders Papers, 60/017, FLI/25, NMM
11 Report on the 'State and Defects of His Majesty's Ship Reliance—Deptford, 8th October, 1800', *HRNSW*, vol. IV, p. 227
12 Flinders, Sr, *Diary and Account Book*, 1 November 1800
13 Banks to Flinders, 16 November 1800, Flinders Papers, 60/017, NMM

CHAPTER 12 ENLIGHTENMENT AND EXPLORATION

1 Archibald Campbell to William Pitt, 18 October 1790, FO 95/7/4. fo. 481, PRO, in Alan Frost, 'The Spanish Yoke, British Schemes to Revolutionise Spanish America, 1739–1807', in *Pacific Empires, Essays in Honour of Glyndwer Williams*, eds Alan Frost and Jane Samson, Melbourne University Press, Melbourne, 1999, p. 33
2 Georg Mortimer, *Engelsmannen Joh. Hinric Cox Resa Genom Söderhafvet Till Ön Amsterdam, Marien-Öarna, Ön-Taheiti, Sandvichs-och-Raf-Öarna, Tinian, Unalaska och Canton in China*, George Mortimer, Nyköping, 1798. Coincidentally, the ship arrived in Tahiti 15 days after the departure of the *Bounty*'s mutineers, to hear a confusing account of events.
3 Alexandro Malaspina to Bernardo del Campo, 9 April 1793, Archivo General de Simancas, Estado, legajo 8159, in Robert J. King, *The Secret History of the Convict Colony, Alexandro Malaspina's report on the British settlement of New South Wales*, Allen & Unwin, Sydney, p. 1
4 Alexandro Malaspina, 'A Political Examination of the English Colonies in the Pacific', in King, *The Secret History*, p. 102
5 Malaspina returned to Spain in 1794. A year later he had fallen victim to the intrigues of the Spanish court, was secretly tried and condemned to ten years' imprisonment, his extensive research and his enlightened recommendations for Spanish colonial reform either suppressed or lost.
6 Christine Cornell, *Questions Relating to Nicolas Baudin's Australian Expedition, 1800–1804*, Libraries Board of South Australia, Adelaide, 1965, p. 26
7 Frank Horner, *The French Reconnaissance: Baudin in Australia 1801–1803*, Melbourne University Press, 1987, p. 181
8 Nicolas Thomas Baudin to Minister of Marine, 29 May 1803, in King, *The Secret History*, pp. 49–50
9 Philip Gidley King to Lord Hobart, 9 November 1802, *HRA*, vol. III, p. 628.
10 King to Banks, 5 June 1802, *HRNSW*, vol. IV, p. 786
11 Henry Bathurst, Earl Bathurst, to Lachlan Macquarie, 19 August 1813, *HRA*, vol. VIII, p. 72

CHAPTER 13 'A SHIP IS FITTING OUT FOR ME'

1 Flinders, Sr, *Diary and Account Book*, 2 February 1801, Flinders 2/fol. 105v, LA
2 Flinders to Flinders, Sr, 9 November 1800, Flinders Correspondence 3/2, LA
3 Flinders, Sr, to Matthew Flinders, 23 November 1800, Flinders Correspondence 3/3, LA
4 Flinders to Flinders, Sr, 29 November 1800, Flinders Papers, 60/017, FLI/25, NMM
5 Elizabeth Flinders, notation in Flinders, Sr, *Diary and Account Book*, 1 May 1802, Flinders 2/fol. 112
6 Flinders to Chappelle, 18 December 1800, Flinders Papers, 60/017, FLI/25, NMM. Partial copy by W. M. F. Petrie in Flinders Papers, LTC
7 ibid.
8 ibid., 16 January 1801
9 ibid.
10 ibid., 27 January 1801
11 Flinders, *A Voyage,* vol. I, p. 4
12 ibid., p. 1
13 Banks to Flinders, 19 February 1801, Flinders Papers 60/017, FLI/1, NMM
14 Flinders to Flinders, Sr, 10 July 1801, Flinders 3/8 Correspondece, LA
15 Evan Nepean, note to Banks, 28 April 1801, *HRNSW,* vol. IV, p. 348
16 Matthew Flinders to Ann Flinders, 5 July 1801, copy by W. M. F. Petrie, Flinders Papers, LTC
17 Peter Good to William T. Aiton, 14 January 1801, in *The Journal of Peter Good, Gardener on Matthew Flinders Voyage to Terra Australis 1801–03,* ed. Phyllis I. Edwards, Bulletin of the British Museum (Natural History), Historical Series vol. 9, London, 1981, p. 29
18 Flinders, *A Voyage,* vol. I, p. 272
19 Banks to unnamed person, probably William Milnes of Ashover, Derbyshire, *HRNSW,* vol. IV, p. 291

CHAPTER 14 A POSSIBILITY OF MARRIAGE

1 Flinders to Flinders, Sr, 3 April 1801, Flinders Correspondence 3/5, LA
2 ibid.
3 Flinders to Chappelle, 6 April 1801, Flinders Papers 60/017 FLI/25, NMM
4 Matthew Flinders to Henrietta Flinders, 10 May 1801, Flinders Papers 60/017, FLI/ 4, NMM
5 Flinders to Flinders, Sr, 14 April 1801, Flinders Correspondence 3/6, LA
6 Statement by W. A. Standert, Matthew Flinders's agent, Flinders Papers 60/017, FLI/6, NMM
7 Isabella Tyler, 'Biographical Outline of Capt. & Mrs Flinders 1852', Flinders Papers 60/017, FLI 107, NMM.
8 ibid.
9 Ann Flinders to Elizabeth Franklin, 17 April 1801, CY Reel 2457, ML Af 2/1–14, 16, ML
10 Smyth, 'A Brief Memoir'
11 Flinders to Henrietta Flinders, 10 May 1801, Flinders Papers 60/017, FLI/4, NMM
12 Flinders, Sr, *Diary and Account Book*, 1 May 1801, Flinders 2/fol. 106v, LA
13 Flinders to Flinders, Sr, 9 May 1801, Flinders 3/7, R. and U. Perry and LA
14 Flinders to Henrietta Flinders, 10 May 1801, Flinders Papers 60/017, FLI/4, NMM
15 Flinders to Flinders, Sr, 9 May 1801, Flinders 3/7, LA
16 Tyler, 'Biographical Outline'

17 ibid.
18 Flinders to Banks, 29 April 1801, ML/DL Banks Papers Series 65.19, ML
19 Matthew Flinders to Navy Board, *Journals of the Investigator, Porpoise and Cumberland, 1801–1803*, 9 May 1801, ML Safe 1/25 CY S1/25 and FM 3/764, ML
20 Banks to Flinders, 21 May 1801, *HRNSW,* vol. IV, p. 372
21 Flinders to Banks, 21 May 1801, Banks Papers, Series 65.19, ML
22 An incident from Banks's own past adds a touch of irony to his opposition now to the presence of a woman on board a naval ship bound for discoveries. In 1772 Banks had withdrawn from his planned participation in Cook's second voyage, and HMS *Resolution* sailed without him. On reaching Madeira Cook was told of a Mr Burnett, who had been waiting there for about three months, and departed suddenly on hearing that Banks was not with the ship. Those who had met Burnett assured Cook that 'Every part of Mr Burnetts behaviour and every action tended to prove that he was a woman ...' James Cook, letter possibly to the Secretary of the Admiralty, 1 August 1772, Georgian Papers, Windsor, in Patrick O'Brian, *Joseph Banks, A Life*, Collins Harvill, London, 1987, p. 163
23 Flinders, *A Voyage*, vol. I, p. 7
24 Flinders, report to the Admiralty, 29 May 1801, ADM 1/1800, vol. 1, CY S1/24 and FM 3/764, Safe 1/24, ML
25 Matthew Flinders, *Journals on the Investigator, Porpoise and Cumberland 1801–1803*, vol. I, 29 May 1801
26 Flinders to Banks, 3 June 1801, *HRNSW,* vol. IV, pp. 380–1
27 Banks to Flinders, 5 June 1801, *HRNSW*, vol. IV, pp. 383–4
28 Tyler, 'Biographical Outline'
29 Flinders, *Journals of the Investigator, Porpoise and Cumberland, 1801–1803*, vol. II, 26 November 1802
30 Flinders to Ann Flinders, 30 June 1801, copy by W. M. F. Petrie in Flinders Papers, LTC
31 Flinders to Ann Flinders, 5 July 1801, Flinders Papers, 60/017, FLI/25, NMM; also copy by W. M. F. Petrie in Flinders Papers, LTC
32 Flinders to Ann Flinders, 7 July 1801, copy by W. M. F. Petrie, Flinders Papers, LTC
33 Banks to Flinders, (n.d.), June 1801, *HRNSW*, vol. IV, pp. 388–9

Chapter 15 The Voyage Out

1 Flinders's instructions from the Admiralty in *A Voyage*, vol. I, p. 10
2 Matthew Flinders, Journal, ADM 7/708, p. 54, PRO
3 Flinders's instructions from the Admiralty in *A Voyage*, vol. I, p. 14
4 Flinders, *A Voyage*, vol. I, p. 36
5 Robert Brown to C. F. Greville, 30 May 1802, *HRNSW*, vol. IV, p. 776
6 Brown to Joseph Banks, Port Jackson, 30 May 1802, *HRNSW*, vol. IV, p. 777
7 Flinders, *A Voyage*, vol. I, p. 19
8 ibid.
9 ibid., p. 28
10 ibid.
11 ibid., p. 29
12 Good, *Journal,* 7 September, p. 40
13 Samuel Smith, 'Diary', 8 September 1801, MSS C222, ML
14 Good, *Journal,* 8 September 1801, p. 40
15 Flinders to Ann Flinders, 3 November 1801, Flinders Papers 60/017, FLI 1/25, NMM
16 Flinders, *A Voyage*, vol. I, p. 39
17 Flinders to Ann Flinders, 3 November 1801, Flinders Papers 60/017, FLI 1/25, NMM
18 Flinders to Flinders Sr, 22 October 1801, Flinders Correspondence 3/10, LA

19 Flinders, *A Voyage*, vol. I, p. 43
20 Matthew Flinders to Willingham Franklin, 27 November 1801, CY 1090 Safe 1/55, Private Letter Book, vol. 1, ML

CHAPTER 16 TERRA AUSTRALIS

1 Flinders, *A Voyage,* vol. I, pp. 48–9
2 Directions from the Admiralty, in ibid., p. 8
3 ibid., pp. lxxiii–lxxiv
4 ibid., p. lxxiv.
5 ibid., p. 53
6 ibid., p. 64
7 ibid., p. 55
8 ibid., pp. 66–7
9 Good, *Journal,* 25 December 1801, p. 51
10 Flinders, *A Voyage*, vol. I, p. 61
11 Smith, 'Diary', 30 December 1801
12 Flinders, *A Voyage,* vol. I, pp. 73–4
13 Flinders to Ann Flinders, 31 May 1802, Flinders Papers 60/017, FLI/25, NMM
14 ibid.
15 Good, *Journal*, 13 January 1802, p. 55
16 Flinders, *A Voyage*, vol. I, p. 86
17 Good, *Journal*, 13 January 1802, p. 55
18 Smith, 'Diary', 14 January 1802
19 Flinders overestimated its height at 500 feet, *A Voyage*, vol. I, p. 93
20 Flinders, *A Voyage*, vol. I, p. 96
21 ibid., p. 97
22 Matthew Flinders, 'Extracts from the Fair Log Book of HMS Investigator', 28 January 1802, in *The Unknown Coast, Being the explorations of Captain Matthew Flinders, R. N., along the shores of South Australia 1802*, ed. H. M. Cooper, s.p., 1953, p. 29
23 Robert Brown, Diary, 3 February 1802, *Nature's Investigator, The Diary of Robert Brown in Australia, 1801–1805*, eds. T. G. Vallance, D. T. Moore and E. W. Groves, Australian Biological Resources Study, Canberra, 2001, p. 125
24 Flinders, 'Extracts', 7 February 1802 in *The Unknown Coast*, p. 35
25 Flinders, *A Voyage*, vol. I, pp. 132–3

CHAPTER 17 TRAGEDY AT NO 12 INLET

1 Flinders, *A Voyage,* vol. I, p. 133
2 Good, *Journal*, 21 February 1801, p. 61
3 Smith, 'Diary', 21 February 1802
4 Flinders, *A Voyage*, vol. I, p. 139
5 Flinders to Ann Flinders, 31 May 1802, Flinders Papers 06/017 FLI/25, NMM
6 Flinders, *A Voyage*, vol. I, p. 142
7 ibid., p. 148
8 Flinders's calculations were based on the supposition that sound travels at the rate of 1142 feet per second
9 Flinders, *A Voyage*, vol. I, p. 148
10 ibid., p. 146
11 ibid., p. 155

12 Good, *Journal*, 10 March, p. 66
13 Flinders, *A Voyage*, vol. I, p. 158
14 ibid., p. 167
15 ibid., p. 169
16 Matthew Flinders, 'Extracts from the Rough Log Book of HMS Investigator', 22 March 1802, in *The Unknown Coast,* p. 78
17 Flinders, *A Voyage*, vol. I, p. 170
18 ibid., p. 181

Chapter 18 Encounter Bay

1 Flinders, *A Voyage,* vol. I, p. 183
2 Brown, Diary, 4 April 1802, in *Nature's Investigator*, p. 174
3 Matthew Flinders, 'Extracts from the Fair Log Book, in *The Unknown Coast*, p. 62
4 Flinders, *A Voyage*, vol. I, p. 189
5 ibid., p. 190
6 Brown, Journal, in *The Unknown Coast*, p. 90
7 Smith, 'Diary', 9 April 1802
8 Brown, Diary, 9 April 1802, *Nature's Investigator*, p. 178
9 Scott, Ernest, *The Life of Captain Matthew Flinders, R.N.*, Angus & Robertson, Sydney, 1914, p. 228
10 Flinders, *Journal*, ADM 7/708, p. 54, PRO
11 Flinders, *A Voyage,* vol. I, p. 194
12 ibid., p. 211
13 Brown, Diary, 27 April 1802, *Nature's Investigator*, p. 190
14 Good, *Journal*, 26 April 1802, p. 75
15 Flinders, *A Voyage,* vol. I, p. 216
16 ibid., p. 226

Chapter 19 Sydney—1802

1 Good, *Journal*, 9 May 1802, p. 79
2 Smith, 'Diary' n.d.
3 Evan Nepean to Governor King, April 1801, *HRNSW*, vol. IV, pp. 360–1
4 Flinders to Banks, 20 May 1802, *HRNSW*, vol. IV, p. 757
5 Flinders, *A Voyage*, p. 228
6 Flinders to the Admiralty, 11 May 1802, *HRNSW*, vol. IV, p. 749
7 Flinders to Banks, 20 May 1802, *HRNSW*, vol. IV, pp. 756–7
8 Banks to King, 8 April 1803, *HRNSW,* vol. V, p. 835
9 Flinders, *A Voyage,* vol. I, p. 232
10 Flinders to Ann Flinders, 31 May–4 June 1802, Flinders Papers 06/017, FLI/25, NMM
11 Flinders to Banks, 20 May 1802, *HRNSW,* vol. IV, p. 757
12 Brown to Banks, 30 May 1802, *HRNSW*, vol. IV, p. 778
13 Flinders, *A Voyage*, vol. I, p. 235
14 ibid.
15 ibid.
16 François Péron, 'Report on Port Jackson', Ernest Scott, *The Life of Captain Matthew Flinders, R. N.*, Angus & Robertson, Sydney, 1914, Appendix B, p. 439
17 ibid., p. 464
18 Flinders to Ann Flinders, 31 May 1802, Flinders Papers 06/017, FLI/25, NMM

19 ibid.
20 ibid.
21 ibid., 20 July 1802

CHAPTER 20 THE CIRCUMNAVIGATION BEGINS

1 Good, *Journal*, 31 July, p. 82
2 Flinders, *A Voyage*, vol. II, p. 24
3 ibid., p, 26
4 Good, *Journal*, 16 August 1802, p. 86
5 ibid.
6 Smith, 'Diary', August 1802
7 John Murray, in Ida Lee, *The Logbooks of the 'Lady Nelson' with the journal of her first commander Lieutenant James Grant, R.N.*, Grafton & Co, London, 1915, p. 174
8 Good, *Journal*, 16 August 1802, p. 86
9 ibid., 15 September
10 Flinders, *A Voyage*, vol. II, p. 49
11 ibid., p. 70
12 Flinders's completed *Charts of Terra Australis by M. Flinders Commr. of H. M. Sloop Investigator, 1799–1803,* 1 January 1814, relied up to this point principally on his own surveys, with small sections from Cook's chart. As Flinders left the coast, the shoreline from the Northumberland Isles to Torres Strait depended entirely on Cook's survey and included a roughly 220-mile (350-km) stretch from just north of Cape Flattery to Cape Weymouth, which Cook, then keeping away from the coast, had not seen. It was a blank space on Flinders's charts, which in 1815 Lieutenant Charles Jeffreys, HM Brig *Kangaroo,* filled in with the results of his own sketch survey.
13 Murray, in Lee, p. 192
14 Flinders, *A Voyage*, vol. II, p. 83
15 ibid., p. 85
16 ibid., p. 84
17 ibid., p. 88
18 ibid., p. 91
19 Flinders, *Journal*, vol. I, 12 October 1802, Adm. 55/57, PRO, p. 323
20 Murray, in Lee, p. 200
21 Flinders, *A Voyage*, vol. II, p. 96
22 Flinders to Ann Flinders, 18 October 1802, 60/017, FLI/25, NMM
23 Brown to Banks, 17 October 1802, *HRNSW*, vol. IV, p. 855
24 Flinders to Banks, 29 April 1801, Banks Papers Series 65.19 ML
25 Flinders, *A Voyage*, vol. II, p. 99
26 ibid., p. 100
27 ibid., p. 104
28 ibid., p. 102

CHAPTER 21 THE STRAIT AND THE GULF

1 Good, Journal, 30 October 1802, p. 97
2 Flinders, *A Voyage*, vol. II, p. 111
3 ibid., p. 110
4 ibid., p. 113
5 ibid., p. 117

6 ibid., p. 118
7 ibid., p. 120
8 ibid., p. 123
9 ibid.
10 Flinders, *A Voyage,* vol. I, p. xlvi
11 Flinders, *A Voyage,* vol. II, pp. 124–5
12 Brown to Banks, March 1803, *HRNSW*, vol. V, p. 82
13 Matthew Flinders, *Chart of Terra Australis, North Coast*, Sheet I, *Atlas, A Voyage to Terra Australis*
14 Flinders, *A Voyage,* vol. II, p. 129
15 ibid.
16 ibid., p. 130
17 Brown to Banks, March 1803, *HRNSW*, vol. V, p. 82
18 Flinders, *A Voyage,* vol. II, p. 132
19 ibid., p.134
20 ibid., p. 138
21 The Investigator Tree was damaged during a cyclone in 1887 and the main section carrying the principal names was brought to Brisbane. It is now on display in the Museum of the Department of Mapping and Surveying. Later inscriptions included *Beagle 1841* (John Lort Stokes). Some virtually illegible marks have been said to show pre-1802 Dutch or Chinese visitors, but if these had existed in 1802 they would undoubtedly have been mentioned by Flinders.
22 Flinders, *A Voyage*, vol. II, p. 141
23 ibid., p. 142
24 Matthew Flinders, *Journals on the Investigator, Porpoise and Cumberland 1801–1803*, vol. II, 26 November 1802
25 Flinders, *A Voyage*, vol. II, p. 143
26 Flinders, *Journals on the Investigator, Porpoise and Cumberland*
27 Smith, 'Diary', 8 September 1802
28 Flinders, *A Voyage*, vol. II, p. 143
29 Flinders, *Journals on the Investigator, Porpoise and Cumberland*
30 Flinders, *A Voyage*, vol. II, p. 142
31 Flinders, *Journals on the Investigator, Porpoise and Cumberland*
32 Flinders, *A Voyage*, p. 154
33 Smith, 'Diary', 8 September 1802
34 Good, *Journal*, 4 December 1802, p. 104
35 Flinders, *A Voyage,* vol. II, p. 161
36 ibid., p. 162
37 Good, *Journal*, 24 December 1802, p. 107
38 Matthew Flinders, *Chart of Terra Australis, North Coast,* Sheet II, *Atlas, A Voyage to Terra Australis*
39 Flinders, *A Voyage,* vol. II, p. 182
40 Good, *Journal*, 3 January 1803, p. 109
41 Smith, 'Diary', 3 January 1803
42 Flinders, Matthew, *A Voyage*, vol. II, pp. 188–9
43 ibid., p. 189

CHAPTER 22 DIVERSE ENCOUNTERS

1 Good, *Journal*, 21 January 1803, pp. 111–2
2 Flinders, *A Voyage,* vol. II, pp. 197–8
3 ibid., p. 208
4 ibid., p. 210

5 ibid., p. 220
6 ibid., p. 225
7 ibid., pp. 226–7
8 ibid., p. 228
9 ibid., pp. 228–9
10 Good, *Journal*, 17 February 1803, p. 118
11 Flinders, *A Voyage*, vol. II, p. 233

CHAPTER 23 THE JOURNEY BACK

1 Flinders, *A Voyage*, vol. II, p. 247
2 Flinders, *Journals on the Investigator, Porpoise and Cumberland*, 6 March 1803
3 ibid.
4 Flinders to Christopher Smith, 1 April 1803, ML MSS 1/25, Private Letter Book, vol. I, ML
5 Flinders to Henrietta Flinders, 2 April 1803, copy by W. M. F. Petrie, Flinders Papers, LTC
6 Flinders to Ann Flinders, 28 March and 4 April 1803, copy by W. M. F. Petrie, Flinders Papers, LTC
7 Brown to Banks, March 1803, *HRNSW*, vol. V, pp. 82–3
8 Instructions from the Admiralty in *A Voyage*, vol. I, p. 10. Although the Trial Rocks were sighted by the brig *Greyhound*, Lieutenant Ritchie, in 1818, they were not identified as these particular rocks until 1935. Marsden Hordern, *King of the Australian Coast, the Work of Phillip Parker King in the* Mermaid *and* Bathurst *1817–1822*, Miegunyah Press, Carlton South, Victoria, 1997. A modern chart puts them at 20°10'S and 115°10'E.
9 Good, *Journal*, 17 May 1803, p. 122
10 Flinders, *A Voyage*, vol. II, p. 269
11 ibid., p. 269
12 Matthew Flinders to Hugh Bell, 27 May 1802, Private Letter Book, vol. I, ML MSS Safe 1/55 CY 1090, ML
13 ibid., 29 May 1803
14 ibid., 39 May 1803
15 ibid., 30 May 1803
16 Flinders, *A Voyage*, vol. II, pp. 270–1
17 ibid., p. 271
18 Smith, 'Diary', 8 September 1801
19 Flinders, *A Voyage*, vol. II, p. 272

CHAPTER 24 THE PORPOISE

1 *New South Wales Advertiser*, vol. I, no. 16, 19 June 1803, in Good, *Journal*, Introduction, p. 28
2 Flinders to Bass, n.d. 1803, CY 1090 Safe 1/55, ML
3 Matthew Flinders to Mrs Elizabeth Flinders, 10 July 1803, ML MSS Safe 1/55, Private Letter Book, ML
4 Flinders to Ann Flinders, 25 June 1803, CY 1090 Safe 1/55, Private Letter Book, vol. I, ML
5 Flinders, *A Voyage*, vol. II, p. 275
6 ibid.

7 ibid.
8 George Bass to Henry Waterhouse, 1 January 1803, Bass/Waterhouse Letters, CY3970, ML
9 Bass to Waterhouse, 5 January 1803, in Keith Macrae Bowden, *George Bass 1771–1803, His Discoveries, Romantic Life and Tragic Disappearance,* Oxford Univerity Press, Melbourne, 1952, p. 123
10 King to Lord Hobart, 9 May 1803, *HRA,* vol. IV, p. 148
11 Flinders to Bass, 8 August 1803, Bass/Waterhouse Letters, CY 3970, ML
12 Matthew Flinders to Eliza Kent, n.d., CY 1090 Safe 1/55, Private Letter Book, vol. I, ML
13 Matthew Flinders to Elizabeth Macarthur, 28 July 1803, in Sidney J. Baker, *My Own Destroyer*, Currawong, Sydney, 1962, Appendix, p. 126
14 Brown to Banks, 6 August 1803, *HRNSW,* vol. V, pp. 181, 183, 184
15 William Westall to Joseph Banks, 31 January 1804, Banks Papers, Series 23.44 ML
16 Orders re the crew of the Investigator, 7 August 1803, *HRA*, vol. IV, p.387
17 Flinders, *A Voyage*, vol. II, p. 279
18 Matthew Flinders, *Log of the Investigator*, Flinders Papers, M5003, Box 141 (2a), LTC
19 Flinders, *A Voyage*, vol. II, p. 297

Chapter 25 Shipwreck

1 Flinders, *A Voyage,* vol. II, p. 297
2 ibid.
3 Matthew Flinders, 'Account of the Wreck of the Porpoise and Cato', Enclosure No. 3 in Governor King's letter to Sir Evan Nepean, 17 September 1803, *HRA,* vol. IV, p. 402
4 Smith, 'Diary', August 1803
5 Flinders, *A Voyage*, vol. II, p. 304
6 Smith, 'Diary', August 1803
7 Flinders, *A Voyage,* vol. II, p. 309
8 Flinders, 'Account of the Wreck of the Porpoise and Cato', p. 404
9 E. M. Palmer, from his account published in *The Orphan*, 3 February 1804, Calcutta, India, in Matthew Flinders, *A Voyage,* vol. II, note, p. 307
10 Williams, Third Officer of the Bridgewater, *Journal*, in Matthew Flinders, *A Voyage*, vol. II, note, p. 308
11 Flinders, *A Voyage*, vol. II, p. 311
12 ibid., p. 312
13 ibid., p. 314
14 Flinders, *Journal*, 1803, ADM 7/ 708, p. 27, PRO
15 ibid.
16 ibid.
17 Flinders, A *Voyage*, vol II, p. 318
18 Flinders, *Journal*, 1803, ADM 7/708, p. 27, PRO
19 ibid.
20 Flinders, *A Voyage*, vol. II, p. 323
21 ibid.
22 ibid.
23 Flinders to King, 24 September–10 October 1803, *HRNSW,* vol. V, 1897, pp. 240–2
24 Flinders, *Journal*, 1803, ADM 7/ 708, p. 36, PRO
25 ibid., pp. 36–7
26 Flinders, *A Voyage,* vol. II, p. 328
27 ibid., p. 323
28 ibid., p. 350

29 Flinders, *Journal*, Flinders Papers, M5003, Box 141/2 (c), LTC
30 ibid.
31 ibid.

CHAPTER 26 MAURITIUS

1 Precise figures are 63 067 slaves, 6 489 Europeans and 909 Free Blacks in 1807; from Edward Duyker, *Of the Star and the Key: Mauritius, Mauritians and Australia*, Australian Mauritian Research Group, Sylvania, New South Wales, 1988, Introduction, p. 1
2 Flinders, *A Voyage*, vol II, p. 353
3 ibid., p. 354
4 Flinders, *Journal*, ADM 7/708, p. 54, PRO
5 Raymond Marrier d'Unienville, *A Story of Some Mauritian Families of European Origin*, privately published, Mauritius, 1995, pp. 38–9
6 ibid., p. 38
7 ibid., p. 39
8 Flinders, *Journal*, ADM 7/708, p. 54, PRO
9 ibid., p. 55
10 ibid.
11 Flinders, *A Voyage*, vol. II, p. 357

CHAPTER 27 DETENTION

1 Flinders, *A Voyage*, vol. II p. 360
2 ibid., pp. 360–1
3 ibid., p. 361
4 ibid.
5 ibid., p. 362
6 Matthew Flinders, *Diary*, 20 December 1803 CY 227 Safe 1/58 ML
7 François Péron, 'Report on Port Jackson,' Ernest Scott, *The Life of Captain Matthew Flinders, R. N.*, Angus & Robertson, Sydney, 1914, Appendix B, p. 464. The French as quoted reads 'seroit de la détruire le plus tot possible'.
8 Flinders's instructions from the Admiralty in *A Voyage*, vol. I, p. 14
9 King to Lord Hobart, 7 August 1803, *HRA*, vol. IV, p. 357
10 ibid., p. 358
11 Flinders, *A Voyage*, vol. II, pp. 368–70
12 ibid., pp. 374–5
13 ibid., p. 377

CHAPTER 28 THE GARDEN PRISON

1 Flinders, *Diary*, 26 February 1804
2 For an explanation of the dollar, see Chapter 2, Note 5
3 Flinders, *A Voyage*, vol. II, p. 382
4 Frank Horner, 'The "Missing" Third Journal of Flinders', *The Great Circle, Journal of the Australian Association for Maritime History*, vol. 20, no. 2, 1998, p. 138

5 Flinders, *A Voyage*, vol. II, p. 460
6 ibid., p. 383
7 ibid., p. 385
9 ibid.
10 ibid., pp. 386–7
11 ibid., p. 387
12 Banks to the Institut National de France. This letter survives as a rough draft without an addressee, but doubtless was directed to the National Institute of France, *HRNSW*, vol. V, p. 455
13 Banks to King, 29 August 1804, *HRNSW*, vol. V, p. 458
14 Banks to Brown, 30 August 1804, *HRNSW*, vol. V, p. 461
15 Flinders, *A Voyage*, vol. II, p. 389
16 *Inventaire Général de la Maison Despeaux*, Mauritius Archives, G. B. 107/140/1811, in Huguette Ly-Tio-Fane Pineo, *In the Grips of the Eagle*, Moka, Mauritius, 1988, p. 204
17 Flinders, *A Voyage*, vol. II, p. 389
18 Flinders, *Trim*, pp. 44–6
19 Davis, Surgeon of American cartel ship *Primrose*, to his wife, 4 August 1804, CY 2457, Af2/1–14, 16, ML
20 Flinders, *Diary*, 18 May 1804
21 ibid., pp. 14–15 May 1804
22 Flinders, *A Voyage*, vol. II, p. 391
23 Matthew Flinders to the Rev. Mr Tyler, 26 April 1804, Flinders Papers, 60/017, FLI/25, NMM
24 Flinders to Tyler, 20 May 1804, transcribed by W. M. F. Petrie, Flinders Papers, LTC
25 Flinders, *A Voyage*, vol. II, p. 393
26 ibid., note, p. 394
27 ibid., p. 395
28 Flinders, *Diary*, 1 June 1804
29 ibid., 3–4 June 1804
30 Flinders, *A Voyage*, vol. II, p. 391
31 Flinders, *Diary*, August 1804

CHAPTER 29 LETTERS

1 Flinders to King, 8 August 1804, *HRNSW*, vol. V, pp. 409, 411–12
2 Flinders to Banks, 12 July 1804, *HRNSW*, vol. V, pp. 397–8
3 Banks to Flinders, 18 June 1905, *HRNSW*, vol. V, p. 646
4 Flinders to Ann Flinders, 13 July, 23 August, 4 November 1804, Private Letter Book, vol. I, CY 1090 Safe 1/55, ML
5 Flinders to Mrs Elizabeth Flinders, 19 June, 25 August, 4 November 1804, Private Letter Book, vol. I, CY 1090, Safe 1/55, ML
6 Matthew Flinders to Samuel Flinders, 25 August 1804, transcribed by W. M. F. Petrie, Flinders Papers, LTC
7 Flinders to Banks, 23 August, redated 4 November, 1804, Royal Greenwich Observatory, Herstmonceux—Board of Longitude Papers RGO 14/51: 18 f. 172, in Ingleton, p. 311
8 Flinders, *A Voyage*, vol. II, p. 400
9 Status as a prisoner from Mauritius Archives, G. B. 79 in Pineo, note 12, p. 112
10 Flinders, *Diary*, 12 August 1804
11 Flinders to Ann Flinders, 31 December 1804, Private Letter Books, vol. I, CY 1090 Safe 1/55, ML
12 Flinders to Ann Flinders, 13 July, 23 August, 4 November 1804, Private Letter Book, vol. I, CY 1090 Safe 1/55, ML

13 Flinders, *A Voyage,* vol. II, p. 400
14 ibid., p. 411
15 Flinders to Banks, 16 May 1805, *HRNSW,* vol. V, p. 623
16 Flinders to Samuel Flinders, 17 May 1805, Private Letter Book, vol. I, CY 1090, Safe 1/55, ML
17 Flinders to Ann Flinders, 7 July and 20 August 1805, *HRNSW*, vol. V, Appendix B, p. 837
18 Flinders, *Diary*, 25 July 1805
19 ibid., 18 August 1805

CHAPTER 30 WILHEMS PLAINS

1 Flinders, *A Voyage*, vol. II, p. 417
2 ibid., p. 418
3 Flinders, *Diary,* 21 August 1805
4 ibid., 22 August 1805
5 ibid., 23 August 1805
6 ibid., 24 August 1805
7 ibid., 26 August 1805
8 ibid.
9 ibid., 27 August 1805
10 ibid.
11 Flinders, *A Voyage*, vol. II, p. 440
12 Flinders to Samuel Flinders, 6 December 1806, Private Letter Book, vol. 2, CY 1090, Safe 1/56, ML
13 Flinders, *Diary*, 4 October 1805
14 ibid., 9 October 1805
15 ibid., 24 October 1805
16 ibid., 11 October 1805
17 Flinders, *A Voyage*, vol. II, p. 440
18 Flinders, *Diary*, 13 October 1805
19 ibid.
20 ibid.
21 ibid., 21 October 1805
22 ibid., 22 October 1805
23 Flinders to Ann Flinders, 20 November 1805, Flinders Papers, 60/017, FLI/25 NMM
24 ibid.
25 Flinders to Ann Flinders, 25 June 1803, Private Letter Book, vol. I, ML
26 Banks to Flinders, 18 June 1805, *HRNSW*, vol. V, p. 647
27 Flinders to Ann Flinders, 20 November 1805, Flinders Papers, 60/017 FLI/25, NMM
28 Banks to Flinders, 18 June 1805
29 Flinders to Ann Flinders, 20 November 1805
30 Flinders, *Diary*, 25 October 1805
31 ibid., 9 December 1805
32 ibid., 3 November 1805
33 ibid., 23 November 1805
34 ibid., 26 December 1805
35 ibid., 6 November 1805
36 Flinders to Ann Chappelle, 18 December 1800
37 Matthew Flinders to Delphine d'Arifat, 1 January 1806, Private Letter Book, vol. I, CY 1090 Safe 1/55, ML
38 Flinders to Samuel Flinders, 29 March 1806, Private Letter Book, vol. I, CY 1090 Safe 1/55, ML

39 Flinders to Banks, 20 March 1806, *HRNSW,* vol. VI, p. 49
40 King to Charles Mathieu Isidore Decaen, 30 April 1805, *HRNSW*, vol. V, pp. 612–13
41 Flinders to King, 3 July 1806, *HRNSW,* vol. VI, p. 105
42 Flinders, *A Voyage*, vol. II, p. 452.

Chapter 31 'They Have Forgotten Me'

1 Flinders to Ann Flinders, 19 March 1806, Private Letter Book, vol. I, CY 1090 Safe 1/55, ML
2 Flinders, *A Voyage*, vol. II, p. 451
3 ibid., p. 453
4 Flinders to Banks, 28 July 1806, *HRNSW,* vol. VI, p. 117
5 Matthew Flinders to Madame D'Arifat, n. d. but late September 1806, Private Letter Book, vol. II, CY 1090 Safe 1/56, ML
6 Flinders, *Diary*, 26–27 September 1806
7 Flinders, *A Voyage*, vol. II, p. 456
8 Matthew Flinders to Thomi Pitot, 21 October 1806, Private Letter Book, vol. II, CY 1090 Safe 1/56, ML
9 Flinders to Ann Flinders, 27 November 1806, Private Letter Book, vol. II, CY 1090 Safe 1/56, ML
10 Survey of HMS *Investigator*, 22 May 1804, *HRA,* vol. V, p. 135
11 Brown, *Journal*, 13 October 1805, in *Nature's Investigator*, p. 598
12 William Kent to Secretary Marsden, 13 November 1805, *HRNSW*, vol. V, p. 230
13 Flinders to Banks, 8 December 1806, *HRNSW,* vol. VI, p. 207
14 ibid., pp. 207–8
15 Flinders to Samuel Flinders, 6 December 1806, Private Letter Book, vol. II, CY 1090 Safe 1/56, ML
16 Flinders to Isabella Tyler, Flinders Papers 60/017, FLI/25, NMM
17 Flinders to Ann Flinders, 11 December 1806, Private Letter Book, vol. II, CY 1090 Safe 1/56, ML
18 Flinders, *Diary*, 20 December 1806
19 ibid., 30 December 1806–2 January 1807
20 Matthew Flinders to William Bligh, 23 March 1807, *HRNSW*, vol. VI, p. 207
21 Flinders to Banks, 1 July 1807, *HRNSW*, vol. VI, p. 274
22 Flinders, *Diary*, 20 January 1807
23 Flinders to Ann Flinders, 31 May 1807, Private Letter Book, vol. II, CY 1090 Safe 1/56, ML
24 ibid.
25 Flinders, *A Voyage*, vol. II, p. 458
26 Flinders, *Diary*, 11 July 1807
27 Flinders to Ann Flinders, 30 June 1807, Flinders Papers 60/017, FLI/25, NMM
28 ibid.
29 Flinders, *Diary*, 19 July 1807

Chapter 32 Intimations of Freedom

1 Flinders, *Diary*, 20 July 1807
2 Flinders, *A Voyage*, vol. II, p. 459
3 ibid., p. 460

4 Flinders to Ann Flinders, quoted in a letter from Ann Flinders to Joseph Banks, 28 March 1808, *HRNSW*, vol. VI, p. 564
5 Matthew Flinders to Charles Desbassayns, 10 October 1807, Private Letter Book, vol. 2, CY 1090 Safe 1/56, ML
6 Matthew Flinders to Sir Edward Pellew, October 1807, Flinders Papers, 60/017, FLI/12, NMM
7 ibid.
8 Flinders, *A Voyage*, vol. II, p. 465; also October 1807, Flinders Papers, 60/017, FLI/12, NMM
9 Matthew Flinders's Journal, p. 209, Flinders Papers 60/017, FLI/12, October 1807, NMM
10 ibid., p. 211
11 ibid., p. 209
12 Flinders, *A Voyage*, vol. II, pp. 465–6
13 Flinders to Banks, 24 January 1808, HRNSW, vol. VI, p. 421
14 Figures from Pineo, p. 136
15 Matthew Flinders to British naval captains, 20 March 1808, Public Letters and Orders, 1804–14, A 1592–6, ML
16 Flinders, *Diary*, 19 October 1808
17 D'Unienville, *A Story*, pp. 39–40
18 Flinders, *Diary*, 7 October 1808
19 Flinders to Ann Flinders, quoted in a letter from Ann Flinders to Joseph Banks, 28 March 1808, *HRNSW*, vol. VI, p. 564
20 Tyler, 'Biographical Outline'
21 Matthew Flinders to Charles Baudin, 25 July 1808, in Baker, Appendix 4, p. 135
22 Flinders, *A Voyage*, vol. II, p. 467
23 Flinders, *Diary*, 3 September 1808
24 Flinders, *A Voyage*, vol. II, p. 427

CHAPTER 33 'SIX YEARS, FIVE MONTHS AND TWENTY-SEVEN DAYS'

1 Flinders, *Diary*, 1 January 1809
2 Flinders, *A Voyage*, vol. II, p. 469
3 Flinders, *Diary*, 7 January 1809
4 Flinders to Banks, 28 February 1809, *HRNSW*, vol. VII, p. 52
5 Flinders, *A Voyage*, vol. II, p. 469
6 ibid., p. 470
7 Flinders, *Diary*, 1 January 1810
8 Flinders, *A Voyage*, vol. II, p. 479
9 ibid., p. 480
10 ibid.
11 Huguette Ly-Tio-Fane Pineo puts forth this last suggestion, p. 146
12 Flinders, *A Voyage*, vol. II, p. 490
13 ibid., p. 491
14 ibid., p. 480
15 Flinders, *Diary*, 6 April 1810
16 André D'Arifat to Matthew Flinders, 2 April 1810, MS 60/017, FLI/2, NMM
17 *Gazette des Iles de France et Bonaparte* No. 19, 9 mai 1810, chapter IV, note 20, in Pineo, p. 148.
18 Flinders, *Diary*, 18 May 1810, selection copied by W. M. F. Petrie, Flinders Papers, LTC

19 ibid., 5 June 1810
20 Flinders, *A Voyage*, vol. II, p. 482
21 ibid., p. 485
22 Flinders, *Diary*, 12 July 1810
23 ibid., 14 July 1810
24 ibid., 15 July 1810

CHAPTER 34 THE RETURN

1 Joseph Banks to Ann Flinders, 25 September 1810, transcribed by W. M. F. Petrie, Flinders Papers, LTC
2 Tyler, 'Biographical Outline'
3 John Franklin to Matthew Flinders, 1 November 1810, Flinders Papers, 60/017, FLI/1, NMM
4 Flinders, *Diary*, 25 October 1810
5 ibid., 27 October 1810
6 'Instructions to Scientific Explorers', *HRNSW*, vol. IV, p. 350
7 William Kent to Matthew Flinders, 17 November 1811, Flinders Papers, 60/017, FLI/1, NMM
8 Flinders, *Diary*, 5 November 1810
9 Flinders, *A Voyage,* vol. II, p. 495
10 Flinders, *Diary*, 7 November 1810
11 ibid., 8 November 1810
12 ibid., 16 November 1810
13 Matthew Flinders to James Wiles, 5 March 1812, State Library of Victoria, Melbourne, in Gavin Kennedy, *Bligh*, Gerald Duckworth, London, 1978, note 4, p. 177
14 Flinders, *Diary*, 20 November 1810
15 ibid.
16 ibid., 3 December 1810
17 'Historical Sketch of the Life of the late Captain Flinders' by an unnamed author was published in 1911 in the *Victorian Geographical Journal*, vol. XXVIII, 1910–1911, pp. 11–39. Discovered in 1903 by a nurse, Jane or Jennie Barnsdale, it was taken to Australia by her sister and her husband when they emigrated. Its authorship was first ascribed to the Rev. Robert Pugh, an earlier vicar of the Church of St Mary and the Holy Rood, Donington, and later to Matthew's brother Samuel Flinders. Documents found at the church in 1999 and other evidence put together by Pamela Cook of Donington now strongly suggest the Rev. John Wilson was the author.
18 Flinders, *Diary*, 4 December 1810
19 ibid., 7 December 1810
20 ibid., 10 December 1810
21 ibid., 15 December 1810
22 Flinders to Desbassayns, 2 February 1811, Private Letter Book, vol. 3, CY 1090 Safe 1/57, ML
23 Flinders, *Diary*, 12 January 1811
24 Frank Horner, 'The "Missing" Third Journal of Flinders', *The Great Circle, Journal of the Australian Association for Maritime History*, Vol. 20, No. 2, 1998. p. 140
25 Flinders, *Diary*, 4 March 1811
26 ibid., 13 March, 1811
27 ibid., 13 April 1811
28 ibid., 21 May 1811
29 ibid., 9 June 1811
30 ibid., 11 June 1811
31 Flinders, *A Voyage,* vol. II, p. 223

CHAPTER 35 A VOYAGE TO TERRA AUSTRALIS

1 Flinders, *Diary*, 13 January 1811
2 It is not clear whether John Arrowsmith was a son or a nephew.
3 Flinders, *Diary*, 26 April 1811
4 ibid., 4 June 1811
5 Flinders to Madame d'Arifat, 7 March 1812, Private Letter Book, vol. 3, CY 1090 Safe 1/57, ML
6 Flinders, *Diary*, 1 May 1811
7 Flinders to Franklin, 20 June 1811, Private Letter Book, vol. 3, CY 1090 Safe 1/57, ML
8 Flinders, *Diary*, 12 August 1811
9 In 1845 Franklin led an Arctic expedition from which he did not return. Fourteen years later a message was found that confirmed his death in 1847.
10 Flinders, *A Voyage*, vol. II, p. 312
11 Flinders, *Diary*, 14 September 1811
12 ibid., *Diary*, 8 August 1811
13 John Barrow to Matthew Flinders, 18 November 1811, *HRNSW*, vol. VIII, p. 640
14 Flinders, *Diary*, 18 November 1811
15 ibid.
16 On his departure from Mauritius Flinders had left with Lebauve a cow, a heifer and a calf of his own, branded with the letter F
17 Flinders, *Diary*, 30 September 1811
18 ibid., 11 October 1811
19 ibid., 7 October 1811
20 Flinders, *A Voyage*, vol. I, Introduction and note, p. iii
21 Flinders, *Diary*, 14 December 1811
22 ibid., 17 December 1811
23 ibid., 26 December 1811
24 ibid., 27 December 1811
25 ibid., 28 December 1811
26 Flinders to Samuel Flinders, 27 December 1811, Private Letter Book, vol. 3, CY 1090 Safe 1/57, ML, Sydney
27 Flinders, *Diary*, 30 December 1811
28 ibid.
29 Flinders to Samuel Flinders, 31 December 1811
30 Samuel Flinders to Board of Longitude, April 1806, Board of Longitude Papers RGO 14/68 f33r, Royal Greenwich Observatory, Greenwich
31 Flinders, *Diary*, 11 February 1812
32 ibid., 17 January
33 ibid., 23 January
34 Flinders to Madame D'Arifat, 7 March 1812
35 Flinders, *Diary*, 1 April 1812
36 Tyler, 'Biographical Outline'
37 Flinders to Mrs Elizabeth Flinders, 2 April 1812, Private Letter Book, vol. 3, CY 1090 Safe 1/57, ML
38 Tyler, 'Biographical Outline'
39 Flinders, *Diary*, 31 May 1812
40 Flinders, *A Voyage*, vol. II, Appendix No II, p. 532

Chapter 36 The Final Years

1 Flinders to Wiles, 2 July 1811, Private Letter Book, vol. 3, CY 1090 Safe 1/57, ML
2 Flinders, *Diary*, 10 January 1813
3 ibid., 17 January 1813
4 ibid., 2 March 1813
5 ibid., 10 May 1813
6 ibid., 27 May 1813
7 ibid., 27 July 1813
8 ibid., 2 August 1813
9 ibid., 17–23 August 1813
10 ibid., 21 May
11 ibid., 14 August 1813
12 ibid., 3 January 1814
13 ibid., 28 January 1814
14 ibid., 31 January 1814
15 ibid., 27 February 1814
16 ibid., 17 March 1814
17 ibid., 20 March 1814
18 ibid., 14 May 1814. The opium poppy (*Papaver somniferum*) bears either blue-purple or white flowers. Opium was used in various forms for a number of illnesses.
19 ibid., June 1814
20 Tyler, 'Biographical Outline'
21 Ann Flinders to Thomi Pitot, 19 September 1814, Private Letter Book, CY 1090, Safe 1/57, ML
22 Flinders, *Diary*, 28 June 1814
23 ibid., 29 June 1814
24 Tyler, 'Biographical Outline'
25 Ann Flinders to Pitot, 19 September 1814
26 *Naval Chronicle for 1814* vol. XXXII, p. 88
27 Flinders, *Diary*, 10 July 1814
28 'Historical Sketch of the Life of the late Captain Flinders', ed. George Gordon McCrae, *Victorian Geographical Journal*, Royal Geographical Society of Australasia, Melbourne, 1911, p. 29 (See Note 7, Chapter 34)
29 Smyth 'A Brief Memoir'. The author described Flinders as calling for 'my papers' just as he dies. A scribbled notation also has Flinders speaking to his officers in his last moments.
30 Tyler, 'Biographical Outline'
31 ibid.
32 Ann Flinders to Charles Hursthouse, 28 December 1814, Private Letter Book, CY 1090, Safe 1/57, ML
33 Ann Flinders to Pitot, 10 October 1814
34 Thomi Pitot to Ann Flinders, 4 December 1818, Flinders Papers 60/017, Fli/29, NMM

Bibliography

Primary sources

Banks, Joseph 1962 *The Endeavour Journal of Joseph Banks—1768–1771*, vols 1 & 2, ed. J. C. Beaglehole, Angus & Robertson, Sydney

Bass, George 1797 'Bass's Journal of the Whaleboat Voyage', *Matthew Flinders' Narrative of his Voyage in the Schooner Francis: 1798, Preceded and Followed by Notes on Flinders, Bass, the Wreck of the Sydney Cove, &c, by Geoffrey Rawson*, ed. Geoffrey Rawson, Golden Cockerel Press, London, 1946

Baudin, Nicolas 1974 *The Journal of Post Captain Nicolas Baudin, Commander-in-Chief of the Corvettes Géograph and Naturaliste*, trans. Christine Cornell, Libraries Board of South Australia, Adelaide

Bligh, William 1791–1793 *A Log of the Proceedings of His Majesty's Ship Providence and the Second Voyage to the South Seas under the Command of Captn William Bligh to carry the Bread Fruit Plant from the Society Islands to the West Indies*, handwritten copy in John Oxley Library, State Library of Queensland

——1976 *The Log of H.M.S. Providence 1791–1793*, facsimile edition, Genesis Publications, Guildford, England

Brown, Robert 2001 *Nature's Investigator—The Diary of Robert Brown in Australia, 1801–1805*, eds T. G. Vallance, D. T. Moore and E. W. Groves, Australian Biological Resources Study, Canberra

Caley, George 1866 *Reflections on the Colony of New South Wales*, ed. J. E. B. Currey, Landsdowne Press, Melbourne

Collins, David 1798 *An Account of the English Colony in New South Wales with remarks on the dispositions, customs, manners, etc. of the native inhabitants of that country, to which are added Some Particulars of New Zealand*, T. Cadell Jun. and W. Davies, London

Cook, James 1969 *An Account of a Voyage round the World with a Full Account of the Voyage of the Endeavour in the year MDCCLXX along the East Coast of Australia by Lieutenant James Cook, Commander of his Majesty's Bark Endeavour*, ed. D. Warrington Evans, W. R. Smith and Paterson, Brisbane

——1968 *Captain Cook's Journal during his First Voyage Round the World made in H.M. Bark "Endeavour" 1768–1771*, facsimile edition, ed. W. J. L. Wharton, Eliot Stock, London, 1893

——*The Journal of Captain James Cook, edited from his original manuscripts by J. C. Beaglehole*, 1955–1974, Hakluyt Society, Cambridge University Press, Cambridge

Dalrymple, Alexander 1770 *An Historical Collection of the Several Voyages and Discoveries in the South Pacifick Ocean*, Nourse, London

Flinders, Matthew 1985 *A Biographical Tribute to the Memory of Trim, Ile de France 1809*, John Ferguson-Halstead Press, Sydney

——1814 *Charts of Terra Australis or Australia, showing the parts explored between 1798–1803 by M. Flinders, Commander of H.M.S. Investigator*, G. & W. Nichols, London

——*Diary* 1803–1814, ML Safe 1/58, Mitchell Library, Sydney

——*Log of HMS Bellerophon Feb. 24 1793 to 10 Feb. 1793–1784*, Flinders Papers, 60/017, FLI/8b, National Maritime Museum, Greenwich

——*Log kept on board HMS Providence, Feb. 24 1793 to 1793*, Admiralty Papers, 55, Public Record Office, London

——*Journals of the Investigator, Porpoise and Cumberland, 1801–1803*, ML Safe 1/25, Mitchell Library, Sydney

——*Matthew Flinders' Narrative of his Voyage in the schooner Francis: 1798, preceded and followed by notes on Flinders, Bass, the wreck of the Sydney Cove, &c, by Geoffrey Rawson*, ed. Geoffrey Rawson, Golden Cockerel Press, Great Britain

——Matthew Flinders' *Narrative of Tom Thumb's Cruise to Canoe Rivulet*, ed. Keith Bowden, Southeastern Historical Association, Brighton, Victoria

——'Narrative of an Expedition in the Colonial sloop Norfolk, from Port Jackson, through the Strait which separates Van Diemen's Land from New Holland, and from thence round the South Cape back to Port Jackson, completing the circumnavigation of the former Island, with some remarks on the coasts and harbours, by Matthew Flinders, 2nd l't, H.M.S. Reliance', *Historical Records of New South Wales,* vol. III, Appendix B

——*Observations on the Coasts of Van Diemen's Land, on Bass's Strait and its Islands, and on Part of the Coasts of New South Wales: intended to accompany the charts of the late discoveries in those countries*, John Nichols, London. Reprinted Australiana Facsimile Editions No. 66, Libraries Board of South Australia, Adelaide, 1965

——*Private Letter Books* 1801–1814, vols 1, 2, 3, ML Safe 1/55, 56. 57, Mitchell Library, Sydney

——1966 *A Voyage to Terra Australis, Undertaken for the Purpose of Completing the Discovery of that Vast Country, and Prosecuted in the Years 1801, 1802, and 1803, in His Majesty's Ship the Investigator, and Subsequently in the Armed Vessel Porpoise and Cumberland Schooner, with an Account of the Shipwreck of the Porpoise, Arrival of the Cumberland at Mauritius, and Imprisonment of the Commander during Six Years and a Half in that Island*, G. and W. Nichol, London, 1814, Australiana Facsimile Editions No. 37, Libraries Board of South Australia, Adelaide

Flinders Sr, Matthew, *Diary and Account Book*, 1775–1803, by kind permission of Robert Perry and Ursula Perry and Lincolnshire Archives, Lincoln, England

Flinders Sr, Matthew, and Matthew Flinders, *Flinders Correspondence c. 1783–1811*, by kind permission of Robert Perry and Ursula Perry and Lincolnshire Archives, Lincoln, England

Good, Peter 1981 *The Journal of Peter Good, Gardener on Matthew Flinders' Voyage to Terra Australis 1801–03*, ed. Phyllis Edwards, Bulletin of the British Museum (Natural History), Historical Series vol. 9, British Museum (Natural History), Melbourne

Hamilton, George 1998 *A Voyage Round the World in His Majesty's Frigate Pandora,* Hordern House, Sydney

Historical Records of Australia, Governors' Despatches to and from England, Series I, vols I, II, III & IV, 1914–1915, ed. Frederick Watson, The Library Committee of the Commonwealth Parliament, Sydney

Historical Records of New South Wales, vols I, II, III, IV, V, VI, VII & VIII, 1892–1901, ed. F. M. Bladen, Government Printers, Sydney

King, Philip Gidley 1980 *The Journal of Philip Gidley King: Lieutenant, R.N. 1797–1790,* eds Paul G. Fidlon and R. J. Ryan, Australian Documents Library, Sydney

Noah, William 1978 *Voyage to Sydney in the Ship Hillsborough 1798–1799 and a Description of the Colony* Library of Australian History, Sydney

Norst, Marlene J. 1989 *Ferdinand Bauer—The Australian Natural History Drawings,* Lothian, Melbourne

Paine, Daniel 1983 *The Journal of Daniel Paine 1794–1797, Together with Documents Illustrating the Beginning of Government Boat-building and Timber-gathering in New South Wales, 1795–1805*, eds E. J. B. Knight and Alan Frost, National Maritime Museum, Greenwich

Péron, François M. 1809 *A Voyage of discovery to the Southern Hemisphere, performed by the order of the Emperor Napoleon, during the years 1801, 1802, 1803, and 1804*, translated from the French, Marsh Walsh, North Melbourne, 1975

Smith, Samuel, 'Diary', MSS C222, Mitchell Library, Sydney

Smyth, William Henry, R. N. (after) 1842 'A Brief Memoir of Captain Matthew Flinders, R. N.' Flinders Papers 60/017 FLI/105, National Maritime Museum, Greenwich; Box 81/3d (No MS number) La Trobe Collections, State Library of Victoria, Melbourne

Suttor, George 1948 *Memoirs of George Suttor, Banksian Collector (1774–1859)*, ed. George Mackaness, privately published for the editor, Sydney

Tench, Watkin 1996 *1788*, ed. Tim Flannery, Text Publishing Company, Melbourne

Tyler, Isabella (after) 1852 'Biographical Outline of Capt. & Mrs. Flinders', Flinders Papers, 60/017 FLI 107, National Maritime Museum, Greenwich

Waterhouse, Henry 1794 'Account of the Battle of the 1st of June 1794', Bass/Waterhouse Letters, CY 3970, Mitchell Library, Sydney

Secondary sources

Aplin, Graeme, ed. 1988 *A Difficult Infant: Sydney before Macquarie*, New South Wales University Press, Kensington

Austin, K. A. 1964 *The Voyage of the Investigator 1801–1803*, Rigby, Adelaide

Badger, Geoffrey 1988, 1996 *The Explorers of the Pacific*, 2nd edn, Kangaroo Press, Kenthurst, NSW

Baker, Sidney J. 1962 *My Own Destroyer—A Biography of Matthew Flinders*, Currawong Publishing, Sydney

Bassett, Marnie 1961 *The Governor's Lady: Mrs. Philip Gidley King*, Melbourne University Press, Melbourne

Beaglehole, J. C. 1966 *The Exploration of the Pacific*, Stanford University Press, Stanford, California

Beasley, A. W. 1975 *Fellowship of Three—The Lives and Association of John Hunter (1728–1793), The Surgeon; James Cook (1728–1779), The Navigator; and Joseph Banks (1743–1820), the Naturalist*, Kangaroo Press, Kenthurst, NSW

Beard, William 1958 *Navigator Immortal*, J. Bell, Glebe, NSW

Bell, Joshua Peter 1988 *Moreton Bay and How to Fathom It*, 9th edn, Queensland Newspapers, Brisbane

Bernier, Olivier 2000 *The World in 1800*, John Wiley, New York

Bickel, Lennard 1991 *Australia's First Lady, The Story of Elizabeth Macarthur*, Allen & Unwin, Sydney

Blainey, Geoffrey 1966, 1983 *The Tyranny of Distance—How Distance Shaped Australia's History*, rev. edn, Sun Australia, Sydney

Bowden, Keith Macrae 1952 *George Bass—1771–1803, His Discoveries, Romantic Life and Tragic Disappearance*, Oxford University Press, Melbourne

Brissenden, Alan, and Charles Higham 1961 *They Came to Australia*, F. W. Cheshire, Melbourne

Brodsky, Isadore 1973 *Bennelong Profile*, University Co-Operative Bookshop, Sydney

Brown, Anthony 2000 *Ill-Starred Captains*, Crawford House, Adelaide

Butlin, S. J. 1968 *Foundations of the Australian Monetary System 1788–1851*, Sydney University Press, Sydney

Cameron, Hector Charles 1952 *Sir Joseph Banks*, Angus & Robertson, Sydney

Carter, Harold B. 1988 *Sir Joseph Banks, 1743–1820,* British Museum (Natural History), London
Chateaubriand, François-René de 1961 *Atala & René*, trans. Walter J. Cobb, The New American Library, New York
Cilento, Raphael 1959 *Triumph in the Tropics,* Smith & Paterson, Brisbane
Clancy, Robert 1995 *The Mapping of Terra Australis*, Universal Press, Macquarie Park
Clark, C. M. H. 1962 *A History of Australia—From Earliest Times to the Age of Macquarie,* Melbourne University Press, Melbourne
——1957 *Sources of Australian History*, Oxford University Press, London
Clune, Frank and P. R. Stephensen, 1954 *The Viking of Van Diemen's Land*, Angus & Robertson, Sydney
Cobley, John 1983 *Sydney Cove 1793–1795—The Spread of Settlement,* Angus & Robertson, Sydney
——1986 *Sydney Cove 1795–1800, The Second Governor,* Angus & Robertson, North Ryde, NSW
Cooper, H. M. 1953 *The Unknown Coast—Being the explorations of Captain Matthew Flinders, R. N. along the shores of South Australia 1802*, published by the author, Adelaide
——1955 *The Unknown Coast (A supplement)* [s.n.] (No publishing details) Adelaide
Cornell, Christine 1965 *Questions Relating to Nicolas Baudin's Australian Expedition, 1800–1804,* Libraries Board of South Australia, Adelaide
Courtaux, Theodore 1892 *Généalogie de la Famille de la Bauve d'Arifat (Languedoc et Ile Maurice) Seigneurs d'Arifat au Comté de Castres, d'aprés les documents conserves dans le dépots publics, Suivie d'une Notice historique ser cette Seigneurie et d'une Table des noms,* Cabinet de L'Historiographe, Paris
Cridland, Frank 1924 *The Story of Port Hacking, Cronulla and Sutherland Shire*, Angus & Robertson, Sydney
Cumpston, J. H. L. 1964 *The Inland Sea and the Great River,* Angus & Robertson, Sydney
Dalrymple, Alexander 1770 *An Historical Collection of the Several Voyages and Discoveries in the South Pacifick Ocean*, Nourse, London
Davidson, Graeme, ed. 1990 *Journeys into History*, Weldon Russell, Willoughby, NSW
Dening, Greg 1992 *Mr. Bligh's Bad Language: Passion, Power and Theatre on the Bounty,* Cambridge University Press, Cambridge
Duyker, Edward 1998 *Nature's Argonaut—Daniel Solander 1733–1783, Naturalist and Voyager with Cook and Banks,* Miegunyah Press, Carlton South, Victoria
——1988 *Of the Star and the Key, Mauritius, Mauritians and Australia,* Mauritian Research Group, Sylvania, NSW
Egan, Jack 1999 *Buried Alive: Sydney 1788–92—Eyewitness accounts of the Making of a Nation,* Allen & Unwin, Sydney
Eisler, William and Bernard Smith, 1988 *Terra Australis, The Furthest Shore,* International Cultural Corporation of Australia, Sydney
Ellis, M. H. 1978 *John Macarthur,* Angus & Robertson, Sydney
Evans, Susanna 1983 *Historic Sydney as Seen by Its Early Artists*, Doubleday, Lane Cove, NSW
Favenc, Ernest 1967 *The History of Australian Exploration from 1788 to 1888,* Meridian, Amsterdam
Findlay, Elisabeth 2000 *Arcadian Quest—William Westall's Australian Sketches,* National Library of Australia, Canberra
Flannery, Tim, ed. 2000 *Terra Australis—Matthew Flinders' Great Adventure in the Circumnavigation of Australia,* Text Publishing Company, Melbourne
Fleming, Fergus 1998 *Barrow's Boys,* Ganta Books, London
Foreman, Laura and Ellen Blue Phillips, 1999 *Napoleon's Lost Fleet—Bonaparte, Nelson and the Battle of the Nile,* Discovery Communications, London
Fraser, Don, ed. 1989 *Sydney—from Settlement to City, An Engineering History of Sydney,* Engineers Australia, Sydney

Frost, Alan 1995 *Botany Bay Mirages: Illusions of Australia's Convict Beginnings,* Melbourne University Press, Melbourne
——1995 *The Precarious Life of James Mario Matra,* Miegunyah Press, Carlton, Victoria
——1998 *The Voyage of the Endeavour: Captain Cook and the Discovery of the Great South Land,* Allen & Unwin, Sydney
Frost, Alan and Jane Samson, eds 1999 *Pacific Empires: Essays in Honour of Glyndwr Williams*, Melbourne University Press, Melbourne
Garran, Andrew, ed. 1886 *Picturesque Atlas of Australia,* vols 1, 2 & 3, Picturesque Atlas Publishing, Melbourne
Gascoigne, John 1994 *Joseph Banks and the English Enlightenment—Useful Knowledge and Polite Culture*, Cambridge University Press, Cambridge
Gill, J. C. H. 1988 *The Missing Coast—Queensland Takes Shape*, Queensland Museum, South Brisbane
Hainsworth, D. R. 1981 *The Sydney Traders: Simeon Lord and His Contemporaries 1788–1821*, Melbourne University Press, Melbourne
Hardy, John and Alan Frost, eds 1990 *European Voyaging towards Australia,* Australian Academy of the Humanities, Canberra
——1989 *Studies from Terra Australis to Australia,* Australian Academy of the Humanities, Canberra
Hazard, Paul 1964 *The European Mind (1680–1715),* Meridian, Cleveland, Ohio
Historical Records of Australia 1914, 1915 ed. Frederick Watson, The Library Committee of the Commonwealth of Australia, Sydney, vols 2, 3 & 4
Historical Records of New South Wales 1892, 1893, 1895, 1896, 1897 ed. F. M. Bladen, Charles Potter, Government Printer, Sydney, vols 1–7
Hoare, Merval 1999 *Norfolk Island—A Revised and Enlarged History 1774–1998,* 5th edn, Central Queensland University Press, Rockhampton, Queensland
Hordern, Marsden 1997 *King of the Australian Coast: The Work of Philip Parker King in the Mermaid and Bathurst 1817–1822* Miegunyah Press, Carlton South, Victoria
Horner, Frank 1987 *The French Reconnaissance: Baudin in Australia 1801–1803* Melbourne University Press, Melbourne
Horton, Helen 1983 *Islands of Moreton Bay,* Boolarong Publications, Brisbane
Hunter, Susan and Paul Carter 1999 *Terre Napoleon—Australia through French Eyes 1800–1804,* Historic Houses Trust in association with Hordern House, Sydney
Ingleton, Geoffrey C. 1944 *The Charting of a Continent,* Angus & Robertson, Sydney
——1986 *Matthew Flinders: Navigator and Chartmaker,* Genesis Publications, Guildford, Surrey, in association with Hedley Australia, Alphington, Victoria
Ireland, Samuel 1791 *Picturesque Views on the River Thames with Observations on the Works of Art in its Vicinity,* T. and I. Edgerton, Whitehall, London
Jardine, Lisa 1999 *Ingenious Pursuits: Building the Scientific Revolution,* Little Brown & Co., London
Jeffreys, Max 1997 *Wreck of the Sydney Cove,* New Holland Publishers, Frenchs Forest, NSW
Jones, Francis Avery and Basil Greenhill, eds *1981 Starving Sailors,* Trustees of the National Maritime Museum, Greenwich
Jones, Michael 1988 *Country of Five Rivers: Albert Shire, 1788–1988* Allen & Unwin, Sydney
'Kangaroo' 1944 *The Spirit of St. George in Action: The Chief Explorer of Australia, Captain Matthew Flinders, R. N., His Life and Times 1774–1814,* The Royal Society of St George, London
Kelly, Celsus, O.F.M. 1965 *Calendar of Documents—Spanish Voyages in the South Pacific and Franciscan Missionary Plans for Its Islanders,* Franciscan Historical Studies (Australia) in association with Archivo Ibera-Americano (Madrid), Madrid
Kelly's Directory of Lincolnshire—1905 1905 Kelly's Directories Ltd, London
Kennedy, Gavin 1978 *Bligh,* Gerald Duckworth, London
Kenny, John 1995 *Before the First Fleet—The European Discovery of Australia 1606–1777,* Kangaroo Press, Kenthurst, NSW
Kiple, Kenneth 1999 *Plague, Pox & Pestilence, Diseases in History,* Phoenix, London

King, Hazel 1980 *Elizabeth Macarthur and Her World,* Sydney University Press, Sydney
King, Jonathan and John King 1981 *Philip Gidley King, A Biography of the Third Governor of New South Wales,* Methuen Australia, North Ryde, NSW
King, Robert J. 1990 *The Secret History of the Convict Colony: Alexandro Malaspina's Report on the British Settlement of New South Wales,* Allen & Unwin, Sydney
Kippis, Andrew 1925 *Captain Cook's Voyages,* Alfred A. Knopf, New York
Krieger, Leonard 1970 *Kings and Philosophers 1689–1789,* W. W. Norton, New York
Lee, Ida 1920 *Captain Bligh's Second Voyage to the South Sea*, Longmans Green, London
——1925 *Early Explorers in Australia*, Methuen, London
——ed. 1915 *The Logbooks of the 'Lady Nelson' with the journal of her first commander, Lieutenant James Grant, R. N,* Grafton, London
Lee, Stephen J. 1978, 1984 *Aspects of European History 1494–1789,* 2nd edn, Routledge, London
Lee, Stuart 1999 *Matthew Flinders and the Discovery of Shoal Bay (Yamba),* Port of Yamba Historical Society, Yamba, NSW
Lenoir, Phillipe n. d. *Mauritius, Former Isle de France,* Editions du Cygne, Port Louis, Mauritius
Lewis, Michael 1960 *A Social History of the Navy, 1793–1815*, George Allen & Unwin, London
——1957 *The History of the British Navy,* Penguin, Harmondsworth, Middlesex
——1948 *The Navy of Great Britain—A Historical Portrait,* George Allen & Unwin, London
Lyte, Charles 1980 *Sir Joseph Banks—18th Century Explorer, Botanist and Entrepreneur,* A. H. and A. W. Reed, Sydney
Mack, James D. 1966 *Matthew Flinders, 1774–1814,* Nelson, Melbourne
Mackaness, George, ed. 1979 *The Discovery and Exploration of Moreton Bay and the Brisbane River, 1799–1828,* Australian Historical Monographs, vol. XLIII (New Series), Review Publications, Dubbo, NSW
——1949 *Fresh Light on Bligh: Some Unpublished Correspondence,* Australian Historical Monographs, vol. V (New Series), Review Publications, Dubbo, NSW
——1931 *The Life of Vice-Admiral William Bligh,* vols I & II, Angus & Robertson, Sydney
——1936 *Sir Joseph Banks—His Relations with Australia,* Angus & Robertson, Sydney
Mackesy, Piers 1984 *War without Victory—The Downfall of Pitt 1799–1802,* Clarendon Press, Oxford
Macknight, C. C. 1969 *The Farthest Coast,* Melbourne University Press, Melbourne
——1998 *Low Head to Launceston—The Earliest Reports of Port Dalrymple and the Tamar,* Historical Survey of Northern Tasmania, Launceston, Tasmania
MacLeod, Roy and Philip F. Rehbock *Nature in Its Greatest Extent,* University of Hawaii Press, Honolulu
Maiden, J. H. 1909 *Sir Joseph Banks—The "Father of Australia"*, William Applegate Gullick, Sydney
Marchant, Leslie R. 1982 *France Australe*, Artlook Books, Perth
Markham, Felix 1963 *Napoleon,* Mentor, New York
Marrier d'Unienville, Raymond 1995 *A Story of Some Mauritian Families of European Origin*, privately published, Mauritius
Martin, Ged, ed. 1978 *The Founding of Australia—The Argument about Australia's Origins,* Hale & Iremonger, Sydney
Masefield, John 1971 *Sea Life in Nelson's Time,* Conway Maritime Press, London
Maurois, André 1956 *A History of England,* Bodley Head, London
McDonald, W. G. 1975 *The First-Footers—Bass and Flinders in Illawarra—1796–1797,* Illawarra Historical Society, Wollongong
McGowan, Ian, ed. 1989 *The Restoration and Eighteenth Century Macmillan Anthologies of English Literature,* Macmillan, Hound Basingstoke, Hampshire
Mee, Arthur, ed. 1949 *The King's England: Lincolnshire, A County of Infinite Charm,* Hodder & Stoughton, London
Miller, David Philip and Peters Hanns Reill, eds 1996 *Visions of Empire: Voyages, Botany and Representations of Nature,* Cambridge University Press, Cambridge

Mortimer, George 1798 *Engelsmannen Joh. Hinric Cox Resa Genom Söderhafvet Till Ön Amsterdam, Marien-Öarna. Ön-Taheiti, Sandvichs-och-Raf-Öarna, Tinian, Unalaska och Canton in China*, George Mortimer, Nyköping, Sweden

Mourot, Suzanne 1969 *This Was Sydney—A Pictorial History from 1788 to the Present,* Ure Smith, Sydney

Mulvaney, D. J. and J. Peter White, eds 1987 *Australians to 1788,* Fairfax, Syme & Weldon, Broadway, NSW

Naval Chronicle for 1814, The General and Biographical History of the Royal Navy of the United Kingdom with a variety of Original papers on Nautical Subjects, vol. xxxii, Joyce Gould, London

O'Brian, Patrick 1987 *Joseph Banks—A Life,* Collins Harvill, London

Oliver, Douglas 1988 *Return to Tahiti—Bligh's Second Breadfruit Voyage,* Melbourne University Press, Melbourne

Ormeling, F. J. 1955 *The Timor Problem—A Geographical Interpretation of an Underdeveloped Island,* J. B. Walters, Groningen, Djakarta and Matinus Nijhoff, Gravenhage

Perry, T. M. 1982 *The Discovery of Australia—The Charts and Maps of Navigators and Explorers,* Nelson, Melbourne

Peters, Merle 1969 *The Bankstown Story, A Comprehensive History of the District,* published by the author, Yagoona, NSW

Pineo, Huguette, Ly-Tio-Fane 1988 *In the Grips of the Eagle: Matthew Flinders at Ile de France, 1803–1810,* Mahatma Gandhi Institute, Moka, Mauritius

Pope, Steve 1998 *Hornblower's Navy—Life at Sea in the Age of Nelson,* Orion Media, London

Powell, Alan 1996 *Far Country—A Short History of the Northern Territory,* Melbourne University Press, Melbourne

Proudfoot, Helen, et al. 1991 *Australia's First Government House*, Allen & Unwin, Sydney

Radcliffe, Ann 1980 *The Mysteries of Udolpho*, Oxford University Press, Oxford

Radok, Rainer 1990 *Capes and Captains: A comprehensive study of the Australian Coast,* Surrey Beatty & Sons, Norton, NSW

Rawson, Geoffrey 1934 *Bligh of the 'Bounty'*, Philip Allan, London

Reed, A. W., ed. 1969 *Captain Cook in Australia—Extracts from the Journals of Captain James Cook, giving a full account in his own words of his adventures and discoveries in Australia,* A. H. and A. W. Reed, Sydney

Retter, Catherine and Shirley Sinclair 1999 *Letters to Ann—The Love Story of Matthew Flinders and Ann Chappelle,* Angus & Robertson, Sydney

Robertson, Anne 1988 *Treasures of the State Library of New South Wales,* Collins with the State Library of New South Wales, Sydney

Russell, R. W. M., ed. 1979 *Matthew Flinders: The Ifs of History*, Flinders University, Adelaide

Schreiber, Roy E. 1991 *The Fortunate Adversities of William Bligh,* American University Studies, Series IX, History, vol. 108, Peter Lang, New York

Scott, Ernest 1929 *A Short History of Australia,* Oxford University Press, London

——1914 *The Life of Captain Matthew Flinders*, R. N., Angus & Robertson, Sydney

Sharp, Andrew 1963 *The Discovery of Australia*, Clarendon Press, Oxford

Smith, Bernard 1992 *Imagining the Pacific—In the Wake of the Cook Voyages,* Miegunyah Press, Carlton South, Victoria

Smith, Keith Vincent 1992 *King Bungaree—A Sydney Aborigine Meets the Great South Pacific Explorers—1799–1830,* Kangaroo Press, Kenthurst, NSW

Stephensen, P. R. and Brian Kennedy 1980 *The History and Description of Sydney Harbour,* A. H. & A. W. Reed, Sydney

Summerson, John 1988 *Georgian London,* new edn, Barrie & Jenkins, London

Taylor, Peter 1982 *Australia—The First Twelve Years,* George Allen & Unwin, Sydney

Thynne, Robert 189? *Matthew Flinders or How We Have Australia, being the first true story of Captain Flinders' explorations and adventures,* John Hogg, London

Tooley, Ronald Vere 1952 *Maps and Map-Makers,* Batsford, London

Walsh, Michael and Colin Yallop, eds 1993 *Language and Culture in Aboriginal Australia,* Aboriginal Studies Press, Canberra

Ward, Russel 1992 *Concise History of Australia,* rev. ed., University of Queensland Press, St Lucia, Queensland

Watt, J., E. J. Freeman and W. F. Bynum, eds 1981 *Starving Sailors: The Influence of Nutrition upon Naval and Maritime History,* National Maritime Museum, Greenwich

Way, Thomas R. and Walter G. Bell 1907 *The Thames from Chelsea to the Nore,* John Lane, Bodley Head, London

Williams, Glynwr and Alan Frost, eds 1988 *Terra Australis to Australia*, Oxford University Press, Melbourne

Wills, Geoffrey 1968 *The English Life Series, vol. IV, c. 1760–1820, George III,* Wheaton, Exeter, UK

Wood, G. Arnold 1922 *The Discovery of Australia,* Macmillan, London

Journals

Austin, K. A. 1962 'Flinders' Hour of Decision', *Walkabout*, Australian National Travel Association, Melbourne, vol. 30, no.7, pp. 29–31

Baldwin, B. S. 1964 'Flinders and the French', *Proceedings of the Royal Geographical Society of Australasia*, Australian Branch, vol. 65, pp. 53–67

Brown, Anthony 1998 'The Captain and the Convict Maid: A Chapter in the Life of Nicolas Baudin', *South Australia Geographic Journal*, vol. 97, pp. 20–32

Burnby, J. G. L. 1988 'The Flinders Family of Donington: Medical Practice and Family Life in an Eighteenth Century Fenland Town', *Lincolnshire History and Archaeology*, vol. 23, pp. 51–58

David, Andrew C. F. ed. 1978 'The Glorious First of June—An Account of the Battle by Peter Heywood', *The Mariner's Mirror*, Society for Nautical Research, London, vol. 64, no. 1, pp. 361–6

Duyker, Edward 1993 'Histoire genéalogique—Mauritius and Family History at the National Library', *National Library of Australia News*, vol. 4, no. 1, pp. 4–6

Fowler, Thomas Walker 1912 'The Work of Capt. Matthew Flinders at Port Jackson', *Victorian Geographical Journal,* Royal Geographical Society of Australasia, vol. XXIX, pp. 20–32

Geeson, N. T. and R. T. Sexton 1970 'H.M. Sloop Investigator', *The Mariner's Mirror*, vol. 56, no. 3, pp. 275–98

Horner, Frank 1998 'The "Missing" Journal of Flinders', *The Great Circle, Journal of the Australasian Association of Maritime History*, vol. 20, no. 2, pp. 138–141

McCrae, George Gordon 1912 'Geographical Discoverers and Explorers of the 18th Century and Earlier Part of the 19th—La Perouse and Baudin in New South Wales and Flinders in Mauritius—Their Experience at the Hands of Colonial Officials', *Victorian Geographical Journal*, Royal Geographical Society of Australia, vol. xxix, pp. 1–18

——ed., 1910–1911 'Historical Sketch of the Life of the late Captain Flinders', *Victorian Geographical Journal*, vol. XXVIII, pp. 11–30

Perry, T. M. 1975 'Seasons for Exploration: The Second Daniel Brock Memorial Lecture 1975', *Proceedings of the Royal Geographical Society of Australasia*, South Australian Branch, Adelaide, vol. 76, pp. 51–8.

Roe, Michael 1987 'New Light on George Bass, Entrepreneur and Intellectual', *Journal of the Royal Australian Historical Society*, vol. 72, Part 5, 1987

Saenger, P. and B. J. Stubbs 1994 'The Investigator Tree, Sweers Island: A Natural Historic Monument', *Proceedings of the Royal Society, Queensland,* vol. 104, pp. 67–78

GENERAL

Australian Dictionary of Biography 1966 vol. 1: 1788–1850, eds A. G. L. Shaw and C. M. H. Clark, Melbourne University Press, London and New York

Australian Encyclopaedia, The 1996 6th edn, Australian Geographic Pty Ltd, Terrey Hills, NSW

Barker, Anthony 1988 *When Was That?—Chronology of Australia* John Ferguson, Surry Hills, NSW

Reader's Digest Guide to the Australian Coast 1983 Reader's Digest Services, Surry Hills, NSW

Tooley, Ronald Vere 1979 *Tooley's Dictionary of Mapmakers,* Map Collector Publications, Tring, Hertfordshire, UK

Index

Page numbers in *italics* refer to illustrations. Page numbers followed by an 'n' indicate a reference to an endnote. 'MF' refers to Matthew Flinders.